BOOKS BY

KENNETH TYNAN

CURTAINS	1961
BULL FEVER	1955
PERSONA GRATA	1953
ALEC GUINNESS	1953
HE THAT PLAYS THE KING	1950

CURTAINS

KENNETH TYNAN

SELECTIONS FROM THE DRAMA CRITICISM AND RELATED WRITINGS

ATHENEUM
1961
NEW YORK

CURTAINS

For permission to reprint most of what follows the author is grateful to the editors of twelve publications, six of them English—THE OBSERVER, THE EVENING STANDARD, THE SPECTATOR, ENCOUNTER, SIGHT AND SOUND *and* BAND WAGON—*and six American*—THE NEW YORKER, HOLIDAY, HARPER'S BAZAAR, HARPER'S MAGAZINE, MADEMOISELLE *and* THE ATLANTIC.

Library of Congress Catalog Card Number 61-6377
Manufactured in the United States of America by Kingsport Press, Inc., Kingsport, Tennessee
Designed by Harry Ford
First Edition

But men must know, that in this theatre of man's life, it is reserved only for Gods and angels to be lookers on.

FRANCIS BACON, *Advancement of Learning*

PREFACE

Since the winter of 1948, when I came floating down from Oxford, I have earned most of my living by writing about the theatre. Long before I became an undergraduate I enjoyed setting down my impressions of plays in performance; it seemed to me unfair that an art so potent should also be so transient, and I was deeply seduced by the challenge of perpetuating it in print. Both at school and at the university I reviewed plays; whenever it was possible, I acted in them and directed them as well. In the autumn of 1950 I brought out a book on the theatre. Its style was ornate, and many of its opinions were outrageous, but it launched me as a drama critic, in which capacity I have since worked for *The Spectator,* the *Evening Standard,* the *Daily Sketch, The Observer,* and—from 1958 to 1960—*The New Yorker.* This volume is a self-compiled anthology of theatre pieces I have contributed, over the past ten years, to these and other newspapers and magazines on both sides of the Atlantic. I have corrected some factual slips, expunged some repetitions and redundancies, and ironed out the odd grammatical flaw; otherwise, the articles (and excerpts therefrom) are reprinted as they originally appeared. I have also included a few studies of film people, and a handful of essays that, for one reason or another, never got into print.

I have tried to arrange these chunks and splinters of prose so that they form a sort of personal mosaic. The order in which they are set out is partly chronological and partly geographical. There are five sections, devoted respectively to the theatres of Britain, the United States, France, Russia and Germany. A special problem was created by articles about British productions of American plays. I have solved it, somewhat arbitrarily, by placing such reviews in the British section except in cases where the emphasis was so exclusively on the playwright that a transfer to the American section seemed logical. Another part of my purpose verges on the autobiographical. Most critics, when they make collections of their work for publication, are astonished to find how consistent they have been; their reviews turn out to be held together by an unbroken thread of conviction that the years have not frayed. My own experience, as I went through my files, was very different. I found a great many inconsistencies, and was not in the least surprised. Since I set up shop as a taster of plays, my palate has undergone a process that some may call a development and others a degeneration; it is, anyway, a process of change. I still have the same hunger for theatre (which is, after all, the art that keeps me off the streets), but to assuage it I nowadays look for a different kind of dramatic *cuisine*.

Ten years ago I was in love with the theatre of fantasy and shock. I wrote in a university magazine that "this sad age needs to be dazzled, shaped, and spurred by the spectacle of heroism. . . . If heroic plays take the stage, life may produce, in honest emulation, its own poor heroes of flesh and fact." I revered poetic plays about the deaths of kings, especially if they had not been performed since the seventeenth century; I suspected that all really first-rate drama was about great men and dying and mourning; beyond that, nothing. It rarely occurred to me that theatre could be more than a combination of technical brilliance (on the part of directors and designers) and personal extravagance (on the part of actors and actresses). For me, in short, drama was apart from life, instead of a part of it.

Since then, like many of my contemporaries, I have swung over to another viewpoint; or, to put it more accurately, I use a wider lens. Travel—in France, America, Russia, and Germany—contributed a good deal to this broadening of outlook; so did the threat and pressure, no longer escapable, of world events; and so, no doubt, did the mere fact of growing up. Whatever the reasons, I became aware that art, ethics, politics, and economics were inseparable from each other; I realised that theatre was a branch of sociology as well as a means of self-expression. From men like Bertolt Brecht and Arthur Miller I learned that all drama was, in the widest sense of a wide word, political; and that no theatre could sanely flourish unless there was an umbilical connection between what was happening on the stage and what was happening in the world. That, roughly, is where I stand today, and this book may give some indication of how I got there.

Most good plays, when you boil them down, deal with the problem of coming to terms with life—of adjusting, without surrender, to hostile and menacing circumstance. Today the theatre itself is confronted by the same problem that has racked so many of its heroes and heroines. Our business is to urge it to face realities, even though the realities in question are more complex and appalling than the worst nightmares of Hamlet or Oedipus.

K T

New York, 1960

CONTENTS

I: THE BRITISH THEATRE

Bartholomew Fair, BY BEN JONSON, AND *Henry V,* BY WILLIAM SHAKESPEARE, AT THE OLD VIC; *The Gay Invalid,* ADAPTED FROM MOLIÈRE'S *Le Malade Imaginaire,* AT THE GARRICK.

The Old Vic sailed, broad-bottomed, into the New Year with Jonson's *Bartholomew Fair,* and went down fighting. The muddled dash and defiance of this play is out of quite another world than that of Shakespeare's lighter pieces—it has its finger on the pulse, its ear at the keyhole, and its nose in the privy: it is, in fact, a documentary. I don't find much of it very hilarious, except the occasional, unexpected use of a long word which has since come to mean something slightly different; but I doubt whether this production, by George Devine, really helped matters. The play, to stand up, certainly needs crutches, but to judge from the crowd Mr. Devine assembles at the fair, nearly everyone in the lower orders of Jacobean England was in dire need not so much of crutches as of stretchers. They all snuffle, limp, or have gap-teeth; and noses this season are going in all directions. The frisky pox, methinks, hath been at them.

Almost everyone uses the same dead device to milk laughs from lines which have ceased to be funny: the actor delivers his collapsed quip as if he alone found it amusing. "What Wyn will, that Wyn's will will win, quotha!" he will say, cackling neurotically, to be greeted by frosty silence from his partner. He then coughs apologetically. This trick is doubtless legitimate from time to time, but I can't believe that Jonson meant all his characters to be played as club bores. It is all very animated and grimy, if a little too much like a drunken leper colony to be really fun. Somebody might make a revue number out of it, though:

I was born in the reign of Queen Bess
And I'm looking a bit of a mess:
I thought it just a little much
When someone gave me that third crutch. . . .

Three actors, each unassisted by nose putty, come well out of it. Robert Eddison, as the *nouveau-riche* Bartholomew Cokes, uses his innate gawkiness to fine effect, and invents for this performance a fat, ingratiating child's laugh—the tense, explosive chuckle of a small boy full of anticipated delights. Then there is Roger Livesey, whose immense sloth is here perfectly matched to his part, that of a perambulant J. P. who, heavily disguised, investigates the "enormities" of the fair. The disguise, of course, renders him about as effectively incognito as a walrus in a ballet-skirt; fearing discovery, he shrinks beneath his cloak, turning up the collar in the manner of a flustered dowager in a high wind. Primly outraged, he looks like Dr. Watson trying clumsily to do a Holmes; the whole performance is portentously Victorian, as if Pinero had written a part for a porpoise.

The third good thing is Alec Clunes' thoroughly eccentric playing of Humphrey Waspe, Cokes' servant. Waspe has a ferocious maternal regard for his young master, which he expresses by reviling him. Clunes behaves as if there were a hornet's-nest in his stomach; he is openly furious, for very little reason, for the greater part of the evening. Intemperately excitable, he jabs and darts about like a galvanic King Rat suffering from ulcers, and wears a perpetual squinting frown which says: "Where did I put those spectacles?" You feel that when he finds them, he will grind them to dust. At times Clunes appears to be crying, so deep-seated is his mysterious anger. And, finally made tipsy, he weaves and lurches through balletic patterns which would not have disgraced Sid Field. But the production elsewhere is wretchedly slow.

Henry V is a much more solid job, perhaps the best all-round Shakespeare production the Vic has presented since the war. The play drives straight to those emotions of soil, birth, and breeding which we all profess to have outgrown, wonderfully spanning the gulf of feeling between Kipling and poems like "No passing bell for us who die as cattle." The mercy and the savagery of war, the peace-lover and the warmonger—each point of view gets a good airing, and the final synthesis seems to me akin in compassion to Binyon's "Recessional." Glen Byam Shaw's production, heraldic, static, and bare, works up a cumulative nobility which convinced me, almost for the first time, that heroic plays need no trimmings. His second-act curtain, with the survivors of Agincourt singing a gruff *"Non Nobis"* as they march away, was a miracle of simple tact.

Alec Clunes' Henry starts out as a ripe rose in the bonnet of kingship. Though this actor can look ominous, he lacks wrath; he respects his own urbanity, and likes most to be at ease, a long-lipped beaming boy of thirty-six or so. Realising intelligently that the fire and bite of battle are beyond him, he chooses to emphasise instead the godliness of this repentant prince: he sanctifies his charm by putting it "in God's hands," and often sounds curiously like Saint Joan. The play warms at once to his touch; but at the end of the first act this graciousness (most strikingly expressed in the huge sigh of regret with which he condemns the traitors at Southampton) was beginning to make me anxious. He could unbend, but could he stand up? And the answer is that he couldn't quite. Persuasively as he presents it, rueful piety alone would not have dragged that bedraggled army back into the breach. But he weakened nowhere else: godliness is next to priggishness, and this Clunes escaped wonderfully, keeping about him the mischief of Henry's youth to soften the holy discipline of his maturity. My only quibble with this triumphantly "gentle gamester" is a look that settles on the actor's face in moments of intense brooding—a bulge-eyed glare which means, to me at least: "I *think* I've swallowed the spoon!"

The Motley sets and costumes were first-rate, preserving a studious contrast between the honest-kersey English and the silken-dalliance French. Roger Livesey (Chorus) moaned quite genially, trotting on and offstage like a St. Bernard; William Devlin was a trenchant and laconic Fluellen; Leo McKern made me laugh at the impossible humours of Nym by presenting him as a frustrated Disney dwarf; and Rupert Davies had a reverent and moving moment as the old soldier who finds that he has unwittingly challenged his king. Maybe the completest performance, apart from Clunes', was Dorothy Tutin's spry little Queen-to-be: a frisk of impertinent babyhood, but a princess withal, with commanding Oriental eyes.

The Gay Invalid, a harlequinade based on Molière's play about a hypochondriac who is pauperised by doctors' bills, might have been jockeyed into a passable evening's fun; but its casting, wasteful and unpleasant, ruined its chances, and for this the blame must rest on Peter Daubeny, the manager responsible.

The play's one joke depends on the fact that Crank, the central character, is an *imaginary* invalid; and we laugh because we can see he is in the prime of life. Mr. Daubeny has called on A. E. Matthews to play the part; and not only is Mr. Matthews, for all his eighty-one years, an actor of the modern school, whose casual method fits Molière about as well as the glass slipper fitted the ugly sisters, he is also, quite obviously, not in the prime of life. It becomes nastily offensive when the quacks besiege this easy, creased old gentleman with his wafer-thin shell of a voice: they hammer him, pound and shake him, and tell him that his lungs are weak and his heart is flimsy. Hereabouts the smell of the bearpit gathers over the evening. Mr. Matthews goes through the hoops with unfussed tact, but he should never have been asked to do it.

I don't wish to be ungallant, but Elisabeth Bergner cannot be a day under twenty-five, and it is nice to record that she has at last decided to stop playing girls in their teens. Miscast as Toinette, Crank's scheming housekeeper, she yet contrived to burrow into my heart as a young and nubile houri: those flowing arms and fingers, that eagerness to beguile, that sheer relish of joy were all as unspoilt as ever. The pity is that Mr. Daubeny's flair for opening cans with diamonds led him to offer her a part which any of a hundred repertory actresses could have played. Someone must soon approach her less wildly and use her special gifts (Bergner open-mouthed, Bergner transported) in some of the parts that belong to her—*Frou-Frou,* for instance, or *Camille*.

The title bestowed on the play is totally misleading: it used to be called *Doctor's Joy,* and I think I trace the hand of Mr. Daubeny in the blithe inaccuracy of *The Gay Invalid*. Why not *The Merry Prank of Mr. Crank?* Or perhaps, for a lark, *They Shoot Horses, Don't They?*

(1951)

The Wedding, BY ANTON CHEKHOV, AND *Electra*, BY SOPHOCLES, AT THE OLD VIC.

In their volatile new offering the Old Vic company prove, to our delight, that both they and Chekhov are still capable of astonishing us. Who, this side of infatuation, would have thought *The Wedding* would act so well, with such *désinvolture?* Certainly nobody since the revolution has given us a more robust, more tenderly destructive vignette of the little bourgeois. The curtain whisks up on a provincial wedding-feast in the banqueting-room of a seedy hotel. With a free flapping of swing-doors and a clinking of bead curtains, the guests, prim and immodest, brimming and parched, swarm in. The gas-brackets spread a derisive, jaundiced glow over them, and as each toast is drunk a mutually indifferent two-piece orchestra obliges with a chord. The bridegroom, fussy as a poodle, pops his eyes and pecks his pinch-faced, quivering wife (Dorothy Tutin); an amiable Greek (Leo McKern) sweats through a wonderfully embarrassing speech, floundering in that vague, repetitious politeness to which the linguistic booby is for ever condemned; meanwhile, mother dithers and father tepidly rambles.

But the chair on the bride's left is empty; the guest of honour is late. Mother is for exploding; has she not sent out Andrey Andreyevitch with twenty-five roubles to capture the nearest available celebrity? At last his approach is announced, the party is fanfared into a stiff receptive group, and, hoar-bearded and mumbling, the lion is shuffled on. He is (praise Heaven) an admiral, and must be cajoled, willy-nilly, into a few words. He speaks, peacefully, endlessly, about his experiences. A chair scrapes; he cries out joyously, discerning a sailor in the throng. Now beside himself, he will demonstrate with what agility naval orders are obeyed. His ancient voice is strained and fluted into delivering a series of gibberish commands which momentarily recall Danny Kaye's excursion into Gogol. Dumbfounded, the sailor stares. The admiral continues. He is seventy-two, he tells us, and a plump girl in green chuckles—not contemptuously, but as a just comment on his senility. Out of an odd gratitude he begins again, an excitable telegraph clerk interrupting to establish his own professional zest by hammering out Morse code on the table. We hear more possessed, moonstruck yells at the rigging. The *dènouement,* in which the admiral, now exposed as a mere captain, stumps off in fury on hearing that his twenty-five roubles have been embezzled by his captor, bears that unmistakable patina of compassion which always, in Chekhov, overlays the jaggedness of farce. The party continues.

In the virtuoso part of the admiral Paul Rogers gives his roundest performance of the season, and George Devine's direction imparts to the whole the speed and wit of the early René Clair comedies. As period piece and as production piece this is a success: at last a light-weight company has found material to match its own excellences. The sets and costumes (by Motley) are most touchingly ugly.

The curtain-raiser, Sophocles' *Electra,* is a valuable example of the kind of work the Old Vic Theatre School has been doing in the past few years. It is naturally a little hard on the audience. There is no doubt that for many centuries after it was written this was a very remarkable play; one may justifiably guess that even at the height of the Renaissance its stringently outspoken treatment of a legendary scandal had some claims on the attention of the new playgoers. But an author does not necessarily add a cubit to his stature with every century that passes; it could be urged that at a certain distance from his own country, time, and conventions his theatrical impact can never be commensurate with the effort required to bulldoze away the mounting drifts of dust and decipher his long-dead zeals and patterns. Michel Saint-Denis' production, slow and curiously unrhythmical, does not succeed in making the iterated griefs of this doomed house of anything more than anecdotal importance. The stock response of terror in the face of matricide has vanished.

The play remains an unrivalled training-ground for novice actors. Its enormous recitations test voice and body to the utmost, without too brutally testing the mind; and there are no awkward props or pieces of furniture to confuse the beginner. Having seen Sophocles at the Vic, one wants to say: "With reservations, splendid. Now let us invite an audience and do a play." Meanwhile Peggy Ashcroft is spanning some amazing arpeggios as Electra, showing unsuspected vocal strength and variety; but she is unable to convince us that the middle part of the play, wholly taken up with lamentations over the reported death of Orestes, is much more than dignified padding. Catherine Lacey (Clytemnestra), perhaps the most striking stylist of our theatre, appears in the costumes, the manner, and even the voice of Gloria Swanson: and it is surely an error, in an age when the platform-sole suggests the shopgirl, to put your tragedy queen into *cothurni*. The Tutor's elaborate lie about Orestes' death is fiercely and unblushingly reeled off by Leo McKern.

(1951)

Caesar and Cleopatra, BY GEORGE BERNARD SHAW, AND *Antony and Cleopatra*, BY WILLIAM SHAKESPEARE, AT THE ST. JAMES.

Overpraise, in the end, is the most damaging kind of praise, especially if you are an actress approaching forty who has already reached the height of her powers. Who now remembers Rose Elphinstoune, of whom it was said in 1865: "Nothing can ever have moved the passions more than her Belvidera in *Venice Preserv'd*"? And in whose head does the name of lovely Lucy Mead, who in 1889 "seemed to attain a fuller greatness with each new performance," now strike a chord?

With these ladies in mind, it may be time for a sober consideration of Vivien Leigh, for whom similarly vivid claims have been made. This summer she celebrates probably the climax of her career, a climax towards which she has climbed, with unflurried industry, for many seasons past. Stoically, she has absorbed her share of ill-judged malice. "Vivien is a galvanised waxwork," gibed an old and bitter friend; and how cunning her detractors have been to point out that the flower-freshness of her face is belied by her sturdy, businesslike wrists and ankles! One cynic, biting his nails furiously, described her as being as "calculating as a slot-machine." In the face of all this her calm has been complete, and we must admire her for it.

Now, with Miss Leigh drawing the town, it is time to scrutinise her dispassionately. Fondly we recall her recent peak, when, in 1945, she held together the shaky structure of Thornton Wilder's *The Skin of Our Teeth.* She used her soul in this display; and was sweet. About this time Laurence Olivier became an actor-manager, and almost at once I felt forebodings that the lady might protest too much and cast her net wider than her special talents would permit. Sir Laurence cast Miss Leigh as Blanche in *A Streetcar Named Desire.* She accepted the responsibility, worked with Trojan intensity, and failed. After the initial shock at hearing Williams' play described by the critics as "a shallow shocker," we shut our eyes tightly and forgave Miss Leigh. This year, emboldened, she has invited the highest kind of judgment by venturing on both Shaw's and Shakespeare's Cleopatras. And several authorities have reached out for the ultimate word in the dictionary of appraisal, and found her "great."

She remains sweet. In all her gentle motions there is no hint of that attack and upheaval, that inner uproar which we, mutely admiring, call greatness; no breath of the tumultuous obsession which, against our will, consumes us. In *Caesar and Cleopatra* she keeps a firm grip on the narrow ledge which is indisputably hers; the level on which she can be pert, sly, and spankable, and fill out a small personality. She does, to the letter, what Shaw asks of his queen, and not a semi-colon more. And how obsequiously Sir Laurence seems to play along with her, never once bowing to the command that most great actors hear, the command to enlarge on the flat symbols of the text.

Antony and Cleopatra is another world. This is a leaping giant of a play which demands "greatness" of its performers and sleeps under anything less. "You were a boggler ever," says Antony at one point to his idle doxy; and one can feel Miss Leigh's imagination boggling at the thought of playing Cleopatra. Taking a deep breath and resolutely focusing her periwinkle charm, she launches another of her careful readings; ably and passionlessly she picks her way among its great challenges, presenting a glibly mown lawn where her author had imagined a jungle. Her confidence, amazingly, never flags. Once or twice in the evening the lines call for a sort of palatial sweetness; and she scents these moments and excels in them.

Yet one feeling rode over these in my mind; the feeling Mr. Bennet in *Pride and Prejudice* was experiencing when he dissuaded his daughter from further pianoforte recital by murmuring that she had "delighted us long enough." Though at times, transported by Shakespeare, she becomes almost wild, there is in Miss Leigh's Cleopatra an arresting streak of Jane Austen. She picks at the part with the daintiness of a debutante called upon to dismember a stag, and her manners are first-rate. "She plays it," as someone said, "with her little finger crooked." This Cleopatra is almost always civil.

Miss Leigh's piercing, candid blankness is superbly pretty; and for several years to come it will not be easy to refrain from wishfully equating her prettiness with greatness. Hers is the magnificent effrontery of an attractive child endlessly indulged at its first party. To play Cleopatra the appealing minx must expand and gain texture; and she puts on a low, mournful little voice (her first wrinkle) to suggest seediness. But for the outrageous, inordinate Queen of Egypt one must return, every few seconds, to the published version.

Miss Leigh's limitations have wider repercussions than those of most actresses. Sir Laurence, with that curious chivalry which some time or other blights the progress of every great actor, gives me the impression that he subdues his blow-lamp ebullience to match her. Blunting his iron precision, levelling away his towering authority, he meets her halfway. Antony climbs down; and Cleopatra pats him on the head. A cat, in fact, can do more than look at a king: she can hypnotise him.

Whenever I see Miss Leigh, an inexplicably frivolous little Rodgers-Hammerstein lyric starts to trot round my head. It goes:

> My doll is as dainty as a sparrow;
> Her figure is something to applaud;
> Where she's narrow she's as narrow as an arrow;
> And she's broad where a broad should be broad. . . .

It is a delightful song, and it gives me great pleasure. But it has nothing to do with the robes of queens; or with gravity; or with greatness.

(1951)

Richard II and *Henry IV*, Part One, by William Shakespeare, at Stratford-on-Avon.

The Shakespeare Memorial Company at Stratford has now launched *Richard II* and the first part of *Henry IV*. Together, these make up the first half of Shakespeare's tetralogy of kingliness, which is to be presented under the joint direction of Anthony Quayle, Michael Redgrave, and John Kidd. The exterior of the Memorial Theatre retains its touching pink ugliness, lapped on one side by the Avon; but inside, Quayle has made great changes, relining the auditorium to look warmer and more inviting, and erecting on the stage a permanent setting (by Tanya Moiseiwitsch) on which the full quartet of history plays will be acted—an imposing arrangement of beams, incorporating rough approximations of the balcony and inner recess of the Elizabethan stage.

Richard II has been less successful than its next of kin. This is a reclining, effeminate play where the "Henry" series are upstanding and male, and Miss Moiseiwitch's timbering is out of key with its lushness. Redgrave, still missing the real heights by an inexplicable inch, makes a fine sketch of Richard, using a shaky tenor voice, a foppish smile, and damp, uncertain eyes to summon up the poor man's instability. In the early scenes, clad in sky-blue doublet and cloak of palest orange, he looked exquisitely over-mothered, a king sculpted in puppy-fat. Alternately malicious and sentimental, Redgrave's Richard is a noble booby, sincerely envious, as well as afraid, of the power to command which is not his. It was not his fault that in the later acts and the slow hysterical slide toward death one tired of him.

There can be no hesitation about *Henry IV,* Part One; oak-beamed and clinker-built, it fits the set perfectly. Memories of Olivier's Hotspur and Richardson's Falstaff inevitably taunt us, but this is undoubtedly a much more thoughtful and balanced production than the Old Vic's. Redgrave now moves into the major key with a rawboned, shockheaded Hotspur, affecting a rasping Lowlands brogue to account for the references to Harry Percy's thickness of speech; and at least three of the best six English juveniles crop up around him. Alan Badel, the intemperately exciting flyweight whose Fool partnered John Gielgud's Lear last year, plays the tiny part of Poins with fastidious distinction; Duncan Lamont, a sour young actor with a swarthy voice, finds a complete character, glowering and long-sighted, in the involved complottings of Worcester; and, finally, a shrewd Welsh boy shines out with greatness—the first this year.

I am speaking of Richard Burton, whom New York saw last fall in Gielgud's *The Lady's Not for Burning.* His playing of Prince Hal turned interested speculation to awe almost as soon as he started to speak; in the first intermission the local critics stood agape in the lobbies. Burton is a still, brimming pool, running disturbingly deep; at twenty-five he commands repose and can make silence garrulous. His Prince Hal is never a roaring boy; he sits, hunched or sprawled, with dark unwinking eyes; he hopes to be amused by his bully companions, but the eyes constantly muse beyond them into the time when he must steady himself for the crown. "He brings his cathedral on with him," said one dazed member of the company. For all his bold chivalry, this watchful Celt seems surely to have strayed from a wayside pulpit. Fluent and sparing of gesture, compact and spruce of build, Burton smiles where other Hals have guffawed; relaxes where they have strained; and Falstaff (played with affectionate obesity by Anthony Quayle) must work hard to divert him. In battle, Burton's voice cuts urgent and keen—always likeable, always inaccessible. If he can sustain and vary this performance through to the end of *Henry V,* we can safely send him along to swell the thin company of living actors who have shown us the mystery and the power of which heroes are capable.

(1951)

His House in Order, BY ARTHUR WING PINERO, AT THE NEW THEATRE.

A young wife, made to feel an intruder in her new surroundings—there are few more rewarding situations. We saw it last in Daphne du Maurier's *Rebecca;* but I cannot promise that *His House in Order* will appeal to quite the same audience. Pinero, writing in an atmosphere thick with Ibsen and with Shaw's didactic drama criticism, concentrates on the ethical implications of the theme with an intensity which lovers of melodrama may refuse to stomach.

Nina, Filmer Jesson's second wife, had entered his house as a governess. His first wife had been a paragon; and her insufferable family now misses no chance to express its resentment that he should have replaced her with one whom they consider a skittish upstart. The discovery of some letters proving that, for seven years before her death, Jesson's paragon had been unfaithful to him puts Nina in a commanding position; and Pinero poses his problem: should she reveal their contents or, by a mighty effort of charity, burn them?

It is a moral as well as a dramatic question, and Pinero, possibly remembering Shaw's homilies about the baseness of sacrificing a conviction in favour of a strong third-act curtain, answers it morally. One of his "dear good old fellows," a sympathetic observer, tries to persuade Nina to conceal her findings. At this point Pinero forgets Ibsen, and dates himself. The action is at its climax; and what reasons does the "good old fellow" propound to restrain Nina's natural impulse to brandish her discovery in the face of the pious snobs who have slighted her? He says that, by holding back, she will join those "people walking the earth who are wearing a halo . . . the people who have made sacrifices." He appeals, in fact, to a nauseating kind of spiritual pride; and Nina succumbs. Whereas your Ibsen counterpart would have said: "Tell him: never mind about his illusions: meet him face to face"; and there would have been a tragic fourth act.

What actually follows is a fascinating compromise, which I conjure you to go and find out. Pinero is so astute a plot-mender that, unless you read the play last week, you will have forgotten. And his flair for summing up a situation in a single piece of stagecraft never deserts him. John Worthing's entrance in mourning in *The Importance of Being Earnest* is not more brilliantly timed than Nina's appearance in flaming pink on the anniversary of her predecessor's death.

Like so many plays by dramatists renowned for their "craftsmanship," this one hinges on a supreme improbability. Nina's stepson, who stumbles on the dusty reticule which contains the incriminating letters, is unable to unfasten the catch; she herself has it open within two minutes. The entire action, one afterwards reflects, depends on the clip of that implausible handbag.

The present performance is good enough to throw a cloak over this central failing. Mary Kerridge brings Nina to life with a desperate impetuousness that never founders in pathos; Sebastian Shaw's nervous urbanity is exactly right for her pompous and fastidious husband—though whether their marriage can ever be more than Mr. Eliot's "best of a bad job" is a matter on which Pinero leaves us in doubt. Godfrey Tearle, as the counsellor-friend, cements the play together; this actor, with his resolute prow of a chin and brave, commiserating eyes, is one of the few who can unfailingly command something like awe. His voice is a moral instrument—a precious attribute for which English drama since the advent of Coward has found less and less use.

(1951)

Othello, by William Shakespeare, at the St. James'.

No doubt about it, Orson Welles has the courage of his restrictions. In last night's boldly staged *Othello* he gave a performance brave and glorious to the eye; but it was the performance of a magnificent amateur. I say this carefully, for I am young enough to have been brought up on rumour of his name, and I sat in my stall conscious that, in a sense, a whole generation was on trial. If Welles was wrong, if a contemporary approach to Shakespeare in his thunderbolt hands failed, then we were all wrong.

What we saw was a tightly limited acting performance in a bound-bursting production. Welles the producer gave us a new vista (based on five permanent golden pillars) for every scene; he used a russet traverse-curtain to wipe away each setting in the same manner that the films would use a dissolve; he sprinkled the action with some striking background music and realistic recordings—in fact, he sacrificed much to give us a *credible* reading of a play which bristles with illogicalities. The presentation was visually flawless—Cassio's drunk scene became a vivid blaze of mutiny, and the killing of Desdemona, with crimson awnings over a white couch, and a high rostrum towering behind, can never have looked more splendid. The St. James's stage seemed as big as a field.

Welles' own performance was a huge shrug. He was grand and gross, and wore some garish costumes superbly. His close-cropped head was starkly military, and he never looked in need of a banjo. But his voice, a musical instrument in one bass octave, lacked range; he toyed moodily with every inflection. His face expressed wryness and strangulation, but little else. And his bodily relaxation frequently verged on sloth. Above all, he never built to a vocal climax: he positively waded through the great speeches, pausing before the key words like a landing-craft breasting a swell. (When dead, his chest went on heaving like the North Sea.) Welles' Othello is the lordly and mannered performance we saw in *Citizen Kane,* slightly adapted to read "Citizen Coon."

I think of Othello as a theatrical bullfight, in which the hero is a noble bull, repeatedly charging the handkerchief in the wristy grip of Iago, the dominating matador. Peter Finch gave us none of this. His Iago is a clipped starveling, puny and humourless, pared to the bone. One can accept a charmless Iago, but a bantam-weight is unforgivable. However, Mr. Finch seemed a little cowed, both by Mr. Welles and the first-nighters, and he will surely improve.

(1951)

Héloïse, BY JAMES FORSYTH, AT THE DUKE OF YORK'S.

I was in some doubt, when the curtain fell, whether I should surrender to rage or compromise on boredom. I knew before I entered the theatre that it would take a master to carve drama out of the strenuous subtleties of twelfth-century theology, and I was ready, too, for a good many over-simplifications about the intransigence of the Catholic Church. I came, then, prepared. Yet within an hour the dykes had burst, and a sort of enraged *ennui* possessed my soul.

Mr. Forsyth justifiably interprets the tale of Héloïse and Abelard as symbolic of the conflict between "blind faith" and rational belief. His cardinal error—perhaps not so much an error as an incapacity—is to have endowed both the lovers with a crushing generic banality which at once stifles any interest we might have taken in what happens to their minds and hearts. Their love scenes kept reminding me of the *aperçu* about Jane Welsh and Thomas Carlyle, that it was as well they married each other, since that meant two unhappy people in the world instead of four. Mr. Forsyth engineers a nocturnal tryst for them by having Abelard awaken Héloïse by knocking something over, and, once they are together, the poetry begins to stand out rather like a vein on one's forehead. Their rapture smells of old, unopened rooms. Abelard crowns one climax of ardour with the remark: "I ask myself—'Whither dogma?' " I found myself repeating Tranio's admonition to Lucentio:

> Let's be no Stoics, nor no stocks, I pray,
> Or so devote to Aristotle's checks
> As Ovid be an outcast quite abjur'd.

But to no purpose. Abelard was duly maimed offstage at the command of Fulbert, here played as a church mouse, and I felt no more regret than when a senile ox goes under the pole-axe. Mr. Forsyth quite fails to engage our compassion for the couple in their subsequent trials, not the least of which is the strain of swimming against a stream of dialogue with the texture of glue. "They have tracked us down like rats in a ship," says Abelard, somewhat loosely; and when, in the final scene, he sums up his entire predicament in the line: "I am utterly weary of this world, and physically I am not well," it is as if Lear, in the fifth act, should come to and demand an aspirin. The play is almost done when Abelard's confidant, having listened in silence to the music of an itinerant minstrel, turns to his drooping friend and says affectionately: "It's your song."

It is usual at this point, when dealing with a new play, to begin one's next paragraph with: "But Mr. So-and-so can certainly write." I am afraid the present evidence denies Mr. Forsyth even that consolation. I commend to his attention the several plays written in the tenth century by Hroswitha, Abbess of Gandersheim. They are as mediaeval as heart could wish, and they have much to teach him in the way of pith, emphasis, and attack.

In such a trap the actors can do little. Siobhan McKenna, flinty of mien, offers a pinched Héloïse which, in its pallor and intensity, recalls the spooky lady in Charles Addams' drawings. Walter Macken invests Abelard with a soft Celtic piety, as soothing and as antiseptic as a bandage. Mervyn Johns, hopefully miscast as Fulbert, is unable to do much more than fuss with a part that culminates in his maniacal exit, shrieking: "The thing, Hugo! The thing!" The direction, by Michael Powell, has a sepulchral reverence of its own, and bears traces of the film studio in that it seemed to be taking a whole working day to get through four minutes of action.

(1951)

The Clandestine Marriage, BY GEORGE COLMAN AND DAVID GARRICK, AT THE OLD VIC.

This plain, brisk, and noisily actable Garrick-Colman comedy is at bottom a comment on *arrivisme*. The penniless Lovewell has secretly married the moneyed Fanny, whose father, a City merchant, wants to buy her a title in exchange for a dowry. By an intricate misunderstanding Lord Ogleby, a senescent rake, is led to believe that he is Fanny's beloved: finally, after headlong nocturnal to-and-froing, love triumphs over the social-profit motive.

The odd thing about the Old Vic production is, in two words, Donald Wolfit; not so much his presence in it as his position. Mr. Wolfit, an actor of the boldly self-made sort, whose skill in playing upstarts is unrivalled in our time, is cast as Lord Ogleby, the senior aristocrat of the whole entertainment. Well, Georges Dandin wanted it; so, it seems, does the Old Vic; and Mr. Wolfit is thus faced with a task akin to that of a craftsman who should be called upon to carve a Sheraton *escritoire* out of Sherwood oak.

The other performances are, in the main, cast strictly to type, and Mr. Wolfit's obtrudes like a pantomime dame in the chorus of a musical comedy. The authors envisaged Ogleby as a flimsy, dew-lapped ruin of a man; Wolfit is as staunch and foursquare as an Olympic wrestler, and what he achieves is a tremendous display of sheer toil, a triumph of art over nature, in which the actor tests all the resources of his paint-box, and coaxes his lordly voice to assume slippery and importunate eld by simulating the whine of a rusty gate-hinge. Possessing not one of the qualities, physical or temperamental, of the part (which have been all but patented by Messrs. Ernest Milton and Ernest Thesiger), he attacks it with the knockdown aplomb that Grimaldi, one imagines, might have brought to Coriolanus. Mr. Wolfit is an actor with a comedian's face and a tragedian's soul, and for this reason nearly always looks mysteriously miscast. He bears his present burden superbly, and rarely groans under it; but the result is a Dickensian pantaloon, not a Garrickian fop.

(1951)

King Lear, BY WILLIAM SHAKESPEARE, AT THE OLD VIC.

This huge, flawed pyramid of a play has a way of collapsing under mere competence. Its *sine qua non* is a Lear who can blast to the mountain's heart and make it volcanic. The present Old Vic production, I am afraid, is disqualified from the start.

There is also a multitude of lesser disqualifications. Hugh Hunt, the director, has kept the action chained to a slow trudge, and very few members of his cast seem vocally capable of competing with the continuous roar of the Old Vic's ventilation system. A whole gamut of inaudibility is painstakingly run, from perfunctory shrieks and grunts to sheer bellows; quite often, listening to Stephen Murray's Lear was like lip-reading Shakespeare by flashes of lightning. Many of the minor characters, notably Ernest Hare's Albany, are bewilderingly miscast. Lee Montague's Edmund is pure butcher-boy, reminiscent of nothing so much as Aubrey's absurd *vignette* of Shakespeare's recitations over the carcasses in the Stratford slaughter-house. John Phillips' Gloucester, stoically resonant, comes off more happily; but the clearest, as well as the most audible, performance is Coral Browne's flamboyant Regan, which is played in this actress' best "Scarlet Empress" vein.

The basic fault of Mr. Murray's Lear is that the actor lacks weight to balance the scales which Shakespeare has loaded so heavily against him. Lear appears in only three of the last eleven scenes, but we must hold him always in mind if we are to forgive the extended clumsiness of the Edmund love-plot. Mr. Murray is unable to bridge this gap, and when he pottered back for the Dover mad scene, my memory of him had blurred almost out of recognition. Another and greater obstacle to the actor is Shakespeare's decision to impose a tragic ending on a story which in every other version (including that in *The Faerie Queene*) had ended happily. Lear comes to die on a stage already corpse-strewn, and must make his death different in kind, wiser and larger than the rest. Here, too, Mr. Murray falls short, becoming just another victim.

Though he ransacks his lungs, drawing speech out as if from a deep well, Mr. Murray lacks breath for the part. The "serpent's tooth" tirade was the first proof of this: he took it laboriously, like a man striding through a swamp. Physically unfitted to take the big speeches by storm, he tries instead to encircle them, as it were, with the spies of his intelligence: a method which is well enough for the smaller things, such as the prose scene with the disgusted Kent, but which will not do for "Howl, howl, howl, howl!" Mr. Murray's performance is a carefully studied picture of senility, based on the fallacy that it is possible to characterise an Alp. In the last act, where Shakespeare calls relentlessly for an Ancient of Days, Mr. Murray gave us Old Moore.

Reece Pemberton's principal setting is a landscape of ragged rocks, and his costumes seem to derive from Tartary, being all fur and feathers. I imagine the inspiration here was Lear's "Robes and furr'd gowns hide all." Alas for the Old Vic, there is much in this production that cannot be covered up.

(1952)

The Deep Blue Sea, BY TERENCE RATTIGAN, AT THE DUCHESS.

Terence Rattigan's new play is a searing study of the destructive zeal of love. It has already been acclaimed as "brilliant theatre," but there is a patronising ring to the phrase which I must set about demolishing. It implies that for a play to suit the theatre is not quite enough; that it is somehow improper to write deliberately for the medium you have selected—not print, not pure sound, but for an upturned host of credulous faces in a darkened hall. *The Deep Blue Sea,* for its first two acts, is a masterly piece of work, and I went out exulting into the second interval, persuaded that I was seeing the most striking new play I could remember, and delighted at having divined a heart-pricking strength of purpose with which I had never before credited Mr. Rattigan.

The play opens with the discovery of a gassed woman whose intended suicide has been foiled by the expiry of the shilling in the meter. And it invites us to piece a jigsaw together, to explore why she wanted to die, to rebuild her past; and by withholding this information until it tells most—by, in fact, beginning his action where most plays of the sort would end—Mr. Rattigan keys us up almost to exploding point. Piece by piece, with seeming idleness, he presents the facts to us. She had left her husband and taken a lover, a clumsy, graceless, but boyishly desirable oaf, of whom she has made possessive demands that he is incapable of meeting. Apprised of her suicide attempt, and appalled by it, he walks out on her; and we leave her, at the second-act curtain, pleading riotously and without shame for him to stay.

I shall never forgive Mr. Rattigan for his last act. It is intolerable: his brilliance lays an ambush for itself, and walks straight into it. If his heroine kills herself, he will merely be repeating the pattern, so he decides to let her live. But he has stated the case for her death so pungently that he cannot argue her out of the impasse without forfeiting our respect. He ekes out ingeniously, lecturing her about the necessity of sublimating her impulses in painting and going to a good Art School. Dishonestly, he makes her insist that she does not *deserve* to live, thus hauling in all kinds of moral implications which are totally irrelevant, since her point was purely that she could not *bear* to live. When, finally, she chooses survival, it is for all the wrong reasons.

The Deep Blue Sea remains the most absorbing new English play for many seasons. And it contains something which no English playwright (save Shaw in *Saint Joan*) has provided since Pinero—a long, straight, emotional part for a young woman. Peggy Ashcroft plays it superbly, as she should, for it is analogous in shape to that of *The Heiress:* deserted by her lover at the end of Act II, she rejects love itself at the end of Act III. And in Kenneth More, who plays her fumbling barfly bedfellow, we have acquired an actor who may become our best retort to Marlon Brando, with the same doubting proviso: can he do anything else?

(1952)

Winter Journey, BY CLIFFORD ODETS, AT THE ST. JAMES'.

"Quite unimportant," said one of my colleagues of this play; and I am sick at heart that no one has thus far ambushed and cudgelled him for a critique so recklessly encapsulated. Mr. Odets' sin, I suppose, is to have written a play that could be described as "sheer theatre"—which is to say, it has a compelling reality within its chosen medium, and does not care to invade the debating-chamber, the library, or the church. And so, by an exercise of sophistry similar to that by which indolent essayists, impatiently discussing an unfamiliar poet, resort to dubbing him "a mere versifier," several popular critics have accepted Mr. Odets' skill in hitting his target as *prima-facie* evidence that his talent is second-rate. I cannot conceive why. "Sheer theatre" (applied disparagingly to Mr. Odets, M. Rostand, and Mr. Rattigan) will hereafter rank in my mind with "How well these old craftsmen knew their jobs!" (applied panegyrically to Pinero or Ibsen) as a moribund cliché beloved of intellectual laziness. The primary business of the theatre is to be theatrical; and I refuse to countenance the argument that a play is unimportant simply because it leaves you nothing to discuss in the intervals. *Winter Journey* (or *The Country Girl,* as it was called on Broadway) is intended not to start you talking, but to *stop* you talking.

It remains well worth talking about. Mr. Odets offers us what amounts to an Ibsenite thesis. A middle-aged actor, after long and willing enslavement to alcohol, is summoned from retirement to play a leading part; we meet his wife, an inscrutable creature who, having devoted herself for a decade to the job of keeping his illusions alive, has become cynically aware of the fact that her principal value to him is as an excuse for his failure. The director of the play for which he is engaged, a spiky and intimidating young idealist, instantly decides that she is the cause of her husband's labefaction; that her apron-strings have strangled him; and his wanton but well-meaning irruption into the actor's domestic life precipitates (as Ibsenites will have guessed) a new, desperate dive into the bottle, after which the play's opening night is all but wrecked. By now both we and the director have realised that the wife is no sorceress, but rather a scapegoat for her husband's infirmity, as well as something of a martyr. Mr. Odets' climax—the Broadway first night—I will not reveal, beyond suggesting that his introduction of an additional theme—the director's love for the wife—is ill-prepared and hangs from the play's body with the irrelevance of a donkey's tail pinned to a fighting bull. Even so, the conclusion, that redemption is a compromise which no amount of idealism can achieve unaided, comes across with unimpaired pungency and passion.

The casting is most imaginative. Michael Redgrave must be as delighted as I am with his playing of the mercurial bibber; it is the best serious performance he has given us for years. Mr. Redgrave has been passing through what his biographers will probably call "a dark period," lapsing often into a semaphoring, half-articulate style of playing which one might call algebraic, and which led him, last year at Stratford, almost to *grope* through his parts in a distracted, unavailing attempt to communicate nuance. Eyes bulging, arms windmilling, he gave the impression of being possessed by an adhesive demon that was fiercely resisting exorcism; it was sometimes as if another man's soul were speaking, ventriloquially, through his reluctant jaws. He seemed, like Coleridge, to be beset by a mixture of hyper-sensitivity and insecurity which was numbing his powers of direct statement.

Frank Elgin, the drunk in Mr. Odets' play, is just such a performer; and in playing him Mr. Redgrave purges himself. "You are not a technical actor," says the director (played by Sam Wanamaker), and Mr. Redgrave, taking a hint from this true word, battles before our eyes to free himself of the technical preoccupations that have been disfiguring his work. He bounds out of his corner, like a recently defeated heavyweight, fighting, lunging, swinging, and counter-punching; but with a revived authority and victory in his eye, for the uncertainties that are Frank Elgin's enemies are Mr. Redgrave's, too. The ensuing duel is convulsive, sudorific, and extremely moving, and the verdict is triumph. Temperamentally, Frank Elgin is a retarded boy, chronically overmothered, and in this aspect of male psychology Mr. Redgrave is deeply versed, as his performance four years ago in Strindberg's *The Father* bore witness. In short, this part is Mr. Redgrave's special pasture; and, the furrow having been ploughed, the transition made, we look to him never to flag again.

Beady-eyed and black-cropped, tautly ironic and especially brilliant in scorn, the young director demands the epithet "combustible." Mr. Wanamaker is downright dangerous. He enjoys smouldering, and when smouldering is not enough, he throws things—among them a medicine bottle, several articles of clothing, and a hail of half-smoked cigarettes. If there is nothing portable to hand, Mr. Wanamaker, profoundly stirred, hits himself on the forehead with a painful and audible smack. This is a most impressive piece of acting. The character itself is fascinating; this director treats his actors in the Buchmanite-cum-revivalist manner popularised by the American Group Theatre, and is satisfied that they have grasped an idea only when one of them is sufficiently moved to hurl a chair halfway across the stage. Mr. Wanamaker pads ferally through the debris, wearing that neurotic, almost poetic look which goes, in America, with acute sinus trouble.

Googie Withers, shiny and bespectacled, gives a blisteringly frank and unchivalrous performance as the actor's wife, whose fundamental loyalty has been ravaged by the frustration of too many dead years. She completes one of the most striking trios I have ever watched on a London stage. Add to this some unassuming and cleverly lit settings by Anthony Holland, and you have what seems to me (and, I hope, to Mr. Wanamaker, who directed the play) quite an important evening in the English theatre.

(1952)

The Dragon's Mouth, BY J. B. PRIESTLEY AND JACQUETTA HAWKES, AT THE WINTER GARDEN.

The Dragon's Mouth, the new foursome reel by J. B. Priestley and Jacquetta Hawkes, is a kind of morality play. Mr. Priestley is not quite accurate in describing it as a return "to the oldest traditions of the drama"; what he has done is to return to the mediaeval morality at precisely the point when it began to die—the point at which it had developed into an interminable debate between moral abstractions. We meet four types—aesthete, materialist, sensualist, and moralist—trapped aboard a plague-stricken yacht in the Caribbean. Ashore, blood samples from each of them are being analysed; and while they await the results of the test the four becalmed souls discuss their respective reasons for living or dying.

Mr. Priestley has hardly bothered to stage his debate: he lines the quartet up in front of microphones and lets us concentrate on the argument. Now, argument for its own sake is only tolerable if one can smoke, drink, nibble at something, or participate—or, exceptionally, when all the participants are men of genius. But when smoking is forbidden and the debaters are cross-sections rather than individuals, argument loses its charm. It ceases, in fact, to be fun; and all drama, no matter how deeply it may later explore the heart-recesses, must first of all be fun to watch.

The Dragon's Mouth should not be compared too closely with the Charles Laughton production of *Don Juan in Hell,* which inspired it. Laughton's experiment had the fascination of a gala charity matinée, since it brought together, on the same stage, Charles Boyer, Cedric Hardwicke, Agnes Moorehead, and the director himself. *The Dragon's Mouth* brings together Michael Denison, Dulcie Gray, Rosamund John, and Norman Wooland, and I beg you not to look at me like that: I am simply suggesting that this is not the most sharply contrasting quartet in existence. There was a moment in which I caught myself echoing Groucho Marx and speculating whether I was looking at four actors with one microphone or one actor with four microphones. When the play ended, I foregathered with three friends, and together, to redress the balance of talk, we sat in total silence for two hours and felt much better.

Mr. Denison, as the arid and tormented aesthete, comes off best; and Miss Gray, savagely miscast as the toast of three continents, tells one intensely exciting anecdote about a seagull. In fact, I had better reveal, furious as I am at having to do so, that *The Dragon's Mouth* contains several flights of the best rhetorical prose I have lately heard on the stage. But make no mistake: Mr. Priestley and Miss Hawkes are misusing the tools of drama, and the logical end of their method would be to distribute scripts to the audience and never to take the curtain up at all. In short, anyone wanting to get away from the theatre for an evening should make straight for the Winter Garden.

(1952)

Timon of Athens, BY WILLIAM SHAKESPEARE, AT THE OLD VIC.

Watching *Timon* was, I found, rather like going to some scandalously sophisticated party at which, halfway through, the host suddenly falls down drunk and begins to rave from under the piano. It starts superbly, a glittering and rapacious satire on big fleas and the little fleas that bite them, and Tyrone Guthrie's clamorous production gallops breakneck to emphasise the luridity of it all, silhouetting Timon's midget pick-thank toadies against the gilded background of his feasts and pomps. Rightly and unsentimentally, he never lets us overlook the upstart element in Timon's too genial distributions of largesse; rightly, too, he abandons all pretence that Shakespeare's Athens has any connection with the town whose walls Isocrates saved from ruin bare. Mr. Guthrie sets us firmly down in Ben Jonson territory, and the senators come mumbling on like a shady conclave of corrupt borough councillors. All this is modern in the best sense.

What follows, of course, is modern in other, less amiable ways. The berserk jeremiads with which Timon responds to the desertion of his erstwhile cronies; his sick and shapeless railings at man's ingratitude—these have a personal, compulsive note in them, a note struck in many of the plays, from *Titus Andronicus* to *Lear,* but elsewhere relieved by grace-notes from other keys. In *Timon,* as we would churlishly put it, the needle seems to have stuck. Admittedly, as Landor conceded of *Paradise Regained,* muscles sometimes stand out from the vast mass of the collapsed; there are moments of wintry, leafless poetry which eat into the mind; and there is a situation of supreme irony when Timon, having banished himself to the wilderness, stumbles in his cave across a cache of gold—the mineral of his whole undoing. But an unhinged hero can, and here does, unhinge an entire play: the final door will not shut, and the conclusion is botched, hasty, and somehow ashamed.

Mr. Guthrie's brilliance in the first half looked like extending itself well into the second, until Andre Morell's Timon laid it low. As the Poet (I do not, of course, mean Shakespeare) says in Act I:

No levell'd malice
Infects one comma in the course I hold

—but I must hold it long enough to insist that Mr. Morell, a sturdy and disarming actor, has nothing like the power and range demanded by Timon's disjointed miseries. Bay though he might, like some locked-out Alsatian, he could not command my sympathy nor even, at the end, my interest. Mr. Morell's eyes seem unable to focus on us; and his voice too lacks grip, being not a little butlerish, and possessed of a hollow, muffled timbre, as if toothache had forced him to thrust cotton-wool into his cheeks. Many lesser things, however, are finely done, among them Leo McKern's squat and spiky Apemantus and John Phillips' robustly effeminate cartoon of a senator. All in all, this is the completest evening the Vic has given us since *Tamburlaine.*

This being a play loaded with references to sums of money, may I add how helpful it would be if the programme were to give some hint of the current exchange-rate in crowns, ducats, and talents? It is much easier, for instance, to form an opinion of a man who owes five talents when you know whether he needs, to restore his credit, a thousand pounds or eight and sixpence. Few bank-managers in the audience, for instance, would be likely to trust a man who owed only eight and sixpence.

(1952)

Macbeth, BY WILLIAM SHAKESPEARE, AT STRATFORD-ON-AVON.

Last Tuesday night at the Stratford Memorial Theatre *Macbeth* walked the plank, leaving me, I am afraid, unmoved to the point of paralysis. It was John Gielgud, never let us forget, who did this cryptic thing; Gielgud, as director, who seems to have imagined that Ralph Richardson, with his comic, Robeyesque cheese-face, was equipped to play Macbeth; Gielgud who surrounded the play's fuliginous cruelties with settings of total black, which is about as subtle as setting Saint Joan in total white; Gielgud who commanded dirty tatters for Macbeth's army and brisk, clean tunics for Malcolm's, just to indicate in advance who was going to win. The production assumed, or so I took it, that the audience was either moronic or asleep; it read us a heavily italicised lecture on the play, and left nothing to our own small powers of discovery.

When, in the banquet scene, a real table and some real chairs, chalices, and candelabra were brought on, life intervened for a moment; but once the furniture had gone, we were back in the engulfing, the platitudinous void, with its single message: "Background of evil, get it?" The point about Macbeth is that the murders in it should horrify us; against Mr. Gielgud's sable scenery they looked as casual as crochet-work.

In the banquet scene, spurred perhaps by the clever handling of Banquo's ghost, which vanished dazzlingly in one swirl of a cloak, Richardson came to life for several consecutive sentences, and I could not help recalling a line he had uttered earlier in the evening: "My dull brain was wrought with things forgotten." Up to this point he had appeared a robot player, a man long past feeling, who had been stumping across the broad stage as if in need of a compass to find the exit. Now, momentarily, he smouldered and made us recall his excelling past, littered with fine things encompassed and performed. And then, and ever after, Sir Ralph's numbness, his apparent mental deafness, returned to chill me: Macbeth became once more a sad facsimile of the Cowardly Lion in *The Wizard of Oz.* At the height of the battle, you remember, Macbeth contemplates suicide, rejecting the thought in the words: "Why should I play the Roman fool, and die on mine own sword?" Sir Ralph, at this juncture, gripped his blade by the sharp end with both hands and practised putts with it; it was as if the Roman fool has been the local pro.

His feathery, yeasty voice, with its single spring-heeled inflection, starved the part of its richness; he moved dully, as if by numbers, and such charm as he possessed was merely a sort of unfocused bluffness, like a teddy-bear snapped in a bad light by a child holding its first camera. Sir Ralph, who seems to me to have become the glass eye in the forehead of English acting, has now bumped into something quite immovable. His Macbeth is slovenly; and to go further into it would be as frustrating as trying to write with a pencil whose point has long since worn down to the wood.

Sleep-walking, which appeared to be this Macbeth's natural condition, had an unexpectedly tonic effect on his lady. Margaret Leighton seized her big solo opportunity, waking up to give us a gaunt, pasty, compulsive reading of the scene which atoned for many of her earlier inadequacies. But two things are required for an effective Lady Macbeth: first, a husband off whom she can strike sparks—and it would be easier to strike sparks off a rubber dinghy than Sir Ralph. Second, she needs to be sexless; Macbeth is unique among the tragedies in that none of the leading characters ever mentions sexuality. Lady Macbeth is painted granite, and to cast a woman as attractive as Miss Leighton in the part is like casting a gazelle as Medusa. In fact, it is probably a mistake to cast a woman at all, since Lady Macbeth offers none of the openings for nostalgia, yearning, and haggard glamour which attach to every other great female part, from Cleopatra to Blanche DuBois. No, Lady Macbeth is basically a man's role, and none of Miss Leighton's sibilant sulks could convince me otherwise.

Now what to praise? Kenneth Rowell's sculptural costumes, which sat well on everyone save, unaccountably, Sir Ralph; Siobhan McKenna's patient Lady Macduff; and the attack, if nothing else, of Laurence Harvey's Malcolm. And that will have to do. The theatre which gave us, last year, so many pretty lessons in Shakespearean acting and production seems, for the time being, to have unlearned them all.

(1952)

The Millionairess, BY GEORGE BERNARD SHAW, AT THE HIPPODROME, COVENTRY.

There have been no new plays this week. A prickly calm, of the kind that precedes summer lightning, has left my playgoing in the doldrums. And so, if you will bear with me, I propose to reminisce. I want to write about something which carried me away like a rocket when I saw it—five weeks ago—at the Hippodrome Theatre, Coventry. It was a play called *The Millionairess;* Katharine Hepburn was playing in it; and, by a happy coincidence, it is opening at the New Theatre tonight.

The Millionairess, as everyone knows, was written by Shaw in 1936 for Edith Evans, but it has never been performed in the West End. And no great wonder, because it is almost without wit, and contains hardly any of those somersaulting paradoxes with which, for so long, Shaw concealed from us the more basic gaps in his knowledge of human behaviour. It is that terrible hybrid, a didactic farce; in it Shaw is grinding an axe, but the sparks refuse to fly. The characters talk interminably, infectiously, and almost interchangeably. It is not even outrageous—nobody, watching it, would ever nudge his neighbour and whisper: "Whatever will he say *next?*" which is the correct response to most Shavian wit. In *The Millionairess,* written in the twilight of a civilisation and of its author's life, the old dexterity and assurance have given place to a querulous fumbling; the dialogue is twice as noisy as Shaw's best, and roughly half as effective.

Its heroine, a steel girder in the play's house of cards, is Epifania

Ognisanti di Parerga, who has inherited from her father £30,000,000 and one piece of advice: she must not marry until she finds a man who can turn £150 into £50,000 within six months. Alastair Fitzfassenden, a mindless athlete, unexpectedly performs the feat, and is duly swallowed up. Tiring of him, Epifania takes to running around with a middle-aged incompetent named Adrian Blenderbland, whose leg, in one of her saucier tantrums, she breaks. At length, still fretful, she meets an eerie Egyptian doctor, who feels her pulse, falls in love with it, and challenges her to go out into the world with thirty-five shillings and earn her living for six months. Nettled, she agrees; and returns six months later to claim her prize, having amassed yet another fortune. She is, you conclude, a shrew past taming, a force beyond resisting, a rich little rich girl with a heart of bullion.

You might think, from my simplification of it, that the play is well constructed. It is nothing of the sort. Its long first act is entirely given over to the exposition of several situations that are never afterwards developed; every scene is plastered with merciless narrative speeches wherein each character tells the others what he or she has been doing while the curtain was down. And the central character is quite hateful. Epifania, described by Shaw as "a born boss," bangs through the play like a battering-ram, living at the top of her lungs, and barking orders like a games mistress run amok. There is something of a crowbar about her charm, and something, too, of a rhinoceros.

The part is nearly unactable; yet Miss Hepburn took it, acted it, and found a triumph in it. She glittered like a bracelet thrown up at the sun; she was metallic, yet reminded us that metals shine and can also melt. Epifania clove to her, and she bestowed on the role a riotous elegance and a gift of tears not of its author's imagining. Her first entrance was as if she had just emerged from the sea and were tossing the spray from her eyes; and it was not one entrance but two, for she had swept in, out, and then in again before I could blink. She used her mink wrap as Hitler is said to have used the Chancellery carpet, hurling it to the floor and falling upon it, pounding her fists in tearful vituperation.

Her voice is a rallying-call to truancy, a downright clarion; "she is," as someone once declared, "that yell—that shriek that is simultaneous with the bell ringing at school"—the bell that provokes the rush into the playground for the break. Miss Hepburn is not versatile; she is simply unique. Like most stars of real magnitude, she can do one or two of the hardest things in the world supremely well; and *The Millionairess* scores a bull's-eye on the target of her talents. It is just hard enough for her, just close enough to impossibility, and from first word to last, star and part are treading common ground. Epifania is written on one note, but it is Miss Hepburn's note, and she makes it sound like a cadenza.

As I could have predicted, she was stark, staring, and scandalously bold, alternately shooting the lines point-blank at us and brandishing them like flags; and she reached a high point in her brazen retort to somebody who inquires, in the second act, whether she throws temperaments merely to make herself interesting. "*Make* myself interesting!" she flings at him. "Man: I *am* interesting." Between outbursts she curls up, cocooned in Balmain's lovely gowns, nipping intently at her sentences with sharp weasel-teeth, relaxing. What is astonishing about her is her warmth. Her grins gleam at you; and as she shapes them, she droops the corners of her eyelids and twinkles like a fire. And in her last long speech, a defence of marriage and all the risks it implies, an urchin quaver invades the determination of her voice, and coaxes the heart. At that moment James Bailey's plushy setting disappeared from my mind, and with it everyone else on stage.

The supporting cast had done much valiant and loving work. Robert Helpmann, rakish under a tarboosh, had padded pop-eyed through the role of the Egyptian doctor and made it eloquent. Cyril Ritchard had lent a flustered dignity, like that of a goosed hen, to the nonentity Blenderbland. But they vanished then, and it was, as it had been meant to be, Miss Hepburn's night. She combines the sparkle of "Kate the Curst" with the attack of Petruchio—that "mad-brain'd rudesby, full of spleen"; she glows like a branding-iron, and marks you her willing bond-slave.

All this, of course, was at Coventry, and many weeks ago. Much may have been changed by now, and the show that arrives at the New Theatre this evening may be quite a different thing. What I have been writing about is strictly past history; but if it should happen to repeat itself, I hope only to be within sound of the cheering.

(1952)

Macbeth, BY WILLIAM SHAKESPEARE, AT THE MERMAID; *Don Juan in Hell*, BY GEORGE BERNARD SHAW, AT THE ARTS.

"If you would see a woman's weaknesses, look into the eyes of her lover" (Wisdom of the East). Now Alec Clunes is transparently in love with *Don Juan in Hell,* as is Bernard Miles with *Macbeth,* and the unfair result is that, in their respective versions of the two plays, Shaw's and Shakespeare's weaknesses are paraded with a new and quite unexpected clarity.

Let us deal first with Mr. Miles, who has opened his little Mermaid Theatre to a production of *Macbeth* spoken entirely in seventeenth-century English pronunciation. By a sad coincidence, this reconstructed dialect bears a violent likeness to Stage Rustic, with a touch of Stage Dublin; and though it helps us to understand rhymes like "heath" and "Macbeth," it does nothing at all that is beautiful. On the contrary, it constantly reminds us that when one kind of standard diction overtakes another, the supplanted dialect invariably becomes debased and thereafter unsuitable for the noblest uses. Macbeth, in fact, is expelled from the court and set down firmly in the farmyard. Balking at further innovation, Mr. Miles has engaged a professional producer, Joan Swinstead, to finish off the job begun by the scholars. Occasionally, and a little wildly, Miss Swinstead experiments: the company is encouraged to act not only on the stage, but throughout the auditorium and once in the garden beyond, and a series of processional entrances is made through a swing-door boldly labelled "Exit." But for the most part the upshot is a feebly conventional picture-stage production in which everyone is mysteriously talking like Uncle Tom Cobley.

Mr. Miles himself embraces the dialect like an old friend (which in his case it is) and goes dourly to work. His Macbeth is a rowdy, shamefaced upstart, a Mummerset Mephistopheles who rarely rises above the spiritual level of the thugs he employs. Gaudy and ostentatious, he struts like a prize rooster, vivid in scarlet and gold. All of which is absolutely faithful to the play; but the poetry, in these accents, rings false, and I realised for the first time why Shakespeare had not bothered to provide death scenes for either Macbeth or his lady. He gave one to each of his other heroes; but in the fate of the Macbeths, he must have decided, there was nothing to regret. I believe he had simply stopped liking them. and so, at the Mermaid, did I.

And now for the Arts Theatre and *Don Juan in Hell.* Like Mr. Miles, Mr. Clunes has enormous respect for his author's intentions; his production, accordingly, is wholeheartedly egocentric. The action is a debate between Don Juan, his ex-mistress Donna Anna, her father, and the Devil about the rival merits of Heaven and Hell; and the trouble with it is that all Shaw's artillery is on the side of the angels. Mr. Clunes seizes on this hint to turn the play into *Saint Juan.* He anoints the part with an overwhelming complacency, wreathed in a halo of weary smiles, and a pointblank refusal to give the Devil his due. David Bird's Satan, all fuss and bluster, is allowed no authority at all: he has only to open his mouth for Mr. Clunes to sigh, shrug, and grin at him as at a truant child. And if he patronises the Devil, Mr. Clunes positively *dandles* the other two. All this is done with a silken, non-creasing technical assurance: and the play emerges as just the outrageously lopsided affair Shaw meant it to be. Don Juan is first, and Hell nowhere.

(1952)

Quadrille, BY NOËL COWARD, AT THE PHOENIX; *The River Line*, BY CHARLES MORGAN, AT THE STRAND; *The Innocents*, BY WILLIAM ARCHIBALD, AT HER MAJESTY'S.

This autumn's comedies are wordier than ever—all festooned with verbal foliage, and no one on hand with a pruning-knife. In almost every case the tree sags groundwards. And here a footnote: all comedy is one, whether the author labels it "farcical comedy," "divertissement," or "romp." Noël Coward's *Quadrille* is described as "a romantic comedy," a phrase to beware of, since it can (and on this occasion does) mean comedy gone flabby, swollen with sentiment and tugging at heartstrings that have slackened long ago with tedium. It is also comedy predictable, comedy suspenseless, comedy that is all situation and no plot. *Quadrille* suggests Oscar Wilde rewritten on a Sunday afternoon in a rectory garden by Amanda McKittrick Ros.

It is 1873: the Marquess of Heronden has run away to the French Riviera with the wife of an American railroad tycoon. Presently their abandoned spouses follow in pursuit, discovering at the end of Act II that they are themselves in love. And that is all. When Griffith Jones (who had been playing the Marquess like a man pushing a pea up a mountain) remarked: "It's no use trying to behave as if nothing had happened," my response was automatic: "But nothing has!" The dialogue throughout has the befeathered sheen of a pheasant's neck; but it is a beheaded pheasant, with no body attached, and no power of movement.

The excuse for this monstrously over-loaded tea-trolley of a play is, of course, the presence in it of Alfred Lunt and Lynn Fontanne, who play together, as the millionaire and the marchioness, like sandpaper on diamond. Mr. Lunt comes off best, since he is not required to sound witty; shambling and guileless, he has the strength and stature of a displaced Zeus. Only his big speech made me cross—a sort of travelogue commentary on the United States that might more appropriately have been set to the tune of "God Bless America." Miss Fontanne, at his side, performs with the crackle and sheen of a new five-pound note; given one sprig of verbal wit to adorn it, this would have been a gorgeous bouquet. Mr. Coward apart, I would nominate Cecil Beaton as the principal culprit in the evening's shame. His costumes and settings reach a standard of elegance so impossibly high that even Oscar Wilde, amid such splendour, would sound lumpishly provincial.

Charles Morgan, being primarily a novelist, is professionally wordy: which is to say that for him to write a play is an effort of compression, not (as so often) of expansion. *The River Line,* his latest, is highbrowism at something like its best, if you accept Virginia Woolf's definition of a highbrow as "a man or woman of thoroughbred intelligence galloping across open country in pursuit of an idea." Three wartime colleagues—a young American, a naval commander, and the latter's French wife—meet again in 1947. They share a common guilt: their lives first intertwined on "the river line," an escape route through France for allied P.O.W's, one of whom—a tall, poetic major nicknamed "Heron"—they killed on suspicion of treachery. In Act II we flash back to the events leading up to his death, and in the last act we discover that he was innocent. More, we learn that the girl whom the American hopes to marry is the dead man's half-sister. Can the brusque, informal savagery of war ever find, in peace, forgiveness? That is the play's problem.

Mr. Morgan solves it in his own remote way, speaking of moral responsibility and the like as if they were dead friends on whom he was conducting a post-mortem. And if you catch a thick, oppressive smell in the air, a trace of embalming fluid, that is all part of the Morgan method: it is the price we pay for the pleasure of hearing him speak, a groping prophet, about "interior grace" and that "creative pause" without which life cannot be more than a bloodstained hurry. The trouble is that Mr. Morgan never sheds his prophet's robes. He cannot unbend even when his characters are discussing dinner or the weather. He avoids direct statements like a saint avoiding Satan. Where other playwrights would say: "What are you looking for?" Mr. Morgan says: "What are you searching for so diligently?" I have heard this dubbed "stylish," but it is really a form of sentimentalism—the thought is burdened with an intensity it cannot support. If Morgan were only less of a master, *The River Line* might be more of a masterpiece. For all its hesitant pomp and ornate ambiguities, however, it is incontestably the finest new play since *The Deep Blue Sea.* Pamela Brown, Virginia McKenna, and, above all, the sweetly eccentric Paul Scofield (a Scofield crew-cut and nasal, of all unlikely sights and sounds!) people it impeccably.

The most wholeheartedly *theatrical* of the recent arrivals is *The Innocents.* This is Henry James' *Turn of the Screw,* transmuted by William Archibald, the adaptor, and Peter Glenville, the director, into a bestial dramatic exercise in artificial fright. "Arresting" is a word critics adore, but at *The Innocents* I was genuinely arrested; I felt the unseen hand on my shoulder, like the man in the story who reached out for the matches in the middle of the night and felt them put into his hand.

The curtain unveils the hall of a country house seventy years back. It is grim and vasty, washed by a pale yellow light that filters through gigantic windows. A new governess is expected for the two children who inhabit it; it is her first job, and when she arrives (played, a little too old for credulity, by Flora Robson), we share her discovery that both the boy and his sister are in constant and intimate contact with evil. We sit, with her, on the tongue of the mouth of hell. The sense of evil is oddly behaved: it can strike you in the silence of an aquarium, in the high corners of an empty room before dawn, and even in Madame Tussaud's. In *The Innocents* you are made to feel it in children. And what performances Jeremy Spenser and Carol Wolveridge are giving! In their dwarf antics you feel something like the chill of watching puppets throw off their strings and beckon to you. *The Innocents* is not the profoundest nor the subtlest play in London, but it is by far the most physically exciting.

(1952)

Romeo and Juliet, BY WILLIAM SHAKESPEARE, AT THE OLD VIC.

I am told that Claire Bloom's performance in the Old Vic's *Romeo and Juliet* is a failure because Miss Bloom ignores the poetry. They say she loses all the music of the verse. To which I can only reply by exposing this alleged defect for the virtue it really is. Let me start by burning my boats and declaring that this is the best Juliet I have ever seen.

"Word-music" is a great maker of reputations. Give an actress a round, resonant voice and a long Shakespearean part, and she will have to enter smoking a pipe to avoid being acclaimed. And everyone will forget (a) that the same voice could turn last year's Hansard into poetry, and (b) that what Shakespeare demands is not verse-speaking but verse-acting. A golden voice, however angelic, is not enough. Whenever a climax looms up, the actor faces a choice between the poetry and the character, the sound and the fury, because you cannot rage mellifluously or cry out your eyes in tune. Edmund Kean, Irving, and Olivier, on whom our whole tradition of heroic acting rests, have one thing in common: they have all been repeatedly accused of lacking poetry. Miss Bloom sins in good company.

The average Juliet sings the part sweetly, chants it demurely, dismissing passion with a stamp of the foot. Nine tenths of Juliet, as Miss Bloom demonstrates, is not in the least demure: she is impatient and mettlesome, proud and vehement, not a blindfold child of milk. And the result is an illumination. The silly lamb becomes a real, scarred woman, and we see that it is the whole character that is poetic, and not just the lines. When she is quiet, as in the balcony scene, Miss Bloom's candour is as still as a smoke-ring and as lovely. "I have forgot why I did call thee back" is spoken with a grave amazement: there are no simpers or blushes in this dedicated young creature. From her first meeting with Romeo, as they touch hands at the Capulets' ball, she is no novice, but an initiate in the stately game of love. In silence, as in speech, her communication with Romeo is complete: their minds fit like hand into glove, and his absence wounds her like an amputation. "Word-music" goes overboard in Miss Bloom's best scene, that in which the Nurse breaks the news of Tybalt's death and Romeo's banishment—first the superb harshness of "Blistered be thy tongue!" after the old crone has reviled Romeo, and then a desolating panic, crowned at the end by an exit suddenly gentle and bereaved, cradling Romeo's rope-ladder to her breast. I have seen no more moving piece of acting this year. Miss Bloom was not quite adequate to the mighty obstacle of the potion speech, and the death scene seemed to catch her off guard. But enough had been done by then to make the golden statue of remembrance, promised by Romeo's father in the last scene, quite unnecessary. We had already seen pure gold.

Alan Badel, her Romeo, is that freak, a young man with an old man's voice, an old man's snicker, and an old man's leer. Couple with these disadvantages a lack of inches and looks, and you have a problem that no amount of intelligence can solve. Mr. Badel is not a romantic actor. He does some daring little things early on, but the later agonies are beyond him. He lingers over them, squirming and yearning, but the total effect is miniature—rather like a restless marmoset.

(1952)

As You Like It and *Coriolanus*, by William Shakespeare, and *Volpone*, by Ben Jonson, at Stratford-on-Avon.

Let me spare a few paragraphs to celebrate the late season at the Stratford Memorial Theatre. I missed *The Tempest,* and wished I had missed *Macbeth,* in which Ralph Richardson gave such a curiously numb performance; but the other three productions were first-rate. Particularly *As You Like It,* where the shift in mood from wintry discord to summery consonance was perfectly reflected in the settings and in Clifton Parker's lovely incidental music. I think with pleasure of those leafless glades because there roamed through them a magical Jaques, proud and sorrowful as the White Knight, and daft as Don Quixote. The actor, Michael Hordern, played him with a marvellous sense of injury, yet beneath the shaggy melancholy you felt a finely tempered mind, drawn still towards wit and beauty, as old racehorses will prick up their ears at the noise of pelting hooves. It was a great performance: rooted in self-disgust, but with a tattered plume of merriment capering always over its head. Meanwhile, Margaret Leighton was giving a highly ornamental exhibition of technique as Rosalind. Fulsomely, she showed us all her tricks, but the impression left was somehow chilly, in the manner of some of Lynn Fontanne's lesser achievements. This Rosalind was a gay and giddy creature—loads of fun, game for any jape, rather like a popular head girl—but a tiring companion, I felt, after a long day.

Coriolanus, also directed by Glen Byam Shaw, is more of a public meeting than a play, but it turned out to be a startlingly modern public meeting. Shakespeare is dealing with the problem of the inordinate man, the public figure so oversized that the law cannot bind him. Coriolanus is a militarist, a Roman Junker, sandwiched between the plebs, whom he spurns, and the patricians, whom he despises. Stratford gave the play what you might call a Tory emphasis. Coriolanus, that is to say, emerged as quite a modest chap, for all his bad temper. This was Anthony Quayle's doing: he played the part as a furious and impatient young bull, but not a mad or treacherous one. I used to think that only Orson Welles could make a perfect Coriolanus; but I am pretty sure that he could not improve on Quayle's delivery of the flamboyant final speech:

> . . . like an eagle in a dovecote, I
> Fluttered your Volscians in Corioli!
> Alone I did it—boy!

The lines rang, as someone once said of Dryden's poetry, like a great brass coin flung down on marble.

It is nobody's fault but Shakespeare's that the play ends with such casual abruptness; but I could find lots of people to blame for the weakness of the supporting cast, who, apart from Mr. Hordern's Menenius, were as uniformly bad as they had been good in *As You Like It.* The women especially belonged much more to the world of RSVP than that of SPQR.

The last production of the season, Ben Jonson's *Volpone,* failed to fill the theatre at matinees, thereby sending Mr. Quayle into a fit of panic. I hope he recovers from it, and I hoot derisively at the idea that he cannot afford to give us one of these non-Shakespearean treats, say, every other year. Pictorially, George Devine's handling of the play would have delighted the heart of Inigo Jones. I thought Richardson's Volpone a little too fantastical and quite deficient in stature and authority. Some of the lines eluded him, others again crept in from other plays, and when he came to the famous "When she came in like starlight, hid with jewels," he got as far as the last word, paused, and firmly made it "gems." You might say, quite fairly, that this was a semi-precious performance: lots of glitter, but not much real worth.

Quayle's Mosca was superb. He turned Volpone's parasite into a mixture of gentleman's gentleman and cad's cad, borrowing for the occasion the exuberantly venomous tones of Eric Blore, the Hollywood butler. And in the small part of Sir Politick Would-Be, which is normally amputated, Michael Hordern lit upon a universal type: the red-faced bore, the man in the know, always bragging of schemes and secrets and contacts—a true ancestor, in short, of poor Apthorpe in Evelyn Waugh's *Men at Arms.*

I am told that Stratford opinion regards this as having been a mediocre season. By 1951 standards it may be so, but that was an exceptional year. The safest introduction to the best in English theatre is still, for my money, the 2.10 from Paddington (change at Leamington for the shrine).

(1952)

The Merchant of Venice, BY WILLIAM SHAKESPEARE, AT THE OLD VIC.

Every play is a party, at which the author is host and the characters are guests. In *The Merchant of Venice* Shakespeare got his invitations badly mixed up, and the party rapidly disintegrates. In one corner Shylock is pulling a knife on Antonio; around the dinner-table, slightly flown with wine, sits a gayer group, headed by Portia and Bassanio; while in the window-seat, oblivious of the rest, Lorenzo and Jessica raptly smooch. The three plots simply do not jell, and no producer is to blame when the play comes to pieces in his hands—I doubt whether all the King's Men, Shakespeare's own company of actors, could put them together again. Hugh Hunt's production fails, but it fails intelligently, attractively, and forgivably.

Its centre-piece, unfortunately, is something of a sore thumb; this is the Shylock of Paul Rogers, who refuses point-blank to admit that he is playing in a comedy at all. Taking his cue from Irving and his methods from the Habima theatre, he erects a wailing-wall on the stage and finds nothing in the character beyond pride and operatic self-pity. Like the tailor who sent Max Beerbohm a final-demand letter, he is in the ungainly position of crawling on his knees while shaking his fist. He demands, in short, an excessive rate of interest on his emotional investments. The length of Shylock's nose is just as vital to *The Merchant* as the length of Cleopatra's was to human history. Enlarge it, and you see Shakespeare's idea of the man: a comic monster, richly and triumphantly witty—a sort of capitalistic Caliban. If the actor grasps that, the pathos will come by itself. Mr. Rogers, by denying the comedy and going all out for the victimisation, is like the man who spoils a fancy-dress party by coming as a leper.

The plot requires all three of its women to impersonate beardless boys, and Roger Furse has rushed to their aid by dressing them up in the knee-breeches and full-bottomed wigs of the Restoration. The disguise is, for the first time in memory, almost credible, particularly in the case of Irene Worth, whose Portia is instantly transformed into a dazzling coffee-house spark. Donning trousers, she seems, like George Sand, to doff primness and mock-modesty; and you begin to understand the fascination male parts held for so many of our early actresses—even poor Mrs. Verbruggen, who possessed what a critic afterwards described as "corpulent and large Posteriours." Peg Woffington's Sir Harry

Wildair, in *The Constant Couple,* was so good that no man dared attempt the part during her lifetime. And did not Mrs. Siddons play Hamlet? Not to mention Mrs. Glover, who went one better and played Falstaff—without padding, or so the rumour went. Only thirty years ago, to crown everything, a certain Lucille Laverne appeared in London as Shylock. Perhaps the influence of film realism has killed the old custom: or can it be that the George Sands of time are running out? At all events, I hope one day to see Miss Worth at it again.

Her beskirted moments rather worried me. Portia's lines are not unremittingly funny, but they are certainly not improved by the frills and flounces which Miss Worth hangs out on them. She repeatedly falls into the classic Old Vic error of supposing that all Elizabethans laughed aloud at their own jokes. For her first entrance she wears an ill-advised, tip-tilted straw hat, such as an amusing aunt might pop on after a few sherries, and within seconds she is practically bursting an appendix with suppressed giggles. I agree that Portia must unbend with her maids, but there is no necessity to go down on all fours. This roguey-poguey style is at present all the voguey-pogue, and I call upon Miss Worth to take a stand against it.

The rest of the cast is a mixed bag. Probably Newton Blick, as old blind Gobbo, comes off best. With a comic finesse more often seen in Molière than in Shakespeare, this fine clown presents a lunatic, dilapidated soul whose nervous tics are always two jumps ahead of his wits. And Jessica? Well, Claire Bloom is a very honest actress who will not put into a part more than she finds there; and in Jessica, of course, she finds hardly anything. She runs tentatively about the stage, striking small attitudes to cover her self-consciousness at having nothing to act. The role makes few positive demands, but it does involve long periods of silence, with which Miss Bloom's technique is not quite ready to cope. If the scene is romantic, she stares, admiringly but disconcertingly, straight into her lover's eyes, like a sea-lion awaiting a fish; if comic, the stare is reinforced with an eager piteous smile, as though she were commiserating with the speaker over the poverty of his material. Miss Bloom has many gifts, but that of acting in a vacuum is not yet amongst them.

(1953)

The Way of the World, BY WILLIAM CONGREVE, AT THE LYRIC, HAMMERSMITH.

William Congreve is the only sophisticated playwright England has ever produced; and, like Shaw, Sheridan, and Wilde, his nearest rivals, he was brought up in Ireland. By sophisticated I mean genial without being hearty, witty without being smug, wise without being pompous, and sensual without being lewd. These attributes, now to be seen in John Gielgud's revival of *The Way of the World,* rarely coincide in an Englishman who has not had the benefit of a Dublin education or, at the very least, of an industrious French governess.

Because they speak precisely and with affection for the language they are using, it is usually taken for granted that Congreve's characters are unreal. Nothing could be more misguided. These people do not bare their souls (that would smack of nudism), but they are real enough. It is the plot which is unreal; and of all plots, none more closely resembles a quadratic equation than that of *The Way of the World.* At the heart of the maze is Lady Wishfort, to whom nearly everyone in the play is related, and in whose money everyone has a consuming interest. But the labyrinth is so brilliantly peopled that you forget the goal. Congreve's genius is for mixing and contrasting human beings, not for taking them anywhere in particular.

And what glorious contrasts Mr. Gielgud has provided! Having assembled what I heard described, in an enviable slip of the tongue, as "a conglamouration of stars," he has let them have their heads. The play sails into life with pennants flying. Mr. Gielgud is at the helm, a crowd of deft character actors like Eric Porter, Richard Wordsworth, and Brewster Mason are manning the rigging, and Eileen Herlie is thrown in for ballast. To pipe us aboard there is Paul Scofield as Witwould, the amateur fop—a beautifully gaudy performance, pitched somewhere between Hermione Gingold and Stan Laurel. Gielgud's galleon would not be complete without a figurehead, and there, astride the prow, she triumphantly is—Margaret Rutherford, got up as Lady Wishfort, the man-hungry pythoness. This is a banquet of acting in itself. Miss Rutherford is filled with a monstrous vitality: the soul of Cleopatra has somehow got trapped in the corporate shape of an entire lacrosse team. The unique thing about Miss Rutherford is that she can act with her chin alone: among its many moods I especially cherish the chin commanding, the chin in doubt, and the chin at bay. My dearest impression of this Hammersmith night is a vision of Miss Rutherford, clad in something loose, darting about her boudoir like a gigantic bumblebee at large in a hothouse.

After which I am sorry to have to end my report on a minor chord. The scenes between Mirabell and Millamant, which should be the play's delicious crown, do not come off at all. The two lovers remain what Johnson called them, "intellectual gladiators," but the strength is all on one side, and the wrong side at that. Mr. Gielgud, an impeccable Mirabell in plum velvet, has Pamela Brown begging for mercy almost before the battle is joined. This is, of course, a ghastly abdication on her part. Millamant must be the empress of her sex, and her words, whether tinkling like a fountain or cascading like Niagara, must always flow from a great height. From Miss Brown's mouth they do not flow at all; they leak, half apologetically, in dribs and drabs. Instead of saving up the revelation that she loves Mirabell, she lets us know it from the outset, thereby dethroning the empress and setting an ogling spinster in her place. Miss Brown, to sum up, sees through Millamant and (what is worse) lets us see through her as well. It is a grave mistake, and I will hear no excuses. All I can offer by way of consolation is this: it is the kind of mistake which only an actress of Miss Brown's intelligence could have made.

(1953)

King Lear, BY WILLIAM SHAKESPEARE, AT THE KING'S, HAMMERSMITH.

It is annoying that the Old Vic did not hold Donald Wolfit in the troupe long enough to show us his *King Lear,* which is now being alternated with *Twelfth Night* at the King's, Hammersmith. His present supporting company explores new horizons of inadequacy. Only Richard Goolden, a macabre Fool with a senile stoop and a child's skipping legs, is of much assistance to the play. Extricate Mr. Wolfit's Lear from the preposterous production and you have a great, flawed piece of masonry, making up in weight what it lacks in delicacy: a tribal chieftain rather than a hereditary monarch. Mr. Wolfit scorns the trick (known to many lesser actors) of flicking speeches exquisitely to leg; he prefers to bash them towards mid-off and run like a stag. In the mad scenes this impatience with finesse is a weakness: the insanity looks too much like tipsiness. And to play the last unearthly act Lear must land, as it were, by parachute on the top of Parnassus. Mountaineering, however dogged, will not take him there. At these moments Mr. Wolfit seems unaccountably grounded.

His mark is still higher up the great slope than anyone else's in our time. He is magnificent in the early scenes, sulking like a beaten dog when Cordelia refuses to play ball with him; and the colloquies with the Fool are horribly moving, with the old man's thoughts staring past his words into the chasm of lunacy. Best of all is the pause that follows his fit of rage at Cornwall's cruelty. "Tell the hot duke—" he begins, and then stops in mid-eruption, veins knotted, fighting hideously to keep his foothold on the tiny ledge which stands between him and madness. Mr. Wolfit's Lear is a brilliant compound of earth, fire, and flood. Only the airy element is missing.

(1953)

The Glorious Days, AT THE PALACE.

The Glorious Days can best be described—to adapt a phrase of George Kaufman's—as Anna Neagle rolled into one. Here she is, anthologised at last, available once nightly in the large economy size; dipping into the fabled store of her talents, she brings up a horn of plenty, from which she pours, with cautious rapture, three dwarf acorns. First, she acts, in a fashion so devoid of personality as to be practically incognito; second, she sings, shaking her voice at the audience like a tiny fist; and, third, she dances, in that non-committal, twirling style, once known as "skirt-dancing," which was originally invented (or so Shaw tells us) to explain the presence on the stage of genteel young women who could neither sing nor act.

The curtain is no sooner up, disclosing a war-time pub, than news arrives that Miss Neagle has been decorated for gallantry; and her entrance is the cue for the opening number, a ragged chorus of "For She's a Jolly Good Fellow," vivaciously led by a Chelsea pensioner. On leaving the pub, Miss Neagle is maliciously greeted by a bomb, and the rest of the entertainment tells, in its own illimitable way, the story of her concussion. For some reason she is being wooed by three men—a rake, a theatrical producer, and a good German—who see her, respectively, as an ideal mistress, an ideal leading lady, and an ideal comrade. Which shall she be? Eliminating obvious improbabilities, you are left, of course, with No. 3, but Miss Neagle's methods are more circuitous. She has hallucinations.

She first imagines herself to be Nell Gwynn, here presented as a scheming social worker using her favours to blackmail Charles II into building Chelsea Hospital. She keeps returning to the subject at crucial moments in their relationship, to the King's understandable annoyance ("That hospital for old soldiers *again?*"); but in the end the unsavoury ruse succeeds. Miss Neagle's Nell (not the broadest of Gwynns) was dressed by Doris Zinkeisen and devised by Robert Nesbitt; the words were put into her mouth by either Mr. Nesbitt, Harold Purcell, or Miles Malleson; her music was composed by—among others—Harry Parr Davies and Henry Purcell, and her dance was arranged by Frank Staff. From their collective guilt I except Miss Zinkeisen alone: her costume designs for the Drury Lane dancers, bold and striking, represent the only contact made by *The Glorious Days* with the living theatre.

Unmoved by her failure to identify herself with pretty Nelly, Miss Neagle goes straight into her second audition: as Queen Victoria, the ideal comrade. While she changes her clothes, three choruses of "The Boys of the Old Brigade" are sung by an army of shuffling baritones, during which time there was some speculation in the house about whether the star had got caught on a nail in the wings. However, we were soon swooning back to Windsor in 1846, where Miss Neagle's idea of the young Victoria was revealed to be a somewhat rowdier version of Mrs. Gwynn. She is pictured singing a drinking song to Albert, accompanying herself on the ivories, and pleading libidinously to be waltzed with. Bang on cue, Johann Strauss drops in, establishes his origin (*"Ach, so"*), and clicks his heels; whereupon the scenery dissolves into the castle ballroom, which turns out to be a nightmare premonition of the casino at Biarritz. To cover another costume change, a curious interlude ensues, of total irrelevance to the action except that it happens twenty years after the preceding scene and twenty years before the next. It is laid in a London supper saloon, and none of the characters or events in it is ever referred to again. The first half ends with an investiture at Windsor.

There was heated division of opinion in the lobbies during the interval, but a small, conservative majority took the view that it might be as well to remain in the theatre. There was always a chance that Miss Neagle might come bowling on as Boadicea, with a knife between her teeth; or that she would be discovered, dressed like Robinson Crusoe, stepping out of a boat and saying: "The Queen of Spain will thank us for this day's work, or she'll have Chris Columbus to reckon with!"

As it was, she spent Part Two playing her mother, meanwhile delegating the job of playing herself to three other actresses. Mother, naturally, was a star of musical comedy who flourished from 1913 to 1937; and Miss Neagle characterises her, with remarkable ferocity, as a well-meaning *diseuse* of appallingly limited technique. We follow her career through the twenties in a series of production numbers that seem to have been recovered from the wastepaper basket of a bankrupt impresario of the period. When this is over, we are back in 1943: Miss Neagle has chosen to marry the producer and decided, against all advice, to become an actress. She departs for Burma with an ENSA troupe; and one cannot help wishing that the whole of *The Glorious Days* could go with her. If not to Burma, then at least to Birmingham.

Its prevailing tone, to sum up, is a mixture of cynicism ("They'll lap it up") and joviality ("God bless them"). *The Glorious Days* demonstrates once and for all that the gap between knowing what the public wants and having the skill to provide it is infinitely wider than most English producers ever dream.

(1953)

The Merchant of Venice, BY WILLIAM SHAKESPEARE, AT STRATFORD-ON-AVON.

Whenever I see *The Merchant of Venice,* I while away the blanker bits of verse by trying to pull the play together in my mind. Does Shylock stand for the Old Testament (an eye for an eye, etc.) and Portia for the New (mercy, etc.)? And if so, what does that make Antonio, the shipping magnate whose bond unites the two plots? Does he represent the spirit of Protestantism? These metaphysical hares chase each other round and round; and when I have done, the play remains the curate's egg it always was. Or, rather, the rabbi's egg, because so much depends on Shylock. Which brings us to the Problem of Michael Redgrave, now, as always, at the turning-point of his career.

The difficulty about judging this actor is that I have to abandon all my standards of great acting (which include relaxation and effortless command) and start all over again. There is, you see, a gulf fixed between good and great performances; but a bridge spans it, over which you may stroll if your visa is in order. Mr. Redgrave, ignoring this, always chooses the hard way. He dives into the torrent and tries to swim across, usually sinking within sight of the shore. Olivier pole-vaults over in a single animal leap; Gielgud, seizing a parasol, crosses by tight-rope; Redgrave alone must battle it out with the current. The ensuing spectacle is never dull, but it can be very painful to watch.

His conception of Shylock is highly intelligent—a major prophet with a German accent, a touch of asthma, and lightning playing round his head. But who cares for conceptions? It is the execution that counts. And here Mr. Redgrave's smash-and-grab methods tell against him. His performance is a prolonged wrestling match with Shylock, each speech being floored with a tremendous, vein-bursting thump; the process also involves his making a noise like a death-rattle whenever he inhales, and spitting visibly whenever he strikes a "p" or a "b."

Some things he did superbly. At the end of the court scene, even after Portia had warned him that to take the pound of flesh would expose him to the death penalty, you felt that this cheated tyrant would be maniac enough to hang the consequences and start carving. There were also hints that Mr. Redgrave did not deny Shylock a sense of humour: he discovered a sensational new pun in his delivery of the speech about "water-rats" and "pi-rates." But he simply could not fuse the villainy of the part with its sardonic comedy. And I begin to think that no English player ever will. It needs a Continental actor to switch from fun to ferocity in a split second: Englishmen take at least half a minute to change gear. And when they are playing in their high-tragedy manner, as Mr. Redgrave is, they find it practically impossible to change gear at all.

Now, Shylock is a proud and successful financier with a chip on his shoulder; he is not an abject slave bearing a yoke of lead. Mr. Redgrave cringes and crumples every time Antonio opens his mouth—you would think he had never seen a Christian before. He should, of course, outsmile the lot of them. Like the other Shakespearean rogues, Richard III, Iago, and Claudius, Shylock must wear a cloak of charm. Even Antonio describes him as "kind," and the bond must seem to be what Shylock calls it, "merry." Mr. Redgrave gives us nothing more merry than a twisted leer. Or perhaps I should say a twisted Lear. Because I shall be much surprised if his performance as the mad king, later in the season, is vocally or physically very different from last Tuesday's Jew. I hope one day to see this actor playing a part insincerely, with his mind on other matters. Then the defences might come down, and the great Shakespearean performance that surges within him might at last be let out.

The jewel of the evening is Peggy Ashcroft's Portia, a creature of exquisite breeding and uncommon sense. She speaks the poetry with the air of a woman who would never commit the social gaffe of reciting in public, with the result that the lines flow out newly minted, as unstrained as the quality of mercy itself. Her handling of the tiresome princelings who come to woo her is an object lesson in wit and good manners; later, in the court-room, we wept at her compassion; and the last act, invariably an anti-climax, bloomed golden at her touch.

Apart from the fiery furnace that is Mr. Redgrave and the cool zephyr that is Miss Ashcroft, the production is pretty tepid stuff. The scenery (flimsy pillars, as usual) looks fine in silhouette, and on one occasion, when the sky inadvertently turned green, assumed extraordinary beauty. But I tire of settings that seek to represent nowhere-in-general; how one longs to see everywhere-in-particular! The trial was well staged—but why must Shylock always be alone? Surely all the Jews in Venice would turn up for his triumph?

I cannot imagine what Donald Pleasence was trying to make of Launcelot Gobbo, who is not, I suggest, an organ-grinder's monkey. Yvonne Mitchell is wasted on Jessica. On the credit side, Tony Britton's Bassanio is an attractive scamp; and Robert Shaw, cast as Gratiano, delighted us and himself by giving a fiery and determined performance of Mercutio.

(1953)

The White Carnation, BY R. C. SHERRIFF, AT THE GLOBE.

R. C. Sherriff, the author of *The White Carnation,* deserves everyone's congratulations on having solved one of the trickiest problems in the contemporary theatre—that of writing a part for Sir Ralph Richardson. Over the last few years the resemblance between Sir Ralph's demeanour on stage and that of a human being in life has been getting progressively more tenuous. He has taken to ambling across our stages in a spectral, shell-shocked manner, choosing odd moments to jump and frisk, like a man through whom an electric current was being intermittently passed; behaving, in short, as if insulated against reality. Mr. Sherriff tried to exploit these limitations in *Home at Seven,* in which Sir Ralph played, if I remember rightly, a man who had been knocked on the head. Seeing that this was not quite enough, Mr. Sherriff has now gone the whole hog. Before the curtain rises on *The White Carnation,* Sir Ralph has been blown to pieces by a flying bomb.

Not to labour the point, he is a ghost, one of a bunch of banshees who annually revisit the suburban house on which the bomb fell, wiping out what seems to have been a very dreary Christmas party. (How the house escaped being demolished is not explained.) Their spooky revels over, they go back to limbo, or wherever small-part actors go in the winter-time—all but Sir Ralph, who is left behind, a 4-D character in a 3-D world. The question is: how will 1951 react to the sudden arrival of a man who was buried in 1944? Mr. Sherriff's reply is to fob us off with an ill-compiled anthology of other ghost plays. He introduces a J. M. Barrie-ish theme, in which the perplexed phantom falls in love with a young librarian (winsomely played by Meriel Forbes). He alternates this with a Priestley-esque *motif,* implying that Sir Ralph has been allowed to slip a cog in time in order to right a wrong performed when he was alive. Finally, he hauls in an Ealing-comedy situation based on the trouble an apparition would have with housing shortages and re-entry permits. Amid such a confusion of moods Mr. Sherriff's play hasn't an unearthly chance of success.

As monarch of the chaos, however, Sir Ralph is perfectly at home. Being a ghost, he can wander about without the disturbing necessity of making human contact with any of the other members of the cast. Freed of this worry, he guides the play through its shallows with the touch of a master helmsman. It is a magnificent performance, and I mean no irony when I nominate Sir Ralph the best supernatural actor of his generation.

Richard III, BY WILLIAM SHAKESPEARE, AT STRATFORD-ON-AVON.

Richard III, like *Hamlet* and *The Wandering Jew,* is generally regarded as a one-man show. I had never realised, until I saw the new Stratford production, that the man in question was the Duke of Buckingham. Not Richard, the riotous medieval usurper, half-Punch, half-Satan, whose murderous progress to the throne is the play's main business: he, in Marius Goring's performance, hardly showed his face. Our interest was focused instead on the rise and fall of his treacherous henchman, Buckingham. Richard, in effect, abdicated, and Harry Andrews walked off with the play.

Other actors may be the heart, brain, and fingertips of English Shakespearean acting: Harry Andrews is the indispensable backbone. His Buckingham is a man of granite, a swaggering butcher with a battleship jaw and no remorse. I have never seen a likelier candidate for the headsman's axe, and when he strode off to the block, hands firmly clasped behind his back, we were in the presence of naked courage as well as first-rate acting. When, earlier on, he uttered the line: "Tut, I can counterfeit the great tragedian," the information was superfluous. He had been doing nothing else all evening.

Marius Goring's Richard is not large enough, vocally or physically, to inspire terror, and you cannot play this tremendous part on mind alone. Where he should have been evil, he was nasty; where misbegotten, he was runtish; where formidable, merely despicable. He sees Richard as a paltry little chap, and to emphasise his unfitness to be king he dresses up for the coronation in oversized robes rather like those Sid Field used to trip over in his sketch about King John. Here he misses the point, which is that though Richard may not be a desirable earthly ruler, he would make an ideal viceroy of hell. It was a revealing slip of the tongue that made the actor refer to "the high-revolving witty Buckingham," instead of "deep-revolving," Buckingham overtopped Richard on Tuesday, and I think Mr. Goring knew it.

(1953)

The Wandering Jew, BY E. TEMPLE THURSTON, AT THE KING'S, HAMMERSMITH.

The present revival of *The Wandering Jew* is one of the most reassuring theatrical experiences in years. Have we really progressed so far? In 1920 the play survived 390 performances; today not a line of it but rings flat and false. Only in village pageants, and in *The Glorious Days,* do traces of its style persist. It is written in four "phases": a trip through time with Donald Wolfit as the legendary Jew who insulted Christ and was doomed to live until the Messiah should return. In the first scene Mr. Wolfit wears a burnous, a shiny red wig, and his usual make-up, a thick white line down the bridge of the nose. As ever, he delivers each line as a challenge, flung in the teeth of invisible foes; his voice roars like an avalanche of gravel; and when he swirled off, girding his rude bathrobe about him, to spit at his Saviour, I fell to wondering exactly where his ponderous, vibrato methods belong.

Not in the little club theatres, I decided; nor in the larger West End houses, where they would soon grow oppressive. Nor yet at the Old Vic—I picture Mr. Wolfit erupting at the very thought. Where, then, is his spiritual home? My answer is nowhere in particular: he is a nomad, part of the great (albeit dead) tradition of the strolling player, who would erect his stage in a tavern yard and unravel his rhetoric to the winds. Mr. Wolfit is not an indoor actor at all. Theatres cramp him. He would be happiest, I feel, in a large field.

Phase two takes us to the Crusades. The Jew has become a marauding knight of uncontrollable sexual appetites. And woe betide the maiden of his choice (I am slipping, as the author incessantly does, into blank verse). The Christian camp, all stripy canvas and flags, seems to be pitched backstage at Bertram Mills' circus, and Mr. Wolfit comes in from jousting in the garb of the human cannon-ball. Throughout the production great stress is laid on headwear: a character in phase two affects a tea-cosy, the guards in phase four go in for tin sombreros, and Mr. Wolfit's jousting kit is topped off by an inverted galvanised-iron bucket with two holes knocked in it. With the morrow he'll be gone, so he chases a young woman around his tent, breathing balefully into her face (having first removed his bucket) and even spitting at her, in a token sort of way. Matheson Lang, a born charmer, might have just carried this scene off. As it was, the scene carried Mr. Wolfit off, prostrate as on a stretcher.

He is back for phase three, tightly encased in a kimono, to play a thirteenth-century Sicilian miser persecuted for his faith. A large trunk in the corner of his villa attracts our curiosity, which is quickly satisfied. He throws it open, and: "What would this be worth in the open market?" he gloats, producing, with a tremendous flourish, a faded horse-blanket. In the final phase the Jew is arraigned by the Spanish Inquisition, which convicts him of un-Catholic activities and sends him to the stake. As the curtain falls, Mr. Wolfit goes up in flames, aged fourteen hundred and some odd years. It is like the annual roasting of an ox on Shakespeare's birthday at Stratford-on-Avon.

(1953)

The Living Room, BY GRAHAM GREEN, AT WYNDHAM'S.

The Living Room is Graham Greene's first play, and also the best first play of its (English) generation. Its subject-matter can be compressed into two texts. One from Shaw: "You can't make a man a Christian unless you first make him believe he is a sinner"; and one from a nameless theatrical manager: "The triangle isn't eternal, but it's good for six months at the box-office." Greene attempts to weld these two propositions, one cosmic and one commercial, into a dramatic unity.

In *The Notorious Mrs. Ebbsmith* Pinero scandalised a Victorian audience by making his heroine throw a Bible into the fire, and immediately comforted them by letting her pull it out again. Greene's heroine, so to speak, chucks it in and leaves it there. She is a young orphan, physically in love with a middle-aged lecturer in psychology who is burdened with a hysterical wife. That is the textbook triangle: Greene now sets about projecting it towards infinity. For the girl is a Roman Catholic. She has come to live with a pair of ancient aunts and an uncle who is a crippled priest. They inhabit a dank suburban house in which strange rituals persist, among them a refusal on the part of the female inmates to admit that they ever go to the bathroom except to take a bath. Greene is a Roman Catholic, but he is also a born rebel; this sepulchral mansion symbolises, I imagine, the obscurantist aspects of the Roman faith. Childishly scared of death, the two aunts have sealed off every room in which anyone has died. The younger of them, a great bulky zealot (fearsomely played by Violet Farebrother), learns of the girl's adultery and threatens her with mortal sin. The wheelchair priest seeks to intensify her feelings of guilt, while her psychiatrist lover seeks to remove them. She vacillates between her lover and her God—between an earthly and a heavenly father-substitute—and finally cries out to the priest, in a striking phrase, that she is one of God's "happy failures."

The play is rising to its climax. The wife, a ravaged neurotic, stages a suicide attempt, which restores to her husband a shamed sense of his responsibilities. And now, on the threshold of triumph, Greene slips and falls. His heroine takes poison. The whole elaborate itinerary of sin and salvation has led us nowhere: she behaves in the crisis like any discarded mistress in a Victorian melodrama. Having tied a modern Catholic knot, Greene cuts it with an old-fashioned theatrical axe. I felt profoundly cheated.

If he stumbles on the highest level, Greene is wonderfully surefooted on the way up. He has given Dorothy Tutin a chance which has been withheld from young English actresses for nearly thirty years: the chance of playing a long, serious part in an important new play. She takes it superbly, as if it were her birthright. Her role is half of what must be the most fully documented love affair in dramatic literature; we are privy to all her secrets, sexual and spiritual alike. Miss Tutin's performance is masterly: the very nakedness of acting. In her greatest sorrow she blazes like a diamond in a mine.

Elsewhere in the cast Peter Glenville (who has directed the play with a midwife's care) is less lucky. John Robinson plays the lover, for instance, in a highly unlovable vein of unctuous rhetoric. And though I applaud Eric Portman's unselfishness in accepting the role of the priest, I must deplore the waste involved. His legs are cut off at the knees, and his temperament is cut off at the mains. Mr. Portman is an active actor miscast in a passive part. His game struggle to repress his natural exuberance produces an effect which I can only describe as vocal costiveness.

To sum up, then: a potentially great dramatist has launched a potentially great actress. He has also transmitted a message, which I can most gracefully summarise in the words of a fellow first-nighter: "Be it ever so lustful, there's no place like Rome."

(1953)

Antony and Cleopatra, BY WILLIAM SHAKESPEARE, AT STRATFORD-ON-AVON.

There is only one role in *Antony and Cleopatra* that English actresses are naturally equipped to play. This is Octavia, Caesar's docile sister, the girl "of a holy, cold and still conversation" whom Mark Antony marries and instantly deserts; and if Shakespeare had done the modern thing and written a domestic tragedy about her disillusionment, generations of English *ingénues* would by now have triumphed in it. But alas! he took as his heroine an inordinate trollop, thereby ensuring that we should never see the part perfectly performed—unless, by some chance, a Frenchwoman should come and play it for us. The great sluts of world drama, from Clytemnestra to Anna Christie, have always puzzled our girls; and an English Cleopatra is a contradiction in terms.

At Stratford, Peggy Ashcroft follows tradition by presenting a lady who, though she goes by Cleopatra's name, is clearly and charmingly an impostor. As she demonstrated in *The Deep Blue Sea,* Miss Ashcroft is expert in suggesting the grief of sexual frustration; but Cleopatra's keynote is the rapture of sexual fulfilment. Even when gorged, she is still ravenous. Miss Ashcroft gave us a ravenous famine victim; just as five years ago Edith Evans gave us a Cleopatra who was really Lady Bracknell, cruelly starved of cucumber sandwiches. The effect of the last act, in which the royal courtesan doffs her baser attributes and proves herself fit for greatness, lost some of its force, because in Miss Ashcroft's performance the baser attributes were never there to begin with.

I missed, too, the infinite variety. To play Cleopatra, as to play

Shylock, you need the Continental actor's ability to juggle with seemingly contradictory emotions; you have to leap from majesty to bawdiness in mid-sentence. For this fitful blaze Miss Ashcroft substituted a steady glow. A nice intense woman, you nearly murmured; such a pity she took up with the head gamekeeper. You could not help thinking of her in local terms like this, for her vowel-sounds (especially that telltale round "o") kept shrieking Sloane Square. Her hair-do was jaunty Chelsea: a red wig gathered into a horse's tail, perhaps in recognition of the line in which she is described as a "ribaudred nag." The summing-up must be that Miss Ashcroft touched with silver a part that needs burnishing with gold. We must record a failure—but a gallant one, in good company. "And," Cleopatra herself reminds me, "when good will is show'd, though it come too short, the actor may plead pardon."

Antony, the superhuman spendthrift, is easier meat. From the play's very beginning he is a sort of historical monument, a ruin testifying to glories long past. Michael Redgrave does not so much fill the part as overflow it. If Miss Ashcroft falls short, he sometimes goes too far. A less decrepit ruin could scarcely be imagined. In their first scene together Mr. Redgrave gave Miss Ashcroft a terrific mauling, clawing at her clothes like a berserk pickpocket. If he can let up a little on the lust and rid himself of a few more mannerisms (among them a nervous trick of uttering everything prison-fashion out of the corner of his mouth), he will be giving a first-rate performance.

(1953)

Venice Preserv'd, BY THOMAS OTWAY, AT THE LYRIC, HAMMERSMITH.

Way out in the smoky suburb of Hammersmith a prodigy has been brought to birth. By which I mean a pure, plain, clear, classical production of the last great verse play in the English language—Thomas Otway's *Venice Preserv'd,* written in 1681, its author's thirtieth year. That it should be performed at all is treat enough; that it should be performed so well is a marvel.

Otway writes grandly, with a sort of sad, nervous power, about a large subject—the ethics of betrayal. Two impoverished Venetian malcontents, Jaffeir and Pierre, join a plot to overthrow the Senate. Their motives are highly personal. Jaffeir's bride is Belvidera, whose miserly father is a senator, and Pierre's mistress is Aquilina, a prostitute whose present keeper is a senator. Rationalising their grudges, they become crusading revolutionaries—the process is not uncommon today. But Pierre is a cynic and a man of action. Jaffeir is a romantic and a man of feeling, and when one of his fellow-conspirators attempts to seduce his wife, the romantic in him subdues the rebel, and he betrays the plot to the Senate. There is another motive for his treachery—his wife's fears for her father's life—but the key to it is private pique, masquerading as public-spiritedness. In the vacillations of poor, uxorious Jaffeir there is magnificent irony. The plotters having been arrested and condemned to torture, he wants desperately to atone. All he can do is to satisfy Pierre's plea for a quick death, and then to kill himself.

The play's major flaw is that Otway allows Jaffeir far too much self-pity, a mood of which John Gielgud, as an actor, is far too fond. The temptation sometimes proves too much for him: inhaling passionately through his nose, he administers to every line a tremendous parsonical quiver. But pictorially, if not emotionally, this is a very satisfying performance. The same goes for Eileen Herlie's Belvidera. The spectacle of Miss Herlie reeling and writhing in coils is both pleasing and appropriate, but something in her voice, a touch of fulsomeness, suggests an energetic saleswoman rather than a tragic heroine.

With the rest of the company I have no quarrel at all. Paul Scofield's Pierre, smouldering under a black wig, is the strongest, surest performance this actor has given since he came to London. Meanwhile, Pamela Brown, pop-eyed and imperious, has recaptured the fluent authority which in *The Way of the World* she seemed to have mislaid. The scene in which Aquilina caters to the masochistic whims of her decrepit senator, Antonio, was written as a scurrilous lampoon of the Earl of Shaftesbury. From this dunghill Miss Brown plucks a daisy of a performance, made up of boredom, contempt, and even a flicker of compassion. Her Aquilina is a definitive drab.

Peter Brook's production and Leslie Hurry's décor go straight to the play's atmospheric point—which is that, while reading it, you get the eerie sensation of being underground, trapped in a torch-lit vault. I shall return to Hammersmith again; but I should do so more than once if Messrs. Gielgud and Scofield could be persuaded to alternate the roles of Jaffeir and Pierre, as Gielgud and Olivier alternated Romeo and Mercutio eighteen years ago.

(1953)

Henry V, BY WILLIAM SHAKESPEARE, AT THE OLD VIC; *Julius Caesar*, BY WILLIAM SHAKESPEARE, AT THE WESTMINSTER.

The martyrdom of William Shakespeare goes on. We have seen him denuded, overdressed, mangled, racked, and up-ended; we have stood by as scholars sampled his blood and pronounced him Catholic, Lutheran, pagan, and Bacon; and yesterday I received from the Middle East a typewritten monograph appealingly headed: "Was Shylock a Jew?" Shakespeare, I suggest, would benefit from a little neglect. In the past week I have seen two of his plays sold into slavery; delivered, that is to say, into the hands of actors whose unreadiness for the responsibility was matched only by their eagerness to accept it.

For the first quarter-hour of the Bristol Old Vic's production in the Waterloo Road I was fascinated by the performance of the leading player, John Neville. Here at last, I felt, was the authentic Richard II: a lithe, sneering fellow, who curdled the milk of human kindness even as he dispensed it, but at whose heart there was abject insecurity. My excitement was marred, however, by the fact that the play being presented was *Henry V*. Mr. Neville's nervous introspection, well suited to one speech—the soliloquy before Agincourt—was elsewhere quite useless.

The rest of Denis Carey's production is solidly second-rate. Sensibly, he refrains from encouraging the French court to behave like a bunch of imbecilic mediaeval clowns—an interpretation which is always being foisted on the play, and to which the text gives not a shred of support. Even so, the war still looks one-sided. English actors are still incapable of playing their ancestors' traditional enemies without implying, by a brutish curl of the lip, that the French were swine and deserved all they got. The comedy scenes come off best. The Bristol Pistol is excellent, and so is the Dame Quickly: in fact, all the evidence suggests that this company, so skilled at amusing us, should stop tiring itself by seeking to move, alarm, inspire, or stun us.

The Elizabethan Theatre Company, who are appearing at the Westminster in a very stage-struck production of *Julius Caesar*, have been cruelly misled. They believe, quite sincerely, that they are achieving a new simplicity in Shakespearean staging. What they are actually achieving is an old complexity. Let me explain.

Most audiences are aware that the action of the play is laid in and around ancient Rome, and the lines inform them, if they do not already know, that much of it takes place at night. Thus equipped, what do they see at the Westminster? Actors in Elizabethan dress with sheets round their shoulders, performing amid a forest of wooden poles resembling a half-dismantled Coronation stand, in a permanent blaze of afternoon sunlight. Now, you and I need no telling that performances at the Globe Theatre were held at tea-time; we also know that the shape of Shakespeare's stage made ornate scenery impossible, and that accurate period costume was almost unknown. But we are the minority: the great majority of spectators will be needlessly confused. The point is that what was simplicity to the Elizabethans is complexity to most of us. A really simple modern production of *Julius Caesar* would be a realistic one, with togas and tents and moonlight. The present production, by Michael Macowan, is obscurantism going by the name of purity.

The programme does not help by insisting that the company is "endeavouring to recapture the spirit in which the original production was presented." Ten actors, between them, play forty parts; "in the theatre of Shakespeare's time," the programme blandly asserts, "this was a necessity." Necessity, it seems, is the mother of convention. It would have been less disingenuous of the programme to have come right out and admitted that it could not afford the extra actors. The ones it could afford look very inexperienced. This young company speaks clearly enough, but acts hardly at all.

(1953)

King Lear, BY WILLIAM SHAKESPEARE, AT STRATFORD-ON-AVON.

Michael Redgrave has played *King Lear* and won. For once the complex armoury of this actor's mind has found a foe worthy of its steel. I say "foe" because Mr. Redgrave approaches his big roles as a hunter stalks big game: he does not march up to them with simple friendship in his eyes. The technical apparatus with which he besieges his parts has sometimes looked a little over-elaborate, recalling the old metaphor about the sledge-hammer and the nut. But Lear is a labyrinthine citadel, all but impregnable, and it needed a Redgrave to assault it. On Tuesday night the balloon went up.

He began finely, conveying grief as well as rage at Cordelia's refusal to flatter him. Physically, already, the whole of Lear was there, a sky-scraping oak fit to resist all the lightning in the world. The second-act decline into madness was perhaps the least impressive stage of Mr.

Redgrave's campaign—Mr. Wolfit effects this transition more eloquently with less fuss. But once Lear was out on the heath, at odds with the elements, Mr. Redgrave found his bearings again, and never lost them to the end. Is it a backhanded compliment to say that this actor is best when maddest? Witness the Dover scene with the eyeless Gloucester: Lear's drifting whims, his sudden, shocking changes of subject, his veering from transcendent silliness to aching desolation were all explored, explained, and definitively expressed. In simple roles Mr. Redgrave is often in the predicament of a higher mathematician asked to add two and two together; he may very well hum and haw and come to the conclusion that in certain circumstances they can make five. But give him a scene, like this at Dover, which is the higher mathematics of acting, and he solves it in a flash; here, and throughout the last act, was the cube root of King Lear, "the thing itself."

Hamlet without the prince is still a fascinating text; *Lear* without the king is something of a bore. How one wishes that Shakespeare had passed the manuscript to someone like Jonson, with instructions to mend the leaks in the Gloucester sub-plot and provide at least some excuse for the unaccountable behaviour of Edgar! The Stratford company treads water energetically. Joan Sanderson and Rachel Kempson are the creepiest, most credible pair of ugly sisters I can remember; but, apart from his physical appearance, which might be captioned "Grimaldi as Caliban," Marius Goring makes a surprisingly ordinary Fool, all too obviously intent on pathos-squeezing. There are some dazzling costumes, of primitive Martian cut, but the setting badly lacks variety. To feel the cold of the heath, we must first have felt the warmth of the hearth. The present décor dumps us out of doors at curtain-rise and leaves us there.

(1953)

The Man with Expensive Tastes, BY EDWARD PERCY AND LILIAN DENHAM, AT THE VAUDEVILLE.

Only a year ago the patrons of the Vaudeville Theatre were briefly privileged to see a play in which Donald Wolfit was visited with a plague of frogs. Last night, under the same roof, something equally bizarre occurred—*The Man with Expensive Tastes,* the theme of which is forgery by hypnosis.

It happens in Mill Hill, where lives Sylvester Ord, a bland epicurean, played with shatteringly dated jollity by George Curzon. His line is graphology, out of which he has made enough money to furnish his house like an antique shop on the eve of a fire sale; he also, for reasons which may have been excised at the third rewrite, has green fingers. His principal lark, however, is forgery, as we learn from his house-guest, an inexpressibly sinister clergyman who is readily identifiable as an international crook. The actor here is Peter Bull, fooling nobody with a silver-grey wig. A self-confessed ex-president of the Oxford Union, he commands what must be the least secretive band of outlaws in the annals of crime. At Mr. Bull's request, Ord explains his technique of forgery. First, you divide your victim's calligraphy into two sections, the capital letters and the rest ("I live with these two alphabets. I saturate myself in them"); you then hypnotise yourself and forge ahead. This satisfies Mr. Bull, who is known in the trade as Monsieur Onyx.

The main action is precipitated by the presence in the neighbourhood of two other graphologists—Ord's daughter, whom he is raising to be a forger, and her American boy-friend, a private eye who has been engaged to investigate the forthcoming forgery coup. M. Onyx, ignoring Ord's helpless protests ("Self-hypnosis twice in one day!"), urges haste; and, fully in the public and private eye, preparations for the coup go forward. The scheme is wrecked by the Corsican girl, who smashes Ord's forging fingers in the door of a safe.

I forgot to mention the Corsican girl. She is a fiery creature named Yrena, highly yrresponsible, whom Ord has adopted and calls his little sparrow. She carries a stiletto, which later proves to be the only rational excuse for her existence on stage. The private eye has meanwhile concluded that he is among thieves; rather than call the police, however, he observes with characteristic obtuseness: "There's one piece of this jigsaw puzzle that doesn't quite fit." The final fitting takes place when Ord agrees to hypnotise his daughter into forging a cheque for £80,000. His alcoholic brother, who collects typewriters, points a torch at the girl; Ord himself intones some Svengali-esque sleepy-talk; in the garden a coloured chauffeur called Spike Munch keeps guard; and upstairs, listening in on the house telephone, is the private eye—or is it the young journalist?

I forgot to mention the young journalist. He came to interview Ord in the first scene and stayed to fall in love with his daughter. I will not reveal, because I can barely recall, the third-act resolution. I remember that Mr. Bull sprang across the stage with, as they say, an agility surprising in one of his bulk; that he ended up with a Corsican stiletto through his jugular; and that Mr. Curzon escaped with a compassionate caution. At all events, those who care about the problems of hypnotic forgery had their pet subject well aired. Others, less intimately concerned, may echo my opinion that *The Man with Expensive Tastes* is the crassest crime play since *The Inn-Keeper's Button,* which disfigured the theatrical season of 1897–8. Peter Bull, a trout among minnows, is magnificently assured; and Philip Stainton bumbles sibilantly through the role of the drunken brother—though even he is unable to save the scenes he shares with the comic Irish housekeeper.

I forgot to mention the comic Irish housekeeper. . . .

(1953)

Hamlet, BY WILLIAM SHAKESPEARE, AT THE OLD VIC; *The Confidential Clerk*, BY T. S. ELIOT, AT THE NEW THEATRE.

Forswearing Hollywood for a season, Richard Burton has joined the Old Vic troupe, with whom, last week, he opened in *Hamlet*. What we had hoped for was a violent, attacking prince who should be a corrective to the fingertip delicacies of the Gielgud tradition; a trumpet instead of a flute. Pale, tough, haunted, and heavy-headed, Burton looked marvels: but vocally the range wasn't there. Without flow or pattern, he jerked from strangled sobs to harsh, intolerant roars, lacking a middle register for contemplation. It was all stubbornly conscientious, rising to something grander in moments of decision, such as the play scene and the duel; but I could not help noting the absence of one essential quality. The absentee was finesse, which Burton can only suggest—to lift a phrase from Guildenstern—"with much forcing of his disposition." Shaw said of Forbes-Robertson that he played Hamlet classically, "as a man whose passions are those which have produced the philosophy, the poetry, the art and the stagecraft of the world, and not merely those which have produced its weddings, coroners' inquests and executions." Burton could never be this kind of hero. He recoils from unpacking his heart in words, and seems uneasy in long, analytical speeches. In fact, I suspect that if they met at a party Burton would find Hamlet a very tiresome companion, all talk and tears.

The women have the best of the production. Polonius is too fidgety, and Claudius a downright sloven; but Fay Compton, abandoning her latter-day manner (trudging and grousing), superbly completes Shakespeare's unfinished portrait of Gertrude, whom she presents as a confused, desperately maternal creature with a fatal gift of lying. And

Claire Bloom's Ophelia is much the best I have seen. Five years ago, when she was seventeen, Miss Bloom played the part at Stratford under the same director (Michael Benthall), and I have never forgotten the moment when, at the end of the dirty doggerel about St. Valentine's day, she screamed: "If—thou—hadst—not—come—to—my—bed!"—driving each word separately home like a coffin nail. She has kept this "effect," and strengthened and deepened the rest of the mad scenes, which are now a miraculous cadenza: the voice flying and plunging, the hair everywhere, the body restless as one of Van Gogh's cypresses, the whole performance a terrible premonition of the jester's grave to which, ironically, Ophelia will finally be committed. Not Polonius' death but Hamlet's (whom she presumes slaughtered in England) is the chief cause of this Ophelia's lunacy. One's impression is of a blind cage-bird suddenly released and beating out its brains against walls and battlements unseen.

Hamlet is easy meat, a welcome febrifuge, after Eliot's new play, which uses devices borrowed from Coward, Pirandello, Wilde, Euripides, and Gilbert and Sullivan to illustrate moral precepts borrowed from nobody. *The Cocktail Party,* which many thought obscure, I found almost painfully simple; but *The Confidential Clerk,* acclaimed in England for its simplicity, strikes me as being one of the most complex pieces of work Mr. Eliot has ever attempted. The language, admittedly, is far from abstruse, and the characters are easy to grasp, but the narrative pattern is staggeringly intricate. It is bizarre; it is "the wrong shape"; it has the weird whorls and intersections one might expect if one's eccentric uncle set about playing with a model railway set. Mr. Eliot has coated a hard moral pill with a myriad layers of theatrical sugar, which cannot but irritate those who, like myself, feel that only children need sugar on their pills.

Although there is little direct action, the play is nearly all plot. The central character is Colby Simpkins, a young ex-organist appointed to replace old Eggerson, a kindly grey-beard, as confidential clerk to Sir Claude Mulhammer, a city financier who believes Colby to be his illegitimate son. The Mulhammer household is full of dynastic discrepancies, including the vivacious Lucasta Angel, another of Sir Claude's bastards, and a breezy stockbroker named Kaghan, who announces himself a foundling. (*Vide* Wilde: "To lose one parent, Mr. Worthing, may be regarded as a misfortune; to lose both looks like carelessness.") An incipient romance between Colby and Lucasta is blighted by Colby's knowledge that they share the same father; at which point, halfway through, the play shifts gear to farce. Sir Claude's wife, the lark-brained Lady Elizabeth, hears Colby's story of his upbringing at the hands of a Mrs. Guzzard in Teddington, and instantly declares that he is *her* illegitimate son, and not her husband's. (*Vide* the *Ion* of Euripides, in which Xuthus and Creusa dispute Ion's parentage, neither of them knowing the truth.) In the third and last scene Mrs. Guzzard herself is summoned to settle the argument: a solid middle-class matron, in whose speeches there are disturbingly oracular overtones, and who may conceivably be Pallas Athene. She is a part-time baby-farmer. (*Vide* Buttercup's song in *H.M.S. Pinafore:*

> A many years ago,
> When I was young and charming,
> As some of you may know,
> I practised baby-farming. . . .
> Two tender babes I nussed;
> One was of low condition,
> The other, upper crust,
> A regular patrician. . . .)

I am not giving away any vital secrets when I divulge that Colby proves to be neither Sir Claude's nor Lady Elizabeth's child, and that a parent is found for the mysterious Mr. Kaghan. Eliot's message has to do with what Mrs. Guzzard calls "wishing wisely": we must all choose vocations that are commensurate with our capacities. What we want to be must tally with what we are. Three acts are spent in establishing *who* the characters are (*vide* Pirandello, *passim*), but more important, Eliot implies, is *what* they are. The conclusion is that geniuses may carve for themselves, reckless of heredity, but the rest, the sublunary lot, must follow their parents.

The dialogue, deliberately flat and explicit, often reminiscent of automatic writing, is much concerned with the difference between imposing terms on life and accepting life's terms, between rejection of routine (the rare, abnormal way) and compromise with it (the sane, usual way). The London critics have agreed that the play is a comedy: but if you subtract Lady Elizabeth, a Cowardesque creature whose first lover was "run over by a rhinoceros," there are precious few laughs in the evening. Truer to say that Eliot invokes the comic spirit, with its attendant mechanism of coincidence and absurdity, to disguise a hard core of sombre theorizing.

The words are physically unexciting to listen to—verse in aspic, you might say. Eliot's gift as a playwright is not to raise the temperature, but to lower it, as spooks are said to do when they enter a room. By the use of an unexpected, hieratic word, he can induce a chill mystery. This is what gives his characters their solitude and remoteness; we are always, the style insists, isolated from one another; there can be no earthly fruition—and, the style being the man, one sympathizes profoundly with the author. In *The Confidential Clerk,* however, he has moved far enough toward mundane humanity to create one warm, complete, stock character: Eggerson, the old retainer, which Alan Webb plays to perfection, interlarding the lines with blinks, coughs, and chuckles enough to outface Mr. Chips himself. The women, Margaret Leighton and Isabel Jeans, are both enslaved to the most potent influence on English actresses since the 1918 armistice—the soaring vocal style of Edith Evans, whose nonchalant music has led our comediennes to believe that to get good notices it is absolutely necessary to mimic Lady Bracknell.

If you look hard, you cannot help noticing that *The Confidential Clerk* nurses, close to its heart, a tiny fictional absurdity. It depends on an undelivered letter sent by Mrs. Guzzard to Sir Claude (conveniently in Canada), informing him that his mistress has died and with her his unborn child. But then, as Mr. Eliot is well aware, the *dénouement* of *Romeo and Juliet* is likewise dependent on postal bungling. No matter how logic may puncture it, *The Confidential Clerk* remains tantalisingly clever—a labyrinth all the more teasing because it leaves you, at curtain-fall, a day's trot away from the centre. It is fascinating in performance, puzzling in retrospect, and, at all times and from whatever angle, unique.

(1953)

A Tribute to Mr. Coward.

To be famous young and to make fame last—the secret of combining the two is glandular: it depends on energy. Someone once asked Demosthenes what was the most important quality in an orator. "Action," he said. And the second? "Action." And the third? "Action." So with a talent.

Noël Coward, who was performing in public at ten, has never stopped being in action; at fifty-three he retains all the heady zest of adolescence. Forty years ago he was Slightly in *Peter Pan,* and you might say that he has been wholly in *Peter Pan* ever since. No private considerations have been allowed to deflect the drive of his career; like Gielgud and Rattigan, like the late Ivor Novello, he is a congenital bachelor. He began, like many other satirists (Evelyn Waugh, for instance), by rebelling against conformity, and ended up making his peace with it, even becoming its outspoken advocate.

Any child with a spark of fantasy in its soul is prone to react against the English middle classes, into which Coward was born. The circumstances of his early upbringing, in Teddington, were "liable," he wrote afterwards, "to degenerate into refined gentility unless carefully watched." He promptly reacted against them, and also against his first school-teacher, whom he bit in the arm—"an action which I have never for an instant regretted." From this orgy of rebellion he excepted his mother, a tiny octogenarian who is now comfortably installed in a flat in Eaton Square. With the production of *The Vortex,* in 1924, notoriety hit him. He had already written two other plays and most of a revue, meanwhile announcing that his own wit and Ivor Novello's profile were the first and second wonders of the modern world.

The Vortex, a jeremiad against narcotics with dialogue that sounds today not so much stilted as high-heeled, was described by Beverley Nichols as "immortal." Others, whom it shocked, were encouraged in their heresy by an unfortunate photograph for which Coward posed supine on a knobbly brass bedstead, wearing a dressing-gown and "looking," as he said, "like a heavily-doped Chinese illusionist." From this sprang the myth that he wrote all his plays in an absinthe-drenched coma; in fact, as he has been patiently explaining for nearly thirty years, he drinks little and usually starts punishing his typewriter at seven a.m. His triumph has been to unite two things ever dissociated in the English mind: hard work and wit. Toil is commonly the chum of serious-mindedness; and though, within Coward, a social historian and philosopher are constantly campaigning to be let out, they seldom escape into his work. His wit in print is variable—he has not written a really funny play since *Present Laughter* in 1942—but in private it is unflagging. It took Coward to describe an American adaptation of *The Cherry Orchard,* set in the deep South, as "A Month in the Wrong Country"; and many other theatrical *mots* have been fathered on him. We may never know, for example, whether it was he who, after seeing a certain actress as Queen Victoria, left the theatre murmuring: "I never realized before that Albert married beneath him."

To see him whole, public and private personalities conjoined, you must see him in cabaret. Just before his first season at the Café de Paris, I noticed him watching his predecessor, whose act was not going too well.

I asked him how he was enjoying the performance, and, with a stark, stunned, take-it-or-leave-it stare, he hissed: "Sauce! Sheer sauce!" A few weeks later he padded down the celebrated stairs himself, halted before the microphone on black-suede-clad feet, and, upraising both hands in a gesture of benediction, set about demonstrating how these things should be done. Baring his teeth as if unveiling some grotesque monument, and cooing like a baritone dove, he gave us "I'll See You Again" and the other bat's-wing melodies of his youth. Nothing he does on these occasions sounds strained or arid; his tanned, leathery face is still an enthusiast's.

All the time the hands are at their task, affectionately calming your too-kind applause. Amused by his own frolicsomeness, he sways from side to side, waggling a finger if your attention looks like wandering. If it is possible to romp fastidiously, that is what Coward does. He owes little to earlier wits, such as Wilde or Labouchère. Their best things need to be delivered slowly, even lazily. Coward's emerge with the staccato, blind impulsiveness of a machine-gun.

I have heard him accused of having enervated English comedy by making it languid and blasé. The truth, of course, is the opposite: Coward took sophistication out of the refrigerator and set it bubbling on the hob. He doses his sentences with pauses, as you dose epileptics with drugs. To be with him for any length of time is exhausting and invigorating in roughly equal proportions. He is perfectly well aware that he possesses "star quality," which is the lodestar of his life. In his case, it might be defined as the ability to project, without effort, the outline of a unique personality, which had never existed before him in print or paint.

Even the youngest of us will know, in fifty years' time, exactly what we mean by "a very Noël Coward sort of person."

(1953)

Some Notes on Stage Sexuality.

The most characteristic English play on the subject of physical love is Shakespeare's *Antony and Cleopatra.* It is characteristic because it has no love scenes. The English, as their drama represents them, are a nation endlessly communicative about love without ever enjoying it. Full-blooded physical relationships engaged in with mutual delight are theatrically tabu. Thwarted love is preferred, the kind Mr. Coward wrote about in *Brief Encounter,* where two married people (married, of course, to two other people) form a sad and meagre attachment without being able to follow it through. At the end of a play on some quite different subject—religion, perhaps, or politics—it is customary for the hero to say, as he does in *Robert's Wife:* "I was deeply in love with a fine woman," and for the wife to reply: "My dear, dear husband"; but there should be no hint elsewhere in the text that they have as much as brushed lips.

In comedies marriage is presented as the high road to divorce. Husband and wife begin the play at Daggers Drawn, their country house, and the whole point of the ensuing exercise is to lure them back into each other's arms. The reconciliation takes place in the last act. Left alone on stage, the two lovers exchange coy salutations:

HENRY: Hello, Sybil.

SYBIL: Hello, Henry.

(*Curtain.*)

Among younger people the technique of courtship is even more rigorously codified. It is always practised on a *chaise-longue*. The girl sits down beside the boy and edges a few inches towards him, whereupon he edges a few inches away. This is repeated *ad lib* until the boy falls off. The purpose of the ritual is to show the English male's terror of sex and his instinctive tendency to yell for mother. He is always bashful and ashamed in the presence of women to whom he is not closely related. At first he addresses them as if they were new and disturbing nannies; later, as the relationship matures, he takes the giant step and treats the girl of his choice as a substitute mother. The plays of the twenties were full of scenes in which the hero, contorted with grief, confessed to his mother that he had transferred his affections to another woman.

A firmly established tenet of English drama is that love which is "only physical" will not last, and is probably ghastly anyway. Englishmen who go to American plays such as *A Streetcar Named Desire* frequently say afterwards: "Perhaps I'm naïve, but all this harping on sex strikes me as awfully boring." (Or "vulgar," or "tasteless," the other key words of English criticism.) They *are* naïve: there is no perhaps about it. Graham Greene's *The Living Room* was one of the few modern plays whose hero admitted to having had and enjoyed an affair. The heroine of Terence Rattigan's *The Deep Blue Sea* made the same dreadful admission. In both cases the penalty for extramarital pleasure was paid. Mr. Rattigan's heroine tried to gas herself and Mr. Greene's took poison. The idea that a man and a woman should fall head over hips in love and sensually exult in their mutual discovery is deeply offensive to English taste. Someone must suffer for it, and our playwrights see to it that someone does, harshly and irrevocably. *That,* it is felt, will teach them to flaunt themselves (the word is always "flaunt"): why can't they be repressed like everybody else?

Proposals are regarded with more tolerance, though the approach to them is often extremely oblique. In country-house comedies it has been known to go like this:

DICK (*blushing*): I have something—rather important to ask you, Miss Godalming.

MISS G.: What is it, Tom? (*I should have explained that there is a mistaken-identity plot going on at the same time.*)

DICK: Well . . . Honestly, I don't know quite how to put it.

MISS G. (*softly*): Is it—so very difficult?

DICK: Well, dash it, Gloria—I mean Miss Godalming—we hardly know each other, and (*business of fiddling with tie*) a fellow feels such a *fool*. . . .

I leave the rest to your imagination, though it is a bequest I wouldn't want left to mine. It comes out, on this occasion, that all Dick wanted was to borrow her razor. The real proposal comes later. Dick trudges down to breakfast with a farcical cold, the result of having climbed a drain-pipe in a hailstorm, clad only in pyjamas, to steal the manuscript of Lady Godalming's scandalous autobiography from its place in the *escritoire*. The emotional climax is now at hand:

DICK: Would you bind passing the bustard?

MISS G. (*primly*): Not in the least, Richard.

DICK: Thag you. Atchoo. (*He munches dolefully, albeit with determination. All stage directions in English farce read like this, albeit worse.*) I say—Gloria!

MISS G.: Yes, Richard?

DICK: I dode suppose it batters a bit eddy bore, but (*wildly*) I love you bost awfully, and—Gloria, will you let me use your razor for always?

MISS G. (*recklessly throwing her toast to the floor*): Of course I will, you darling chump!

Their embrace is interrupted by the French maid Marie, pronounced Murray, and the title of the piece, a miracle of catarrhal euphony, is *Barry Be Todight.*

English romantic drama is built around interrupted or frustrated embraces. Uninterrupted embraces only take place years before the

to grip his ten-year-old boy by the shoulders and say: "Don't know how it is, son, but we never seem to—to *get through* to each other," the child would assume that he was drunk. In an American play the child would burst into tears and take to drink himself.

The function of English stage children is usually to teach their elders the rudiments of good behaviour, on the out-of-the-mouths-of-babes-and-sucklings theory. If junior starts wearing a shoulder-holster and spitting in church, it is a hint to Mums and Dads that they had better set about patching up their marriage. If Sensitive Type spends her nights sulking in the rabbit-hutch, it is because she is being deprived of love. If a whole batch of sucklings flies off to a peace conference (as in Roger MacDougall's *Escapade*), it is to teach their parents the foolishness of war. Modern kid plays are always cautionary plays.

The smallest category is that devoted to Juvenile Delinquents. It takes as its text the words "Society is the Real Criminal." This quickly grows wearisome, not because it is not true, but because it tends to rob the child of any capacity for individual choice, which is the life-blood of drama. Whatever he does, it is never his doing: he is a pawn in a game of sociological chess. For recent examples, see *Cosh Boy* and *Murder Story*.

We next find, loitering in the toils of adolescence, a listless battalion of Sensitive Types. These are the direct descendants of the children in Victorian plays, who existed only for the purpose of dying young or being orphaned. The girls get tragic crushes, from which they are gently dissuaded: "You must remember, darling, Robert is fifty years older than you. When you're twenty-five, he'll be seventy-nine. Had you thought of that?" The oldest inhabitants in this group are the Constant Nymph and Young Woodley. These two, by a sort of box-office mating, have bred dozens of equally tormented offspring. Before Mummy can announce in the last scene that "Our little girl has become a woman," her little girl must spend at least two acts hating Mummy's guts. Traumatic experiences are not uncommon. The heroine of *The Seventh Veil* was blighted as a concert pianist by a school caning, while *The Girl Who Couldn't Quite* was fixated by a wart on her nanny's nose. The latter, by the way, was the last ingenue on the English stage to utter the time-honoured line: "I'm going to keep crying till there's no more cry left in me."

Though a little short on cry, the dominant variety of child's play is undoubtedly school drama. It is always a public school; no other kind of education is known to the English theatre. Only three types of men need apply for jobs on the staff: breezy young half-wits (to teach Sports), thin-lipped sadists (to teach Latin or Science, according to the author's politics), and genial old bumblers (to teach a Broad Understanding of Humanity). Sadists and bumblers alike address their charges in polysyllables: "And what has the egregious Watson minor to say for himself? Come, come, boy, say not that the omniscience of yesternight has vanished with the snows of yesteryear!" Latin tags are also in evidence, a favourite being the one beginning "*Tempora mutantur. . . .*"

Every school has its Swot, who is named Crump or Pilkington and wears clothes that are slightly too small for him. Primitive Swots were always buffoons, but with the dawn of the liberal conscience they have become semi-sympathetic characters: "Do they rag you," the leading lady may enquire, "for reading Swinburne in the dorm?" But the great majority of stage schoolboys, now as in the past, are Wide-Eyed Bouncers. These bounce like the kind of beach-ball one longs to throw out to sea. They begin every sentence with "I say!" and their vocabulary of slang has survived unchanged from the era of Jack Harkaway and the horseless carriage. To them the Swot is "a complete smear" who talks "bilge," and they express derision in such terms as "Three groans for the Beak!" Stool-pigeons are said to "split," and no self-respecting Bouncer ever gets through a scene without using "funk it," "shirty," or "lazy slacker." Bouncers never leave a room: they "cut along." One of the finest recent snatches of Bouncer dialogue was contributed by Warren Chetham Strode: "No decent chap mentions soccer at a rugger school"—though it is strongly challenged by someone else's masterly line: "What rot, Sholto! Nobody sacks a man for blubbing!"

Every now and then our playwrights try their hand at the boy-born-to-be-king theme, in which the hero is a child with an aura of mystery surrounding him. J. M. Barrie's *The Boy David* is a fair example of this sort of thing. David tells Samuel that he has just had an important thought while minding the sheep. Invited to share it, he recites the opening verses of the Twenty-third Psalm. "You must finish that some day," says Samuel sagely. These chosen children, destined in later life to become prophets, poets, or inventors of the spinning-jenny, are regarded by their families—for the first act, at least—with resentment and hostility. They are the Cinderellas of the household, and represent the apotheosis of the Sensitive Type. Suddenly they perform a miracle or write a symphony. Their parents are appalled and beat them; but before long the mighty of the earth, having heard of the wonder, are besieging the little mud hut. The child is uncomfortably dressed in his best, and one of the visitors is sure to remark: "Your son, my good woman, stands in no need of external finery. His power is within." Emlyn Williams' *The Wind of Heaven* has all the earmarks of the breed, which has proved extremely prolific.

The classic, all-round English urchin is still, of course, Peter Pan. Pan is no Swot, but he combines the characteristics of all the other types. He is Wide-Eyed, he is Sensitive, and he is murderous enough at times to be classed as a Juvenile Delinquent. The only adult thing about Barrie's play is its unctuous sentimentality; the rest shows real insight into the cruelty and wantonness of childhood. It also gives a disquieting picture of the nanny-worship and mother-complexes which turn so many English children into interesting psychological wrecks. The "Wendy bird" is first wounded and then deified as mother; the villain of the piece is Father, who ends up literally in the dog-house.

If someone were to undertake a full Freudian analysis of Pan, I have a feeling that it would teach us a great deal about all English dramatists who write about children. For they share with him one basic quality: a rooted aversion to growing up.

(1954)

Prose and the Playwright.

Where the modern poetic drama is concerned, I have always been for the man Bacon quotes who, when asked his opinion of poets, said he thought them the best writers, next to those that wrote prose. But lately, among my friends, I have been finding myself in a beleaguered minority; the post-war vogue of T. S. Eliot and Christopher Fry has brought back into play that ancient battering-ram of criticism, the assumption that the upper reaches of dramatic experience are the exclusive province of the poet. This kind of talk is probably giving the prose playwrights a brutal inferiority-complex, and I have a mind to contest it. For if Eliot is right in suggesting that there are certain subtle and rarefied states of being which can achieve theatrical expression only in verse, then a great battle has been lost, almost by default.

We tend to forget how long it took to make prose socially acceptable in the theatre. Up to the last quarter of the nineteenth century it remained a slightly dingy poor relation; the Greeks sniffed at it, Shakespeare reserved it mostly for persiflage, Molière shunned it whenever (as in *Tartuffe* or *Le Misanthrope*) he had anything ambitious in hand, and in the long eighteenth-century debates about the relative fitness of blank verse and heroic couplets for tragedy, prose seldom got more than a passing and perfunctory mention. The English romantics carried on the tradition of bardolatry: Shelley, Byron, Wordsworth, Keats, and Coleridge all wrote unactable verse tragedies, thus delivering what might easily have been the death-blow to serious drama in English. Nobody seemed to have noticed that ever since Shakespeare's death poetic tragedy had been languishing and prose comedy flourishing; and it occurred to no one that the latter's prosperity might be due not so much to its being comic as to its being prose. In the Elizabethan era, before drama had been clearly distinguished from other literary forms, it naturally contained a good deal of the epic, much of the lyric, and a strong flavor of what A. B. Walkley called "that element of mixed philosophy and rhetoric which was soon afterwards to be diverted into other channels, in England by Sir Thomas Browne, in France by the great pulpit orators." By the beginning of the last century the process of differentiation had taken place, and the drama stolidly ignored it.

The three gigantic musketeers of prose were, of course, Ibsen, Chekhov, and Shaw; they made it respectable, and Chekhov even went so far as to show that prose, by means of what it implied rather than what it stated, could reproduce the effect of poetry in purely theatrical terms. By 1900 it began to look as if prose had gained its point—and pretty tardily, too, since the novel had started to replace the verse epic two centuries earlier, It would have surprised the drama critics of the period to be told that within fifty years the old medium would once more be asserting its claim to dramatic supremacy. Yet that is what has happened. Just as prose has started to test its wings, we are asked to believe that it can never fly. The powers of the line that stops short of the margin are again being hymned and its mysteries celebrated.

This seems to me grossly unhistorical and based on an alarming number of unproven assumptions. For an irrevocable change has been overtaking language in the last three hundred years. Poetry and colloquial prose, which are now (in spite of Wordsworth) linguistically divorced, shared in the sixteenth century rich champaigns of vocabulary and image. Elizabethan pamphlets are as generous with metaphor as Elizabethan plays; and a dramatist could inject a shot of colloquialism into a tragic aria without courting bathos. Nobody titters when Hamlet, in mid-soliloquy, exclaims, "Why, what an ass am I!"; but when Aaron, in Christopher Fry's tragedy *The Firstborn,* says of Moses that "he took me by the scruff of my heart," it is comic in much the same way as Abe Burrows' parody of the "sophisticated-type" love song: "You put a piece of carbon-paper under your heart, and gave me just a copy of your love." Everyone agrees that formal poetic diction is dead; yet if you spike a dramatic verse-form with the vernacular, the experiment invariably fails—unless a comic or ironic effect was what you had in mind. Auden, Isherwood, Eliot, and Fry have all exploited this trick of bathos; and it may be that the wheel has come full circle, that poetry in the theatre should be confined to comedy, where its potency still lingers.

The customary plea for verse is summed up in this extract from one of Dryden's essays: "All the arguments which are formed against it, can amount to no more than this, that it is not so near conversation as prose, and therefore not so natural. But it is clear to all who understand poetry, that serious plays ought not to imitate conversation too nearly." And once you admit that "naturalness" is not enough, he continues, you are halfway to accepting poetry: "You have lost that which you call natural, and have not acquired the last perfection of Art." But Dryden's antithesis is a false one. The perfection of art in the theatre depends neither on naturalism nor on poetry. Drama has in its time borrowed tricks from both, but what it has built is a new and separate structure, whose foundation stones—the last acts of *The Master Builder* and *The Three Sisters*—are architectural triumphs of prose over naturalism.

On naturalism I shrink from pronouncing, because I have never (has anyone?) seen a completely naturalistic play—I doubt if one exists. What bothers me is the way in which the higher criticism equates prose with poverty of dramatic expression. "What is the prose for God?" cries one pundit, quoting from Granville-Barker and forgetting that the answer to the question is on almost every page of the Bible. Nobody wants to banish luxury of language from the theatre; what needs banishing is the notion that it is incompatible with prose, the most flexible weapon the stage has ever had, and still shining new. Those playwrights who have followed the Ibsen-Chekhov lead are in the main stream of modern drama. Giraudoux for prime example; *La Folle de Chaillot* and *La Guerre de Troie* represent prose exulting in its own versatility, embracing slang and stateliness, gutter and glitter, in one enormous grasp. Synge and O'Casey stand beside Giraudoux in the great line; and when, earlier this year, Dylan Thomas' *Under Milk Wood* was published, nobody could doubt that only death had robbed us of another to join them. *Under Milk Wood* was commissioned by BBC for sound broadcasting, but two Sunday-night stagings of it at the Old Vic proved that it could enmesh the watcher as well as the listener. Here, unfolding in the talk and thoughts of its inhabitants, was a day in the life of a Welsh coastal town, a devout and mischievous celebration of the sea, soil, wind, and wantonness of Wales. Prose went into battle rejoicing. Take, for instance, this exchange between Mrs. Cherry Owen and her errant husband:

MRS. CHERRY OWEN: Remember last night? In you reeled, my boy, as drunk as a deacon with a big wet bucket and a fish-frail full of stout and you looked at me and you said, "God has come home!" you said, and then over the bucket you went, sprawling and bawling, and the floor was all flagons and eels.

CHERRY OWEN: Was I wounded?

MRS. CHERRY OWEN: And then you took off your trousers and you said, "Does anybody want to fight?" Oh, you old baboon.

Or the letter written by Mog Edwards, "a draper mad with love," to his "Beloved Myfanwy Price, my Bride in Heaven":

> I love you until Death do us part and then we shall be together for ever and ever. A new parcel of ribbons has come from Carmarthen today, all the colours in the rainbow. I wish I could tie a ribbon in your hair a white one but it cannot be. I dreamed last night you were all dripping wet and you sat on my lap as the Reverend Jenkins went down the street. I see you got a mermaid in your lap he said and he lifted his hat. He is a proper Christian. Not like Cherry Owen who said you should have thrown her back he said. Business is very poorly . . . If this goes on I shall be in the workhouse. My heart is in your bosom and yours is in mine. God be with you always Myfanwy Price and keep you lovely for me in His Heavenly Mansion. I must stop now and remain, Your Eternal, Mog Edwards.

The whole play is a tumult of living, and its burden is compressed into the remark of Polly Garter, the town tart: "Isn't life a terrible thing, thank God!" Philip Hope-Wallace, writing in the *Manchester Guardian,* sent his thoughts to the right place when he said: "Not since *Juno and the Paycock* have we heard in a theatre words coming up thus, not chosen but compelled: a fountain from the heart."

Thomas side-stepped the snare which besets the prose playwright who, though he abjures verse, secretly aspires to the condition of poetry. This fatal urge is responsible for the solemn, booming cadences, the sentences lying in comatose state, which one sometimes finds in the plays of Charles Morgan. *The Burning Glass* is a forest of prose on stilts, opulently teetering. Morgan's excuse, of course, is that Thomas had a head start on him, since (like O'Casey) he was putting words in the mouths of a people essentially imaginative. Morgan's characters are drawn from the English upper class, whose vocabulary is crippled by the restraints of social usage (no tears, no ecstasies), and about whom it is today practically impossible to write a great play. The spirit is not in them; or if it is, their tight lips firmly repress it. I doubt if even Arthur Miller or Tennessee Williams, the prose masters of the contemporary English-speaking theatre, could construct a tragedy around the country homes of Berks and Bucks. It is significant that the most successful passages of *The Cocktail Party* were those in which Eliot exposed the vacuity of *haut bourgeois* chatter:

> JULIA: . . . The only man I ever met who could hear the cry of bats.
>
> PETER: Hear the cry of bats?
>
> JULIA: He could hear the cry of bats.
>
> CELIA: But how do you know he could hear the cry of bats?
>
> JULIA: Because he said so. And I believed him.

Eliot is here using verse to show how resolutely, how comically unpoetical his characters are; and, wryly but appropriately, it works.

One of the handicaps of poetry is that penumbra of holiness, the legacy of the nineteenth century, which still surrounds it, coaxing us into tolerating sentimental excesses we would never forgive in prose:

> O God, O God, if I could return to yesterday, before I thought that I had made a decision. What devil left the door on the latch for these doubts to enter? And then you came back, you, the angel of destruction—just as I felt sure. In a moment, at your touch, there is nothing but ruin.

Exit, you might expect, into snowstorm; but you would be wrong. The lines come not from Victorian melodrama but from *The Cocktail Party,* printed as prose. Their lameness is particularly vexing because Eliot has shown himself capable of writing intensely muscular dramatic prose. So has Fry: one has only to read his lecture, "An Experience of Critics," parts of which are as speakable as a Giraudoux tirade. Much of his latest play, *The Dark Is Light Enough,* is infinitely less dramatic. Its construction rules out of court the old argument that poetic plays are deficient only in plot; *The Dark Is Light Enough* abounds in plot and incident, yet remains as static as a candle-lit tableau or darkling waxwork. It happens in a chateau on the Austro-Hungarian border. The Hungarian rebellion of 1848 has just begun, and a crisis is precipitated by the Countess Rosmarin, who decides to give shelter to Gettner, a deserter from the revolutionary army. The play's main action is the regeneration of Gettner, nihilist and traitor, by the Countess, who stands for divine charity, the justification of God's circuitous ways to man.

The first great drawback is the fact that Rosmarin, being by definition perfect, is incapable of development; in spite of Dame Edith Evans' vocal exertions, she can scarcely avoid resembling a benignly crinolined soup-kitchen. The second and greater drawback is, I am afraid, Fry's style, which—though it is noticeably less sportive than it used to be—seems now to have taken on the texture of diatomite, a substance used in the manufacture of pipestems which contains thousands of fossils to the cubic inch. The characters studiously express different attitudes towards life, but they use interchangeable rhythms and identical tricks of speech in which to do so. They *tell* us, with ruthless fluency, what kind of people they are, instead of letting us find out for ourselves. I needn't say that there are some fine set pieces of rhetoric; but the best of them—that in which Rosmarin likens Gettner to a blue plucked goose shivering on the water's brink—embodies in itself the germ of poetry's weakness: it describes in repose rather than illustrates in action. And one regrets the readiness with which Fry has succumbed to padding and jingle, in phrases like "for my sake, if my sake is worthy," "a coward, if a coward is what you are," "splendidly sleeping," "precariously promising," and "inconsolable inclination."

It is good to learn that he is at present making prose adaptations of Anouilh's *L'Alouette* and Giraudoux' *La Guerre de Troie;* perhaps the experience will lure him across the frontier into the large Gothic landscapes of prose. The chance of converting Eliot is, I imagine, much slimmer; but it may not be impertinent to suggest that even in his best play, *Murder in the Cathedral,* the most impressive pages were those which contained the speeches of self-exculpation by the four knights and the sermon delivered by Becket on Christmas Day. And these were all prose:

> I have spoken to you today, dear children of God, of the martyrs of the past . . . because it is fitting, on Christ's birth day, to remember what is that Peace which He brought; and because, dear children, I do not think I shall ever preach to you again; and because it is possible that in a short time you may have yet another martyr, and that one perhaps not the last. . . .

In poetry, Fry gilds where Eliot anoints; in neither procedure are there seeds of real dramatic vitality. If they, the foremost heretics, can be persuaded off their crosses, away from their martyrdom in a lost cause, the theatre would immediately benefit. Mallarmé once said, in lapidary despair: *"Pour moi le cas d'un poète, en cette société qui ne le permet de vivre, c'est le cas d'un homme qui s'isole pour sculpter son propre tombeau."* But he was slightly in error. It is not our society but our theatre which rejects the poet; "nowadays," as Walkley said, "we expect a drama to be purely dramatic." If poetic playwrights did not exist, it might be an agreeable caprice to invent them; but it would no longer be a necessity. And in a theatre starved by the cinema and besieged by television, necessities must come first.

(1954)

Rattigan in Two Volumes.

Reading Terence Rattigan's ten collected plays is an experience not unlike reclining on the bank of a suavely trickling stream in hot weather. One basks, stretches, is lulled by the swift, interminable murmur; one's reflexes are neutralised, and life pauses. Except when, at long intervals, the roar of a distant waterfall obtrudes, one's pleasure is negative, derived wholly from that marketable quality known to cynics as ingratiation and to romantics as charm.

It is a charm closely related to that of Bing Crosby, in that it looks deceptively, guilelessly imitable; indeed, it would not be too unfair to call Rattigan the bathtub baritone of the drama. So steadily does he aim to please that in his whole *oeuvre* there is but one "unpleasant" character—the rapacious Mrs. Crocker-Harris in *The Browning Version,* which stands beside the first two acts of *The Deep Blue Sea* as his most impressive work for the theatre. Elsewhere the negative virtues predominate: tact, understatement, avoidance of cliché—the hallmarks, in fact, of the "gentleman code" which holds so much of West End playwrighting in curious thrall.

The very title of Rattigan's play about Alexander of Macedon is significant: *Adventure Story*. Is it a modest shrug, or a form of insurance against the terrible charge of pretentiousness? After reading the play one is forced to conclude that Alexander's real crime, in Rattigan's eyes, was to have been guilty of conduct which would get him expelled from any decent club. His pagan legionaries move like gods and talk like prefects: "Been cheeking Alexander again, I expect," says a general of his son; the language will not rise to the occasion. Rather than risk the embarrassment of rhetoric, Rattigan, like many other English playwrights, has developed a talent for drawing undramatic people, and for deriding people who take life "dramatically," such as the actor-manager in *Harle-*

quinade, the sulky, Hamletesque son in *Love in Idleness,* or the little Frenchman in *While the Sun Shines,* with his talk of "a white-hot burning of the heart." There is no question that if Cyrano de Bergerac were to turn up in a Rattigan play, he would be laughed off the stage in two minutes.

The author's long preface to the two volumes must be one of the most articulate confessions of faith ever penned by a popular playwright. Much of it is an unexceptionable defence of "good theatre." What demands refutation is the way in which Rattigan generalises from his own example. It is a pity that he feels it necessary to ironise at the expense of dramatists whose plays fail to please the million—there is, after all, such a thing as a minority audience, and it is a matter of shame, not of self-congratulation, that there is less minority theatre here than in Paris. Nor is it true to assert that "A play does not fail because it is too good; it fails because it is not good enough." Thornton Wilder's *Our Town* failed in London seven years ago: for whom, one wonders, was it not good enough? The answer is that many plays fail because they are not bad enough.

I understand, though I cannot applaud, Rattigan's allegiance to a mythical, middle-class admirer called "Aunt Edna," whom he holds to be the backbone of the theatre. Confusion arises when, blind to her failings, he credits Aunt Edna with having been the first to decide that *Hamlet* was a better play than *Timon of Athens;* the truth, of course, is that she goes to *Hamlet* because generations of highbrows have told her to. She follows, never leads, intelligent taste; nor does she abandon for an instant her inner conviction that *Hamlet* is a far less suitable play than *Quiet Weekend.* In his loyalty to the old lady, as in his subsequent declaration that the theatre is not the place in which to express "ideas," Rattigan is rationalising to the top of his bent. The fact that Aunt Edna is collectively flocking to see *The Sleeping Prince* (described by an American visitor as "a breath of old caviare") will doubtless do much to comfort him.

Whatever his shortcomings as a theorist, nobody can deny Rattigan's supreme agility as a craftsman. His mastery of exposition is complete: give one of his characters a telephone, and within a minute, imperceptibly, the essentials of the situation will have been clearly sketched in. To the complaint that there is nothing quotable in his work, he has prepared an elaborate answer. He refers in the preface to an "element of the pioneering and the experimental" in his comedies, by which he means their verbal economy; he believes that "Yes," in context, can be more effective (i.e., funnier) than an ornately turned paragraph—which, if one judges comedies entirely on the number of sides they split, is indisputable. But in setting his face against what he calls "the 'gilded phrase' school" (Congreve and his contemporaries), Rattigan overlooks a vital point, which is that Congreve was writing about men and women of exceptional wit: and extraordinary people do tend to speak extraordinarily, even memorably.

The greatest plays are those which convince us that men can occasionally speak like angels. The rest, which conspire to imply that angels speak exactly like men, deserve and achieve respectable acclaim, but they must not repine if, finally, their passports to immortality are found invalid. The Grand Duchess in *The Sleeping Prince* is the first exceptional human being Rattigan has invented. We must now hope for more. He has already given us two striking tragedies of understatement, a vivid *drame à thèse,* and a clutch of likeable comedies, but I doubt whether he will long be content with a position, however secure and widely acknowledged, at the head of the second rank. Meanwhile, I commend to him Shaw's dictum: "the drama's laws the drama's patrons do *not* give: that is the prerogative of the dramatist, and of the dramatist alone."

(1954)

A Note on Criticism.

Critics in the past have seen themselves variously as torch-bearers, pall-bearers, and lighthouses shining over unmapped seas; I see myself predominantly as a lock. If the key, which is the work of art, fits snugly into my mechanism of bias and preference, I click and rejoice; if not, I am helpless, and can only offer the artist the address of a better locksmith. Sometimes, unforeseen, a masterpiece seizes the knocker, batters down the door, and enters unopposed; and when that happens, I am a willing casualty. I cave in *con amore.* But mostly I am at a loss. It is a sombre truth that nowadays our intellectuals go to the cinema and shun the theatre. Their assistance is sadly missed; but their defection is my opportunity.

(1954)

Hedda Gabler, BY HENRIK IBSEN, AT THE LYRIC, HAMMERSMITH; *Macbeth*, BY WILLIAM SHAKESPEARE, AT THE OLD VIC.

Let me court peril with a generalisation: that good drama, of whatever kind, has but one mainspring—the human being reduced by ineluctable process to a state of desperation. Desperate are the cornered giants of Sophocles; desperate, too, as they huddle in their summer-houses, the becalmed gentry of Chekhov; and the husband of French farce, with a wife in one bedroom and a mistress in another, is he not, though we smile at his agony, definably desperate? The clown in the haunted house and the prince on the haunted battlements have this in common, that their drama heightens as they are driven to the last ditch of their souls. How, in this extremity, will they comport themselves? It is to find out that we go to theatres: to *Hedda Gabler* at Hammersmith, or to *Macbeth* at the Vic.

What a match, one muses, these two fiends would have made! Hedda is all rapacious sterility, a perfect embodiment of the philosophy of de Sade, which Mr. Geoffrey Gorer has described as one of "pleasure in the ego's modification of the external world." Power over life is what she and Macbeth seek, and he achieves it with the satanic flourish, the "vine-leaves in his hair," to which Eilert Lovborg could never aspire. It is for Macbeth's world that Hedda, a locust at large in a grove of Pooters, perennially pines.

One knows with what ballast Sardou would have loaded her story. Ignored by an ageing husband, she would have seduced an ex-lover (Lovborg), lost him to another woman, and blackmailed him into suicide. Shamed by the nobility of Tesman's forbearance, she would then have killed herself "to atone." Ibsen takes this raw meat and deliberately removes the romantic element. Hedda's destructiveness springs not from passion but from sexual frigidity. Not otherwise would she have married Tesman, whom George Devine plays with an exquisite, lumbering donnishness; not otherwise repel the advances of Brack (Michael MacLiammoir, a trifle uneasy in the mysteries of cicisbeism); not otherwise stiffen at every mention of motherhood, or burn Eilert Lovborg's manuscript, his "child" by Mrs. Elvsted. *Hedda Gabler* is what Hazlitt called Kemble, "an icicle upon the bust of tragedy."

Peter Ashmore's production is the finest tribute to Ibsen since Michael Benthall's *Wild Duck* in 1948. Your weather-beaten British playgoer, who likes his entertainment warmed by the blue skies of Verona,

Nice, or Siam, has immemorially shunned Ibsen, with his grim galoshes and abiding rain. Aware of this, Mr. Ashmore's designers, Motley, have dulcified Hedda's habitat: the Tesman villa is a costly pleasance, baked in a blinding sun. The centrepiece is Peggy Ashcroft's Hedda, a flinty, marvellously impartial performance. How many temptations this actress resists! She makes no play for sympathy; nor does she imply that she despises the woman she is impersonating. Her vocal mannerisms, cool and tinkling as teaspoons twirled in china cups, are exactly fitted to Hedda's malice; and the whole display is a monument to *nymphomanie de tête,* which might roughly be translated as the nymphomania of Hedda.

The Old Vic *Macbeth* offers nothing as good. Mr. Benthall's production is a bellowing-match, with every other word, how harmless soever its meaning, spat in a pet at the audience's face. My impression was of an operatic transcription of the cartoons of Charles Addams. One of the play's few quiet lines, "It will be rain to-night," fell from the mouth of Eric Porter's Banquo like manna on the starved. Rachel Roberts is the best witch for years; John Wood's Lennox cuts like a razor through the stubble of fustian; and Ann Todd makes a piercing Lady Macbeth. As her distracted helpmeet, Paul Rogers amalgamates all the vital characteristics of the First, Second, and Third Murderers. The part needs lungs plus genius; Mr. Rogers does all that lungs can, and is at his best in the last act, which he plays all out for wild white hair and bellicose ecstasy.

(1954)

Second-rateness.

Every critic, tiring of perfectionism, acquires an uncritical self. This is the self which he, a happy truant, brings to the consideration of striptease, pantomime, amateur performances of Shakespeare, and professional performances of English farce. Such trivia, he feels, are beneath criticism; their frailty must be tolerated. Should his skilled, observant, critical self rise up and dismember a foolish farce, he is at once accused of being a spoilsport. Obediently he anaesthetises the very faculty that governed his choice of profession, and when faced with nonsense, he dubs it "unpretentious" and lets it pass.

But at times, out of sheer overwork, the uncritical self rebels. The familiar phrases—"a harmless romp," "for children of all ages," "should pack the theatre for years"—trot less readily from the typewriter. And the critic discerns that someone has taken advantage of him. Incubated by his lenience, the second-rate things—Thalia's failures—have flourished and multiplied until they crowd his horizon, roaring with laughter and pushing from sight the few obstreperous oddlings who had hoped to tell him of life and pain, of love and death. When this happens, he must call a halt.

Some weeks ago Walter Kerr, the American critic, arrived at a snap diagnosis of the West End theatre. Where Broadway has one standard of playcraft, he said, London has two, equally successful: a primary drama, including respectable revivals and new plays by established authors, and a secondary drama, comprising tea-cup comedy and kitchen farce. Politeness forbade him to draw the obvious conclusion: that critics and public alike lower their sights whenever a "secondary" play is presented. We *expect* our farces to be bad, and are outraged when Broadway, which insists that its farces be good, sends us a specimen as celestially gay as *The Seven Year Itch.*

The results of our culpable tolerance surround us. No playwright rises above his audience's expectations for very long. Why should he do his best work when *Dry Rot* and *The Love Match* are delighting the public with their worthlessness? Nobody wants to see the secondary theatre abolished, but it is imperative that it should be judged by higher critical standards. Twenty-seven West End theatres are at present offering light comedies and musical shows, of which perhaps a dozen are good of their kind. The number of new plays with the slightest claim to serious discussion is three: *A Day by the Sea, The Dark Is Light Enough,* and *I Am a Camera.* One need not be a purist to be ashamed of the discrepancy. Our garden is beset with weeds, and "the coulter rusts that should deracinate such savagery." The secondary theatre must put forth better shoots—and fewer. It is so easy, as the elder Dumas said, not to write plays.

(1954)

Separate Tables, BY TERENCE RATTIGAN, AT THE ST. JAMES'.

(The scene is the dining-room of a Kensington hotel, not unlike the Bournemouth hotel in which Separate Tables, *Terence Rattigan's new double bill, takes place. A Young Perfectionist is dining; beside him, Aunt Edna, whom Mr. Rattigan has described as the "universal and immortal" middle-class playgoer.)*

AUNT EDNA: Excuse me, young man, but have you seen Mr. Rattigan's latest?

YOUNG PERFECTIONIST: I have indeed.

A.E.: And what is it about?

Y.P.: It is two plays about four people who are driven by loneliness into a state of desperation.

A.E. (sighing): Is there not enough morbidity in the world . . . ?

Y.P.: One of them is a drunken Left-wing journalist who has been imprisoned for wife-beating. Another is his ex-wife, who takes drugs to palliate the loss of her looks. She revives his masochistic love for her, and by curtain-fall they are gingerly reunited.

A.E. (*quailing*): Does Mr. Rattigan analyse these creatures?

Y.P.: He does, in great detail.

A.E.: How very unwholesome! Pray go on.

Y.P.: In the second play the central character is a bogus major who has lately been convicted of assaulting women in a cinema.

A.E.: Ouf!

Y.P.: His fellow-guests hold conclave to decide whether he should be expelled from the hotel. Each contributes to a symposium on sexual deviation. . . .

A.E.: In pity's name, stop!

Y.P.: The major reveals that his foible is the result of fear, which has made him a hermit, a liar, and a pervert. This revelation kindles sympathy in the heart of the fourth misfit, a broken spinster, who befriends him in his despair.

A.E. (*aghast*): I *knew* I was wrong when I applauded *The Deep Blue Sea.* And what conclusion does Mr. Rattigan draw from these squalid anecdotes?

Y.P.: From the first, that love unbridled is a destroyer. From the second, that love bridled is a destroyer. You will enjoy yourself.

A.E.: But I go to the theatre to be taken out of myself!

Y.P.: Mr. Rattigan will take you into an intricately charted world of suspense. By withholding vital information, he will tantalise you; by disclosing it unexpectedly, he will astound you.

A.E.: But what information! Sex and frustration!

Y.P.: I agree that the principal characters, especially the journalist and the major, are original and disturbing creations. But there is also a tactful, omniscient *hôtelière,* beautifully played by Beryl Measor. And what do you say to a comic Cockney Maid?

A.E.: Ah!

Y.P.: Or to Aubrey Mather as a whimsical dominie? Or to a pair of opinionated medical students? Or to a tyrannical matriarch—no less than Phyllis Neilson-Terry?

A.E.: *That* sounds more like it. You console me.

Y.P.: I thought you would feel at home. And Peter Glenville, the director, has craftily engaged for these parts actors subtle enough to disguise their flatness.

A.E. (*clouding over*): But what about those difficult leading roles?

Y.P.: Margaret Leighton plays two of them, rather externally. Her beauty annihilates the pathos of the ex-wife, who should be oppressed with crow's-feet. And her mousy spinster, dim and pink-knuckled, verges on caricature. It is Eric Portman who commands the stage, volcanic as the journalist, but even better as the major, speaking in nervous spasms and walking stiff-legged with his shoulders protectively hunched. He has the mask of the true mime, the *comédien* as opposed to the *acteur*.

A.E.: Yet you sound a trifle peaky. Is something biting you?

Y.P.: Since you ask, I regretted that the major's crime was not something more cathartic than mere cinema flirtation. Yet I suppose the play is as good a handling of sexual abnormality as English playgoers will tolerate.

A.E.: For my part, I am glad it is no better.

Y.P.: I guessed you would be; and so did Mr. Rattigan. Will you accompany me on a second visit tomorrow?

A.E.: With great pleasure. Clearly, there is something here for both of us.

Y.P.: Yes. But not quite enough for either of us.

(1954)

Arden of Faversham, AUTHORSHIP UNKNOWN, AT THE THEATRE ROYAL, STRATFORD-ATTE-BOWE.

Who wrote *Arden of Faversham?* Kyd, perhaps; or that hack of the shades, George Wilkins. But plainly its authorship lies as far from Shakespeare as Stratford-atte-Bowe (where Theatre Workshop are reviving the piece) lies from Stratford-on-Avon. The epilogue speaks of "this naked tragedy," adding that:

> . . . simple truth is gratious enough
> And needs no other points of glozing stuff.

But for Shakespeare, twenty-eight years old when the play was published, simple truth was not enough; he would have glozed over the nakedness with poetry. All in all, I think George did it.

One wonders whether critics three centuries hence will be ransacking Mrs. Christie's thrillers for traces of Mr. Fry's "hand of glory." The analogy is not inept, for *Arden* is shameless blood and thunder, an account of an actual Tudor homicide enlivened by the thrusting pulse of blank verse. It reeks of documentary realism. And do you hear that whiffling detonation? That is T. S. Eliot snorting. Mr. Eliot holds that since *Arden* English drama has declined into a "desert of exact likeness to the reality which is perceived by the most commonplace mind." But it takes a mind more than commonplace to perceive and transcribe *any* sort of reality; and our national nose for the details of human behaviour won't, as our literature proves, stop quivering. We have an incontinent passion for fact, and George satisfies it.

He shows us Alice Arden wantoning with a base steward named Mosbie, enlisting the help of a pair of Cheapside assassins to slay her husband, and finally, after fearful delays and frustrations, having her will. *Arden* asserts what Elizabethan drama as a whole denies, that murder is a hard thing to accomplish. "When," moans Black Will, the hired bravo, "was I so long in killing a man?" The play's failing is a long central sag, during which we leave the lovers and follow their victim on a trip to London; but the climax, with Arden stabbed and dragged out into the fields, tingles with grimness. The blood must be scrubbed away, all must be set at rights, and Alice rounds suddenly on Mosbie with an accusing shriek: " 'Twas thou that made me murder him!" But hereabouts, to my grief, Joan Littlewood's production went off the rails, dislodged by false economy. John Bury had already provided two excellent settings, a gloomy prospect of trees and a cramped vista of London alleys; but the third, Arden's kitchen, was not forthcoming. Which meant an alfresco killing, and the excision of the lines in which Franklin, the dead man's friend, reveals himself as the first detective in English fiction:

> I fear me he was murdered in this house
> And carried to the field, for from that place
> Backwards and forwards may you see
> The print of many feet within the snow. . . .

Worse still, the retribution scene was omitted, so that we did not see what the title-page promised, "the shameful end of all murderers." I urge Miss Littlewood not to deprive her company of these opportunities. Perhaps George Cooper overplays Black Will's braggartry; but the rampant *Bovarysme* of Barbara Brown's Alice could hardly be bettered, and Harry Corbett plays Mosbie with a dark, cringing bravura which recalls the Olivier of *Richard III*. Lady Chatterley and Strindberg's

Miss Julie must, one feels, be looking down with approval on these premonitions of their plight.

(*1954*)

Saint Joan, BY GEORGE BERNARD SHAW, AT THE ARTS THEATRE.

"Swagger and fustian" was Shaw's phrase for the minor Elizabethans, and it applies all too easily to much of his own charmless masterpiece, *Saint Joan,* which John Fernald has restaged at the Arts Theatre. This is the first of his plays into which Shaw's senility creeps. The jokes misfire; the debates languish; and Shaw's passion for penal reform obtrudes to the detriment of the end. Joan withdraws her confession only when she finds that the alternative to death is perpetual incarceration away from the sun and the sky. If Shaw's Joan had lived in an age of prisons without bars, her recantation would have gone through and the calendar would lack a saint.

She suffers as a dramatic creation from the weakness of having no weaknesses. A divinely illuminated simpleton, she is incapable of change or development. Or so it seems on the page. And this is where Siobhan McKenna comes in. *"La vie,"* said Rémy de Gourmont, *"est un dépouillement,"* and this actress lets us see life stripping Joan down to her spiritual buff. The beaming clown of the opening scenes has undergone, by the end, an annealing: all that was mortal about her is peeled away, and sheer soul bursts through. "God is alone" had tears flowing everywhere in the house, and during the epilogue one scarcely dared look at the stage. Miss McKenna's voice, with its brave Connemara twang, must somehow acquire a middle register between *pp* and *ff;* but this is my only quibble with the richest portrait of saintliness since Falconetti shaved her head for Dreyer's film *La Passion de Jeanne d'Arc.*

(*1954*)

The Bishop's Bonfire, BY SEAN O'CASEY, AT THE GAIETY, DUBLIN.

The Irish never forgive those they have insulted. Back from long exile came Sean to Dublin, and his compatriots hissed his play at curtain-fall. At the first night of Mr. O'Casey's *The Bishop's Bonfire* there were more stage Irishmen in the house than in the cast, and by the first interval venomous tongues were already lamenting the play's failure. Those who had uprooted the author now charged him with having forgotten his roots; those who had expelled him from the parish charged him with being too parochial. How, they jeered, could a man from an urban working-class Protestant family write well about a rural middle-class Catholic family? Some blamed the director, picturing Tyrone Guthrie as an ambulance which had run over the man it was summoned to help. Others excoriated the cast. In this congress of feud and polemic the play was forgotten.

And what were the facts? That Mr. O'Casey's genius, once tragicomic, had declined into a state best described as manic-depressive; that his hand had lost its sureness in shifting from mood to mood; and that here were two plays, one ghastly, one gorgeous, in unhappy juxtaposition. The depressive (or serious) theme is youth's subservience to authority, as reflected in the plights of Councillor Reiligan's two daughters. One of them is cheated of fulfilment because her impoverished lover allows class-consciousness to intimidate him. The other follows her man into the Church, from which he defects; and the tension between the spoiled priest and the reluctant nun ends in murder.

The rigid formulae of society and religion, Mr. O'Casey argues, are strait-jackets which warp youth's love of life; but the argument is blurred by the floridity of the author's style. Where every image is a new crimson splash on a verbal Turner sunset, the expression of ideas becomes impossible. Like most Irish playwrights, Mr. O'Casey risks self-parody when he tries to write seriously. The shades of Dion Boucicault and Amanda Ros seem to guide his pen, coupled with the inflated Oriental metaphors and tiresome alliterations of the Authorised Version, on which (unlike most Irish playwrights) he was brought up.

What matters is the manic half of the play. Here, dealing with the wild inconsequent rustics who are redecorating Ballyoonagh for the bishop's impending visit, Mr. O'Casey hits his full stride as the old mocker and fantastic ironist, ever happier with tongue in cheek than with hand on heart. Broad comedy of protest was always the best Irish vein, and Mr. O'Casey strikes it rich, extracting from Eddie Byrne, Seamus Kavanaugh, and Harry Hutchinson performances of preposterous gaiety; and if Cyril Cusack fails to make the ancient Codger plausible, it is because the author has chosen to philosophise the part as well as drivel it. The elation of these quarrelsome, gin-swigging scenes is tremendous; you feel Mr. O'Casey had to get the characters drunk to account for the boldness of their utterance. Phrases so "shockin' massive" fall seldom from sober lips. The passage in which the handymen debate the chances of saving Ireland from the Reds by persuading the Americans to drop thousands of jeeps by parachute is pure comic uproar, the notion being twisted, squeezed, and up-ended until it has yielded its last drop of laughter.

And why are these hirelings so free of speech? Because, as one of them says: "Me soul's me own particular compendium. Me soul's me own spiritual property, complete an' entire, verbatim in all its concernment." They abound in their own sense, and while they are about, shouting loud or muttering "sotto vossie," the play magnifies life as gloriously as it magnifies language. Mr. O'Casey was never a great thinker; he is no longer a great craftsman; but he remains a great singer.

(1954)

West-End Apathy.

"And how," ask my friends, having debated the opera, the ballet, politics, and the Italian cinema, "how is the theatre getting along?" The very set of their features, so patiently quizzical, tells me I am being indulged; after the serious business of conversation, they are permitting themselves a lapse into idleness. I shrug cheerily, like a martyr to rheumatism. A wan, tingling silence ensues. Then: "De Sica's new film is superb," says somebody, and talk begins again, happy and devout. I stew, meanwhile, in what Zelda Fitzgerald once called "the boiling oil of sour grapes."

The bare fact is that, apart from revivals and imports, there is nothing in the London theatre that one dares discuss with an intelligent man for more than five minutes. Since the great Ibsen challenge of the nineties, the English intellectuals have been drifting away from drama. Synge, Pirandello, and O'Casey briefly recaptured them, and they will still perk up at the mention of Giraudoux. But—cowards—they know Eliot and Fry only in the study; and of a native prose playwright who might set the boards smouldering they see no sign at all. Last week I welcomed a young Frenchwoman engaged in writing a thesis on contemporary English drama. We talked hopefully of John Whiting; but before long embarrassment moved me to ask why she had not chosen her own theatre as a subject for study. She smiled wryly. "Paris is in decline," she said. "Apart from Sartre, Anouilh, Camus, Cocteau, Aymé, Claudel, Beckett, and Salacrou, we have almost nobody."

If you seek a tombstone, look about you; survey the peculiar nullity of our drama's prevalent *genre,* the Loamshire play. Its setting is a country house in what used to be called Loamshire but is now, as a heroic tribute to realism, sometimes called Berkshire. Except when someone must sneeze, or be murdered, the sun invariably shines. The inhabitants belong to a social class derived partly from romantic novels and partly from the playwright's vision of the leisured life he will lead after the play is a success—this being the only effort of imagination he is called on to make. Joys and sorrows are giggles and whimpers: the crash of denunciation dwindles into "Oh, stuff, Mummy!" and "Oh, really, Daddy!" And so grim is the continuity of these things that the foregoing paragraph might have been written at any time during the last thirty years.

Loamshire is a glibly codified fairy-tale world, of no more use to the student of life than a doll's-house would be to a student of town planning. Its vice is to have engulfed the theatre, thereby expelling better minds. Never believe that there is a shortage of playwrights; there are more than we have ever known; but they are all writing the same play. Nor is there a dearth of English actors; the land is alive with them; but they are all playing the same part. Should they wish to test themselves beyond Loamshire's simple major thirds, they must find employment in revivals, foreign plays, or films. Perhaps Loamshire's greatest triumph is the crippling of creative talent in English directors and designers. After all, how many ways are there of directing a tea-party? And how may a designer spread his wings in a mews flat or "The living-room at 'Binsgate,' Vyvyan Bulstrode's country house near Dymsdyke"? Assume the miracle: assume the advent of a masterpiece. There it crouches, a pink-eyed, many-muscled, salivating monster. Who shall harness it? We have a handful of directors fit to tame something less malleable than a mouse, and a few designers still capable of dressing something less submissive than a clothes-horse. But they are the end, not the beginning, of a tradition.

Some of us need no miracles to keep our faith; we feed it on memories and imaginings. But many more—people of passionate intellectual appetites—are losing heart, falling away, joining the queues outside the Curzon Cinema. To lure them home, the theatre must widen its scope, broaden its horizon so that Loamshire appears merely as the play-pen, not as the whole palace of drama. We need plays about cabmen and demi-gods, plays about warriors, politicians, and grocers—I care not, so Loamshire be invaded and subdued. I counsel aggression because, as a critic, I had rather be a war correspondent than a necrologist.

(1954)

Directors and Directions.

The English have never really warmed to theatrical directors. Not for them the despotism of a Meyerhold or a Reinhardt, nor yet the prophetic zeal of a Gordon Craig, who, spurned by the scorn of true democrats, fled to France for refuge. Granville-Barker, tolerated for his scholarship, left no successors, and though Continental directors such as Komisarjevsky and M. Saint-Denis have sojourned here, they have all retired in confusion. Our native maestro, Tyrone Guthrie, occasionally gladdens the West End by shaking from his mane such a dewdrop as *The Matchmaker,* but he is mostly abroad, working in the real laboratories of his craft.

In his new book, *The Director in the Theatre,* Hugh Hunt attempts, sanely and temperately, to state the case for creative direction. "Can we," he asks, "have a work of theatrical art which is at the same time a distortion of the author's intention? The answer is, of course, yes; just as we can have a fine portrait which bears no resemblance to the sitter." I happen to agree with Mr. Hunt; you may not; but, as Englishmen, we are both arguing from ignorance.

Two schools of thought dispute the field of Western acting. One, derived from the deep-burrowing naturalism of Stanislavsky, is practised in America by directors like Elia Kazan and actors like Marlon Brando; the other, based in East Berlin, is the "Epic Theatre" of Bertolt Brecht. Stanislavsky, emphasising illusion, taught his actors to immerse themselves in their parts; Brecht, rejecting illusion, teaches detachment, employing a sort of stylised shorthand whereby the actor makes no pretence to be a real "character" expressing "emotion," but declares himself instead a professional performer illustrating a general theme. "You are in a drawing-room," says Stanislavsky to his audience, "witnessing life." "You are in a theatre," says Brecht, "witnessing actors."

That, roughly, is the conflict. We in London hear the distant thunder of the guns, but how shall we judge of the outcome? We know Stanislavsky only in genteel, dramatic-school dilution, and of Brecht, whose plays have captured central Europe, we know nothing at all. We are like those complacent anglers who, as A. B. Walkley said, "continued to fish for gudgeon under the Pont-Neuf while the Revolution raged overhead."

Dramatists utilise acting styles, and playhouses preserve them, but directors create them. If our theatres are filled with the kind of hollow semi-realism for which our authors write, much of the blame must rest with our directors. Many of them are affable, intelligent men, but none measures up to the Continental definition—a dynamic compound of confessor, inquisitor, and sage. "The real art of the director," it has been sardonically observed, "is his ability to get a script to direct"—which involves charming a management and at least one star, who is quite likely, if the motivation of his performance is even remotely questioned, to round on the director with a chill request that he go easy on "that Stanislavsky stuff."

The trouble is that neither of our greatest pioneers was primarily an actors' director. Craig cared most for design and William Poel for Elizabethan stagecraft. Thus, they distracted the theatre from naturalism at the very moment when, given encouragement, it might have stormed and fertilised our acting. Many scenic artists still bear Craig's thumbprint, but Poel survives only in the fallacy of arena staging, a method which overrates the importance of "intimacy" in the theatre and, by citing the circus in vindication of its creed, overlooks the fact that of the two most exciting things that happen in a circus one takes place behind bars and the other hundreds of feet in the air.

Apart from Granville-Barker and, intermittently, Guthrie, no English director has had much perceptible influence on English acting. We pride ourselves on our "stylishness," by which we mean an addled mating of Victorian rhetoric with Du Maurier realism—life above stairs seen through the eyes of a housemaid. Modishly, we rejoice that the era of naturalism is over. But we err: in this country it has hardly begun. Let us, by all means, dismiss Stanislavsky and Brecht; but let us first engage a few foreign directors to give our actors instruction. Then, perhaps, we shall know what we are dismissing.

(1954)

Richard II, BY WILLIAM SHAKESPEARE, AT THE OLD VIC AND AT THE THEATRE ROYAL, STRATFORD-ATTE-BOWE.

Truly, an embarrassment of Richards. On my right, the Old Vic's *Richard II,* a well-scrubbed fighter of spare physique; very much on my left, Theatre Workshop's version of the play, a crowding south-paw. The Old Vic wins, as it was bound to do, on points. For one thing, it has a larger company, which means no toil and trouble with double doubles. For another, it has a Bolingbroke (Eric Porter) who brings a proper queasiness to the job of usurpation, which is tackled by George Cooper at Stratford with the businesslike aplomb of a public executioner. Indeed, the whole anti-Richard faction at Stratford behave like rodent-exterminators enamoured of their work: Howard Goorney's Gaunt is a very Isaiah of rebuke, and one almost expected Wat Tyler's rebellion to be staged as a mimed prologue.

Between the two settings there is little to choose. Stratford's sombre castellation is stronger though less graceful than Leslie Hurry's ramped promontory at the Vic, but neither really fits the play's geographical restlessness. In the matter of production style Theatre Workshop makes up in barn-storming what it lacks in finesse. And there one would leave the subject, were it not for the astounding disparity between the two Richards.

Theatre Workshop, keeping well off the beaten path, offers instead a beaten psychopath. I guessed beforehand that Harry Corbett, a natural choice for the third Richard, might make heavy going of the second; I could never have guessed to what extremes his temperamental wrongness would lead him. The part is played in a frenzy of effeminacy. This Richard is a senile Osric, a flutter of puff-pastry, his voice a quavering falsetto which suggests Ernest Milton as Andrew Aguecheek. Whimpering with rage, he flies at Gaunt's throat and hurls him to the ground, recoiling at once, with tremulous lips, like a child caught in the pantry and torn between defiance and contrition. The return from Ireland and what follows are conceived as a switchback-ride into lunacy, culminating in the dungeon at Pomfret, round which Mr. Corbett raves and reels, chained by his ankle to the floor. The deposition of intellect is complete.

I take Mr. Corbett's to be a highly effective rendering of a totally false idea. The inference that Richard was a pervert rests on a few ambiguous lines wherein Bolingbroke condemns the caterpillars for having

> Made a divorce betwixt his queen and him,
> Broke the possession of a royal bed—

which might mean no more than that Richard took concubines. The charge against Mr. Corbett is that he has acquiesced in the modern trick of equating dandyism and love of verse with sexual abnormality. Certainly Richard loved show, and there is much truth in C. E. Montague's picture of him as a conscious verbal artist, tipsy with grief. What we forget is that in Shakespeare's age a passion for finery in speech and dress was regarded as the natural outward expression of virility. The image to clutch is that of the peacock. Your pallid, shrinking-violet Richard derives from (a) *fin-de-siècle* aestheticism, (b) memories of Marlowe's

Edward II, and—most misleadingly—(c) the assumption that the king is the same man at the beginning of the play as he is at the end. Richard must begin headstrong and arrogant, a spirited tyrant rather than a spiritless poet. York gives the clue when he speaks of him as a "young hot colt," and Gaunt clinches the case by referring to "his rash, fierce blaze of riot." Where in the Richards of Messrs. Guinness, Redgrave, and Corbett were the "violent fires" which would impel a king to war in Ireland? Would not all three, rather than face battle, have curled up with a good tapestry?

The events of the later acts reveal Richard a moral coward; they denude him, peeling away the layers of bluster and caprice that have formerly protected him. Yet in the end he is annealed by calamity. Of course, there are long spasms of self-pity wherein, as Agate said, Richard "plunges his nose with zest into the bouquet of humiliation." But the prime stroke of irony, grotesque and neglected, is that Richard grows up at the very moment when he is about to be cut down. "I wasted time, and now doth time waste me": knowing himself at last, he speaks his own best epitaph. He dies a dishonoured king but an honourable man. We have seen his wings clipped, but the dramatic point is that they were an eagle's wings, not a butterfly's.

John Neville, at the Vic, takes firm steps in the right direction. He overweens, rejoicing in the manipulation of power; his sneer is steely and unforced, and he fails only where he could not have succeeded—he has no gift for pathos, and the vital later speeches coldly congeal. Nonetheless, this is a clear diagrammatic outline for the definitive performance, as yet unseen. For the rest, Michael Bates does a glum play the service of making York a comic sketch for Polonius. Which prompts a footnote on one of Shakespeare's recurrent messages: never trust uncles. Of Richard's uncles, Gloucester detests him, Lancaster reviles him, and York betrays him. Someone must soon write a monograph on "Evidences of Uncle-Fixation in Hamlet."

(1955)

The Lost Art of Bad Drama.

Night-nurses at the bedside of good drama, we critics keep a holy vigil. Black circles rim our eyes as we pray for the survival of our pet patient, starved and racked, the theatre of passion and ideas. We pump in our printed transfusions—"honest and forthright," "rooted in a closely observed reality"—but so avidly do we seize on signs of relapse that we fail to observe that, for the moment at least, the cripple is out of bed and almost convalescent. He can claim, this season, three successes: *Hedda Gabler,* Anouilh's *Time Remembered,* and Pirandello's *Rules of the Game*—and he had a vestigial hand in *Separate Tables.* (Mr. Rattigan is the Formosa of the contemporary theatre, occupied by the old guard, but geographically inclined towards the progressives.) Further tonics lie ahead, among them a Giraudoux and another Anouilh before spring is out. Implausible as it may sound, good drama may be able to walk unaided within a year or so.

But what of bad drama, the kind which repudiates art and scoffs at depth, which thrives on reviewers who state themselves "shocked, but I rocked with laughter"? We assume that it is healthy; in fact, it looks extremely frail. Many a frankly "commercial" play has come smiling to town in recent months and walked straight into an upper-cut from both critics and public. Take *The Night of the Ball,* for instance—a knightly piece, glib and well-nourished, star-bright and silk-swathed, yet see how scarred and blunderbussed the critics left it! And is old *Happy Holiday* dead? As any doornail. Jesu, Jesu, the bad plays that I have seen! and to think how many of my old acquaintance are dead! How a good yoke of starlets at Cambridge Circus? Truly, cousin, I was not there.

It is now, in fact, a risky proposition to back plays that twenty years ago would have swept the boards unopposed. One imagines a box-office mogul bewailing his lot in Justice Shallow's vein: "By the masses I was call'd everything. . . . There was I, and little Noël Coward of Teddington, and black Ben Travers, and Frederick Lonsdale, and Vernon Sylvaine, a Manchester man—you had not four such rib-crackers in all of Shaftesbury Avenue again; and, I may say to you, we knew where the bona-robas were, and had the best of them all under two weeks' notice. . . . Is old *double-entente* of your town living yet?" Dead, sir, dead.

One begins to suspect that the English have lost the art of writing a bad successful play. Perhaps some sort of competition should be organised; the rules, after all, are simple enough. At no point may the plot or characters make more than superficial contact with reality. Characters earning less than £1,000 a year should be restricted to small parts or exaggerated into types so patently farcical that no member of the audience could possibly identify himself with such absurd esurience. Rhythm in dialogue is achieved by means either of vocatives ("That, my dear Hilary, is a moot point") or qualifying clauses ("What, if you'll pardon the interruption, is going on here?"); and irony is confined to having an irate male character shout: "I am perfectly calm!"

All plays should contain parts fit to be turned down by Gladys Cooper, Coral Browne, Hugh Williams, and Robert Flemyng. Apart from hysterical adolescents, nobody may weep; apart from triumphant protagonists, nobody may laugh; anyone, needless to say, may smile. European place-names (Positano and Ischia) are romantic; English place-names (Herne Bay and Bognor Regis) are comic. Women who help themselves unasked to cigarettes must be either frantic careerists or lustful opportunists. The latter should declare themselves by running the palm of one hand up their victim's lapel and saying, when it reaches the neck: "Let's face it, Arthur, you're not exactly indifferent to me." The use of "Let's face it" in modern drama deserves in itself a special study. It means that something true is about to be uttered, and should strike the audience with the same shock as the blast of the whistle before the train plunges into a tunnel. . . .

But I falter. I cannot convince myself that these rules, archaic already, will assure success. For bad plays, dependent on what is topical and ephemeral in mankind, are much harder to write than good ones, for which the rules are permanent and unchanging. The commercial writer must blind himself to history, close his eyes, stop his ears, shutter his mind to the onslaught of reality; he must ignore all the promptings which instinct tells him to be valid, about unity of action and the necessity of reducing one or more of his characters to a logical crisis of desperation; he must live the life of a spiritual hermit. Such self-abnegation is seldom found. The great age of the thoroughly bad play seems to be over, and it behoves the critic to sing a requiem.

A thermometer, meanwhile, might be left in the mouth of good drama. Our season's tally is certainly encouraging, but it pales by comparison with last season's record in Sweden. There, according to the report in *World Theatre,* one might have seen four Strindbergs, four Shakespeares, three Chekhovs, three Pirandellos, two Molières, two Shaws, two Ibsens, two Giraudoux, and one each from Vanbrugh, Wycherley, Lorca, Kafka, Brecht, Ugo Betti, Arthur Miller, Anouilh, Eliot, Bernanos, and Samuel Beckett—not to mention the *Oresteia* of Aeschylus. Yet "the season," mourns the compiler of the report, "was not a milestone." We have a long way to go.

(1955)

Sailor Beware!, BY PHILIP KING AND FALKLAND CARY, AT THE STRAND.

Sailor Beware! is a surprisingly realistic parlour farce on which Philip King has collaborated with Falkland Cary. The situation, a working-class wedding threatened by a heavy-weight mother-in-law, is as ancient as its development, whereby the husband-to-be jilts his bride; but the dialogue is authentic suburban poetry. And in Peggy Mount, a newcomer from repertory, London has acquired a comedienne fit to be floodlit, whose effigy should be raised above the grave of the mother-in-law joke, which, by her peerless exertions, she must surely have killed.

Emma Hornett, as played by Miss Mount, is not your rock-like, immovable virago, like the Marx Brothers' Margaret Dumont. She scorches the earth about her with ceaseless physical activity, charging as she cleans, swooping as she dusts; even out of sight she intimidates, like the distant thunder of hooves. She is frankly a beast of a woman, a mobile fortress, a sadistic *dompteuse,* compound of basilisk and earth-mother, of Gorgon and Zola. And her face is heaven-sent for its job, a broad, baleful mask whose worst fears are constantly being confirmed: she told us so, and now, if we don't mind, we'll listen to her and stop fidgeting. The savage impatience of Miss Mount's acting must be seen to be believed. The first-night intervals were unwontedly short, and there must have been many in the audience who pictured Miss Mount viciously stabbing the warning-bell and growling: "What did I tell you? There they are, up in the bar drinking, when I've got work to do. . . ." I ask of this magnificent player only that she will one day consider appearing in *Tristan and Isolde* opposite Wally Patch. The house rightly rose to her at the curtain: a house full of roarers who clearly cared for the name of King.

(1955)

Henry IV, Parts One and Two, BY WILLIAM SHAKESPEARE, AT THE OLD VIC.

I suspected it at Stratford four years ago, and now I am sure: for me the two parts of *Henry IV* are the twin summits of Shakespeare's achievement. Lime-hungry actors have led us always to the tragedies, where a single soul is spotlit and its agony explored; but these private torments dwindle beside the Henries, great public plays in which a whole nation is under scrutiny and on trial. More than anything else in our drama they deserve the name of epic. A way of life is facing dissolution; we are in at the deathbed of the Middle Ages. How shall the crisis be faced? The answer takes us to every social and geographical outpost: to Eastcheap drunks and Gloucestershire gentry, to the Welsh and the Scots, to the minor nobility and the crown itself.

There is much talk of death; to the king it comes as a balm, Falstaff sags at the mention of it, Shallow is resigned to it, and Hotspur meets it with nostrils flared. The odd, irregular rhythm wherein societies die and are reborn is captured as no playwright before or since has ever captured it. In Hal's return to honour and justice the healing of a national sickness is implied. Implied: that is the clue—for there is no overt exhortation in these plays, and no true villain, no Claudius or Iago on whom complacent audiences can fix their righteous indignation. Hotspur is on the wrong side, yet he is a hero; Prince John is on the right one, yet his cynical perfidy at the disarmament conference would have astonished Hitler. Only a handful of plays in the world preserve this divine magnanimity. To conceive the state of mind in which the Henries were written is to feel dizzied by the air of Olympus.

We knew from Douglas Seale's handling of the *Henry VI* trilogy that he was a director of rare historical imagination; and the Old Vic company, which lacks star quality, exactly fits a pair of plays which lack star parts. Note how cleverly Mr. Seale lets the two evenings illuminate each other. He gives Falstaff a page in Part I as well as Part II, using the boy as mute audience to the knight's soliloquies; taking his cue from a phrase in Part II—"wearied and out-breathed"—he makes Hotspur and Hal in Part I so stricken with battle fatigue that they can scarcely lift their swords. The tavern scenes, writhing with squalor and pulsing with visual wit, transport us straight to pre-Crookback England.

Paul Rogers' Falstaff is fussy and perhaps too easily discomfited, but vocally it is a display of rich and immaculate cunning. Rachel Roberts hits off Mrs. Quickly to perfection, and few Pistols have been fired more powerfully than John Neville's. The same actor's Hotspur was hampered by a stammer needlessly borrowed from Sir Laurence Olivier; and the best double was that of Paul Daneman, whose malign Worcester was followed by a goatish Justice Shallow, giddy with snobbery and agog with innocence.

Mr. Seale's hand seems to stiffen at contact with royalty: his groupings in the court scenes were static, and the episode of the purloined crown was badly staged on a remote rostrum, high and half-visible. Eric

Porter gave us all of Henry's guilt but little of his grandeur; and in Robert Hardy's Hal there was too great a show of intelligence. Mr. Hardy is rightly proud of his technique, but he is in danger of developing it at the expense of his acting "innards": the performance was well-timed but soft-centred. Ann Todd and Virginia McKenna intrude briefly and softly into what has been called the smoking-room of Shakespearean drama —though Miss Todd's irruption into the middle of the curtain-call was, to say the least, presumptuous. Audrey Cruddas' permanent setting is both rugged and regal. To sum up, Mr. Seale has put the Old Vic in particular and Shakespearean production in general on the right realistic track.

(1955)

Notes on a Dead Language.

When the London theatre takes to its bed, the habit of criticism is to scourge the invalid; the sick-room resounds with bullying cries of "Who are the new English playwrights?" A more acute inquiry might be: "Who were the old ones?" For the brute fact is that no Englishman since the third decade of the seventeenth century has written an acknowledged dramatic masterpiece. Note that I say "acknowledged"; I might make claims for Otway or Dryden, you for Pinero or Maugham, but in the general censure we should be outvoted. The truth would out: that the legend of English drama springs partly from Shakespeare, our luminous accident, and mostly from an Irish conspiracy to make us ashamed of our weakness. English drama is a procession of glittering Irishmen: Farquhar, Goldsmith, Sheridan, Shaw, Wilde, Synge, and O'Casey are there; and even Congreve slips in on a quibble, since his Irish upbringing served to correct the fault of his English birth. We should not mourn that there are no great English playwrights; we should marvel that there are any English playwrights at all.

Come closer; observe how few fine plays have been written *about* the English in the last three hundred years. High drama presupposes high colloquial speech, which, since Cromwell, has been a rarity on English lips. We will accept eloquence from a Tartar emperor, a Dublin pickpocket or a New York taxi-driver, but we would rightly baulk at verbal beauty in a Yarmouth policeman. When Shakespeare was born, our language was being pelted with imports, from France, from Italy, from classical translations; "thought," as Virginia Woolf said, "plunged into a sea of words and came up dripping." A stock-pot was bubbling which everyone tasted and tried out in speech; and drama evolved out of an epidemic of logorrhoea.

For half a century we have watched a similar process in America, where a clash of immigrant tongues has produced the same experimental play of language. In England the riot is over. Lexicography has battened on the invaders, and our dictionaries swell with the slain; a memorable phrase flies sometimes from a typewriter into print, but seldom from a larynx into a listening ear. Christopher Fry has performed prodigies of artificial respiration; the words are there, and richly he deploys them; but do they not resemble the bright, life-stimulating dyes which American morticians apply to the faces of the dead? To gain admission to drama, words must be used; they must put on flesh, throng the streets, and bellow through the buses. Dylan Thomas' *Under Milk Wood* was one of the last outposts of the living vernacular, a memory of a time when a phrase was as concrete a thing as a brick; and Thomas, remember, was not English, but a Welshman writing about Welshmen.

The sudden onslaught of a million immigrants of mixed nationalities might help. Until then, I propose an agonising reappraisal of our theatrical status, which is now that of a showroom for foreign goods. A swarm of Continental plays crowds our stage-door; our part, as hosts, is to provide for them translators of genius. Mr. Fry, who is now adapting Anouilh's *L'Alouette* and Giraudoux' *La Guerre de Troie n'aura pas lieu,* has set a noble, instructive, and realistic example.

(1955)

Tiger at the Gates, BY JEAN GIRAUDOUX, TRANSLATED BY CHRISTOPHER FRY, AT THE APOLLO.

In spite of a few bad performances and a setting uniquely hideous, I do not believe that anyone could emerge from *Tiger at the Gates* unaware that what had just hit him was a masterpiece. For this is Giraudoux' *La Guerre de Troie n'aura pas lieu,* brought to us at last, after twenty years of impatience, in a methodical translation by Christopher Fry. It remains the final comment on the superfluity of war, and the highest peak in the mountain-range of modern French theatre. At the lowest estimate, it is a great occasional play, in the sense that its impact might be doubled if war seemed imminent; but to call it dated because nowadays we are at peace is to ignore its truest warning, which is that nothing more surely rouses the sleeping tiger of war than the prospect of universal tranquillity.

What is to engage us is the process whereby the Trojan war nearly failed to happen. Returning disillusioned from one campaign, Hector finds another impending; to send Helen back to the Greeks he will undergo any humiliation, even the dishonour of his wife. Paris, his brother, gives in to him easily, but Helen is harder to persuade. The fates, in choosing her for their instrument, have endowed her with an icy indifference to Hector's enormous compassion. "I'm sure," she says, "that people pity each other to the same extent that they pity themselves." Yet she, too, puts herself in his hands.

Breaking all precedents, Hector refuses to make the traditional speech of homage to his fallen soldiers; instead, we have the majestic tirade in which he rejoices with those who survived, the cowards who live to make love to the wives of the dead. His last stumbling-block is Ulysses, wily and circumspect, who reminds him, as they amicably chat, that a convivial "meeting at the summit" is always the preamble to war; but even he agrees to gamble against destiny and take Helen home in peace. In the play's closing moments, war is declared. To reveal how would be an insult to those who know the text and a terrible deprivation to those who do not. Enough to say that history passes into the keeping of (Max Beerbohm's phrase) "those incomparable poets, Homer."

I cannot but marvel at the virtuosity of Giraudoux' prose. It embraces grandeur and littleness in one gigantic clasp; having carved a heroic group in granite, it can turn to the working of tiny heads on cherry-stones. No playwright of our time can change gear so subtly, from majestic gloom to crystalline wit. Sometimes, in the mass debates, the verbal glitter is overpowering, but in duologues Giraudoux has no rival. Hector's scenes with Helen in the first act and with Ulysses in the second ring in the mind like doubloons flung down on marble. Is it objected that English actors jib at long stretches of ornate prose? Or that they are unused to playing tragic scenes for laughs and comic scenes for tears? If so, they had better relearn their craft. The player who thinks Giraudoux unactable is in the wrong profession. Harold Clurman, the director, has tried hard to teach old dogs new tricks, but the right note of vocal aristocracy is only intermittently struck. Listening to Giraudoux should be like watching a series of lightning water-colours, dashed off by a master; some of the present company make do with ponderous cartoons, licking the lead and plunging it deep into the paper. This is the case with Walter Fitzgerald's Ulysses, a dour and laboured performance; and Diane Cilento, though fetchingly got up in what I can best describe as a Freudian slip, gives us paste jewellery instead of the baleful diamond Giraudoux had in mind for Helen. It is Michael Redgrave, as Hector, who bears the evening's brunt. He is clearly much happier in the emotional bits than in the flicks of wit which spark and speckle them; but, even so, this is a monumental piece of acting, immensely moving, intelligent in action, and in repose never less than a demi-god. In the presence of such an actor and such a play, I will forgive much. Especially do I feel for anyone unlucky enough to have to stumble and clamber over the obstacle-course of Loudon Sainthill's set. It is enough to make a chamois nervy.

(1955)

Macbeth, BY WILLIAM SHAKESPEARE, AT STRATFORD-ON-AVON.

Nobody has ever succeeded as Macbeth, and the reason is not far to seek. Instead of growing as the play proceeds, the hero shrinks; complex and many-levelled to begin with, he ends up a cornered thug, lacking even a death scene with which to regain lost stature. Most Macbeths, mindful of this, let off their big guns as soon as possible, and have usually shot their bolt by the time the dagger speech is out. The marvel of Sir Laurence Olivier's reading is that it reverses this procedure, turns the play inside out, and makes it (for the first time I can remember) a thing of mounting, not waning, excitement. Last Tuesday Sir Laurence shook hands with greatness, and within a week or so the performance will have ripened into a masterpiece: not of the superficial, booming, have-a-bash kind, but the real thing, a structure of perfect forethought and proportion, lit by flashes of intuitive lightning.

He begins in a perilously low key, the reason for which is soon revealed. This Macbeth is paralysed with guilt before the curtain rises, having already killed Duncan time and again in his mind. Far from recoiling and popping his eyes, he greets the air-drawn dagger with sad familiarity; it is a fixture in the crooked furniture of his brain. Uxoriousness leads him to the act, which unexpectedly purges him of remorse. Now the portrait swells; seeking security, he is seized with fits of desperate bewilderment as the prize is snatched out of reach. There was true agony in "I had else been perfect"; Banquo's ghost was received with horrific torment, as if Macbeth should shriek "I've been robbed!," and the phrase about the dead rising to "push us from our stools" was accompanied by a convulsive shoving gesture which few other actors would have risked.

The needle of Sir Laurence's compass leads him so directly to the heart of the role that we forget the jagged rocks of laughter over which he is travelling. At the heart we find, beautifully projected, the anguish of the *de facto* ruler who dares not admit that he lacks the essential qualities of kingship. Sir Laurence's Macbeth is like Skule in Ibsen's chronicle play *The Pretenders,* the valiant usurper who can never comprehend what Ibsen calls "the great kingly thought." He will always be a monarch *manqué.*

The witches' cookery lesson is directed with amusing literalness; the Turk's nose, the Jew's liver, and the baby's finger are all held up for separate scrutiny; but the apparitions are very unpersuasive, and one felt gooseflesh hardly at all. On the battlements Sir Laurence's throttled fury switches into top gear, and we see a lion, baffled but still colossal. "I 'gin to be a-weary of the sun" held the very ecstasy of despair, the actor swaying with grief, his voice rising like hair on the crest of a trapped animal. "Exeunt, fighting" was a poor end for such a giant warrior. We wanted to see how he would die; and it was not he but Shakespeare who let us down.

Vivien Leigh's Lady Macbeth is more niminy-piminy than thundery-blundery, more viper than anaconda, but still quite competent in its small way. Macduff and his wife, actor-proof parts, are played with exceptional power by Keith Michell and Maxine Audley. The midnight hags, with traditional bonhomie, scream with laughter at their own jokes: I long, one day, to see whispering witches, less intent on yelling their sins across the country-side. The production has all the speed and clarity we associate with Glen Byam Shaw, and Roger Furse's settings are bleak and serviceable, except for the England scene, which needs only a cat and a milestone to go straight into *Dick Whittington.*

(1955)

Mother Courage, BY BERTOLT BRECHT, AT THE DEVON ARTS FESTIVAL.

Bertolt Brecht's *Mother Courage,* which had its English *première* last week, is a chronicle play about warfare in which warfare scarcely appears. It is *Henry V* without the dear friends and the breach and the nonsense about not wishing one man more. Brecht's subject is the decimating tumult of the Thirty Years' War, yet no plumes nod from his heroes' helmets and no rhetoric glitters on their lips. Instead we have rags and curses, for we are dealing with the underside of battle, the rowdy hordes of parasites whose only care is the strategy of survival. They batten on war, profiting when they can, and suffering if they must, but knowing always that the price of their wares, drink and food and clothing, varies in direct ratio to the fury of the fighting. We see war reflected in the eyes of a nomadic camp-follower called Mother Courage, her three children, and the guests who share her covered wagon—a fugitive priest and a lecherous cook.

It is well known that Brecht leans eastward in his politics: must we therefore expect Mother Courage's family to be downtrodden peasants oppressed by Fascist beasts? Nothing of the sort. Mother Courage is a bawdy cynic who can barely recall the names of the men who sired her children. Her code of honour is Falstaff's, and her moral code Doll Tearsheet's. She is in the war for what she can make out of it; and in return the war robs her of her children, the very reasons for her avarice. Her younger son is shot for theft. Her elder son commits a murder during a moment of truce, and is executed for his error in timing. And her daughter, a mute, dies at the end of the most tremendous scene to have enriched the drama for many years.

Sheltering in a lonely farmhouse, she overhears soldiers plotting to massacre the townsfolk sleeping below. She seizes a drum, climbs onto the roof of the barn, pulls the ladder up behind her, and beats out a frenzied tattoo of warning. The troop commander begs her to stop, promising immunity for her friends on his honour as a gentleman. There is a pause: and she beats harder, until a musket is fetched to silence her. The aftermath is written in the same vein of dispassionate, ironic tragedy. Mother Courage is keening a lullaby over her dead child when the sound of a marching army is heard. The war is moving on; and she goes with it, hauling her wagon and singing her song of defiance. There is no room for self-pity in drama like this.

By any definition, the play is an epic: a tale of endurance set in the open air (there are no interior scenes) of any war-bruised country. It is also a folk opera. Its earthy language, dotted with imagery as mountains are dotted with edelweiss, takes frequent flight into song, accompanied by Paul Dessau's trenchant music. Theatre Workshop, the company chosen to play it, was dismally unequal to the strain. Ants can lift objects many times their size and weight, but actors cannot. Mother Courage is a role calling for the combined talents of Anna Magnani and Siobhan McKenna: Joan Littlewood plays it in a lifeless mumble, looking both over-parted and under-rehearsed. Lacking a voice, she has had to cut Mother Courage's song, which is like omitting the Hallelujah Chorus from the *Messiah*.

As director, she has sought to present, with fourteen players in a concert hall, a play which the author intended for a company of fifty in a fully equipped theatre with a revolving stage. She has made a vice of economy by allowing her actors to change the scenery in full view of the audience, a device at which Brecht would boggle. Some of her blunders are attributable not so much to financial straits as to sheer perverseness. She adds music where Brecht indicates none, uses Dessau's score in the wrong places, and has it sung badly where she uses it rightly. The result is a production in which discourtesy to a masterpiece borders on insult, as if Wagner were to be staged in a school gymnasium. Barbara Brown does well as the mute Kattrin, and Harry Corbett's decaying chaplain abounds in hints of the performance this actor might have given in more favourable surroundings.

(1955)

Waiting for Godot, BY SAMUEL BECKETT, AT THE ARTS.

A special virtue attaches to plays which remind the drama of how much it can do without and still exist. By all the known criteria, Samuel Beckett's *Waiting for Godot* is a dramatic vacuum. Pity the critic who seeks a chink in its armour, for it is all chink. It has no plot, no climax, no *dénouement;* no beginning, no middle, and no end. Unavoidably, it has a situation, and it might be accused of having suspense, since it deals with the impatience of two tramps, waiting beneath a tree for a cryptic Mr. Godot to keep his appointment with them; but the situation is never developed, and a glance at the programme shows that Mr. Godot is not going to arrive. *Waiting for Godot* frankly jettisons everything by which we recognise theatre. It arrives at the custom-house, as it were, with no luggage, no passport, and nothing to declare; yet it gets through, as might a pilgrim from Mars. It does this, I believe, by appealing to a definition of drama much more fundamental than any in the books. A play, it asserts and proves, is basically a means of spending two hours in the dark without being bored.

Its author is an Irishman living in France, a fact which should prepare us for the extra, oddly serious joke he now plays on us. Passing the time in the dark, he suggests, is not only what drama is about but also what life is about. Existence depends on those metaphysical Micawbers who will go on waiting, against all rational argument, for something which may one day turn up to explain the purpose of living. Twenty years ago Mr. Odets had us waiting for Lefty, the social messiah; less naïvely, Mr. Beckett bids us wait for Godot, the spiritual signpost. His two tramps pass the time of day just as we, the audience, are passing the time of night. Were we not in the theatre, we should, like them, be clowning and quarreling, aimlessly bickering and aimlessly making up —all, as one of them says, "to give us the impression that we exist."

Mr. Beckett's tramps do not often talk like that. For the most part they converse in the double-talk of vaudeville: one of them has the ragged aplomb of Buster Keaton, while the other is Chaplin at his airiest and fairiest. Their exchanges are like those conversations at the next table which one can almost but not quite decipher—human speech half-heard and reproduced with all its *non-sequiturs* absurdly intact. From time to time other characters intrude. Fat Pozzo, Humpty Dumpty with a whip in his fist, puffs into sight with Lucky, his dumb slave. They are clearly going somewhere in a hurry: perhaps they know where Godot is? But the interview subsides into Lewis-Carrollian inanity. All that emerges is that the master needs the slave as much as the slave needs the master; it gives both a sense of spurious purpose; and one thinks of Laurel and Hardy, the ideal casting in these roles. Commanded to think, Lucky stammers out a ghostly, ghastly, interminable tirade, compounded of cliché and gibberish, whose general tenor is that, in spite of material progress and "all kinds of tennis," man spiritually dwindles. The style hereabouts reminds us forcibly that Mr. Beckett once worked for James Joyce. In the next act Pozzo and Lucky return, this time moving, just as purposefully, in the opposite direction. The tramps decide to stay where they are. A child arrives, presenting Mr. Godot's compliments and regretting that he is unable to meet them today. It is the same message as yesterday; all the same, they wait. The hero of *Crime and Punishment* reflects that if a condemned man "had to remain standing on a square yard of space all his life, a thousand years, eternity, it were better to live so than to die at once. . . . Man is a vile creature! and vile is he who calls him vile for that!" Something of this crossed my mind as the curtain fell on Mr. Beckett's tatterdemalion stoics.

The play sees the human condition in terms of baggy pants and red noses. Hastily labelling their disquiet disgust, many of the first-night audience found it pretentious. But what, exactly, are its pretensions? To state that mankind is waiting for a sign that is late in coming is a platitude which none but an illiterate would interpret as making claims to profundity. What vexed the play's enemies was, I suspect, the opposite: it was not pretentious enough to enable them to deride it. I care little for its enormous success in Europe over the past three years, but much for the way in which it pricked and stimulated my own nervous system. It summoned the music-hall and the parable to present a view of life which banished the sentimentality of the music-hall and the parable's fulsome uplift. It forced me to re-examine the rules which have hitherto governed the drama; and, having done so, to pronounce them not elastic enough. It is validly new, and hence I declare myself, as the Spanish would say, *godotista.*

Peter Hall directs the play with a marvellous ear for its elusive rhythms, and Peter Woodthorpe and Paul Daneman give the tramps a compassionate lunacy which only professional clowns could excel. Physically, Peter Bull is Pozzo to the life; vocally, he overplays his hand. Timothy Bateson's Lucky is anguish made comic, a remarkable achievement, and perfectly in keeping with the spirit of the play.

(1955)

Titus Andronicus, BY WILLIAM SHAKESPEARE, AT STRATFORD-ON-AVON.

I have always had a soft spot for *Titus Andronicus,* in spite of the fact that I have often heard it called the worst thing Marlowe ever wrote. Whoever wrote it, whether a member of the Shakespeare syndicate or the chairman himself, he deserves our thanks for having shown us, at the dawn of our drama, just how far drama could go. Like Goya's "Disasters of War," this is tragedy naked, godless, and unredeemed, a carnival of carnage in which pity is the first man down. We have since learned how to sweeten tragedy, to make it ennobling, but we would do well to remember that *Titus* is the raw material, "the thing itself," the piling of agony on to a human head until it splits.

It is our English heresy to think of poetry as a gentle way of saying gentle things. *Titus* reminds us that it is also a harsh way of saying harsh things. Seneca's Stoicism, in which the play is drenched, is a cruel doctrine, but it can rise to moments of supernal majesty. Lear himself has nothing more splendid than:

> For now I stand as one upon a rock,
> Environ'd with a wilderness of sea. . . .

The parallel with Lear is sibling-close, and Peter Brook cleverly strengthens it by having the fly-killing scene performed by a wanton boy. But when all its manifold excellences have been listed, the play still falls oddly short. One accepts the ethical code which forces Tamora to avenge herself on Titus, and then Titus to avenge himself on Tamora; it is the casualness of the killing that grows tiresome, as at a bad bullfight. With acknowledgements to Lady Bracknell, to lose one son may be accounted a misfortune; to lose twenty-four, as Titus does, looks like carelessness. Here, indeed, is "snip, and nip, and cut, and slish, and slash," a series of operations which only a surgeon could describe as a memorable evening in the theatre. When there enters a messenger "with two heads," one wonders for a lunatic instant whether he is carrying them or was born with them.

Much textual fiddling is required if we are to swallow the crudities, and in this respect Mr. Brook is as swift with the styptic pencil as his author was with the knife. He lets the blood, one might say, out of the bath. All visible gore is eliminated from the play, so that Lavinia, tongueless and handless, can no longer be likened to "a conduit with three issuing spouts." With similar tact, Mr. Brook cuts the last five words of Titus' unspeakable line, "Why, there they are both, baked in that pie," as he serves to Tamora his cannibalistic speciality—*tête de fils en pâte* (*pour deux personnes*).

Adorned by a vast, ribbed setting (the work of Mr. Brook, designer) and accompanied by an eerie throbbing of *musique concrète* (the work of Mr. Brook, composer), the play is now ready for the attentions of Mr. Brook, director. The result is the finest Shakespearean production since the same director tackled *Measure for Measure* five years ago. The vocal attack is such that even the basest lines shine, like Aaron the Moor, "in pearl and gold." Anthony Quayle plays the latter role with superbly corrupt flamboyance, and Maxine Audley is a glittering Tamora. As Lavinia, Vivien Leigh receives the news that she is about to be ravished on her husband's corpse with little more than the mild annoyance of one who would have preferred foam rubber. Otherwise, the minor parts are played up to the hilt.

Sir Laurence Olivier's Titus, even with one hand gone, is a five-finger exercise transformed into an unforgettable concerto of grief. This is a performance which ushers us into the presence of one who is, pound for pound, the greatest actor alive. As usual, he raises one's hair with the risks he takes. Titus enters not as a beaming hero but as a battered veteran, stubborn and shambling, long past caring about the people's cheers. A hundred campaigns have tanned his heart to leather, and from the cracking of that heart there issues a terrible music, not untinged by madness. One hears great cries, which, like all of this actor's best effects, seem to have been dredged up from an ocean-bed of fatigue.

One recognised, though one had never heard it before, the noise made in its last extremity by the cornered human soul. We knew from his Hotspur and his Richard III that Sir Laurence could explode. Now we know that he can suffer as well. All the grand unplayable parts, after this, are open to him: Skelton's Magnificence, Ibsen's Brand, Goethe's Faust—anything, so long as we can see those lion eyes search for solace, that great jaw sag.

(1955)

The Water Gipsies, BY A. P. HERBERT AND VIVIAN ELLIS, AT THE WINTER GARDEN.

When a man misses one target by yards, it is kinder to assume that he was aiming at another. And so, instead of measuring the miles by which *The Water Gipsies* fails as a modern musical comedy, let me point out to the authors, Sir Alan Herbert and Vivian Ellis, the inches by which they have failed to turn out a matchless museum-piece.

Their enterprise, beyond doubt, was to write a Cockney pastoral. I had better explain that I use the word "pastoral" in William Empson's sense: as a form in which the working classes are presented as helpless and semi-literate but full of a simple wisdom denied to sophisticates. They are happy with their lot, and the spectator (to quote Mr. Empson slightly out of context) "is put into a mood in which one would not try to alter it." Cockney pastoral derives from Dickens and reached, in the *Punch* cartoons of the eighties, the state of flawless unreality which Sir Alan has striven to preserve. And how nearly he has succeeded! Hammersmith, as he conceives it, is a rural hamlet peopled with quaint barges whose joys are homely and whose destiny (they are jovially reminded) is perforce obscure. They are born to blush unseen; and how they blush when the kindly swell from "up West" reproves them for displays of bad temper! Yet we forgive them: laughter is a great healer, and who could forbear smiling at the hoyden who takes an "aperient" before her meal, followed by a bottle of "Bummery"? Her sister, the heroine, is played by Pamela Charles, a newcomer who strikes a note of artless servility exactly right for the song wherein she pledges her allegiance to "the state of life to which it pleases God to call me." And Vivian Ellis' music, chiming like cowbells over the meadow, is bang in the pastoral tradition.

Yet, sniper that I am, I still find room for improvement. Two major errors of casting should be speedily reconsidered. Dora Bryan, to begin with, does not know her place at all; to the role of the hoyden she brings resources of wit, audacity, and vocal finesse which have the deplorable effect of making everything around her seem old-fashioned. And the robust intelligence of Laurie Payne, as the jolly bargee, is nothing short of shocking: one almost suspects him of aspirations to a state of life unsanctified by the divine summons. Both these performances need humbling and broadening. By some oversight, several members of the cast are clad in what is unmistakably modern dress; this should be modified at once. The Communist villain, who stresses the second syllable of "capitalist," might be merged, with amusing results, into the Jewish gambler—I coquetted for a moment with the picturesque idea of giving him a hump back as well. Jerry Verno might be encouraged to spit occasionally. The scene in which the heroine does a strip-tease and then kneels in prayer would gain in continuity if she were to hum some well-known hymn as she undressed. Finally, I feel that if Peter Graves must offer her a "treat," he might accede less readily when she requests a hotel room "wiv a barf." Some tactful proviso should be made. "Only," he might admonish her, "if you promise not to put coal in it."

(1955)

Ondine, BY JEAN GIRAUDOUX, AT THE BRISTOL OLD VIC.

Why, during his lifetime, did we so sorely neglect the author of *Ondine?* If we picture European drama between the wars as a house, Jean Giraudoux was the decorator, and he did it up so imposingly that only Shaw, Brecht, Pirandello, and O'Casey could live in it without feeling dwarfed. We travel through his plays as through a luminous grotto, glimpsing murals of time-suspending wit and loveliness; and it would be churlish, after such a journey, to complain that the labyrinth seemed shapeless, that there were too many blind alleys, or that every picture did not tell a story. As well might one condemn the Uffizi Gallery for lacking narrative impact.

Life as Giraudoux perceived it was life as it appeared to Mr. Huxley while mescalin was tickling his cerebral cortex: cleansed, pure, alive with colour, and so transformed in the matter of dimensions that a turn of phrase was as tangible as a column of alabaster. Though he preferred what Thomas Mann called the "finer and much less obvious rhythmical laws" of prose, Giraudoux was arguably the greatest theatrical poet of his time. As a prose architect he easily eclipsed Shaw in the art, now forgotten but once obligatory, of providing long speeches for crucial moments. Not for him the clipped, chopped scurry of most modern dialogue. At regular intervals Giraudoux feels a set-piece coming on, and the plot must pause while it blazes; when this occurs, we get marvels like the Madwoman's account of her daily ritual in *La Folle de Chaillot,* or the Judge's speech in the present play, which describes the unearthly calm that hung over the world one summer afternoon when all the attendant spirits, celestial and infernal alike, ran off for a few hours and left mankind to its solitude.

A playwright is a man who can forget himself long enough to be other people; and a poet is a man who can forget other people long enough to be himself. In Giraudoux, as in few others, the two vocations are fused like Siamese twins. The playwright sets the scene, and in the *tirades* the poet takes over; and by a miracle of collaboration the poet's eloquence nearly always crowns an arch which the playwright has built. So it is with the Judge's speech in *Ondine.* The play has been making one of Giraudoux's pet points, that once humanity acquires knowledge of the supernatural it is lost. A brave but doltish knight-errant has married a water-sprite, unaware that if he is unfaithful to her he must die. We have squandered much time in the second act on glittering trivialities, Giraudoux in his rhinestone vein; but now, in the third, we return to the main theme. The loyal Ondine is on trial; but it is the disloyal knight who will die. One thinks of the warning delivered to the heroine of *Intermezzo: "Ne touchez pas aux bornes de la vie, à ses limites."* We have to live in the same universe as the agents of the supernatural; but we must beware of trying to live on the same plane.

The tone of this beautiful play is half festal seriousness and half momentous levity. It gets from John Moody and his Bristol troupe a far better production than the pantomime extravaganza, directed by Alfred Lunt, which bore its name on Broadway two seasons ago. And this, amazingly, in spite of having no Ondine to speak of. In New York Audrey Hepburn flouted the text by having hair which was short and dark instead of long and blonde, and menaced the mood by wearing fish-net tights; yet she gave the character its one vital quality: a destructive innocence. Beyond the charm of her sepulchral little voice, one saw the ruthlessness of the troll. Moira Shearer has the harmless innocence of Miranda in her brave new world, and her voice issues not from the anteroom of eternity but from the pump-room at Bath. It is the cool, collected voice of a Jane Austen heroine. Miss Shearer's dancing had a lyricism which her acting has not, and henceforth she had better steer clear of naiads. Her real line, I suspect, is comedy, and contemporary comedy at that.

(1955)

The Queen and the Rebels, BY UGO BETTI, AT THE HAYMARKET.

As one who has whined incessantly about the paucity of serious plays in the London theatre, I must admit at once that Ugo Betti's *The Queen and the Rebels* is as serious as anything London has seen since Marie Corelli's *The Sorrows of Satan* in 1897. It is exactly what large numbers of people (most of them non-playgoers) expect a serious play to be. So was the same author's *The Burnt Flower-Bed;* so are all plays about frontier incidents in unnamed countries torn by revolution. It deals with the dilemma of the contemporary conscience, and with a crisis of self-determination in the individual soul. I know this because the author will not let me forget it; he rubs it in as often and as explicitly as his fondness for rhetoric will allow.

It would be frivolous to dismiss his play as a mere melodrama about a tart with a heart of gold. It would be frivolous, firstly, because melodrama has outgrown that particular theme; secondly, because modern melodrama is not so mere that it would countenance a scene in which two people plot the death of a third person at the top of their voices in the third person's presence; and, thirdly, because Betti's style (or that of his translator, Henry Reed) forbids me to harbour thoughts so low. Only the heights will do.

Now, I should have thought that there was a good, compact little play, with plenty of implications in it for those who wanted them, in the situation of a prostitute who takes pity on a fugitive queen and offers herself to the revolutionaries as a substitute martyr. But Betti was a pupil of Pirandello, as Pinero was a pupil of Ibsen, and for him implications are not enough. Heaven forbid that he should be caught forgetting to philosophise! Or that a moment should pass without some evidence of high seriousness! If someone observes that corpses stink, someone else must be on hand to remark: "It's the smell of history." Not trusting us to recognise in his Commissar the Inquisitors and Interrogators we have already met in numberless plays and novels, Betti blunts his point by pressing it: the Commissar must define himself as a "fury" who thinks of human beings as grubs wriggling in cheese. We are familiar with the inconveniences of the slut's vocation, but this does not spare us a series of speeches in which the heroine explains the nausea she feels at the touch of sweaty, prying hands.

The higher redundancy comes later: not content with impersonating a queen, she must *become* one. At this point it becomes impossible to take Betti's seriousness seriously. To object that people do not talk like that would be naïve; the real objection is that conventional symbols do. When a playwright manages to create characters larger than life, nobody is happier than I. But this is just where Betti fails. He has taken the tritest figures of old-fashioned melodrama and inflated them, which is by no means the same thing. Inevitability, the strong pull of life towards death, is an attribute of many fine plays; but in a puppet's inevitable march towards a cardboard scaffold I find it hard to take much interest.

Seriousness has indeed returned to the West End stage, and I can imagine Mr. Rattigan's Aunt Edna splitting a bottle of tonic wine to celebrate the occasion. But I begin to suspect that "serious" is the wrong epithet. Mr. Hemingway made an instructive distinction when he said: "A serious writer may be a hawk or a buzzard or even a popinjay, but a solemn writer is always a bloody owl."

Correctly deciding that realism would be out of place, Frank Hauser and his company go all out for the grand manner—or, rather, for that echo of it which often passes, in countries without playwrights, for great acting. (One remembers how Mrs. Brown-Potter took South Africa by storm in 1907.) This is not to sniff at Mr. Hauser's troupe; I cannot see what else they could have done with dialogue so incompatible with the known facts of human behaviour. The more brutish characters (Alan Tilvern and Duncan Lamont) savagely button-hole us, showing full sets of clichés as they do so. As the Commissar, Leo McKern has the unfair advantage of coming straight from another Betti play at the Arts Theatre, from which he has learned the value of starting on a quieter note; but before long this excellent actor is bellowing with the rest.

A cynical director and a cynical leading lady might perhaps, by discreet underplaying, have coaxed pure pathos from Betti's heroine. It stands to the credit of Mr. Hauser and Irene Worth that they attempt no such evasion. Up to the moment of her conversion Miss Worth presents a prostitute so noisily world-weary that it is a bore for her even to deafen us; and afterwards, when the switch to queenship has been made, she becomes full-bloodedly operatic. A younger actress (Julie Harris, for instance) might have touched us, even to tears, with the tremulous aspirations of a tart to regality. Miss Worth gives the author what his lines demand, a display of technique which is grandiose, heartfelt, marvellously controlled, clear as a crystal, and totally unmoving. The house exploded in cheers when she had done, which was only natural. Having been roared at for two and a half hours, it restored the balance by roaring back.

(1955)

Hamlet, BY WILLIAM SHAKESPEARE, AT THE PHOENIX.

As he proved seven years ago at Stratford, no living actor is better equipped for Hamlet than Paul Scofield. On him the right sadness sits, and also the right spleen; his gait is a prowl over quicksands; and he can freeze a word with an irony at once mournful and deadly. He plays Hamlet as a man whose skill in smelling falseness extends to himself, thereby breeding self-disgust. He spots the flaw in every stone, which makes him either a born jeweller or a born critic. He sees through Gertrude, Claudius, Rosencrantz, Guildenstern, Polonius, and Ophelia: what remains but to see through himself? And this Mr. Scofield does superbly, with a mighty bawl of "O vengeance!" followed by a rueful stare at his own outflung arms and a decline into moans of derisive laughter. His eulogy of Horatio is not only a hymn to the only honest man in Denmark, it is the tribute enviously paid by complexity to simplicity.

Mr. Scofield's outline is impeccable. What is surprising is the crude brushwork with which he fills it in. Vocally and physically he is one long tremendous sulk; a roaring boy is at large, and not (as when he played the part before) a scholar gipsy. The new Mr. Scofield protests much too much. The note struck on "Vengeance!" is thrice repeated, with diminishing returns; too many speeches are mechanically gabbled; and the actor's face is a mask devoid of pathos. To hold our attention he will hit wrong notes or leap up the scale halfway through a line, but the grip seems artificial, as if he had decided that what could not be coaxed into life had better be shouted to death. Potentially, Mr. Scofield is still Sir Laurence Olivier's natural heir, but in the technique of realistic acting he is badly out of practice. We have fed him on rhetoric and starved him of life, and if he fails to move us, it is as much our theatre's fault as his.

Peter Brook's production moves like the wind. In a permanent setting (by Wakhevitch) which overhangs the action like a great stone bird-cage, he achieves changes of scene which are both swift and stunning. Yet, though movement is there, destination is lacking. Mr. Brook thrives on plays long unopened, such as *Venice Preserv'd* and *Titus Andronicus. Hamlet,* his first attempt at a major tragedy, seems to have overawed him. In the crowd scenes—the play and the duel—he brings off grand slams, but elsewhere his direction is oddly tentative, with niggling cuts and ear-distressing transpositions, and when he seeks to play a trump—by giving the court musicians toy drums and trumpets—one is merely conscious that he has revoked.

Broad fun was never Mr. Brook's strong suit. Hence Osric falls flat; Ernest Thesiger's praying-mantis Polonius is annoyingly restrained; and the gravediggers, despite the earthiness of Harry H. Corbett, miss their true *Galgenhumor.* The Gertrude is droopy, the Laertes stiff and hysterical; and though Mary Ure is helped by the substitution of wild flamenco chants for the traditional jingles of Ophelia's madness, her playing has about it a cool calculation which points rather to comedy than to tragedy.

I reserve until last the bloat king, the *bonne bouche* which swallows up the rest. Alec Clunes is not only the best Claudius I have seen, but in most respects the only one. Hamlet speaks of the king as a "remorseless, treacherous, lecherous, kindless villain," and every Claudius in my memory has played him as such. Mr. Clunes, returning to the basic principle of acting, plays Claudius from Claudius' own point of view: as a man who committed a *crime passionnel* after an internal battle which has left scars on his conscience. Into this reading the prayer scene, normally an excrescence, perfectly fits; and the line about Gertrude—"I could not but by her"—rings a bell-note of pure pathos. We watch the slow crumbling of a man of action who has created through crime a new universe which now falls, stone by stone, about his ears. "O Gertrude, Gertrude! When sorrows come, they come not single spies, but in battalions!" is a heart-cry rendered doubly moving by the actor's refusal to overstress it and by Gertrude's rejection of his outstretched hand.

To quell Laertes' rebellion, he collects himself, weary yet still majestic. This lonely man engages once again in plotting, of which he is still a master, like the gouty Napoleon at Waterloo. "That we would do, we should do when we would": this is not only an echo of Macbeth, but a tacit condemnation of Hamlet, who could not when he would. Yet when the plot is laid, a premonition clouds the king's mind, a sigh ominous with defeat. In these scenes of conspiracy (usually regarded merely as a rest for the star) Mr. Clunes performs miracles of reclamation which one is lucky to see once in a lifetime of Shakespearean playgoing. For long periods he was the only actor on stage who seemed, supply and subtly, to be listening.

It is objected that he whitewashes Claudius? He shows us a man who has tried and failed to rationalise his faults—and if that is whitewashing, it is how most of us spend our lives. Under his influence *Hamlet* is the tragedy not only of a prince but of a whole doomed family. If my thoughts on Thursday turned to the House of Atreus, it was Mr. Clunes' magnificent doing. This is a superb performance.

(1955)

The Wild Duck, BY HENRIK IBSEN, AT THE SAVILLE.

Ibsen at Christmas, *The Wild Duck* instead of the tame turkey! John Clements is the manager who has set the bird before us, the master ironist who has presented, in the season of good will, the greatest attack on good will ever penned. He deserves nothing but thanks. The time is past when Ibsen was staged only for short summer runs, and Firbank wrote of a certain Mrs. Steeple:

> One burning afternoon in July, with the thermometer at 90, the ridiculous woman had played "Rosmersholm" in Camberwell. Nobody had seen her do it, but it was conceivable that she had been very fine.

Everyone, I hope, will see Mr. Clements' company, who are very fine indeed and almost give the impression of a team. I say "almost" because Emlyn Williams is by ancient bent and recent practice something of a lone wolf. Of course, Hjalmar Ekdal is a man of straw, but this is a point that Ibsen himself can be trusted to make; the actor need not be at such pains to show that he too sees through the character. Mr. Williams exposes Hjalmar's paltriness with the cool competence of an accountant tabulating forged entries in the firm's books, but he does not feel for the man; nor, in consequence, can we. Though full of mimetic cunning, this is a less memorable Hjalmar than Anton Walbrook's, seven years ago. Nor does Dorothy Tutin, an eager Hedvig, divest herself of years as movingly as Mai Zetterling did in the old St. Martin's production. But this is Christmas: let me emit but one peep of complaint. Since Hedvig's sight is failing, why does she not wear spectacles?

Nothing else at the Saville blurs the impact of a play which is not only a supreme tragedy but a supreme comedy to boot. Its theme, the destructiveness of idealism, is timeless enough to have appealed to Graham Greene, who used it, albeit ingenuously, in *The Quiet Ameri-*

can. And its technique, the Swiss-watch glibness of the plotting, still works as smoothly and hypnotically as ever. The play was best described by Shaw as "a tragi-comic slaughtering of sham Ibsenism," an assault by the great grouch of Skien on those idealists who are really egoists *manqués*. Gregers, the son whose desire to wound father takes the form of a compulsive passion to help others, is still very much with us; and so is Hjalmar, the weak vessel which the new wine of idealism shatters.

Some charge the play with preaching moral expediency, but what it really preaches is charity. Let the Hjalmars of the world keep their illusions: no price is too high for the postponement of despair. Politically, Munich may be indefensible, but few of us could live without frequent Munichs of the conscience. Michael Gough, imaginatively cast, is a perfect Gregers, oozing sincerity whilst letting the man's neuroses seep through the façade.

(1955)

Henry V, by William Shakespeare, at the Old Vic.

Harry of Monmouth, butcher and sophist, is a figure hard to love for himself alone. When he protests envy of the common man, who "all night sleeps in Elysium," we cannot but jeer, for we have just seen three common men kept up till dawn by his persistent quarrelling. By stressing the "gentle gamester" aspect of the part and delivering the rest as a trumpet voluntary, many actors have been able to blind us to the barbarity of *Henry V*. Richard Burton takes a steeper path. He gives us a cunning warrior, stocky and astute, unafraid of harshness or of curling the royal lip. The gallery gets no smiles from him, and the soldiery none but the scantest commiseration. Though it sometimes prefers rant to exuberance, this is an honest performance, true and watchful and ruthless.

The job of creating sympathy for Henry's cause thus falls to the director, and here Michael Benthall lets us down. Bowing to the "tradition" inaugurated by Sir Laurence Olivier's film, he presents the French as fluttering mountebanks. Charles VI is a girlish fumbler, the Dauphin an affected lout; this being so, the goal is kept by fops and Henry has nothing to beat. Instead of bearding a pride of lions, the armed might of England is employed to drown a basket of kittens. That the English were a happy few we know, but to stir our hearts they must challenge a triumphant many. We expect splendour from our Frenchmen, a robust assurance, a pomp and a power, not a weedy and beribboned defiance. Great battles may be won on the playing-fields of Eton, but not when the first fifteen is playing the third.

Apart from this central *gaffe,* there is little wrong with the production that a National Theatre and a more experienced company could not cure. Derek Francis' dogged Gower, Dudley Jones' brisk Fluellen, and Job Stewart's Nym, irretrievably glum, are perfect, as is the cosy, careworn sketch which Rachel Roberts makes of Mrs. Quickly. If I devote more space to John Neville, it is because this actor implicitly demands it. He has shown in the past that he has strong and curious views on the play. Some years ago, as Henry V, he gave a compelling performance of Richard II; now, as Chorus, he is giving a princely and effusive performance of Henry V, old style. How the plumbing stands out in his neck! And how romantically he snatches each word from the air! Yet, as Sainte-Beuve said, *"l'écueil particulier du genre romanesque, c'est le faux,"* a remark amplified by the American critic Stark Young when he condemned English actors for "a certain sweetish piety peculiarly their own and peculiarly false." Here we recognise Mr. Neville, who played so piously to the loftier seats that they begged him, at the end, to take the "star" curtain. The *compère* who steals the show is by definition a bad *compère*. Mr. Neville's failure is pretty, seductive, "actorish," and complete.

(1955)

Notes on the National Theatre.

Since today begins a New Year, it is fitting that the English should be reminded of a resolution that was made in their name on January 21, 1949. That, as the fervent will remember, was the day of the Giant Step, when the drama received its greatest (and almost its only) official boost since Charles II created the patent theatres. It was the day on which the House of Commons unanimously approved the National Theatre Bill, empowering the Treasury to spend a million pounds on building a home for the nation's drama.

Seven years have passed, and what has become of that august and imaginative resolve? One stone has been regally laid; and that, by mischance, in the wrong place. Having expressed our will, we, the people, left things to them, the National Theatre Executive Committee, and shortly afterwards relapsed into what Matthew Arnold bitterly called "our favourite doctrines of the mischief of State interference, of the blessedness of leaving every man to do as he likes, of the impertinence of presuming to check any man's natural taste for the bathos and pressing him to relish the sublime."

Why? Has the theatre forgotten the long passion that brought its dream to the brink of fact? Surely the classic arguments, endorsed always by the few and seven years ago by the many, need no reiteration. Must it again be urged that Britain is the only European country with a living theatrical tradition which lacks a national theatre; and that the public money which gave us a visual library, the National Gallery, is needed just as vitally to provide (in Benn Levy's phrase) a "living library" of plays? But the points were all made in the Commons debate. The general impotence of our theatre, as opposed to the individual excellence of our actors, is the laughing-stock of the Continent; and it is unthinkable that anyone nowadays would sink to the crassness of saying, as a daily paper did in 1938: "To have no National Theatre is a tribute to our liberty." To whom, one wonders, is the following quotation still controversial? "I consider it a pity, and even a folly, that we do not make some national effort to aid and assist dramatic representation. . . . Think with what excitement and interest this people witnesses the construction or launching of a Dreadnought! What a pity it is that some measure of that interest cannot be turned in the direction of the launching, say, of a National Theatre!" The speech from which these extracts are taken was delivered by Sir Winston Churchill in 1906.

Geoffrey Whitworth, the pioneer of the National Theatre, died in 1951; one regrets that he did not live to see and surmount the ironies with which time has festooned his vision. One recalls William Archer and Granville-Barker, in the first flush of certainty, graciously smiling on the idea of a subsidised opera-house, but never doubting for an instant that the theatre would come first, since "England possesses a national drama but does not as yet possess a national opera." Well, that was in 1904. We now have a subsidised opera-house; we are soon to have a second concert-hall on the South Bank; and the L.C.C. has just agreed to spend seven million pounds on the "rehabilitation" of the Crystal Palace. And still that lonely, misplaced stone is all we have of our theatre.

But what, the diehards may ask, will the National Theatre give us that Stratford and the Old Vic do not? Firstly, a really modern theatre, comparable with those abroad and capable of staging the widest variety of plays. Secondly, not a cast of underpaid second-stringers, like the

Old Vic, nor yet a starry, short-term band, like Stratford, but a large, experienced, permanent company, drawn from our finest talent and paid accordingly. Of the several objects prescribed for the National Theatre, Stratford and the Old Vic fulfil but one—that of presenting Shakespeare. The others (those of reviving the rest of our classical drama, presenting new plays and the best of foreign drama, and preventing recent plays of merit from rusting in oblivion) have no roof at all over their heads. At the X Theatre the play is good; at the Y, the acting; and the decor at the Z is magnificent. But there is nowhere we can send our guests, confidently saying: "This is our theatre's best. On this we stand."

Our theatre has always been dogged by poverty; it is now dangerously close to being bitched by it. In 1880 Matthew Arnold concluded his great germinal essay with the words: "The theatre is irresistible; organise the theatre!" To which one would add: "The Act is irresistible; implement the Act!"

(1956)

Art for Our Sake.

Riffling through my colleagues' comments on M. Sartre's *Nekrassov,* I see that, while most of them found it witty, nearly all of them deplored the way in which it "resorted to propaganda"—as if the presence of propaganda in a play automatically condemned it. I used to share this assumption myself. None was readier than I to chide the proselytising playwright, to mock at the zeal of the determined homilist. But now, in this arid theatrical season, I begin to wonder whether I was right. In demanding an end to propaganda, was I not depriving the drama of one of its most ancient sources of energy?

Nobody denies that there are bad propaganda plays, just as there are bad poetic plays. But to hold that all plays containing propaganda are by definition bad is to run counter to a theory of art on which much great drama is based and which nobody seriously challenged until the nineteenth century. I mean the notion that the purpose of art was "to instruct through delight," the idea set forward in Sidney's *Defence of Poesie*. Early playwrights would have been shocked by the suggestion that they were not propagandists. The whole of Greek tragedy (and all satire from Aristophanes through Ben Jonson to M. Sartre) is admonitory in intent, and admonition is nothing if not moral propaganda.

Everyman is a propaganda play. So is *Henry V;* so are *An Enemy of the People, A Doll's House,* and *Ghosts;* so is the entire *oeuvre* of the greatest living European playwright, Bertolt Brecht.

At this point we had better define propaganda and distinguish between good and bad forms of it. A melodrama is a play whose author is more interested in the impact events are having on his audience than in their impact on his characters. A propaganda play is the same, with "ideas" substituted for "events." Its aim is to start you thinking; and, though I agree that the effect of the greatest plays is to present an action so complete that only silence can succeed it in the mind, I cannot understand by what logic this rules out the theatre of parable, polemic, and pamphlet. Propaganda plays are admittedly distortions of life, but so are cartoon films, and they are all the better for it.

I know many good minor playwrights whose view of life is biased but clear, tendentious but honourable. Fear of being dubbed "propagandist" prevents them from stating it. Instead, they give us feeble "mood" plays with no point of view at all. This fear of commitment, of being thought *engagé,* accounts for the rash of pseudo-Chekhovs that has broken out all over the contemporary theatre. Don't comment, just record: kindly stick to the news. And this attitude is encouraged by the terminological vagueness which led one eminent British critic to dismiss Giraudoux's *La Folle de Chaillot* as "a misty piece of Socialist propaganda." Only a madman would wish that Chekhov had written didactically, yet it seems even madder to argue from this that the stage should never be used by lesser men as a political platform or as a pulpit. The logical end of that dispute is to exact from every playwright a guarantee that he holds no convictions strongly enough to let them influence his writing. And that is like demanding a certificate of intellectual impotence.

Bad propaganda plays occur when the idea being propagated is trite and too repetitively stressed, or when the author's tone is either embittered or sentimentally fulsome. But it is irrelevant to indict a propaganda play on the ground that it is "unfair." Morality plays are "unfair" to the Devil; *Henry V* is "unfair" to France. The self-indulgent hero of Mayakovsky's satire, *Klop,* is treated with formidable unfairness, yet the play prodded me, spurred me, irritated me into thought. Before calling him "preacher" or "sermoniser," remember the handicaps under which the propagandist works. He is a judge passing sentence on the strength of evidence which he has himself manufactured, and if the sentence is too harsh or too shrilly delivered, the audience will be quick to unmask him as a bigot. The finest and rarest sort of theatrical teacher is that defined in a dictum of Howard Lindsay's: "If you are going to write a propaganda play, you had better not let any of your characters know what the propaganda is." Brecht's *Mother Courage* falls into this category. Behind its every line, as behind every line of *Everyman,* there beats a passionate desire to improve the human condition. Honestly felt and truly expressed, this passion can generate a special and unique dramatic excitement, an irreplaceable theatrical heat. It brings us into contact not only with a man's power of narrative invention, but with the mind of the man himself.

There are many other kinds of theatrical excitement. All I seek to establish is that propaganda has a place in the hierarchy. Brecht once drew an analogy which I think worth quoting. Some surgeons, he said, are content to supply merely a diagnosis; others feel it their duty to recommend a cure. Most propaganda plays, admittedly, offer quack remedies. The danger is that our hatred of quacks may lead us to despise the true healers.

(1956)

The Face of Love, BY IAN DALLAS, AT THE ROYAL ACADEMY OF DRAMATIC ART; *Darkling Child*, BY W. S. MERWIN AND DIDO MILROY, AT THE ARTS.

The hegemony of verse drama ended when Chekhov proved that in the theatre words were not paramount but auxiliary, not tyrants but collaborators; working alongside atmosphere and the movement of character, they could achieve a poetic effect in prose. The claim that high drama could only be written in lines of unequal length was exposed overnight as an archaic fraud. Chekhov and Shaw completed the revolution that Ibsen had begun, and prose, thereafter, was liberated in the serious theatre. Beside these three giants, Messrs. Eliot and Fry suggest nothing so much as a pair of energetic swimming instructors giving lessons in an empty pool.

These truths I had thought self-evident, but it seems I was wrong. A penumbra of holiness, a promise of access to realms otherwise inaccessible, still hangs over verse plays; and in the past week two talented young writers have swooned to the lure. One is Ian Dallas, who wrote *The Face of Love;* the other is W. S. Merwin, the co-author (with Dido Milroy) of *Darkling Child*. Let me say at once that Mr. Dallas' play, a scathing surview of the Trojan War, is acted with notable assurance, especially by Albert Finney, the smouldering young Spencer Tracy who plays Troilus; here is an actor who will soon disturb the dreams of Messrs. Burton and Scofield. But why, having garbed his Trojans in modern dress and chosen as his theme the contagious faithlessness of war, does Mr. Dallas drape his climaxes in verse—and bombastic, quasi-Marlovian verse at that? To the Elizabethans, poetry was a stone's throw from actual speech. Now it is light-years removed, and once Mr. Dallas embarks on it, his characters start to speak interchangeably, in a vein of vague and generalised emotion. Versified pap is infused into a subject which cries out for precise, ironic prose.

Darkling Child is a similar case: beneath its poetry a good play lies smothered. A wild Restoration witch poisons her godless father in order to escape to the arms of a rigid young clergyman, who rejects her when he learns of her crime. Some hint here of the sexual motive behind religious ecstasy: yet see how Mr. Merwin obscures it, in a style how memorably cute, how ruinously studded with distracting phrases! We pause, and think: "How clever!" and in that instant drama flees. I do not feel cold shudders running down my spine; instead, "a keel of cold scales slithers between my shoulders." You do not knit your brows; instead, "there's a dwarf hand twitching like nervous fire between your eyes." No line, however commonplace, is allowed to go free without its compulsory metaphor, its pause for irrelevant embellishment. This is Philistine art, art for ostentation's sake, like an overcrowded junk-shop on the eve of a fire-sale. It conforms to Nietzsche's definition of literary decadence as a thing which occurs when the phrase jumps out of the sentence, the sentence out of the paragraph, and the paragraph out of the chapter. Margaret Whiting, the militant firebrand who plays the murderess, swoops on her long speeches like a ski-jumper at Cortina; how she would fare on a level course one cannot tell. I admit that she has a quality which has lifted many people to stardom: the ability to speak swiftly and powerfully without contorting her lips. She has been called a young Siddons. I would rather, and more warily, dub her an early Herlie.

(1956)

Othello, BY WILLIAM SHAKESPEARE, AT THE OLD VIC.

Even in prospect, the double *Othello* of John Neville and Richard Burton looked fairly black. The roles of Othello and Iago were to be alternated by two born Cassios: how could they manage overnight the switch from black outside to black inside? And in part one's qualms were justified. The Moor came lame from the struggle, as he must when age is absent. Messrs. Burton and Neville are the youngest Othellos the town has seen this century, and if they reply that both Garrick and Kean played the part before reaching thirty, my counter-charge must be that the audience which swallowed the fourteen-year-old Master Betty as Hamlet would swallow anything.

Temperament alone is not enough for Othello, nor is physical beauty. The essence is that unfeignable quality which some call weight and others majesty, and which comes only with age. Frederick Valk had it, a great stunned animal strapped to the rack; but neither Mr. Burton, roaring through his whiskers, nor Mr. Neville, a tormented sheikh, could give the Moor his proper magnitude. In the grace-notes Mr. Neville was exemplary, the moments of sacrificial tenderness; he conveyed, even at the raging climax, a sense of pain at the treachery of Iago, whom once he had loved. The part's quiet dawn and its quiescent sunset were both there. What escaped the actor was the intervening tempest.

Tuesday's performance, with Mr. Burton blacked up and Mr. Neville a capering spiv, was a drab squabble between the Chocolate Soldier and the Vagabond King. Only the best things in Michael Benthall's production held one's attention: Rosemary Harris' Desdemona, a moth of peace who might profitably have beaten her wings more vigorously, and Richard Wordsworth's Roderigo, a wholly credible ninny. On Wednesday we were in a different world. Mr. Burton was playing Iago, and the production rose to him.

Paradoxically, the only way to play Iago is to respect Othello. Let Iago mock the Moor with cheap laughs, and the play collapses: it becomes the farce of an idiot gull instead of the tragedy of a master-spirit. Mr. Burton never underestimates Othello; nor, in consequence, do we. His Iago is dour and earthy enough to convince any jury in the world. He does not simulate sincerity, he embodies it; not by the least wink or snicker does his outward action demonstrate the native act and figure of his heart. The imposture is total and terrifying. Like his author, Mr. Burton cares little for the question of Iago's motive: mere jealousy of Cassio's rank is not enough, else why should Iago go on hounding Othello after he has supplanted Cassio? Discarding this, Mr. Burton gives us a simple, dirty, smouldering drive towards power without responsibility. With a touch more of daemonism in the soliloquies, this will be an incomparable performance.

We may now define this actor's powers. The open expression of emotion is clearly alien to him: he is a pure anti-romantic, ingrowing rather than outgoing. Should a part call for emotional contact with another player, a contemptuous curl of the lip betrays him. Here is no Troilus, no Florizel, no Romeo. Seeking, as Othello, to wear his heart upon his sleeve, he resorts to forced bellowing and perfunctory sobs. Mr. Burton "keeps yet his heart attending on himself," which is why his Iago is so fine and why, five years ago, we all admired his playing of that other classic hypocrite, Prince Hal. Within this actor there is always something reserved, a secret upon which trespassers will be prosecuted, a rooted solitude which his Welsh blood tinges with mystery. Inside these limits he is a master. Beyond them he has much to learn.

(1956)

Tabitha, BY ARNOLD RIDLEY AND MARY CATHCART BORER, AT THE DUCHESS.

There is a kind of Englishman who regards all drama that is powerfully exciting as a gross invasion of his privacy; who likes his plays eked out with long stretches of eventless time in which he can meditate undisturbed on the nature of his destiny. For such playgoers *Tabitha* might have been written. At discreet intervals a "plot point" is made; between points the characters brew tea, drink whisky, and chat quietly among themselves. During these interludes, I submit, it would be a courtesy on the part of the management to turn on the house lights and serve tea and whisky to the audience, but I suppose one cannot have everything.

With the plot I shall not long detain you. It rears its head only intermittently, signalling for attention like the hamburger stands that (I assume) enliven one's journey across the baking plains of Arizona. Three impoverished gentlewomen (well played by Janet Barrow, Christine Silver, and Marjorie Fielding, though Miss Fielding's aloofness suggested at times that she had not been formally introduced to the rest of the cast) consider murdering their landlady, who has lately poisoned their pet cat, Tabitha. Should she continue to pilfer their liquor, they decide, she will find it lethally laced. Squeamishly they abandon the plan, and yet the landlady is poisoned. How? The answer, like a hamburger stand, is visible far off, so that the last scene is about as suspenseful as the Coronation ceremony. The authors, Arnold Ridley and Mary Cathcart Borer (I will repeat that), show an interesting ineptness in the management of entrances and exits, but by these technical matters only specialists are likely to be absorbed. For the most part, the audience is left to its own devices.

Constructive as ever, I feel moved to propose a few thoughts with which ticket-buyers might while away the long pauses between points. They might, for instance, think over someone's observation that, whereas the characters in American realistic drama drink whisky which is really cold tea, the characters in English artificial comedy drink tea which is really warm whisky. They might also revolve the question of stage nomenclature. What is it about the name "Mary Trellington" that brands it at once as fiction, not fact? Cats, too, might come into this. Mr. Thurber has expressed his mistrust of people who call their twin puppies Fitz and Startz; I myself have an irrational fear of cat-owners who give their pets names like Ella Wheeler Wilcox or Nina Mae McKinney. (Mary Cathcart Borer, in this whimsical context, would be an excellent name for a blue Persian.)

Another distraction might be to work out an appropriate epigraph for *Tabitha*. The best I could summon up was: "Home is where you hang your cat." More soberly, one might ask oneself how far the excitement generated by murder plays depends on the existence of the public hangman. And one might reasonably ponder the anomaly by which, though we campaign to abolish the death penalty for murderers, we happily retain the death penalty for plays. I refer, of course, to the Lord Chamberlain, who creates his own precedents and is accountable to no one, and from whom there is no court of appeal. Moreover, his sentences are carried out pre-natally, before the play is produced—a crime for which, in the medical world, many a doctor has been struck off the register. The Lord Chamberlain's refusal to grant a licence to Tennessee Williams' *Cat on a Hot Tin Roof* is already notorious; now, it is buzzed, the axe has fallen on Arthur Miller's latest success, *A View from the Bridge;* we are thus neatly cut off from the finest two playwrights at present writing in English. When M. Anouilh's *The Waltz of the Toreadors* transfers from the Arts Theatre to the West End, it is conceivable that his lordship will demand some verbal changes. If so, it would be a bold, gay, and instructive experiment to substitute the phrase "Lord Chamberlain" for every word deleted.

Does the reader complain that I have offered nothing in the way of constructive criticism? With all respect, he errs. My chase has an end in view. I have sought to illustrate, in the foregoing, an art which is integral to the writing of mystery plays and in which the authors of *Tabitha* are notably deficient: the art of intelligent padding.

(1956)

Social Drama.

The American edition of Arthur Miller's latest work, *A View from the Bridge,* is prefaced by a long essay which Mr. Miller entitles: "On Social Plays." At which we wince, those of us who remember what the thirties meant by "social plays"—tracts hoarse with rage and hungry for martyrdom, dramatic tumbrils from which the authors yelled their prophetic curses on us, the complacent *tricoteuses.* Sombre and embittered social plays led us to equate responsibility with solemnity, which we loathed, and irresponsibility with gaiety, which we loved. Mr. Miller's purpose is to show us that this dichotomy was false—that there are such things as festal seriousness, responsible gaiety, and triumphant tragedy. He defines theatre in the Greek manner, as "a dramatic consideration of the way men ought to live," and thence takes off into an artistic credo as stimulating as any of our time.

Just as *Pravda* decries the "cult of the individual" in politics, Mr. Miller decries it in drama. Defying Donne, our modish playwrights see their heroes as islands doomed to be swamped by an impersonal and vanquishing sea. Their prevalent theme is frustration; the hero is either defeated by society or reduced by it to a negative conformity. What has vanished is the positive concept of men living fruitfully together. Modern heroes die sadly in the dark; they "go gentle into that good night," a pitiful spectacle which has bred in modern audiences an appetite for pathos that amounts to an addiction. Tragedy, by contrast, should happen in sunlight. The hero bends in desperation beneath his burden, but he dies in the service of something larger than himself, and the sun shines the more brightly for his suffering. Ancient tragedy puts the question: "How are *we* to live?" Modern tragedy asks: "How am *I* to live?" That is the vital difference.

The first English play to set up personal fulfilment as a tragic ideal happened, unfortunately, to be a masterpiece: *Hamlet.* Here, for the first time, the hero was an outcast, both divorced from and superior to the society around him; for the first time an audience was invited to sympathise with a man's apartness and to ignore his "togetherness." Lear stands boldly for England; but Hamlet stands only for Hamlet, the first tragic protagonist to despise and reject every value by which his society lives. One echoes Shaw's stricture:

> *Hamlet* is the tragedy of private life—nay, of individual bachelor-poet life. It belongs to a detached residence, a select

> library, an exclusive circle, to no occupation, to fathomless boredom, to impenitent mug-wumpism, to the illusion that the futility of these things is the futility of existence. . . .

Hamlet spurns the old idols, dies in the dark, and leaves only a shambles behind him; it is magnificent, but it is not tragedy. As Mr. Miller says:

> I can no longer take with ultimate seriousness a drama of individual psychology written for its own sake, however full it may be of insight and precise observation. Time is moving: there is a world to make . . . a world in which the human being can live as a naturally political, naturally private, naturally engaged person, a world in which once again a true tragic victory can be scored.

I shall continue to applaud all plays that are honestly frivolous, devoutly disengaged; but I shall reserve my cheers for the play in which man among men, not man against men, is the well-spring of tragedy.

A View from the Bridge is a double bill, in the second half of which one character accuses another of homosexuality; the accusation is false, but it is made clearly enough to have convinced the Lord Chamberlain that the play should be banned in this country. Thus deprived of Mr. Miller, where else shall we search for a social playwright? No further, one suggests, than Bertolt Brecht's company in East Berlin, which is acknowledged to be the best theatre company in Europe and has been heavily tipped as the best in the world. Paris has twice capitulated to them; and it is time someone brought them to London, so that we might see in practice what Mr. Miller so eloquently preaches—the powerful exhilaration of a true "social theatre."

(1956)

The Power and the Glory, ADAPTED BY DENIS CANNAN AND PIERRE BOST FROM GRAHAM GREENE'S NOVEL, AT THE PHOENIX.

To my shame, I never finished reading Graham Greene's *The Power and the Glory*. About midway through the book I began to feel emotionally coerced, unable any longer to "identify" with the hero, a fugitive priest in Communist Mexico. I tried shutting my eyes and concentrating on Saint Sebastian, but it was no use; when I reopened them, there was the begging-bowl again, and the sign above it: "Hopeless Alcoholic, Chronic Non-Celibate and, if that doesn't move you, Catholic as well." One closed the book with a sense of having experienced not so much a dark night of the soul as a lost week-end. Buy your martyr's kit here, it seemed to be saying, and don't miss the special bonus, given away free with every package: a whiff of lechery, a bottle of Scotch, and your money back if persecution does not immediately follow purchase. You may be 20,000 leagues below the Holy See, but you are yet the elect, ever to be preferred to the merely elected, who are egalitarian bullies and unquestionably damned. (At this stage of Mr. Greene's development Satan had a Communist face. Now he has an American face. Students of double-think will recognise the process.)

Since Mr. Greene was writing about a country where, as Marx might have said, religion is the mescalin of the people, I cannot understand why he did not make his whisky-priest a dope-fiend as well; but one cannot have everything, and it is a considerable feat, scarcely equalled by Nigel Dennis in *Cards of Identity,* to have invented a character who is at the same time soak, seducer, and saint. I am not, I hope, without charity for the fallen: it is just that when virtue is presented to me so whorishly garlanded and vice is defined as the manure in which salvation flowers, I begin to suspect that I am in the presence of special pleading.

This personal digression may help to account for my failure to be moved by the stage version of the novel, an expert condensation by Denis Cannan and Pierre Bost. Through six vivid scenes we accompany the priest on his search for communion wine in a land of prohibition. We see his vocation leading him irrevocably to his death, and still, and yet, the tears will not come. Part of the trouble lies in the difficulty of reconciling English accents with Mexican make-ups. The physical production is assuredly not at fault. Using a "sound-track" of his own composition and five glorious settings by Georges Wakhevitch, Peter Brook plants us firmly in Mexico; but few of the large cast seem really at home south of the border.

This objection does not apply to Paul Scofield, who brings off a prodigious success as the trudging, wizened hero-victim. Puffing on a cheroot, with lines of resignation etched as if by acid on to his cheeks and forehead, Mr. Scofield exudes, drunk or sober (he gets most delicately drunk), a Goyaesque melancholy. This is the authentic face of Mexico, fly-blown and God-bitten. No matter though the actor's voice sometimes recalls the plummier inflections of Richard Haydn, the fish mimic: if the play fails to touch us, the blame is not his. It is probably mine, for choking over Mr. Greene's message. But who, one wonders, will swallow it? Non-Catholics certainly won't; nor will many Catholics, and the godless are presumably immune to it. Which leaves—well, who?

(1956)

Troilus and Cressida, BY WILLIAM SHAKESPEARE, AT THE OLD VIC.

Directors with a talent for self-expression traditionally get short shrift from English critics. "Exhibitionism" and "straining after effect" are the cult-cries, bandied about by people who should be well aware that if exhibitionism were a criminal offence, the entire theatrical profession would now be in gaol, and that a man who strains after an effect not infrequently achieves it. Tyrone Guthrie is the latest victim. He has mounted *Troilus and Cressida* in turn-of-the-century costumes, the trappings of the last epoch which thought war glamorous; and already hackles have risen and hecklers are busy. Now, it is true that many of the lines are spoken with numbing sloppiness and that this must be remedied; but to imagine a straight production of the piece with the Vic's present underpowered company is to thank God incontinently for Mr. Guthrie's intervention.

Out of the play's many styles he has chosen one—broad satire—and let the rest go hang. His Trojans are glass-smashing cavalry officers who might pass for British were it not for the freedom with which they mention Helen's name in the mess; their leader is Hector, game but ageing, and ripe for any exploit which will endear him to the young bloods he commands. Pandarus (Paul Rogers) becomes a Proustian *voyeur* and Cressida (Rosemary Harris) a militant flirt, an interpretation that throws romanticism out of the window and, incidentally, turns Troilus into a besotted half-wit.

John Neville, the actor in question, is the production's chief casualty, and he is further handicapped by one of Mr. Guthrie's most anarchic whims—the idea of playing "I am giddy: expectation whirls me round" as if the giddiness were due to alcohol. The Greeks, scarred and monocled, are all graduates of Heidelberg. The scenes between Achilles and Patroclus are played as classic expositions of sado-masochism; Ulysses, as one might guess, is an admiral of the fleet; and Dudley Jones' Nestor, a terrifically bearded toy martinet, is a refreshing change from the usual dotard. After ten minutes of protest one surrenders to a masterly joke, a lusty "newborn gaud" that Mr. Guthrie, to whom praise be, has "made and moulded of things past."

(1956)

The Chalk Garden, BY ENID BAGNOLD, AT THE HAYMARKET.

On Wednesday night a wonder happened: the West End theatre justified its existence. One had thought it an anachronism, wilfully preserving a formal, patrician acting style for which the modern drama had no use, a style as remote from reality as a troop of cavalry in an age of turbo-jets. One was shamefully wrong. On Wednesday night, superbly caparisoned, the cavalry went into action and gave a display of theatrical equitation which silenced all grumblers. This engagement completed, the brigade may have to be disbanded. But at least it went out with a flourish, its banners resplendent in the last rays of the sun.

The occasion of its triumph was Enid Bagnold's *The Chalk Garden,* which may well be the finest artificial comedy to have flowed from an English (as opposed to an Irish) pen since the death of Congreve. Miss Bagnold's style recalls Ronald Firbank's *The Princess Zoubaroff;* it has the same exotic insolence, the same hothouse charm. We eavesdrop on a group of thoroughbred minds expressing themselves in speech of an exquisite candour, building ornamental bridges of metaphor, tiptoeing across frail causeways of simile, and vaulting over gorges impassable to the rational soul.

The heroine of *Zoubaroff,* entreated to wear a smile, replied that it was too hot to wear another thing; and boy met girl with the exchange: "We slept together"—"Yes. At the opera. 'Bérénice.' " Like Firbank, Miss Bagnold evokes a world full of hard, gem-like flame-throwers, a little room of infinite riches. "Of course I'm affected," Aubrey Beardsley is rumoured to have said: "Even my lungs are affected!"; but there is nothing affected, or snobbish, about Miss Bagnold, unless verbal precision is a mark of snobbery.

London gives her the actors she needs. Dame Edith Evans, exasperated by "this *mule* of a garden," suggests a crested wave of Edwardian eccentricity vainly dashing itself on the rocks of contemporary life. Peggy Ashcroft is, beautifully, the dumpy governess who leads Dame Edith's granddaughter, a pretty pyromaniac ferociously played by Judith Stott, to forsake the sterility of her grandmother's house and rejoin her errant mama—a role in which Rachel Gurney shows once again how foolish our theatre has been to neglect her.

Something is being said about the necessity of rescuing young people from the aridity of a rich, irresponsible life; but it is being said wittily, obliquely, in a manner that one would call civilised if one thought civilisation was worthy of the tribute. *The Chalk Garden* probably marks the end of an era; Miss Stott's farewell to Dame Edith, as irrevocable as Nora's departure in *A Doll's House,* represents the future taking leave of the past. But the past has its joys. In this production (by Sir John Gielgud) we see English actors doing perfectly what few actors on earth can do at all: reproduce in the theatre the spirited elegance of a Mozart quintet.

(1956)

Suez and the Theatre.

English drama is like the Suez Canal during Eden's war, a means of communication made hazardous by a myriad sunken wrecks. There, scarcely visible above the ooze, is the mighty hulk that was Pinero; and there, stranded on a sand-bar, the flimsy outrigger Stephen Phillips. Salvage work is being carried out on the doughty tanker Priestley, but it remains a peril to navigation; and a whole stretch of waterway has been declared unsafe because of the presence, just on the surface, of the first aluminium leviathan; the captain has not yet abandoned his ship, on whose prow may be read the legend: "Noël Coward. Teddington." The lighthouse at Shaw's Corner is out of action, and traffic at any point is likely to be menaced by the sudden appearance of the deserted Esther McCracken, whose crew are thought to have jumped overboard in the middle of tea, which is laid in every cabin—a veritable mystery of the sea. And the ghost-frigate Eliot still provokes the superstitious to chant:

> But why drives on that ship so fast,
> Without or wave or wind?
> The air is cut away before,
> And closes from behind. . . .

The fledgling pilot has many such dangers to avoid. Yet there is—there must be—a way through.

(1956)

Hotel Paradiso, BY GEORGES FEYDEAU, AT THE WINTER GARDEN.

Georges Feydeau's *Hotel Paradiso,* revived, translated, and directed by Peter Glenville, is a sixty-year-old farce of clockwork cunning and, once you accept its postulates, impregnable plausibility. A henpecked husband (like you, I wish there were a synonym) takes his best friend's wife to a shady hotel on the very night when events are conspiring to bring almost everyone he knows to the same squalid rendezvous, which is run by an Italian *voyeur* who drills peepholes in the walls. Verbally, little is memorable: what matters is the dazzling economy of the construction. Feydeau wastes nothing. If an elderly barrister (well fooled by Douglas Byng) has a habit of stammering whenever it rains, be sure that this infirmity will play a vital part in the *dénouement*. The naked offstage woman who demands a pack of cards is not merely funny in herself; she also establishes at a stroke the atmosphere of the hotel.

Yet the kind of laughter that greeted the play was not unlike that which greets Sir Laurence Olivier, Vivien Leigh, and Danny Kaye when they dress up in sailor-suits and sing "Triplets" for charitable purposes. We laugh, that is to say, not at the song itself, nor yet at the skill with which it is done, but at the very idea of such august persons doing it at all. An element of charade intrudes.

Irene Worth, for example, is an actress whom we associate with the roles of women interestingly doomed. Here she appears with a top-hat jammed down over her chin. In the same way, Martita Hunt is formidably funny, swooping about like a wounded pterodactyl and indulging in regal, dismissive gestures which suggest that she is conducting an invisible symphony orchestra; yet when she is made to fence with a hatpin, one gets the same triplettish feeling as when Miss Worth wears her topper or when Alec Guinness is compelled to put his head up a chimney and emerge fuliginous. The joke is not so much on the characters in the play as on the dignity of the people who are playing them, an outrageous humiliation which . . .

But here the scales tip and qualms vanish, for Mr. Guinness is giving a display of such exquisite stealth that it transcends all objections. We have seen him in this vein before: the chubby, crafty little fellow obsessed by an urge to break out and show the world his mettle. Twinges of remorse occasionally contort his face, but, once resolved, he will hold his course, he will sleep out and around, he will live dangerously. What though his plans miscarry? He will have made his tiny protest, like that respectable resident of the Ritz in Paris who one day smuggled into his room five white mice in a paper bag and set them free in the corridor with cries of "Mice in the Ritz! Mice in the Ritz!"—cries, alas, which nobody heard.

Not the least wonderful thing in Mr. Guinness' performance is its sheer physical dexterity. In the "morning-after" scene he is almost unmasked as the black-faced sweep of the night before. "He was about your size," says someone suspiciously. "Oh, no—much taller!" cries Mr. Guinness, crumpling into a chair and shrinking before our eyes to the dimensions of a pickled walnut. This most creative *farceur* is notably assisted by Kenneth Williams as a blond prig and by Osbert Lancaster's happily unprettified settings.

(1956)

Look Back in Anger, BY JOHN OSBORNE, AT THE ROYAL COURT.

"They are scum" was Mr. Maugham's famous verdict on the class of State-aided university students to which Kingsley Amis' Lucky Jim belongs; and since Mr. Maugham seldom says anything controversial or uncertain of wide acceptance, his opinion must clearly be that of many. Those who share it had better stay well away from John Osborne's *Look Back in Anger,* which is all scum and a mile wide.

Its hero, a provincial graduate who runs a sweet-stall, has already been summed up in print as "a young pup," and it is not hard to see why. What with his flair for introspection, his gift for ribald parody, his excoriating candour, his contempt for "phoneyness," his weakness for soliloquy, and his desperate conviction that the time is out of joint, Jimmy Porter is the completest young pup in our literature since Hamlet, Prince of Denmark. His wife, whose Anglo-Indian parents resent him, is persuaded by an actress friend to leave him; Jimmy's prompt response is to go to bed with the actress. Mr. Osborne's picture of a certain kind of modern marriage is hilariously accurate: he shows us two attractive young animals engaged in competitive martyrdom, each with its teeth sunk deep in the other's neck, and each reluctant to break the clinch for fear of bleeding to death.

The fact that he writes with charity has led many critics into the trap of supposing that Mr. Osborne's sympathies are wholly with Jimmy. Nothing could be more false. Jimmy is simply and abundantly alive;

that rarest of dramatic phenomena, the act of original creation, has taken place; and those who carp were better silent. Is Jimmy's anger justified? Why doesn't he *do* something? These questions might be relevant if the character had failed to come to life; in the presence of such evident and blazing vitality, I marvel at the pedantry that could ask them. Why don't Chekhov's people *do* something? Is the sun justified in scorching us? There will be time enough to debate Mr. Osborne's moral position when he has written a few more plays. In the present one he certainly goes off the deep end, but I cannot regard this as a vice in a theatre that seldom ventures more than a toe into the water.

Look Back in Anger presents post-war youth as it really is, with special emphasis on the non-U intelligentsia who live in bed-sitters and divide the Sunday papers into two groups, "posh" and "wet." To have done this at all would be a signal achievement; to have done it in a first play is a minor miracle. All the qualities are there, qualities one had despaired of ever seeing on the stage—the drift towards anarchy, the instinctive leftishness, the automatic rejection of "official" attitudes, the surrealist sense of humour (Jimmy describes a pansy friend as "a female Emily Brontë"), the casual promiscuity, the sense of lacking a crusade worth fighting for, and, underlying all these, the determination that no one who dies shall go unmourned.

One cannot imagine Jimmy Porter listening with a straight face to speeches about our inalienable right to flog Cypriot schoolboys. You could never mobilise him and his kind into a lynching mob, since the art he lives for, jazz, was invented by Negroes; and if you gave him a razor, he would do nothing with it but shave. The Porters of our time deplore the tyranny of "good taste" and refuse to accept "emotional" as a term of abuse; they are classless, and they are also leaderless. Mr. Osborne is their first spokesman in the London theatre. He has been lucky in his sponsors (the English Stage Company), his director (Tony Richardson), and his interpreters: Mary Ure, Helena Hughes, and Alan Bates give fresh and unforced performances, and in the taxing central role Kenneth Haigh never puts a foot wrong.

That the play needs changes I do not deny: it is twenty minutes too long, and not even Mr. Haigh's bravura could blind me to the painful whimsey of the final reconciliation scene. I agree that *Look Back in Anger* is likely to remain a minority taste. What matters, however, is the size of the minority. I estimate it at roughly 6,733,000, which is the number of people in this country between the ages of twenty and thirty. And this figure will doubtless be swelled by refugees from other age-groups who are curious to know precisely what the contemporary young pup is thinking and feeling. I doubt if I could love anyone who did not wish to see *Look Back in Anger*. It is the best young play of its decade.

(1956)

The Family Reunion, BY T. S. ELIOT, AT THE PHOENIX.

After *Hamlet* and *The Power and the Glory,* the Peter Brook–Paul Scofield season of sin and damnation has entered on its last anguished lap with Mr. Eliot's *The Family Reunion.*

To Mr. Scofield, who has hardly had a cheerful line to speak in the past six months, one's heart goes out; having worked like a Trojan, he is now called on to impersonate a tormented pseudo-Greek. He does it yeomanly. On Mr. Eliot's Orestean hero he bestows a sleepless mien, gently haggard, and an anxious warmth of utterance that very nearly cures the character of its priggishness. As he is softened by Mr. Scofield, we almost come to like Harry. Almost, we believe that he might exist.

This, of course, is just a trick of mimetic *trompe-l'oeil*. Harry has no real blood in his veins. He is merely a projection of the obsessive guilt (often connected with the death of a woman) that constantly recurs in Mr. Eliot's work. "Sweeney Agonistes" gives the clue:

> I knew a man once did a girl in
> Any man might do a girl in
> Any man has to, needs to, wants to
> Once in a lifetime, do a girl in.

Harry returns to his aunt-haunted ancestral home convinced that he has done his wife in. Through his sibylline Aunt Agatha he discovers that the true culprit was his father, who sought and failed to knock off his mother. Harry embarks, enlightened, on a pilgrimage of atonement; but the suddenness of his departure has the ironic effect of striking his mother dead. Now, if Mr. Eliot had admitted that Harry was a rare and special case, all might have been well. Instead, he insists that we accept him as a timeless and universal symbol. We are to identify ourselves with Harry when he decides to embrace the Furies, saying that "my business is not to run away but to pursue." But at this point I could not help recalling a sentence from Manès Sperber's essay on Freud: "In the circle of his actions the neurotic is as much in pursuit of the Furies as he is pursued." Harry is an interesting upper-class neurotic (more New England than North Country, by the way), but he is nothing more, except to those who still retain an objective belief in fate. Mr. Eliot has dressed him in borrowed classical robes, but he sinks beneath their weight.

To preserve Harry from disaster as he swings about on the metaphysical high trapeze, Mr. Eliot has thoughtfully installed a safety net. He has given him two stupid aunts and two stupid uncles who cannot understand what he is driving at. In them the obtuseness of Philistia is incarnate; they suspect that Harry's spiritual garments have come from the Emperor's tailor; and if we agree with them, that makes us Philistines too.

The play contains two splendid jokes (in prose) and many passages of bony analytic precision. It also demonstrates Mr. Eliot's gift for imposing a sudden chill, as ghosts are said to do when they enter a room. Images of vague nursery dread insistently recur—the attraction of the dark passage, the noxious smell untraceable in the drain, the evil in the dark closet (which was really, as Dylan Thomas used impiously to say, the school boot-cupboard), the cerebral acne in the monastery garden, the agony in the dark, the agony in the curtained bedroom, the chilly pretences in the silent bedroom. (One of these phrases is my own invention. Entries by Ash Wednesday.) But though Mr. Eliot can always lower the dramatic temperature, he can never raise it; and this is why the theatre, an impure assembly that loves strong emotions, must ultimately reject him. He is glacial, a theatrical Jack Frost; at the first breath of warmth, he melts and vanishes.

This has-been, would-be masterpiece is magnificently revived by Peter Brook, who also designed the setting, an eerie upholstered vault. Apart from Mr. Scofield, Sybil Thorndike as the doomed matriarch and Gwen Ffrangcon-Davies as Agatha the oracle perform magisterially, and fine work is done by Nora Nicholson and Patience Collier. The whole cast inhales Mr. Eliot's thin air as if it were nourishing them; or as if it held some scent more refreshing than that of dry bones.

(1956)

A Critic of the Critics.

A few weeks ago there thudded through my letter-box a thunderbolt, postmarked "Boston, Massachusetts." Duly unwrapped, it turned out to be a book, shiny, pocket-sized, and unsummoned. Its stark title was: *"Precious Rubbish,* as raked out of current criticism by Theodore

L. Shaw." The fly-leaf revealed that Mr. Shaw had also written such elder blasts as *War on Critics* and *The Hypocrisy of Criticism*. This led me to expect some pretty jazzy polemic, and I was not disappointed. Mr. Shaw's avowed intent is to destroy criticism as we know it. His arch-enemy is "the absolutist," by which he means the reviewer who judges works of art by ideal and immutable standards, drawing artificial distinctions between "major" and "minor" poets, between "poetry" and "verse," between "almost first-rate" and "haplessly second-rate" writing. He dubs the absolutist a Shig—"a blend of Snobbery, Humbug, Ingratitude and Gas."

Shigs take it for granted that complex art is *per se* superior to simple art, and it is this assumption that riles Mr. Shaw. His watchword is Relativism. Relativists believe, with George Jean Nathan, that the only rule is that there are no rules. Their final criterion is the pleasure-principle, and they scorn the notion that there is such a thing as "timeless" art. In time, we tire of everything. "Fatigue," according to Mr. Shaw, is "the decisive factor in every merit appraisal of art works." After twenty hearings of *The Beggar's Opera* we weary and yearn for *Guys and Dolls*. "A mountain is something to climb, a continent something to explore, and a masterpiece something to get tired of—and the sooner the better." If we jib at this, Mr. Shaw declares, we are flying in the face of fact; we are refusing to admit that at one stage this, at another stage that, kind of art is aptest to please us. Art exists for us: we do not exist for art. Mr. Shaw clinches his case in a pamphlet I have not yet read, entitled *Art Is a Giant Drug Store*.

Mr. Shaw may be truculent, but he is no fool. He scores a bull's-eye when he rebukes Lewis Mumford for having said that fine art should not be available in postcard reproduction. "There are paintings by Van Gogh and Matisse and Picasso," cried Mr. Mumford, "that are descending the swift, slippery slope to oblivion by reason of the fact that they are on view at all times and everywhere." At which Mr. Shaw leaps in, hopping with rage, to ask: Why shouldn't they descend? Why shouldn't we be allowed to tire of them? And in seeking to restrict their availability, isn't Mr. Mumford tacitly admitting that greatness in a work of art depends entirely on how often you look at it? When he puts questions like this, Mr. Shaw has the absolutists on the ropes.

Yet in the long run he errs. Rightly, he wants art to be therapeutic, to produce healthful pleasure; but he fails to see that the purpose of good criticism is identical. Theatre critics, as Walkley said, "are consumers of one art, the art of drama, and producers of another art, the art of criticism." What counts is not their opinion, but the art with which it is expressed. They differ from the novelist only in that they take as their subject-matter life rehearsed instead of life unrehearsed. The subtlest and best-informed of men will still be a bad critic if his style is bad. It is irrelevant whether his opinion is "right" or "wrong": I learn far more from G.B.S. when he is wrong than from Clement Scott when he is right. The true critic cares little for here and now. The last thing he bothers about is the man who will read him first. His real rendezvous is with posterity. His review is a letter addressed to the future—to people thirty years hence who may wonder exactly what it felt like to be in a certain playhouse on a certain distant night. The critic is their eye-witness; and he has done his job if he evokes, precisely and with all his prejudices clearly charted, the state of his mind after the performance has impinged on it. It matters little if he leans towards "absolutism" or "relativism," towards G.B.S. or Hazlitt. He will find readers if, and only if, he writes clearly and gaily and truly; if he regards himself as a specially treated mirror recording a unique and unrepeatable event.

(1956)

Romanoff and Juliet, BY PETER USTINOV, AT THE PICCADILLY.

"He is our greatest narrative expert on the ways in which countries differ from one another. On the things they have in common he is, at the moment, less secure." Such, three years ago, was my judgment on Peter Ustinov. *Romanoff and Juliet* leaves it substantially unrevised. Comedy, for this Protean polyglot, derives from the clash of national attitudes. When Greek meets Greek, Mr. Ustinov is bored; but let Greek meet Dane (or Turk or Finn), and at once he is alert, ready to explode into the furry, compassionate chuckle which is his unfailing response to the bewildering legacy of Babel.

In his new play America confronts Russia, two embassies arguing (in Sydney Smith's phrase) from opposite premises, facing each other across the central square of the smallest country in Europe. Soviet son falls in love with Yankee daughter, an outbreak of peace which shocks and appals their respective families. Simple fun is made of the mighty opposites: the Americans conventionally bluster, while the Communists are presented as po-faced kill-joys, in accordance with the theatrical rule that all countries hostile to the British way of life are by definition humourless.

What have Russia and America in common? Romance, says Mr.

Ustinov—a conclusion that will start few riots by its novelty. But where, you may ask, is the evidence of his expertness in national differences? Don't we know already that America is Ford-fixated and that Russia is the home of Marxmanship? You forget that a third country is involved, the microscopic domain where the crisis takes place, a tiny homeland which differs radically from any other under the sun, but especially from Russia and America. Mr. Ustinov himself plays its President, a fussy pacifist general whose cardinal point of policy is to maintain "the balance of feebleness" by delaying his declarations of war until he is quite sure which side is going to lose. The author's comic expertise lies in the contrast he draws between the great grim certainties of East and West and the happy vagueness of his midget Utopia. Gaiety here is a national duty, since the place has been conquered and liberated so many times that every other day is Independence Day.

Mr. Ustinov's dwarf dreamland is authenticated with lavish detail. We learn something of its religion: it has a sect of penitents called the Mauve Friars, who neither sit nor stand but walk about on their knees, and a deaf little archbishop, played in a world of his own by Edward Atienza. We learn something of its history, notably of the boy king Theodore the Uncanny, whose cunning marriage to a Spanish Infanta "led to the eventual expulsion of the Albanians from our soil." Mr. Ustinov presides over our enlightenment with a sort of ruffled tact that combines the best features of Chorus, Pandarus, and fleet-footed Mercury. It has been said of this elusive author that he writes not so much plays of ideas as ideas for plays. In *Romanoff and Juliet* the idea has come out happy and whole, a blithe Ruritania with echoes for all of us, a satirical touchstone against which to test the pretensions of both Eastern bloc and Western alliance. Michael David and Katy Vail (Judy Holliday *en vacances*) make a charming pair of red-star-crossed lovers; William Greene is lankily wistful as a rejected fiancé: and Frederick Valk, the Russian spokesman, pays a brief, massive, and memorable tribute to the glories of old St. Petersburg.

(1956)

The Quare Fellow, BY BRENDAN BEHAN, AT STRATFORD-ATTE-BOWE.

"Bloddy sparklin' dialogue," said a pensive Irishman during the first interval of *The Quare Fellow*—and sparkle, by any standards, it amazingly did. The English hoard words like misers; the Irish spend them like sailors; and in Brendan Behan's tremendous new play language is out on a spree, ribald, dauntless, and spoiling for a fight. In itself, of course, this is scarcely amazing. It is Ireland's sacred duty to send over, every few years, a playwright to save the English theatre from inarticulate glumness. And Irish dialogue almost invariably sparkles. But now consider the context of Mr. Behan's hilarity. His setting is an Ulster prison, and one of its inmates is shortly to drop, rope-necklaced, through the untender trap.

> To move wild laughter in the throat of death?
> It cannot be: it is impossible.

But Berowne was wrong. To a countryman of Swift many things are possible, and this among them; this, perhaps, especially.

In adversity the Irish always sparkle. "If this is how Her Majesty treats her prisoners," said one of them, handcuffed in the rain *en route* for gaol, "she doesn't deserve to have any." With this remark of Oscar Wilde's, Mr. Behan, who has spent eight years of his life in prison for sundry acts of I.R.A. mischief, entirely agrees; and his protest is lodged in the same spirit of laconic detachment. The Irish are often sentimental about causes and crusades, but they are hardly ever sentimental about human beings. So far from trying to gain sympathy for the condemned man, an axe-murderer known as "the quare fellow," Mr. Behan keeps him off-stage throughout the action. All he shows us is the effect on the prison population of the knowledge that one of their number is about to be ritually strangled.

There are no tears in the story, no complaints, no visible agonies; nor is there even suspense, since we know from the outset that there will be no reprieve. Mr. Behan's only weapon is a gay, fatalistic gallows-humour, and he wields it with the mastery of Ned Kelly, the Australian bandit, whose last words, as the noose encircled his neck, were: "Such is life." Mr. Behan's convicts behave with hair-raising jocularity, exchanging obscene insults even while they are digging the murderer's grave. An old lag feigns a bad leg in order to steal a swig of methylated spirits; a newcomer anxious to raise bail is blithely advised to "get a bucket and bail yourself out." Even the hangman is presented serio-comically as a bowler-hatted publican with a marked addiction to the wares he sells. The tension is intolerable, but it is we who feel it, not the people in the play. We are moved precisely in the degree that they are not. With superb dramatic tact, the tragedy is concealed beneath layer after layer of rough comedy.

Meanwhile, almost imperceptibly, the horror approaches. Two warders, chosen to share the murderer's last eight hours of life, thoughtfully discard their wrist-watches in anticipation of his inevitable demand: What time is it? His last letters are thrown unopened into his grave: better there than in the Sunday papers. Dawn breaks, accompanied by the ghastly, anguished clatter of tin cups and plates against iron bars that is the tribute traditionally paid by the thousand convicts who will see tomorrow to the one who will not. The empty exercise yard now falls silent. The hush is broken by a unique *coup de théâtre,* Mr. Behan's supreme dramatic achievement. An unseen humorist, bawling from some lofty window, embarks on an imaginary description, phrased as racily as a Grand National commentary, of the hundred-yard dash from condemned cell to scaffold. They're coming into the straight now; the chaplain's leading by a short head. . . . A young warder, new to the ceremony, faints and is carried across the stage for treatment. A sad, bawdy ballad filters through from the punishment block. The curtain falls, but not before we have heard the swing and jerk of the drop. I left the theatre feeling overwhelmed and thanking all the powers that be for Sydney Silverman.

John Bury's two sets exactly capture the aridity of confinement. And Joan Littlewood's production is the best advertisement for Theatre Workshop that I have yet seen: a model of restraint, integrity, and disciplined naturalism. Glynn Edwards, Brian Murphy, and Maxwell Shaw, as three of Her Majesty's guests, and Dudley Foster, as one of the same lady's uniformed hosts, stand out from an inspired all-male company. Miss Littlewood's cast knows perfectly well what it is doing. She must now devote a few rehearsals to making sure that we can understand precisely what it is saying. That done, *The Quare Fellow* will belong not only in such transient records as this, but in theatrical history.

(1956)

Cards of Identity, BY NIGEL DENNIS, AT THE ROYAL COURT.

> "I must know who I am, mustn't I?"
>
> "Surely your own play isn't going to tell you?"
>
> "Of course not, dear; it's the critics who'll tell me. At the moment I don't exist; I don't even know what to *become*. But once my play's done, I'll know. . . ."
>
> —NIGEL DENNIS, *Cards of Identity*

Vain hope. Having seen the play that Mr. Dennis has excavated from his novel, I will be keel-hauled if I know what to tell him. At his true identity I cannot guess. I know him for a master satirist, and also for a stylist. To boot, he is a conjurer, a card-manipulator who has yet to learn that a straight flush in the hand may look somewhat repetitive when laid face upward, card by card, on the stage; may even, such is the waywardness of theatre, fail to vanquish a full house. But one thing is certain: for all his talents, Mr. Dennis does not yet belong in the company of those writers the very tone of whose voices, urgent and hypnotic, at once sets our minds shaping the question: "And then what happened?" The power to do this is not the highest of dramatic skills, but it is one of the hardest; and whenever he lays claim to it, whenever he assumes the identity of story-teller, Mr. Dennis lets us down. I do not know what he essentially is; but I do know what he is not.

The novel was an extravagant *bal masqué* whose theme was: "Come as you aren't." Three formidable frauds, closely reminiscent of Subtle, Face, and Doll in *The Alchemist,* commandeer a derelict country house in the name of the Identity Club. Triumphantly they test the club's maxim, that modern man no longer knows exactly who he is and can easily be persuaded that he is someone else; a man in whom arrogance and servility alternate can, for example, be transformed overnight, to his entire satisfaction, into a butler. The idea is to cram the largest possible number of mutually exclusive qualities into the same new personality. (The club's *chef d'oeuvre* is a Catholic Communist who is also an alcoholic.) Perhaps by chance, Mr. Dennis stumbled on the notion that the basic symbol of our time was not the atom scientist but the actor, the *histrio,* the man of multiple selfhood who had a brave new face for each sad new situation.

The idea that human personality is neither absolute nor immutable is no novelty: it was Pirandello's obsession, and we find it in the changeable masks used by the people in O'Neill's *The Great God Brown.* Nor is it a stranger to the novel: we are in its presence when Mr. Amis' Lucky Jim puts on his "Edith Sitwell face." Mr. Dennis' contribution was to elaborate it into a whole philosophy of life.

His book was a series of firework displays, each of which illuminated the same thesis. It had a plot, something to do with a conspiracy to assassinate the Club's President, but this was an appendage that wise readers skipped. We now approach the vital distinction between novel and play. A novel is a static thing that one moves through; a play is a dynamic thing that moves past one. Mr. Dennis has made the mistake of supposing his plot robust enough to haul his parade of set-pieces across the stage. Observe, for instance, the gorgeous tableau in which two dandies, Edwardians born too late, find fulfilment in the twin sinecures of Co-Wardens of the Badgeries, where their only duty is to parade an imaginary badger on State occasions. Superb! But now poor Plot comes puffing back to drag the next float into view. This is Father Orfe's account, delivered by George Devine with the most squalid unctuousness, of how modern religion is not only reconcilable with but inseparable from the basest debauchery: "I stink, therefore I am." *Éclatant!* Then in plods Plot again, trudging and sweating and patently loathing the job.

The spectacle grows painful. In the novel, Plot works only a seven-hour day; but in the theatre it must work overtime, from dawn to dusk, nudging and sheep-dogging the action into its predestined fold. Mr. Dennis' Plot is too frail to stand the strain; instead of being vigilant, it dozes, snores, and then awakens, quite unexpectedly, in alarming convulsions. If Mr. Dennis were to cut the whole of Act Two, Scene Three, and most of the last act, he would ease the burden on Plot and allow us to concentrate on the set-pieces, which bristle with wit, style, perception, audacity, malice, and profundity.

Tony Richardson's production brings Mr. Dennis' nightmare to pungent life. As the Machiavellian hero, Michael Gwynn excels himself; this is a display of caddishness at once rich and racy, genial and sinister, false-faced and multi-faceted. Joan Greenwood repeats her well-known impersonation of a baby theatrical Dame with "strep throat"; and who should turn up, wearing false sabre-teeth and a hairless dome, but John Osborne, ruthlessly funny as the Custodian of Ancient Offices! The Royal Court's captive playwright stands out from an excellent supporting cast.

(1956)

Visit to the Past.

I went to see Gordon Craig partly because he is among the last of the great Edwardians and partly because a blue-haired and brilliant American authoress had spent several hours exhorting me with considerable violence to meet the ageing giants of art while yet they lived. "Don't just read their books," she had said. "That's like just eating the meat of the lobster. Be a gourmet; go to the head and suck the brains. There's tasty chewing there!" Spurred by this daunting advice, I drove up from Nice one Sunday this midsummer to talk to a man who was born in the same year as Aubrey Beardsley.

Although he is eighty-four years old and has published little for a quarter of a century, Gordon Craig is still several lengths ahead of the theatrical *avant-garde*. Ideas that he expounded fifty years ago, in his breathless prophetic prose, are nowadays bearing fruit all over Europe. He anticipated Bert Brecht when he said of actors: "To-day they *impersonate* and interpret; to-morrow they must *represent* and interpret. . . . " His notion that true drama was a one-man responsibility, in which words, direction, décor, lighting, and music should all proceed from the same organising brain, once seemed a fatuous vanity; yet last year Peter Brook, directing *Titus Andronicus,* undertook all these tasks save that of writing the play. Nor would Craig hold this omission against him, since he regards the hegemony of the writer as the supreme tragedy of theatrical history: literary men, he says, are intruders, despoilers of the purity of theatre as a separate art. Dismissed as a crank, he none the less brought modern staging to birth with his productions, a memorable few which include *Hamlet* at the Moscow Art Theatre and Eleanora Duse in *Rosmersholm*. If today we call "stage-managers" directors and "scene-painters" designers, it is largely Craig's doing.

He last saw England in 1929, when C. B. Cochran invited him to take on a new production of his own choice. There was a dispute over expenditure, after which Craig left the country in a permanent huff. He lived in France until the Nazis arrived and shut him up in an internment camp. A few months later a German intelligence officer, asking for one of his books at a Paris store, learned from the assistant that its author was imprisoned; shocked, he contrived to have Craig released. For the rest of the war the old theorist worked unmolested in his Paris studio. He now occupies a single cluttered room in a modest *pension de famille* at Vence, high in the hills that overlook Nice. Here, last spring, he learned that a tardily grateful nation had created him a Companion of Honour. He was flattered, but at the same time embarrassed, because he could not afford to come to London and be royally congratulated. His only regular income derives from investments made by his mother, Ellen Terry. It amounts to just over £6 a week.

I arrived in fear of finding a testy sage steeped in pathos and embittered by neglect. As soon as the car drew up in front of the *pension* I knew my error. The figure that greeted me was surely bowed and slightly crumpled, but what it exuded was neither pathos nor rancour, but mischief. You might have taken him for the oldest truant schoolboy alive—or, more extravagantly, for an indomitable old lady who had just, by some constitutional fantasy, been elected President of the French Republic. He wore a snuff tweed suit with six pens clipped to the breast pocket, a neat cream stock around his neck, a shawl-like garment draped across his shoulders, and a broad-brimmed hat on top of wild white curls.

He clambered into the car, crowing with conspiratorial glee, and told the driver to take us down to a nearby inn for lunch. *"Prenez garde!"* he cried as we moved off. "Bad corner! Hoot, hoot!" Grinning wickedly and waving his mottled, curry-coloured hands, he began to talk in a voice of such vagrant music that I found myself listening as much to its cadences as to its meaning. He peeped at me from time to time across a nose as sharp as a quill. I was already reassured. There was no bitterness here: only resilience, magnanimity, and a great appetite for joy.

"You have the right face for a critic," he said as we disembarked. "You have the look of a blooming martyr." Having ordered the meal in genial and execrable French, he opened the briefcase he was carrying: it contained two razor-edged knives, in case the management had been slack in sharpening its cutlery. We were talking vaguely about Edward Lear when Craig whisked me back eighty years in a single sentence. "One day," he said, "when I was very small, that man Charles Dodgson came to tea. Tried to divert me with a puzzle about ferrying six cows across a river on a raft. Very tiresome . . ."

Trowelling sauce-drenched food ("I hate a dry plate") into his mouth, the almost toothless lion avidly reminisced. Irving was the greatest director he had ever known, and as an actor: "We've had no one so *dangerously* good." The Terrys, he said, were always a slapdash sort of family: the Irvings were precision instruments. Granville-Barker was "a small man among giants"—this in a whisper, as if Barker himself might spectrally be eavesdropping on the conversation. "Rather an affected man," said Craig, securely merry and patriarchal.

Far from being pent up in the past, Craig keeps in touch with every new development in theatre, cinema, and even television. He was soon urging me to see the new French underwater documentary, *Le Monde du Silence:* "It's like nothing you've ever dreamed of. Or, rather, it's like *everything* you've ever dreamed of." He showed a keen interest in "this fellow Orson Well-ess," of whose films he had heard much. "I'll tell you a thing about Well-ess," he said. "A Paris paper published an interview with him, in which he said that one day he was standing in the American Express in Paris when the door *flew* open to reveal a cloaked figure in a funny hat. *Me!* He threw himself to the ground in veneration. I gathered him up and took him to my studio and spent six months teaching him the art of the theatre." Craig was now shaking with glee. "Magnificent, isn't it? *Because I've never met the fellow in my life!*" He nudged me and we rocked.

After lunch he conducted me on foot round the baked medieval village of Tourrette, leading the way in his rangy shuffle and talking of his memoirs, extracts from which are to be published in the autumn under the title *Index to the Story of My Days.* He spoke glowingly of Picasso ("Those eyes!" he said, stabbing two fingers at me like prongs), and gaily of his own poverty: "I'm as poor as a fish!"

He has a collection of theatrical souvenirs—books, prints, letters, and designs—which is worth around £20,000. So far he has rejected all offers for it, mostly because he suspects the buyers of planning to break up the collection and resell it piecemeal. "A few years ago," he confided, "an American made a handsome bid. But I knew as soon as we started to talk business that he wasn't quite the man. He said to me: 'Please sit down, Mr. Craig.' And I said: 'It's *my* room—*you* sit down!' Not quite the fellow, you see. . . ." I reflected that it would be a generous thing if the Arts Council were to purchase his treasures; and the sooner the better. "I count my life in days now, not in years or months or even weeks."

Back in the *pension,* he led me up to the dark little room where he sleeps and works. Masks of his own carving hung on the walls (there is more than a touch in him of William Morris); day-books and journals were piled on the floors; implements for painting and writing littered the tables. On a shelf beside the brass bedstead stood a cork into which was stuck a photograph of a composed and smiling beauty: "My mother," said Craig. He talked, as he pottered, of his plans for the future. He is making a collection of English farces of the last century; "and," he said, "I'm beginning to solve the problem of staging the cauldron scene in *Macbeth.* I'm not certain yet, mind you, but it's getting clearer. It's getting clearer every day. . . ." Suddenly: "Did you ever think that Shakespeare had a cat? Look at the sonnets. Most of them aren't written to a woman or a boy. They're addressed to a *cat.*"

But there was one thing he especially wanted to show me, and he flipped through his scrapbooks to find it. He raced past priceless letters from Irving and Stanislavsky until: "There!" he said. Following his finger, I stared at an advertisement, cut out of an American magazine, for stainless steel. "Stainless steel!" he cried. "There's something serious there!" I pictured towering settings of steel taking shape in that restless, hungry mind. From one of his journals, volume after volume of fastidious, spidery script, there floated to the floor a newspaper cutting. I picked it up. Its headline ran: "£105 m. for New Schools." In the margin was an annotation in Craig's hand: "Why not educate by the stage?" Seeing that I had read it, he laughed joyously. "We only need five millions for our theatre," he said, "but they'll never let us have it. Never."

I took my leave, exhausted, though he was not. He explained that he had much to do: there were some new ideas about *The Tempest* that needed his attention. As I drove away, he waved, winked, and loped back to his den. The theatre is not yet ripe for Gordon Craig. Perhaps, indeed, it will never be. But meanwhile, at Vence, work is still in progress. When the theatrical millennium arrives, he will be its first harbinger and surest witness.

(1956)

Timon of Athens, by William Shakespeare, at the Old Vic.

The best that can be said of Michael Benthall's production of *Timon of Athens* is that its cuts and transpositions are clever. The rest is aimless improvisation. Leslie Hurry's settings are as coarse as his costumes, a dissonance of sequins, Pepsi-Cola purple, and desiccated mud. And to those who imagined the play to be a study of benevolence warped by ingratitude, Mr. Benthall administers a succinct slap: it is, by his curious lights, the story of a scoutmaster betrayed by his troop. To the role of the scoutmaster Sir Ralph Richardson brings his familiar attributes: a vagrant eye, gestures so eccentric that their true significance could be revealed only by extensive trepanning, and a mode of speech that democratically regards all syllables as equal. I select, for instance, Sir Ralph's thanks to the Amazons for enlivening his feast. "You have added," he said distinctly, "worth, and toot, and lustre." It took a trip to the text to reveal that "and toot" meant "unto't." Yet there was in his performance, for all its vagueness, a certain energy, and it was a relief to hear Timon's later tirades spoken with irony instead of fury. The stone-throwing scene with Apemantus was the best thing of the night.

Some of the junior members of the troop carry on very oddly: killingly painted and draughtily dressed, they besiege one with an epicene intensity. Mr. Benthall must really curb his love of moralising. In a play set in Greece, there is no need to plug so savagely the reasons which pious historians adduce to explain the fall of Rome. As Sydney Smith said when Mrs. Grote tried to lure him to the theatre: "All this class of pleasures inspires me with the same nausea as I feel at the sight of rich plum-cake or sweetmeats; I prefer the driest bread of common life."

(1956)

Under Milk Wood, BY DYLAN THOMAS, AT THE NEW THEATRE.

Future historians may well pronounce *Under Milk Wood* one of the last outposts of the ear in a period ruled by the eye. But I am not a future historian, and I gaze appalled on those who insist that works meant to be heard should not also be seen: do they, I wonder, go blindfold to symphony concerts?

The truth is that all words intended to be spoken gain from the sight of the speaker, which is why I endorse the present experiment. Watching it, I recalled the fashionable charges against Dylan Thomas' play: that it approaches sex like a dazzled and peeping schoolboy, and that Llaregyb, so far from being a real village, is a "literary" village that Thomas has adorned with a false moustache of lechery—Cranford, in fact, with the lid off. The characters duplicate one another: Mae Rose Cottage equals Polly Garter, Mrs. Ogmore-Pritchard equals Mrs. Pugh, and Gossamer Beynon equals Myfanwy Price. The end is a perfunctory tapering-off: the town takes twenty-three pages to wake up but is packed off to bed in less than ten.

To all these accusations Thomas must plead guilty. Yet we, the jury, rightly acquit him. He *talks* himself innocent: on two dozen occasions he gets past the toughest guard and occupies the heart. And the manic riot of his prose outdoes even the young O'Casey. He conscripts metaphors, rapes the dictionary, and builds a verbal bawdy-house where words mate and couple on the wing, like swifts. Nouns dress up, quite unselfconsciously, as verbs, sometimes balancing three-tiered epithets on their heads and often alliterating to boot. Hopkins with a skinful? Tap-room baroque? However we sum up the play's style, it lights up the sky as nothing has since *Juno*.

Douglas Cleverdon and Edward Burnham, the directors, have let a large young company loose on the text. Some caricature their roles, revue-fashion, thereby bringing out the worst in Thomas; but many hit the right note of reverent ribaldry, among them William Squire, T. H. Evans, Diana Maddox, and all the children who skip and pout through the kissing-game. As the narrator, Donald Houston is as unobtrusive and omnipresent as a good chorus should be, and more exquisitely spoken than one could imagine. Michael Trangmar's multiple setting, though it answers the mechanical questions posed by the play, does so rather grudgingly, in curt visual monosyllables: the décor is ingenious but dull.

Yet we are held: why? Nothing happens. The play is a montage of static snapshots, its only action the movement of the sun across the village. The characters certainly talk, but they seldom converse. Each lives in a cocoon of fantasy which the outside world can hardly penetrate. Organ Morgan, for example, when asked whether he prefers Fred Spit to Arthur, unhesitatingly replies: "Oh, Bach without any doubt. Bach every time for me." But is not this the secret? We are gripped, as in comedy we have immemorially been gripped, by a bunch of characters with one-track minds who, though they incessantly collide with one another, never make real contact. Not less than *Bartholomew Fair, Under Milk Wood* is a true comedy of humours.

(1956)

The Good Woman of Setzuan, BY BERTOLT BRECHT, AT THE ROYAL COURT.

"What is style?" asked Cocteau, and answered: "For many people, a very complicated way of saying very simple things. According to us, a very simple way of saying very complicated things."

Many local critics have roundly consigned *The Good Woman of Setzuan* to the first category. Why, they demand, does Brecht need three hours, fourteen scenes, and thirty actors to prove that poor people are often a grasping lot? And, indeed, if that were all he was saying, we could write the play off and turn to something more important—a musical, perhaps, needing three hours, fourteen scenes, and thirty actors to say precisely nothing. But in fact the rapacity of the poor is a point made only in the play's first act. Shen Te, a genial harlot whose goodness the gods reward with a large cash prize, is instantly fleeced by the neighbours she has been enjoined to love, and is saved from bankruptcy only by the ruse of inventing and impersonating a ruthless male cousin named Shui Ta.

So far, so simple. Now watch the plot proliferate, burgeoning into paradoxes that only a simpleton could find simple. Shen Te falls in love with a shiftless airman who needs money to buy himself a job, and how better can she supply it than in the guise of the go-getting Shui Ta? Only this time it is not she alone who suffers: she raises the money, but learns that "you cannot help one poor man without trampling down twelve others." Pregnant and deserted, betrayed by two kinds of love, she devotes herself to a third—love for her unborn child, to safeguard whose future she once more summons Shui Ta. With fearful results: she rapidly becomes the richest inhabitant of Setzuan, and the most diligently hated.

The final trial scene is one of those high moments of art when character and symbol coalesce. Shui Ta is accused of murdering Shen Te. "You were her greatest enemy!" shouts an angry peasant. "I was her only friend," is the sad reply. Irony as august, as bitterly conclusive, as this is seldom heard anywhere, least of all in the theatre. A fallacy has been exposed: that of seeking to be perfect in an imperfect society. Hastily mumbling a few vague exhortations, the gods who rewarded Shen Te nip back to heaven. Their commandments clearly don't work—but whose will? Must good ends always be achieved by base means? An epilogue, rashly omitted in the present production, poses the question to the audience, inviting it to choose between changing human nature and changing the world. Brecht implies, of course, a Marxist solution: let us change human nature *by* changing the world; and China embarked on just such an experiment several years after he wrote the play.

First fill a man's stomach and then talk to him about morality—that is Brecht's springboard, as it was in *The Threepenny Opera;* but the new dive is far more sophisticated. Macheath, after all, was a criminal; Shui Ta causes far more pain without ever breaking the law. Rather the opposite: "he" is regarded by the authorities as a pillar of society. Similarly, the worthless pilot earns promotion in Shui Ta's sweat-shop by an impeccably moral act; he refuses to accept from a kindly timekeeper more money than is his due, and thereby wins the boss's eternal respect. This is a scene of the most biting subtlety.

At every turn emotion floods through that celebrated dam, the "alienation-effect." More and more one sees Brecht as a man whose feelings were so violent that he needed a theory to curb them. Human sympathy, time and again, smashes his self-imposed dyke: when Shen Te meets her airman on a park-bench in the rain; when she learns (disguised as Shui Ta) that he means to abandon her; when, alone on the stage, she shows her unborn son the glory of the world; and, most poignantly, at the close, when she begs the gods for aid and enlightenment.

In George Devine's production the great challenge is partly muffed. Honourably bent on directing his cast along cool, detached Brechtian lines, Mr. Devine forgets that the Brechtian method works only with team-actors of great technical maturity. With greener players it looks like casual dawdling. Conscious of my heresy, I wish he had chosen an easier style and presented the play as a sort of *Teahouse of the October Revolution.* Teo Otto's tubular setting would still have fitted, and Eric Bentley's clumsy translation would, I hope, have come in for drastic revision. Anything would be preferable to hearing Mr. Bentley's Americanisms spoken with North Country inflections.

Peggy Ashcroft, in the taxing central role, is only halfway fine. As Shui Ta, flattened by a tight half-mask which helps her to produce a grinding nasal voice, she is superb; nothing tougher has been heard since Montgomery last harangued the troops. Yet her Shen Te won't do. Sexily though she blinks, all hints of whorish earthiness are expunged by those tell-tale Kensingtonian vowels. What remains is a portrait of Aladdin as it might be sketched by Princess Badroulbadour.

All the same, the production must not be missed by anyone interested in hearing the fundamental problems of human (as opposed to Western European) existence discussed in the theatre. In the context of our present prosperity, these problems may appear irrelevant. They are still cruelly relevant to more than half of the inhabited world.

(1956)

Nude with Violin, BY NOËL COWARD, AT THE GLOBE.

When Sir John Gielgud appears in modern dress on the London stage for only the second time since 1940, selecting as his vehicle Noël Coward's *Nude with Violin,* one's expectations are naturally low. Sir John never acts seriously in modern dress; it is the lounging attire in which he relaxes between classical bookings; and his present performance as a simpering valet is an act of boyish mischief, carried out with extreme elegance and the general aspect of a tight, smart, walking umbrella.

The play of his choice is at once brief and interminable. Its target is modern art. The three celebrated "periods" of a great modern painter, recently dead, are exposed as the work of three untalented hirelings—a mad Russian princess, a tipsy chorus-girl and (culminating joke) a Negro. Kathleen Harrison's Cockney chorine is game, and Patience Collier's rambling Russian is game, set, and match; but the rest of the cast resembles a cocktail party at which the gin has run out. The conclusion recalls those triumphant Letters to the Editor which end: "What has this so-called 'Picasso' got that my six-year-old daughter hasn't?"

When not boggling, my imagination went in for speculation. Mr. Coward's career can also be divided into three periods. The first began in the twenties: it introduced his revolutionary technique of "Persiflage," the pasting of thin strips of banter on to cardboard. In the early thirties we encounter his second or "Kiplingesque" period, in which he obtained startling effects by the method now known as "kippling"—i.e., the pasting of patriotic posters on to strips of banter pasted on cardboard. (The masterpieces of this period, *Cavalcade* and *In Which We Serve,* have been lost. The damp got at the cardboard.)

In 1945 a social holocaust destroyed all but a few shreds of the banter. In the third and final phase a new hand is discernible. *Is it Mr. Coward's?* The question must be faced. Where Mr. Coward was concise, the newcomer brandishes flabby polysyllables; and the clumsiness of his stagecraft was described by one expert last week as "a dead give-away." An American student of the last three "Coward" plays has declared that they may have been written by Ethel M. Dell. *Nude with Violin,* on the other hand, with its jocular references to at least thirty place-names, both homely and exotic, tends to support the theory that the new crypto-Coward is in reality a Departures Announcer at London Airport. I take no sides. On this last, decisive period I reserve judgment. We are too close to it. Much, much too close.

(1956)

The Bald Prima Donna AND *The New Tenant*, BY EUGÈNE IONESCO, AT THE ARTS.

The new double bill of plays by Eugène Ionesco is explosively, liberatingly funny. Its first half is a maniacal assault on the banality of English suburbia. A family is discussed, every member of which, past or present, is named Bobby Watson; a young couple are alarmed to find, after lengthy mutual cross-examination, that they have been married for years; and the arrival of the Captain of the Fire Brigade completes a *reductio* that is not only *ad absurdum* but way beyond it.

Yet this is not the untethered nonsense of Lear; rather, it is a loony parody of the aunts and uncles in *The Family Reunion,* uncertain of who they are and of why they exist. M. Ionesco's *petits bourgeois* are so wildly confused that quite often they get their sexes mixed: the only person secure in her identity is the maid, who sternly declares: "My name is Sherlock Holmes." For such people words have no verifiable meaning, since they relate to nothing real, and the climax is an orgy of *non-*

sequiturs, at the height of which someone screams: "Stop grinding my teeth!" Acted with a swifter abandon, and stripped of the cuckoo-clock with which its director, Peter Wood, has facetiously seen fit to adorn it, this little masterpiece would be irresistible.

The New Tenant is a macabre anecdote about a man who moves into an attic room and fills it with so much furniture that all access to the outside world is blotted out; happy and submerged, his last wish is that the light should be turned off. The nature of sanity is to move out into the world; the nature of disease is to be drawn back into the womb, to which dark constriction M. Ionesco's hero is inescapably attracted. Nowhere is there a fuller and funnier portrait of introversion. Robert Eddison plays the part to perfection, and splits with Michael Bates the lion's share of a memorable evening.

(1956)

The Demolition Expert.

He is six years dead, and the old saw holds truer than ever: nobody who did not know Shaw personally ever loved him. The Memorial Fund in his honour aimed at £250,000: it received £407. One doubts if Shaw would have cared. He was the Bradman of letters: he scored all round the wicket off all kinds of ideological bowling; he hit centuries off all causes and men that were idle or unrealistic; but though he took great pains to command respect, he took none at all to inspire affection.

In most writers, style is a welcome, an invitation, a letting-down of the drawbridge between the artist and the world. Shaw had no time for such ruses. Unlike most of his countrymen, he abominated charm, which he regarded as evidence of chronic temperamental weakness. (Much the same is true of Swift, who likewise despised emotional cheating: and both men, by coincidence, found an outlet for their repressed feelings by using baby-talk in letters to women named Stella.) We may admire Shaw, but, in public at least, he will not allow us to embrace him.

He praises little except at something else's expense. What spurred him was his capacity for being outraged. Righteous indignation at the follies of mankind infallibly roused his adrenal glands: the more indignant he became, the more he rejoiced; and the more he rejoiced, the more brilliant he became. But human folly was always the key to his treasures. "Fifty million Frenchmen," he once said, "can't be right."

Whatever the majority believed, Shaw derided; whatever it rejected, he applauded. At a time when most people assumed that arms manufacturers were cynical profiteers, Shaw gave them Undershaft, an arms manufacturer who was also a radical philosopher; and revolutionaries, in Shavian plays, usually turn out to be capitalists at heart. Whenever he found that he had fifty million people behind him, he would abruptly change sides and denounce his supporters as servile dupes. He did this more and more in his later years, when many of the causes he championed had been won. Hating to be one of a crowd, he would deliberately isolate himself by defending dictatorship and condoning, in the preface to *Geneva,* the extermination of minorities.

The only lyrical thing about Shaw is his fury: his attacks on Irving and Shakespeare are prose poems of Olympian invective. His style on such occasions flashes like a scythe. It is when he goes in for affirmations that he makes us qualmish. His vision of the future, in *Back to Methuselah,* is frankly repellent: creative evolution, he enthusiastically predicts, will produce a race of oviparous Struldbruggs who live for ever and whose only joy is pure cerebration.

As a private citizen, he loved the arts, but as a public playwright, he could not create an artist. Dubedat is a parasite, and Marchbanks a hollow fraud—Shaw could not conceal his impatience with them. His puritan, muscular, moor-tramping soul (superbly mirrored in Higgins' hymn to the intellect in *Pygmalion*) bred in him a loathing of all things, whether poems or gadgets, that were designed to comfort the human condition without actively trying to improve it. "Think and work" was his only positive advice. It is a doctrine often heard from the mouths of those who are scared to feel.

Yet he was without doubt a great writer, greater than many whose emotional range was far wider and deeper than his. In the years of his maturity—between 1895, when he wrote his first piece of drama criticism for *The Saturday Review,* and 1919, when *Heartbreak House* was published—he attempted, and almost pulled off, two mountainous tasks: he cleared the English stage of humbug, and the English mind of cant. (They both returned later, but as guests, not as residents.) As a demolition expert he has no rivals, and we are being grossly irrelevant if we ask a demolition expert, when his work is done: "But what have you created?" It is like expecting a bull-dozer to build the Tower of Pisa, or condemning a bayonet for not being a plough. Shaw's genius was for intellectual slum-clearance, not for town planning. As far as modern society is concerned, he came to scoff, and remained to scoff.

We sit through his plays unshocked by most of what he meant to be shocking, embarrassed by his efforts to make us exclaim "Whatever next!" but continuously diverted by the sheer mad Irishness of the man: by his crazy irrelevancies, his sudden interpolations of surrealism—as when, in *Misalliance,* a young assassin hides in a portable Turkish bath from which he emerges to declare: "I am the son of Lucinda Titmus." Shaw's sanity nowadays tends to be tiresome. His lunacy will always be irresistible.

But does he ever move us? Only once, I think: with the speech in which St. Joan reminds herself that "God is alone." That came from Shaw's heart, and goes straight to ours. Otherwise, if Chaucer is the father of English literature, Shaw is the spinster aunt. By this I do not mean to imply that he was sexless—St. John Ervine's new biography, if it does nothing else, should squash that myth for ever. It is only in his writing that the aunt in him rises up, full of warnings, wagged fingers, and brandished umbrellas. How many of his letters contain phrases like: "It is no good your trying to excuse your infamous conduct . . ."!

This is the true auntly note, and the psychiatrists may not be wrong when they describe it as filial revenge. Shaw's mother, a cold woman, ignored and neglected him; and he was bent on outdoing her in indifference to the common code of human sympathy; on proving that his heartlessness could exceed even hers. As a man, he was often generous and compassionate. As a writer, the chill sets in. You thought *that* was cruel and clinical? he seems to be saying; just wait till you hear *this*—it will show you that I love you all even less than you ever suspected.

Shaw was unique. An Irish aunt so gorgeously drunk with wit is something English literature will never see again. But there is fruit for the symbolist in the fact that, prolific as he was, he left no children.

(1956)

Oh! My Papa!, AT THE GARRICK.

The most memorable feature of *Oh! My Papa!,* an imported Swiss musical of multiple authorship, is that it contains no yodelling. Otherwise it conforms exactly to the English image of the Swiss as a nation of merry, gluttonous half-wits, full of *Gemütlichkeit* and boomps-a-daisy. Since my Swiss friends are few, I have no idea whether the picture is faithful; but I am sure that a monograph must some day be written on the subject of non-English-speaking national stereotypes in the English theatre. The Teutonic nations alone would be a rewarding field of study. I have carried out a preliminary survey, and I pass on the results to anyone contemplating a full-length thesis.

In English plays, good Teutons are Teutons who express themselves with the utmost awkwardness, using only the shortest words: e.g., "I am here now three days. There is hate." The bad Teuton gives himself away every time by the presumptuous fluency with which he speaks English. "You will forgive me if I indulge myself in a cognac before dinner? It is—how do you say?—unsmart, but, in the words of one of my country's proverbs, it kennels the black dog of despair." Any Teuton who talks like that will be up to no good before the act is over; if German, he will probably turn out to be a spy.

Exceptions are sometimes made in the case of Austrians, who are allowed to be literate because they are so harmlessly gay. All stage Austrians were born in Ruritania. They have a child-like enthusiasm for everything they see, and at most of what they see they wink. They trip over the hazards of our so difficult language (*vide Autumn Crocus, passim*), but beneath their accents they are reasonable fellows, ready to fight for the right they adore. Comic Teutons, of any nationality, are always provided with phonetic dialogue that suggests a mad mating of Greta Garbo and Tony Weller: e.g., "I vos joose vondering. 'Ow would ze wife react if, vun day, you bring 'ome—a strange vooman?" That is a verbatim quote from a recent and very successful farce, Samuel French edition. Later in the same play the English hero threatened to "brechen das necken" of the alien upstart, and no vonder.

To assist the playwrights of the future, I have compiled a speech that can be used, with appropriate variations, by any good, safe, simple Teuton—i.e., any native of Austria, Switzerland, Scandinavia, or the Low Countries. It goes like this:

> Ach yes, my little Elizabet. It is good to be at home in the spring-time. It is good to look up at the sky and hear the cow-bells [goat-bells, reindeer-bells] across the valley. My father, he say that all of life is like the bursting of a crocus [tulip, edelweiss] bud; and when comes the spring, we make the great festival in the village. All the young boys and maidens, they dance by the lake [dike, fjord], and when the moon is high they are making the *dumsplacket*. Ach, I forget, you do not know what is the *dumsplacket*. It is—you permit?—like this. (*He tilts a lighted candle directly above Elizabet's head. As the wax drips onto her brow he smiles and kisses her gently.*) And then—they shout and dance, dance until the legs can no more carry them. These are my people, little Elizabet. There I belong.

(1956)

Precious Lillie.

Debrett's Peerage, a thick, comely, and infallible volume, correctly refers to Beatrice Gladys Lillie by her married name, Lady Peel. *Who's Who in the Theatre* is also thick and comely, but it is not quite infallible, and one of the most fallible things about it is its habit, in edition after edition, of describing Miss Lillie as an "actress." Technically, I suppose the blunder might be defended, since she has been known to impinge on the legitimate stage; in 1921 she appeared in *Up in Mabel's Room* and eleven years later played the Nurse in Shaw's *Too True to Be Good.* But these were transient whims. To call her an actress first and foremost is rather like calling Winston Churchill a bricklayer who has dabbled in politics. If acting means sinking your own personality into somebody else's, Beatrice Lillie has never acted in her life. There may be some mechanical means of disguising that true and tinny voice, or of suppressing that cockeyed nonchalance; but the means might very well involve the use of masks and gags, and the end would not be worth it. She would never be much good at impersonation. One of her recurrent delusions is that she is a mistress of dialects, but in fact the only one she has really mastered is her own brand of Berkeley Square Canadian; and she can hardly open a door on stage without squaring up to the operation as if she were about to burgle a safe.

To some extent, an actress can be judged by measuring her performance against the character she is meant to be playing; but there is nothing against which to measure Miss Lillie. She is *sui generis.* She resembles nothing that ever was, and to see her is to experience, every time, the simple joy of discovery that might come to an astronomer who observed, one maddened night, a new and disorderly comet shooting backward across the firmament. But if she is not an actress, no more is she a parodist, as some of her fans insist; she parodies nothing and no one except herself. Nor does she belong in the main stream of North American female comics. Almost without exception, American comediennes get their laughs by pretending to be pop-eyed, man-hunting spinsters. Miss Lillie is as far removed from these as a butterfly is from a guided missile. The miracle is that this non-acting non-satirist has managed to become the most achingly funny woman on earth.

Twentieth-century show business has a small and incomparable élite: the streamlined international entertainers of the twenties and thirties. Noël Coward, Gertrude Lawrence, Maurice Chevalier, Alfred Lunt and Lynn Fontanne were among the founder-members of this shining and exclusive gang. Miss Lillie is the Commonwealth representative. She was born fifty-eight years ago in Toronto, the second daughter of John Lillie, a volatile Irish schoolmaster who had served in the British Army under Kitchener. The first recorded event in her life was her summary ejection, at the age of eight, from the choir of the local Presbyterian church. It seems she upset the congregation by pulling faces during the hymns. Both her father, who died in 1933, and her mother, who lives in a Thames-side house near London, achieved an early and lasting tolerance of their child's eccentricities. Sensing that she had something to express, but not knowing exactly what it was, they sent her to a man named Harry Rich—of whom nothing else is known—for lessons in gesture. She loathed the lessons, but they stuck, and many of the odder poses in which she nowadays finds herself are directly attributable to Mr. Rich.

At fifteen she left school and embarked with her mother and sister for England, with the idea of becoming a child soprano. Her official repertoire included such ballads as "I Hear You Calling Me" and "Until," but secretly she and her sister Muriel were rehearsing something a little wilder, entitled "The Next Horse I Ride On I'm Going to Be Tied On." This clandestine seed was later to bear lunatic fruit; for the moment, however, it got nowhere.

Her career as a straight singer languished until the summer of 1914, when she was engaged for a week at the Chatham Music Hall on the outskirts of London. Here she sang Irving Berlin's "When I Lost You," and the audience reaction indicated that she had lost them for good. Without much hope, she attended an audition held by the Anglo-French impresario André Charlot. Idly, she guyed a serious romantic number, smiled wanly, and was about to leave the theatre when Charlot, in a state verging on apoplexy, seized her arm and offered her forty-two dollars a week to appear in his next revue, *Not Likely!* She accepted, and soon the panic was on. Charlot adored and fostered the madness of her method, constantly giving her bigger spots, and it was under his banner that she made her triumphant Broadway debut in *Charlot's Revue of 1924*.

Around this time she had her hair cut off, for reasons that may give some hint of the devious way her mind works. With Michael Arlen, H. G. Wells, Frederick Lonsdale, and Lonsdale's two daughters, she was cruising on Lord Beaverbrook's yacht. The Lonsdale girls were close-cropped, and Miss Lillie, who favored plaits, was powerfully impressed by the advantages of short hair for swimming. Back in London she ordered her coiffeur to give her what would now be known as a brush cut. Only when he had finished did it occur to her that there was more to life than swimming. For a while she wore false plaits attached to her ears by rubber bands. One day the elastic snapped, and she has remained, ever since, cropped for immersion. Nowadays she hides her hair beneath a bright pink fez. There is no good reason for this, either. It is just one *idée fixe* on top of another.

Meanwhile, she had fallen in love. In 1920 Robert Peel, a young and toweringly handsome great-grandson of Sir Robert Peel, resigned his commission in the Guards and married Charlot's zany soubrette. They spent a raffish honeymoon at Monte Carlo, winning $25,000 at the tables a few hours after arriving and losing $30,000 a few hours before departing. In 1925 Robert's father, the fourth baronet, died, and Miss Lillie became Lady Peel. Her husband, a man of devouring energies, was at various times a sheep farmer in Australia and a race-horse owner in England. During the slump he generously formed an orchestra of unemployed miners and toured the country with it, often losing as much as £500 a week. He died in 1934, leaving one son. Eight years later the young Sir Robert, who had just passed his twenty-first birthday, was killed when the British destroyer *Hermes* was sunk by Japanese dive bombers in the Indian Ocean. His mother received the news in a Manchester dressing room, where she was putting on make-up to appear in a new Cochran revue. It is one of the paradoxes of the theatre that though every actor's ambition is to stop the show, his instructions are that it must go on. The revue went on that night with Miss Lillie clowning on schedule and wishing herself ten thousand miles away. Thereafter an inner withdrawal took place; since her son's death she has entered into no binding personal relationships with anyone.

In forty years on the stage she has been seen in nearly forty shows, many of them bearing prankish, exclamatory titles like *Cheep!* and *Oh! Joy!* and most of them remembered chiefly for her part in them. Apart from the war years, when she sang for the troops in the Mediterranean area, she has seldom been far away from the big money. The movies have intermittently attracted her, but, like Coward and the Lunts, she has never thought of depending on them for a living. Pre-war residents of Hollywood remember her vividly, swinging an enormous handbag within which there rattled a motley haul of jewelry known as "The Peel Poils." For a talent so deeply spontaneous, the stage was always the best place. In New York, just before the war, she was paid $8,000 for a week at the Palace, and today one imagines even Las Vegas baulking at her cabaret fee.

Her title sits drolly on her, like a tiara on an emu, and for a certain kind of audience there is an irresistible savour in the spectacle of a baronet's wife shuffling off to Buffalo. There have, however, been moments of embarrassment. In 1936, billed as Lady Peel, Miss Lillie appeared in an Ohio city and rashly chose as her opening number a travesty of a suburban snob. "Ladies and gentlemen," she began, "I'm sure you will appreciate what a comedown this is for me—me that's always 'ad me own 'orses. . . ." Few acts can have fallen flatter. Many women in the house began to sniff audibly, and at the end of the monologue, according to Miss Lillie, some attempt was made to take a collection to sustain her in her fight against poverty.

Offstage she leads a fairly intense social life, and has arguably slept through more hours of daylight than of dark. Her conversation is an unpunctuated flow of irrelevancies which only acute ears can render into sense. As a maker of epigrams her rating is low. It is rumoured that she once said of a tactless friend that "he doesn't know the difference between tongue-in-cheek and foot-in-mouth," but remarks like that need a degree of premeditation to which she is a stranger. She excels at the casual impromptu, as when a pigeon flew in at the window of her apartment and she, looking up, briskly inquired: "Any messages?" To surprise her friends, she will go to considerable lengths. Her last Christmas present to Noël Coward was a baby alligator, to whose neck she attached a label reading: "So what else is new?" Last year she stood for several hours on a draughty street corner in Liverpool in order to wave maniacally at the Duke of Edinburgh as he drove by with the Queen. She received from the carriage a royal double-take, which she regarded as ample compensation. At parties, with a little pressing, she will try out her newest hallucinations, nursery rhymes villainously revamped or bizarre attempts at mimicry; I once saw her spread-eagled on top of an upright piano, pretending to be Marilyn Monroe.

Some of her leisure time is spent painting, a difficult art for which she has evolved impossible working habits. "I do children's heads out of my nut," she told an interviewer. "I paint on the floor and show my work on the piano in the dark. I call myself Beatrice Van Gone." She habitually uses as canvasses the cardboard lids of laundry boxes. One of her sitters was the child actor Brandon de Wilde. He is also one of her closest confidants. Whenever Miss Lillie is in New York, she calls up Brandon and the two journey to Coney Island, where they frequently end up in the Tunnel of Love. A radio commentator once asked Brandon what Miss Lillie did in the tunnel. "It's very dark in there," the child explained, as to a child, "so naturally she doesn't do anything."

De Wilde's ingenuous imagination appeals strongly to Miss Lillie, who has a great deal of urchin in her and very little *grande dame.* She also has the kind of knockdown spontaneity that one associates with Zen masters, together with something much more mysterious—that ambiguous, asexual look that so often recurs among the greatest performers.

Her last show, *An Evening with Beatrice Lillie,* took three quarters of a million dollars at the Broadway box office three seasons ago, and then ran for eight successful months in Britain. It enshrined her art in what seems likely to be its final form. The rebuke to Maud for her rottenness, the lament about wind round my heart—they were all there, presented with a relaxed finesse that astonished even her oldest eulogists. She looked like Peter Pan as Saul Steinberg might sketch him, and the only phrase for her face was one that a French critic used many years ago to describe Réjane—*"une petite frimousse éveillée,"* which means, in James Agate's rough translation, "a wide-awake little mug." A supreme economy distinguished all she did. By twirling four Oriental fingers, she could imply a whole handspring, and instead of underlining her gags in red pencil she could bring down the house with a marginal tick. For any line that struck her as touching on the sentimental she would provide a withering facial comment, as if to say (the expression is one of her pets): "Get *me!*" She would survey the audience with wintry amazement, until it began to wonder why it had come; she would then overwhelm it with some monstrous act of madness, such as wearing an osprey feather fan as a hat, banging her head against the proscenium arch, or impersonating Pavlova and a roller-skating bear, one after the other, in a sketch bearing no relation either to ballet or zoology.

Once, in an effort at self-analysis, she said: "I guess it's my nose that makes them laugh," but the explanation is as perfunctory as the nose. One thing is certain: she wrecks the old theory that all great clowns have a breaking heart. Miss Lillie has no more pathos than Ohrbach's basement. Nothing on stage seems to her tragic, though many things arouse in her a sort of cool curiosity. If a ton of scenery were to fall at her feet, she would regard the débris with interest, but not with dismay; after a light shrug and a piercing little smile, she would go on with whatever she was doing. (In wartime this insouciance was a rare asset. Quentin Reynolds, who was often her companion during the blitz, testifies that in the midst of the bombing her demeanour was positively sunny.) She reminds one of a bony, tomboyish little girl attending what, if her behavior does not improve, will surely be her last party. Her attitude toward events, if she has one, might be summed up in the comment: "Hmmmm . . ."

I have two theories about her: one about what she does, and another about the way she does it. What she has been doing for the last forty years is conducting guerrilla warfare against words as a means of communication. Having no message to convey, she has no need of language as most of us understand it, so she either abandons words altogether or presents them in combinations aberrant enough to crack a ouija board. Faced with the drab possibility of consecutive thought, she draws herself up to her full lunacy. She will do anything to avoid making sense—lapse into a clog dance, trap her foot under an armchair, or wordlessly subside beneath the weight of a mink coat.

Mime attracts her as an alternative to words. This imperial urchin can let winsome candour, beady-eyed tartness, and appalled confusion chase each other across her face in a matter of seconds. Consider the frosty, appraising regard she bestows on the waistcoat of the huge baritone who suddenly interrupts her act to sing "Come into the Garden, Maud" straight down her throat. Though she takes an early opportunity to seize a chair in self-defence, she betrays none of her apprehension in words.

The traditional comic formula is: Tell them what you're going to do; do it; then tell them you've done it. Miss Lillie's is: Tell them what you might do; do something else; then deny having done it. Even the famous purchase of the double-damask dinner napkins embodies her basic theme: the utter futility of the English language. Nobody is a more devout anthologist of the whimpers, sighs, and twitters than the human race emits in its historic struggle against intelligibility. It is not surprising that she turns to French when delivering her demented salute to the home life of cats: *"Bonjour,* all the little kittens all over the world!" When someone in another number fails to understand a question, she tries German, brusquely demanding: *"Sprechen Sie Deutsch?"* And once, into a Cockney sketch already obscured by her inability to speak Cockney, she inserted a sudden moan of Italian. If ever a monument is erected to her, it should be modelled on the Tower of Babel. She is like Eliza Doolittle at Mrs. Higgins' tea party in *Pygmalion,* using what seems to her perfectly acceptable verbal coinage but to everyone else counterfeit gibberish. In certain moods she becomes quite convinced that she is an authority on bird talk. Coward once wrote for her a comic folk song that contained the line: "And the robin sings ho! on the bough." Every time she reached it she would pause. "The robin," she would firmly declare, "does *not* say ho."

In 1954, on a trip to Japan, she visited the Kabuki Theatre and was fascinated by what she saw: the colour, the weirdness, and the elaborate stylization. The idea of using Kabuki technique in a sketch at once took hold of her mind, and she was not in the least perturbed when someone pointed out that British audiences (for whom the sketch was intended) might be slightly befuddled by a parody of something they had never seen. Following instinct, she devised a number called "Kabuki Lil." When it was still in the formative stage, by which I mean a condition of nightmarish inconsequence, she described it to me:

"These Kabuki plays, you see, they go on for six months with only one intermission. All the women are men, *of course,* and they're simply furious most of the time, waving swords round their heads and *hissing* at each other. They take off their boots when they come on, and kneel down on cushions. There's a lot of work done with cushions, so I shall have cushions too. And they play some kind of musical instrument that goes right round the back of my neck, only one string, but I expect I shall manage. I don't think I shall say a word of English—after all, *they* don't—but I wish I could get hold of one of those terrific rostrums they have in Tokyo that sail right down the aisle and out of the theatre. I think they have rollers underneath them, or perhaps it's men? Anyway, I think I've got the spirit of the thing. . . ."

Something was dimly taking shape in the chaos of her mind, but what emerged on stage was beyond all imagining. It varied notably from night to night, but the general layout remained the same. Miss Lillie shuffled on attired as a geisha, with a knitting needle through her wig and a papoose strapped to her back. After performing some cryptic act of obeisance, she sat cross-legged on a pile of cushions. Thereafter, for about ten minutes, she mewed like an asthmatic sea gull: the sketch contained not one recognizable word. Tea was served at one point, and the star produced from her sleeve a tiny bottle of Gordon's gin with which to spike it. From time to time she would grasp a hammer and savagely bang a gong, whereupon music would sound, jittery and Oriental. This seemed to placate her; until the sixth bang, which evoked from the wings a sudden, deafeningly amplified blast of "Three Coins in the Fountain," sung by Frank Sinatra.

It was while watching this sketch, so pointless, yet so hysterical, that I hit on the clue to her method. I reveal it without hesitation, because I do not believe that anyone could copy it. The key to Beatrice Lillie's success is that she ignores her audience. This is an act of daring that amounts to a revolution. Maurice Chevalier was speaking for most of his profession when he said in his autobiography: "An artist carries on throughout his life a mysterious, uninterrupted conversation with his public." To get into contact with the dark blur of faces out front is the Holy Grail of every personality performer except Miss Lillie, who converses not with her public but with herself. Belly laughter, for which most comedians sweat out their life's blood, only disconcerts her; it is an intrusion from another world. She is uniquely alone. Her gift is to reproduce on stage the grievous idiocy with which people behave when they are on their own: humming and mumbling, grimacing at the looking glass, perhaps even singing into it, hopping, skipping, fiddling with their dress, starting and stopping a hundred trivial tasks—looking, in fact, definably batty. At these strange pursuits we, the customers, peep and marvel, but we are always eavesdroppers; we never "get into the act."

The theatre is Miss Lillie's hermitage. It is an empty room in which she has two hours to kill, and the audience, like Alice, is "just a thing in her dream." She is like a child dressing up in front of the mirror, amusing herself while the grownups are out. The fact that we are amused as well proves that she has conquered the rarest of all theatrical arts, the art of public solitude, which Stanislavsky said was the key to all great acting. To carry it off, as she does, requires a vast amount of sheer nerve and more than a whiff of genius, which is really another word for creative self-sufficiency. One might add that it probably helps to have had experience, at an early age, of pulling faces in church.

Her future, like her act, seldom looks the same from one day to the next. She would like to take her solo show to South America and Asia, with a split week in Tibet, where she feels she has many fans. A musical has been written for her, based on the life of Madame Tussaud. Its title, which she finds hauntingly seductive, is *The Works*. But wherever her choice falls, the queues will form. There is no substitute for this magnetic sprite. She alone can reassure us that from a theatre increasingly enslaved to logic the spirit of unreason, of anarchy and caprice, has not quite vanished.

(1956)

End of a Twelvemonth

At this time of thanksgiving and convalescence, when all is hushed save for the gentle pop of bursting facial capillaries, it is somehow fitting that we should look back on the past year and on to the new. (We can uncross our eyes later.)

1956 was full of good theatrical auguries. At the Comedy Theatre the Lord Chamberlain was smilingly flouted, while from the Royal Court there issued a distinct sound of barricades being erected. The Berliner Ensemble came, was seen, and overcame; and Angus Wilson, Nigel Dennis, Dylan Thomas, Brendan Behan, and Eugène Ionesco were exposed for the first time to London audiences. Tyrone Guthrie made *Troilus and Cressida* seem like a new play, and Edith Evans made *The Chalk Garden* seem like a classical revival. Fewer people forgave John Gielgud for appearing in *Nude with Violin* than would have forgiven him five years ago. And the play of the year, over which families were split in almost the same way as they were split over Suez, was John Osborne's *Look Back in Anger,* an oasis of reality, as Arthur Miller rightly said, in "a theatre hermetically sealed off from life."

By putting the sex war and the class war on to one and the same stage, Mr. Osborne gave the drama a tremendous nudge forwards. Much of modern thought outside the theatre has been devoted to making Freud shake hands with Marx; within the theatre they are mighty incompatibles. Social plays are traditionally sexless, and plays about sex are mostly non-social. Jimmy Porter is politically a liberal and sexually a despot. Whether we like him or not, we must concede that he is a character with a full set of attitudes, towards society as well as personal relations. Others may solve Jimmy's problem: Mr. Osborne is the first to state it. No germinal play of comparable strength has emerged since the war.

Assuming that the year's good things bear fruit, what else can one predict for 1957? A lot, quite safely. Someone will present a play about a homosexual athlete with a millionaire father, whereupon many citizens will write to the papers mysteriously complaining that they get enough of that sort of thing in everyday life without going to the theatre for it. A new play by J. B. Priestley will have its *première* in Danzig. A famous actor, drawing on the rich experience of having played two modern roles in ten years, will declare that the Stanislavsky method ("all this soul-searching and pretending to be a lettuce") is ruining modern drama. The London Shakespeare method will meanwhile ruin fifty-six young actors, several of whom will be signed on for a second season at the Old Vic. A farce entitled *Giblets on Parade* will begin a four-year run at the Whitehall Theatre. Noël Coward will announce the successful completion of his five-hundredth Atlantic crossing.

The establishment of drama chairs at English universities will be triumphantly opposed on the grounds that the practical study of drama neither encourages nor requires intellectual discipline: by this means will be perpetuated the philistine myth that drama is best when most brainless. The suggestion that actors, like singers, should keep in training will be dismissed as a transatlantic extravagance, like good plumbing; and the virtues of muddling through will be illustrated by reference to the Elizabethan theatre. ("So far as actors are concerned, they, as I noticed in England, are daily instructed, as it were in a school, so that even the most eminent actors have to allow themselves to be instructed by the dramatists, which arrangement gives life and ornament to a well-written play . . ."—Johannes Rhenanus, writing in 1613.) In spite of everything, about four good native plays will be performed and supported. None of them, however, is likely to deal seriously with Suez, Cyprus, Kenya, the United Nations, the law, the armed forces, Parliament, the Press, medicine, jazz, the City, English cities outside London, or London postal districts outside the S.W. and N.W. areas. Two thousand wish-fulfilling plays will be written about life after the next war. Ten will be staged. One will be good.

(1957)

Acting from the Inside.

The British attitude towards acting is what I would call Olympic. If we were to win too many gold medals, we would somehow forfeit our amateur status; we would rather have one eccentric, preposterous victory ("A steeplejack by trade, Les Bowkett trains on cabbage") than sweep the board by means of vast, scientific training programmes. Similarly, we prefer actors who spring seemingly from nowhere to actors who come off the "assembly-line" of a school or method.

Among senior theatricals mistrust of "Method" acting verges on hysteria. Actors, they boast, are born, not made: beyond a certain stage, training is both useless and undesirable, as futile as trying to educate the Bantu. The intensity of this feeling, particularly along the Coward-Gielgud axis, hints at a disquiet that has recently spread throughout the *derrière-garde* of the profession. Young actors are abroad, of appalling seriousness and assurance, speaking an impenetrably alien language with every appearance of understanding it. Reports filter through of acting classes, held (if you please) in the morning and attended, incredibly, by actors who are not out of work.

The main stronghold of this fifth column is the London Studio, founded in August of 1956 by Al Mulock and David de Keyser. Mr.

Mulock, an American, served his apprenticeship at the Actors' Studio in New York, that envied cradle where Lee Strasberg teaches his version of the Stanislavsky Method to a select gaggle of alumni that includes Marlon Brando, Julie Harris, Eli Wallach, Marilyn Monroe, Rod Steiger, and many others who have lately changed the face of Broadway and Hollywood. They might, of course, have succeeded anyway. The Method does not claim to create talent: it merely teaches talent how to keep fit, how to relax, concentrate, and develop with the minimum of wasted energy. In a word, it helps the actor to know himself.

Neither Mr. Mulock nor Mr. de Keyser has a personality as massively compelling as that of Mr. Strasberg or Elia Kazan. Their purpose is to lay foundations. Twice a week, on Mondays and Thursdays, they give professional actors the chance of exposing their craft to the vicarious scrutiny of Stanislavsky. Already some seventy actors have accepted the challenge, among them Geraldine Page, Dorothy Bromley, Denholm Elliott, and Kenneth Haigh. Prepared snippets and improvised *vignettes* are performed; after each item Messrs. Mulock and de Keyser interrogate the players, and the audience, about twenty strong, joins in the inquisition. It is like being present at a public rehearsal: on all sides one can hear English reserve cracking, and the noise is healthy.

The direction of plays has too long been regarded as a furtive, magical rite, to be carried out in secret behind locked doors—something too fragile to be opened to public inspection. This merely encourages the enfeebling heresy that actors are unaccountably different from other people, that they shrivel outside a specially protective environment, and wince and blink in daylight. The London Studio brings acting out into the open. It may thus dispel the self-consciousness, the reluctance to make a fool of oneself, the desperate clinging to inhibitions, that account for the non-committal tentativeness of so much English acting.

Its second great virtue is that it gives actors a common vocabulary. It stringently outlaws the grand vague cries of the past, such as "Give it more feeling!" and "Don't be so intense!" In matters of terminology it is logical and positive. Every scene has a total "action" and every actor has a clear "objective." At the climax of *Of Mice and Men,* for instance, George's objective is "to kill Lennie." It is never "verbalised" (i.e., expressed in words) or "externalised" (i.e., expressed in action), and it must be conveyed without "signalling" or "indicating" (i.e., revealing to the audience more than is truthful of what one intends to do). Emotions must never be "general" but always "specific." And the basest error of all is to take as one's objective the urge "to finish the scene"—i.e., to get through it as quickly and violently as possible. (Old Vic, please note.)

Technical terminology is always ugly and usually precise. A famous American director of the old school recently said to me: "The switch is purely verbal. I used to tell actors to be quicker on their cues. Now I have to tell them to reach their objectives sooner." But the Method means more than that: it insists on knowing why. And this rouses the giant, hydra-headed problem. Nobody doubts that Stanislavsky is the perfect mentor if we are discussing plays written in the last hundred years. But what of the classics? Questions of motive seldom worried the Elizabethans. When Othello asks Iago "why he hath thus ensnared my soul and body," the answer is succinct and daunting:

> Demand me nothing: what you know, you know:
> From this time forth I never will speak word.

Nor does he. We must judge for ourselves. Perhaps Iago was clumsily suckled by a Negro nurse; but it is hard to see how such an inference would help the play.

To go back even further in time: the Method dwells on the word "specific," but the strict and single intent of ancient dramatic art was to be "general." Jacques Barzun defines romantic act as "an art of particulars, of individual exploration and report, of local colour and all-embracing diversity—or, as we should say to-day, an art that aimed at realism." For this kind of art the Method is magnificently equipped. Its efficacy in drama between Marlowe and Sheridan is something that London Studio actors, most of whom have been brought up on Shakespeare, are uniquely fitted to explore. But for actors who cherish antiquity, who dream of hitting the headlines in Greek tragedy or Japanese Nō plays, the answer must be a discreet and regretful no. The Method is not for them. Which is no great pity, for such fellows are a backward few.

(1957)

The Purist View.

Last Sunday at the Old Vic, John Whiting, whose place among the most eminent living English playwrights is secure everywhere but in England, delivered the annual lecture on "The Art of the Dramatist." It was an historic occasion. In the annals of the theatre it may indeed come to be regarded as Romanticism's Last Stand, the ultimate cry of the artist before being engulfed by the mass, the final protest of individualism before being inhaled and consumed by the ogre of popular culture. One pictured, as each phrase of Mr. Whiting's elegant jeremiad came winging out into the dark, some attenuated hermit saint bravely keeping his chin up while being sucked through the revolving doors of a holiday camp. Even before he began, I felt I was in the presence of a condemned man. There was resignation in the very set of his gentle, scolded face, and the expression in his large dark eyes seemed to anticipate, even to embrace, defeat. He stood before us like one lately descended from an ivory tower, blinking in the glare and bustle of day.

He spoke exquisitely of the threats to integrity that nowadays encircled the playwright. He rejected with scorn the idea that a writer should see himself as the spokesman of a group or class. "The cult of the individual," he declared, "is the basis of all art." Today the artist was obliged to speak in a "collective voice"; he was obliged to compromise with "the masses," who lived in a second-hand world filled with "colour prints of Van Gogh."

Everything, we swiftly gathered, militated against Mr. Whiting's concept of pure drama. All we were offered in the modern English theatre were plays of "social significance," plays set in concentration camps, plays made up of "the idiot mumblings of the half-wit who lives down the lane." Instead of looking within themselves for their own unique modes of utterance, playwrights were content to reproduce the "direct, unornamented speech" of everyday life. Austerity was no longer prized. Instead, fashionable authors (Mr. Whiting did not actually name John Osborne) allowed their characters to indulge in long, dishevelled, emotional outbursts. Three years, he reminded us without rancour, had passed since one of his plays had been seen in London; even so, he found himself as convinced as ever that it was no part of the author's job to surrender to his audience by approaching it on its own terms. A play, he said, "has nothing to do with an audience."

It was hereabouts that I began to wonder whether we were talking about the theatre at all. Were we not rather talking about poetry or the novel, private arts intended to be sampled by one person at a time? Had we not somehow strayed from the drama, a public art which must be addressed to hundreds of people at the same time? Somewhere in Mr. Whiting's imagination there glows a vision of an ideal theatre where the playwright is freed from the necessity of attracting customers, where his fastidious cadences are not tainted by exposure to rank plebeian breath. It is a theatre without an audience. And it exists—again in Mr. Whiting's imagination—as a gesture of defiance against those other, equally mythical London theatres where socially significant plays about concentration camps are constantly being staged to the vociferous approval of "the masses." (Anyone not a playwright belongs, in Mr. Whiting's mind, to the masses—who belied, by the way, their imputed stupidity by turning up in force to hear his lecture, and by asking at the end a number of surprisingly literate questions.) On the whole, I find Mr. Whiting's theatrical dream-world extremely seductive. He says it exists, and wishes it didn't. I know it doesn't, but rather wish it did. There would be few complaints from me if the West End were full of realistic contemporary plays enthusiastically acclaimed by mass audiences.

At one point in his lecture, to illustrate the deadness of naturalism, Mr. Whiting read out an invented snatch of dialogue such as one might hear in a bus-queue. How repetitive! he implied. How drab and dull! It was in fact infectiously and rivetingly alive. One longed to hear more. I realised then, with a sense of wild frustration, that Mr. Whiting was a born playwright determined at all costs not to be a playwright at all.

(1957)

Amédée, BY EUGÈNE IONESCO, AT THE ARTS, CAMBRIDGE.

Many good plays, as James Agate used to say, are built in two storeys—a ground floor of realism and a first floor of symbolism. M. Ionesco goes further than that: farcical at street level, he is tragic one flight up. *Amédée* is a perfect example of this unique architectural audacity.

On the ground floor the play is a macabre farcical anecdote about a married couple with an unusual problem. There is a corpse in their flat. Neither of them can recall how it got there or who killed it, but its presence has kept them indoors for the best part of fifteen years. In one corner of the living-room Amédée sits working on a play (average annual output: one word). In the opposite corner, at the top of her voice, his wife operates a busy telephone switchboard. Meanwhile, the corpse, recumbent in the bedroom, begins to grow; and, as if this were not inconvenient enough, its growth is accompanied by a sickening proliferation of poisonous mushrooms all over the walls of the apartment. For Amédée's wife, a short-tempered woman at the best of times, it is the last straw when the bedroom doors burst open to admit a pair of outsize, cadaverous, and extremely unwelcome feet.

Before long the room is full of mushrooms, feet, and furniture, a scenic demand brilliantly met by Peter Zadek's production and Feliks

Topolski's designs; and the harassed couple are discussing "How to Get Rid of It" (the play's alternative title) in tones that are certainly exasperated, but no more so than if the problem in hand were a dead mouse or a smell in the sink. Their very imperviousness to calamity is what makes Amédée and his wife so persistently funny. The horror of their plight simply does not occur to them; if they are irritated, it is more with each other than with the corpse. The whole mood of the play is like Alexander Woollcott's famous tale of the housemaster who, coming upon a mutilated torso in the school boot-cupboard, briskly remarked: "Some dangerous clown has been here."

The *dénouement*, never Ionesco's strongest point, is a messy phantasmagoria that is probably as unstageable as Mr. Zadek makes it seem. The upshot of it is that Amédée pulls the house down and plunges to his death, in which condition he takes on the appearance of the corpse he was trying to extricate.

And now, if you will just step upstairs to the symbolic level, watching out for the dustbins that Mr. Beckett has carelessly left on the landing, we will examine the meaning of what we have just been laughing at; for up here sits Ionesco the puppet-master, inscrutably pulling the strings. Something, in the bourgeois marriage whose last hours we have witnessed, died long ago. Neither partner will take the blame for it; but the wife protests her innocence a thought too shrilly; and this, coupled with the fact that the victimised male is a pet Ionesco figure, is enough to convince me that she is the principal culprit. But what has she killed? What is the dead thing that won't lie down, that so hilariously tumesces? A tableau from the play springs to mind: Amédée, the writer unable to communicate, vainly repeating the two lines which represent fifteen years' work, while his wife sits at the switchboard, communicating like mad in glad contrapuntal cries of: "I'm putting you through! I'm putting you through!" What has died is the creative spark that was the real Amédée, and the tragedy is that he doesn't know it. In the loveless hothouse of his marriage the dead tissue has flowered into a cancerous life of its own, which eventually destroys him. Only as he dies does he realise that the corpse in the bedroom was himself.

If I have made the play sound obscure, I have blundered. Its meaning is always there, staring at us through the veil of glittering farce that disguises it; and such is Ionesco's mastery that we are most aware of it when our laughter is loudest. This, the best of his plays that I have seen, is also the neatest proof that his philosophy of despair is pure humbug. A man who triumphantly succeeds in communicating his belief that it is impossible to communicate anything is in the grip, I cannot help thinking, of a considerable logical error. The scratch cast is led ably by Kathleen Michael and unforgettably by Jack MacGowran, who resembles (if you can imagine such a thing) a panicky Manolete.

(1957)

Pausing on the Stairs.

Would you know the shortest way to bad playwriting? I will tell you. It is to begin with a great theme, a Grand Purpose, in the hope that it will throw forth, of its own essential energy, such desirable by-products as character and dialogue. Woe to him who so far misunderstands the nature of drama as to suppose that abstractions can breed human beings! The diary of such a man might read: "Really must decide on Theme tomorrow. Torn between Problems of Power, Loneliness, Colour, H-Bomb Threat, and Revolutionary Spirit in Eastern Europe. All major, surely? At least they can't say I'm ignoring the crisis of our time. Have worked out just what I feel about all five Themes, so the big creative effort is over. All that remains is the donkey-work of filling in dialogue and characters. But which Theme to choose? Went out for walk to clear head. Strange encounter with landlady on stairs: she said I looked like George III and tittered. Silly woman."

Useless, of course, to point out that the genesis of good plays is hardly ever abstract; that it tends, on the contrary, to be something as concrete and casual as a glance intercepted, a remark overheard, or an insignificant news item buried at the bottom of page three. Yet it is by trivialities like these that the true playwright's blood is fired. They spur him to story-telling; they bring on the narrative fit that is his glory and his only credential. Show me a congenital eavesdropper with the instincts of a peeping Tom, and I will show you the makings of a dramatist. Only the makings, of course: curiosity about people is merely the beginning of the road to the masterpiece: but if that curiosity is sustained you will find, when the rules have been mastered and the end has been reached, that a miracle has happened. Implicit in the play, surging between and beneath the lines, will be exactly what the author feels about the Major Issues of his Time.

To take off from a generality is an infertile exercise, as if a man should carry about with him the plan of some mighty edifice, hoping that if he stares at it long enough the human beings needed to build it will spring full-grown from the parchment. Vain hope, for the secret of life is not there. It hides where it has always hidden, in the most obvious and unguarded place. It lies somewhere within that staircase eccentric, my diarist's landlady, who likened him to George III and tittered. Study her, or your wife, or the grocer; probe them patiently; and you will find, to your resounding amazement, that you have written a play about power, loneliness, colour, bomb-fright, and revolution to boot. Would you know the shortest way to good playwriting? Pause on the stairs.

(1957)

Speaking Out.

In the past twenty years the great majority of successful playwrights have abandoned the idiocy of pretending that the audience does not exist. It is there: why not speak to it? *Our Town, I Remember Mama, The Glass Menagerie, Teahouse of the August Moon, A View from the Bridge, No Time for Sergeants, Edward, My Son, Bobosse,* and *L'Oeuf* (Félicien Marceau's new Paris success) are a few of many recent examples. Messrs. Wilder and Miller use the technique for choric purposes; the speaker is only peripherally involved in the action. The others take a bolder course; the speaker is the protagonist.

I have heard this device described as "fish fur," a phrase employed by advertising men to denote irrelevant adornment. I disagree. It seems to me a necessary return to the well-spring of drama, which began when one articulate man sought to share his experiences with his fellows, acting out the bits that were actable, and narrating the rest. When a man steps out from the curtain and addresses me, I feel at once welcome and engaged. In the theatre of realistic illusion the curtain often rises on an empty room, and it generally takes me at least twenty minutes to feel completely at home. Playwrights who follow the first-person trend are not merely aping a vogue: they are moving with history.

(1957)

The Balcony, BY JEAN GENET, AT THE ARTS.

The great virtue of Jean Genet's *The Balcony* is that it seeks to relate sexual habits to social institutions. According to M. Genet, the bishop's mitre, the monarch's sceptre, the judge's robes, and the general's jackboots are symbols that inspire common men to sexual fantasies of domination and submission. In Madame Irma's House of Illusions their dreams become facts. The man from the gas company, episcopally garbed, forgives a penitent her sins; a repressed bank clerk defiles the Virgin Mary, while other clients prefer to disguise themselves as flagellant judges or victorious warriors. M. Genet regards these scabrous rituals with a sort of furious pity. What else, he implies, can we expect of a society whose only absolute values are those of conquest and authority?

That is the indictment. M. Genet dramatises it by setting his quaint bordello in the midst of a revolution that has already wiped out all the real holders of power save one, the Chief of Police, who now enlists the regular customers to play out their fantasy roles in earnest. Overnight, the revolt is quelled; and soon afterwards a new figure takes its place in the mythology of the brothel. A stranger asks permission to dress up as the Chief of Police, in which guise he promptly gelds himself. This horrific act completes M. Genet's argument. The image of power is erotic, but power itself is sexless. The reality survives by enslaving mankind to the symbol.

To object that the play's view of life is extremely personal is merely to say that only one man could have written it. Some power symbols are clearly more erotic than others. I myself would not place Sir Winston's cigar in quite the same category as Mussolini's fasces, but Baldwin's pipe is a disquieting thought; and the histories of Roman Catholicism and English Protestantism alike attest to the fact that the idea of female virginity is a potent and highly seductive thing. Nor can one rationally object to the violence of M. Genet's language: only dolts would contend that playgoers, who are numbered in thousands, should be protected against words and situations with which library subscribers, who run into millions, have long been familiar. The true objection to the play is that, although nobody but M. Genet could have written the first half at all, almost anyone else could have written the second half better.

The first, or expository, half is flawless; out of an anarchic, unfettered imagination there emerges a perfect nightmare world. But the second half is argumentative, and logic is necessarily a fettered thing, bound by rules to which M. Genet, who has flouted rules all his life, is temperamentally opposed. Just when the play cries out for an incisive, satiric mind like M. Sartre's, it branches off into a confusion so wild that I still cannot understand what the scenes in the rebel camp were meant to convey. As an evoker, M. Genet is magnificent; as an explainer, he is a maddening novice. He cannot think in cold blood—as witness his statement that the Arts Theatre had coarsened his play, when in fact (if Bernard Frechtmann's translation is to be trusted) it had softened it.

Apart from Selma Vaz Dias and Hazel Penwarden, Peter Zadek's cast is shamelessly feeble; but many good actors, one guesses, took one look at the text and turned it down in a huff. For all its faults, this is a theatrical experience as startling as anything since Ibsen's revelation, seventy-six years ago, that there was such a thing as syphilis.

(1957)

Tea and Sympathy, BY ROBERT ANDERSON, AT THE COMEDY.

Tea and Sympathy is one of those studies of victimisation that American authors write so well and so often, the victim on this occasion being a teen-age schoolboy who has long hair, likes music, swims in the nude with a friendly master, and is usually cast as the female lead in the end-of-term play. His descent into despair is hastened by the glib pep-talks of his uncomprehending father and the bleak hostility of his housemaster, whose strident maleness is merely a cloak for long-suppressed homosexual tendencies. It is the housemaster's wife, most feelingly played by Elizabeth Sellars, who resolves the boy's doubts by going to bed with him. Young Would-if-he-Could-ley is saved; and so tactful and responsive is Tim Heely's performance that the process is never mawkish and often extremely moving. John Fernald's direction, superb at the top, diminishes in strength as the parts get smaller; but no director could make this a wholly serious play. Always it takes the easy, conciliatory course. There is never any possibility that the hero might in fact be an invert. The wife's adultery is triply excused: her husband neglects her, she was once an actress, and the boy reminds her of her first, dead love. The villain of the piece is the unmasked queer, and the message is that it's all right not to conform as long as you're not really a nonconformist. Yet it makes a good middlebrow evening, and I look forward to an English counterpart—in which, of course, the positions would be reversed: the hero would be a hearty extrovert persecuted by a schoolful of dandified eggheads.

(1957)

The Entertainer, BY JOHN OSBORNE, AT THE ROYAL COURT; *Camino Real*, BY TENNESSEE WILLIAMS, AT THE PHOENIX; *Comedy in Music* AT THE PALACE.

This has been one of the most varied, nourishing, and provocative weeks that the London theatre has known since the war. Let me but list its riches—Olivier working with John Osborne, Peter Hall directing Tennessee Williams, and the West End début of the funniest one-man show on earth. For once, I felt mine was an enviable *métier*.

To begin at the deep end: Mr. Osborne has had the big and brilliant notion of putting the whole of contemporary England on to one and the same stage. *The Entertainer* is his diagnosis of the sickness that is currently afflicting our slaphappy breed. He chooses, as his national microcosm, a family of run-down vaudevillians. Grandad, stately and retired, represents Edwardian graciousness, for which Mr. Osborne has a deeply submerged nostalgia. But the key figure is Dad: Archie Rice, a fiftyish song-and-dance man reduced to appearing in twice-nightly nude revue. This is the role that has tempted Sir Laurence to return to the Royal Court after twenty-nine years.

Archie is a droll, lecherous fellow, comically corrupted. With his blue patter and jingo songs he is a licensed pedlar of emotional dope to every audience in Britain. The tragedy is that, being intelligent, he knows it. His talent for destructive self-analysis is as great as Jimmy Porter's. At times, indeed, when he rails in fuddled derision at "our nasty sordid unlikely little problems," he comes too close to Jimmy Porter for comfort or verisimilitude. He also shares the Porter Pathological Pull towards bisexuality, which chimes with nothing else in his character, though it may be intended to imply that he has made a sexual as well as a moral compromise.

But I am carping too soon. To show the ironic disparity between Archie's mind and the use he makes of it, Mr. Osborne has hit on a stunningly original device. He sets out the programme like a variety bill, and switches abruptly from Archie at home, insulated by gin, to Archie on stage, ogling and mincing, joshing the conductor, doing the chin-up bit and braying with false effusiveness such aptly named numbers as "Why Should I Bother to Care?," "We're All Out for Good Old Number One," and "Thank God We're Normal." In these passages, author, actor, and composer (John Addison) are all at peak form. A bitter hilarity fills the theatre, which becomes for a while England in little: "Don't clap too hard, lady, it's an old building."

Archie has abdicated from responsibility. He despises his wife, sleeps out nightly, and morally murders his father by coaxing him back into grease-paint: yet he can still button-hole us with songs and routines that enjoin us to share the very couldn't-care-less-ness that has degraded him. The death of his son, kidnapped and killed in Egypt, restores him for a while to real feeling. He has just been reminiscing, with drunken fervour, about a Negress he once heard singing in a night-club, making out of her oppression "the most beautiful fuss in the world." Now, shattered himself, he crumples, and out of his gaping mouth come disorganised moans that slowly reveal themselves as melody. Archie the untouchable is singing the blues.

With Sir Laurence in the saddle, miracles like this come often. At the end of the first act Archie is struggling to tell his daughter about the proudest encounter of his life, the one occasion when he was addressed with awe. "Two nuns came towards me," he says. "Two nuns . . ." All at once he halts, strangled by self-disgust. The curtain falls on an unfinished sentence. Sir Laurence brings the same virtuosity to Archie's last story, about a little man who went to heaven and, when asked what he thought of the glory, jerked up two fingers, unequivocally parted. The crown, perhaps, of this great performance is Archie's jocular, venomous farewell to the audience: "Let me know where you're working tomorrow night—and I'll come and see *you*."

When Archie is offstage, the action droops. His father is a bore and his children are ciphers: the most disquieting thing about the play is the author's failure to state the case of youth. There is a pacifist son who sings a Brechtian elegy for his dead brother, but does little else of moment. And there is Jean, Archie's daughter, a Suez baby who came of age at the Trafalgar Square rally but seems to have lost her political ardour with the passing of that old adrenalin glow. She is vaguely anti-Queen and goes in for loose generalities like "We've only got ourselves"; beyond that, *nada*. Rather than commit himself, Mr. Osborne has watered the girl down to a nullity, and Dorothy Tutin can do nothing with her.

This character, coupled with Archie's wife (Brenda de Banzie, bedraggled-genteel), reinforces one's feeling that Mr. Osborne cannot yet write convincing parts for women. He has bitten off, in this broad new subject, rather more than he can maul. Although the members of Archie's family incessantly harangue each other, they seldom make a human connection, and you cannot persuade an audience that people are related simply by making them call each other bastards. Tony Richardson's direction is fairly lax throughout, but I cannot see how any director could disguise either the sloth of the first act or the over-compression of the third.

In short: Mr. Osborne has planned a gigantic social mural and carried it out in a colour range too narrow for the job. Within that range he has written one of the great acting parts of our age. Archie is a truly desperate man, and to present desperation is a hard dramatic achievement. To explain and account for it, however, is harder still, and that is the task to which I would now direct this dazzling, self-bound writer.

Tennessee Williams' *Camino Real* is likewise microcosmic, but in a stricter sense; it takes on the whole world. The message shrieked by Mr. Williams' garish symbols is that life is diseased and curable only by innocence. It issues from a dingy, timeless coastal town where Spanish is spoken, the police are in charge, and "hermano" is a dirty word. On one side of the plaza is an hotel for decayed romantics such as Casanova; on the other, a squalid flophouse where people like the Baron de Charlus find what is modishly known as their adjustment. The proles are kept happy by frequent festivals, among them a burlesque fertility rite wherein a tart is ceremonially declared a virgin. Idealism is mirrored in Don Quixote, emblem of the pure romantic quest, and in Kilroy, a vagrant American prize-fighter who loves people so perilously much that the police force him to dress up as a clown.

At this stage the play goes off the rails. Its middle stretch is devoted to the tedious courtship of Casanova and Marguérite Gautier; and when we get back to Kilroy, it is merely for a comic seduction scene with the pseudo-virgin—gay in itself, but essentially irrelevant. He finally decides to venture, with Quixote, into the desert that surrounds the town's sleazy chaos, but by then we have stopped taking him seriously. Mr. Williams has beckoned us into too many gaudy sideshows. Some of his inventions are extremely bright—Freda Jackson as a gipsy brothel-keeper, Ronald Barker as her beskirted bouncer, Elizabeth Seal as her daughter, who thinks, feels, and wears as little as the law will allow—but they do not really advance the author's simple thesis: that purity can survive corruption as long as it gets the hell out.

There are three attitudes that a serious writer can adopt towards the world. He can mirror its sickness without comment; he can seek to change it; or he can withdraw from it. Mr. Williams, by recommending withdrawal, places himself in the third batch, along with the saints, the hermits, the junkies, and the drunks. The attitude is defensible, but it somehow sounds better in diaries and autobiographies than in a place as social and public as a theatre.

About Peter Hall's direction, however, I have no doubts, and this despite a Kilroy (Denholm Elliott) who can manage neither the accent nor the dumbness of the part. Judged as a frenetic pageant, a circus of noise and colour, a three-ring freak show, the production generates an excitement that London has not felt in a theatre since the early extravagances of Peter Brook. The use of sound—nasal bullfight music and bleating fairground spiels—is especially striking. Mr. Williams, champion of the fly-blown, the man who sold solitude to the gregarious, has never found in London a director half so bold, half so loyal.

The art of public solitude reaches a high water-mark in Victor Borge's solo recital, *Comedy in Music.* From his first entrance, bowing gravely and releasing from his mouth a cryptic puff of smoke, the beady-eyed Danish pianist had a doubting house in the palm of his hand. To dub him a soloist is perhaps inept. He has two mechanical stooges, the piano and the microphone—especially the piano, which he describes at various times as "grinning" and "non-segregated." His is the technique of the infinitely delayed climax. Always promising to play, he teases us for minutes on end before actually doing so. The comedy of self-interruption has never been more subtly explored.

Between key-tickling bouts, he talks. About what? Mostly about families: about the philoprogenitive Bachs, and the fated Debussys (all wiped out, just like that); about Joe E. Brahms and Harry S. Beethoven; about his own parents, who had three children, "one of each." Students of American humour will by now have identified the style. It is Benchley set to music, with the master's suave irrelevance, his dangerous cosiness, and his habit of telling insane historical anecdotes with enormous gravity (cf. Mr. Benchley's radio account of the man who invented jazz: "Johann Sebastian Gesundheit was born in Japan in 1789. He was a backward child but very friendly . . ."). Mr. Borge, who is here for six more weeks, is by several miles the funniest man in London. If, as J. B. Morton says, Wagner is the Puccini of music, Victor Borge is the Danny Kaye of comedy.

(1957)

The Chairs, BY EUGÈNE IONESCO, AND *L'Apollon de Bellac*, BY JEAN GIRAUDOUX, AT THE ROYAL COURT.

The two prime assumptions of French literature are that there is no humour without satire and no truth without logic. Eugène Ionesco denies both propositions, and hence the French adore him. He flouts both of their household gods. The words he utters are those of an anarch, of a logical negativist who believes that nothing in the dictionary has a verifiable meaning. In his plays the light of verbal communication is extinguished. People collide in the dark; and when, fleetingly, a phrase kindles the heart, it is as if a match had been struck and we glimpsed, for a second, a human face, lonely and deeply appalled.

In England, where satire and logic lost their literary hegemony two centuries ago, we are less likely than the French to be overwhelmed by the originality of a style based on nonsense-humour and nonsense-logic. That it is virtuoso nonsense nobody denies: Ionesco is a poet of double-talk. But this is at best a minor gift. It does not explain why *The Chairs* is such an enthralling experience.

It is night on an island. In a round house of many doors sit a nonagenarian couple who will soon fling themselves suicidally into the river. At first, however, all is tranquil. Mad scraps of reminiscence are swapped, the old man bemoans his failure in life, the old woman babies and consoles him. From their moonstruck chatter we gather that he has a message to the world which he has bidden everyone to hear. The guests start to arrive, at first singly, then in pairs, soon in unmanageable droves, until the old-age *pension* resembles Groucho's cabin in *A Night at the Opera*. With this difference: that all the guests are invisible. They are creatures of the old man's dream, and before long he and his wife are plunging in and out of doors with yet more chairs for the unseen multitude, whom they engage, from time to time, in phantom conversation.

The audacity of the idea is breathtaking; here is pure theatre, the stage doing what only the stage can do. As the doorbell rings and the numbers crazily swell, one sees that Ionesco is more than a word-juggler. He is a supreme theatrical conjurer. And what does the trick mean? A hired orator, at the end, speaks the old man's message to the listening throng. Or rather, he would speak it, were he not dumb; and they would listen, if they existed. Moral: truth is a tale told without words to people who cannot hear it. Communication between human beings is impossible.

I mention this facile and despondent philosophy because it leads us to Ionesco's second great virtue. He knows the secret of creating comic people. It derives from the Jacobean comedy of humours; and there are hints of it in Bergson, who says somewhere that the comic character "slackens in the attention that is due to life . . . in some way or other he is *absent";* but what it boils down to is that a person who pursues an obsession, who sees life through the blinkers of a fixed idea, who is blind to the world and the people around him, is by definition comic. If I stroll into a peace conference and quietly apply hot feet to the assembled statesmen, I am comic; but the moment I apologise and begin to explain myself, the joke is over. I must not hesitate: my special bent must be at once irrational and unreasonable-with.

The Old Man in *The Chairs* is such a character; so is the hero of Ionesco's *The New Tenant;* so are Jacques Tati and the amiable zanies of *La Plume de Ma Tante,* not to mention most of the great drolls of world literature. Each is gripped by an obsession he cannot be bothered to account for. If they paused to give a rational explanation of their actions, the comedic contrast between their private world and the observable world would be irretrievably lost. It is precisely because they don't "communicate," either with us or with each other, that Ionesco's people are funny. As a thinker he is banal; as a word-trickster he is no more than ingenious; but as a comic inventor he is superb and classical.

Tony Richardson's direction has the right, spooky enthusiasm. The Old Man really needs an actor less *voulu* in his eccentricity than the dogged George Devine; but Joan Plowright, all boggling fervour and timorous glee, makes a wonderful North-Country mouse of the Old Woman. The same director does considerable damage to the curtain-raiser, Giraudoux's *Apollon de Bellac,* which you would be wise to miss, in spite of a summery performance by Heather Sears. At one point Miss Sears informs a chandelier that it is beautiful. According to Giraudoux, "Le lustre s'allume de lui-même"; according to Mr. Richardson, Apollo switches it on at the door. Thus can poetry, in a single gesture, become irrevocable prose.

(1957)

The Summer of the Seventeenth Doll, BY RAY LAWLER, AT THE NEW THEATRE.

In a recent film called *A Man Is Ten Feet Tall* a startling precedent was created. Never before, save in pictures with all-coloured casts, had a Negro actor played a leading character who was neither a droll imbecile nor a victim of racial hatred, but a simple human being, the colour of whose skin was scarcely mentioned in the whole course of the film. This radical departure, spotted at once in America, passed largely unnoticed in England. I cite it here lest anyone should overlook a comparable development that took place last week in the London theatre. In Irish, American, and Continental drama it took place long ago; but our own drama lost sight of it in the fifteenth century, since when many attempts have been made to revive it, most of them over-anxious, all of them failures.

Last Tuesday, against all augury, the lost cause was suddenly won. One of Her Majesty's subjects turned up with a play about working people who were neither "grim" nor "funny," neither sentimentalised nor patronised, neither used to point a social moral nor derided as quaint and improbable clowns. Instead, they were presented, like the Negro in the above-lauded movie, as human beings in their own right, exulting in universal pleasures and nagged by universal griefs. They were poor only in passing, as the Negro is only incidentally black. The play that pulled off the feat is *The Summer of the Seventeenth Doll,* and if Ray Lawler, its Australian author, is aware of the magnitude of his achievement, I shall be the most astonished critic in London, for I am sure revolution was not in his mind when he wrote it. He was merely born with something that most English playwrights acquire only after a struggle and express only with the utmost embarrassment—respect for ordinary people.

It takes more than that, of course, to make a good play. The exciting thing about Mr. Lawler is that he can also construct. Out of unremarkable gaieties and regrets, out of everyday challenges and defeats, he has composed a story as gripping in the theatre as it would be in life. It has to do with the reluctance of people to grow up, to prepare for age, to exchange immaturity for responsibility. For sixteen years two canecutters—little, ebullient Barney and burly, taciturn Roo—have lived their lives to a pattern: seven months of hard work, followed by five months of pleasure with Nancy and Olive, their unmarried wives. Sixteen souvenir dolls brighten the walls of the house.

At the height of the seventeenth summer—Australia's sweltering December, with the windows open all night and Christmas a great day for swatting mosquitoes—the idyll collapses. Nancy has found herself a safe husband, and her substitute is a dawdling middle-aged barmaid whose enthusiasm sags sharply when she learns that Barney has already scattered three bastards across the continent. And Roo, the bulging sun-god whom Olive first loved, has begun to bald and weaken; his supremacy in the cane-fields has been smashed by a younger man, and with it his self-respect. Both the buccaneering cutters are themselves cut down: Barney descends to street-corner pick-ups, Roo to the ultimate disgrace of a factory job. When the curtain falls, reality has demolished the romantic myth of the past; but we have laughed too much in the process to call the play a tragedy. It records a mischance that has befallen a special group of people whom, since we love them, we regard with unique compassion.

At first blink, most of the characters look like stereotypes—two rugged outdoor heroes and two soft-hearted indoor heroines, one of whom has a tetchy and disgruntled mother. What redeems them is the penetrating freshness of Mr. Lawler's vision: he has perceived the realities that underlie the stereotypes and made them exuberantly new. He himself plays Barney with rather exaggerated perkiness. Otherwise the Australian cast cannot be reasonably knocked. Ethel Gabriel's wary Mama, who removes her ring before playing the piano, is a wonderfully intimidating portrait; and June Jago, all angles, teeth, and gush, must by now have relaxed into a performance as heart-caressing throughout as the moment on Tuesday night when she leapt into Roo's arms crying: "If you hadn't come, I'd have gone looking for you with a razor!" Madge Ryan's Pearl is flawless—the infinitely suspicious newcomer, jibbing in stately dudgeon at the slightest hint of orgy; and no actor in England could play Roo with the bulk, the dignity, and the uncomplicated assurance of Kenneth Warren.

Mr. Lawler has been strangely described as the Australian Tennessee Williams. The comparison is just only in that both writers deal with people who live in a hot climate and speak rawly and freely about their emotions. But where Mr. Williams concerns himself with odd men out, Mr. Lawler concerns himself with even men in. The results, though different, are not less rewarding. In short, we have found ourselves a playwright, and it is time to rejoice.

(1957)

Henry VI, Parts One, Two, and Three, by William Shakespeare, at the Old Vic.

Superficially, the three parts of *Henry VI* seem jingoistic and Churchillian: history is made by martial patriots engaged in a series of ardent brawls. It takes a director as sharp as Douglas Seale to unearth the vein of savage irony that runs through the plays, and to reveal that in this hindsight view of the century before his own Shakespeare was more than a reporter: he editorialised as well. Beneath the almighty hubbub of clanking potentates angrily swopping genealogies and hurling roses, gauntlets, and place-names ("Detested Salisbury!") at each other, one seems to hear the uncertain voice of Michael Williams: "I am afeard there are few die well that die in battle."

Henry V, who led England to that "finest hour" still blindly cherished by many merry Englishmen, is dead. No sooner is he underground than we plunge straight into the lower depths. Everyone betrays everyone else: the greater the patriot, the more vehement his ratting. One is fascinated to hear the number of cast-iron excuses these people can find for decimating their relations. War, for them, is a virile hobby that gets you out and about instead of frowsting in the keep all day; it is, you might say, fox-hunting writ large. In Part One France slips through the nerveless hands of Henry VI, conchie and bookworm. In Part Two, noisily harassed by Queen Margaret, York steps in to fill the power vacuum, with diversionary aid from Jack Cade and his mutinous underdogs. In Part Three Margaret makes her come-back, and York's head duly rolls; but his sons, their blood boiling, live on to keep the blood flowing, and by curtain-fall Edward is king, unaware as yet that his hunchback brother has marked fratricidal tendencies.

These lurid broils, of course, all stem from the fatal act which for Shakespeare and his contemporaries was the great turning-point of history: Bolingbroke's dethronement of Richard II, the replacement of a king *de jure* by a king *de facto.* The bloody reverberations of that moment are the subject-matter of both cycles of history plays. The grand debate on the ethics of usurpation was far from over in Shakespeare's day—it had, indeed, an acid relevance to the opportunistic methods of the Tudors—and it went on haunting the drama until Ibsen settled it once and for all in *The Pretenders,* the last great play in which kings were heroic.

In *Henry VI* Shakespeare exploits it with brutal sensationalism, yet leaves one with the irrational conviction that he cannot have been a warlike man. He spends too much time lamenting the innocent dead. After the ranting has faded, the scene that stays most tensely in the mind is one in which nobody's voice is raised above a regretful plea: the despised king yearns for a shepherd's life, flanked on either side by those two strange, symbolic figures of grief, "a Son that has kill'd his father" and "a Father that has kill'd his son." Red rose and white are forgotten. "A plague on both your roses," we mutter; and so, I hazard, did Shakespeare.

Mr. Seale's boldly stylised treatment of this scene is still as powerful as it was in his famous Birmingham Repertory production four years ago. Now, as then, one gapes at the ease with which he clarifies the intricate family relationships of a trilogy snarled and studded with lines that frequently sound like: "And does thou now presume, base Leamington, to scorn thy brother's cousin's eldest son?" Most of the time one actually knows who is kin to whom, and how closely.

But it was an error to compress the first two parts into one evening. The upshot is confusion, since the French scenes in Part One, to which reference is constantly being made, have vanished completely; Talbot is axed *in toto,* and with him that splendidly besotted witch, Joan La Pucelle. But Part Three makes amends. As staged by Mr. Seale, it stands up in its own right, shoulder-high at least to the twin peaks of *Henry IV*. The final curtain is a magnificent stroke of textual audacity. Alone on stage after the pomp of Edward's coronation, Gloucester embarks on the opening soliloquy of *Richard III*. Before long his voice is drowned by an offstage clamour of loyalty to the new king: obliviously he goes on, and is still, when the curtain falls, grimacing and gesturing, an inaudible power-driven puppet, the authentic agent of death.

This year's good Vic company is just the right weight for plays like these, in which the main requirements are pace, energy, vocal attack, and reasonable swordsmanship. I took exception to a couple of very grubby prelates, and in the Cade scenes the crowd ran a little too picturesquely riot; but in such basic bits of Shakespearean expertise as running up and down flights of stairs in the dark and looking vicious or resolute or both, the whole troupe is exceptionally fly—as, with a setting as heavily booby-trapped as Leslie Hurry's, it needs to be. There is plenty of exemplary doubling: from Ronald Fraser, for instance, as a blood-thirsty Kentish butcher, later Lewis XI of France; and from Derek Godfrey, no sooner slain as Suffolk than revived as crookback Gloucester. In the latter role he at first seemed too flippant, but he grew in daemonism and towards the end was bringing off some really fruity Olivier cadences.

Among the singles champions I would name Rosemary Webster's sedate young queen; Derek Francis' black-avised Cade; and—a leather-lunged trio—Barbara Jefford's fire-breathing Margaret, Oliver Neville's Warwick, and Jack Gwillim's York. Both Messrs. Neville and Gwillim, pillars of the trilogy, reminded me of Donne's "grim eight-foot-high iron-bound serving-man": here were the robber-barons of childhood nightmares come dragonishly to life. As Henry, the point of rest in the midst of chaos, Paul Daneman contrived a touching bewilderment, muted intentionally in Parts One and Two and involuntarily in Part Three. "Let us our lives, our souls, our debts, our careful wives, our children and our sins lay on the king." Our laryngitis, too, it seems.

(1957)

The Making of Moo, BY NIGEL DENNIS, AT THE ROYAL COURT.

"As to that detestable religion, the Christian . . ." Thus would Shelley, speaking gently and uncontentiously, strike up conversation at the dinner-table, causing among his fellow-guests much the same affronted consternation that seems to have been felt last Tuesday by many of the critics who witnessed Nigel Dennis' *The Making of Moo*. Few of them, of course, admitted that they had been shocked, but whenever critics use words like "old-fashioned" and "tasteless" you may begin to suspect that they have been outraged to the core of their being; and if "undergraduate joke" is the phrase qualified by "tasteless," you can be absolutely sure.

Now I will not slander my colleagues by supposing that what shocked them was the play's intellectual content. Mr. Dennis is a straightforward rationalist who regards organised religion as an insult to human intelligence. My own guess would be that he leans rather to atheism than agnosticism, that cloak under which atheists gain admission to the Royal Enclosure; but I cannot see how any of his ideas could really startle even the seventy-one per cent of our population who, according to a recent poll, believe that Jesus Christ was the Son of God. No: what shocked my colleagues was not the novelty of Mr. Dennis' ideas, but the novelty of hearing them in a theatre. *"Pas devant les enfants!"* was the essence of their reaction to a play which, for all its faults, is a milestone in history: the first outright attack on religion ever to be presented on the English stage.

It is Mr. Dennis' simple belief that God, as human beings envisage him, is a thoroughly bad influence on society. And he has had the audacity not only to state his belief in a theatre, but to state it *without reverence*—thereby offending against the rules of fair play. The militant sceptic, according to this curious code, is permitted to disbelieve only as long as he disbelieves reverently; as long as he shows respect for that which he is sworn to demolish. Mr. Dennis violates this hypocrisy by showing no respect at all. He is by turns skittish and savage. His final advice to those contemplating religion is: "Stop when you come to a pool of blood." Stop, in fact, when you come to a ritual sacrifice, a massacre of heretics, a holy war, or a God-sanctioned nuclear weapon; in other words, don't start. To compare Mr. Dennis with Shaw, as several critics have, is to miss the point completely. Even at his most iconoclastic, Shaw always made it clear that he was only kidding. Mr. Dennis, by contrast, is in earnest: he means what he says, and expects us to act on it. If his play is crude, it is the forgivable crudity of all pioneer work.

The first act is mild enough. A pompous English dam-builder discovers that he has inadvertently flooded and destroyed the ancestral home of Ega, a native god. Deciding to replace what he has destroyed with (as the novel has it) "something of value," he invents a new deity, Moo. His wife takes on the job of writing suitable scriptures, and his secretary, an amateur musician, sets about composing appropriately intimidating hymns. In the second act the cult is really rolling, with a garish liturgy of its own and thousands of adherents blissfully shouting their affirmative answer to the solemn question: "Have you taken leave of all your senses?" The curtain falls on a tableau at which Shaw would certainly have jibbed: the ritual murder of two casual visitors from the old country. The last scene whisks us into the future. The inventor of the myth has now become a senile patriarch, wheeled daily on to the balcony to receive homage, and his son, a new character, quickly discloses that passionate interest in pain and guilt that stamps the true Protestant.

Mr. Dennis makes his points with reckless pungency and eldritch wit. He is more concerned, of course, with ideas than with character, and it takes all the efforts of George Devine, Joan Plowright, and John Osborne to persuade us that a dim trio of suburban expatriates would be capable of such bloody excesses. But my main criticism of the piece is that, for a *soi-disant* "history of religion," it omits altogether too much. Is Christianity really what Rémy de Gourmont called it, "a machine for creating remorse"? Is a sense of sin a natural endowment or a conditioned reflex? These questions Mr. Dennis does not discuss; nor does he investigate the political influence exerted by the Church in such matters as convincing the poor that poverty is a virtue.

But, in spite of these and other gaps, Mr. Dennis deserves all our thanks for having introduced the full gaiety of blasphemy to the English theatre, and our apologies for having welcomed him with reviews that paid no attention to whether his ideas were true or false but devoted themselves instead to the totally irrelevant question of whether or not they would "give offence." To "give offence," it seems, is to be "in bad taste." A healthy state, I should judge, to be in. To a theatre that is perishing of decorum, a few more truly offensive, sincerely tasteless plays would come as a reviving boon.

(1957)

Hamlet, BY WILLIAM SHAKESPEARE, AT THE OLD VIC.

O, there has been much throwing about of brains.
Hamlet, Act II, Scene 2

Michael Benthall has directed *Hamlet* no fewer than three and a half times. On the first occasion he collaborated with Tyrone Guthrie, many of whose ideas rubbed off on him and have stayed rubbed. Then came the famous "Victorian" production at Stratford in 1948, with Paul Scofield's incomparable Scholar-Gipsy prince. In 1953, distracted perhaps by the burdens of his new job as Director of the Vic, Mr. Benthall revived the play drably, and one thought him exhausted on the subject. One was wrong. His new production in the Unlucky Horseshoe of Waterloo Road discards the dross while retaining the gold of its predecessors. Textually and conceptually it is as near to a definitive *Hamlet* as anything I have ever seen.

With imperious intelligence Mr. Benthall has brought off a minor Shakespeare revolution. He has taken his scene-order not from the Folio but from the First Quarto of 1603. Line for line, as everyone knows, the Quarto is a bad text, frequently verging on parody; all the same, it is an actors' text, rushed into print (or so scholarship conjectures) by two opportunistic members of the original cast. Their memory of the other players' lines was hazy, but they remembered the order of the scenes as acted; and in this respect their testimony is valuable. One vital transposition makes it revolutionary. "To be or not to be," which we know as the fourth soliloquy, is in their text the third. Together with the ensuing nunnery scene, it is jerked out of the third act and shoehorned into the second.

The improvement, in dramatic logic as well as sheer actability, is enormous. Hamlet's progressive disillusionment with humanity—first Gertrude and Claudius, then Ophelia and Polonius, then Rosencrantz and Guildenstern—is presented as an uninterrupted whole, leading up to the arrival of the players and the switch from inertia to action. He has met the ghost and cursed his fate. We have next seen him pondering suicide and rejecting the frail, corrupted Ophelia; he has reviled Polonius for having used her to pump him and he has unmasked his old college chums as spies. He now works out his conscience-catching plot and goes straight ahead with it. Compare this logical sequence with the incoherent Folio text, wherein "The play's the thing" is immediately followed by "To be or not to be," an inexplicable *volte-face* that halts the actor just when the movement of the play demands swiftly unfolding action. It is like driving through a green light into a road-block. This ludicrous blockage, hitherto regarded with veneration as part of a grand inscrutable design, has now been removed to its proper functional place. The play is still, as it should be, full of mystery and dark corners; but now at least its signposts fulfil what they promise.

The production has the clean physical dexterity I associate with Mr. Benthall at his best. The costumes—mid-nineteenth-century Mittel-Europa—are those of an intrigue-ridden court on the eve of the 1848 upsets; and Audrey Cruddas' setting, a semi-circle of columns, easily manages the abrupt switches from interior to exterior. The ghost scenes quite froze my youngish blood. By projecting shifting cloud-images on to the dead king, Mr. Benthall makes him dissolve, solidify, and redissolve before one's eyes, while the voice that issues from him suggests not the usual visiting fireman (with built-in loudspeaker) but an outraged, anguished human being, peremptory in his wrath and Claudius' true brother. Jack Gwillim's Claudius is an iron-headed general at the awkward age, slightly ashamed of having fallen in love—an original conception, of which Coral Browne's maternally voluptuous queen makes splendid sense.

At the end of the play scene Mr. Benthall blows, as they say, his top. "The king rises" is an awed, edged whisper, followed by a pause; and only after half a dozen more whispers and pauses does Claudius break the tension with a final shattering cry—all of which is much more credible than the usual inchoate hurly-burly of rhubarbing extras. Nor shall I forget the ensuing hunt for Hamlet, which was like the Congress of Vienna run mad—a paranoid nightmare in silks and satins, bristling at first with veiled threats and later with cold steel. It is a tribute to Mr. Benthall's stagecraft and timing that I was held almost all the way. At no point, however, was I moved. Against the blackness of the cyclorama, the play's bare bones danced before me, macabre and mesmerizing, yet always remote, like a phosphorescent skeleton in a puppet show.

The Ophelia, Judi Dench, is a pleasing but terribly sane little thing, and there is little in the way of a Hamlet; John Neville resists agony with lips prefectorially stiff, and simply won't let go of his voice. Always there is effort, audible vocal effort, with the actor pushing for climaxes he might be able to reach if only he would stop pushing. He is first-rate, however, in the hysteria that follows the interview with the ghost, which I have never seen better done. *À propos* of the ghost scenes, and before leaving an immensely convincing production: has anyone noticed the striking relevance of Hamlet's "vicious mole" speech to the Wolfenden proposals for reforming the laws against homosexuality?

(1957)

A Lack of Weight.

In many ways our theatre is what we think it to be—a republic run by actors. No British director has anything like the power that is wielded in America, over authors and players alike, by such men as Joshua Logan and Elia Kazan. With very few exceptions, the drawing-power of West End authors and directors is easily eclipsed by that of the actors they employ. In younger players our strength is formidable and brightly auspicious, ranging from Paul Scofield, our senior *jeune premier,* to such promising debutants as Peter O'Toole of the Bristol Old Vic and Albert Finney of Birmingham Rep. There may not be an outright Meggie Albanesi among the girls, but Dorothy Tutin, Mary Ure, Barbara Jefford, and Jill Bennett will do to be going on with; and intramural reports speak ecstatically of Sian Philips, the R.A.D.A. champion.

We are similarly rich in older actresses. Dame Edith and Dame Sybil regally contend for the title of *doyenne,* beadily observed from the wings by a platoon of competitive juniors, all of whom (especially Margaret Rawlings) are ready to pounce on the crown should deadlock between the queenpins at any time be reached. And, though she has confined her incalculable gifts to Broadway for the past two seasons, I have an uneasy feeling that Siobhan McKenna may at any moment land with an army at Milford Haven.

Yet there is a gap in the ranks. You will spot it at once when I ask:

where in Britain is the automatic choice for Lear? I do not think he exists. What we lack, in a phrase, is the older actor of *weight:* which means not avoirdupois but presence, assurance, and power. For some cryptic reason, conceivably connected with diet, the older English actor tends to wither. He contracts instead of expanding. He develops a fine sensibility and the nicest comic finesse, but in such qualities as weight, stature, and sheer psychological bulk he declines disastrously. Examples are plentiful. Consider A. E. Matthews, Ronald Squire, Ernest Thesiger, Ernest Milton, the late Esmé Percy—all admirable players, but none of them equipped to deliver those sledge-hammer blows to the solar plexus of an audience that came so effortlessly from the lamented Czech tragedian Frederick Valk.

An American critic once sourly observed that any actor who spoke his lines slowly in a deep bass voice was sure to be hailed as an actor of "authority." True enough: but the fact remains that many of the great roles, ancient and modern, demand the threat of thunder, a threat which our senior players simply cannot supply. The erratic Wilfrid Lawson can manage it in intermittent bursts, but what is one Lawson beside the glowering battalions of oak-like elders who adorn the Russian theatre? Two years ago I attended a performance of Tolstoy's comedy *The Fruits of Enlightenment* at the Moscow Art Theatre. Halfway through it, at a peak of gaiety, my English companion turned to me and said: "There are ten men on that stage who could play King Lear." I looked, and it was true. The same company will be visiting London next May, when those lucky enough to grab tickets will be able to test my impressions.

I am speaking, remember, of actors well into or past their fifties: that is the time at which, in England, the mysterious marcescence sets in. It is probable that Olivier will retain into age the exceptional powers that now distinguish his prime. There is hope, too, for Redgrave and even the fantastic Richardson. But where else? I admit the brilliance of Gielgud and Guinness, but neither can be described as a heavyweight in the real, pile-driving sense.

If the Russians excel at the kind of acting I miss, the Germans are not far behind, with players like Krauss, Bassermann, Gründgens, and Busch. I do not myself respond to the extravagance of Pierre Brasseur, but at his best he is an actor of weight in every sense of the word, and one sees why Paris flocks to him. In another medium Raimu was a perfect example of "authority" achieved without bellowing; even without raising the voice. Spencer Tracy is a comparable performer in the American cinema, while from Broadway I could cite such a display as that of Fredric March in *Long Day's Journey into Night.* Alfred Lunt, if only he would take himself seriously; Orson Welles, if only he would take anyone else seriously; and Lee J. Cobb, who looks like Lear even when chewing a hamburger—these are three more exemplars of what we lack. I do not say that there is anyone in America who could play Macbeth, Brand, Halvard Solness, and Micawber in a single repertory season; but there are several who can play (and have played) Big Daddy in Tennessee Williams' *Cat on a Hot Tin Roof*.

And this is very much a case in point, for Mr. Williams' play is to be produced next month in London. The role of Big Daddy, an exuberant sixtyish titan of oxlike stature, has been given to Leo McKern, a young actor in his thirties. I will not say *faute de mieux,* for Mr. McKern is an extremely skilled performer. He is not, however, what I or Mr. Williams would call obvious casting for the part. And I repeat: who in England is?

(1957)

Flowering Cherry, BY ROBERT BOLT, AT THE HAYMARKET.

No doubt about it, Sir Ralph Richardson gave an amazing performance of *something* at the Haymarket last Thursday. No actor in England is more interesting to watch. He is interesting all the time, without respite; even when he plays a dull man, that dull man is never permitted a dull moment. Sir Ralph will spruce him up and set him frisking, running the gamut from manic to depressive; the fellow's neuroses will get a thorough airing, as if they were dogs being taken out for a walk. Everything about him will be written, in a flowing hand, all over Sir Ralph's face, and his simplest remark will seem eccentric when the Richardson voice, waltzing and skating from syllable to syllable, has finished with it. (What is the word for that voice? Something between bland and grandiose: blandiose, perhaps.) Characters played by this actor are too busy to have an inner life, which is why his Peer Gynt was so good, and why I should like to see him as Azdak, the flamboyant rogue of *The Caucasian Chalk Circle*. To any role that gives him half a chance he brings outsize attributes, outsize euphoria, outsize dismay. Those critics who hold that he excels in portraying the Average Man cannot, I feel, have met many Average Men.

Bearing all this in mind, let us look at Sir Ralph's latest part, the hero of *Flowering Cherry,* a remarkable new play by Robert Bolt. Jim Cherry, who lends his name to the silly punning title, is an insurance man whose adjustment to reality leaves a lot to be desired. Everything in his domestic life takes second place to an obsessive dream of one day throwing up his job and living in the country, where he was brought up. This fantasy, once mild, has grown cancerous and now infects his whole world. He is for ever hymning the lost green days of his youth, days spent in the sun among great bronzed labourers as strong as they were shrewd. Next year, he declares, he will plant his orchard; already he is writing to nurserymen, selecting trees for an estate we know he will never buy.

Like most neurotics, he misinterprets his nostalgia. What he takes to be a manly preference for the outdoor life is in fact an unhealthy yearning for the secure irresponsibility of childhood. At the climax he is offered a practical chance of buying an orchard, of realising his dream. He rejects it: the dream itself was a lie. And at this point Mr. Bolt's spiky, provocative play dissolves into abject melodrama: sudden death instead of a dying fall. Attempting to prove his virility by a feat of strength, Cherry succumbs to a wretchedly predictable heart attack. By a single stroke (if Mr. Bolt can pun, so can I) the play moves down from alpha minus to beta plus. All the same, in a desert of gammas it is a considerable oasis.

Sir Ralph's performance, engrossing though it is, should properly be considered apart from the play. It is conceived, for one thing, on a scale much grander than the environment Mr. Bolt has provided for it: you feel that Sir Ralph could eat six Jim Cherrys for breakfast without getting indigestion. He rides, not rough-shod but with spring-heeled lightness, over everyone else on stage. Mr. Bolt's hero is an apparently normal suburbanite who lives in a world of fantasy: Sir Ralph gives us all of the fantasy and none of the normality. Like all actors driven by instinct, he sometimes brings off effects which "reason and sanity could not so prosperously be deliver'd of." I concede that at such moments Sir Ralph is a genius. What I seriously doubt is whether this is a part for a genius.

(1957)

The Angry Young Movement

It all came to a head one May evening in 1956 at the Royal Court Theatre in Sloane Square. There had of course been plenty of preliminary rumbles. A group of young British writers had recently published a series of picaresque novels featuring a new sort of hero—a lower-class intellectual with a ribald sense of humour, a robust taste for beer and sex, and an attitude of villainous irreverence towards the established order. A butterfly-theorist named Colin Wilson had written an apocalyptic best-seller about the necessity of being an "outsider." An attack had just been launched by the younger movie critics and directors against the genteel vacuity of the British cinema: their new watchword was "commitment," by which they meant commitment to reality and social truth. A similar rebellion was taking place in the world of painting, where the new "kitchen-sink school" (so called for its alleged preoccupation with domestic squalor) had begun to move into the lead. Even before the events of that May evening it was clear that the post-war generation in Britain had a good deal to say and was in quite a hurry to say it.

Most of the new rebels were leftish-liberal or outright Socialist; a few, like Colin Wilson, had religious aspirations; but on one point nearly all of them agreed. They detested "the Establishment," a phrase that had lately been coined to describe the hard core of top people—professional monarchists, archbishops, press barons, Etonian Tories, and *Times* leader writers—who still seemed, in spite of a war and a social revolution, to be exerting a disproportionate influence on the country's affairs. Protest against these apparent immovables was very much in the air. So it was, of course, in the 1930's. But the intelligentsia of that period were mostly rebelling against their own class; many of them were Etonians and most came from solid Establishment backgrounds. The new malcontents were chiefly state-educated lower-middles. Their feeling about the country-house class, which had survived into their era like some grotesque coelacanth, was not one of filial resentment. It was closer to outraged boredom.

Into this combustible atmosphere John Osborne, a lean, esurient actor in his twenty-seventh year, flung a play called *Look Back in Anger,* which summed up what many of his contemporaries were feeling about their rulers and elders. It opened, unheralded, at the Royal Court Theatre; and the explosion of that spring night two years ago is still reverberating through the decorous anterooms of English culture. It was as if, in the tiptoe hush of a polite assembly, someone had deafeningly burped. The theatre's press-agent, asked for a description of the iconoclastic young gate-crasher, said he was first and foremost "an angry young man." Before long the phrase, in itself not particularly striking, had snowballed into a cult. It did so because it defined a phenomenon that was nationally recognisable. It gave a name to a generation of young intellectuals who disliked being called intellectuals, since they thought the word phoney, affected, and "wet."

There is nothing new in young men being angry: in fact, it would be news if they were anything else. Byron and Shelley were classically angry young men. American writing in the 1930's was on fire with anger: Dos Passos, Steinbeck, and Odets come to mind, all brandishing their fists. The very phrase was used in 1951 by an English social philosopher named Leslie Paul as the title of his autobiography: it is the story of a devout left-wing agitator who lost his faith in Russia during the 1930's and turned, like so many others, to a vague sort of Christian humanism. What distinguishes the modern English "young angries" is that they all came of age around the time that their elders invented the hydrogen bomb. How could they revere "civilisation as we know it" when at any moment it might be transformed into "civilisation as we knew it"? How could they carry the torch of freedom when to do so meant running with it into the ammunition dump? These unanswerable questions set up feelings of uselessness and impotence, which led in some to apathy, in others to a sort of derisive detachment, and in still others to downright rage. And these feelings were intensified by the knowledge that Britain no longer had a voice strong enough to forbid chaos if, by some horrific chance, it should impend.

Somebody, in short, had to say that many young Britons were fed up; that to be young, so far from being very heaven, was in some ways very hell. Osborne was the first in the theatre to say it; and, the theatre being the naked, public place it is, the statement caused a considerable bang. What made it even more shocking was that both the author and his hero, Jimmy Porter, came from low social shelves, yet had the cheek to be highly articulate on a wide variety of subjects, including the sex war, the class war, and war itself. There was no mistaking the portents. A break-through was beginning. The new intelligentsia created by free education and state scholarships was making its first sizeable dents in the façade of public-school culture.

A few months before, in a Christmas message to the readers of the London *Sunday Times,* Somerset Maugham had expressed his opinions of state-aided undergraduates. It was simple and unequivocal: "They are scum," said the Old Party. He was in fact referring to Jim Dixon, the hero of Kingsley Amis' immensely successful novel, *Lucky Jim.* Dixon, who lectures at a minor university, is a frankly comic character, much less ferocious than Jimmy Porter; he keeps his anger in check by drinking and pulling dreadful faces; but he shares with Osborne's hero a defiant provincialism, semi-proletarian origins, and the kind of blithe disgruntlement that inspires such phrases as "the interminable facetiousness of filthy Mozart." By Mr. Maugham's standards *Look Back in*

Anger was the apotheosis of scum. The letter columns of the more pompous dailies were soon filled with similar opinions. These young men (said one correspondent) were just envious upstarts: in a decently run society they would have been sent out to work at fourteen with no time to brood about ideas above their station.

Despite his greater violence and dogmatism, it was clear that Jimmy Porter was speaking essentially the same idiom as Lucky Jim and the heroes of John Wain's *Hurry on Down* and Iris Murdoch's *Under the Net*. Both these novels, the work of writers under thirty, had been grouped with Amis' and achieved a comparable celebrity. Wain's hero was a young provincial iconoclast whose occupations included, at various times, window-cleaning and dope-running: Miss Murdoch's was an aimless pub-crawler with a mordant sense of humour and a talent for sponging. Both were obvious forerunners of Jimmy Porter. All the same, to most of the London critics he was a new and unheard-of disease. They reacted to the play with flustered disapproval; while acknowledging Osborne's command of dialogue, they dismissed his hero as "a young pup."

The salient thing about Jimmy Porter was that we—the under-thirty generation in Britain—recognised him on sight. We had met him; we had pub-crawled with him; we had shared bed-sitting-rooms with him. For the first time the theatre was speaking to us in our own language, on our own terms. Most young people had hitherto regarded the English theatre as a dusty anachronism which, as Dylan Thomas said of a certain Welsh museum, ought to be in a museum. Osborne showed them their error; and some of them even began to write plays.

The under-thirties responded to many qualities in Jimmy Porter—his impulsive, unargued leftishness, his anarchic sense of humour, and his suspicion that all the brave causes had been either won or discredited. For too long British culture had languished in a freezing-unit of understatement and "good taste." In these chill latitudes Jimmy Porter flamed like a blowtorch. He was not, like Jean Cocteau, *"trop occupé pour être engagé";* he cared, and cared bitterly. On the one hand, he represented the dismay of many young Britons whose childhood and adolescence were scarred by the depression and the war; who came of age under a Socialist government, yet found, when they went out into the world, that the class system was still mysteriously intact. On the other hand, he reflected the much wider problem of what to do with a liberal education in a technological world. In Britain, as elsewhere, the men who count are the technocrats of whom Sir Charles Snow writes. Jimmy Porter's education fitted him for entry into the intelligentsia at the very moment when the intelligentsia were ceasing to matter. He lurks, a ghostly, snarling dodo, in the scientists' shadow.

In Europe as on Broadway, it is difficult to escape *Look Back in Anger*. Nearly every repertory company in Britain has performed it, and it is being played all over Germany and Scandinavia. Osborne followed it up in 1957 with another hit, *The Entertainer,* which repercussed almost as widely. In just eighteen months an obscure repertory actor had become one of the most prosperous playwrights of the century, with a weekly income in the neighbourhood of £3,500. Osborne married his leading lady, Mary Ure, and moved into a smart little Chelsea backwater, at least a class and a half above Fulham, the suburb of his birth, where he and his mother (a contented barmaid) at one time subsisted on a joint income of less than a pound a week. Once, as a boy, he was out walking with his grandfather, who surprised him by indignantly cutting a passer-by who greeted them. "That man's a Socialist," said grandfather in explanation. "That's a man who doesn't believe in raising his hat." Osborne has never found a better definition of his own Socialism: its emblem is an untugged forelock rampant. When a master slapped his face at school, he at once riposted by slapping the master; and this, in Britain, takes preternatural guts.

He is passionate in his refusal to venerate what he calls "the idiot heroes" of patriotic movies; and his fervent republicanism recently led him to describe the British royal family as "the gold filling in a mouthful of decay." He will probably always be a bad belonger, to any party or group; his real talent is for dissent. But when his enemies complain that all his opinions are negative, I think they forget that nowadays there is a positive value in merely standing against a current of events which you believe is moving towards suicide. Osborne is a disconcerting, rather impenetrable person to meet: tall and slim, wearing his shoulders in a defensive bunch around his neck; gentle in manner, yet vocally harsh and cawing; sharp-toothed, yet a convinced vegetarian. He looks wan and driven, and is nervously prone to indulge in sudden, wolfish, silly-ass grins. Sartorially he is something of a peacock, and his sideburns add a sinister touch of the Apache. A dandy, if you like: but a dandy with a machine-gun.

Unlike Jimmy Porter, Osborne never went to a university. This is about all he has in common with Colin Wilson, the brash young metaphysical whose first book, *The Outsider,* was hailed as a masterpiece by several middle-aged critics who saw in its philosophy of salvation through despair an antidote to their own disillusion. Although a playwright can get along without the disciplines of higher education, a philosopher cannot, as Wilson's book awfully proved. As one ploughed through its inconsistencies, repetitions, and flights of paranoid illogic (an experience rather like walking knee-deep in hot sand), all one could state with any certainty was that an "outsider" was anyone whose books happened to have been on the author's recent library list. "We read Anatole France," said a French critic, "to find out what Anatole France has been reading"; and the same is true of Wilson. He was angry, all right, but his anger was more presumptuously cosmic than that of Osborne and the rest. For him we were not just misguided: we were rotten to the core. As far as I could make out, Wilson's philosophic position was somewhere between existentialism and Norman Vincent Peale; but his talk of a spiritual revival, with an élite of outsiders leading the world out of chaos, exerted a hypnotic charm on the lonely and maladjusted, who are always enticed by the promise of words like élite. Shaw was posthumously enrolled in the cult: not Shaw the Fabian Socialist and wit, but that later, lesser Shaw whose belief in the "life force" led him to condone dictatorship. This, cried Wilson, was the greatest religious thinker of modern times.

In 1957, fresh from unsuccessful flirtations with acting and playwriting, a twenty-four-year-old Yorkshireman named Stuart Holroyd climbed on the Bund-wagon by writing a philosophical work called *Emergence from Chaos,* which more or less followed the Wilson line. According to Holroyd, democracy was "a myth" and government was best left to "an expert minority"; but by now it was beginning to dawn on many people that such ideas, if not consciously fascist, were certainly the soil in which fascism grew. Wilson's second book, *Religion and the Rebel,* appeared last autumn. It proved to be a road-company version of the first, and was obliteratingly panned.

Not all the prominent young Britons of today are self-taught. Many of them were at Oxford when I was there, during the four years immediately after the war. As undergraduate generations go, it was disorderly and a bit piratical, but full of gusto and wildfire. There was plenty of gaiety about, but not of the fox-hunting, cork-popping, bounder-debagging kind that followed World War I; most of the new undergraduates were ex-servicemen living on government grants, for whom upper-class prankishness held very little appeal. Kingsley Amis and John Wain both come from the Oxford of that period. Neither of them had an Oxford accent, which is ordinary speech pushed through a constipated flute: that sort of "poshness" was emphatically out. Both Amis and Wain were (and are) poets and critics as well as novelists, and after graduation both taught at provincial universities; and it is this all-round academicism that makes their writing at once saner and tamer than, for instance, Osborne's. Another post-war Oxonian was Lindsay Anderson, whose anger with the *status quo* has not been off the boil for at least ten years. A formidable film critic, director, and polemicist, he has done more than anyone else to bring the idea of "committed art" into public controversy. Many Continental critics today speak of Anderson as if he were the dominant force in British cinema. According to one reporter, the party thrown by Mike Todd after the Cannes *première* of *Around the World in Eighty Days* was entirely made up of people anxiously whispering, in eighteen languages: "Lindsay didn't like it." He won an Academy Award in 1955 for *Thursday's Children,* a documentary about the education of deaf-mutes, and a Venice Grand Prix two years later for a forty-minute exploration of life in Covent Garden market; and though he has yet to make a feature film, his position as a critical moralist and spokesman for life-embracing cinema is unique in Britain. Quite apart from its A.Y.M.'s, the post-war Oxford vintage was a heady one. It also produced Tony Richardson, who directed both of Osborne's plays in London and on Broadway; Sandy Wilson, author of *The Boy Friend,* the most successful of post-war British musicals; and Roger Bannister, the first four-minute miler. In Labour politics it turned out the virulent back-bencher Anthony Wedgwood Benn; and on the Tory side, Sir Edward Boyle, who was the youngest member of the Eden cabinet when he resigned as a protest against the Franco-British invasion of Egypt.

The flag-wagging, wog-flogging assault on Suez was a great promoter of anger. Passions long thought extinct flared everywhere; people who had prided themselves on their detachment suddenly found themselves clobbering their best friends. Reasonably enough, those who were anti-Suez also tended to be supporters of *Look Back in Anger*. In the heat of the crisis, while smoke-bombs were bursting in Downing Street and mounted police charged the crowds in Whitehall, Osborne conceived his second play, *The Entertainer*. When it opened last April, the leading role was played—and played to the hilt—by Sir Laurence Olivier. Significantly, it was he who approached Osborne for a part, presumably on the principle of joining what you can't lick. This was the Establishment's first bow to the "angries." It meant that they had officially arrived.

It also established the Royal Court Theatre as the home of forward-looking British drama. Angus Wilson's first play had its London *première* there; so did Nigel Dennis' Swiftian satire, *Cards of Identity,* and the same author's furious parable, *The Making of Moo,* which is the only overtly atheistic play in the English language. Newcomers like Michael Hastings, the ambitious East End teen-ager, saw their work conscientiously staged; and the whole venture throve, and thrives still, in a heady intellectual ferment. Its fiscal keystone, however, was Osborne, who has proved against all augury that you can make a fortune by telling an audience the very things about itself that it wants least to hear.

On the other side of the Thames the National Film Theatre has developed into a comparable oasis of progressive cinema, with the pugnacious film magazine *Sight and Sound* acting as its ally and interpreter. Nor have I yet mentioned such associated phenomena as the rhetorical left-wing poet Christopher Logue or the stoutly committed art critic John Berger, whose influence on the graphic arts is roughly commensurate with Lindsay Anderson's on the cinema.

The newest angry is a fleshy Yorkshireman named John Braine, whose novel *Room at the Top,* an analysis of the means used by an amoral young opportunist to break into the upper stratum of provincial society, was among the larger English best-sellers of 1957. Shrewd and deliberate of speech, Braine has the stamina of a youthful J. B. Priestley, plus a vein of bizarre, unfettered humour that will probably seep into his next novel: its title, *The Vodi,* is the name of a monumentally batty secret society which has figured in his private fantasies for many years. He is at heart a plain old-fashioned Socialist with a common-sense regional brogue, but there is wildness in his background. He was connected, during the war, with a mildly anarchist group in Yorkshire that published a mimeographed broadsheet with an unprintable name. (One of its members, hating regimentation, gathered together a number of cans and fixed them with wire to selected lamp-posts in the town where he lived. On each can he painted the words: "Please put your Identity Cards in here." Before the police removed the cans he had collected, and subsequently burned, nearly five thousand cards.)

Braine exudes ambition and may easily outlast many of his fellow angries. His egotism is extremely disarming. After a long conversation some months ago he warned me not to be surprised if much of our talk turned up in his next book. "And if you complain of being plagiarised," he said gustily, with his little finger admonitorily raised, "I shall expose you to the world as one who tried to climb to fame on the back of that colossus of letters—*Braine.*"

In many directions, a lot of unequal talent is exploding. Certain things, however, seem to be agreed on, certain attitudes towards the relationship of the arts to living. The ivory tower has collapsed for good.

The lofty, lapidary, "mandarin" style of writing has been replaced by prose that has its feet on the ground. And the word "civilised," which had come to mean "detached, polite, above the tumult," is being restored to its old etymological meaning: to be civilised nowadays is to care about society and to feel oneself a responsible part of it. The books, plays, poems, films, and paintings that the young Britons are trying to turn out may well be ham-fisted and un-Englishly crude, but they will be based on the idea that art is an influence on life, not a refuge from it or an alternative to it. That, really, is what the anger is all about. It is anger that our kind of world is so chary of that kind of art.

If you object that you have heard this sort of thing before, I urge you to remember that the day you stop hearing it will be the day on which art shrugs its shoulders, gives up the ghost, and dies. Britain's angry young men may be jejune and strident, but they are involved in the only belief that matters: that life begins tomorrow.

(1958)

A Resounding Tinkle, BY N. F. SIMPSON, AT THE ROYAL COURT.

About the highest tribute I can pay N. F. Simpson's *A Resounding Tinkle,* which was tried out at the Royal Court last Sunday, is to say that it does not belong in the English theatrical tradition at all. It derives from the best Benchley lectures, the wildest Thurber cartoons, and the cream of the Goon Shows. It has some affinities with the early revues of Robert Dhéry and many more with the plays of M. Ionesco. In English drama it is, as far as I know, unique. It is also astonishingly funny, and a superb vindication of the judicial acumen that placed it third in *The Observer* play competition.

To sustain anarchic humour for a full evening is among the hardest things a playwright can attempt. Once having espoused the illogical, the irrelevant, the surreal, he is committed: a single lapse into logic, relevance, or reality, and he is undone. A playwright of Mr. Simpson's kind comes defenceless to the theatre. He has voluntarily discarded most of the dramatist's conventional weapons. He can have no plot, since plots demand logical development. Lacking a plot, he can make no use of suspense, that miraculous device which, by focusing our attention on what is going to happen next, prevents us from being intelligently critical of what is happening now. Mr. Simpson can never free-wheel like that. At every turn he must take us by surprise. His method must be a perpetual ambush. All playwrights must invent, but he must invent incessantly and unpredictably. It is the only weapon left him—he is otherwise naked. As naked, perhaps, as a British Foreign Secretary without an H-bomb; yet unilateral disarmament, even in the theatre, is an extremely disarming thing. At least, the audience seemed to find it so.

What they saw, hilarious though it was, notably differed from the play to which we of *The Observer* awarded the prize. Mr. Simpson had revised and reshuffled it, and there were moments when I felt like the American director who, revisiting one of his old productions, found it necessary to call an immediate rehearsal "to take out the improvements." The original text began in the suburban home of Bro and Middie Paradock, a young married couple disturbed by the presence, in their front garden, of an elephant they had not ordered. The question soon arose of how to name it. Middie conservatively favoured "Mr. Trench," their usual name for unexpectedly delivered animals, a suggestion which the radical Bro countered with bravura alternatives such as " 'Tis-Pity-She's-A-Whore Hignett." The debate was interrupted by the arrival of two Comedians, who were lodged in the kitchen, from which they emerged from time to time to discuss, with examples, the nature of comedy. This arrangement set up what I may call, with a deep breath, a sort of counterpoint. Mr. Simpson has since decided to lump all the Comedian scenes together into his first act, while reserving the Paradock scenes for the second. I take this to be a back-breaking error, and when the English Stage Company decides (as it surely must) to put on the play for a run, I hope it will amalgamate the two texts and insist on a new ending.

Even as it stands, this is a revolutionarily funny piece of work. In a programme note Mr. Simpson declares his indebtedness to the simple fact that the earth, given luck, can support life for another twelve hundred thousand years. How, for so long, are we to keep ourselves amused? This is the problem that faced the tramps in *Waiting for Godot.* An astonished patience is Mr. Simpson's answer, as he implies when one of the Comedians doubts the audience's ability to sit through a play full of pauses and the other replies by asking him whether he has ever complained of buying a sponge full of holes.

I prefer Mr. Simpson's assumption, which is that we are all on the brink of boredom, to that of most comic writers, which is that we are all on the brink of hilarity. Bro Paradock (Nigel Davenport) is a splendidly sour creation, drab, leather-elbowed, and disgruntled, comic because he reacts with no surprise to circumstances of absolute fantasy. Neither he nor his wife, Middie (Wendy Craig, a pretty study of controlled disgust), is perturbed when their Uncle Ted turns out to be a woman; and he has nothing but quiet scorn for the man who calls and asks him, at six o'clock in the evening, to form a Government. (As he says, that's the Prime Minister's job.)

About a fifth of Mr. Simpson's family portrait is *voulu,* polysyllabic, and of a determined quaintness. The rest is pure plutonium, by which I mean something that is rarer than gold.

(1957)

Hazards of Playgoing.

There are a good many inconveniences attached to the simple act of going to a theatre. The greatest of these is usually the play itself, and on this most critics rightly concentrate. In an empty week, however, I have been pondering those minor irritations, peas under the mattress, that ought to be removed if playgoing is to take its proper place among life's softer options.

One such pea, in London at least, is the difficulty of finding out what theatre is housing the play you want to see. The list of attractions used by West End managers to advertise their wares in the newspapers is primarily a list of theatres, not of plays. If your choice is *Divorce Me, Darling,* you may have to run through the names of forty playhouses before finding what you want. In New York you would simply look under "D," and there, after *Dig My Gallows Deep* and before *Dreyfus and Son,* it would be, followed by the name and address of the theatre. The London system harks back to the days of the actor-managers, when you went to the Lyceum to see Irving without caring very much what you were going to see him in. Nowadays, when the play and not the playhouse is the thing, the New York arrangement is clearly more sensible.

Having identified the theatre, you next have to get there. Here London has the advantage of both Paris and New York, especially if you travel by taxi. Seen from the air around curtain-time, Broadway resembles a war of caterpillars; rows of cabs, minutely jerking forwards, clog the whole area. In Paris, of course, all taxis vanish from the streets for half an hour before the curtain goes up. You occasionally catch sight of one roaring out to keep a date with destiny or dinner at Courbevoie, but the chance of its stopping is remote; the most you can expect is a tragic shrug from the driver as he flashes by, the slave of fate or his stomach.

Assuming you arrive at the theatre, you must then dispose of your coat. You will almost certainly be wearing one. Indoor drama thrives only in cold weather; few people in hot climates would be foolish enough to spend a whole evening indoors with neither wine nor words on their lips. The cloakrooms of most London theatres are mere holes in the wall, wardrobes occupied by five hundred coats and one human being, and it is amazing that M. Ionesco has not written a play about them. Berlin and Moscow are the only cities known to me that have solved the garment-reclaiming problem. At the Schiller-Theater in Berlin there are two long walls of cloakrooms in the foyer, staffed by twenty attendants, and the same is true of the Moscow Art.

The scandal of London theatre programmes is notorious and seemingly incurable. Whenever I watch British audiences happily paying sixpence for eight pages of text, six of which are devoted to advertisements, a quotation from Brecht leaps to my mind: "I can see their divine patience, but where is their divine fury?" In Paris, at the very least, you get a little booklet for your money; and in New York you get a rather larger booklet for nothing. *Playbill,* the Broadway programme, is published and edited by a private company; it is in fact a forty-page weekly magazine, with critical articles on international drama, and full biographies of the author, director, and actors. The only London theatre to have taken even a tentative step in this direction is the Westminster, where the programmes tell you not only who the actors are but where you last saw them. Unfortunately, in many of the plays produced at this theatre the information is not encouraging.

Interval amenities vary from capital to capital. In New York (as in Paris) I tend to doze, drugged by the heat: the reviving draughts that sweep across London theatres are unknown in these upholstered ovens. The New Yorkers themselves, forbidden liquor in theatres, obey laconic commands to "get your orange drinks, get your refreshing orange drinks." The French make unhurried bee-lines for the longest, best-stocked theatre bars on earth. Meanwhile the Englishman is barking his elbows in a tiny, thronged snuggery where warm gin is dispensed by surly, glaring, female teetotallers.

The final hazard of London playgoing is the playing of the National Anthem, during which we stand to attention, while gloves, scarves, and programmes fall unregarded to the floor. This compulsive display of patriotism (unknown outside Britain and the Commonwealth) is today almost classifiable as a game. People with at least one hand on the exit-door when the drum-roll begins are held to be exempt from standing through Dr. Bull's little melody. The rest must stay rooted to the spot, staring vaingloriously at the curtain; if they move, some undefined forfeit is payable.

Only two British theatres have departed from this nightly habit of sending the Queen happy. One is Theatre Workshop, where (says the programme) "the National Anthem will be played only in the presence of royalty or heads of States." The other is the Royal Opera House, Covent Garden, where it is played once a year, at the beginning of the season. This seems a sane procedure. I might add that royalist hymns can be extremely irksome to foreigners. Some years ago the Americans in the London production of *Guys and Dolls* were requested to sing the anthem after the opening performance. All agreed except one, who shook his head and said: "It ain't my toon." Besought to change his mind, he declined. "It's a matter of principle," he said. "I'm for the people. *They* oughta get sent."

One thing about the London theatre, though: you can get into it. Contrast this with the Palais de Chaillot in Paris, the home of the Théâtre National Populaire and the most impenetrable playhouse on earth. You have, let us say, booked a seat and go to the *contrôle* to collect it. But no, this is the agency *contrôle;* you must go to the other, which handles private reservations. You sprint across, while a voice barks through a loudspeaker that unless you take your seat in three minutes you will be excluded from the performance.

You seize your ticket and dart (*"Deux minutes"*) towards the escalator that leads to the vast subterranean auditorium. You scuttle, skidding, down two marble staircases (*"Une minute"*), whereupon the full Kafkaesque horror is unleashed on you: not a warning bell, but a deafening fanfare of hunting horns blares out of the wall at your ear. You run along echoing corridors, to cries of *"Au bout, monsieur, et puis à gauche."* More trumpets shriek, and you fling yourself into your seat. Ten minutes pass, during which nothing happens. At length the curtain rises and you realise, too late, that you have no programme.

(1958)

The Iceman Cometh, BY EUGENE O'NEILL, AT THE ARTS; *Cat on a Hot Tin Roof*, BY TENNESSEE WILLIAMS, AT THE COMEDY.

Paul Valéry once defined the true snob as a man who was afraid to admit that he was bored when he was bored; and he would be a king of snobs indeed who failed to admit to a *mauvais quart d'heure* about halfway through *The Iceman Cometh.* But perhaps, as a colleague suggests, all great art should be slightly boring. A vast structure is to be built, and in the long process there are bound to be moments of tedium: they are the price we pay for size and splendour, and we pay it gladly once the architect has convinced us that we can trust him. O'Neill convinced last Wednesday's audience in thirty minutes flat, after which no doubts remained. This was no crank, planning a folly dependent on sky-hooks: we were safe in the hands of the American theatre's nearest counterpart to Frank Lloyd Wright.

But how did he hold us in our seats through four hours and more of circular alcoholic conversation? By means of verbal magic? I think not. O'Neill writes clumsily and top-heavily. He never achieves the luminous, crystallising phrase, nor has he the opposite virtue of earthy authenticity: his gin-mill dialogue has the stagey swagger of melodrama. If it isn't the language, then, is it the universality of the theme? Again, no. Most of the characters are special cases, confirmed alcoholics out of touch with any kind of reality that cannot be bottled. When Hickey, the reformed drunk, urges these red-eyed wet-brains to abandon their pipe-dreams and face the truth about themselves, we know that the cure will kill them; but we cannot relate this knowledge to our own lives as we can, for instance, when Gregers Werle strips Ekdal of his illusions in *The Wild Duck*. Many of us, like Ekdal, have a dark-room of the soul where we develop dreams that the light of day would obliterate. But very few of us actually live in the dark-room, so enslaved to our fantasies that we would rather have D.T.'s than give them up.

No, what holds us about the play is the insight it gives us into O'Neill himself. It is a dramatised neurosis, with no holds barred, written in a vein of unsparing, implacable honesty. "Speak, that I may see thee," said Ben Jonson; and when O'Neill speaks, he hides nothing. Instead of listening to a story, we are shaking hands with a man, and a man whose vision of life is as profoundly dark as any since Aeschylus. It is this autobiographical intensity that grips us throughout the *longueurs* of the narrative and the gawkiness (I had almost said Gorkiness) of the style. For O'Neill, a pipe-dream is not just one alternative to despair: it is the only alternative. His bar-room derelicts comfort and sustain one another as long as each tolerates the others' illusions. Once Hickey has removed the illusions, nothing remains but guilt and mutual accusation. One may not agree with O'Neill's conclusions, but one cannot escape the look in his eye, which is as magnetic as the Ancient Mariner's. He speaks like a man who has touched bottom himself; for whom words like "inferior" no longer have meaning. He is one of the few writers who can enter, without condescension or contempt, the world of those whom the world has rejected.

The play demands and gets superb direction. Peter Wood's production is better in many respects than the New York version I saw and admired last spring. Like all good directors, Mr. Wood is loyal to the text; he is also constructively disloyal to the hysterical punctuation and overheated stage-directions of which American playwrights are so fond. His cast deserves individual attention. Nicholas Meredith plays a cashiered Blimp, making a character out of a caricature by discreet understatement; Lee Montague is funny, dour, and truthful as an Italian barkeep who cannot bring himself to admit that he is also a pimp; and Jack MacGowran, pinch-faced and baggy-trousered, plays the tetchy proprietor with a weasel brilliance I have not seen since the heyday of F. J. McCormick. In the sketchily written role of a drunken Harvard alumnus, Michael Bryant gets closer to the raw nerve of reality than any West End débutant I can remember. The pale, shaky smile, the carefully preserved sophistication, the glib, hectic delivery all converge to make a rounded, original whole, half clown, half martyr.

Of the three central characters, Patrick Magee does not quite get the rock-sombre melancholy of Larry, the disgusted nihilist who has deserted anarchism for drink; but the other two are perfect—Vivian Matalon as a guilty young stool-pigeon, pathetically ripe for suicide, and Ian Bannen, as Hickey, the manic salesman, driving his friends to destruction with the enthusiasm of a revivalist. I winced a bit at the Kensington cosiness of Mr. Wood's three waterfront tarts. Otherwise, the production is flawless. It makes a wonderful worrying evening.

By a useful coincidence, *Cat on a Hot Tin Roof* also explores the impact of truth on illusion, the difference being that where O'Neill thinks pipe-dreams necessary, Tennessee Williams condemns them under the generic heading of "mendacity." A world war separates the two plays. In jazz terms, *The Iceman Cometh* (1939) is a collective improvisation on a traditional blues theme. *Cat on a Hot Tin Roof* (1954) belongs to the modernist school, its three acts being in essence three long introspective solos (by, respectively, Maggie, Big Daddy, and Big Mama), accompanied throughout by the ground-bass of Brick's pervasive melancholy.

The first act lays bare a breaking marriage: Brick, the liquor-loving son of a Southern millionaire, can no longer sleep with Maggie, his wife. The second act tells us why, in the course of a scorching duologue between father and son which reveals that Brick is a latent homosexual, consumed with guilt because he spurned a college friend who loved him and died, shortly after the spurning, of drink. Brutally reacting to this harsh dose of truth, Brick ripostes in kind, and Big Daddy learns what the rest of the family already knows: that he is suffering from inoperable cancer. In the last act the relations gather round Big Mama to batten on the inheritance. Maggie wins it by pretending to be pregnant. To support her lie, Brick must sleep with her; and thus mendacity breeds mendacity.

A magnificent play: but modern jazz, to pursue the metaphor, calls for much greater technical virtuosity than Dixieland. Williams' quasi-tragedy needs superlative soloists, superlatively directed. After seeing Peter Hall's production I feel I owe an apology to Elia Kazan. I still prefer the author's third act (here played for the first time) to the modified version approved by Mr. Kazan; but I missed, more than I would ever have thought possible, the galvanic inspiration of Mr. Kazan's direction. Mr. Hall's pace is lethargic: he stresses everything except what needs stressing. General sloth may account for the cutting of (among others) Big Daddy's best speech; but I cannot think what could account for the omission of the play's last vital line, in which Brick ironically queries Maggie's protestations of love, unless it was the inadequacy of the actor playing the part. Paul Massie, to whom I refer, is callow and absurdly unprepared for a searching test like Brick. All the same, he ought to have been allowed to utter, however lamely, the final clinching statement of the play.

Leo McKern, with crudely padded shoulders, uses enormous vocal exertions to become Big Daddy; but the more he tries, the more he fails, for the whole point about the character is that his cynical, animal zest should flow without effort. Which leaves us with Kim Stanley, the gifted Broadway actress who plays Maggie the Cat. Miss Stanley has all the qualities for the part, an anxious lyricism, a limpid voice, tear-puffed eyes, and indomitable gallantry; but, as pregnant women are said to be eating for two, she found herself quite early on acting for four. It was like watching a first-rate squash player hammering away at a court without walls.

(1958)

Epitaph for George Dillon, BY JOHN OSBORNE AND ANTHONY CREIGHTON, AT THE ROYAL COURT.

The second act of *Epitaph for George Dillon,* written four years ago by John Osborne and Anthony Creighton, contains a long duologue which in terms of human contact and mutual exploration is better than anything in Mr. Osborne's later unaided works. One of the participants

Dillon himself, a *farouche* young actor-dramatist currently sponging on a suburban family straight out of Mr. Coward's *Fumed Oak.* (Subject for a thesis: estimate the influence on Mr. Osborne's later plays of *The Vortex* and *Red Peppers,* also bearing in mind that the dismissive use of "little," favoured by Mr. Osborne in a plethora of phrases beginning "nasty little," "feeble little," "sordid little," etc., was pioneered by Mr. Coward in the twenties.) Dillon has walked out on his wife, a prosperous actress whom he venomously accuses, *à la* Jimmy Porter, of having "betrayed" him. In his new suburban bolt-hole he meets, as Jimmy never did, his intellectual match.

This is Aunt Ruth, the family outsider, whose life has hit the emotional doldrums. She has just ended two affairs, one of them with Communism and the other with a young writer skilled in the neurotic art of extorting love by means of pathos. The job of playing Marchbanks to her Candida is temporarily vacant. George volunteers for the part, and the scene in which they come to grips (or, rather, fail to come to grips) is an object lesson in meaty, muscular, dramatic writing.

Ruth, the born giver, slowly recognises in George a born taker. He savages her cliché-ridden family, whom he regards as part of a universal conspiracy to destroy him. "I attract hostility," he declares in a paranoid ecstasy, "I'm on heat for it." (Note the female sexual image: one would love to let a good analyst loose on George.) Whenever he goes too far, he resorts to spasms of little-boy charm and bursts of comic improvisation; but though Ruth laughs with him and is sorry for him, she has lived through such scenes before. No more of that sickness for her; no more diving to the rescue of people who scream for help while lying in puddles, achieving by the pretense of drowning a voluptuous fusion of self-pity and power over others. George's only justification for his behaviour is his talent. But where, as Ruth piercingly reminds him, is the evidence that he has any talent at all? And at length George admits to a terrible doubt. He has all the popular symptoms of genius, but perhaps not the disease itself. The admission, however, cuts no ice with Ruth, and George has to console himself by jumping into bed with her teen-age niece.

Up to this point, apart from a few glaring crudities in the handling of flashbacks, the play is entirely successful—powerful, honest, and transfixing. The spirit of suburbia is lovingly captured in Stephen Doncaster's setting and the performances of Alison Leggatt, Wendy Craig, and especially Avril Elgar, whose dowdy spinster daughter, merry as a jerboa, is twin sister to Alec Guinness' unforgotten Abel Drugger. William Gaskill's direction drives shrewdly throughout.

Yvonne Mitchell, though she lacks the years for the part, plays Ruth with a steely, sad directness that is exactly right; and one could not wish for a better George than Robert Stephens, one of the new "red-brick actors," neither actorish in aspect nor conventionally po-voiced, to whom the English Stage Company has introduced us. Mr. Stephens makes George both wolfish and wan, and there is in his voice a cawing note that may even have been modelled on Mr. Osborne himself. This is the cleverest portrait I have seen of a certain kind of neurotic artist.

But what kind? Good or bad? And this is where the authors let us down. In the third act George makes one of his plays a provincial hit by spiking it with sex; simultaneously he recovers from an attack of T.B. and agrees to marry Ruth's niece, who is pregnant by him. He ends in tears. But are they the tears of a good writer frustrated by the commercial theatre and suburban morality? Or the tears of a bad writer who has at last met himself face to face? We are given no clue. If George is seriously intended to be a persecuted genius, then the whole play, not just the hero, is paranoid to the point of hysteria. If, on the other hand, he is a mediocre writer forced at length to accept his own mediocrity, it is a play of astounding courage and strength. The authors shrug and allow us to guess which answer is right, which is as if one were to write a play about the crucifixion of a miracle healer without giving the smallest hint as to whether the cures worked. Have we been rooting for a phoney or the real thing? The mere fact of doubt indicates that the play has misfired. Yet the fire is there, boiling and licking, however neurotically; and you must not miss that second act.

(1958)

The Potting Shed, BY GRAHAM GREENE, AT THE GLOBE.

The time is ten years hence, a decade after the London opening of Graham Greene's *The Potting Shed*. A Failed Drama Critic lies abed in his dingy lodgings, up to here in Scotch. Around him are the bleak and grimy symbols of his faith—the cobwebbed bust of Brecht, the mildewed model of the National Theatre, the yellowing autograph of Stanislavsky, the drab little pot of clotted Eulogy, the rusty Panning Pen. He looks somehow void and empty, though of course, as we know, he is up to here. A young Psychiatrist is interrogating him.

P.: But in that case why do you still go to the theatre?

C. (*simply, if indistinctly*): It's my job. Once a critic, always a critic. It's my half of the promise. Sometimes I fall down during the Anthem and disappear for acts on end, and then they have to take my pen away for a while. But I always come back. The people need critics, and a whisky-critic's better than none.

P.: Even if he's lost his vocation?

C.: Even then. But don't misunderstand me. I'm not a bad critic. I go through the motions. I get out of bed every day at seven o'clock in the evening and go to the theatre. Sometimes there isn't a play on, but I go anyway, in case I'm needed. It's a matter of conscience. Have another slug of fire-water.

P.: Not just now. Can you remember exactly where you lost your faith? When did you last have it with you?

C.: I didn't lose it. It was taken away from me one night ten years ago at the old Globe Theatre, before they turned it into a car-park. John Gielgud was in the play. Very wrought-up he was, very curt and brusque—you know how he used to talk to other actors as if he was going to tip them? Irene Worth played his ex-wife. Then there was Gwen Ffrangcon-Davies, very fierce, and a clever little pouter called Sarah Long. And Redmond Phillips—he played a frocked sot on the brink of the shakes. He was the best of a fine lot. No, you couldn't complain about the acting. But somehow that made it worse. (*He sobs controllably.*)

P. (*controllingly*): Tell me about the play. Force yourself back into the theatre. Slump now as you slumped then in D16.

C. (*in a hoarse whisper*): Graham Greene wrote it. It began with the death of a famous atheist, head of a rationalist clan. Greene made them out to be a bunch of decrepit puritans, so old-fashioned that they even enjoyed the company of dowdy dullards like Bertrand Russell. But fair enough: Greene's a Catholic, and the history of Catholicism shows that you can't make an omelette without breaking eggheads. Anti-intellectual jokes are part of the recipe. At first I thought I was in for a whodunit. The old man's son—Sir John—was kept away from the deathbed because of something nameless that had happened to him in the potting shed at the age of fourteen. There were clues all over the place. For one thing, he had recently lost his dog. . . .

P. (*shrewdly*): Dog is God spelled backwards.

C.: The same crude thought occurred to me, but I rejected it (pity my complexity) as being unworthy of the author. How wrong I was! The hero's subsequent investigations into his past revealed that we were indeed dealing not with a whodunit but a God-dunit. He had hanged himself in the dread shed, and demonstrably died. And his uncle, the priest, had begged God to revive him. Make me an offer, haggled the Deity. My faith in exchange for the boy's life, said the priest:

and so the repulsive bargain was struck. The boy lived, and uncle lost his faith. My first impulse on hearing these farcical revelations was to protest by the only means at my disposal: a derisive hiccup. But then I looked about me and saw row after row of rapt, attentive faces. *They were taking it seriously!* And suddenly, in a blaze of darkness, I knew that my faith in the theatre and the people who attend it had been withdrawn from me.

P.: But why?

C.: You may not now remember the theatre as it was ten years ago. It seemed on the brink of renaissance. I was one of many who were newly flushed with a great conviction. We recklessly believed that a theatre was a place where human problems could be stated in human terms, a place from which supernatural intervention as a solution to such problems had at long last been ousted. Drama for us was an affirmation of humanism, and its basic maxim was not: "I die that you may live," but: "I *live* that you may live." *The Potting Shed,* financed by two normally intelligent managements at a highly reputable theatre, shot us back overnight to the dark ages.

P.: But what about Gibbon? "The Catholic superstition, which is always the enemy of reason, is often the parent of the arts"?

C.: Art that is not allied with reason is today the enemy of life. And now you must excuse me. You have kept me in bed long after my usual time for getting up. And I have a first-night to attend. The play, I understand, is a fearless indictment of a priest who refuses to accompany a murderer to the scaffold because of stupid, heretical, rationalist doubts about the efficacy of prayer to bring the man back to life. The bounder will no doubt be shown his error. Meanwhile (*he takes a deep draught of red-eye*), here's to good old G.G.! Who said the Pope had no divisions? (*He departs, half-clad and half-cut, to perform in a spirit of obedient humility the offices laid down for him by providence and the Society of West End Theatre Managers.*)

(1958)

A Resounding Tinkle AND *The Hole*, BY N. F. SIMPSON, AT THE ROYAL COURT.

Two years ago last Tuesday there was no English Stage Company. What a dull theatre we must have had! And what on earth did we playgoers find to argue about? After only two years I can scarcely remember the theatrical landscape as it was before George Devine set up shop in

Sloane Square and called in John Osborne, the Fulham flamethrower, to scald us with his rhetoric. The climate, on the whole, was listless. We quarrelled among ourselves over Brecht and the future of poetic drama; in debates with foreign visitors we crossed our fingers, swallowed hard, and talked of Terence Rattigan; but if we were critics, we must quite often have felt that we were practising our art in a vacuum.

In two years and twenty-eight productions the Royal Court has changed all that. To an extent unknown since the Ibsen riots, it has made drama a matter of public controversy. It has button-holed us with new voices, some of them bawdy, many of them irreverent, and all of them calculated to bring gooseflesh to the evening of Aunt Edna's life. It has raised hackles, Cain, laughs, and the standards of English dramaturgy. It has given the modern repertoire a permanent London address. At times, perhaps, it has appealed too exclusively to the *côterie*-votaries (Chelsea offshoots of the North American culture-vultures). Yet in spite of this it has reached out and captured popular audiences on television and Broadway and in the West End. Once or twice, quite spectacularly, the Court has fallen on its face, but this is one of the occupational hazards you must expect if you set out to climb mountains. For the most part it has given my mind a whetstone, and my job a meaning, that the English theatre of five years ago showed few signs of providing. If (and the if is crucial) it can hold its present nucleus of talent together, it may very well change the whole course of English drama.

It has celebrated its second birthday by giving us a present: a dazzling new playwright. On the strength of his double bill, *A Resounding Tinkle* and *The Hole,* I am ready to burn my boats and pronounce N. F. Simpson the most gifted comic writer the English stage has discovered since the war. The first of his two plays, which has been drastically cut and revised since it won a third prize in *The Observer* competition, I reviewed when the Court gave it a Sunday showing last year. I indicated its affinities with M. Ionesco, M. Dhéry, and the late Robert Benchley. I tried to explain how and why it had convulsed me, this casual surrealist sketch of a suburban couple with an elephant at their front door; and, had space allowed, I would have applied to Mr. Simpson what Sir Max Beerbohm said of humorists in general:

> The jester must be able to grapple his theme and hang on to it, twisting it this way and that, and making it yield magically all manner of strange and precious things, one after another, without pause. He must have invention keeping pace with utterance. He must be inexhaustible. Only so can he exhaust us.

But I wondered at the time how Mr. Simpson would follow his *tour de force*. Could he bring it off again without repeating himself? *The Hole* proved triumphantly that he could; that he was no mere flash in the pen, but a true lord of language, capable of using words with the sublime, outrageous authority of Humpty Dumpty.

People who believe with John Lehmann that English writers have lost interest in verbal and stylistic experiment should see Mr. Simpson's work and recant. Indeed, everyone should see it: for it is not a private highbrow joke, but pure farce, wild and liberated, on a level accessible to anyone who has ever enjoyed the radio Goons (Peter Sellers and Spike Milligan, especially) or treasured the memory of W. C. Fields. I suspect, in fact, that Goon-lovers, who are accustomed to verbal firework displays at which logic is burnt in effigy, may get more sheer pleasure out of Mr. Simpson than professional intellectuals, against whose habit of worrying about the meaning of things the play is essentially directed. At heart it is a riotous satire at the expense of people who deal in pigeonholes, categories, and generalisations, seeking to pin down to a consistent pattern the unrepeatable variety of human existence, working out comprehensive philosophic and religious systems in which somehow one vital thing gets forgotten: the glorious uniqueness of everything that is.

A tramp, who describes himself as "the nucleus of a queue," is peering into a hole in the road. Others join him, among them a rabid authoritarian, a drifting rubberneck, and a student philosopher: each has a fantastic vision of what is going on down the hole and tries to impose it on the others. They are interrupted, from time to time, by two housewives, one with a husband who desperately wants to be the same as everyone else ("There's nothing Sid wouldn't do to be *identical* with somebody"), the other with a husband who wants, equally desperately, to be different. . . . But here I must stop, for I am falling into the very trap Mr. Simpson has laid for us intellectuals. I am explaining instead of experiencing. And I am in danger of letting you forget that Mr. Simpson is ceaselessly, mortally, and unpredictably funny. With Michelet, he cries: *"Mon moi! Ils m'arrachent mon moi!"*—and if that is bourgeois individualism, long may it thrive.

(1958)

The Party, BY JANE ARDEN, AT THE NEW; *A Taste of Honey*, BY SHELAGH DELANEY, AT THE THEATRE ROYAL, STRATFORD-ATTE-BOWE.

In principle, it is an admirable thing for an established star to lend a helping hand to a struggling novice. In practice, however, everything depends on the nature of the grip. A helping hand can imperceptibly become a half-Nelson, and the newcomer may find himself in the position of the tragic mouse that was petted to death by John Steinbeck's Lennie. When this happens it is nobody's fault, since the star always means well, but it certainly makes life hard for the critic. Take, for example, Jane Arden's *The Party*.

As far as I could tell on Wednesday night, Miss Arden's play is a dim family drama which might, given shrewd casting, cohesive direction, and the immediate withdrawal of *Flowering Cherry,* have groped its way towards a modest but respectable success. It may have other qualities, such as a sense of place and a feeling for suburban reality; if so, they have perished at the over-zealous hands of Miss Arden's benefactor, Charles Laughton, to whose Lennie she plays mouse. Mr. Laughton's admiration for the play, though to my mind excessive, is clearly genuine—why else would he have chosen it to celebrate his return, as actor and director, to the West End theatre? Yet almost every step he takes, in either capacity, treads on the toes of its few, mild merits.

Mr. Laughton the actor is still what he always was: Mr. Laughton the outsize human being. Baby LeRoy with elephantiasis could not sulk more eloquently, and no player alive (with the possible exception of Robert Morley) knows more about the nuances of bluster. An expert at cringing and cajoling, he can make miracles of wit out of lines which in other mouths would seem mere explosions of petulance. But he is not a realist; and Miss Arden's play is nothing if not realistic. Mr. Laughton's role is that of a downtrodden Kilburn solicitor with a history of alcoholism, vaguely stemming from incestuous feelings towards his daughter, who despises him. His premature return from a mental home compels her to cancel her birthday party, lest he should get drunk and wreck it. An actor like Wilfrid Lawson might have made the man real, dangerous, and defeated, and shown us why the girl might fear him. Mr. Laughton offers neither danger nor defeat, just an extravagant booby harmlessly letting off steam. On top of this, he plays the part in a *faisandé* Cockney accent straight out of Bruce Bairnsfather's Old Bill cartoons. All of which is fascinating, but has nothing to do with solicitors, Kilburn, or observable reality.

Mr. Laughton the actor has not appeared in London for twenty-two years, and Mr. Laughton the director is here to prove it. The action seems to unfold in a timeless nowhere. The hero has a wife who speaks perfect Schools Programme English and is his junior by about twenty-five years, yet the disparities in age and accents are never even mentioned, let alone explained. They are broke, yet manage, with only one lodger, to run the kind of mansion, all bookcases and pale beaming, that you would expect a visiting film-star to take near Henley for the summer. Their closest friend is a rowdy coquette who talks like the late Suzette Tarri and owns what everyone weirdly calls "the nylon shop."

I do not blame Joyce Redman for making nothing of the wife; nothing, after all, will come of nothing; but Elsa Lanchester makes far too much of the nylon-huckster, and for this I blame Mr. Laughton. I blame him, too, for not having queried the feyness of the dialogue, and its lapses into idioms—like "to make over" in the sense of "to change"—that are blatantly American and oceans away from N.W.6. Most of the production is simply out of touch, not only with the play, but with English life in general.

This does not apply to Ann Lynn as the mutinous daughter (though her final reconciliation with dear old dad rings ruinously false), nor to Albert Finney, who has brought to London from Birmingham Rep those qualities of technical assurance and latent power that are the fruits of hard training and the buds of great acting. Mr. Finney, playing Miss Lynn's boy-friend, shares the best scene of the evening with Mr. Laughton, who rises like a salmon to the occasion: few young actors have ever got a better performance out of their director. But the cause as a whole is lost. It is too late now for anyone to come to the aid of *The Party*.

Miss Arden's heroine resents her soak of a father. Shelagh Delaney's heroine, in *A Taste of Honey,* resents her tart of a mother. And there the analogy ends, for Miss Delaney brings real people on to her stage, joking and flaring and scuffling and eventually, out of the zest for life she gives them, surviving. Suffering, she seems to say, need not be tragic; anguish need not be neurotic; we are all, and especially if we come from Lancashire, indestructible. If I tell you that the heroine was born of a haystack encounter between her mother and a mental defective; that a Negro sailor gets her pregnant and deserts her; and that she sets up house, when her mother marries a drunk, with a homosexual art student—when I tell you this, you may legitimately suspect that a tearful inferno of a play awaits you. Not a bit of it.

The first half is broad comedy (comedy, perhaps, is merely tragedy in which people don't give in); almost too breezily so; and Joan Littlewood's direction tilts it over into farce by making Avis Bunnage, as the girl's brassy mother, address herself directly to the audience, music-hall fashion. The second half is both comic and heroic. Rather than be lonely, the gusty young mother-to-be shares her room (though not her bed) with a skinny painter who enjoys mothering her and about whose sexual whims ("What d'you do? Go on—what d'you do?") she is uproariously curious. Together they have what amounts to an idyll, which is interrupted by mother's return with her puffy bridegroom, who likes older women and wears an eyepatch—this brings him, as he points out, at least halfway to Oedipus. By the end of the evening he has left, and so, without rancour, has the queer. A child is coming: as in many plays of this kind, life goes on. But not despondently: here it goes on bravely and self-reliantly, with a boisterous appetite for tomorrow.

Miss Delaney owes a great deal to Frances Cuka, her ribald young heroine, who embraces the part with a shock-haired careless passion that suggests an embryonic Anna Magnani. This is an actress with a lot of love to give. There are plenty of crudities in Miss Delaney's play: there is also, more importantly, the smell of living. When the theatre presents poor people as good, we call it "sentimental." When it presents them as wicked, we sniff and cry "squalid." Happily, Miss Delaney does not yet know about us and our squeamishness, which we think moral but which is really social. She is too busy recording the wonder of life as she lives it. There is plenty of time for her to worry over words like "form," which mean something, and concepts like "vulgarity," which don't. She is nineteen years old: and a portent.

(1958)

Variations on a Theme, BY TERENCE RATTIGAN, AT THE GLOBE.

Let us suppose that Terence Rattigan's Muse, a brisk, tweedy travelling representative of Thalia-Melpomene Co-Productions Ltd., has just returned home after four years' absence. We find her reading the reviews of Mr. Rattigan's *Variations on a Theme*. After a while she flings them impatiently down. Her tone, as she addresses us, is querulous:

MUSE: This would never have happened if I'd been here. We get *Separate Tables* launched, I go off on a world cruise, and as soon as my back's turned, what happens? He tries to write a play on his own. Oh, he's threatened to do that before now, but I've always scared him out of it. "Look what happened to Noël Coward," I'd say. *That* usually did the trick. "Just you wait till I'm ready," I'd say. "Inspiration doesn't grow on trees, you know." But Master Terence Slyboots knows better. Thinks you can write plays just like that, haha. The minute I heard what he was up to I came beetling back, but they were already in rehearsal.

"What's the meaning of this?" I said, and I can tell you I was blazing. "Well, darling," he said, "four years is a long time, and—" "Don't you darling me," I said. "I'm a busy Muse. I've got my other clients to consider. You're not the only pebble on the Non-Controversial Western Playwrights' beach, you know. Now let's get down to cases. What's this play about?" "Well," he said, "the central character, who's rich and bored and lives in a villa near Cannes, gets desperately fond of a cocky young boy from the local ballet company, and—" "Hold your horses," I said. "We've never had a play banned yet, and, by George, we're not starting now. Make it a cocky young *girl*." "The central character," he said, very hoity-toity, "is a *woman*."

Black mark to me, I must admit. But once I'd grabbed hold of the script and taken a good dekko at it, my worst fears were confirmed. About the best you could say about it was that it wouldn't be banned. This heroine (he calls her Rose Fish and then, if you please, makes jokes about whether or not she has gills) started out as a typist in Birmingham. She's married four men for money before she meets this ballet-boy. He's been keeping company with a male choreographer, but give the devil his due, Master Terence knows his Lord Chamberlain well enough to keep *that* relationship platonic.

Egged on by the choreographer, Rose gives the lad up for the good of his career. He reforms overnight, but returns to her just as she's in the last throes of succumbing to a wonky lung. And in case you haven't cottoned on to the fact that it's Marguérite Gautier all over again, Rose has a daughter whose pet author is Dumas *fils*. Master Terence makes no bones about his sources. Trouble is, he makes no flesh either. That's where I should have come in. Honestly, I could slap the scamp.

"Interesting subject, don't you think?" he said when I gave the script back to him. "No," I said, "but you've made a real Camille of it, haven't you?" He ignored my barbed word-play. Ruthlessly I pressed on. "Whatever became," I asked, "of that subtle theatrical technique of yours we hear so much about? T.B., indeed, in this day and age! And making the boy symbolically sprain his ankle. And having Rose leave her farewell message to him on a tape-recorder. And giving her a *confidante* I'd have been ashamed to wish on Pinero. And what about that Sherman lover of hers who is talking the so comic English? If you'd written the play well, it would have been bad enough. As it is—" "I thought the theme would carry it," he said, "a young boy living off an older woman." That made me plain ratty. "You're not Colette," I said, "and don't you think it."

Anyway, I've told Master Terence that from now on he can whistle for his Muse. I'm not going to come crawling back to him. He thinks the play will succeed in spite of me, in spite of its lack of inspiration. He thinks it's what the public wants. But that reminds me of what Groucho Marx said when three thousand people turned up at the funeral of a rich Hollywood mogul whom everyone loathed. "You see what I mean?" he said. "Give the public what they want, and they'll come to see it." I hope Master Terence heeds the warning. I can get along without him, thank you very much. But he can't get along without me.

(1958)

Hamlet, BY WILLIAM SHAKESPEARE, AT STRATFORD-ON-AVON.

The case of Michael Redgrave is perennially absorbing, even to those who deny that he is a great actor. On he plunges, struggling and climbing and stumbling, bursting with will and intelligence, and seeking always to widen the range of his remarkable physical and vocal equipment. Never, to my knowledge, has he run away from an acting problem: he'll wrestle with them all. A serious actor, in short.

Yet something is missing. We admire, but are not involved. "I wish thar was winders to my Sole," said Artemus Ward, "so that you could see some of my feelins." Mr. Redgrave's trouble is that his windows are opaque—one might even say frosted. Sir Laurence Olivier once said he would rather lose his voice or his arms than his eyes. Watch Mr. Redgrave's: no matter how he rolls and darts them about, they remain somehow glazed and distant. We know from the evidence of our own that he has two of them, yet something about him persistently suggests the Cyclops. When he looks at other people, either actors or audience, it is as if he saw them only in two dimensions. They are simply "things in his dream." Try as he may (and God knows he tries), he cannot establish contact with them as human beings. Just as we think he is about to break through to us, something within him shies and bolts. He withdraws into his solitude, and when next we look, the windows are shuttered again.

Now this business of "connecting," of getting into emotional touch with others, is at the heart of all acting. It is the very touchstone of the craft. And that is Mr. Redgrave's paradox. He has in abundance all the attributes of a great actor, without the basic quality necessary to be a good one.

Even so, he is always fascinating to watch. His present *Hamlet* is a packed, compendious affair, much richer in detail than the one he gave us eight years ago at the Vic. At fifty, Mr. Redgrave is the oldest Hamlet to have been seen in England since 1938, when Esmé Beringer struck a glancing blow for feminism by playing the part in her sixty-fourth summer; and it must be conceded that the actor sometimes resembles less a youth approaching murder for the first time than a seasoned Commando colonel suffering from battle fatigue. Nor is the illusion helped by a Gertrude who looks even younger than Googie Withers—a surprising achievement, considering that Miss Withers herself plays the part. Sheer intellectual agility, of which he has plenty, is what Mr. Redgrave relies on. He knows the text inside out, and when he offers new readings (such as "Nilus" for "eisel" in the grave scene), we trust him as we would trust a walking Variorum Edition of the play. No subtlety of inflexion or punctuation escapes him; at times, indeed, he seems to be giving us three different interpretations of the same line *simultaneously,* which is a bit flustering.

In terms of character, Mr. Redgrave presents a man fearful of rousing the sleeping demon within him. Cocteau described the artist as a kind of prison from which works of art escape. This Hamlet is a prison from which fury escapes, in wild frustrated spasms. His lips quake with the effort of containing it. Bottled hysteria is this actor's speciality, as the cellarage scene brilliantly proves. Mr. Redgrave's Hamlet, like his Lear, is most convincing when closest to madness. It is, however, entirely, unmoving, for the reason mentioned above.

Dorothy Tutin's Ophelia, a mouse on the rack, makes some illuminating minor points, chief among them her horrified reaction, in the play scene, to the mimic death of the Player King. I liked Edward Woodward's Laertes, Paul Hardwick's Rosencrantz (a nervous hearty), and the notion of playing the Second Gravedigger as a supercilious bureaucrat. Almost everything else in Glen Byam Shaw's production is dismal. The courtiers line up like mechanical waxworks, raising their hands in polite embarrassment when the royal family is exterminated before their eyes. The music is Victorian, the costumes are fussy, and the setting, an arrangement of shiny hexagonal pillars, appears to have been inspired by the foyer of the old Paramount Cinema in Birmingham. The best piece of business (Claudius' slapping the face of the Player Murderer) comes from Hugh Hunt's 1950 production. About two of the major performances my feelings are neutral: Cyril Luckham's sane, plodding Polonius and Mark Dignam's Claudius, which very nearly makes up in practical shrewdness what it lacks in dignity and sensuality.

(*1958*)

The Hostage, BY BRENDAN BEHAN, AT THE THEATRE ROYAL, STRATFORD-ATTE-BOWE.

At the end of N. F. Simpson's *A Resounding Tinkle* there is a passage, aberrantly omitted from the Royal Court production, in which four B.B.C. critics discuss the play. It reads, in part:

CHAIRMAN: Denzil Pepper—what do you make of this?

PEPPER: This is a hotchpotch. I think that emerges quite clearly. The thing has been thrown together—a veritable rag-bag of last year's damp fireworks, if a mixed metaphor is in order.

MISS SALT: Yes, I suppose it *is* what we must call a hotchpotch. I do think, though—accepting Denzil Pepper's definition—I do think, and this is the point I feel we ought to make, it is, surely, isn't it, an *inspired* hotchpotch?

PEPPER: A hotchpotch de luxe. . . . A theatrical haggis.

CHAIRMAN: Isn't this what our ancestors would have delighted in calling a gallimaufry?

(*Pause*)

MUSTARD: Yes. I'm not sure that I don't prefer the word gallimaufry to Denzil Pepper's hodgepodge.

PEPPER: Hotchpotch. No, I stick, quite unrepentantly, to my own word. . . .

The satanic accuracy of all this is enough to make any critic's elbow fly defensively up. I quote it because it has a chilling relevance to Brendan Behan's *The Hostage*. He would, I fancy, be a pretty perjured critic who could swear that no such thoughts infested his mind while watching Mr. Behan's new (careful now)—Mr. Behan's new *play*. I use the word advisedly, and have since sacked my advisers—for conventional terminology is totally inept to describe the uses to which Mr. Behan and his director, Joan Littlewood, are trying to put the theatre. The old pigeon-holes will no longer serve.

From a critic's point of view, the history of twentieth-century drama is the history of a collapsing vocabulary. Categories that were formerly thought sacred and separate began to melt and flow together, like images in a dream. Reaching, to steady himself, for words and concepts that had withstood the erosion of centuries, the critic found himself, more often than not, clutching a handful of dust. Already, long before 1900, tragedy and comedy had abandoned the pretence of competition and become a double act, exchanging their masks so rapidly that the effort of distinguishing one from the other was at best a pedantic exercise. Farce and satire, meanwhile, were miscegenating as busily as ever, and both were conducting affairs on the side with revue and musical comedy. Opera, with Brecht and Weill, got into everybody's act; and vaudeville, to cap everything, started to flirt with tragi-comedy in *Waiting for Godot* and *The Entertainer*.

The critic, to whom the correct assignment of compartments is as vital as it is to the employees of Wagons-Lits, reeled in poleaxed confusion. What had happened was that multi-party drama was moving towards coalition government. Polonius did not know the half of it: a modern play can, if it wishes, be tragical-comical-historical-pastoral-farcical-satirical-operatical-musical-music-hall, in any combination or all at the same time. And it is only because we have short memories that we forget that a phrase already exists to cover all these seemingly disparate breeds. It is Commedia dell'Arte. *The Hostage* is a Commedia dell'Arte production.

Its theme is Ireland, seen through the bloodshot prism of Mr. Behan's talent. The action, which is noisy and incessant, takes place in a Dublin lodging-house owned by a Blimpish veteran of the Troubles whose Anglophobia is so devout that he calls himself Monsieur instead of Mr. His caretaker is Pat (Howard Goorney), a morose braggart who feels that all the gaiety departed from the cause of Irish liberty when the I.R.A. became temperate, dedicated, and holy. Already, perhaps, this sounds like a normal play; and it may well sound like a tragedy when I add that the plot concerns a kidnapped Cockney soldier who is threatened with death unless his opposite number, an I.R.A. prisoner sentenced to be hanged, is reprieved. Yet there are, in this production, more than twenty songs, many of them blasphemously or lecherously gay, and some of them sung by the hostage himself. Their authorship is attributed to Mr. Behan, his uncle, and "Trad." Nor can one be sure how much of the dialogue is pure Behan and how much is gifted embroidery; for the whole production sounds spontaneous, a communal achievement based on Miss Littlewood's idea of theatre as a place where people talk to people, not actors to audiences. As with Brecht, actors step in and out of character so readily that phrases like "dramatic unity" are ruled out of court; we are simply watching a group of human beings who have come together to tell a lively story in speech and song.

Some of the speech is brilliant mock-heroic; some of it is merely crude. Some of the songs are warmly ironic; others are more savagely funny. Some of the acting is sheer vaudeville; some of it (Murray Melvin as the captive, and Celia Salkeld as the country girl whom, briefly and abruptly, he loves) is tenderly realistic. The work ends in a mixed, happy jabber of styles, with a piano playing silent-screen music while the Cockney is rescued and accidentally shot by one of the lodgers, who defiantly cries, in the last line to be audibly uttered: "I'm a secret policeman, and I don't care who knows it!"

Inchoate as it often is, this is a prophetic and joyously exciting evening. It seems to be Ireland's function, every twenty years or so, to provide a playwright who will kick English drama from the past into the present. Mr. Behan may well fill the place vacated by Sean O'Casey. Perhaps more important, Miss Littlewood's production is a boisterous premonition of something we all want—a biting popular drama that does not depend on hit songs, star names, spa sophistication, or the more melodramatic aspects of homosexuality. Sean Kenny's setting, a skeleton stockade of a bedroom surrounded by a towering blind alley of slum windows, is, as often at this theatre, by far the best in London.

(1958)

The Elder Statesman, BY T. S. ELIOT, AT THE LYCEUM, EDINBURGH.

Last week, for the third time in twelve years, the Edinburgh Festival presented the world *première* of a play by T. S. Eliot. It has not always been the same play, though sometimes it has seemed so: in this author's imagination the same themes compulsively (and not always compellingly) recur, among them a guilt-bearing death in a man's past, the human need for contrition and absolution, and the paradox whereby true selfhood can be attained only through self-abnegation.

The Elder Statesman contains all these, together with a rich haul of familiar stylistic devices. Images calculated to evoke well-bred dread cluster together ("The laughter in the doorway, the snicker in the corridor, the sudden silence in the smoking-room"); percipient aphorisms alternate with verbal horseplay, as when an old lag remarks:

> Forgery, I can tell you, is a mug's game.
> I say that with conviction. Ha ha! yes, with conviction.

And Mr. Eliot's trick of iteration frequently verges on outright parody:

> I see more and more clearly
> The many many mistakes I have made
> My whole life through, mistake upon mistake,
> The mistaken attempts to correct mistakes
> By methods which proved to be equally mistaken.

At moments like this *The Elder Statesman* comes dangerously near to the competition pages of the *New Statesman.*

But if the old Eliot is well in evidence, the voice of a new Eliot is also heard, unexpectedly endorsing the merits of human love. It is a safe bet that the word "love" occurs more often in the present play than in all the author's previous work put together: the new Eliot has majored in the Humanities as well as the Eumenides. Often in the past, as the latest Eliot unfolded chill and chaste before us, we have inwardly murmured: "Poor Tom's a-cold." Now, by comparison, he is positively aflame.

Encouraging though we may find this step in his spiritual development, it is not by itself enough to make good theatre. In some ways, indeed, it has the opposite effect: Mr. Eliot's Indian-summer love-lyrics have little distinction, either literary or dramatic. A new simplicity has certainly entered his style, but so has simplicity's half-wit brother, banality; and at times one longs for the old equivocations, for just one kind of characteristic ambiguity.

This banality extends to the plot. Lord Claverton, politician and tycoon, has retired to a convalescent home, accompanied by his beloved and adoring daughter. Two figures from his past return to plague him, each a reminder of an occasion when he behaved dishonourably. One of them, a prosperous crook from Latin America, was with him when, as an undergraduate motorist, he ran over a man and failed to stop; true, the victim was dead already, but technical innocence, as Claverton knows, is poles apart from moral innocence. His second tormentor is a rich, ageing *chanteuse* whom long ago he seduced and paid off in order to avoid a breach-of-promise action. Other, affiliated sins come home to him. The crook might not have turned to crime, might even have got a First, had not Claverton introduced him to the pleasures of the *luxe* life. Moreover—last item in the catalogue—the old man has sought to dominate his son, who has become in consequence a mutinous wastrel.

By way of expiation Claverton makes a full confession of his misdeeds to his daughter and her fiancé. Duly absolved, having found his true self by sloughing off the sham, he goes off to die mysteriously beneath a great beech tree in the grounds of the sanatorium. He has learned patience and strength; the two lovers, left alone, celebrate their union in language more suggestive of Patience Strong.

It does not help to point out that Mr. Eliot has based his play on *Oedipus at Colonus,* in which the guilty, discredited king journeys with his faithful daughters to the sacred grove. Translated into a world of board-rooms and pin-striped trousers, Sophocles becomes Pinero on stilts—the old story of the great man whose past catches up with him, the hero who has Lived a Lie. The more we remember the Sophoclean background, the more we are conscious of the disparity between Claverton, with his puny sins and facile absolution, and the tremendous obsessing agonies of Oedipus. One's conclusion must be that out of the wisdom of his years and the intensity of his cerebration Mr. Eliot has come up with a gigantic platitude. Towards the end, to be sure, he casts over the play a sedative, autumnal glow of considerable beauty, and here and there a scattered phrase reminds us, by its spare precision, that we are listening to a poet. On the whole, however, the evening offers little more than the mild pleasure of hearing ancient verities tepidly restated.

The production, by E. Martin Browne, is careful and suave, with settings by Hutchinson Scott that loyally hint at Attic temples and holy grottoes. Paul Rogers lends Claverton a fine shaggy sonority and the right look of stoic dismay, as of a man staring past the fire into his thoughts. Anna Massey, of the beseeching face and shining eyes, is a first-rate stand-in for Antigone, and Alec McCowen is bonily brilliant as the rebel son.

(1958)

Long Day's Journey into Night, BY EUGENE O'NEILL, AT THE GLOBE.

Eugene O'Neill died five years ago. The eclipse of reputation that commonly befalls great men as soon as they die has not yet happened to him; and now that *Long Day's Journey into Night* has followed *The Iceman Cometh* into London, I doubt if it ever will. O'Neill has conquered. We have the measure of him at last, and it is vast indeed. His work stretches like a mountain range across more than three decades, rising at the end to these two tenebrous peaks, in which the nature of his immense, hard-pressed talent most clearly reveals itself. As Johnson said of Milton, he could not carve heads upon cherry-stones; but he could cut a colossus from a rock. Sometimes the huge groups of his imagination stayed stubbornly buried within the rock; worse, they would sometimes emerge lopsided and unwieldy, so that people smiled at them—not without reason, for it is widely felt that there is nothing funnier than a deformed giant.

Many charges, during his lifetime, were levelled at O'Neill by the cherry-stone connoisseurs of criticism. That he could not think; that he was no poet; that his attempts at comedy were even more pathetic than his aspirations to tragedy. The odd thing is that all of these charges are entirely true. The defence admits them: it does not wish even to cross-examine the witnesses. Their testimony, which would be enough to annihilate most other playwrights, is in O'Neill's case irrelevant. His strength lies elsewhere. It has nothing to do with intellect, verbal beauty, or the accepted definitions of tragedy and comedy. It exists independently of them: indeed, they might even have cramped and depleted it.

What is this strength, this durable virtue? I got the clue to it from the American critic Stark Young, into whose reviews I have lately been dipping. Mr. Young is sometimes a windy writer, but the wind is usually blowing in the right direction. As early as 1926 he saw that O'Neill's theatrical power did not arise from any "strong dramatic expertness," but that "what moved us was *the cost to the dramatist of what he handled.*" (My italics.) Two years later, reviewing *Dynamo,* he developed this idea. He found in the play an "individual poignancy" to which he responded no matter how tritely or unevenly it was expressed. From this it was a short step to the truth. "Even when we are not at all touched by the feeling itself or the idea presented," he wrote, "we are stabbed to our depths by the importance of this feeling to him, and we are all his, not because of what he says but because saying it meant so much to him."

Thirty years later we are stabbed in the same way, and for the same reason. The writing of *Long Day's Journey* must have cost O'Neill more than Mr. Young could ever have conceived, for its subject is that rarest and most painful of all *dramatis personae,* the dramatist himself. No more honest or unsparing autobiographical play exists in dramatic literature. Yet what grips us about it is not the craft of a playwright. It is the need, the vital, driving plaint, of a human being.

We are watching a crucial day in O'Neill's late youth, covered with a thin gauze of fiction; events are telescoped, and the family's name is Tyrone. They live in a gaunt, loveless New England house. Father is a rich retired actor, now beetle-browed with drink, whose upbringing as an immigrant Irish pauper has made him a miser: he recognises the fault, but cannot cure it. His wife suffered badly at the birth of their second son (Edmund, otherwise Eugene), and he hired a cheap quack to ease her pain, with the result that she has become a morphine addict. The elder boy is a failed actor, something of a whoremaster, and a great deal of a drunk. His brother, Edmund, who has been to sea and is ambitious to be a poet, also drinks and detests more than he wholesomely should.

We catch the quartet on the desperate day when mother, after a long abstinence, returns to drugs, and Edmund learns that he has T.B. With these urgent, terrible realities the family cannot cope. Old rows, old resentments keep boiling up; the pressures and recriminations of the past will not let the present live. Every conversation leads inexorably to the utterance of some sudden, unforgivable, scab-tearing cruelty. At every turn O'Neill points the contrast between official Irish-Catholic morality and the sordid facts of drink and dope. The family goes round and round in that worst of domestic rituals, the Blame Game. I blame my agony on you; you blame yours on her; she blames hers on me. Father blames his past; mother blames father; elder son blames both; and younger son blames all of them. If the play has a flaw, it is that O'Neill, the younger son, lets nobody blame him—though I recall, as I write this, the moment when his mother cries out that she would not be what she is had he never been born. The wheel, coming full circle, runs over all of them. Shortly after the events covered in the play, O'Neill entered a sanatorium, where, he wrote later, "the urge to write first came to me." It was more than an urge, it was a compulsion.

The London production is much shorter than those I saw in Berlin and New York; about a quarter of the text has been cut away. This is shrewd pruning, since a non-American English-speaking cast might not have been able to carry the full four-hour burden. Alan Bates, shock-haired and forlorn, approaches Edmund with just the right abandon. Once inside the part, however, he stumbles over a distracting North Country accent. Ian Bannen, on the other hand, gets easily to the heart of the elder brother, especially in the last-act debauch when he confesses to Edmund how much he hates and envies him: what he lacks is the exterior of the seedy Broadway masher. He falls short of his New York counterpart, Jason Robards, Jr., just as far as Anthony Quayle falls short of Fredric March. Mr. March, with his corrugated face and burning eyes, looked as weighty as if he were made of iron. Mr. Quayle, though he conveys every syllable of the part's meaning, never seems to be heavier than tin.

By West End standards, let me add, all these performances are exceptionally good. That of Gwen Ffrangcon-Davies is by any standards magnificent. In this production mother is the central figure: a guileful, silver-topped doll, her hands clenched by rheumatism into claws, her voice drooping except when drugs tighten it into a tingling, bird-like, tight-rope brightness. Her sons stare at her, and she knows why they are staring, but: "Is my hair coming down?" she pipes, warding off the truth with a defensive flirtatiousness. At the end, when the men are slumped in a stupor, she tells us in a delicate quaver how the whole mess began. "Then I married James Tyrone, and I was happy for a time. . . ." The curtain falls on a stupendous evening. One goes expecting to hear a playwright, and one meets a man.

(1958)

Krapp's Last Tape AND *End-Game*, BY SAMUEL BECKETT, AT THE ROYAL COURT.

Slamm's Last Knock, a play inspired, if that is the word, by Samuel Beckett's double bill at the Royal Court:

The den of Slamm, the critic. Very late yesterday. Large desk with throne behind it. Two waste-paper baskets, one black, one white, filled with crumpled pieces of paper, at either side of the stage. Shambling between them—i.e., from one to the other and back again—an old man: Slamm. Bent gait. Thin, barking voice. Motionless, watching Slamm, is Seck. Bright grey face, holding pad and pencil. One crutch. Slamm goes to black basket, takes out piece of white paper, uncrumples it, reads. Short laugh.

SLAMM (*reading*): ". . . the validity of an authentic tragic vision, at once personal and by implication cosmic . . ."

Short laugh. He recrumples the paper, replaces it in basket, and crosses to other—i.e., white—basket. He takes out piece of black paper, uncrumples it, reads. Short laugh.

SLAMM (*reading*): ". . . Just another dose of nightmare gibberish from the so-called author of *Waiting for Godot* . . ."

Short laugh. He recrumples the paper, replaces it in basket, and sits on throne. Pause. Anguished, he extends fingers of right hand and stares at them. Extends fingers of left hand. Same business. Then brings fingers of right hand towards fingers of left hand, and vice versa, so that fingertips of right hand touch fingertips of left hand. Same business. Breaks wind pensively. Seck writes feverishly on pad.

SLAMM: We're getting on. (*He sighs.*) Read that back.

SECK (*produces pince-nez with thick black lenses, places them on bridge of nose, reads*): "A tragic dose of authentic gibberish from the so-called implication of *Waiting for Godot.*" Shall I go on?

SLAMM (*nodding head*): No. (*Pause.*) A bit of both, then.

SECK (*shaking head*): Or a little of neither.

SLAMM: There's the hell of it. (*Pause. Urgently.*) Is it time for my Roget?

SECK: There are no more Rogets. Use your loaf.

SLAMM: Then wind me up, stink-louse! Stir your stump!

Seck hobbles to Slamm, holding rusty key depending from piece of string round his (Seck's) neck, and inserts it into back of Slamm's head. Loud noise of winding.

SLAMM: Easy now. Can't you see it's hell in there?

SECK: I haven't looked. (*Pause.*) It's hell out here, too. The ceiling is zero and there's grit in my crotch. Roget and over.

He stops winding and watches. Pause.

SLAMM (*glazed stare*): Nothing is always starting to happen.

SECK: It's better than something. You're well out of that.

SLAMM: I'm badly into this. (*He tries to yawn but fails.*) It would be better if I could yawn. Or if you could yawn.

SECK: I don't feel excited enough. (*Pause.*) Anything coming?

SLAMM: Nothing, in spades. (*Pause.*) Perhaps I haven't been kissed enough. Or perhaps they put the wrong ash in my gruel. One or the other.

SECK: Nothing will come of nothing. Come again.

SLAMM (*with violence*): Purulent drudge! *You* try, if you've got so much grit in your crotch! Just one pitiless, pathetic, creatively critical phrase!

SECK: I heard you the first time.

SLAMM: You can't have been listening.

SECK: Your word's good enough for me.

SLAMM: I haven't got a word. There's just the light, going. (*Pause.*) Are you trying?

SECK: Less and less.

SLAMM: Try blowing down it.

SECK: It's coming! (*Screws up his face. Tonelessly.*) Sometimes I wonder why I spend the lonely night.

SLAMM: Too many f's. We're bitched. (*Half a pause.*)

SECK: Hold your pauses. It's coming again. (*In a raconteur's voice, dictates to himself.*) Tuesday night, seven-thirty by the paranoid barometer, curtain up at the Court, Sam Beckett unrivalled master of the unravelled revels. Item: *Krapp's Last Tape,* Krapp being a myopic not to say deaf not to say eremitical eater of one and one-half bananas listening and cackling as he listens to a tape-recording of twenty years' antiquity made on a day, the one far gone day, when he laid his hand on a girl in a boat and it worked, as it worked for Molly Bloom in Gibraltar in the long ago. Actor: Patrick Magee, bereaved and aghast-looking grunting into his Grundig, probably perfect performance, fine throughout and highly affecting at third curtain-call though not formerly. Unique, oblique, bleak experience, in other words, and would have had same effect if half the words *were* other words. Or any words. (*Pause.*)

SLAMM: Don't stop. You're boring me.

SECK (*normal voice*): Not enough. You're smiling.

SLAM: Well, I'm still in the land of the dying.

SECK: Somehow, in spite of everything, death goes on.

SLAM: Or because of everything. (*Pause.*) Go on.

SECK (*raconteur's voice*): Tuesday night, eight-twenty by the Fahrenheit anonymeter, *End-Game,* translated from the French with loss by excision of the vernacular word for urination and of certain doubts blasphemously cast on the legitimacy of the Deity. Themes, madam? Nay, it *is,* I know not themes. Foreground figure a blind and lordly cripple with superficial mannerisms of Churchill, W., Connolly, C., and Devine, G., director and in this case impersonator. Sawn-off parents in bins, stage right, and shuffling servant, all over the stage, played by Jack MacGowran, binster of this parish. Purpose: to analyse or rather to dissect or rather to define the nature or rather the quality or rather the intensity of the boredom inherent or rather embedded in the twentieth or rather every other century. I am bored, therefore I am. Comment, as above, except it would have the same effect if a quarter of the words were other words and another quarter omitted. Critique ended. Thesaurus and out.

SLAMM: Heavy going. I can't see.

SECK: That's because of the light going.

SLAMM: Is that all the review he's getting?

SECK: That's all the play he's written.

Pause.

SLAMM: But a genius. Could you do as much?

SECK: Not as much. But as little.

Tableau. Pause. Curtain.

(1958)

The Ages of Man, AT THE 46TH STREET THEATRE, NEW YORK.

I have always felt that Sir John Gielgud is the finest actor on earth from the neck up, and, having heard his Shakespearean recital, *Ages of Man,* I am in no mood to revise that opinion. Whenever I think of Sir John, I remember what C. E. Montague (my favourite drama critic next to Shaw) said of Coquelin; namely, that "his power was simply the sum of the three strict elements of great acting—a plastic physical medium, a finished technical cunning, and a passion of joy in the thought of the character acted." Sir John has the last two qualities in abundance, and is almost entirely deficient in the first; when in motion, he is constricted, hesitant, and jerky, enmeshed in unseen cords of inhibition. His exceptional virtues of mind and voice stand out most clearly in repose, and for this reason the present display at the Forty-sixth Street Theatre seems to me one of the most satisfactory things he has ever done. Now and then, when the impulse of a speech demands it, he takes a step or two to right or left and permits his hands, which spend much of the evening protectively clasping each other, to fly up in gestures that claw the air, but for the most part he is still, and all the better for it; the voice flows freely among us, a thrilling instrument that commands the full tonal range of both viola and 'cello. Brass is absent, and this may explain why he gives us nothing of *Henry V* or *Antony and Cleopatra* and only the briefest snatch of *Macbeth*—all of them plays that cannot readily be scored for unaccompanied strings. But what he can do he does peerlessly. Never before have I followed Richard II's slow ride down to despair with such eager, pitying attentiveness (Sir John himself wept, as Richard should), and the excerpts from *Hamlet* were delivered with a mastery of *rubato* and a controlled energy that put one in mind of Mozart. The speech before the duel ("Not a whit, we defy augury . . .") was in the nature of an epiphany, the last phrases falling on the ear in cadences of overwhelming tenderness and serenity.

I had expected successes like these from Sir John; what I had forgotten was his narrative virtuosity. To passages that tell a story—Clarence recounting his nightmare, Hotspur describing a brush with a fop on the battlefield, Cassius tempting Brutus with splenetic anecdotes about Caesar—he brings a graphic zeal that is transfixing. Like the spider's touch in Pope's poem, his voice "feels at each thread, and lives along the line." The impact of the performance is not, however, exclusively aural; as I've said, Sir John's physical inexpressiveness does not extend above the collar stud. Poker-backed he may be; poker-faced he certainly isn't. Wherever pride, scorn, compassion, and the more cerebral kinds of agony are called for, his features respond promptly, and memorably. The whole programme, I should add, is an abridgement of George Rylands' Shakespeare anthology *The Ages of Man,* which, in the process of compression, has lost its definite article, presumably so that it can be listed in the daily press high up, under "A," rather than low down, under "T."

(1959)

Summing Up: 1959.

As recently as five years ago, popular theatre in the West End of London was virtually dominated by a ruthless three-power coalition consisting of drawing-room comedy and its two junior henchmen, murder melodrama and barrack-room farce. Although competitive among themselves, the members of the combine were united in their determination to prevent the forces of contemporary reality from muscling in on their territory. The average playwright had ceased trying to hold the mirror up to nature, and the fashionable playwright could not possibly hold a mirror up to anything, since genteel idiom demanded the use of the word "looking-glass." Nightly, in dozens of theatres, the curtain rose on the same set. French windows were its most prominent feature, backed by a sky-cloth of brilliant and perpetual blue. In the cheaper sort of production, nothing but the sky was visible through the windows, and the impression was conveyed that everyone lived on a hill. There was also a bookcase, which might even—if the producer was in a devil-may-care frame of mind—be three-dimensional and equipped with real books. If we were not at Mark Trevannion's country house in Berkshire, we were probably at Hilary Egleston's flat in Knightsbridge, and, wherever we were, we ran into the same crowd—Rodney Curzon, feeling frightful; a "really rather nice" American named Kip, Joe, or Calvin McIlhenny III; and, of course, that audacious young Susan Mainwaring, accompanied by her Aunt Gertrude, an obligatory dragoness with strong views about modern youth, the welfare state, and her senile rip of a husband, referred to as "your poor Uncle Edgar," who never appeared. Offstage characters like Uncle Edgar continually cropped up in remarks such as "This reminds me of that ghastly evening when Priscilla Mumbles took her owl to the Ritz for cocktails." Nobody except the gardener was ever called Sidney or Bert, and names like Ethel and Myrtle were reserved for housemaids, paid companions, and pets. To pour the drinks, there was usually somebody's tweedy, middle-aged stick of a husband, who grinned tolerantly at his wife's caprices, offered brandy to her lovers, and never raised his voice above street level; a symbol of sanity in a collapsing world, he was described by the other characters as "damn decent" or "rather dim," and by the critics as "that admirable actor, Cyril Raymond." (Or any of a dozen other admirable actors.) The language of drawing-room drama was of a rigid deformity. People never just *went* anywhere; they beetled down to Godalming, hurtled up to town, nipped round to Fortnum's, and staggered off home. All bores were cracking, all asses pompous, and the dialogue was sprinkled with epithets of distaste, mostly drawn from the vocabulary of English nannies; for example, "horrid," "dreadful," "nasty," "sickening," "disgusting," and "nauseating." These were often reinforced by the additional disparagement of "little," as in "dreadful little man," "disgusting little creature," or "nasty little mind." (In other contexts, "mind" was replaced by the classier "mentality"; e.g., "You have the mentality of a day-old chick." For similar reasons, "visualize" was generally preferred to "imagine.") At some point in every play, the hero was required to say, "That, Celia, is a thoroughly immoral [or "perfectly revolting"] suggestion." Minor English place names were relied upon to tinge the baldest statements with wit. A line like "I am spending the summer in the country" could convulse a whole audience if revised to read "I am spending the summer at Sidcup/Herne Bay/Budleigh Salterton."

Five years ago, anyone whose knowledge of England was restricted to its popular theatre would have come to the conclusion that its standard of living was the highest on earth. British plays about people who could not afford villas on the Côte d'Azur were very nearly as rare as

British people who could afford them. The poor were seldom with us, except when making antic contributions to broad farce or venturing, tongue-tied with embarrassment and clutching cloth caps, into the gracious salons of middle-class comedy, where they were expected to preface every remark with "Beggin' yer pardon, Mum." To become eligible for detailed dramatic treatment, it was usually necessary either to have an annual income of more than three thousand pounds net or to be murdered in the house of someone who did. This state of affairs did not apply during the war years, when everyone pulled together and even Noël Coward wrote tributes to the patriotism of the working classes; otherwise, however, it had persisted since the mid-thirties and *Love on the Dole*. And it had been noticed much earlier than that.

> If our dramatists will condescend to make our acquaintance (or rather cease from trying to persuade themselves that they don't know us), they will find that we, too, the unmentioned by Debrett, the jaded in aspect, have brains and hearts. They will find that we, too, are capable of great joys and griefs, and that such things come our way quite often, really.

Max Beerbohm wrote that in February 1907. It might easily have been written in 1954. I do not think it could be written today.

A change, slight but unmistakable, has taken place; the English theatre has been dragged, as Adlai Stevenson once said of the Republican Party, kicking and screaming into the twentieth century. Only an Englishman, probably, would notice the difference. In the middle of summer there were twenty-one straight plays running in London. Sixteen of them were farces, light comedies, or detective stories, and one at least of the remaining five was a borderline case. I refer to Graham Greene's *The Complaisant Lover,* which bears the same relationship to Mr. Greene's earlier plays that his "entertainments" bear to his more serious novels. It deals with a suburban dentist whose wife has just started to sleep with a local bookseller. The adulterous pair arrange to spend a week-end in Amsterdam, which is interrupted—in a scene of the bitterest farce—by the sand-blind, unsuspecting cuckold. To force the issue, the lover informs the husband, by letter, of his wife's infidelity. The trick misfires. It drives the dentist to tears but not to divorce; instead, he cannily proposes a *ménage à trois*—a solution that satisfies him, assuages his wife's guilt, and utterly disconcerts the bookseller. Perhaps because John Gielgud's antiseptic direction failed to convince me that the lovers had achieved any significant carnal contact, perhaps because Ralph Richardson performed in a vein of fantasy that seemed incompatible with dentistry, I could not believe a word of it. Or, rather, I believed in many of the words—Mr. Greene's lines have a startling, casual candour— but not in the people who were uttering them. Mastery of dialogue, I reflected afterward, is no substitute for mastery of characterization.

Apart from *The Complaisant Lover,* plays are thriving in central London with titles like *The French Mistress, Caught Napping,* and *Simple Spymen.* How, then, can I support my claim that the English theatre is growing up? I do so by reference to a three-pronged suburban assault that has lately been launched on the central citadel. As in a Shakespeare history play, the western region is all afire with deep-revolving zeal, led by the English Stage Company, which set up shop in 1955 at the Royal Court Theatre, in Sloane Square, where it has since presented, in addition to well-known texts by Arthur Miller, Brecht, Giraudoux, and Ionesco, the first plays of Angus Wilson, Nigel Dennis, Doris Lessing, N. F. Simpson, and John Osborne. The Court is run by a stuffy committee and aided by a meagre subsidy from the Arts Council; even so, it managed to stage, during the 1958–9 season, two remarkable plays that would never five years ago have transferred—as these did—to the West End. One was *The Long and the Short and the Tall,* by a thirty-year-old television writer named Willis Hall. In construction this was a wartime anecdote of fairly familiar mould. A reconnaissance patrol, cut off by a Japanese advance in the middle of the Malayan jungle, debates its chances of getting back to base by breaking through the enemy lines. The argument is complicated by the fact that the men have taken a Japanese prisoner; should they let him accompany them, or shoot him out of hand? As in most British war stories, the cast is a cliché microcosm, a "cross-section of the community" that includes a Scot, a Welshman, a North Countryman, a Cockney, a trigger-happy sadist, and a tough, warmhearted sergeant. They are all, however, deeply individualized; each speaks a language so abundant in racy local metaphor that I could have kicked myself for having acquiesced in the popular myth that the British vernacular is dull wherever it is not Americanized. Mr. Hall's play is not only boisterous, exuberant, and accurate; it is also beautifully written. Moreover, it is performed in what, for the London theatre, is a new style of acting. Until a few years ago the English drama schools devoted much of their energy to ironing out of their pupils' accents all trace of regional origin and to replacing it with the neutral, official dialect spoken by B.B.C. announcers. Suddenly, however, a group of plays has sprung up for which B.B.C. English is utterly useless. Out of nowhere—or perhaps out of everywhere—an ambitiously talented bunch of young provincial actors has emerged, ideally fitted to embody the new drama, which treats ordinary people not as helpless victims, stoical jingoists, or clownish vulgarians but as rational human beings. Only two of the eight men in Mr. Hall's cast had appeared in the West End, and their director, Lindsay Anderson, had no previous experience of the professional stage, although he has a high reputation as a documentary-film maker. With his actors—Kenji Takaki, Robert Shaw, Edward Judd, Ronald Fraser, David Andrews, Emrys James, Bryan Pringle, and Peter O'Toole—I could find no fault, and in the case of Mr. O'Toole, as the cynical Cockney who befriends the Japanese captive, I sensed a technical authority that may, given discipline and purpose, presage greatness. To convey violence beneath banter, and a soured, embarrassed goodness beneath both, is not the simplest task for a young player, yet Mr. O'Toole achieved it without sweating a drop. The play lacked stars, and it had a downbeat (that is, anti-war) ending, in which the patrol was decimated. These facts may explain why, despite enthusiastic notices, it ran in the West End for only three months. It will, anyway, be remembered as a portent.

The same can be said of *Roots,* a new piece by Arnold Wesker, who is twenty-seven years old and was born in the East End of London. The subject of his play, which opened at the Court in June and has since moved to the West End, is ignorance. The daughter of a family of agricultural laborers comes home, after a long stay in London, full of progressive ideas she has learned from her lover, who works (as Mr. Wesker once worked) in the kitchen of a West End restaurant. Fruitlessly, she tries to explain art and politics to her kinfolk, who regard her with compassionate bewilderment; she plays classical music to her mother on the phonograph, and embarks on a wild dance to illustrate the release it has brought to her. Mother nods, smiling but uncomprehending; how should she care for art, fed as she is by radio pabulum, living as she does with no electricity, an outdoor toilet, and water from a garden tank, on less than thirteen dollars a week? Beatie, the daughter, has returned with a vocabulary that succeeds only in alienating her from her background. In the last scene a family gathering is reluctantly convened to welcome her urban boy friend, who fails to turn up. A smug reaction of I-told-you-so prevents anyone from comforting the shattered Beatie. If this were an English play of the traditional kind, the jilted girl would at this point recognize the futility of her intellectual aspirations and snuggle back to the bosom of the family. Not so Beatie. She rounds on her relatives, blaming their conservatism and their suspicion of independent thought for her own inability to communicate with intelligent people. She has failed because of the *mystique* of humility that has taught her since childhood to keep her place and not waste time on books. At the end of this tirade she realizes that for once she has not been parroting the opinions of her lover but has been thinking for herself. With the wonder that is cognate with one's first sense of identity, she cries, "I'm beginning. *I'm beginning!*" And the play is over. I stumbled out in a haze of emotion, on a sticky, baking July evening. The theatre, I noticed, was full of young men and women who had been distracted from the movies, from television, and even from love-making by the powerful lure of a show that concerned them and that could help as well as amuse. Joan Plowright played the awakened rustic, and the director was John Dexter, and in neither case can I think of an alternative half as good.

What the future has in store for the Royal Court is anyone's guess. *Roots* was followed by Vivien Leigh in *Look after Lulu!,* Noël Coward's adaptation of Feydeau's *Occupe-toi d'Amélie,* which flopped last season on Broadway. The London critics politely detested it, and I cannot imagine why it was ever staged at that address. John Osborne told me that he walked into the theatre early in July and found it full of Miss Leigh, Mr. Coward, and Hugh Beaumont, the most powerful of West End producers. He wondered for a second if he had come to the wrong place. The original idea had been that the Royal Court should conquer Shaftesbury Avenue; instead, Shaftesbury Avenue seemed to have conquered the Royal Court.

Whatever doubts one may have about the Sloane Square assault on the West End, the two other spearheads look pretty formidable. It is too early yet to pass judgment on the Mermaid Theatre, at Puddle Dock, which was conceived by a dedicated actor-impresario named Bernard Miles, built by public subscription on the brink of the Thames in the financial heart of London, and opened with fanfares last spring. A great concrete hangar, with a raked auditorium, a revolving stage, and an acting area that extends from wall to wall, the Mermaid is physically a director's dream. Its inaugural production—an immediate success—was a free adaptation, augmented by music and song, of *Rape upon Rape,* an eighteenth-century comedy by Henry Fielding, a satirist whose mordancy was such that it impelled Walpole, the Prime Minister, to bring all stage performances under the censorship of the Lord Chamberlain. (Fielding subsequently took up the novel, and England, according to Shaw, was thereby deprived of its finest playwright between Shakespeare and himself.) Intended as a sour indictment of corrupt judges, the play has been adulterated by the addition of insipid tunes and acting of a prevailing coyness; perhaps only Brecht and Weill could have given Fielding the kind of musical staging he needed. The new title, *Lock Up Your Daughters,* indicates the degree of compromise that was involved. But Mr. Miles has some valiant plans for his new playhouse. Once this hit has run its course, *on verra.*

By far the most damaging dent in the West End structure has been made by Joan Littlewood, the artistic director of the company known as Theatre Workshop. Two of the smartest playhouses in London—Wyndham's and the Criterion—are occupied, as I write this, by productions that originated at the Theatre Royal, Stratford-atte-Bowe, the East End headquarters of Miss Littlewood's extraordinary troupe. At the Criterion there is *A Taste of Honey,* a first play by Shelagh Delaney, a Lancashire girl who is well over six feet tall and just over twenty years old. It deals joyfully with what might, in other hands, have been a tragic situation. The teen-age heroine, who lives in a ratty tenement bed-sitter, is deserted by her nagging, peroxided mother, who is unaware that her daughter is pregnant by a Negro sailor. Played with tenderly cheeky impulsiveness by a young actress named Frances Cuka, the girl accepts the fact that her child is likely to be fatherless and makes a temporary home with a slender art student whose sexual bent is toward his own sex. Her only qualm is that her own father was mentally deficient: "He lived in a twilight land, my dad, the land of the daft." Eventually her mother comes home, the student is summarily evicted, and the curtain falls on preparations for the impending birth. I don't know that I like all of Miss Littlewood's production tricks; I don't see why the mother should address all her lines to the audience, like a vaudeville soloist, and I can't understand why the original ending, in which she accepted the Negro paternity of her daughter's baby, has been altered to permit her to make unattractive jokes about pickaninnies and "bloody chocolate drops." All the same, we have here quite a writer, and quite a director.

Brendan Behan's *The Hostage,* currently playing at Wyndham's Theatre, is a perfect embodiment of Miss Littlewood's methods, and well deserved the prize for the best production of the 1959 Paris International Theatre Festival. It is a babble of styles, devoid of form yet full of attack—*Hellz-a-Poppin,* you might say, with a point of view. The scene is a Dublin bawdy-house in which a British serviceman is held as hostage for an I.R.A. soldier condemned to death for shooting a policeman. As in *A Taste of Honey,* what sounds tragic turns out to be uproariously comic. The brothel becomes a sort of music hall. The actors chat to the audience, send themselves up in the mock-heroic manner that is Ireland's least imitable contribution to world literature, and sing a number of outstandingly villainous songs, including a devastating tribute to England—

> Old ladies with stern faces,
> And the captains, and the kings

—and a life-embracing chorus called "There's no place on earth like the world." No dramatic unity is achieved or aimed at; the players wander in and out of character whenever they, or the events of the play, feel like it. The jokes are unpredictable and often genuinely rude. The brand name of a whisky is clarified as "Vat 69—the Pope's telephone number," one of the principal clowns is a male transvestite named Princess Grace, and I particularly liked the Negro prizefighter who, in a moment of exceptional tumult, strolls across the stage bearing a sign that reads "Keep Ireland Black." Finally, the hostage—beautifully played by Alfred Lynch—is accidentally killed in a raid, but no time is allowed for mourning. Mr. Lynch jumps up again and joins all the rest of the cast in a rousing number entitled "Oh death, where is thy sting-a-ling-a-ling, oh grave, thy victor-ee!"

Miss Littlewood demands players who can improvise not only in rehearsal but before an audience. She likes the morning's headlines to be incorporated into the evening's performance—a habit that caused her last year to be haled into court and fined for contravening the censorship regulations, which insist that every word spoken on a public stage must first be submitted for approval to the Lord Chamberlain's office. Whether it is desirable for actors to usurp the writer's job and invent their own lines is something I seriously doubt. Whenever I raise the subject, Miss Littlewood starkly replies that as soon as a production is fixed, it is dead, and that she would prefer anything to the inflexible monotony of what she sees in the West End. A stocky, trenchant woman in her forties, she was born in a working-class district of South London and educated at a convent school. She went to the Royal Academy of Dramatic Art on a scholarship, and founded Theatre Workshop in 1945, warning her actors that regular salaries were out of the question; all she could promise them was that the box-office receipts would be equally divided at the end of each week. The company toured England, Germany, Norway, Sweden, and Czechoslovakia for eight years before settling down at the Theatre Royal. To Miss Littlewood's dismay, the local proletariat failed to support her enterprise, and it was not until her productions of *Arden of Faversham* and *Volpone* were thunderously acclaimed at the 1955 Paris International Theatre Festival that the senior London critics began to take her seriously. Her recent conquest of the West End pleases her, but only because it means more money with which to realize her life's obsession—a people's theatre outside the West End. Politically, she stands well to the Left. This is not, I might add, a fact of much significance; it applies to nearly every theatre company in Europe of any contemporary importance.

Stratford-on-Avon is celebrating this year its hundredth season, with a troupe of actors led by Dame Edith Evans, Sir Laurence Olivier, Paul Robeson, Charles Laughton, and Sam Wanamaker. A stylistic chaos swirled around nearly everything I saw; it was like an all-star benefit show run mad in doublet and hose and lacking, for the most part, either unity or purpose. The five guest stars seemed remote from the rest of the cast—and not surprisingly, when you consider that Dame Edith and Mr. Laughton are playing only two roles apiece in a total of five plays, while Sir Laurence and the Messrs. Robeson and Wanamaker are confining themselves, respectively, to Coriolanus, Othello, and Iago. Moreover, it takes a closely knit company and dynamic direction to offer consistently good work to an audience that is mainly composed of uncritical tourists and a town that is frankly apathetic toward theatre. Peter Bull, the English character actor, has lately recorded—in a highly diverting autobiography called *I Know the Face, But . . .* —his impressions of the place:

> I am here to say, with prejudice, that I personally loathe Stratford-on-Avon. . . . The atmosphere of old Tudory and brass ornaments brings my bile to boiling-point, and I did fancy during my short stay there that no one in the town seemed frightfully keen on the actors, who are largely responsible for bringing the shop ladies and gentlemen their revenue.

Mr. Bull's testimony may be slightly loaded, since he was fired during rehearsals; all the same, he has a point.

All's Well That Ends Well, the first Stratford production I saw this year, is directed by Tyrone Guthrie with his familiar, infuriating blend of insight and madness. On the one hand we have the great conductor, the master of visual orchestration, conceivably the most striking director alive when there are more than six people on stage; on the other hand we have his zany *Doppelgänger,* darting about with his pockets full of fireworks and giving the members of the orchestra hot-feet whenever genuine feeling threatens to impend. He has done to *All's Well* what he did a few seasons ago to *Troilus and Cressida* at the Old Vic; that is, set it in a Shavian Ruritania faintly redolent of *Arms and the Man.* This, of course, would have delighted Shaw, who always held that Helena, the lady doctor who pursues and ensnares the man of her choice, was a harbinger of his own aggressive heroines. Mr. Guthrie's modernization enables him to make some telling points that Elizabethan costume often obscures. When Helena, having worked her miracle cure on the king's fistula, claims as her reward the hand of Bertram, the young man's initial reaction is to treat the whole thing as a joke; he cannot believe that the daughter of a medical practitioner could seriously contemplate marrying into the aristocracy. Meanwhile, the braggart Parolles becomes a breezy, overdressed roadhouse cad, foredoomed to failure in his social climbing by the possession of an accent that is ever so slightly "off." What Mr. Guthrie has done is to make subtle class distinctions where Shakespeare made broad ones; one wonders whether the idea could have occurred to anyone but an Englishman. Until the evening was halfway through, I was beguiled and fascinated. Afterwards Mr. Guthrie's love of horseplay obtrudes, and we get—among other things—a long scene, performed mainly in mime, wherein a deaf general reviews the French troops and exhorts them to battle through a faulty public-address system. Two hours of this can be fun; three and a quarter is too much. Lavache, the Countess of Roussillon's clown, who has some of the most haunting prose in Shakespeare, is entirely omitted; to cut a play, yet make what remains last longer than the whole, must argue, I suppose, a kind of dotty genius. The role of the Countess, curiously described by Shaw as the most beautiful old woman's part ever written (it is in fact merely the only old woman's part in Shakespeare that is neither a scold nor a murderess), is played by Dame Edith in her characteristic later manner—tranquillized benevolence cascading from a great height, like royalty opening a bazaar.

Peter Hall, the young man who will next year assume the direction of the Stratford theatre, has staged *A Midsummer Night's Dream* in a manner just as personal as the Guthrie *All's Well.* With sound historical justification, he sees the play as an occasional piece, intended for the celebration of a well-bred marriage; accordingly, he deploys the action in the great hall of an Elizabethan manor house, which gradually, through the cunning of Lila de Nobili's décor, sprouts greenery and develops into a more or less credible forest. Foolishly, the lovers' scenes are played for broad comedy; Mr. Hall's sense of stage humour is not of the subtlest, and too many people stumble and fall unfunnily down. His positive contribution is in his handling of the fairies. Fatigued by sinister Oberons with sequins on their eyelids and by Junoesque Titanias attended by sinewy girls flapping romantically about to Mendelssohn, I was delighted by Mr. Hall's fresh approach. His fairies are closely related to the lost boys of *Peter Pan,* with Titania as their prim, managing Wendy. Admittedly, they are clad somewhat like insects, and one of them is without doubt a diminutive old lady. But Oberon himself is pure Peter—a petulant, barefoot boy, well-meaning and genuinely magical. Puck, in this interpretation, is not so much his slave as his kid brother. Finally, we have Charles Laughton, a ginger-wigged, ginger-bearded Bottom. I confess I do not know what Mr. Laughton is up to, but I am sure I would hate to share a stage with it. He certainly takes the audience into his confidence, but the process seems to exclude from his confidence everyone else in the cast. Fidgeting with a lightness that reminds one (even as one forgets what the other actors are talking about) how expertly bulky men dance, he blinks at the pit his moist, reproachful eyes, softly cajoles and suddenly roars, and behaves throughout in a manner that has nothing to do with acting, although it perfectly hits off the demeanour of a rapscallion uncle dressed up to entertain the children at a Christmas party.

Othello, as directed by Tony Richardson, is full of factitious life—jazz drumming between scenes, rampageous crowds, gestures toward symbolism, like making the Duke of Venice a cripple who has to be carried offstage by a Negro servant, and bizarre climatic effects, as when Othello disembarks on Cyprus in a thick fog and a high wind—and totally devoid of emotional reality. Shakespeare's great indictment of circumstantial evidence comes almost suavely across, without passion or impact. None of the three leading players seems to be operating on the same wave-length as the others, or even to be speaking the same language. Two of them—Mr. Robeson and Mr. Wanamaker—have had very little Shakespearean experience, and the third—Mary Ure—is vocally ill-equipped for either tragedy or poetry. Miss Ure primly flutes; Mr. Wanamaker clips and swallows, playing Iago in a style one would like to call conventional if only he were doing it well. Iago, above all, should be disarming. Mr. Wanamaker, to coin an epithet, is profoundly arming. In more appropriate company, I am sure, Mr. Robeson would rise to greater heights than he does. As things are, he seems to be murdering a butterfly on the advice of a gossip columnist. His voice, of course, is incomparable—a foundation-shaking boom. It may, however, be too resonant, too musically articulated for the very finest acting. The greatest players—Kean and Irving, for example—have seldom been singers as well. Their voices were human and imperfect, whereas the noise made by Mr. Robeson is so nearly perfect as to be nearly inhuman.

We will skim over the inessentials of the Stratford *Coriolanus* as quickly as possible. Boris Aronson's setting is mountainous, which is fine, and full of mountainous steps, which is not—I recalled Alec Guinness' remark, *à propos* of Shakespearean productions in general, that he himself had very few conversations on the stairs of his own house. Harry Andrews is a stolid, muscular Menenius. As Volumnia, the hero's stifling mother, Edith Evans looks overpowering, but her fussy, warbling vibrato swamps all too often the meaning of the lines. Peter Hall's direction is straight and vigorous, with hardly any ideological slanting—a good way with a play that is best served when either everything is slanted or nothing. The lesson to be learned from *Coriolanus* is that although Shakespeare was willing to condemn anyone in the social order, no matter how low or high his position, he would never have condemned the order itself. Any rung in a ladder may be rotten, but there must be a ladder, and rungs.

We can now get down to the heart of the production, which is Olivier's performance of Coriolanus. The first thing to praise is its sheer, intuitive intelligence. Olivier understands that Coriolanus is not an aristocrat; he is a professional soldier, a *Junker,* if you like, reminiscent in many ways of General de Gaulle—a rejected military saviour who returns, after a long and bodeful silence, with an army at his back. Fully aware of the gap between Coriolanus and the patricians he is serving, Olivier uses it to gain for the man an astounding degree of sympathy. With the delicacy that is his hallmark as much as power—few actors are physically as dainty, and none rolls eyes that are half as calf-like—he emphasizes Coriolanus the hater of phoneyness, the plain military man embarrassed by adulation, the awkward adult boy sickened equally by flattery and by the need to flatter. A cocky, jovial commander, he cannot bring himself to feign humility in order to become Consul, and his sulky refusal to apologize to the people takes on, in Olivier's hands, the aspect of high political comedy. We cannot applaud the man, but we like him, and thus the battle of the part is halfway won. What spurs him to betray Rome is not pride but a loathing of false servility.

Olivier also seizes on the fact that Coriolanus was brought up under his mother's thumb. "There's no man in the world/More bound to 's mother," says Volumnia. Her opinion always comes first. "I muse my mother/Does not approve me further" is our initial hint that Coriolanus is doubtful whether he is right to be so intransigent toward the plebeians. Under her persuasion, he consents to make his peace with them, and it is Volumnia who finally dissuades him from sacking Rome, the paternal city. Olivier's ashamed, hesitant collapse is among the truest moments of his performance. Sidling toward Volumnia, he grasps her hand and murmurs, "Oh—*my mother. . . .*"

This Coriolanus is all-round Olivier. We have the wagging head, the soaring index finger, and the sly, roaming eyes of one of the world's cleverest comic actors, plus the desperate, exhausted moans of one of the world's masters of pathos. But we also confront the nonpareil of heroic tragedians, as athletically lissome as when he played Oedipus a dozen years ago. No actor uses *rubato,* stealing a beat from one line to give to the next, like Olivier. The voice is soft steel that can chill and cut, or melt and scorch. One feels the chill in the icy tirade that begins "You common cry of curs" and ends "There is a world elsewhere." And one is scorched by the gargled snarl of rage with which Olivier rams home, by a wrenching upward inflexion on the last syllable, "The fires i' th' lowest hell fold in the peo*ple!*" At the close, faithful as ever to the characterization on which he has fixed, Olivier is roused to suicidal frenzy by Aufidius' gibe—"thou boy of tears." *"Boy!"* shrieks the overmothered general, in an outburst of strangled fury, and leaps up a flight of precipitous steps to vent his rage. Arrived at the top, he relents and throws his sword away. After letting his voice fly high in the great, swingeing line about how he "flutter'd your Volscians in *Cor-i-o-li,"* he allows a dozen spears to impale him. He is poised, now, on a promontory some twelve feet above the stage, from which he topples forward, to be caught by the ankles so that he dangles, inverted, like the slaughtered Mussolini. A more shocking, less sentimental death I have not seen in the theatre; it is at once proud and ignominious, as befits the titanic fool who dies it.

The image, and the echo, of this astonishing performance have taken root in my mind in the weeks that have passed since I witnessed it. The dark imprint of Olivier's stage presence is something one forgets only with an effort, but the voice is a lifelong possession of those who have heard it at its best. It sounds, distinct and barbaric, across the valley of many centuries, like a horn calling to the hunt, or the neigh of a battle-maddened charger.

(1959)

II: THE AMERICAN THEATRE

South Pacific, BY RICHARD RODGERS AND OSCAR HAMMERSTEIN II, AT DRURY LANE, LONDON.

I wept, and there is nothing in criticism harder than to convey one's gratitude for that. I had better begin with a few calming facts about *South Pacific*. First, this "musical play" is quite alien in tone and method to what we understand by "American musical comedy"; secondly, its treatment is realistic, which at once precludes ballet and chorus-girls; and, thirdly, to compare it with *Oklahoma!* is as unhelpful as to compare a novel with a ballad. So much, I am afraid, must be stated to temper the innocence of some of my colleagues, who seem to have blamed the show for not living up to the inaccurate puffs it had received in their own newspapers.

This is the first musical romance I have ever seen which was seriously involved in an adult subject. It concerns a young nurse, serving on an American-held island in the Pacific war, who falls inextricably in love with a middle-aged French expatriate. He is, we discover, a murderer, and the father of two coloured children. She can forgive the first, and the narrative concentrates on her fierce struggle to forgive the second. Clearly, your song-and-dance experts could never sustain this, so Joshua Logan, the director, has assembled—amazingly at Drury Lane—a company of fine singers who are also, down to the last perspiring and frustrated marine, absorbed and accomplished actors.

Already, then, we have reason to be grateful. But when to so much originality one adds the real *raisons-d'être* of the evening—the peasant graces of Mr. Rodgers' music and the boldness of Mr. Hammerstein's lyrics—one recoils from the attitudes of complaint as from a sickroom. After the first act I heard astringent voices insisting irrelevantly that the war against Japan was won in Europe, arguing that it was especially tasteless to bring racial problems into large theatres, and loftily wondering why the producers had not seen the theatrical advantages of erupting volcanoes and tribal rituals. I was unable to take part in any of these conversations, being transparently embarrassed by the huge sob of delight of which I was the all too witting custodian. For this I hold Mary Martin responsible. Skipping and roaming round the stage on diminutive flat feet, she had poured her voice directly into that funnel to the heart which is sealed off from all but the rarest performers, and which was last broached, I believe, by Yvonne Printemps. After one burst of morning joy she explains that "it's an American-type song, but we sort of put in our own words," and this artful spontaneity is in everything she does. Later, with a straw hat pulled over her eyes and a beam comically broad, she stands astride, turns up her toes, and sings: "I'm in love with a wonderful guy." Aldous Huxley once wrote of the Caroline poets that "they spoke in their natural voices, and it was poetry." Miss Martin's style is similar; the technique is informal, and the effect, unless we are to imprison the poor word, poetic.

Not that her achievement is all. There is Muriel Smith as a Rabelaisian Tonkinese pedlar called Bloody Mary; and there is Ray Walston, magnificent as a proudly cynical naval engineer, padding suspiciously through his lines as if he were bent on despising every word of them, and curdling each final syllable with a whirring baritone growl. There is Betta St. John, gravely glowing in the tiny part of a French-speaking native girl, and Wilbur Evans, who, as Miss Martin's elderly suitor, has all the good qualities of wool.

Amid so much excellence the few lapses glare. Jo Mielziner's settings, for example, are undistinguished, and in the second half you may balk at such a steady flow of plot. But, these flaws noted, I have nothing to do except thank Messrs. Logan, Rodgers, and Hammerstein and climb up from my knees, a little cramped from the effort of typing in such an unusual position.

(1951)

The Consul, BY GIAN-CARLO MENOTTI, AT THE CAMBRIDGE, LONDON.

Gian-Carlo Menotti, who wrote and composed that striking double bill, *The Medium* and *The Telephone,* has invaded the Cambridge Theatre with his new piece, *The Consul,* a deeply felt exercise in sung melodrama, bearing marked traces everywhere of the influence of Gian-Carlo Menotti. This time there is a thesis, to the effect that there should be no national boundaries and that bureaucracy is a dead hand. The efforts of a youngish wife to cross a frontier in search of her fugitive husband are frustrated by the agents of an unnamed Consul, whom nobody ever sees. The resemblance to Kafka is violent but shallow, since Kafka's symbols are wrapped in that sham-repelling mystery which often envelops valid intuitions, while Menotti's (black leather gloves and a crazy conjuror) belong ineradicably to a Hitchcock movie. Much of *The Consul* looks and sounds like a slow American second-feature with heavy background music, against which the actors unexpectedly sing instead of talk. Squirming to escape banality, Menotti occasionally returns to the tunes of his youth, which were nice; his newer style, pruned and streamlined, has a kind of sincere slickness which would fool nobody.

There is no very good reason for seeing it except Patricia Neway, who would be reason enough to see one's mother's execution. Miss Neway sings, acts, evokes, communicates, and transcends the part of the bereft wife: her second-act aria ("My name is woman") is the most heart-gouging piece of dramatic singing I have ever heard. Miss Neway is that rarest kind of actress in whom all the impulses and forms of womanhood are, quite unselfconsciously, incarnate: she is woman generalised yet microscopically observed; symbol and individual fuse together in a perfect and passionate mating. Miss Neway glows; she is stricken with a pure anger; she is instinctively honourable. Her large, capable hands stroke your heart; she stands, raw-boned and transfixed, and her hard grey face speaks intelligent anguish; and she is handsome. Part of her appeal is sensual, for in Miss Neway spirit and sex flatteringly commingle: she is most men's dream mistress. All the social guilts of Europe in the last ten years are purified by her sacrifice, and when she kills herself, it is like standing by at the death-bed of personal responsibility. In all she does, Miss Neway has the long-sighted look of a woman who could wash nappies or burn at the stake without a change of vocation. On a lower level, she is the Thurber woman: no man could ever hold a stage with her.

(1951)

The Constant Wife, BY W. SOMERSET MAUGHAM, AT THE NATIONAL; *I Am a Camera*, BY JOHN VAN DRUTEN, AT THE EMPIRE.

One of the Broadway season's least inspiring achievements has been a lame and static revival of Maugham's *The Constant Wife,* which represents Katharine Cornell's coming-of-age as an actress-manager. Miss Cornell, once the first and now almost the last lady of the American theatre, makes her every entrance with the martyred look of a woman who has just swept out the attics, put two dozen children to bed, finished the washing-up, and painted the scenery as well. Her stock-in-trade mingles quizzical charm with gusty bossiness, her forehead sags wearily over her eyes, and at high moments her simulation of courage and wisdom in extremity gives her a strong resemblance to an industrious district nurse in the Orkneys. Her method with Mr. Maugham's flimsy witticisms is to bellow them with an expression of incipient nausea; to paraphrase Wilde, she bears distinct traces of what must once have been a quite intolerable condescension.

John van Druten's adaptation of Christopher Isherwood's *Berlin Stories,* presented under the title of *I Am a Camera,* suffers a little from the fact that its hero (being a camera) contributes nothing to the action. This is a mood piece about Berlin in 1930; about two second-rate expatriates, not in love, who manage to ignore the rising Nazi storm outside their window. Yet the dialogue stings, and there is one performance of indelible accomplishment: that of Julie Harris, who plays Isherwood's Sally Bowles as a sort of Daisy Ashford gone to seed, with frank, piercing eyes and the softness of a marshmallow. Miss Harris' Sally is a frail, alcoholic adolescent with grubby fingers. She bursts with unrealised affectations, and is for ever latching herself on to a bullrush-length cigarette-holder, like a peignoir suspended from a clothes-hook. She brings with her an aura of cigarettes stubbed out in pots of cold cream; of moths and flames; and of a most touching wit. I expect Miss Harris to mature astonishingly, and to become, very shortly, one of the nobler ladies of the modern stage. Already she has the orphaned look of greatness.

(1952)

Ruth Draper, AT THE CRITERION, LONDON.

I am sure that what happened to me at the Criterion Theatre on Tuesday night was happening to very few other people in the house. I was seeing Ruth Draper for the first time. The rest of her audience were annual loyalists, ancient friends of her art; for some of them, I afterwards discovered, she has all but ruined the pleasures of normal playgoing, since her large supporting cast, which exists only at her mind's fingertips, is so much more satisfactory than any which makes the vulgar mistake of being visible.

I cannot content myself with a few perfunctory references to the familiar, inimitable etcetera with which she presents her well-loved gallery of etceteras: she must have enough notices of that kind to paper a palace. I want to declare Miss Draper open to the new generation of playgoers, and to trample on their suspicions, which I once shared, that she might turn out to be a museum-piece, ripe for the dust-sheet and oblivion. She is, on the contrary, about as old-fashioned and mummified as spring, and as I watched her perform her thronging monologues the other night, I could only conclude that this was the best and most modern group acting I had ever seen. It seems, in passing, absurd to use a singular verb in connection with so plural a player. Let me put it that Ruth Draper are now at their height of their career, and add that you have only six weeks in which to see them.

She works her miracles benignly and unfussed; and do not be misled by her aquiline nose and razor-edged eyes into taking her for one of those prima donnas who prefer to give solo performances merely because their egos cannot abide competition. I have an idea that, at the back of her mind, Miss Draper is hoping still to find a company of actors skillful enough to stand up to comparison with the accuracy, tact, and wisdom of her technique. She is actually doing her contemporaries a great kindness by not exposing them to such a hazard. The riches of her style lie in its quietness; it is a peaceful spawning of microscopically observed details, each of which does the work of an explanatory paragraph in a novel. Within the space of a short story, she manages to sketch in enough background for an epic.

Her first and wittiest study is of a dowager opening a bazaar and pausing in her inspection of the stalls to inquire cautiously: "Is that a rose or a tomato?" Next she is a fisherman's wife, wrinkled in granite, gossiping on the porch while her rheumatic husband ("an awful heavy man to rub") complains from within the house. Then follows the fabled procession of the women in Mr. Clifford's life—tireless secretary, dry-hearted wife, and patient mistress. The patience of the last-named, by the bye, seemed to me a little too monumental; we were almost, for a moment, in the swamps of sentimentalism, and I caught echoes of the almighty cooing of Dame Sybil Thorndike on an off day. With the finale, however, we are back on the peaks: the Parisian actress preparing for a world tour. During this exhibition the audience broke out into applause, amazingly when you consider that Miss Draper had just concluded a long tirade blazing with charm and avarice, but spoken entirely in Russian.

Watching her is like being present at a successful audition for the role of a theatrical immortal. I can pay her no higher compliment than to say that the best plays of Chekhov read as if they had been written at her express commission. To older playgoers I must apologise for dwelling on so much that they already knew. Younger ones will form an orderly queue outside the Criterion, and need not cross their fingers.

(1952)

Jack Benny, AT THE LONDON PALLADIUM.

There is a rumour about to the effect that Jack Benny, who has returned to the Palladium for three weeks, is a great clown. This is a dreadful slur on his reputation, so let us dispose of it at once. Mr. Benny is not a clown at all; he is a straight man, or stooge, and possibly the subtlest in the history of comedy. Funny men surround him, but they are there purely for the purpose of leaving him cold. It is he who, in all good faith, asks the questions; the others provide the punch-lines. He is the duck's back; they pour the water. He receives their slights with a mask of bland resignation; his eyes glaze to a blood-curdling blue, and inwardly he meditates mayhem. At length, adjusting his smile with an effort and shrugging faintly, like an injured diplomat, at the audience, he passes on to other, happier things. He gets his laughs, in fact, not by attacking, but by suffering in silence.

Benny's is a character performance, with a clear and considered attitude towards humanity. He wants to cheat and rob it. Calm, sunburnt, and ingratiating, he is forever pondering devices by which the bite may suddenly and simultaneously be put on his wife, his family, his friends, and the United States Treasury. His fabulous repose is shaken, his small fine hands start to expostulate, only when he is accused of avarice. This hurts and disgusts him, and his eyebrows, tired and deprecating, start upwards. Benny's whole act is that of a man fatigued with protesting his innocence to a court which is disposed to hang him out of hand: it is a long yawn, with an eye to the main chance.

To be as fond of Benny as I am may easily be an eccentric taste: he is technically a buffer-state, a rarity in this country, where comedians are generally aggressors. But no one with an eye for the craft of comedy should miss the chance of studying the ease and timing of his minutely rehearsed ad-libs. His company includes a nest of three hopeful songbirds, who fail repeatedly to win his heart; and a guileless Irish tenor, looking appropriately starved, called Dennis Day. Mr. Day, incidentally, ventures for several minutes on end into the special hell reserved for people who impersonate Sir Harry Lauder singing "Roamin' in the Gloamin'," complete with gestures and stick. Someone should tell him that Danny Kaye is in the Lauder business too, and that it is getting tough at the top.

(1952)

Frankie Laine, AT THE LONDON PALLADIUM.

Like Sir Max Beerbohm—whose eightieth birthday we are celebrating this week-end—I am quite indifferent to serious music. But I find it practically impossible to be indifferent to Frankie Laine, the American singer, who is currently at the Palladium, calling the cattle home across the sands of D flat. Nobody could spend an hour in the same room as Mr. Laine's amplified voice without getting a very pronounced reaction. I came out of the theatre feeling slightly clubbed.

Mr. Laine takes us back on a nostalgic journey to the half-forgotten era of Johnnie Ray and "Cry." He is a beefy man with a strangler's hands and a smile like the beam of a lighthouse, but he sings almost exclusively about tears and regrets. You form a mental picture of him sobbing into his pillow, hammering it with his fists until the bed collapses under him. His approach to the microphone is that of an accused man pleading with a hostile jury. He complains of betrayals, and shouts his defiance of faithlessness. It is like the day one's elder brother was dropped from the first eleven. I am not sure what the opposite of bashfulness is—bashlessness, I suppose—but, whatever it is, Mr. Laine is loaded with it. He spreads his arms out like a wrestler and then hits a mad, toneless headnote, holding it so long that you expect him to drop like a stone at the end of it. Seizing a bull-whip and grinning intimately, he can even get passionately excited over mules—a rare thing in the modern theatre, or any other, for that matter.

The applause, like the act, was deafening, chiefly taking the form of a sustained wailing from upstairs. Mr. Laine, you see, is not content with mere handclaps: once satisfied that he has the audience in the palm of his hand, he goes one further and clenches his fist. Cruel it may be, but it gets results. You would have thought they were holding a witches' sabbath in the gallery. Myself, I eluded his grip. Except in one spooky little ballad called "High Noon," he showed none of the lyrical fire and sensitivity of Johnnie Ray, who is a much more finished exponent of the new art of heartfelt yell.

After singing five numbers, Mr. Laine sprang into the wings, returning when the panic had subsided to announce: "After my fifth song I always come back anyway!" This simple message of reassurance had a weird and impressive effect on one of my colleagues, who reported Mr. Laine as having said: "After my fifth song I always go bang anyway." The truth is that, while he showed no signs of blowing up in our faces, Mr. Laine quite definitely kept on coming back. Again and again and again.

(1952)

Guys and Dolls, BY FRANK LOESSER, AT THE COLISEUM, LONDON.

Guys and Dolls, at which I am privileged to take a peek last evening, is a hundred-per-cent American musical caper, cooked up out of a story called "The Idyll of Miss Sarah Brown," by the late Damon Runyon, who is such a scribe as delights to give the English language a nice kick in the pants.

This particular fable takes place in and around Times Square in New York City, where many citizens do nothing but roll dice all night long, which is held by one and all, and especially the gendarmes, to be a great vice. Among the parties hopping around in this neighbourhood is a guy by the name of Nathan Detroit, who operates a floating dice game, and Miss Adelaide, his ever-loving pretty, who is sored up at this Nathan because after fourteen years engagement, they are still nothing but engaged. Anyway, being short of ready scratch, Nathan lays a bet with a large gambler called Sky Masterson, the subject of the wager being whether The Sky can talk a certain Salvation Army doll into joining him on a trip to Havana. Naturally, Nathan figures that a nice doll such as this will die sooner, but by and by she and The Sky get to looking back and forth at each other, and before you know it she is his sweet-pea. What happens next but The Sky gets bopped by religion and shoots craps with Nathan and the boys for their immortal souls. And where do the sinners wind up, with their chalk-striped suits and busted noses, but at a prayer meeting in the doll's mission house, which hands me a very big laugh indeed. The actors who nab the jobs of playing these apes and essences of 42nd Street have me all tuckered out with clapping them.

Nathan Detroit is Sam Levene, who expostulates very good with his arms, which are as long as a monkey's. Stubby Kaye, who plays Nicely-Nicely Johnson, the well-known horse-player, is built on lines which are by no means dinky, for his poundage maybe runs into zillions, but he gives with a voice which is as couth as a choir boy's or maybe couther. He commences the evening by joining in a three-part comedy song about the nags. In fact, it is a fugue, and I will give you plenty of eleven to five that it is the first fugue many patrons of the Coliseum ever hear. Miss Vivian Blaine (Miss Adelaide) is a very choice blonde judy and she gets to sing a song which goes as follows: "Take back your mink to from whence it came" and which hits me slap-dab in the ear as being supernaturally comical. Myself, I prefer her to Miss Lizbeth Webb, who plays the mission doll, but, naturally, I do not mention such an idea out loud.

The Coliseum is no rabbit hutch, and maybe a show as quick and smart as this *Guys and Dolls* will go better in such a sized theatre as the Cambridge Theatre. Personally, I found myself laughing ha-ha last night more often than a guy in the critical dodge has any right to. And I am ready to up and drop on my knees before Frank Loesser, who writes the music and lyrics. In fact, this Loesser is maybe the best light composer in the world. In fact, the chances are that *Guys and Dolls* is not only a young masterpiece, but the Beggar's Opera of Broadway.

(1952)

The Crucible, by Arthur Miller, at the Bristol Old Vic.

Convictions, as Nietzsche said, are prisons: they exclude from life the fun of doubt and flexibility. In *Death of a Salesman* Arthur Miller observed mankind in detached, compassionate surview; in *The Crucible* he takes sides. And the strength of his convictions breeds the ultimate weakness of his play.

He re-creates the Salem witch-hunt of 1692, which began when a clutch of flighty wantons, discovered dancing naked by moonlight, absolved themselves by accusing others of sending the devil into them. Were they really practising witchcraft, that fertility magic which Christian theology has taught us to call black? Mr. Miller evades the issue. For him all oppression is vile, and we must assume that in Salem there was smoke but no fire. A fearful town believes the girls' charges, whereat Mr. Miller skins history alive, revealing beneath the surface the familiar ugliness of McCarthyism. Silence is evidence of guilt; he who testifies to a prisoner's innocence is himself suspected. Abigail Williams, the leader of the crypto-coven, seeks to ensnare her ex-lover, John Proctor, by naming his wife as a witch. "Is the accuser always holy now?" he cries, and, to prove Abigail's malice, confesses his infidelity to the court. But his wife, thinking to shield him, denies it, thereby ensuring her own and her husband's condemnation.

The fierce narrative thrill of the action depends mostly on Mr. Miller's mastery of period dialogue. The prose is gnarled, whorled in its gleaming as a stick of polished oak, an incomparable dramatic weapon. Witness Abigail's speech, swearing her friends to secrecy:

> Let either of you breathe a word, or the edge of a word . . . and I will come to you in the black of some terrible night, and I will bring a pointy reckoning that will shudder you. . . . I saw Indians smash my dear parents' heads on the pillow next to mine, and I have seen some reddish work done at night, and I can make you wish you had never seen the sun go down.

What pity, then, that Mr. Miller's convictions so crucially imprison him! He presents Deputy-Governor Danforth, the judge, as a motiveless monster, which is as if Shaw had omitted the Inquisitor's speech from the trial scene of *Saint Joan*. The enemy is allowed no appeal. Mr. Miller writes wrathfully, a state in which the creative muscles tend to seize up; and a hard human tragedy, which one hoped to see irrigated, is desiccated instead. "For the Poet," said Sidney, "he nothing affirmeth, and therefore never lyeth." Mr. Miller affirmeth plenty, and to support his affirmations he is forced to restrict his sympathies—a fatal abdication from truth. He prejudges those whom he accuses of prejudice, and the last scene, in which Proctor goes to the noose, plays like old melodrama; the words ring heroically hollow, because dramaturgy has declined into martyrology. Men are never wholly right or wholly wrong. The witch-hunters at Salem thought they were, and Mr. Miller, the hunters' hunter, flaws a magnificent play by sharing their fallacy.

Rosemary Harris exactly catches the wan aridity of Proctor's wife; and Proctor himself is Edgar Wreford, who, sniffing melodrama in the air, lets the part play him, replacing the firm reins of realism with the loose bit of rhetoric.

(1954)

Moby Dick, ADAPTED BY ORSON WELLES FROM HERMAN MELVILLE'S NOVEL, AT THE DUKE OF YORK'S, LODNDON.

At this stage of his career it is absurd to expect Orson Welles to attempt anything less than the impossible. It is all that is left to him. Mere possible things, like Proust or *War and Peace,* would confine him. He must choose *Moby Dick,* a book whose setting is the open sea, whose hero is more mountain than man and more symbol than either, and whose villain is the supremely unstageable whale. He must take as his raw material Melville's prose, itself as stormy as the sea it speaks of, with a thousand wrecked metaphors clinging on its surface to frail spars of sense. (You do not dip into Melville, you jump in, holding your nose and praying not to be drowned. If prose styles were women, Melville's would be painted by Rubens and cartooned by Blake: it is a shot-gun wedding of sensuousness and metaphysics.) Yet out of all these impossibilities Mr. Welles has fashioned a piece of pure theatrical megalomania—a sustained assault on the senses which dwarfs anything London has seen since, perhaps, the Great Fire.

It was exactly fifty years ago last Wednesday that Irving made his last appearance in London. I doubt if anyone since then has left his mark more indelibly on every second of a London production than Mr. Welles has on this of *Moby Dick.* He serves Melville in three capacities: as adapter, as director, and as star. The adaptation, to begin with, is beautifully adroit. Captain Ahab's self-destructive revenge on the albino whale that tore off his leg is over in less than a hundred and fifty minutes. And two brilliant devices reconcile us to the lushness of Melville's style. Firstly, seeing how readily Melville falls into iambic pentameters, Mr. Welles has versified the whole action. Secondly, to prepare us for the bravura acting which is to come, he "frames" the play as a rehearsal held sixty years ago by a tyrannical brandy-swigging American actor-manager. My only criticism must be that the role of Pip, the mad cabinboy, has been rather too heavily expanded. Mr. Welles clearly sees Ahab as Lear and Pip as a cross-breed of the Fool and Cordelia, but the duologue between them was a very ponderous affair, not helped by the agonised inadequacy of the actress to whom Pip's ramblings were given.

The real revelation was Mr. Welles' direction. The great, square, rope-hung vault of the bare stage, stabbed with light from every point of the compass, becomes by turns the Nantucket wharf, the whalers' chapel, the deck of the *Pequod,* and the ocean itself. The technique with which Thornton Wilder evoked "Our Town" is used to evoke "Our Universe." The whaling-boat from which Ahab flings himself at Moby Dick is a rostrum projecting into the stalls, and the first-act hurricane is a model of imaginative stagecraft: ropes and beams swing crazily across one's vision, while the crew slides and huddles beneath. Mr. Welles' films have already established his mastery of atmospheric sound: here the crash and howl of the sea is alternated with a brisk little mouth-organ theme and strange, foreboding chords played on a harmonium. Dialogue is overlapped, words are timed, syllables are pounced on with a subtlety we have not heard since *The Magnificent Ambersons.* Gordon Jackson, a much-neglected actor, gives Ishmael just the right feeling of perplexity, and Patrick McGoohan as Starbuck, the mate who dares to oppose Ahab's will, is Melville's "long, earnest man" to the life, whittled out of immemorial teak. His is the best performance of the evening.

When I say that, I am not excepting Mr. Welles, who now comes before us as actor. In aspect, he is a leviathan plus. He has a voice of bottled thunder, so deeply encasked that one thinks of those liquor advertisements which boast that not a drop is sold till it's seven years old. The trouble is that everything he does is on such a vast scale that it quickly becomes monotonous. He is too big for the boots of any part. He reminds one of Macaulay's conversation, as Carlyle described it: "Very well for a while, but one wouldn't *live* under Niagara." Emotion of any kind he expresses by thrusting out his chin and knitting his eyebrows. Between these twin promontories there juts out a false and quite unnecessary nose. Sir Laurence Olivier began his film of *Hamlet* with the statement that it was "the tragedy of a man who could not make up his mind." At one point Mr. Welles' new appendage started to leave its moorings, and *Moby Dick* nearly became the tragedy of a man who could not make up his nose.

Let me now turn about and say that, though Mr. Welles plays Ahab less than convincingly, there are few actors alive who could play it at all. Earlier in the evening, as the actor-manager, he makes what seems to be a final statement on the relationship of actor to audience: "Did you ever," he says, "hear of an unemployed audience?" It is a good line; but the truth is that British audiences have been unemployed far too long. If they wish to exert themselves, to have their minds set whirling and their eyes dazzling at sheer theatrical virtuosity, *Moby Dick* is their opportunity. With it, the theatre becomes once more a house of magic.

(1955)

AMERICAN BLUES
The Plays of Arthur Miller and Tennessee Williams.

"Since 1920," Arthur Miller has said, "American drama has been a steady, year-by-year documentation of the frustration of man," and the record supports him. Between the wars most of the serious American playwrights—Odets, for instance, Elmer Rice, Maxwell Anderson, Irwin Shaw, and Lillian Hellman—did their best work in the conviction that modern civilisation was committing repeated acts of criminal injustice against the individual. Their heroes were victims, such as Mio in *Winterset,* and they devoted themselves to dramatising the protests of minorities; it was thus that they ploughed the land cleared for them by O'Neill, the solitary pioneer bulldozer. For his long-sightedness they substituted an absorption in immediate reality; where he was the admonitory lighthouse, they were the prying torches. During the war their batteries ran out: since 1945 none of them has written a first-rate play. The mission of martyrology has been taken up by the younger generation, by Arthur Miller and Tennessee Williams.

Miller and Williams seem, on the face of things, to have even less in common than Ibsen and Bjørnson. Miller, a man of action, belongs to the thirties' tradition of social drama, while Williams, a poet *manqué,* looks ahead to a lyrical, balletic *Gesamtkunstwerk* in which (though I doubt whether he fully recognises the fact) words as such are likely to have less and less importance. Yet the two men share much. Both echo Jacob in *Awake and Sing,* who says: "We don't want life printed on dollar bills." Miller is a rebel against, Williams a refugee from the familiar ogre of commercialism, the killer of values and the leveller of men. "You know, *knowledge*—ZZZZpp! *Money*—zzzzpp! POWER! Wham! That's the cycle democracy is built on!" exults the Gentleman Caller in *The Glass Menagerie*. But this is not their only joint exploit. Both reserve their most impassioned utterance for one subject, into which they plunge headlong, sometimes floundering in self-pity, sometimes belly-diving into rhetoric, but often knifing straight and deep: the subject of frustration. Lady Mulligan, in Williams' latest play *Camino Real,* complains to Gutman, the proprietor of her hotel, that he has chosen to shelter some highly undesirable guests. Whereupon:

GUTMAN: They pay the price of admission the same as you.
LADY M.: What price is that?
GUTMAN: Desperation!

Techniques change, but grand themes do not. Whether in a murder trial, a bullfight, a farce like *Charley's Aunt,* or a tragedy like *Lear,* the behaviour of a human being at the end of his tether is the common denominator of all drama. When a man (or woman) arrives at self-knowledge through desperation, he (or she) has become the raw material for a great play. The stature of the work will depend on the dramatist's honesty and skill, but its cornerstone is already laid. Though they take the same theme, Miller and Williams build very differently. In European terms, Miller is the Scandinavian: he has in fact translated Ibsen, whose fierce lucidity, humourlessness, and "odour of spiritual paraffin" he shares. Williams, on the other hand, is the Mediterranean, the lover of Lorca and D. H. Lawrence, sensuous, funny, verbally luxuriant, prone to immersion in romantic tragedy. Miller's plays are hard, "patrist," athletic, concerned mostly with men. Williams' are soft, "matrist," sickly, concerned mostly with women. What links them is their love for the bruised individual soul and its life of "quiet desperation." It takes courage, in a sophisticated age, to keep faith with this kind of love, and their refusal to compromise has led both Miller and Williams into some embarrassing pseudo-simplicities. Their reward is in characters like Joe Keller of *All My Sons,* Willy Loman of *Death of a Salesman,* John Proctor of *The Crucible,* Blanche DuBois of *A Streetcar Named Desire,* Laura of *The Glass Menagerie,* Kilroy of *Camino Real,* who live together in the great theatrical line of flawed, victimised innocents.

Arthur Miller, who was born in Brooklyn in 1915, achieved his first Broadway production at the age of twenty-nine. The play, *The Man Who Had All the Luck,* had a framework which Miller (himself a second son) later elaborated in *All My Sons* and *Death of a Salesman:* the relationship of two sons with their father. The protagonist is David, the elder, an unskilled garage hand in a midwestern town. His brother, Amos, forcibly trained by Pat, a jealous and protective father, to become a baseball pitcher, gets nowhere, while the ignored David thrives, financially as well as maritally. His inability to fail makes David neurotic, and to deaden his sense of unworthiness he falls into the habit of ascribing his success to luck. In the final scene he is made to understand that "luck" is merely a word used by men less diligent than himself to explain his triumphs. "You made it all yourself," cries his wife. "It was always you." His hired man, the immigrant Gus, puts the play's case: a man must believe, he says, "that on this earth he is the boss of his life, not the leafs in the teacups, not the stars. In Europe I seen already millions of Davids walking around, millions. They gave up already to know that they are the boss. They gave up to know that they deserve this world." The point of the *drame à thèse* is weakened because the principal characters are too obviously pawns in Miller's hands; what stays in the mind is the craggy candour of the dialogue. Miller, like Williams, is committed to prose drama, in which both men have uncovered riches which make the English "poetic revival" seem hollow, retrogressive, and—to use Cyril Connolly's coinage—praeteritist.

Pat, David's father, is guilty only by implication. Joe Keller in *All My Sons,* staged by Elia Kazan in 1947, is a criminal in the legal sense. Shadily, he has been acquitted of manufacturing faulty aircraft parts during the war, and when the play opens, his partner is in gaol, taking the rap for him. Of Joe's two sons, one has been killed in action, and the other, Chris, intends to marry his brother's ex-fiancée, the convicted partner's daughter. Chris is a militant idealist ashamed of having survived the war; material possessions sicken him unless they have been purely and honourably acquired—"Otherwise what you have is loot, and there's blood on it." Miller concentrates on two shifting relationships: between Chris and his girl, and between Chris and his father. Joe Keller (like Willy Loman) had to compromise in order to live; and Chris (like Biff in the later play) is overwhelmed by the revelation of paternal guilt. How can he marry the daughter of a man who was imprisoned because of his father's perjury? Miller solves this classic impasse with a smart stroke of melodrama: unconvincingly, Keller accepts the burden and shoots himself.

"I'm his father," says Keller at one point, "and he's my son, and if there's something bigger than that I'll put a bullet in my head." This message, more symphonically orchestrated, reappears in Miller's best play, *Death of a Salesman,* which Kazan directed in 1948. *All Our Fathers,* as Daniel Schneider suggested, would be an appropriate alternative title. Willy Loman and his two sons, the sensualist Happy and the mysteriously retarded Biff, are ruined by their belief in "the wrong dream," the mystique of salesmanship. "What are you building?" says Ben, Willy's millionaire brother. "Lay your hand on it. Where is it?" Unlike most hero-victims, Willy is not cynical about the values which are corrupting him; he is pathetic because, brightly and unquestioningly, he reveres them. As the play begins, Biff, the quondam college hero, has returned penniless to his Brooklyn home, where he finds his father going crazy with failure to sell. The ensuing action covers the next twenty-four hours: in a series of beautifully welded interlocking flashbacks we pursue Willy's thoughts into the past, back to the germinal moment of calamity when he was surprised by Biff in a hotel room with a half-dressed tart. This encounter, with its implied destruction of the father-god, stunted Biff's career and left Willy with a load of remorse redoubled by the fact that he, too, was the unsuccessful one of two brothers. Memory explodes the cocoon of illusions within which he preserves his self-respect, and (ostensibly for the insurance money) he commits suicide.

The play is Miller's triumph in the plain style; it rings with phrases which have entered into the contemporary subconscious. "He's liked, but he's not—well liked"; "The woods are burning, boys"; Ben's complacent "The jungle is dark but full of diamonds, Willy." More memorably, there is Mrs. Loman's anguished rebuke to her sons for having scorned their father:

> Willy Loman never made a lot of money. His name was never in the papers. He's not the finest character that ever lived. But he's a human being, and a terrible thing is happening to him. So attention must be paid. He's not to be allowed to fall into his grave like a dog. Attention, attention must be finally paid to such a person.

Charley, Willy's neighbour, speaks an epitaph over him which has the same groping, half-articulate power:

> And for a salesman, there is no rock bottom to the life. He don't put a bolt to a nut, he don't tell you the law, or give you medicine. . . . Nobody dast blame this man. A salesman is got to dream, boy. It comes with the territory.

There is a fair amount of otiose breast-beating in the script, and Miller's prose sometimes slips into a sentimental rhythm of despair which could be convicted of glibness. But the theatre is an impure craft, and *Death of a Salesman* organises its impurities with an emotional effect unrivalled in post-war drama.

Willy Loman goes to his fate without knowing exactly why it has overtaken him. The heroes of Miller's last two plays are also defeated, but they know what forces have beaten them: the enemy in each case is identified. In 1950 he adapted *An Enemy of the People,* turning it into a racy contemporary pamphlet. His temperament chimed with what he describes as Ibsen's "terrible wrath," and the dilemma of Stockmann, the betrayed crusader, duplicated Miller's own, that of the life-long democrat who learns, from the example of his own country, that majority rule is not infallible. Stockmann is vanquished by the pusillanimous stupidity of the mob, on which, in the original, he launches a furious attack. Miller softens it in translation, thereby forfeiting the objectivity which allowed even Ibsen's heroes their weaknesses. Anger is a great simplifier, and Miller is an angry writer. *An Enemy of the People* marks his decision to weight the scales in favour of the oppressed minority man.

"Before many can know something, *one* must know it"—Stockmann's affirmation steers us towards *The Crucible,* Miller's most recent play, produced in New York last January. The bird's-eye compassion of *Salesman* has now been replaced by a worm's-eye sympathy which extends only to the "right-minded" characters. Though it draws plain contemporary parallels with its subject, the witch-hunt at Salem, it is not an overtly political play: it deals with the refusal of a stubborn intellect to enter into enforced allegiances. "I like not the smell of this 'authority,' " says Proctor, the hero. In Salem, as in Stockmann's township, nonconformity was allied with sin, an attitude which Miller detests so savagely that the play often resembles the trial scene from *Saint Joan* with the Inquisitor's speech deleted. The inquisitors in *The Crucible* are unmotivated fiends, and the atmosphere in which they flourished is never explored or accounted for.

The action stays close to historical fact. A group of flighty wantons, charged with engaging in mildly orgiastic rites in a wood near Salem, hit on the notion of exculpating themselves by accusing their neighbours of having sent the devil into them. Their accusations are believed; a tribunal is set up; and the hangings begin. Proctor's wife is arrested, and his attempts to exonerate her lead to his own arrest. In a fine, clinching line he demands: "Is the accuser always holy now?" If he confesses, giving a list of those who infected him with diabolism, he will be freed; if not, he will be executed. At their last meeting his wife tells him how another of the condemned died:

> Great stones they lay upon his chest until he plead aye or nay. They say he give them but two words. "More weight," he says. And died.

Head high, as the drums roll, Proctor sacrifices himself for his principles, a commonplace "Victorian" martyrdom worthy of a mind much less subtle than Miller's. *The Crucible* is disturbing because it suggests a sensibility blunted by the insistence of an outraged conscience: it has the over-simplifications of poster art.

In *The Devils of Loudun,* a much more searching analysis of witch-hunting, Aldous Huxley mentions the euphoria of the "adrenalin addict," a type to which Miller seems at present to belong. "There are many people," Huxley says, "for whom hate and rage pay a higher dividend of immediate satisfaction than love," this satisfaction being derived from "their psychically stimulated endocrines." Bad temper, which produces cramp in the creative muscles, is an enemy of art; and though *The Crucible* is on the right side morally, socially, and politically, it is the artistic equivalent of a closed shop. Full of affirmations, it is also full of emotional half-truths; which will do for a leader-writer, but not for a playwright of Miller's giant stature.

Tennessee Williams' genius has no social commitments, but many aesthetic ones. His faults, like Miller's, are the defects of his virtues. The present cast of Miller's mind traps him in the present, the male preserve wherein history is shaped, and the universal preoccupation is with action and incident; Williams trades in nostalgia and hope, the past and the future, obsessions which we associate most strongly with the great female characters—Marguérite Gautier, Cleopatra, Hedda Gabler, and Chekhov's women, none of whom cares for today half as much as she cares for yesterday or tomorrow. His plays thus have the static quality of dream rather than the dynamic quality of fact; they bring the drama of mood to what may be its final hothouse flowering.

Williams is a Southerner, born forty years ago in Columbus, Mississippi, and his work first reached Broadway when his "memory play," *The Glass Menagerie,* was produced in 1945. It turns a burning-glass on to a storm-proof family unit, insulated against life by its careful preservation of gentility. A stage direction reads:

> The apartment faces an alley, and is entered by a fire-escape, a structure whose name is a touch of accidental poetry, for all of these huge buildings are always burning with the slow and implacable fires of human desperation.

Here live Amanda, garrulous and suffocatingly maternal, her cynical son, Tom, and her crippled daughter, Laura. Retrospectively, Tom tells the story of how he invited a Gentleman Caller to dinner as a possible beau for Laura, and how the Caller, affable though he was, revealed that he was already spoken for. Laura's spinsterhood is confirmed; Amanda's hopes are dashed; but neither of these minor disasters is made to sound mawkish. Williams' wry wit acts as a caustic to the wounds. In Amanda, fussy and conversationally archaic, he shows the perfection of his ear for human speech, and also the extent of his tact: she never becomes a grotesque. The play is not a major achievement, but its opacity is as precise and marvellous as a spider's web.

You Touched Me!, on which Williams collaborated with Donald Windham, is of interest only because it dealt (like *The Glass Menagerie*) with the impact of reality on illusions, in this case on two isolated, mutually infectious virgins; and because it was adapted from the short story of the same name by D. H. Lawrence, one of Williams' heroes. It was followed in 1947 by *A Streetcar Named Desire,* which was directed by Kazan, who seems to have an instinct for the best of both Miller and Williams. It is perhaps the most misunderstood of his plays: the English and French productions were both so blatantly sensationalised that Williams' underlying lyric fibre passed unnoticed. If Willy Loman is the desperate average man, Blanche DuBois is the desperate exceptional woman. Willy's collapse began when his son walked into a hotel apartment and found him with a whore; Blanche's when she entered "a room that I thought was empty" and found her young husband embracing an older man. In each instance the play builds up to a climax involving guilt and concomitant disgust. Blanche, nervously boastful, lives in the leisured past; her defence against actuality is a sort of aristocratic *Bovarysme,* at which her brutish brother-in-law Stanley repeatedly sneers. Characteristically, Williams keeps his detachment and does not take sides: he never denies that Stanley's wife, in spite of her sexual enslavement, is happy and well-adjusted, nor does he exaggerate the cruelty with which Stanley reveals to Blanche's new suitor the secrets of her nymphomaniac past. The play's weakness lies in the fact that the leading role lends itself to grandiose overplaying by unintelligent actresses, who forget that when Blanche complains to her sister about Stanley's animalism, she is expressing, however faintly, an ideal:

> Such things as art—as poetry and music—such kinds of new light have come into the world since then! . . . That we have to make *grow!* And *cling* to, and hold as our flag! In this dark march toward whatever it is we're approaching . . . *Don't—don't* hang back with the brutes!

When, finally, she is removed to the mental home, we should feel that a part of civilisation is going with her. Where ancient drama teaches us to reach nobility by contemplation of what is noble, modern American drama conjures us to contemplate what might have been noble, but is now humiliated, ignoble in the sight of all but the compassionate.

In 1948 Williams reworked an earlier play, *Summer and Smoke.* Its heroine, Alma, is Blanche ten years younger: a Southern virgin concealing beneath "literary" affectations a sense of inadequacy in the presence of men. Her next-door neighbour, a notorious rake, tries to seduce her and is boldly repulsed. He shows her an anatomy chart, and explains that the human body is a tree inhabited by three birds, the brain, the belly, and the genitals. Where, he asks, is the soul of which she speaks and for which, in Spanish, her name stands? Ironically, he ends up reformed, whereas Alma, her sexual instincts newly awakened, moves to the other extreme. They exchange attitudes, passing almost without contact. *Summer and Smoke,* a needlessly symbolic morality play, is sentimental in that its characters are too slight to sustain the consuming emotions which are bestowed on them.

Nobody could say that *The Rose Tattoo* (1950) did not contain large characters. It is the most thoroughgoing star vehicle of the last ten years, expressly written for Anna Magnani, whose shaky acquaintance with English unfortunately prevented her from playing the lead in the stage production. Here Williams pleads the cause of sexual love as its own justification. "So successfully," he says in his preface, "have we disguised from ourselves the intensity of our own feelings, the sensibility of our own hearts, that plays in the tragic tradition have begun to seem untrue." At a time when Miller's plays were growing colder and more intellectualised, Williams' blazed hotter and more sensuous. His heroine is a poor Sicilian immigrant whose husband, a truck-driving smuggler with a fabulous capacity for sexual devotion, has been shot. She learns to her horror that her man had been faithless to her, but the realisation does not prevent her from joyously taking as her new lover a man who physically resembles the dead ideal. The play's complex structure—short scenes linked by evocative snatches of music—is too poetic for its theme, but the virtuosity of the writing, alternately ribald and pathetic, is tremendous. Does it alternate between tragedy and farce? That is because it was meant for a great actress whose gift it is to switch emotional gear, change from a Siddonsesque pose to a bout of nose-picking without a moment's hesitation. Williams' fault, as in *Streetcar,* was to have overestimated English-speaking actresses. It would take a Magnani to play the scene in which Serafina, the heroine, entertains her new lover, out of whose pocket, as the poetic tension mounts, there falls a neatly packaged contraceptive. Sardou never asked as much of Bernhardt, nor D'Annunzio of Duse.

Kazan renewed his association with Williams in the spring of 1953, when he directed the violently controversial *Camino Real*. This is a phantasmagoria of decadence, as limpidly rebellious to modern civilisation as a Bix Beiderbecke solo is to a Paul Whiteman orchestration. The published text has a unity never achieved by the acting script. It carries to its conclusion Williams' dictum: "I say that symbols are nothing but the natural speech of drama." In a preface he adds: "I have read the works of 'thinking playwrights,' as distinguished from us who are permitted only to feel. . . ." The result is a tranced play of hypersensitivity, a weird drug-work of wit, terror, and inertia.

It is set in a mythical Central American coastal town. Stage left is the Seven Seas Hotel, where live Byron, Casanova, and Marguérite Gautier, ghosts of the aristocratic way of life; stage right are a pawnbroker's shop, a fortune-teller's tent, and a flophouse, where, among the outcasts, we encounter the Baron de Charlus. Upstage is an arch, giving on to a desert, where a hot wind blows and whither no one dares travel. Williams' hero is Kilroy, the new arrival at this fetid microcosm of modern life: the embodiment of youth and enterprise, he was once a prizefighter but had to abandon his career because "I've got a heart in my chest as big as the head of a baby." He is elected the town butt, and the police deck him out in a clown's costume, complete with electrically sparking nose. How does this simpleton fit in with the filth of the Camino Real? Williams answers the question in writing which seems too often to have been composed in a state of *kif*. He indulges in vague, roseate aphorisms; nor can he resist theatrical shortcuts such as a noisy aeroplane crash and *two* chases down the aisles and into the boxes of the theatre, devices which assist the play about as tellingly as a consignment of heroin would help an anti-narcotics campaign. Yet out of the strident blare of the action, Williams' faith in Kilroy's truth, in a child's mistrust of phoneyness, emerges with overwhelming clarity. For those anarchists who escape he has undisguised sympathy. Byron, for example, says of his later works: "They seem to improve as the wine in the bottle—dwindles. . . . *There is a passion for declivity in this world"*; but when, having roused himself, he departs into the murderous desert, Williams gives him a splendid epitaph: *"Make voyages!—Attempt them!*—there's nothing else!"

Kilroy, too, attempts the voyage, but only after a serio-comic encounter with a character called the Gypsy, who organises and advertises the local fiesta, at which her daughter, in a loony parody of a fertility ritual, annually recovers her virginity. The Gypsy's garish cynicism ("File this crap under crap") struck the New York critics as the most recognisable thing in the play, along with Kilroy's seduction of the Gypsy's daughter, a grossly comic scene in which the two young people repeat to each other eight times the talismanic words: "I am sincere." Surviving a brisk attempt to murder him, Kilroy journeys through the perilous arch, accompanied by Don Quixote, that other liegeman of the lost cause, who ends the play with a movingly symbolic cry: "The violets in the mountains have broken the rocks!"

Many charges can be brought against *Camino Real.* It has too many italics, too many exclamation marks; it depends too much on boozed writing and aureate diction. Its virtue is in its affectionate championing of the flyblown, inarticulate stratum of humanity. Perhaps when Quixote and Kilroy reach the snowy upper air of the unnamed mountains, they will become subjects for a play by Miller, whose artistic life is dedicated, like Shaw's, to a belief in progress towards an attainable summit. Williams' aspirations are imaginative and hence unattainable; and therein lies the difference between them.

Complementary, yet irreconcilable, Miller and Williams have produced the most powerful body of dramatic prose in modern English. They write with equal virtuosity, Williams about the violets, Miller about the rocks. The vegetable reinforces the mineral; and the animal, a dramatic element feared or ignored in the English theatre, triumphantly reinforces both.

(1954)

Valentine to Tennessee Williams.

In Spain, where I saw him last, he looked profoundly Spanish. He might have passed for one of those confidential street dealers who earn their living selling spurious Parker pens in the cafés of Málaga or Valencia. Like them, he wore a faded chalk-striped shirt, a coat slung over his shoulders, a trim, dark moustache, and a sleazy, fat-cat smile. His walk, like theirs, was a raffish saunter, and everything about him seemed slept in, especially his hair, a nest of small, wet serpents. Had we been in Seville and his clothes been more formal, he could have been mistaken for a pampered elder son idling away a legacy in dribs and on drabs, the sort you see sitting in windows along the Sierpes, apparently stuffed. In Italy he looks Italian; in Greece, Greek; wherever he travels on the Mediterranean coast, Tennessee Williams takes on a protective colouring which melts him into his background, like a lizard on a rock. In New York or London he seems out of place, and is best explained away as a retired bandit. Or a beachcomber: shave the beard off any of the self-portraits Gauguin painted in Tahiti, soften the features a little, and you have a sleepy outcast face that might well be Tennessee's.

It is unmistakably the face of a nomad. Wherever Williams goes he is a stranger, one who lives out of suitcases and has a trick of making any home he acquires resemble, within ten minutes, a hotel apartment. Like most hypochondriacs, he is an uneasy guest on earth. When he sold the film rights of his play *Cat on a Hot Tin Roof* for half a million dollars, he asked that the payment should be spread over ten years, partly out of prudence but mostly out of a mantic suspicion, buzzing in his ears, that in ten years' time he might be dead. He says justly of himself that he is "a driven person." The condemned tend always to be lonely, and one of Williams' favourite quotations is a line from a play which runs: "We're all of us sentenced to solitary confinement inside our own skins." He says such things quite blandly, with a thick chuckle which is as far from cynicism as it is from self-pity.

To be alone at forty is to be really alone, and Williams has passed forty. In a sense, of course, solitude is a condition of his trade. All writing is an anti-social act, since the writer is a man who can speak freely only when alone; to be himself he must lock himself up, to communicate he must cut himself off from all communication; and in this there is something always a little mad. Many writers loathe above all sounds the closing of the door which seals them up in their privacy. Williams, by contrast, welcomes it: it dispels the haze of uncertainty through which he normally converses, and releases for his pleasure the creatures who people his imaginings—desperate women, men nursing troublesome secrets, untouchables whom he touches with frankness and mercy, society's derelict rag dolls. The theatre, he once said, is a place where one has time for the problems of people to whom one would show the door if they came to one's office for a job. His best-loved characters are people like this, and they are all, in some way, trapped—Blanche DuBois, of *Streetcar,* beating her wings in a slum; Alma of *Summer and Smoke,* stricken with elephantiasis of the soul; Brick in *Cat,* sodden with remorse. As we shall see, much of what has happened to them has also happened to him. He is the most personal of playwrights. Incomplete people obsess him—above all, those who, like himself, have ideals too large for life to accommodate. There is another, opposed kind of incompleteness, that of materialists like the Polack in *Streetcar* and Big Daddy in *Cat;* and in most of Williams' work both kinds are to be found, staring blankly at each other, arguing from different premises and conversing without comprehension. In his mental battlefield the real is perpetually at war with the ideal; what is public wrestles with what is private, what drags men down fights with what draws them up. This struggle is an allegory, by which I mean that it reflects a conflict within Williams himself. He cannot bring himself to believe that the flesh and the spirit can be reconciled, or to admit that the highest emotion can spring from the basest source. As Aldous Huxley has put it: "Whether it's passion or the desire of the moth for the star, whether it's tenderness or adoration or romantic yearning—love is always accompanied by events in the nerve endings, the skin, the mucous membranes, the glandular and erectile tissue. . . . What we need is another set of words. Words that can express the natural togetherness of things." For Williams they remain stubbornly apart, and it is this that gives his writing its odd urgency, its note of unfinished exploration. Alone behind the door, sustained by what one critic called the "comradeship of his introspection," he seeks to bridge the gap between his two selves. His work is a pilgrimage in search of a truce. His typewriter stands on the glass top of a hotel table, and most likely neither he nor it will be there tomorrow.

Though he does not need company, he does not shun it. Leaning back on a bar stool, one of a crowd, he can simulate ease with a barely perceptible effort. Mostly he is silent, sucking on a hygienic cigarette holder full of absorbent crystals, with a vague smile painted on his face, while his mind swats flies in outer space. He says nothing that is not candid and little that is not trite. A mental deafness seems to permeate him, so that he will laugh spasmodically in the wrong places, tell you the time if you ask him the date, or suddenly reopen conversations left for dead three days before. Late at night, part of him may come to life: in shreds of old slang ("We're in like Flynn") or bursts of old songs, remembered from St. Louis in the twenties and unexpectedly proceeding, in a voice at once true and blue, from his slumped figure, which you had thought slumbering, in the back seat of somebody else's car. This is Williams on holiday, and you may be sure that his mind is not far from a blank.

He longs for intimacy, but shrinks from its responsibilities. Somewhere in the past, before he became famous, lies the one perfect passion; its object parted from him and afterward died of cancer. Since then, too cautious to spoil perfection by trying to repeat it, he has kept all emotional relationships deliberately casual. He will incur no more emotional debts, nor extend any more emotional credit. His friendships are many and generous, ranging from Mediterranean remittance men to Carson McCullers; but love is a sickness which he will do anything to avoid. If his deeper instincts crave release, you may find him at a bullfight—or even writing a play.

He was born forty-four years ago in Columbus, Mississippi, the son of an itinerant shoe salesman known throughout the territory as a fiery and accomplished poker player. As a child he lived in Columbus with his mother, his elder sister, and his younger brother at the home of his maternal grandfather, a highly respected Episcopal rector. Here an image took root which has haunted much of his work: the South as a fading mansion of gentility. The first great wrench of his life occurred when he was still very young. His father took a desk job in St. Louis and the family left Columbus to join him. "We suddenly discovered," Williams says, "that there were two kinds of people, the rich and the poor, and that we belonged more to the latter." It was here, in a stuffy, backstreet apartment, that his world split, amoeba-like, into two irreconcilable halves—the soft, feminine world of the room that he and his sister filled with little glass animals, and the cruel, male world of the alley outside, where cats fought and coupled to a persistent screaming. He entered the University of Missouri and at the age of sixteen got a story into *Weird Tales,* but the depression sent him to work for three memorably detested years in a shoe factory. The result was a heart attack, followed by a complete physical breakdown. He returned to his studies and in 1938 took a B.A. at the University of Iowa. By now his imagination was alive with human voices, and two of his plays had been performed by the St. Louis Mummers. The future offered by his father meant going back to the shoe factory. Subjecting his life to its second great wrench, he left home.

"And it don't look like I'm ever gonna cease my wanderin'. . . ." He waited on table in New Orleans and worked on a pigeon ranch in California; then a one-act play won him a prize of a hundred dollars and attracted the attention of a Broadway agent, Audrey Wood. He sent her the script of *Battle of Angels,* an ambitious survey of "the sometimes conflicting desires of the flesh and the spirit." To his amazement, the Theatre Guild bought it. It opened in Boston in December 1940 and closed without reaching New York. On top of that, and perhaps because of it, Williams developed a cataract in his left eye. The next two years found him a vulnerable and myopic vagabond in Bohemia, always the victim of a hectic nervous system, which alarmed him by expressing its disquiet as often in illness as in imaginative visions. Back to New Orleans, living from pawnshop to mouth; then to Greenwich Village, where he worked as a waiter, wearing a black eyepatch which someone adorned with a surrealistic white eyeball.

In 1943 Audrey Wood got him a six-month contract in Hollywood. He spent most of it writing *The Glass Menagerie,* in which his twin worlds of fact and dream came out for the first time distinct and dovetailed. Its Broadway success a year later gave him security: but "security," he was soon writing, "is a kind of death. . . ." To escape it he returned to New Orleans, to cheap hotels and rented apartments. On a trip to Taos, New Mexico, he came down with what proved to be a ruptured appendix; but he heard a nun whisper that it might be cancer, and, spurred by the death sentence, he fled from the hospital. Feverishly he composed what was meant to be his last message to the world.

A new friendship helped him to obey Hemingway's dictum and "get it out whole." This was with Carson McCullers. In his own words: "Carson came to me in the summer of 1946 at the height of my imaginary dying, she came to Nantucket Island, which I had chosen to die on, and the moment she came down the gangplank of the ship from the mainland, in her baseball cap, with that enchantingly radiant crooked-toothed grin of hers, something very light happened in me. I dropped my preoccupation with the thought that I was doomed, and from then on there was a process of adjustment to the new situation, and by the late fall of 1947 I was able to release all the emotional content of the long crisis in *Streetcar*." The play was produced in the same year and fully deserves Williams' description of it: "saturated with death."

More studies in desperation followed: *Summer and Smoke* and *The Rose Tattoo,* perhaps the fullest expression of Williams' special kind of romanticism, which is not pale or scented but earthy and robust, the product of a mind vitally infected with the rhythms of human speech. When overheated, however, it can give off lurid fumes, some of which clouded the air in his next play, *Camino Real*. This was Williams' gaudiest rebellion against materialism, conceived in terms of symbols and carried out mainly in italics. Directed by Elia Kazan in the spring of 1953, the play flopped. There ensued one of those low-energy spells from which Williams frequently suffers. Work became a depressant instead of a stimulant; he kept losing sight of the impulse that sent him to the typewriter and felt that his ideas were being smirched and dog-eared by the well-meaning interference of agents, producers, and directors. *Cat on a Hot Tin Roof* was eighteen months in the writing. I now think it his best work, but when I first saw it, it struck me as an edifice somehow tilted, like a giant architectural folly. It was august, all right, and turbulent, but there were moments of unaccountable wrongness, as if a kazoo had intruded into a string quartet. When I saw the published text and read, side by side, the original third act and the version that was presented on Broadway, I guessed at once what had happened. The kazoo was Kazan.

Cat is a birthday party about death. The birthday is that of Big Daddy, a Southern millionaire dying of cancer. His son Brick is a quiet, defeated drinker; and the cat of the title is Maggie, Brick's wife, whose frayed vivacity derives from the fact that she is sexually ignored by her husband. The play deals with the emotional lies that are shockingly exposed as people try to "reach" each other, to penetrate the inviolable cell in which the soul lives. Williams' trade-marks are all there: the spectre of disease, the imminence of death, the cheating implicit in all emotion, the guilt bound up with sex—plus the technical ability to make tragic characters immeasurably funny. But a play might have all these things and still be bad; what distinguishes *Cat* is the texture of its writing. This is dialogue dead to the eyes alone. It begs for speech so shrilly that you find yourself reading it aloud. "When you are gone from here," says Big Daddy, "you are long gone and no where!"—the words fall from the tongue like "snow from a bamboo leaf," the image by which Zen Buddhists teach their pupils that "artless art" which is the goal of contemplation.

But Kazan was not satisfied. He felt that Brick should undergo a change of heart after the showdown with his father; and into Brick's lines a certain hollowness began to creep. In a stage direction Williams had spoken of "the thundercloud of a common crisis"; with stupefying literalness, Kazan introduced a full-tilt symbolic thunderstorm. Maggie's big lie, uttered to win Big Daddy's inheritance, originally ran: "Brick and I are going to have a child." Inflated by Kazan, the line became: "A child is coming, sired by Brick and out of Maggie the Cat!" The bitterness of the final tableau, when Brick prepares to sleep with Maggie to sustain her lie, was sweetened until the scene seemed to betoken a lasting reconciliation. Williams in no way resents these adjustments, which, he says, "did not violate the essential truth of the play." For him, Kazan is "a very big man, the biggest artist in the theatre of our time." He is at present working on a film script, which Kazan will direct; but some of his admirers feel that a less creative collaborator might, in the long run, be more helpful.

Discussing the incidence of genius, Somerset Maugham once remarked: "The lesson of anatomy applies: there is nothing so rare as the normal." Williams' view of life is always abnormal, heightened and spotlighted, and slashed with bogey shadows. The marvel is that he makes it touch ours, thereby achieving the miracle of communication between human beings which he has always held to be impossible.

Yet he looks anonymous. One ends, as one began, with the enigma. Arthur Miller, after all, looks Lincolnesque, and Anouilh looks hypersensitive, and Sartre looks crazy. Williams, alone of the big playwrights, seems miscast. From that round, rubbery face, those dazed eyes which nothing, no excess or enormity, can surprise—from here the message comes, the latest bulletin from the civil war between purity and squalor. It will always, however long or well I know him, seem wonderfully strange.

(1956)

Waiting for Godot, BY SAMUEL BECKETT, AT THE GOLDEN.

Ten days ago *Waiting for Godot* reached New York, greeted by a baffled but mostly appreciative press and preceded by an advertising campaign in which the management appealed for 70,000 intellectuals to make its venture pay. At the performance I saw, a Sunday matinée, the eggheads were rolling in. And when the curtain fell, the house stood up to cheer a man who had never before appeared in a legitimate play, a mighty and blessed clown whose grateful bewilderment was reflected in the tears that speckled his cheeks, a burlesque comic of crumpled mien and baggy eyes, with a nose stuck like a gherkin into a face as ageless as the Commedia dell' Arte: Bert Lahr, no less, the cowardly lion of *The Wizard of Oz,* who played the dumber of Samuel Beckett's two timeless hoboes, and by his playing bridged, for the first time I can remember, the irrational abyss that yawns between the world of red noses and the world of blue stockings.

Without him, the Broadway production of Mr. Beckett's play would be admirable; with him, it is transfigured. It is as if we, the audience, had elected him to represent us on stage; to stand up for our rights; to anticipate our reactions, resentful and confused, to the lonely universe into which the author plunges us. "I'm going," says Mr. Lahr. "We can't go," snaps his partner. "Why not?" pleads Mr. Lahr. "We're waiting for Godot," comes the reply; whereat Mr. Lahr raises one finger with an "Ah!" of comprehension which betokens its exact opposite, a totality of blankest ignorance. Mr. Lahr's beleaguered simpleton, a draughts-player lost in a universe of chess, is one of the noblest performances I have ever seen.

(1956)

The Caine Mutiny Court-Martial, BY HERMAN WOUK, AT THE HIPPODROME, LONDON.

The Caine Mutiny Court-Martial is a fine ephemeral play disfigured at the end by a brute stroke of tendentious illogic. We have just left the court-room where the main action takes place: we have seen Captain Queeg exposed as a paranoiac and Lieutenant Maryk acquitted of the charge of having improperly deposed him at the height of a typhoon.

Now, at a party given to celebrate the verdict, the author's underlying message, a complete *volte face,* is delivered by Barney Greenwald, counsel for the defence. Greenwald's view is that the real villain was not Queeg but Maryk's best friend, an enlisted intellectual in whose mind the first hint of mutiny took root. Where, asks Greenwald, was this seditious egghead until war broke out? In college, reading Proust and Joyce. And where was Queeg? Patrolling the high seas, and thereby discouraging Hitler from liquidating Greenwald's Jewish mother. Greenwald clinches his case and brings down the curtain by throwing a glass of champagne at the college-boy's face.

The inferences from this tirade are extremely nasty: that the egghead ought to have run away from school and joined the Navy, that a truculent paranoiac is a better citizen than a pacific intellectual, and that a wartime commander must be blindly obeyed even when he is demonstrably gaga and a danger to the lives of his men. I should be mightily relieved to learn that Herman Wouk, who adapted the play from his own novel, introduced this scene purely for cheap effect. For we find, if we take it seriously, that Mr. Wouk's standards of human conduct differ from those of the Nazi Party only in that Mr. Wouk is not anti-Semitic. One wonders, neither idly nor for the first time, just how many thinkers of his stamp would have opposed Hitler if Hitler had not indulged in racial persecution.

Chop off its poisonous tail, and the play is mesmeric and enthralling. It breaks all the superficial rules of drama in that it is static and chiefly devoted to retrospective narration. But it happens in a courtroom, which means that it conforms to the fundamental rule of all theatre: it deals with human beings who are driven, by a chain of events both logically and morally acceptable, to a plight from which there is no apparent escape. A man in a drawing-room, faced with searching and intimate questions, can always grab his hat and leave. But a man in a witness-box must answer them; and whether he speaks truth or falsehood, there will be in the manner of his answering the naked stuff of drama. We talk of drama as a baring of souls. It is more honestly an extortion of confessions—not by torture, since that would be morally unacceptable, but by logical pressure, either of law or circumstance. The truest civic theatre is a democratic court-room.

Mr. Wouk's witnesses are marvellously characterised. Maryk, played by Nigel Stock as a nice, perplexed bull-calf, is thrown neatly into relief by the contrasting methods of the two opposing counsels, one (Peter Dyneley) all gruff directness, the other (David Knight) all circuitous guile. I shall never forget the skill with which Lloyd Nolan, two years ago in New York, outlined the collapse of Queeg: the glib plausibility with which he took the stand, and the self-justifying hysteria with which he left it. Shipped into a larger theatre, Mr. Nolan has slightly coarsened his performance, and I hope he will soon restore the terrible moment when Queeg turns toward the judges' bench with a frantic, appealing smile and knows, from the row of grave and troubled faces that confront him, that he has lost his case.

(1956)

In the Family.

FATHER (heartily concerned): How come we never get to talk to each other, son?

SON (*sullenly*): We're talking now, aren't we?

FATHER: We're talking, but we're not saying anything, goddammit!

Sometimes it is father and daughter, sometimes mother and son, but that, in a nutshell, is what modern American drama is about. It takes place either in a transparent doll's-house with a porch (the porch is obligatory) or in the past; or both. In this house live a pathetic, ill-matched couple. Mom is driven near-crazy, as she puts it, by dad, who goes on periodical bats. Meanwhile, the porch is full of the children to whom they cannot get through. They are two in number, of whom one is a confused adolescent boy, just awakening to the eternal mysteries of stud poker. There is a strange, stammering poetry in this off-beat child: indeed, it is coming out of his ears. He is about to undergo an emotional upheaval that will scar him for life. Comic relief, for the first half at least, will be provided by friends and neighbours. After that we discover that their lives too are founded on pain and insecurity and lack of togetherness.

Don't mistake me: the failure of generations to communicate with each other is not a bad thing for drama to be about. But there are other things for it to be about, and in the American theatre the theme has become obsessive. Plays lacking it are just not "serious"; plays with it can usually count on extracting from at least one critic a review beginning: "With this production the Broadway theatre becomes a palace of truth again." My present visit to the palace of truth has so far yielded three plays of this breed. All of them have moments of extreme poignancy. All contain performances of the utmost power and subtlety. All of them are as intellectually flabby as they are emotionally redundant.

The most ambitious, already the winner of the New York critics' award for the year's best play, is *Look Homeward, Angel,* adapted from Thomas Wolfe's autobiographical novel. This is a portrait of the artist as a young martyr. The boy here is Wolfe, painfully preparing to be a prose Whitman. The house is a shabby Southern hotel run by his parents. His mother, a covetous drudge, has no time for him. His father, a monumental mason, understands him but, being also a monumental drunk, can all too seldom see him. He has a frustrated love affair and runs away from home. Comic relievers, acting wildly in all directions, round off the play, which is written in starry-eyed, deep-breathing prose that resembles melting butter. Anthony Perkins, pale and filled with tentative fire, is a beautiful sight as Wolfe, and Hugh Griffith comes rowdily freebooting in as his father, albeit from another world.

With the second play, William Inge's *The Dark at the Top of the Stairs,* we move from 1916 to the early twenties. The mood again is personal and reminiscent. The house now is in Oklahoma. Father is a travelling salesman, for ever battling with a suspicious wife. The boy is a tow-haired tot alternately neglected and mother-smothered; his sister has an abortive flirtation with a hypersensitive young Jew who kills himself. This time it is father who runs away. The actor in question behaves throughout as noisily as if he were in *Oklahoma!* rather than Oklahoma; but on the whole, this being a production by Elia Kazan, the performances are electric and intense, especially that of Eileen Heckart, the best thin actress alive. Sharp writing, yet a remote and somehow unnecessary ordeal.

The third, and abysmally the dimmest example of the genre, is called *Blue Denim,* which at times verges on parody. The house, complete with porch, has shifted to Detroit and today. The boy, sensitive as a snail's horn, traditionally gangles. Father is a militant back-slapper, mother a helpless fussbudget. Unable to get through to either of them, he gets a girl pregnant and procures for her an illegal operation. The whole exercise is conducted in dialogue that recalls the Hardy Family films. This one might be called *Abortion Comes to Andy Hardy.*

Why do these plays, even the best of them, seem so ingrowing, so unchallenging, so constricted? I trace the trouble to that house, which is not a house at all but a hothouse. It is an island of shuttered anxieties unrelated (except cursorily) to the society that created it. All criticism, all protest is directed inwards, towards the parents: everything outside is accepted with nothing more rebellious than a shrug. The result is one-eyed drama with a squint induced by staring too long down domestic microscopes and never looking out of the window. If, as these writers allege, the infant bloom is diseased, it is no use merely blaming the stem. It is time to analyse the soil. Arthur Miller did just that in *Death of a Salesman,* striking a balance between soil-analysis and flower-pressing which still awaits a true successor.

(1957)

Requiem for a Nun, BY WILLIAM FAULKNER, AT THE ROYAL COURT, LONDON.

The curtain has just fallen on William Faulkner's *Requiem for a Nun.* It has been performed with imposing devoutness by Ruth Ford, Bertice Reading, Zachary Scott, and John Crawford. The production (by Tony Richardson) and the settings (by Motley) have been austerely hieratic. Let us now imagine that there steps from the wings the Stage Manager of Thornton Wilder's *Our Town.* Pulling on a corn-cob pipe, he speaks.

S.M.: "Well, folks, reckon that's about it. End of another day in the city of Jefferson, Yoknapatawpha County, Mississippi. Nothin' much happened. Couple of people got raped, couple more got their teeth kicked in, but way up there those faraway old stars are still doing their old cosmic criss-cross, and there ain't a thing we can do about it. It's pretty quiet now. Folk hereabouts get to bed early, those that can still walk. Down behind the morgue a few of the young people are roastin' a nigger over an open fire, but I guess every town has its night-owls, and afore long they'll be tucked up asleep like anybody else. Nothin' stirring down at the big old plantation house—you can't even hear the hummin' of that electrified barbed-wire fence, 'cause last night some drunk ran slap into it and fused the whole works. That's where Mr. Faulkner lives, and he's the fellow that thought this whole place up, kind of like God. Mr. Faulkner knows everybody round these parts like the back of his hand, 'n' most everybody round these parts knows the back of Mr. Faulkner's hand. But he's not home right now, he's off on a trip round the world as Uncle Sam's culture ambassador, tellin' foreigners about how we've got to love everybody, even niggers, and how integration's bound to happen in a few thousand years anyway, so we might just as well make haste slowly. Ain't a thing we can do about it.

(*He takes out his watch and consults it.*)

Along about now the good folk of Jefferson City usually get around to screamin' in their sleep. Just ordinary people havin' ordinary nightmares, the way most of us do most of the time.

(*An agonised shrieking is briefly heard.*)

Ayeah, there they go. Nothin' wrong there that an overdose of seconal won't fix.

(*He pockets his watch.*)

Like I say, simple folk fussin' and botherin' over simple, eternal problems. Take this Temple Stevens, the one Mr. Faulkner's been soundin' off about. 'Course, Mr. Faulkner don't pretend to be a real play-writer, 'n' maybe that's why he tells the whole story backwards, 'n' why he takes up so much time gabbin' about people you never met—and what's more, ain't going to meet. By the time he's told you what happened before you got here, it's gettin' to be time to go home. But we were talkin' about Temple. Ain't nothin' special about her. Got herself mixed up in an auto accident—witnessed a killin'—got herself locked up in a sportin' house with one of those seck-sual perverts—witnessed another killin'—got herself married up 'n' bore a couple of fine kids. Then, just's she's fixing to run off with a blackmailer, her maid Nancy—that's the nigger dope-fiend she met in the cathouse—takes a notion to murder her baby boy. That's all about Temple—just a run of bad luck that could happen to anyone. And don't come askin' me why Nancy murders the kid. Accordin' to Mr. Faulkner, she does it to keep him from bein' tainted by his mother's sins. Seems to me even an ignorant nigger would know a tainted child was better'n a dead one, but I guess I can't get under their skins the way Mr. Faulkner can.

(*He glances up at the sky.*)

Movin' along towards dawn in our town. Pretty soon folks'll start up on that old diurnal round of sufferin' and expiatin' and spoutin' sentences two pages long. One way or another, an awful lot of sufferin' gets done around here. 'Specially by the black folk—'n' that's how it should be, 'cause they don't feel it like we do, 'n' anyways, they've got that simple primitive faith to lean back on.

(*He consults his watch again.*)

Well, Temple's back with her husband, and in a couple of minutes they'll be hangin' Nancy. Maybe that's why darkies were born—to keep white marriages from bustin' up. Anyways, a lot of things have happened since the curtain went up tonight. Six billion gallons of water have tumbled over Niagara Falls. Three thousand boys and girls took their first puff of marijuana, 'n' a puppy-dog in a flyin' coffin was sighted over Alaska. Most of you out there've been admirin' Miss Ruth Ford's play-actin', 'n' a few of you've been wonderin' whether she left her pay-thos in the dressing-room or whether maybe she didn't have any to begin with. Out in Hollywood a big producer's been readin' Mr. Faulkner's book and figurin' whether to buy the movie rights for Miss Joan Crawford. Right enough, all over the world, it's been quite an evening. 'N' now Nancy's due for the drop.

(*A thud offstage. The Stage Manager smiles philosophically.*)

Ayeah, that's it—right on time.

(*He re-pockets his watch.*)

That's the end of the play, friends. You can go out and push dope now, those of you that push dope. Down in our town there's a meetin' of the Deathwish Committee, 'n' a fund-raisin' rally in aid of Holocaust Relief, 'n' all over town the prettiest gals're primping themselves up for the big beauty prize—Miss Cegenation of 1957. There's always somethin' happenin'. Why—over at the schoolhouse an old-fashioned-type humanist just shot himself. *You* get a good rest, too. Good-night."

(*He exits. A sound of Bibles being thumped momentarily fills the air.*)

(*1957*)

Garden District, BY TENNESSEE WILLIAMS, AT THE ARTS THEATRE, LONDON.

Suddenly Last Summer, the longer of the two plays Tennessee Williams has put together under the joint title of *Garden District,* has about it a strangely truncated look. It does not end, it stops—leaving us suspended amid loose ends that trail like lianas.

We have just listened to one of the longest, most febrile *récits* in modern drama. A Southern spinster, her tongue loosened by a truth drug, has described how she witnessed the death of her cousin Sebastian, a homosexual poet who was set upon and in part devoured by a mob of enraged Spanish street-urchins. The audience for this bloody tale consists of the poet's mother, a decaying witch bent on avoiding scandal; the young doctor whom she hopes to bribe into performing a silencing operating on the girl's brain; and the girl's mother and brother, who fear that the old lady will somehow cheat them out of the money Sebastian has left them. The recital ends, and three or four lines later the curtain comes sighing down.

It comes down not on a play but on a short story recited to a group of lay figures. Once the girl has finished, the curtain must fall, since we care nothing about the others. The ogress-mama (Beatrix Lehmann at her most ghoulish) is a conventional caricature of maternal rapacity. The doctor functions solely as interlocutor, and Mr. Williams' interest in the girl's greedy relations is so slight that he fails to explain why or how her brother's inheritance could possibly be endangered. Above all, there is the dead poet. The failure here is of a different kind. The picture we get of him is all too clear: a pampered dandy, patrolling the Riviera with mama on his arm, whispering flatteries and Dubedatteries into her ear while his eye roves the beaches for likely lads. The trouble is that we do not see him with Mr. Williams' eyes, in which all aesthetes are sacred. It is one thing to sympathise with a man who has been garrotted by the old umbilical cord. It is quite another when we are asked to see in his death (as Mr. Williams clearly wants us to) a modern re-enactment of the martyrdom of St. Sebastian.

If Mr. Williams had really dramatised his subject, this might not have mattered. But he hasn't: his approach is strictly literary, a series of teasing diversions leading up to the girl's big monologue. His purpose is not to tell us a story but to have someone else tell it, and a long retrospective narrative, no matter how impassioned, is not the same as a play. I must pause here to salute Patricia Neal, the American actress who plays the girl. The power and variety of her dark-brown voice, on which she plays like a master on the 'cello, enable her to separate the cadenza from its context and make of it a plangent cry from the depths of memory. Rhetoric and realism, in this harrowing performance, not only fuse but fertilise each other, and I was more than once reminded of Maria Casarès' incomparable Phèdre. We need more actresses like this in the West End, that garden where a hundred Blooms flower. Mr. Williams, whose speciality is hysteria precariously held in check by formal habits of speech, has given Miss Neal some of his richest prose—a *symphonie en blanc majeur,* in which image after image of blazing pallor evoke the climate of Sebastian's death.

"What a writer!" one murmurs during these passages. But one cannot honestly add: "What a play!" Nor can one feel that it represents an extension of Mr. Williams' talents. Rather, it is a narrowing-down. It picks out, like a torch in a charnel-house where a jewel has been lost, one quick bright thing in a world of hatred, cupidity, and squalor, exclusively dedicated to the persecution of purity. Nature is destructive, mother is destructive, families are destructive; even the nun who acts as the heroine's nurse is a sadist. We are in a world where mighty black conspires to victimise puny white; and any black-and-white world is dramatically a dull one. After this excursion to the brink of paranoia, we must pray for Mr. Williams' return to the true dramatic world of light and shade, where the easy violence of melodrama is softened by compassion.

Herbert Machiz' direction is thick with atmosphere, and (apart from Miss Neal's outburst) there are assured performances by David Cameron and Philip Bond. What Mr. Machiz has done to *Something Unspoken,* the shorter of the two pieces, is nobody's business except perhaps that of Mr. Williams and his lawyers. Unsubtle is the gentlest word for this triumph of misunderstanding. Mr. Williams wrote a compact study of a tyrannous Lesbian matriarch who appears to be dominating her mouselike companion, until we realise that the mouse is in fact the cat: vengefully, and blandly, she has decided not merely to reject her employer's advances but to ignore their existence. Mr. Machiz, who may have read too many of those reviews which portray Mr. Williams as a coarse-grained shock-vendor, sees the play as broad farce. The companion (Beatrix Lehmann, more ghoulish than ever) becomes a Charles Addams woman, bristling with *tics;* and Beryl Measor gets nowhere near the monstrous pathos of the Lesbian despot. A civilised, oblique, relentlessly funny piece of writing is entirely blunted. It is like seeing vintage Strindberg performed by Punch and Judy.

(1958)

West Side Story, by Leonard Bernstein, Stephen Sondheim, and Arthur Laurents, at the Winter Garden.

American musicals traditionally divide into two opposed categories: folksy optimism (Rodgers and Hammerstein) versus city cynicism (Rodgers and Hart)—rural versus urban, grass roots versus asphalt jungle. The king of the jungle is *West Side Story,* which comes screaming out of the tall island's Western tenements, where Puerto Ricans carve and are carved by bands of less recent immigrants. A "P.R." girl falls in love with a boy from the enemy gang, and the tragedy of Verona, with appropriate adjustments, is retold. He kills a member of her family; a rumour is spitefully spread of her death; and as he sees her across a square and runs to grasp her, he is cut down by a volley of Puerto Rican bullets.

The score, by Leonard Bernstein, is as smooth and savage as a cobra; it sounds as if Puccini and Stravinsky had gone on a roller-coaster ride into the precincts of modern jazz. Jerome Robbins, the director-choreographer, projects the show as a rampaging ballet, with bodies flying through the air as if shot from guns, leaping, shrieking, and somersaulting; yet he finds room for a peaceful dream-sequence, full of that hankering for a golden age that runs right through American musicals, in which both gangs imagine a paradise where they can touch hands in love, without fear or loss of face. The jokes are necessarily few and sardonic, as when the delinquents express their scorn of social therapists who regard them as symptoms rather than as individuals:

> My sister wears a moustache,
> My brother wears a dress—
> Goodness gracious, that's why I'm a mess!

Mr. Robbins has probably over-stylised a situation too fresh and bloody to respond to such treatment. The boys are too kempt; their clothes are too pretty; they dope not, neither do they drink. This makes them unreal, and gives the show an air of sociological slumming. Yet it compromises only on the brink of greatness; and that, surely, is triumph enough.

(1958)

My Fair Lady, BY FREDERICK LOEWE AND ALAN JAY LERNER, AT DRURY LANE, LONDON.

"Was all the hysteria justified?" one read on Thursday morning, *à propos* of the uproar at Drury Lane last Wednesday night. The nerve of the question took one's breath away, coming as it did from the very journalists who had created the hysteria. Those who beat drums are in no position to complain of being deafened. Let us forget about the hysteria associated with *My Fair Lady* and point instead to the rare, serene pleasure it communicates, a pleasure arising from the fact that it treats both the audience and *Pygmalion* with civilised respect.

This winning show honours our intelligence as well as Shaw's. It does not bully us with noise: the tone throughout is intimate, light, and lyrical, and even Doolittle's *lion-comique* numbers are sung, not shouted. It does not go in for irrelevant displays of physical agility: the dustman's pre-nuptial rout at Covent Garden is the only choreographic set-piece. Following the film, it restores Eliza to Higgins at the end, but no other sentimental concessions are made: the score contains only two love songs. Never do we feel that numbers have been shoe-horned, with a beady eye on the hit parade, into situations that do not concern them. Where most musical adaptations tend to exploit their originals, this one is content to explore.

Everything in the score grows naturally out of the text and the characters; the authors have trusted Shaw, and we, accordingly, trust them. Consider the four solo numbers they have provided for Higgins. In the first he rails against the English for neglecting their native tongue; in the second he congratulates himself on the sweetness of his disposition. In the third he damns women for their refusal to behave like men; and in the fourth, a wonderful blend of rage and regret, he furiously acknowledges his attachment to a woman who is unlike him in every respect. All four songs are right in character, and all four are written more to be acted than sung. Rex Harrison, performing them in a sort of reedy *Sprechgesang,* is not merely doing the best he can; he is doing just what the authors wanted. For all its grace and buoyancy, what holds the show together at the last is its determination to put character first.

On this resolve all its talents converge. A feeling of concord positively flows across the footlights. In a sense, the outstanding thing about the evening is that there is nothing outstanding about it, no self-assertion, no sore thumbs. The keyword is consonance. Oliver Smith's décor, lovely in itself, both enhances and is enhanced by Cecil Beaton's dashing dresses. Frederick Loewe, the composer, and Alan Jay Lerner, the lyricist, have produced a score as sensitive to Shavian nuance as litmus to acid. They have drawn song out of Shaw's people, not imposed it on them. Mr. Lerner's words are wily enough for Gilbert, and Mr. Loewe's contribution, enriched by the creative arrangements of Robert Russell Bennett, is far more than a series of pleasant songs: it is a tapestry of interwoven themes, criss-crossing and unexpectedly recurring, so that a late number will, by a sudden switch of tempo, echo an apt phrase from an earlier one. Apart from all this, the cast itself, directed by the hawk-eyed Moss Hart, is among the best ever assembled for *Pygmalion.*

Stanley Holloway is the fruitiest of Doolittles, Robert Coote the most subtly pompous of Pickerings. Nothing in Julie Andrews' Cockney becomes her like the leaving it; but she blossoms, once she has shed her fraudulent accent, into a first-rate Eliza, with a voice as limpid as outer space. And I don't doubt that Mr. Harrison, who seemed a bit edgy on Wednesday, is by now giving the effortless, finger-tip performance I saw last year on Broadway. The moment when he, Miss Andrews, and Mr. Coote erupt into that ecstatic, improvised tango, "The Rain in Spain," is still the happiest of the night. Ten years ago, I learn, Shaw was approached for permission to turn his play into a musical. Outraged, he replied: "If *Pygmalion* is not good enough for your friends with its own verbal music, their talent must be altogether extraordinary." In this instance, it is.

(1958)

The Critical Scene.

Of the seven accredited Broadway critics, Walter Kerr, of the *Herald Tribune,* is the cogent best. There is no one in London quite like him; no one, I mean, who combines a style that is vivid and popular (in the best sense of the word) with a background of scholarship that comes from having taught drama for many years at a university. Mr. Kerr vaults over the barrier we erect between "serious" and "light" journalism; and after reading *Pieces at Eight,* his new collection of theatrical essays, I am forced to conclude that if he sought critical employment on an English national daily he would be most unlikely to find it. The mass-circulation papers would think him over their readers' heads; the middle-brow liberal papers, those precarious survivors, could not give him the space he needs to develop his arguments; and the "quality" dailies, which have the space, would sniff at the brisk informality of his style.

New York journalism is primarily aimed at an audience that is not national but local and metropolitan. No London morning paper aims at this audience; and none, in consequence, has room for the kind of style that appeals to it. This style, nimble, flexible, and informed, is Mr. Kerr's. Its target is the sort of reader who has reached a good median level of sophistication; who can take a wise-crack in one sentence and a reference to Scaliger or Castelvetro in the next. Being a director as well as a critic, Mr. Kerr can write with authority of the ulcerous tensions that precede a Broadway opening and the verbal prophylactics, born of despair, that are ritually employed to palliate bad notices—e.g., "Well, we know one thing—we've got an audience show," and "Well, they weren't laughing, but they were enjoying it." (The latter remark, Mr. Kerr suggests, might pleasantly be rephrased to describe audience reactions to the cruder kind of bedroom farce—viz.: "Well, they were laughing, but they weren't enjoying it.") Swiftly and statistically he disposes of the myth that the Broadway critics are omnipotent: their word, it seems, is law only when all seven of them concur either in rave or blame.

At times his enthusiasms slip the leash and begin to caper, as when he says of a musical comedy that it "opened the theatre's childlike bag of tricks and tossed them at our heads in a high, happy, bubbling good humour" (who wants to have his head pelted?); and sometimes, though less often, we catch on his face the apologetic smile of an Honest Joe anxiously disclaiming egghead pretensions. "Although it may not seem very likely, I have been having a wonderful time with a book called *Sources of Theatrical History*"—as if this were not just the sort of book that a respectable critic *ought* to be enjoying. But for most of the time he is quite shamelessly intelligent. His study of Buster Keaton is a brilliant piece of extended interpretative eulogy, and in dyslogy he can be wickedly compact: how did that actor ever recover whom Mr. Kerr summed up as "suffering from delusions of adequacy"?

But I must not claim too much for Mr. Kerr: the pressure under which journalists work necessarily makes them more attentive, in Sir Desmond MacCarthy's phrase, to the minute hand of history than to the hour hand. Mr. Kerr's championing of verse drama as the salvation of the modern theatre is a case in point. He argues fluently, adopting some astonishingly acrobatic postures to defend Christopher Fry *in toto,* yet never does he face the point made thirty-five years ago by his revered compatriot Stark Young: "Dramatic poetry is not the dramatic situation poetically expressed; it is the dramatic expression of the poetic that lies in a situation." And there is no more need for this to be in verse than for it to be in Esperanto or blue suede shoes.

Another hazard of Broadway criticism, even at its wisest, is its tendency to become parochial. To be metropolitan is a virtue; its defect is to be insular. Mr. Kerr has travelled, as his remarks on the London theatre prove; yet working, as he diurnally does, in the most commercially geared theatre on earth, he cannot help absorbing, and in part regurgitating, its values. His final dictum, however he may qualify it, is that the audience knows best. He cites with approval Mr. Rattigan's defence of Aunt Edna. "The critic," he says, "who attempts to reverse the judgment of an audience, to 'instruct' it in taste, is the critic who deals in lost causes . . . a bore and a fool." From the near-sighted viewpoint of the morning after, this is probably true; but a decade later such boring fools as Shaw and Agate, who dared to challenge the public for its indifference to Ibsen and Chekhov, have sometimes reversed the roles. They proved the audience wrong—which is why, in the long perspective of history, we call them first-rate critics.

I quite understand Mr. Kerr's purpose, which is to rebuke the fanatics for whom no play can be an artistic success unless it has been a commercial disaster. But the opposite extreme, which equates box-office success with art, is equally indefensible, and this is the position towards which Mr. Kerr is moving. It is significant that in the current issue of *Variety* Mr. Kerr is hailed as the "rightest" Broadway critic: i.e., his opinions, last season, coincided most often with those of the public. The most alarming gap in his otherwise lively and sensible book is that it nowhere gives us any reason to suppose, or argument to prove, that *Worm's Eye View, Mister Roberts,* or *Abie's Irish Rose* are plays less great than *Ghosts, Troilus and Cressida,* and *The Playboy of the Western World.*

(1958)

The Shadow of a Gunman, BY SEAN O'CASEY, AT THE BIJOU; *Edwin Booth,* BY MILTON GEIGER, AT THE 46TH STREET THEATRE.

A great deal of dedicated work has clearly gone into the new revival of Sean O'Casey's *The Shadow of a Gunman.* For the most part, unfortunately, it is work of a kind that belongs somewhere else. I yield to no fan in my respect for the stimulus, frequently galvanic, that has been applied to the acting styles of Broadway and Hollywood by members of the Actors' Studio. Their approach to the mimic craft may be tortuous and time-consuming by the standards prevailing around Times Square, but it gets results, often of a shattering subtlety and power. In *The Shadow of a Gunman,* which is being presented under the Studio's auspices, both director and principals are Studio-fledged. They have come up with a production that makes one think not so much of a mountain bringing forth a mouse as of mice bringing forth a mountain. The play itself is short enough to be performed (as it often is) with a thirty-minute curtain-raiser. At the Bijou it seems bloated, leaden, and interminable.

Before we take up the fascinating question of what went wrong, a glance at the text may be helpful. O'Casey's first play is set in a Dublin tenement at the height of the Troubles. Outside, in the streets of the city, the future of Ireland is being fought out; that is the real action, but right in the middle of it are two men who think it none of their business and ask only to live in what little peace they can find. One is Seumas, who sells defective suspenders at street corners on the rare occasions when he is not in bed bewailing the shiftlessness of the Irish. His roommate, Donal, is a distracted young poet whom the whole tenement aberrantly believes to be an I.R.A. gunman. The error at first breeds comedy, as mistaken identity usually does. Donal's neighbors and fellow lodgers bring him their wrongs to be righted, vow solidarity with the cause, and boast of their acquaintance with him, while one of them, an awe-struck girl named Minnie, falls hesitantly in love with his borrowed glamour. Toward the end, the grin on the play's face fades; it clenches its fist and lets us have it, with Irish abruptness, straight in the solar plexus. The world outside begins to close in. The house is raided by the Black and Tans, whereupon Donal finds himself the custodian of a bagful of bombs left on the premises by one of Seumas' friends. When Minnie volunteers to hide them under her bed, both Donal and Seumas consent. She is subsequently shot. The poet survives, transfixed by the guilt that is reality's revenge on those who seek to escape responsibility.

The tempo of the piece, up to the last minute, is exuberantly comic —sometimes to the point of naïveté, as when the author indulges his fondness for jokes based on working-class malapropisms. O'Casey called his play a tragedy, but by that he meant nothing more than that it did not end happily. (When the Irish want to compose pure tragedies, they generally do so in Gaelic.) O'Casey belongs in the boisterous gallery of Irish satirists, comedians, ironists, and mock-heroic wits who, since the death of Shakespeare, have written nearly everything of lasting importance in what is sardonically known as the English drama. He means us to laugh at the plight of two men trapped in a lie, and he expects of his small-part players the pace and timing of vaudeville. And this is where the Actors' Studio lets him down. Instead of expedition, they give us exploration. Where O'Casey prescribes panic, they offer rational concern. Under Jack Garfein's direction, they present a number of thoughtful investigations into character, entirely ignoring the element of volatile caricature that is the glory of the play, its essence and its life. Lines that in print are winged like Mercury are uttered as if they were shod in concrete. I do not doubt that Mr. Garfein's actors have achieved exactly what they set out to achieve. The trouble is that O'Casey was aiming at a different target. Gerald O'Loughlin (Seumas) is a gifted actor, but he is far too stolid and brow-beetling to supply the twitches, flurries, and stammers for which the part cries out. Susan Strasberg, who should wipe off half her smile and at least one layer of make-up, plays Minnie, the little simpleton who blunders into martyrdom, as if she were a sort of incipient tart, a misconception that may account for some of the actress' painful self-consciousness. The poet is a tougher task, since O'Casey never tells us how good a poet he is, or whether we are to take his outbursts of grief seriously. William Smithers settles for the kind of lithe, confused, disconsolate hero one sees in adult Westerns. His performance is slow and has nothing to do with Ireland, but it is not actively objectionable. George Mathews, in two short scenes as a lumbering drunk, gets nearest to the O'Casey flavour. Peter Larkin's cluttered set is perfect, and so are the sound effects. Every word, I should add, is audible. If Mr. Garfein's production does nothing else, it should quash the rumour that the Actors' Studio teaches actors to mumble. Regrettably, not to mumble is not enough.

Apart from the writing, which has the quality of mildewed plush, there is little wrong with *Edwin Booth,* Milton Geiger's chronicle play at the Forty-sixth Street Theatre, that is not equally wrong with every other stage biography of a great dead actor. The thing to hold on to is that *all* such actors invented "the natural style." What the rise of the middle class is to political history the rise of the natural style is to theatrical history—an event of ubiquitous date that has taken place roughly twice in every century from the sixteenth onward. Betterton, about whom nobody writes plays, was a ranter; then along came Garrick, who staggered the public by the naturalness of his manner. He was superseded by Edmund Kean, whose command of natural speech revolutionized a theatre inured to Garrick's rantings. Before long, Kean's absurd rhetoric was supplanted by the newer, more natural techniques pioneered by Irving and Booth. Breaking decisively with the past, the Moscow Art Theatre under Stanislavsky inaugurated an acting method so radical that it made hams like Irving and Booth sound like Betterton. It was founded on the cataclysmic idea that actors should act natural.

The main problem in presenting plays about great actors is casting. Edwin Booth, unless the record lies, was deeply introspective. His father was an alcoholic tragedian, partly insane, who sired him out of wedlock. His first wife died of tuberculosis, his second went mad, and one of his brothers murdered Lincoln. He drank compulsively. His chief quality as an actor seems to have been a burning, withdrawn magnetism. "He *is* Hamlet," said his brother, the antic assassin, "melancholy and all." Booth's comment on himself was that he was "too damned genteel and exquisite." This is the role in which José Ferrer, the director of the play, has chosen to cast himself. Now, Mr. Ferrer is a man of varied talents, but he is not, to put it suavely, the first actor in the world who leaps to my mind in connection with exquisite melancholy. At his most characteristic, he is a bustler, a kidder, a crafty extrovert, and whenever the script allows him to perform in these capacities he is splendid—once when he is heckled by his first wife (Lois Smith) at a rehearsal of *Romeo and Juliet,* and again when he wards off lionizers at a smart supper party by getting impenetrably tight. But for most of the evening he is frankly at a loss. Quite often one has the impression that, with the best will in the world, his mind is not wholly focussed on the matter at hand. He looks impatient, too busy to be wasting his time acting; you feel you are imposing on him, keeping him from some vital engagement that he would much rather not have postponed. He did, however, provide me with one flash of inspiration. This occurred when he stumbled on, complete with leer, limp, and golliwog wig, to recite a snatch of *Richard III*. Instantly I had a vision of what Mr. Ferrer's true vocation might be. If I am right, he should make it his business to corner the market in stage biographies not of great tragedians but of great clowns. What a Bert Lahr, for instance, he would make! And if anyone ever writes a play about the Marx Brothers, Mr. Ferrer will be my first choice for all three.

(1958)

Flower Drum Song, BY RICHARD RODGERS AND OSCAR HAMMERSTEIN II, AT THE ST. JAMES.

Ever since Marco Polo, the Orient has exerted a steady and growing influence on the Western imagination. I need only mention the names of Stevenson, Gauguin, Lafcadio Hearn, Sax Rohmer, and W. C. Fields to indicate how much our civilization owes to the ancient cultures of the East. Our debt was increased last week by the arrival at the St. James Theatre of *Flower Drum Song,* the new musical by Richard Rodgers and Oscar Hammerstein II. In this case, I fear, what we owe is not gratitude but an apology. I am not so demented as to expect from a Broadway show any profound insights into the Chinese temperament. All the same, it was something of a shock, and rather more of a bore, to find the country that cradled Lao-tse, Confucius, and Zen Buddhism treated as if our only clues to its way of life were those provided by the lyrics of "Limehouse Blues" and "Chinatown, My Chinatown."

The authors' attitude toward exotic peoples in general seems to have changed hardly at all since they wrote *South Pacific* and *The King and I.* If friendly, the natives have a simple, primitive, childlike sweetness. If girls, they do not know how to kiss, but once they have been taught they are wild about it. They also beg to inquire, please, just what it is that is said with flowers. In their conversation, as you may have gleaned, there is more than a smidgen of pidgin, and I should not have been surprised in the least if the heroine of the present work, which is elsewhere full of self-plagiarism, had at some point embarked on a lyric beginning, "Baby talk, keep talking baby talk." It seems to have worried neither Mr. Rodgers nor Mr. Hammerstein very much that the behaviour of war-torn Pacific islanders and nineteenth-century Siamese might be slightly different from that of Chinese residents of present-day California, where *Flower Drum Song* is fictionally sung. So little, indeed, has it worried them that they have entrusted the principal female roles to Japanese actresses. Their assumption, which may be justified, is that the audience will not notice the difference. It will, however, unless nostalgia has rendered it purblind, notice a marked difference between this and the better Rodgers-and-Hammerstein shows. They may all look alike to the authors, but not, I am afraid, to me.

The plot, promising in itself and based on a popular novel by C. Y. Lee, concerns a conflict of values between those inhabitants of San Francisco's Chinatown who have embraced Americanization and those who have resisted it. The first group includes a jolly stripper who lusts after Thunderbirds, and her part-time lover, a raffish type named Sammy Fong, who has foolishly summoned from Formosa a mail-order bride of stupefying ingenuousness. The passive resisters are represented by a strait-laced family on to whose son Sammy attempts to unload his pretty but unwanted import. She wins over the boy's father by declaring, in song, that "a hundred million miracles are happening every day," but has more trouble with the lad himself, who has leanings toward the stripper. On this four-cornered framework the action rests, so complacently that halfway through the second act it falls asleep and topples into somnolent implausibility. This would not matter as much if the encircling *chinoiserie* sounded authentic instead of synthetic, or if anything in the score came so leapingly to life that it banished all memories of former triumphs in the same vein. But no. The ring of this coin, at almost every throw, is counterfeit. The same fingers, to switch the metaphor, are at the typewriter, but two carbons have sadly blurred the impression. The elders sing a mournful plaint about the decadence of their children, and, sure enough, five minutes later the children troop on and deplore, to the same tune, the decadence of their parents. The dream ballets and the silken Oriental processions likewise reinforced my sense of *déjà vu,* and my suspicion, amounting at length to a conviction, that what I saw before me was simply a stale Broadway confection wrapped up in spurious Chinese trimmings. Perhaps as a riposte to Joshua Logan's *The World of Suzie Wong,* Rodgers and Hammerstein have given us what, if I had any self-control at all, I would refrain from describing as a world of woozy song.

(1958)

The Cold Wind and the Warm, BY S. N. BEHRMAN, AT THE MOROSCO; *J. B.,* BY ARCHIBALD MACLEISH, AT THE A.N.T.A. THEATRE.

"The play is memory." These four words, which occur in the opening speech of Tennessee Williams' *The Glass Menagerie,* may stand as an epigraph for a considerable segment of post-war American drama. They are uttered by a character who represents the author as a younger man, and they introduce an incident from his past, seen through a semi-transparent fictional veil. This technique—the use of what might be called the first person once removed—cropped up again in *I Am a Camera,* whose hero was the youthful Christopher Isherwood, and since then there has been no escaping it. In play after play we have accompanied writer after writer on a series of formative strolls down memory lane, that broad highway leading from the wrong side of the tracks to the anterooms of Perry and Pulitzer. We have been lashed by storms, and dampened by drizzles, of autobiographical emotion, recollected sometimes in tranquillity and sometimes, one suspects, with the aid of tranquillizers. William Inge revisited his childhood for us in *The Dark at the Top of the Stairs; Look Homeward, Angel* invited us to share the growing pains of Thomas Wolfe, *Winesburg, Ohio* those of Sherwood Anderson; and we gained from *Long Day's Journey into Night* a profound and tenebrous insight into the adolescence of Eugene O'Neill. The latest excursion into nostalgia is *The Cold Wind and the Warm,* which offers an elaborate report on how it felt to be the young S. N. Behrman.

Mr. Behrman's play is founded on episodes from his book *The Worcester Account,* a collection of reminiscent *contes* whose quality I cannot judge, since I have not read them. There is always, however, a sizeable gap between the printed page and viable drama, and it does not seem to me that Mr. Behrman has succeeded in bridging it. Prose in stiff covers (or soft, for that matter) is addressed to only one reader at a time; drama, by contrast, is aimed at a thousand spectators simultaneously assembled. Where a bored reader would skip, a bored audience walks out. To prevent this, the playwright must concentrate his action, narrow his focus, and resolutely shun those digressive details that are at once the novelist's province and his pride. "In the play," said Virginia Woolf, "we recognize the general . . . in the novel, the particular." The dangers of getting too particular are multiplied when drama verges on autobiography. Fondly ransacking the attics of his mind, the author grows more and more reluctant to throw anything away, and frequently ends up by convincing himself that nothing could be more fascinating to an audience than a lengthy procession of the most unforgettable characters he has ever met, including, of course, himself. The result, almost invariably, is something that might have achieved a modest sale as a volume of memoirs but has about as much to do with drama as a police line-up. The awkward art of writing a good memory play demands far more in the way of self-discipline and condensation. The two great examples of the genre are *The Glass Menagerie* and *Long Day's Journey into Night,* and it is significant that neither of them was adapted from a book. In each case the author, looking back on his life, singled out a turning point—a crucial, indelible event that somehow determined the course of his maturity. Mr. Behrman is inspired by a similar conception; where he falters is in the matter of execution. Both Williams and O'Neill confined their *dramatis personae* to people who were actively involved in the crisis—in Williams' play, his mother, his sister, and the latter's "gentleman caller"; in O'Neill's, his parents and his elder brother, plus a harmless necessary maid. And both of them were careful to select incidents in which they themselves figured not merely as observers but as participants, not just recording but contributing. Mr. Behrman slips up on both counts. Not only is his plotting vagrant and diffuse; he has imposed on it a character who does nothing but impede it—to wit, himself as a child. This is a camera-type (or perhaps I should say daguerreotype) play that has been thrown off balance by the photographer's insistence on being in the picture.

The situation, once we have peeled off its nostalgic slough, is the old one in which an ambitious boy is forced to choose between a nice girl and a flamboyant flirt. All three are members of the Jewish community in Worcester, Massachusetts, half a century ago. Willie, the hero, is an enthusiastic student whose zeal for research and inquiry extends to his private life, which he devotes first to Myra, the dazzling blonde widow he pursues to New York, and later to Leah, the docile homebody whose child, in a moment of erethism, he fathers. (Under the International Convention of Theatrical Conventions, annually ratified by the Society of Authors, one night's cohabitation is enough, irrespective of the calendar, to guarantee a pregnancy.) Unwilling to marry the girl, he commits suicide, by means that are not revealed, after a scene with Myra that we do not see and an internal struggle that is never exposed to us.

There might have been time to repair these omissions if Mr. Behrman had kept himself out of the play; as I should have pointed out, Willie represents not the author but the author's best friend and elder counsellor. The young Behrman appears in the guise of Tobey, a would-be composer in knee pants who utters a great many lines, takes no part in the action, and might with advantage have been jettisoned. His relatives are all designed to accord with the popular theatrical image of Jews as warmhearted clowns who get their sentences back to front. One of them, a matchmaking aunt, is played with uproarious, upholstered aplomb by Maureen Stapleton, who can cock an eyebrow and purse a lip with more wit than many actresses find in the whole of Oscar Wilde, but there are limits to the joy one can derive from lines like "I could tear you from each limb." Morris Carnovsky, shrugging as to the manner trained, performs wearily and well as Mr. Behrman's fictional father, a rabbinical grocer, while theatrical *chutzpa* of a more shameless kind is displayed by Sig Arno, all popeyed apology, and Sanford Meisner, whose parody of a foxhunting *nouveau riche* makes me long to see him in a farce by Feydeau or Labiche. Apart from Suzanne Pleshette, the prim unmarried mother, and Carol Grace, who pitches Myra somewhere between a pallid fawn and a Southern belle, almost everyone is joke-Jewish. As Willie, Eli Wallach is interestingly miscast. Instead of an ingenuous face that betrays precocious intelligence, he shows us a sophisticated face through which boyishness occasionally peeps. What is needed here is not a better actor but a slightly younger one. The direction, which is by Harold Clurman, struck me as markedly stale.

Elia Kazan, who staged Archibald MacLeish's *J.B.,* is the best man alive to direct plays that rumble with passion, blaze into violence, and flower in a climate of frenzy. Whether he has the lightness of touch and the affection for grace that are required by works of less febrile content, I have no means of knowing; it is enough to say here that he can raise whirlwinds, and that whirlwinds are exactly what Mr. MacLeish wants raised. The cast is a strong one. It is led by Pat Hingle, a specialist in portraying the American male as a lusty, overgrown boy, given perhaps to blustering but inherently goodhearted. He is flanked on the one hand by Raymond Massey, as imposing as a riven oak, and on the other by Christopher Plummer, the flexible, saturnine young Canadian whose range, widening every season, has already put him within striking distance of most of the light-heavyweight roles in the American and European repertoires. Boris Aronson's setting, a desolate, cavernous circus tent, is one of the most majestic I can remember; it prepares the heart for events of towering grandeur and cosmic repercussion. In every department the presentation is flawless. The same, unfortunately, cannot be said of the thing presented.

Never one to waste his time on trivialities, Mr. MacLeish has taken on the Miltonic task of justifying the ways of God to man. *J.B.* is the Book of Job, that greatest of hard-luck stories, retold in the form of a morality play. The characters are modern, but speak in bumpy alliterative verse, and the narrative technique is similarly medieval. God and Satan are embodied in, respectively, a peddler of balloons and a popcorn vendor (Mr. Massey and Mr. Plummer), who wander down the aisle of the theatre, pick up a couple of masks, and act as joint masters of ceremonies, commenting on Job's story (which unfolds in the circus ring) from the vantage points assigned to them by tradition—stage left for Evil, stage right for Good. Mr. Massey, high up on a funambulist's platform that Mr. Aronson has cunningly turned into a pulpit, gets the best of the bargain. Beneath him Job, in the person of J.B., a "perfect and upright" businessman, takes the ghastly battering that is to test his faith in the benevolence of the Deity. In a series of scenes as predictable as they are repetitive, he loses most of his family and all of his fortune. War and an automobile accident dispose of four of his children, while the fifth and last is murderously assaulted by a juvenile psychopath. To cap everything, a bomb falls on his bank, leaving him not only penniless but afflicted by an unpleasant skin condition—Mr. MacLeish's substitute for the boils in the Bible, and presumably to be diagnosed as the result of exposure to atomic blast. After each new body-blow God's chosen sparring partner staggers back off the ropes for more, to the delight of Mr. Massey and the chagrin of Mr. Plummer, whose purpose is to make Job curse his creator. Up to this point the play falls into a clear-cut sociological category: it represents the apology of American capitalism for its astonishing prosperity. Job knows he has not sinned, yet feels permanently and inexplicably guilty; he cannot bring himself to deny that God is just. His first Comforter, a Marxist, tells him that historical necessity is punishing him; the second, a psychoanalyst, that he is punishing himself; the third, a gloating cleric, that he is being punished for the unpardonable crime of having been born. He rejects all three, but still feels terrible. Why? And here the argument disconcertingly swerves. God takes off the gloves and restores to Job, as a guarantee of good will, his affluence and his wife, who has left him in disgust at his refusal to defend himself. He accepts these favours with an eagerness that shocks Mr. Plummer and even perturbs Mr. Massey. Job's explanation, offered in a brief epilogue, is that there is no divine justice; there is simply human love. He and his wife will be content hereafter to live together and, in a phrase worthy of an Abe Burrows parody, "blow on the coal of the heart." To say that this ending cheats is to put it mildly. The play rests on the assumption, everywhere endorsed by the text, that we are judged by God. It then poses the question: why are we judged so harshly? The answer, which destroys everything that has preceded it and entirely demolishes the original premise, is that he does not judge us at all. Having bothered us for more than two hours with an apparently insoluble problem, Mr. MacLeish blithely shrugs and confesses that it was the wrong problem to begin with.

The truth, of course, is that he has stated the right problem in the wrong way. We are all of us vitally concerned in any search for the causes of human pain, but when needless agony is inflicted (as it is on J.B.) by bombs, bullets, drunken drivers, and lunatic adolescents, our first impulse, if we are rational beings, is surely to seek an explanation in human terms—to ask how the war could have been avoided, why the man drank, what pressures sent the boy mad. Not many of us, I think, immediately ascribe our sufferings to the judicial acumen of the Old Testament God, who could never be ranked among the more sympathetic characters in world literature, and who appears in the Book of Job at his worst—arrogant, bombastic, and casually cruel. Yet Mr. MacLeish's hero thinks of nobody else. The emphasis on guilt is obsessive:

> We have no choice but to be guilty.
> God is unthinkable if we are innocent.

And, again:

> Guilt matters. Guilt must always matter.
> Unless guilt matters the whole world is
> Meaningless.

Long before the final curtain I was bored to exasperation by the lack of any recognizable human response to calamity. Above all, I yearned for the intervention of just one character from an alien—preferably an Oriental—culture. It would have clarified so much. Mr. MacLeish's postulate is that we expect God to be just, since we think of him not only as our creator but as our judge, a maker of moral laws that we break at our eternal peril. If we defy them, we feel what Alan W. Watts, my authority on comparative religion, calls "a sense of guilt so preposterous that it must issue either in denying one's own nature or in rejecting God." This is Job's dilemma, and it is relevant only to a civilization that equates the Creator with the Legislator. Oriental tradition separates the two functions. Justice, which distributes punishments and rewards, is a human invention that can err and be corrected; to be wrongly chastised by it is a misfortune, not an evidence of sin. The process of creation itself, meanwhile, is above and beyond justice. It neither punishes nor rewards, and cannot be lauded or offended; it merely exists. This is the attitude toward which Mr. MacLeish seems to be veering at the end of *J.B.* Had he reached it sooner, he might have written a better play, or no play at all, sparing us, in either case, lines as pompously hollow as "Death is a bone that stammers." But he seems to have been determined to wound nobody, even in passing, and to keep up, at all costs, the appearance of devotion to an antique and extravagant concept of the deity. Even at curtain-fall we do not know where he really stands. As Samuel Johnson said to Boswell in the spring of 1776, "Sir, there is no trusting to that crazy piety."

(1958)

Directors as Writers.

A mediocre drama critic may be defined as a man who is content merely to review plays. He comes to the theatre as a high-school gourmet to a restaurant, equipped with nothing more positive than an open mind and a clean palate; having tasted the dish that is set before him, he pronounces it pleasant or unpleasant and then goes home to gargle. He is now ready to approach his next meal in the same state of artificial innocence, uncontaminated, as far as possible, by any noxious taint of experience. His mind, like his mouth, hangs open and empty, a fact of which he is quietly proud, since it proves beyond a doubt that he is unprejudiced. In other words, he judges plays in a condition that would unfit him for almost any human activity except sunbathing. Intellectually, he is self-gelded, for he has deliberately erased from his thinking all sense of continuity with the past, together with all those aspects of the present that lie outside the theatre's walls. His task, or so he conceives it, is to keep out of his criticism the values and convictions that govern his life and shape his attitude, if he has one, toward society. The great test comes when he brings out a book (imaginably entitled *Rogues and Vagabonds*) of his collected reviews. Considered singly, they may glitter; *en masse,* they resemble nothing so much as a bag of unstrung beads.

Another, rarer kind of criticism is exemplified in *Lies Like Truth,* a compilation of articles on the theatre written by Harold Clurman between 1947 and 1957, mostly for the *New Republic* and the *Nation.* I mean to sound complimentary when I say that Mr. Clurman reads better in bulk than he does in weekly instalments. Few of his reviews have literary pretensions; the prose is brusque, spasmodic, and excitable, frequently falling over its own feet in its haste, and many of the items have the fragmentary quality of bulletins from the front line. Yet the book as an entity holds up. The pieces fit together into a consistent pattern; the beads, in short, are strung. Mr. Clurman sees plays in terms of their environment in time and place. Faced with a new work, he asks himself not only whether he likes it and why, but where it stands in relation to the author's development, where the author stands in relation to the theatre he writes for, and where that theatre stands in relation to society as a whole. There is something in him of the child who, addressing a letter to a friend, begins with the name, the street, the city, and the state, and then cannot stop until he reaches the hemisphere and, finally, The World. Mr. Clurman's horizon is similarly uncontracted. This is literally as well as figuratively true; few modern critics have travelled so far in search of theatre. And none, it is safe to say, is better informed about the practical side of the business than Mr. Clurman, who was a director of the Group Theatre for ten palpitating years and is still volcanically active, having staged two Broadway productions in the past five months. This first-hand knowledge is what keeps his idealism firmly nailed to reality. His theories, impassioned and exalted, about what the theatre ought to be are not dreams but workable extensions of what it actually is.

Two themes, so tightly plaited that they sometimes appear one, recur throughout the book. One of them is the sickness inherent in a theatre that equates merit with profit, and the corresponding need for a remedy in the form of subsidized playhouses in which talents, rather than investments, can mature. The other is the nature of merit itself. In Mr. Clurman's eyes, every stage production makes both a statement and an emotional impact, and the critic's job is to decide not merely what the statement is, but whether it has value—or, as Mr. Clurman would say, whether it is "humanly relevant." At first glance his admirations look wildly disparate, ranging, as they do, from Giraudoux to Judy Garland. Always, however, the touchstone is value: are we being offered an enrichment that will outlive pleasure? In the least restrictive sense of the word, Mr. Clurman is a moralist. "Theatre," he says, in a congested but expressive phrase, "is philosophy in a fleshed design of action." The difference between him and the clean-palate dilettantes is that he knows what he expects of the drama. They go to the theatre ready for anything. He goes ready for something.

Mr. Clurman is an impatient, untidy writer who throws off his pearls as perfunctorily as a dog shaking itself after a swim, and for this reason it is hard to do him justice in quotation. Here, all the same, are a few *aperçus* that may help to convey the flavour of his shrewdness. Of the tirelessly eclectic Thornton Wilder: "He arranges flowers beautifully, but he does not grow them." Of O'Neill, with special reference to *Long Day's Journey into Night*: "Every character speaks in two voices, two moods—one of rage, the other of apology." Of Ibsen: "A graph of Ibsen's thematic material would show him oscillating between the determined idealism of 'no compromise' and the more modern question of how much to compromise." Of certain French *avant-garde* playwrights: "Their rebellion is a little like . . . a revolt in an orphanage." Of Miss Garland: "The tension between the unctuously bright slickness which is expected of her medium . . . and the fierceness of what her being wants to cry out produces something positively orgiastic in the final effect."

The best piece of sustained criticism in the book is Mr. Clurman's analysis of *A Streetcar Named Desire* as directed on Broadway by Elia Kazan. His conclusion, which I find unassailable, is that the "intense, introspective, and almost lyric personality" of Marlon Brando turned the play's values upside down by gaining so much sympathy for the brutish Kowalski that the audience could not help seeing Blanche DuBois through his eyes—as a posturing fraud who deserved most of what she got. Mr. Clurman's account of how an actor's natural creativeness can inadvertently contradict the spirit of a text without departing from the letter of it could have been written only by a practising director. With that thought in mind, let us agree to bury the popular notion, fostered in self-defense by generations of reviewers, that backstage *expertise* is at best irrelevant and at worst inimical to good criticism.

On the Stanislavsky Method, which achieved full American citizenship through the diligence of the Group Theatre, Mr. Clurman is concise and authoritative. "The grammar of acting," as he calls it, is now securely enthroned on Broadway and needs no defence except against bad actors and imbecile publicity. Not without weariness, Mr. Clurman reminds us that Stanislavsky was concerned just as much with external technique as with "inner truth": "I have never heard anyone speak as long or as dogmatically on the importance of the voice and diction as did Stanislavsky to me on the several occasions of our meeting in Paris and Moscow. As for posture, physical deportment, correctness of carriage, discipline of manner: on these subjects Stanislavsky was almost fanatic."

The same line is taken by Robert Lewis, another Group graduate, in *Method—or Madness?,* which preserves in permanent form a series of chatty, flossy, but basically sensible lectures delivered by the author to an audience of theatre people two years ago. Mr. Lewis' thesis, clearly visible through a small forest of exclamation points, is that too much emphasis has been laid on the Stanislavsky of *An Actor Prepares,* which deals mainly with the "insides" of acting, and too little on the Stanislavsky of *Building a Character,* which concentrates on the outward, or visible and audible, aspects of the craft. He attributes this imbalance to the fact that the latter book was not published in America until 1949—thirteen years after its companion volume—by which time the older testament had been accepted as the whole of the law and its high priests had grown deaf to new doctrine. Mr. Lewis supports his argument with some wily anecdotes and a superbly daunting chart, translated in 1934 from Stanislavsky's own copy, of the entire Method process, from the conception of a role to its perfect execution. By stressing the executive side of the chart, which contains panels labelled "Dancing," "Rules of Speaking," "External Tempo and Rhythm," and so forth, Mr. Lewis is able to serve the cause of fair play while at the same time putting in a suave plug or two for the kind of poetic, semi-stylized drama that lies, I suspect, nearest to his affections.

I read his little book with pleasure; even so, I could not help wishing that he had been too busy to write it. Mr. Lewis is one of the most active New York directors, and yet in the twenty years that have passed since he staged William Saroyan's *My Heart's in the Highlands* for the Group he has directed only fourteen Broadway shows—among them no classics, and nothing written more than a quarter of a century ago. By Continental standards, he is scarcely more than a beginner. Nor is his a special case; it applies, *mutatis mutandis,* to Broadway as a whole. The American theatre is alive with talent, most of which, culturally speaking, is marking time. None of it is employed as such talent ought to be—in permanent companies, where it might try its hand at everything from Aeschylus to Axelrod and grow by constant use. By a bizarre paradox, the barely competent performers do far more theatrical work than the most strikingly gifted; prestige deters the latter from taking artistic risks that might land them in a flop, while conscience forbids them to indulge in the kind of *Kitsch* that would guarantee a hit. From the directors' point of view as well as the actors', there is not much doubt that the healthiest theatres are those of Sweden, Russia, and Germany. If there were a Staattheater in the neighbourhood of Times Square, Mr. Lewis would long since have celebrated his fiftieth production and Mr. Brando might have played thirty stage roles in ten years, instead of one.

Compared to the playhouses of Germany, Mr. Clurman wrote from Berlin in 1956, "the American, English, French stages look like little-theatre activities." It is not that the grass grows greener there but that it is more systematically nourished. When the Group Theatre broke up, in 1941, Mr. Clurman made a significant, though ill-phrased, comment: "The basic defect in our activity was that while we tried to maintain a true theatre policy artistically, we proceeded economically on a show-business basis. Our means and our ends were in fundamental contradiction." That is still the dilemma of the Western theatre.

(1959)

Requiem for a Nun, BY WILLIAM FAULKNER, AT THE GOLDEN.

Having been pursued by William Faulkner's *Requiem for a Nun* across half a continent and the whole of an ocean, I begin to understand how Francis Thompson must have felt when the Hound of Heaven picked up his spoor. In three years the play has tailed me from Berlin to New York, via Paris, Madrid, and London; wherever I go into hiding, it goes into rehearsal. Last week it got its man for the fourth time. (I contrived to miss the Spanish production by lying about my health. According to Mr. Faulkner, we pay for our sins through the suffering of others. Judging by the expression on the face of my companion at the Broadway opening, I have paid in full.) My long international association with the piece has taught me a lot about the mental processes of the people who like it. They are usually ready to concede that the writing is dense and prolix, the characterization crucially inconsistent, and the construction primitive, but what do these superficial considerations matter, they ask, in a work that goes to the very roots of the human condition?

The short answer is (a) a great deal and (b) it doesn't. To start by enlarging on (a), Mr. Faulkner's play is essentially undramatized. It is a sequel to his novel *Sanctuary,* which dealt with the early life of a girl named Temple Drake and her springtime awakening to nymphomania. A mean, moody, and munificent premonition of Lolita, Miss Drake got herself involved, while still at college, in a car crash, with a drunken lover at the wheel. After witnessing a murder, she was kidnapped by a midget voyeur called Popeye and imprisoned in a Memphis brothel, where she liked the work so much that she fell in love with a regular customer, who was regrettably slain on his way to her bed. Before the play begins, she has married the drunken driver, now dried out into respectability, and borne him two children, one of whom has been murdered by her maid, Nancy, a "nigger dope-fiend whore" she befriended in captivity. All this comes under the heading of "what has gone before," and the problems of putting it across are gigantic. Mr. Faulkner tackles them by wasting most of the evening on exposition in its least dramatic form—retrospective narration in the first person. One swift flashback breaks the monotony; otherwise, we are wearied by detailed descriptions of events we have not seen and people we have not met. And what descriptions! Sentences as interminably woolly as unravelled sweaters alternate with moral saws that are either turgid restatements of platitudes or stammering attempts at paradox; for the most part the style nags the thought to death. It frankly enraged me, but, as Mr. Faulkner might say, man may not utter in anger, or wrath, or what passes with him for anger and wrath, if anything does, and not be defiled, or tarnished, or lastingly unstrung.

The play's basic flaw, however, is its handling of Nancy. For one thing, we are never told how the dope-hooked prostitute of the exposition developed into the model of glowing piety that we see on the stage. For another—and this is where we verge on (b)—Mr. Faulkner's explanation of why Nancy committed infanticide seems to me profoundly unreal, if not inhuman. Temple, we learn, was about to leave her husband for a new lover; Nancy slaughtered the baby to keep it from being tainted by its mother's sins, and also to dissuade Temple from wrecking her marriage. I should have thought that a live child, however tainted, was worthier of preservation than a dying marriage, but Nancy goes to the noose contentedly singing spirituals, with the author's full approval of her self-sacrifice. At the core of Mr. Faulkner's eerie, specialized philosophy I stumbled on a dumbfounding linguistic confusion. Nancy's defence counsel insists at one point that when Christ said "Suffer the little children to come unto me," he meant that the children's parents should really suffer—literally agonize—to achieve salvation. What can one say except that he didn't? A writer who is unaware that "suffer," in that context, means simply "allow" is obviously beyond the reach of verbal persuasion. Toward the end, just before she slow-marches offstage right, into the eye of a spotlight, Nancy replies to an inquiry about her faith by saying that though she believes nothing in particular, she "believes." Shortly afterward Temple, who asked the foolish question that got the foolish answer, marches offstage left, similarly lighted. The residue from two hours of mimetic pain is no more than that—the sort of faery food that will serve, I don't doubt, to nourish those who admire Mr.

MacLeish's *J.B.*, of which Mr. Faulkner's work is in some respects the segregated version.

Tony Richardson's direction is, to put it gently, unobtrusive, or, to put it truly, limp; the text is intoned rather than embodied. Bertice Reading, with wide eyes and a face full of tears, makes a nobly symbolic figure of the incredible Nancy, and Zachary Scott grinds meatily away as her lawyer, but Ruth Ford is an arid, anonymous Temple ("What a personality that girl needs!" I said to myself, echoing a famous impromptu of Richard Haydn's), and I assure the actor who plays her husband that it is possible to convey passion without inhaling audibly through the nose twice in every sentence.

(1959)

The Rivalry, BY NORMAN CORWIN, AT THE BIJOU.

By conventional Broadway standards, Norman Corwin's *The Rivalry* is not a play at all. Yet it is unquestionably theatre. To see it is to realize, with a shock of disquiet, how many theatrical weapons our authors have lately allowed to rust. A stage is a platform that can serve a multitude of purposes, most of which we neglect or ignore. The legitimate theatre of today deals mainly in domestic anecdote. Devoted to the manufacture of imaginary storms in family teacups, it demands of its audience no mental effort more exacting than that involved in reading the tea leaves. Mr. Corwin has other ideas, one of them being that ideas themselves are exciting. He also believes that non-fiction can be as potent on the stage as it is in the library. His new show is a mixture of polemical drama, which bases its appeal on argument, and documentary drama, which pins its faith to facts. By taking as his subject the Lincoln-Douglas debates on slavery, Mr. Corwin has voluntarily thrown away the twin crutches of surprise and suspense on which most plays are thankful to lean; the facts are familiar, and everyone knows how the argument came out. Apart from a few glimpses of the Douglases at home, a couple of chance encounters between Lincoln and Mrs. Douglas, and some scattered remarks from party campaigners, the bulk of the text comes verbatim from the stenographic record of 1858. It is a tribute to the power of authenticity and the fascination of controversy, as much as to Mr. Corwin's editing skill, that the play is continuously absorbing. The set, a wooden rostrum decked with flags, stands for any and all of the outdoor stages on which the combatants conducted their seven sessions of mutual dissent. They address their speeches directly to us. Not only are we present at the making of history, we are also helping to make it. The combination is hard to resist.

This particular slice of history, however, presents the playwright with special problems, some of which Mr. Corwin has failed to solve. No matter how you condense the debates, the verdict must go to Lincoln; it is inconceivable that anyone outside Saudi Arabia could nowadays endorse Douglas' attitude toward slavery. This being so, I feel that Mr. Corwin might have strengthened the conflict without blunting his point if he had reminded us that Lincoln was a canny politician as well as an idealist. "I am not, nor ever have been, in favour of bringing about in any way the social and political equality of the white and black races"—thus Lincoln at Charleston, in the southern half of Illinois. In the same debate he declared that "there must be the position of superior and inferior, and I as much as any other man am in favor of having the superior position assigned to the white race." When Douglas taxed Lincoln with varying his opinions according to his geographical position, he had a good logical case, and I am sure Mr. Corwin would not have damaged his play if he had let us hear it. But the greatest difficulty facing anyone who tries to dramatize the rivalry is the fact that the two adversaries spoke different rhetorical languages, and hence never truly communicated with each other. Douglas, the racial bigot and champion of states' rights, took the short, legalistic view; Lincoln, the verbal magician and champion of human rights, took the long, philosophic view. If the former cited law in his support, the latter riposted with the Bible; a quibble from Douglas would be met by a joke from Lincoln; and although it is clear that Douglas was consistent but wrong while Lincoln was inconsistent but right, their dispute produced no durable answers to the mighty questions it raised. At what precise point does self-government become misgovernment? How can democracy, the rule of the majority, be prevented from discriminating against minorities? The antagonists wander around these issues, yet never tackle them head on; the argument is circular rather than progressive.

It is bootless, however, to blame on Mr. Corwin the shortcomings of history; for all its flaws, I relished the evening and hope to spend more like it. He has directed his own play superbly. Richard Boone is a raw-boned, ruminative Lincoln, swathed in the melancholy that we associate with the man, yet suggesting beneath it a moral certitude as unswerving as a planet's course. Mr. Boone's voice, alternately musing and impassioned, matches in richness the prose it is called on to enounce. Martin

Gabel, as the squat and virulent Douglas, booms and cajoles to great effect, though at times he cannot help betraying the fact that he disapproves of the character he is impersonating. This is an error: Douglas must be played from his own point of view, not from ours. If Mr. Gabel can bring himself to cut down on the sneering, his performance will be faultless, as it already is in the epilogue, which covers Douglas' reconciliation with his old enemy as well as the hectic campaign in support of the Union that ended his short life. Nancy Kelly plays Mrs. Douglas, patience married to a monument, and Woodrow Parfrey, fumbling and perspiring, says a few endearing words as a fervent Lincolnista. As I left the theatre, a news item caught my eye. Snaking its way in electrified capitals around a building on Times Square, it announced that a federal judge had turned down a petition to exclude nine Negroes from Southern schools. The debate continues.

(1959)

Look after Lulu, BY NOËL COWARD, AT THE HENRY MILLER.

What is style in the theatre? A happy consonance of manner with matter, of means with end, of tools with job. Style is the hammer that drives in the nail without bruising the wood, the arrow that transfixes the target without seeming to have been aimed. It makes difficult things—and on the stage everything is difficult—look simple. When a strenuous feat has been performed without strain, it has been performed with style. The essence of it all is tact. *"La perfection du style,"* said Taine, *"c'est la disparition du style."* I would not labour the point in this unstylish way if it were not for the fact that a new definition of the word has lately been plaguing the theatre. According to this, style is a special kind of galvanic treatment to be meted out indiscriminately to all artificial comedies written before World War I. Having picked your play, you first overdress it and then overstress it, so that unimportant lines are delivered as if they were italicized, and important ones as if they were printed in capitals and followed by three exclamation marks; finally, you keep the characters whirling about the stage like the ingredients in a Waring Blendor. When the show closes after five performances, you are apt to become a sage, shaking your head wisely and pitying the inability of modern audiences to recognize style when they see it. The truth, of course, is that what you have offered them is not style at all but its antithesis. Your production said, in effect, "See how hard it is to be entertaining!" Style, on the other hand, would have shown how easy it is, and kept its mouth shut.

The false definition is currently getting a thorough workout at the Henry Miller Theatre, where Georges Feydeau's classic fifty-year-old farce *Occupe-toi d'Amélie* opened last week, in an adaptation entitled *Look after Lulu.* The direction, which is by Cyril Ritchard, appears to be based on the postulate that the play is unactable and must therefore be parodied. The result is that supreme theatrical redundancy, a burlesque of a burlesque. We are encouraged to laugh not so much at the piece itself as at the period in which it was thought funny. Forget about the lines, Mr. Ritchard seems to implore us; concentrate instead on the physical energy, the facial contortions, and the vocal mannerisms with which they are delivered. If we are still unconvulsed, he bids us chortle at Cecil Beaton's "amusing" scenery—those erotic murals in the bedroom scene, for instance, which make female nudity so mysteriously unattractive. And what about Mr. Beaton's costumes, those glittering bandages that swathe the mummified text, those hats like hatboxes, those cloaks like tents? The effort that has gone into the staging is prodigious, but it is of the frenzied kind that betokens lack of conviction. The company subsides, waving, grimacing, and gesticulating, into what it clearly believes to be a swamp.

It has been grossly misled. The play can be directed—as Jean-Louis Barrault proved some years ago—in a manner that is at once effortless and utterly convinced. Like all good productions, M. Barrault's was an act of faith in the dramatist. Feydeau's intrigue concerns a malleable cocotte whose fidelity is put to the test by the temporary absence of her lover, a jealous young Army officer. The latter returns unexpectedly (nobody in farce ever returns expectedly) to find her sharing a bed with his best friend, a good-natured idler, on whom he forthwith plans a signal revenge. Aware that the traitor will inherit a pile of money if he marries, and also that he is in love with a married woman, the chafing cuckold offers to stage a mock ceremony wherein his erstwhile chum will appear to have wedded the cocotte. But the offer is a cheat; what was promised to be false turns out to be real, and the last act deals with the victim's stratagems for getting an annulment. Meanwhile, a predatory noblewoman prowls around grumbling, and a lubricious prince arrives from Salestria, determined to occupy himself with Amélie—or, in the present version, to look after Lulu. As performed by the Barrault troupe, these trivial events took on something more than volatile skittishness. They seemed—thanks to such players as Madeleine Renaud, Jean Desailly, and Pierre Bertin—to imply a tolerance of human frailty and a sympathy with human gullibility. We were smiling at people we knew and liked. It was Stanislavsky who said, "Characters in vaudeville are ordinary and realistic. One should not consider them strange creatures. . . . Their only strangeness is their absolute credulity about everything." This credulity, for which another word is innocence, is what is missing from Mr. Ritchard's production. Tammy Grimes, the husky, pop-eyed little pouter who plays Lulu, might have achieved it in circumstances less frantic; so might Roddy McDowall, her reluctant husband, who is halfheartedly perturbed where M. Desailly, in the same role, was wholeheartedly appalled. Kurt Kasznar, as the unsleeping prince, comes off best, but even he lacks the weight and seniority that the part demands. Polly Rowles is a close second, though her clothes envelop her so completely and get so many rounds of applause that it is not always possible to see her and hear her at the same time. Most of the other performances are either antic or dull, or both.

It would, however, be unfair to blame the failure of the evening entirely on Mr. Ritchard. Much of the responsibility belongs to the adapter, whom the programme astonishingly alleges to be Noël Coward. This cannot, I feel, be the Mr. Coward I know, the eagle-eyed, teacup-clutching yachtsman on whose calves the breakers of Jamaica incessantly beat. The script contains a few lines that are redolent of the real Mr. Coward—especially in the second act, which takes place behind blinds closed against the midday sun—but most of the gaiety is dependent on jokes about smelling salts and Epsom salts, doubts about whether a Great Dane is a Scandinavian lover or a dog, puns derived from homophones like "chaste" and "chased," and visiting Russians who, having "come down all those frightful steppes," remark that "the peasants are always revolting." Either Mr. Coward has fallen among sycophants too affectionate to gainsay him or he has at his fingertips an open-and-shut imposture case.

(1959)

Sweet Bird of Youth, BY TENNESSEE WILLIAMS, AT THE MARTIN BECK; *Raisin in the Sun*, BY LORRAINE HANSBERRY, AT THE ETHEL BARRYMORE.

Apart from the performance of Geraldine Page, a display of knock-down flamboyance and drag-out authority that triumphantly quells all doubts about this actress' ability to transcend her mannerisms, almost everything connected with *Sweet Bird of Youth,* Tennessee Williams' new play at the Martin Beck, dismayed and alarmed me. The staging, by Elia Kazan, is operatic and hysterical; so is the writing; and both seem somehow unreplenished, as if they had long been out of touch with observable reality. A dust bowl, one feels, is being savagely, obsessively ploughed, in defiance of the known facts about soil depletion and the need for irrigation. The heroine (Miss Page) is a decaying movie queen, querulous, doped, alcoholic, hypochondriac, and exorbitantly sexed. She fears heart attacks, and admits, like her author, that she has been "accused of having a death wish." Her current gigolo is a blond lad whose past history includes a spell in the chorus of *Oklahoma!* and a brief, reluctant participation in the Korean War; since then he has devoted himself to selling his virility to the highest bidder. He escorts Miss Page on a trip to his home town on the Gulf Coast. His purpose is to see once more a girl named Heavenly, whom he loved, seduced, and photographed in the nude when she was barely fifteen. He is not, however, aware that his youthful attentions left the girl physically tainted, so virulently that the curative operation has robbed her of the power to bear children. Heavenly's father, a political boss, has determined to avenge his daughter by gelding her seducer. In the second act we meet the boss—Big Daddy rewritten in the deep dyes of Victorian villainy—and see him delivering, for reasons that may have to do with directorial panache, a racist speech on a TV screen that covers the whole cyclorama. The obvious and unmistakable *scène à faire,* between his daughter and her ex-lover, never takes place and appears to have been forgotten. And after the first act the film star contributes nothing to the plot beyond offering her boy friend a lift to the next town; he turns it down, out of an obscure awareness that he must stay and surrender himself to be castrated. He begs us, in parting, to understand him, and to recognize ourselves in him.

For my part, I recognized nothing but a special, rarefied situation that had been carried to extremes of cruelty with a total disregard for probability, human relevance, and the laws of dramatic structure. My brain was buzzing with questions. How does it happen that the boy has not heard about the operation to which his beloved has submitted herself? Come to that, why is he ignorant of his mother's death? Can the postal service be that bad? And why is it emphasized that the action begins on Easter Sunday? Is castration to be equated with resurrection? By what convention, moreover, are weighty rhetorical asides, pages long, addressed directly to the audience while the other characters on stage freeze and pretend not to listen? Are Jo Mielziner's settings bleak and wall-less for symbolic reasons or because the lines would have been unspeakable against décor more realistic? Are we, in short, listening to anything more significant than antique melodrama pepped up with fashionable details about tape-recorders, coronaries, happy pills, and the price of diamond clips? Frankly, I doubt it. And I suspect that *Sweet Bird of Youth* will be of more interest to Mr. Williams' biographers than to lovers of the theatre. The hero of *Orpheus Descending,* his play before last, was torn to shreds by dogs. In *Suddenly Last Summer,* which succeeded it, the poet was slain and partly devoured by Spanish urchins, and the heroine was threatened with mental castration in the form of brain surgery. Now, it seems, the urge is out in the open; in *Sweet Bird of Youth* the *ingénue* has lost the use of her sexual organs before the curtain rises, and an analogous deprivation awaits the hero immediately after it falls. Let us hope that the theme is at last exhausted, that by exhausting it Mr. Williams has achieved some kind of personal fulfilment, and that in the future he will be able to write with fewer nerve ends trailing and in a style less dependent on the dictates of inner anguish. "The age of some people," says Paul Newman, as the gigolo, doing everything possible to clothe a symbol in credible flesh, "can only be calculated by the level of rot in them." In *Sweet Bird of Youth* the level is dangerously high; none of Mr. Williams' other plays has contained so much rot. It is as if the author were hypnotized by his subject, like a rabbit by a snake, or a Puritan by sin. Under hypnosis a man may reveal much about himself that would otherwise remain hidden, but the process of revelation involves the loss of his ability either to control what he is doing or to relate it to objective reality. And without this ability art is impossible.

On the evidence of *Sweet Bird of Youth,* Mr. Williams seems at present to be wholly alienated from the tangible, diurnal world that formerly nourished his talent. The supreme virtue of *A Raisin in the Sun,* by Lorraine Hansberry, is its proud, joyous proximity to its source, which is life as the dramatist has lived it. I will not pretend to be impervious to the facts; this is the first Broadway production of a work by a coloured authoress, and it is also the first Broadway production to have been staged by a coloured director. (His name is Lloyd Richards, and he has done a sensible, sensitive, and impeccable job.) I do not see why these facts should be ignored, for a play is not an entity in itself, it is a part of history, and I have no doubt that my knowledge of the historical context predisposed me to like *A Raisin in the Sun* long before the house lights dimmed. Within ten minutes, however, liking had matured into absorption. The relaxed, freewheeling interplay of a magnificent team of Negro actors drew me unresisting into a world of their making, their suffering, their thinking, and their rejoicing. Walter Lee Younger's family lives in a roach-ridden Chicago tenement. The father, at thirty-five, is still a chauffeur, deluded by dreams of financial success that nag at the nerves and tighten the lips of his anxious wife, who ekes out their income by working in white kitchens. If she wants a day off, her mother-in-law advises her to plead 'flu, because it's respectable. ("Otherwise they'll think you've been cut up or something.") Five people—the others being Walter Lee's progressive young sister and his only child, an amiable small boy—share three rooms. They want to escape, and their chance comes when Walter Lee's mother receives the insurance money to which her recent widowhood has entitled her. She rejects her son's plan, which is to invest the cash in a liquor store; instead, she buys a house for the family in a district where no Negro has ever lived. Almost at once white opinion asserts itself, in the shape of a deferential little man from the local Improvement Association, who puts the segregationist case so gently that it almost sounds like a plea for modified togetherness. At the end of a beautifully written scene he offers to buy back the house, in order—as he explains—to spare the Youngers any possible embarrassment. His proposal is turned down. But before long Walter Lee has lost what remains of the money to a deceitful chum. He announces forthwith that he will go down on his knees to any white man who will buy the house for more than its face value. From this degradation he is finally saved; shame brings him to his feet. The Youngers move out, and move on; a rung has been scaled, a point has been made, a step into the future has been soberly taken.

Miss Hansberry's piece is not without sentimentality, particularly in its reverent treatment of Walter Lee's mother; brilliantly though Claudia McNeil plays the part, monumentally trudging, upbraiding, disapproving, and consoling, I wish the dramatist had refrained from idealizing such a stolid old conservative. (She forces her daughter, an agnostic, to repeat after her, "In my mother's house there is still God.") But elsewhere I have no quibbles. Sidney Poitier blends skittishness, apathy, and riotous despair into his portrait of the mercurial Walter Lee, and Ruby Dee, as his wife, is not afraid to let friction and frankness get the better of conventional affection. Diana Sands is a buoyantly assured kid sister, and Ivan Dixon plays a Nigerian intellectual who replies, when she asks him whether Negroes in power would not be just as vicious and corrupt as whites, "I *live* the answer." The cast is flawless, and the teamwork on the first night was as effortless and exuberant as if the play had been running for a hundred performances. I was not present at the opening, twenty-four years ago, of Mr. Odets' *Awake and Sing,* but it must have been a similar occasion, generating the same kind of sympathy and communicating the same kind of warmth. After several curtain calls the audience began to shout for the author, whereupon Mr. Poitier leaped down into the auditorium and dragged Miss Hansberry on to the stage. It was a glorious gesture, but it did no more than the play had already done for all of us. In spirit, we were up there ahead of her.

(1959)

First Impressions, AT THE ALVIN; *Masquerade*, BY SIGMUND MILLER, AT THE GOLDEN.

They said it couldn't be done, and it couldn't. That, I'm afraid, must be the verdict on Abe Burrows' attempt to turn *Pride and Prejudice* into a musical play. Let me make it clear that I don't wish to impugn Mr. Burrows' integrity. A self-proclaimed Janeite, he has tackled the task of adaptation on his knees, in a spirit of outright reverence. To avoid confusion with an earlier dramatization, he has called his show *First Impressions,* which was Miss Austen's original title for the novel. As writer, he has kept verbal anachronisms down to a minimum; as director, he has fought back the temptation to whoop things too boisterously up. The level of decorum on the stage of the Alvin is enough to stagger anyone who remembers the Mr. Burrows of a few years ago, author and interpreter of such rowdy works as "Upper Peabody Tech" and "The Girl with the Three Blue Eyes." The dances, deftly supervised by Jonathan Lucas, are few and graceful, and the lively elegance of Peter Larkin's décor succeeded in undermining a conviction I have held for years—namely, that the only people who can design English period pieces are French. The music and lyrics, on which Robert Goldman, Glenn Paxton, and George Weiss have collaborated, understandably fail to measure up to the perfection of Miss Austen's prose architecture; even so, their efforts are discreet and praiseworthy. Mozart, the right man for the composer's slot, was unavailable, but at least we are spared anything in the nature of "Doing the Regency Rag," "Strut Miss Lizzie Bennet," or—a possible theme song for Darcy—"Playing It Cool." There are several spirited numbers, among them the duet in which Mr. Collins proposes to Elizabeth, who contrapuntally rejects him, and though I doubt whether the score is going to haunt my memory, I shall take no especial pains to exorcise it if it does. Let me add, on the credit (or, anyway, non-debit) side of the production, that it contains stylish supporting performances by Christopher Hewett, as Collins; James Mitchell, as Wickham the cad; and Phyllis Newman, as the eldest of the Bennet girls. Yet, despite its merits (or, anyway, non-demerits), the show as a whole is a fiasco. The reasons for this have to do partly with characters that have been misconceived or miscast, or both, but mostly with a single, vital character who has been omitted altogether.

The misconceptions and miscastings, unfortunately, include all the principal roles. Farley Granger, who plays Darcy, has none of the surly, magnetic arrogance that should make the man unbearable until at length we realize that his sourness is a defensive, and not an aggressive, tactic. Darcy must have a sense of innate, unquestioned superiority to the country gentry among whom he is temporarily thrown; Mr. Granger, by contrast, seems merely uppish. The nuances of class distinction, so maddeningly integral to the English way of life, escape him utterly. Polly Bergen, his partner, is a pert and wholesome performer, but she is Mr. Granger's Elizabeth rather than Mr. Darcy's; instead of the candour, the mockery, the sheer combative intelligence that properly belong to Mr. Bennet's second daughter, she gives us nothing more than a warm-hearted flirt. The fault here is not entirely Miss Bergen's. In the novel Elizabeth is her father's favorite; their relationship is one of mutual respect, and most of her attitudes toward life and love derive from the affectionate tuition of this witty, sardonic, defeated man, who has immersed himself in his library in order to avoid the company of his wife—"a woman," as Miss Austen tartly observes, "of mean understanding, little information, and uncertain temper." In Mr. Burrows' version Elizabeth is deprived of her paternal mentor. Mr. Bennet is a bewhiskered nullity, bug-eyed, henpecked, and amiably feeble, and the balance of the household tilts precipitously in favor of his lady. Mother, in fact, takes over from father, in accordance with accepted Broadway practice. As played by Hermione Gingold, Mrs. Bennet is no longer the vague, fussy provincial matchmaker of Jane Austen's imagination but a burbling dragoness fully capable (as she never is in the novel) of withering her husband with a single fire-darting glare. Needless to say, much of what Miss Gingold does is strangely hilarious. No actress commands a more purposeful leer; and in nobody's mouth do vowels more acidly curdle. But she upsets the equilibrium of the Bennet family, and hence of the play. Rather than Mrs. Bennet, she suggests Lady Catherine de Bourgh, slightly tanked up and ready to take on Prinny at midnight skittles. Mention of the latter beldam prompts me to query another of Mr. Burrows' alterations. In his adaptation the servile Mr. Collins, Lady Catherine's creature and dependent, is not a clergyman but a librarian —a change that utterly destroys Miss Austen's satiric intent, which was to show what could happen to a servant of God if he started to identify God with the existing social hierarchy. I would hate to believe that Mr. Burrows was scared of offending the church, but I can't think of any other excuse for what he has done. It is as if he had adapted *Ghosts* and made Pastor Manders a Scoutmaster.

All these are errors that rewriting or recasting might correct. We come now to the fault that is beyond remedy—the omission of the protagonist, in whose absence the tale loses its moral edge and becomes a featherweight account of a stiff man's unbending to a brisk young woman. The absentee and unseen heroine is, of course, Jane Austen herself. The theatre is admirably equipped to present her characters in action—talking, smiling, and sedately loving—but it cannot reproduce the running commentary, sometimes malicious, sometimes approving, that she keeps up on their behavior; and it is precisely this scrutiny, this relentless concern with motivation, that makes her a novelist, as opposed to a social reporter. *First Impressions,* like every other adaptation of Jane Austen, gives us the people and the dialogue but not the interpretative captions, the shell but not the core. The same would probably be true of any attempt to put a first-rate novel on the stage. In fact, if a novel works in the theatre, it is fairly safe to assume that it wasn't first-rate to begin with.

I am always gladdened by Donald Cook. He is as much a part of middlebrow comedy as the chandelier, the French windows, and the lighters by Ronson. It rejoices me to see him make one of his bustling entrances, rubbing his hands and heading straight for the drinks table, around which he sniffs like a bloodhound until, as customarily happens, somebody urges him to go ahead and help himself. (It is invariably someone else's house or apartment. I can't imagine Mr. Cook at home; he is one of nature's guests.) His manner exudes the insatiable lechery of the perpetually hung-over. Even his voice—a wry, disenchanted gurgle—sounds bloodshot. Yet it has alchemic powers; by merely *leaning* on a key syllable, it can create wit where no wit was. The sunnier literature of the twenties is full of Mr. Cook; the character he habitually plays—a kind of dapper black-sheep uncle, compounded in equal proportions of suavity and depravity—might have walked right out of the pages of P. G. Wodehouse or Donald Ogden Stewart. Mr. Cook represents *l'homme* rather more than *moyen sensuel,* contentedly enslaved to what Ben Jonson called "the fury of his gullet and groin."

During the second act of Sigmund Miller's *Masquerade,* which opened (and closed) last Monday, Mr. Cook dropped in for cocktails and delivered a short burst of erotic reminiscence that momentarily turned the limp play into a sort of bawdier *Claudia.* Soon afterward, to my bitter regret, the plot got under way again and steered the evening back into the doldrums from which Mr. Cook had briefly reclaimed it. Mr. Miller's heroine was a young wife with a problem. It took him nearly an hour to tell us what her problem was (sexual frigidity) and another hour to explain how she came by it (her mother taught her, as a child, to hate men). In the closing minutes she decided on suicide and actually had one leg over a second-storey balcony before her husband hauled her unceremoniously back to safety. Henceforth, we were suddenly and illogically informed, they would be able to look each other in the eye, and this ocular confrontation would make their marriage work. As a solution of the girl's difficulty, this seemed to me to be on a par with warm milk as a cure for deafness, but it was perfectly in keeping with the listless inconsequence that hung over the show as a whole. Gene Lyons, for example, who played the heroine's brother-in-law, is a man of robust build, yet she referred to him, not once but three times, as "skinny." And since she was alleged to have fooled her husband by feigning voluptuousness in his arms, it struck me as an odd caprice on the author's part to have made the hero a qualified medical man, who would surely have spotted that something was wrong. Later, however, I realized that this choice of profession had been governed by reasons of dramatic technique. If a lazy playwright wants a good excuse to get his hero offstage whenever two other characters need to exchange confidences, the easy answer is to give him an M.D.; the telephone rings, Mrs. Jukes has shingles, he grabs his bag, and the coast is clear. I can offer little to the cast except a shrug of commiseration. Cloris Leachman, a lithe and tender young actress, has already found and will find again better roles than that of the doctor's reluctant bedfellow. Glenda Farrell played her mother, one of those baleful matrons who throng the annals of American drama, turning their children into psychological messes by using them as ventriloquists' dummies. Mr. Cook appeared as an ex-husband of Miss Farrell's, and it was obvious that nothing in his marriage became him like the leaving it.

(1959)

A Desert Incident, BY PEARL S. BUCK, AT THE GOLDEN.

It would be awfully easy to write a flip, sardonic review of Pearl S. Buck's *A Desert Incident,* which succumbed last week after seven performances. By any standards, its plot was a weird one. The setting, if I may drop into the historic present, is an atomic-research establishment in the middle of an American desert, where an eager team of scientists is working on an experimental project that will, if successful, give the United States a clear lead in the battle for supremacy in thermonuclear weapons. Alternatively, the discovery could be developed peacefully, to the material benefit of the world at large. The problem of choice, however, does not immediately arise, since the experiments cannot be completed without the assistance of a young English physicist who knows the answers to several vital questions that baffle the Americans. Flown out to the desert H.Q., the Englishman is naïvely horrified to hear that his co-operation is being sought for possible military purposes. A familiar debate is joined, the newcomer asserting that scientists are morally responsible for the uses to which their knowledge is put, while Dr. Ashley, the man in charge of the laboratory, ripostes with the doctrine of science for science's sake. But before long Miss Buck abandons argument in favor of implausible and essentially irrelevant action. The Englishman has brought with him an oaken chest full of jazz records, which he plays incessantly. Some of them, he innocently remarks, comes from behind the Iron Curtain, and this revelation results in his being investigated for subversive activities, on the ground that the discs may contain rhythmically coded messages. At the same time he reopens an old love affair with Dr. Ashley's wife, a wartime refugee from Poland, to whom he addresses remarks like "Your eyelashes are tipped with gold." A number of peripheral characters have meanwhile been introduced, all of them symbolic, in one way or another, of the life force, or fertility. They include a bulbously pregnant Indian housemaid, a couple of children who are fascinated by the mystery of procreation, a company wife in a desperate state of sexual neglect, and an ageing professor—Miss Buck's spokesman, and a sort of would-be Robert Graves—who believes that history began to go awry when women made the fatal error of assuming that men could govern the world. Eventually, after a confused triangular discussion, Mrs. Ashley converts both her husband and her lover to the old man's point of view, and the two scientists bow to her will. As the curtain falls, they are both on the telephone, urging their colleagues to convene in protest, with the aim of postponing for as long as possible the extinction of that unique biped, man.

The writing throughout is clumsy, and, as I've said, it would be easy to poke fun at Miss Buck's notions of dramaturgy. Large numbers of people would also quarrel with her reasoning, or at least with its implications. Her assumption is that the human race must go on existing, at any cost. From this she argues, or seems to be arguing, that the scientists of the West should decide, unilaterally, to withhold from their governments any information that might possibly be used to prosecute a war. This, of course, is a fairly extreme position to take, and until a few days ago I would not have worried very much about the rejection of a play that advocated it. Since then, however, I have encountered the opposite extreme, and I have begun to worry quite a lot. To explain why, I shall have to embark on a personal digression.

Last week, on a sunny morning of this momentous spring, I was invited to lunch with a tall, smiling young man, happily married and extraordinarily well read, who has risen in a very short time to one of the highest executive posts in American journalism. During the conversational preliminaries I mentioned that I had been rather disturbed by the news, reported in all the Sunday papers, that radioactive fallout is heavier in the northern United States than anywhere else on earth, and I added that I had been especially unnerved by James E. Warner, of the *Herald Tribune,* who wrote on March 22, "There appears to be no immediate cause for worry, however, as experts appear to be agreed that the chance of any individual getting a deadly dose of Strontium 90 is only about one in 500,000." Assuming that there are roughly eighty million people in the northern United States, I took this statement to be tantamount to an admission that about a hundred and sixty murders were going to be committed in the near future, and I asked my host whether he did not think this an "immediate cause for worry." He shrugged and said it was all a matter of ends and means. I inquired what he meant, and I must confess that he gave me a full and elaborate answer. To begin with, he told me that for many months he and a number of influential friends had been swapping views on the ethics of thermonuclear war. Their deliberations had been based on the premise that diplomatic approaches to the summit were useless. "My wife and children know what to expect, and they've accepted it," he said. "I've told them that there'll probably be an exchange of hydrogen bombs before the end of June, and I've explained to them that it will probably mean the death of all of us." His voice was calm, even gallant; he was not arguing a case but regretfully defining a position. He said that whenever he boarded a plane and flew over the towers of Manhattan, he could not help feeling a pang of melancholy at the thought that this proud and festive city, this dynamic cluster of energy and aspiration, was so soon, and so inexorably, to be demolished, and, with it, all the cities around the globe where its name was known. In his mind the holocaust was not only imminent but necessary. "I'm in love with America," he said, with a sincere and poignant grin. "I guess you could call me a conservative." I suggested to him that since a conservative is, by definition, one who seeks to conserve things—i.e., to keep them from harm or decay—he might be able to find a more precise term to describe himself. He genially conceded that I "had a semantic point there." Returning to the main theme, I said that while I recognized his right as an individual to commit suicide rather than live under alien rule, I could not understand his equanimity at the thought that the whole of mankind would perish with him. At this, he smiled a deep, forgiving, historian's smile. Other forms of life, he said, had been destroyed; what was so special about the human race, which was doomed to ultimate annihilation anyway by the cooling of the earth? Whatever happened in the coming war, he went on, life itself would not be annihilated; certain autotrophic bacteria, for instance, would be likely to survive, particularly if they lived beneath the polar icecap, where the effects of fallout would be minimal, and who could say that in the course of billenniums they would not evolve into a species superior to ours? "Life renews itself," he declared, but, to hasten the process of renewal, it would, he felt, be a kindly act on our part to bury, miles beneath the earth's surface, caskets containing a few vital theorems ("Pythagoras, and so on") that would help our successors over their initial hurdles.

I asked my host, who was eating heartily, how he had managed to reconcile himself so philosophically to the imminent destruction of his kind. His reply was lengthy, but it can be reduced to a simple statement: he believed the concept of human liberty to be more valuable than the human beings who invented it. To preserve the freedom of mankind, he was ready to sacrifice mankind itself. In defense of an idea, he was prepared to condone the slaughter not merely of himself and his compatriots but of all thinking creatures, in whose minds alone the idea could exist. By now luncheon was over, and we quitted the restaurant.

In parting, I asked him, as casually as I could, to give my regards to his wife and children, whom I had never met. He thanked me and walked off, smiling, down the ugly, clamorous, irreplaceably precious street.

I do not know how many there are of him scattered across the countries of the world. There may be only a few, but even a few would be enough to carry out that deadly dream of June and make this our farewell summer. I realize that considerations like these are not supposed to affect the judgment of a theatre critic. All the same, as long as there are men like my host at luncheon, I cannot imagine myself pouring scorn on any play that challenged their opinions, however cloudily and with whatever disregard for *Realpolitik*. Miss Buck botched her attempt, partly out of inexperience (this was her first work for the theatre) and partly because her cast, except for Shepperd Strudwick and Cameron Prud'homme, was frankly amateurish and in some instances embarrassing. Yet she chose the most important subject in the world, and though she handled it vaguely and emotionally, she came down on the side of life, while the detached, historical viewpoint of my smiling friend led him to espouse the cause of death. Because of her choice, and her commitment, I am prepared to forgive Miss Buck a great deal.

(1959)

The Backstage Jungle.

William Gibson's *The Seesaw Log,* published in a volume that also contains the text of Mr. Gibson's Broadway hit *Two for the Seesaw,* is a blow-by-blow, cut-by-cut account of an ordeal that occupied two years of the author's life and left him, at the end, financially enriched and spiritually depleted. In short, it is a success story. At the same time it is a study of defeat. In the course of a hundred and forty pages, the rugged-individualist theory of art, which regards the author's intentions as sacrosanct, is eroded and finally overwhelmed by the rugged collectivism of an industry in which nothing is more sacred than the will of the audience. *Per se,* the struggle is old stuff. The cry of the betrayed dramatist ("That's not my play!") is among the more easily identifiable night sounds of Broadway, and if the theme of ideals versus commercialism were to be banished from literature today, a tidy heap of American writers would be out of work tomorrow. Mr. Gibson's book, however, has three qualities that, conjoined, give it a special fascination. One is the sturdy excellence of its prose. The second is its attention to detail;

this is the fullest factual record I can remember of the daily hazards involved in getting a Broadway show on the road and bringing it back alive. Thirdly, and personally, I was fascinated by the ambiguity of Mr. Gibson's conclusions. By a strange exercise of doublethink, he seems to have felt simultaneously fulfilled and frustrated when his play became a hit. While resenting the changes he had been called on to make, he was grateful to those who had asked him to make them. After a characteristic agony of rewriting in Philadelphia, he describes himself as suffering "the paradoxical experience of seeing his work improve by becoming poorer." No student of semantics could resist a phrase like that.

For non-playgoers, let me explain that *Two for the Seesaw* is a dialogue for two lovers—a Nebraska lawyer on the brink of divorcing a rich wife, and an ebullient girl from the Bronx with whom he has a temporary, solacing affair. When Mr. Gibson finished the first draft, in April 1956, he was in his early forties; he had already written five unstaged plays, a novel, a television script, and a lot of poetry, but Broadway was new to him—just how new he learned seven months later when a New York producer bought an option on his dramatized duet. In the fall of 1957 Henry Fonda agreed to play the lead opposite an unknown *gamine* named Anne Bancroft. Rehearsals started in November, whereupon all hell, quietly at first but rapidly mounting to tantrum intensity, began to break loose. Mr. Fonda, on whose presence in the cast the show's backing depended, belatedly realized that the hero was not only dull by comparison with the heroine but pretty nasty in his own right. Accordingly, changes were suggested, and Mr. Gibson's attempts to reconcile his own convictions with those of the star, the director, the producer, and the audience kept him sweating until the Broadway opening on January 16, 1958. By this time he had been—by turns—sick, furious, conciliatory, disgusted, delighted, and sick again. He had slept through performances of rewrites that had cost him sleepless nights, and he had entered in his diary such confidences as this, written during the Washington tryout:

> The play grew more and more effective, and I felt less fulfilled as a writer.

After Washington he went back to his home in Massachusetts, where he lacerated himself for his subservience and decided that we—every man jack of us—had lost "some religious component in ourselves, and this component was the difference between art and entertainment." Yet a few days later, when the Philadelphia critics had expressed approval of the production, we read:

> The fact was unblinkable, after such reviews, that the hammering my script and head had undergone . . . had issued in a much better play.

His conclusion, after the New York dailies had conceded him a hit, is that the American theatre is "primarily a place not in which to be serious, but in which to be likable."

As acted, *Two for the Seesaw* is funny, accurate, and often poignant. Since Mr. Gibson offers no specific examples of the alterations he was required to make, and since he informs us that the printed text contains elements of several versions, it is almost impossible to tell whether we have lost a masterpiece or gained a smash. For a fledgling playwright, Mr. Gibson seems to have gone in for an awful lot of backstage hectoring, lecturing, and quasi-directing, so that one is tempted to wonder how much his own behaviour contributed to the general uproar. Be that as it may, his main point is that he was forced to modify his original conception under pressure from his co-workers and his audience. How humiliating that sounds! Yet Chekhov rewrote at the behest of Stanislavsky, and Bertolt Brecht, perhaps the most original dramatist of our century, was not only ready but positively eager to learn from his spectators and to incorporate into his work the suggestions of fellow intellectuals. It was Brecht who spoke of what he called "the romantic concept of individual creation," by which he meant that nobody can write a play singlehanded; it emerges from, and is aimed at, a particular social, political, and historical climate, and in its final form, if it is a good play, all the influences implied in those adjectives will coalesce. No dramatist, in other words, is an island. To think otherwise is a form of solipsism.

Mr. Gibson writes as if only two choices lay open to the playwright; he can either make compromises for the sake of the box office or refuse them in the name of artistic integrity. There is in fact a third choice—that of adapting one's play so that it will have the maximum impact on the audience, small or large, dumb or smart, for which it was intended. That, unfortunately, is feasible only in a non-commercial subsidized theatre. Mr. Gibson, meanwhile, is trapped in a false antithesis. The true source of his torment is not that he was asked to make his play appeal to its own audience but that he was asked to make it appeal to *every* audience. His tale is hypnotically readable, and I urge him, in the light of what I have said, to dramatize it. It would make a provocative and alarming evening.

It is disturbing to reflect that to a Russian about three quarters of

The Seesaw Log would seem either mad or meaningless. In the Soviet theatre there are no tryouts and no investors to consider. No star's reputation is at stake, nor is there a first-night panic, since the Moscow critics seldom review a play until they have seen it at least twice. Russian theatres are institutions, and institutions sometimes turn into museums. Our theatres are shopwindows, and shopwindows sometimes turn into peepshows. The danger with the Russian system is that economic security has been known to breed complacency; the trouble with ours is that economic insecurity frequently breeds hysteria. Of both worlds, one cannot help feeling, there must be a borrowable best.

(1959)

Gypsy, BY JULE STYNE, STEPHEN SONDHEIM, AND ARTHUR LAURENTS, AT THE BROADWAY.

Quite apart from considerations of subject matter, perfection of style can be profoundly moving in its own right. If anyone doubts that, he had better rush and buy a ticket for *Gypsy,* the first half of which brings together in effortless coalition all the arts of the American musical stage at their highest point of development. So smooth is the blending of skills, so precise the interlocking of song, speech, and dance, that the sheer contemplation of technique becomes a thrilling emotional experience. It is like being present at the triumphant solution of some harsh architectural problem; stone after massive stone is nudged and juggled into place, with a balance so nice that the finished structure seems as light as an exhalation, though in fact it is earthquake-proof. I have heard of mathematicians who broke down and wept at the sight of certain immaculately poised equations, and I have actually seen a motoring fanatic overcome with feeling when confronted by a vintage Rolls-Royce engine. *Gypsy,* Act I, confers the same intense pleasure, translated into terms of theatre. Nothing about it is superfluous; there is no display of energy for energy's sake. No effort is spared, yet none is wasted. Book, lyrics, music, décor, choreography, and cast seem not—as so often occurs—to have been conscripted into uneasy and unconvinced alliance but to have come together by irresistible mutual attraction, as if each could not live without the rest. With no strain or dissonance, a machine has been assembled that is ideally fitted to perform this task and no other. Since the task is worth while, the result is art.

As everyone must surely be aware, the show is based on the memoirs of Gypsy Rose Lee, the renowned kimonophobe (to use a word of George Jean Nathan's) whose intellectual aspirations were gently pinked by Rodgers and Hart in a song called "Zip." Miss Lee's account of her early life in vaudeville and her subsequent transition to burlesque stripping was dominated by the eccentric, outspoken, and wildly propulsive figure of Rose, her mother. The latter, a nightmare incarnation of Noël Coward's Mrs. Worthington, put her two daughters on the stage as soon as they could walk, and kept them there, as a coy and piping child act, until both were well into their teens. They had no formal—and very little informal—education. Their parents were divorced when Gypsy, the elder of the sisters, was four years old, and although their mother afterward ran through two other husbands, the liaison in each case was brief, and it cannot be said that the girls ever felt truly fathered. Rose's pride and cynosure was her younger daughter, Baby June, who has recently published, under her present stage name of June Havoc, an autobiography in which her mother appears as a total monster, forever pressing the children's noses to the grindstone of her own frustrated ambitions. The show at the Broadway takes Miss Lee's view, which is rather more temperate; the element of vicarious fulfillment is unmistakably there, but we are encouraged to admire Rose's shrewdness as much as to dislike her possessiveness. The miraculous first half deals with her obsessive attempts to make Baby June a star, and ends when the child elopes, at the age of fourteen, with one of the boys in the act. As the curtain comes down, Rose has erased June from her mind and transferred her fantasies of fame to the gauche, neglected elder sibling. I don't know that I shall ever forget the way Sandra Church, as Gypsy, quails and shakes when she encounters her mother's beady, appraising stare and guesses what is in store for her. It is like watching a rabbit petrified by the headlights of a silently onrushing car.

Although Miss Church happens to be acting better than anyone else of her age on Broadway, a lot of people are equally responsible for the wonder of that first act. Jule Styne, the most persistently underrated of popular composers, has contributed to it nine songs, all of which are both exciting in themselves and relevant to the action—from the opening chorus, "May We Entertain You?", a splendid pastiche of ragtime vapidity, to "Everything's Coming Up Roses," in which Rose, whistling in the dark, tries to persuade herself that life without June is going to be just peachy. In addition, we have "Small World," an elastically swaying tune used by Rose to seduce Herbie, the agent who becomes her lover; "Little Lamb," sung by Gypsy to one of her mother's menagerie of pets; "You'll Never Get Away from Me," Rose's jovial assertion of her man's dependence; "If Momma was Married," in which the daughters complain about their enslavement; and "All I Need Is a Girl," a song-and-dance number in the Astaire manner, performed by a young man who wants to leave Momma's troupe and go out on his own. He demonstrates his routine to Gypsy and invites her to dance with him. This being a musical, she does, but, this being no ordinary musical, she does not know the steps, and the partners end up in a state of mild, enjoyable confusion. The credit for this stroke, and for the whole physical gesture of the evening, belongs to Jerome Robbins, who, as director and choreographer, has poured into *Gypsy* the same abundance of invention with which he galvanized *West Side Story*. From the latter show he has borrowed a lyricist, Stephen Sondheim, and a librettist, Arthur Laurents, both of whom have brought to their new jobs an exemplary mixture of gaiety, warmth, and critical intelligence. A passing genuflection will suffice as tribute to Jo Mielziner, who must by now be aware that he is a superlative scenic designer, but I feel I should dwell longer on the cast. On Jacqueline Mayro, for instance, who plays Baby June, the cavorting tot, with a mask of dutiful glee and an absolute mastery of applause-milking devices, such as the pretense of breathlessness after a not particularly exhausting routine. On Lane Bradbury, too, who plays June grown up and ready to bolt. (The ageing process is handled superbly, like a movie dissolve; the children dance in a flickering spotlight and are replaced, one at a time, by their adolescent selves.) And, above all, we must linger on Ethel Merman, the most relaxed brass section on earth, singing her heart out and missing none of her own inimitable tricks, among them her habit of sliding down to important words from a grace note above, which supplies the flick that precedes the vocal whip-crack. But Miss Merman not only sings; she acts. I would not say that she acts very subtly; Rose, after all, with her dreams of glory, her kleptomania, her savage parsimony, and her passion for exotic animals and Chinese breakfasts, is scarcely a subtle character. Someone in the show describes her as "a pioneer woman without a frontier," and that is what Miss Merman magnificently plays.

The second half, which is briefer, is also less effective. There are several reasons for this. One has to do with plot; having seen the grooming of Baby June, we now watch the grooming of Gypsy, and this makes for redundancy. Another is that Act II contains only three new songs; the rest are reprises. A third is the lack, felt ever more urgently as the hours tick by, of a good, solid male singer; Jack Klugman, the show's nearest approach to a hero, is an amiable actor, but his voice is no more than an amplified snore. Fourth, Sandra Church is too chaste in demeanour to reproduce the guileful, unhurried carnality with which the real Gypsy undressed. Fifth, we have the finale. Rejected by both her daughters, Miss Merman plods on to the empty stage and bursts into a song about how she could have been better than either of them, given the chance. No sooner has she embarked on what promises to be a burlesque routine of staggering panache than the authors cut in to remind her of their purpose, which is to demonstrate the beastliness of managing mothers. Accordingly, she breaks off in mid-phrase and sets about lacerating herself in prose. This, I felt, was a case of integrity carried too far. Once Miss Merman has started to sing, nothing short of an air-raid warning should be allowed to interrupt her. To mute her at this point is an act of presumption, and the evening suffers from it. The latter half has in its favour a flamboyant trio of strippers, one of whom peels with her left hand while playing a trumpet with her right. But I don't see how anyone could deny that the show tapers off from perfection in the first act to mere brilliance in the second.

(1959)

The Great God Brown, BY EUGENE O'NEILL, AT THE CORONET.

For a short season at the Coronet, the Phoenix Theatre Company is presenting a revival of O'Neill's *The Great God Brown.* It makes a fascinating evening. When the play was first performed, in 1926, most of those who took the trouble to analyze it came to the conclusion that the author was writing about the conflict between Art, symbolized by Dion Anthony, and Crass Materialism, represented by Billy Brown. And so, on the surface, he was. Anthony, painter and compulsive lush, has all the attributes we popularly associate with genius. He is hypersensitive and converses, for the most part, either in sentences ending with exclamation marks or in elaborate rhetorical questions, such as "Why was I born without a skin, O God, that I must wear armour in order to touch or to be touched?" His power over women is infallible, as witness the ease with which he defeats Brown, poor baffled clod, in their rivalry over the girl Margaret. Once married, he goes in heavily for night-long tippling and afternoon rising, thus providing further evidence that he has an artist's soul; it was, I think, Desmond MacCarthy who said that whenever he turned up at someone's house for tea and found his host shaving in front of the drawing-room mirror, he was tempted to believe that he might be among bohemians. Still conforming to aesthetic type,

Anthony spends much of his spare time—and his time is mostly spare—in the company of a bovine tart named Cybel, who mothers him, and to whom he skittishly refers as Mother Earth, Old Filth, or "you sentimental old pig." Utter the phrase "a characteristic O'Neill hero," and at once I see a tearful, ageless adolescent with his face buried in the lap of a prostitute. (There's nothing like a bordello for a man who needs a captive audience.) To complete the picture, Anthony habitually addresses his intimates in the self-pitying, ponderously ironic manner of a drunken Irish tragedian—a sure sign that O'Neill means us to accept him as a frustrated genius. Brown, on the other hand, is just as obviously the incarnation of material success. He lacks imagination, toils all day at his desk, and smoothly passes off Anthony's ideas as his own. Envious of his friend's sexual magnetism, he uses his wealth to buy Cybel's affection, and when Anthony dies in his presence, of a heart attack, he carries his envy to the maniacal extreme of deciding to impersonate the dead man and thus to sleep with his wife. In the last (and by far the worst) act he is shot down by the cops as an escaping murderer.

That, in outline, is the play O'Neill's early admirers thought he had written—a straight fight between a frail introvert full of hidden love and a hardy extrovert full of hidden hate. But did he mean no more than that? Today, looking back on the body of O'Neill's work, we know better. Consider Anthony's speech—his best, and least exclamatory—at the close of the first act. He is speaking of his father:

> What aliens we were to each other! When he lay dead, his face looked so familiar that I wondered where I had met that man before. Only at the second of my conception. After that, we grew hostile with concealed shame. And my mother? I remember a sweet, strange girl, with affectionate, bewildered eyes, as if God had locked her in a dark closet without any explanation. I was the sole doll our ogre, her husband, allowed her and she played mother and child with me for many years in that house until at last through two years I watched her die with the shy pride of one who has lengthened her dress and put up her hair. And I felt like a forsaken toy and cried to be buried with her, because her hands alone had caressed without clawing. She lived long and aged greatly in the two days before they closed her coffin. The last time I looked, her purity had forgotten me, she was stainless and imperishable, and I knew my sobs were ugly and meaningless to her virginity; so I shrank away, back into life, with naked nerves jumping like fleas. . . .

This is the voice of O'Neill himself, bursting through the artifice of the play like a bareback rider plunging through a paper hoop. These parents, as we know from his later work, are his parents, and *The Great God Brown* reveals itself as one of the many tentative sketches he made for the final, brutal family portrait, *Long Day's Journey into Night*. Billy Brown, the pseudo-chum who loathes Anthony under the guise of love, is O'Neill's first attempt to express what he felt about his elder brother, the secret enemy with whom he constantly competed—not, however, for the love of Margaret but for the affection of his mother. One of the sternest objections to *The Great God Brown* is that it fails to establish its postulate; we meet Anthony's parents only briefly, in a prologue, and this short acquaintance does not explain why he feels so furious, bereft, and forlorn. The truth is that the prologue itself needs a prologue, in the shape of *Long Day's Journey into Night*.

In the light shed by the latter play, the first two acts of *The Great God Brown* make sharp dramatic sense. Freud and Ibsen, O'Neill's joint literary progenitors, are supplemented by loans from Pirandello and the Greeks; property masks are donned to indicate the social self, as opposed to the private self. To protect himself against society, Anthony wears a mask of cynical sensuality; when he removes it, exposing the naked face beneath, his wife is terrified. Similarly, she herself, who needs no disguise with her husband, puts on a mask of idealized girlhood when talking to Billy Brown. Only to Cybel, the whore, can Anthony speak freely without a false face; on one occasion he visits her masked, which prompts her to inquire, "Haven't I told you to take off your mask in the house?" The reproach might have been better phrased, but I don't think it destroys the validity of the convention. The destruction occurs later, when Brown steals the mask of the dead Anthony; and it wrecks the last two acts. A device hitherto employed to explore character is suddenly enlisted to advance the plot. I am ready to concede that a man might assume an alien façade in order to deceive the world, but that a wife might allow an old friend to pass himself off as her husband is totally incredible. We are transported into a soggy realm of bad fantasy; either Billy is a brilliant mimic or Margaret is a blockhead. If the former is the case, I simply don't believe it; if the latter, I lose interest.

(1959)

The Tenth Man, BY PADDY CHAYEFSKY, AT THE BOOTH.

The redemption of a cynic through religion is one of the oldest themes known to Western drama. Latterly in retirement, it has come bounding back to the theatre in *The Tenth Man,* by Paddy Chayefsky. It has done so, needless to say, in heavy disguise. Despite all the evidence to the contrary, there are limits to what modern audiences will swallow, and Mr. Chayefsky has been clever enough to conceal what he is up to until the very last moment, with the result that he is already being congratulated in some quarters on having attempted something previously untried in the theatre. His ostensible subject is the problem of a young Jewish girl who is suffering from an advanced case of schizophrenia. Persuaded that her mental disorder has been caused by daemonic possession, the girl's grandfather takes her to the local synagogue, where a few middle-aged members of the congregation are preparing for morning prayers. At first they are inclined to scoff at the old man's talk about dybbuks, but his granddaughter's ravings—she insists, among other things, that she is "the whore of Kiev"—help to tip the scales, and before long they are agreed on the necessity of performing the ceremony of exorcism. Finding themselves one short of the quorum demanded by tradition for the casting out of dybbuks, they dispatch the sexton in search of a volunteer. He returns accompanied by a young Jewish lawyer whom he has buttonholed on the street.

It is here that Mr. Chayefsky begins to unveil his purpose. The lawyer is a hollow man, drained of faith and disillusioned with humanity. He has been through a painful divorce; he has tried to kill himself; he is in the throes of psychoanalysis (I should have mentioned that the play is set in the twentieth century); and, to round off the catalogue of symptoms, he is an ex-Communist. His present creed is one of bitter nihilism. It requires no great powers of clairvoyance to predict that this state of affairs cannot be allowed to continue, and that what lies in store for the misguided fellow is come-uppance or conversion, or both. He develops a strange kinship with the deranged girl and decides that she needs psychiatric care rather more urgently than exorcism, but the white-haired rabbi who is in charge of the performance soon puts him right about that. Having ascertained that he is dealing with a nihilist, he says it is better to believe in dybbuks than to believe in nothing. It may, of course, be better still to believe in neither, but since it is no part of Mr. Chayefsky's scheme to appeal to reason, he has equipped none of his characters with the ability to argue thus rationally, and hence the rabbi's extremely loaded statement goes unchallenged. The ceremony takes its course, and in the upshot it is the lawyer, and not the girl, who is cleansed of an evil spirit. Hitherto he has claimed to be incapable of love, which has been tainted for him, as for a multitude of other fictional protagonists, by the squalor of zip fasteners and creaking bedsprings. He now declares himself purged of this deficiency, and out of this double negative Mr. Chayefsky fashions a positive ending. The lawyer falls in love with the girl; she is still, presumably, as schizoid as when we first met her, but what does that matter beside the overriding fact of the hero's spiritual rebirth?

Intellectually, I am always affronted by plays that present the human condition as a choice between God and Freud—the church and the couch—but, whatever his shortcomings as a thinker, Mr. Chayefsky is a wonderfully creative listener. The best of his Jewish dialogue is as meaty as any I have heard since the heyday of Clifford Odets. Lou Jacobi, as a belligerent atheist who jettisons his principles in order to participate in the climactic ritual, gets the funniest lines, and every word uttered by Arnold Marlé, the ancient exorcist, shines and quivers with conviction. Donald Harron, who plays the saved lawyer, makes the thin ice of his part seem as solid as concrete, and the sexton, David Vardi, is a model of exasperation, as well he might be, considering that the congregation includes such obstreperous members as George Voskovec and Jacob Ben-Ami. (I failed to understand all the Jewish expressions employed by Mr. Ben-Ami, but, like most Gentiles, I laughed anyway.) Risa Schwartz endows the heroine with little more than a fiery monotony, but Gene Saks takes full advantage of the finest speech in the play —a telephone conversation wherein a young rabbi instructs an even younger colleague in the art of making a synagogue pay. Yet for most of the evening I felt I was watching an image of the Jewish people that was as limited in its way as the image of Uncle Tom. These were stage Jews, whose innocence, congenital stoicism, and inverted sentence structure displayed the same kind of folksiness that one finds, and abhors, in stage Irishmen. There is plenty of charm in Mr. Chayefsky's writing, but I wish he had not wasted so much of it on stereotypes. The direction is by Tyrone Guthrie—a comparative stranger to realistic drama, though clearly a quick learner—and the cramped, dusty setting was designed by David Hays.

(1959)

Heartbreak House, BY GEORGE BERNARD SHAW, AT THE BILLY ROSE; *The Miracle Worker*, BY WILLIAM GIBSON, AT THE PLAYHOUSE.

One of the attractive things about Shaw is that the play he set out to write was seldom the play he wrote. He could never follow patterns, even when they were his own; Shaw the rationalist was putty in the hands of Shaw the Dubliner, always ready to be lured into those riotous byways of irrelevance and inconsequence that are among the glories of Irish literature. Nowhere is this clearer than in *Heartbreak House*. What Shaw had in mind was a stern indictment of the English leisured classes, whom he saw as a bunch of feckless loafers, drifting blindfold to perdition while flirting irresponsibly with culture, ideas, and each other's spouses. The house itself was meant to symbolize their anarchic inertia —a landlocked ship run by a senile tosspot who is insanely bent on concocting an explosive powerful enough to destroy every upstart money-grubber on earth. Captain Shotover and his family inhabit a world of twilit confusion where nothing is certain, not even individual identity. The old man fails to recognize his own younger daughter, and persistently mistakes one of his female guests for the offspring of a pirate. (The pirate himself turns up later, in the guise of a burglar.) Lies and impostures, illusions and hypocrisies litter the household. Everything is topsy-turvy; the women rule like men, and the men weep like women. What an aimless existence—and how full of *taedium vitae!*

That, at any rate, was what Shaw intended us to feel. He did not succeed. The dialogue is abundantly alive and utterly devoid of tedium; at quite an early stage he must have decided to give the characters their heads and let them rattle on wherever their angelic tongues led them. The result is that, despite their shiftlessness and stupidity, we cannot dislike them. They are frank, shameless, and entirely madcap; like everyone in a good Shaw play, they speak in the accents of their author, which may explain why he was never able to create a wholly convincing villain. Their plight may be gloomy, but they themselves are without melancholy, because—like all of Shaw's characters, in bad plays as well as good—they are deficient in human emotion. They can say anything to each other, however cruel, however painful, because none of them has any feelings to be hurt; theirs is the candour of the heartless. The finale is characteristically ruthless and unexpected. A zeppelin, cruising over England during the First World War, excretes a bomb that slays two of the cast—the burglar and a millionaire. Until this instant there has been no mention at all of the fact that a war is being waged; improvisation, founded on the air raids that were going on while the play was in the works, brings down the curtain. The author always claimed that *Heartbreak House* was an English version of Chekhov, and he was right to the extent that it could no more have been written without *The Cherry Orchard* as a model than *You Can't Take It with You* could have been written without *Heartbreak House*. In treatment, of course, the three plays are utterly dissimilar; Chekhov's pathos is worlds away from the high comedy of Shaw and the domestic farce of Kaufman and Hart. But they are all concerned with the same situation—that of a picturesque and eccentric family cut off from reality and the mainstream of history—and where they most instructively differ is in their attitudes toward this kind of wilful escapism. Both Chekhov and Shaw, at bottom, deplore it; Kaufman and Hart, writing rather later in the twentieth century, think it a thoroughly sensible idea.

The present production is fittingly operatic. Harold Clurman, the director, has instructed his cast to line up in a bold white light and belt the words across loud and fast. At times he is over-explicit; when Mangan, the industrialist, declares that he is going to take off all his clothes, Shaw restricts the stripping to a coat half doffed, but in Mr. Clurman's version the trousers are removed as well. (Sam Levene is the actor involved, and he may have needed some such encouragement; this gifted comedian specializes in playing underdogs, whereas Mangan is a top dog laid low. The result is that Mr. Levene is most like Mangan when Mangan is least like himself.) But Diana Wynyard, as Mrs. Hushabye, is all warmth and melting wit, and Pamela Brown brings gloating eyes and effortless vocal authority to her portrait of Lady Utterword, as lordly as a mermaid who has been trained to walk on her tail. Alan Webb's Mazzini Dunn is a model of anxious sincerity, and Maurice Evans gets all the grumbling capriciousness of Shotover, though he misses some of the prophetic wildness that makes the man more than just an ageing zany. (Mr. Evans has chosen to disguise himself as Shaw. "Why not?" you may ask, to which I answer, "Why?") The insolent, indolent uppishness that the text demands is sometimes absent. Hector is a more extravagant creature than Dennis Price imagines, and Diane Cilento, as Ellie Dunn, goes in for strident honking, where the lines call for a devastating demureness. (Miss Cilento, by the way, is the victim of a curious textual change. She says she would be prepared to marry somebody like Othello, "only, of course, English, and very handsome." What Shaw wrote was "white, and very handsome." Too much sensitivity, I suggest, is as bad as too little.) Ben Edwards, the designer, has cunningly compressed Shaw's two sets into one; the interior and exterior scenes both take place on a sort of canopied sun deck, which provides a sumptuous background for the finest comic writing at present available on Broadway.

William Gibson's *The Miracle Worker* deals with the childhood of Helen Keller, and how she was saved from the lifelong solitary confinement that is the accustomed lot of those who are deaf, mute, and sightless. The rescue was performed by a young Irish-American nurse named Annie Sullivan, who had once been blind herself and knew from her own experience the horrors of life inside a state institution. She came, seventy years ago, to the Keller home in Alabama, where she was able, by a mixture of patience, intuition, brute force, and love, to gain the confidence of a child who seemed at first little better than an animal, scratching and clawing in the silence and the dark. At length she coaxed this tiny, hostile creature up to human stature by teaching her how to communicate with other people, and thereafter, as we know, there was no stopping Miss Keller. That is the story Mr. Gibson has to tell, and it could scarcely be nobler, or more squarely affirm the dignity of our wayward species. He does not sentimentalize the struggle between Annie and her charge. Chairs are flung about, plates smashed, arms wrenched, and faces slapped; short of maiming Patty Duke, the resilient child who plays Helen, the combat could hardly be more violent. Arthur Penn's direction is honest and lucid, and Anne Bancroft, all scrubbed cheeks and glowing purpose, performs devoutly as the Irish catalyst. Yet, apart from the moment when Miss Duke, sniffing and groping, met Miss Bancroft for the first time, I was unmoved throughout. A few years back I saw a documentary film about handicapped children. It was called *Thursday's Children,* and it touched me more deeply inside ten minutes than *The Miracle Worker* did in two and a half hours.

My resistance to Mr. Gibson's play is partly due to the fact that it shocked me. It is, to begin with, very nearly describable as a barrel of laughs; some of the stage business that has been worked out for the child borders closely on the cute, and her guardian seldom lets a line go by without a snappy, indomitable Irish comeback. You feel that an agonizing process is being sweetened, discreetly softened, and made publicly palatable. Moreover, to add "dimension" to the exercise, the nurse is constantly being addressed by ghostly voices; the reproduction was so poor that I lost many of the words, but their general tenor seemed to be hortatory. Helen's family consists of an irascible father (Torin

Thatcher), a wailing mother (Patricia Neal), and a scapegrace half-brother (James Congdon), all of whom behave like characters out of a bad nineteenth-century play. Stereotypes themselves, they cast doubt on other aspects of the piece, which may, for all I know, be authentic. By the end of the second act Annie Sullivan has taught her pupil to sit at table and fold her napkin. Just before the final curtain she brings off a much greater feat; Helen learns to connect physical objects with the digital symbols that spell out their names. But a few seconds afterward, with no aid from her tutor, the child manages the infinitely harder jump from finger talk to speech; she pronounces the word "water." This certainly ends the play with a decisive thump, yet Mr. Gibson did not convince me that it happened like that—so swiftly, so simply, so conveniently. The events he is handling are too delicate to be submitted to Broadway tailoring, however well-intentioned. Perhaps inevitably, there hangs over the whole production a faint aura of exploitation. One of the early scenes, for instance, takes place in a home for the blind. The inmates are played by blind children. There is no logical reason why I should find this as objectionable as I do, but, equally, there is no logical argument against casting a tuberculosis victim as Marguérite Gautier.

(1959)

The Sound of Music, BY RICHARD RODGERS AND OSCAR HAMMERSTEIN II, AT THE LUNT-FONTANNE.

In their new operetta Richard Rodgers and Oscar Hammerstein II introduce to us a young woman who takes a job as governess in the household of a surly, authoritarian gentleman with a large family. She proves to have a miraculous way with the children; when a storm alarms them, for example, she allays their fears by teaching them a little song. Eventually her employer himself melts to the extent of joining her in a little dance, during which they discover that they are in love with each other. Meanwhile, from the sidelines, the tyrant's former favourite glumly surveys her rival's success.

The entertainment whose first act I have just outlined is not, as you might suppose, a revival of *The King and I,* though there is ample excuse for wishing that it were. It is called *The Sound of Music,* and it may come to be known in the annals of Broadway as Rodgers' and Hammerstein's Great Leap Backward. When I say this, I am not referring to the fact that the partners have indulged in self-plagiarism; ironically, the borrowings from *The King and I* seem less dated than anything else in *The Sound of Music.* It is the rest of the show that constitutes the real throwback, and what it throws us back to, fantastically enough, is the defunct tradition of English musical comedy as it was embodied (and interred) in the works of the late Ivor Novello. Romantic melodrama spiced with honey and bolstered by uplift was the genre in which Novello excelled, and nothing pleased him more than to contrive a love affair between a Middle European nobleman and a winsome commoner. I confess I never thought I would see the day when the two brave innovators who wrote *Oklahoma!* would turn out the very kind of musical they had laboured so hard, and so successfully, to abolish. But this is what has happened. It is as if the years that separate *Pal Joey* from *Gypsy* had dropped out of history and we were back in the musical and dramatic idiom of *White Horse Inn.* Listening to *The Sound of Music,* one begins to suspect that the collaborators have succumbed to a sort of joint amnesia and forgotten everything that Broadway learned, partly under their tutelage, in the forties and fifties.

The plot of their exercise in atavism is based on the early career of the Trapp family, who slipped out of Austria in 1938 and later became famous for their singing in America. The basing is admittedly loose, and I think I had better confine myself to the vaguely fictionalized version that is presented by the Messrs. R. and H. and their librettists, Howard Lindsay and Russel Crouse. The hero is the Baron von Trapp, a rich widower and retired naval captain whose obsession with discipline is such that he summons his seven children not by name but by means of blasts from a boatswain's pipe. Like Theodore Bikel, who plays the part, he is an expert guitarist. The heroine is Maria, a curly-haired postulant who is turned out of a nearby nunnery because of her irrepressible high spirits. This is Mary Martin, who can still brandish a note as blithely and suddenly as the best of them, though the sunlight of her voice is somewhat dimmer than it used to be. Engaged as tutor to the Trapps, she plunges at once into a series of numbers that spring half-grown from the score of *The King and I.* As a substitute for "Getting to Know You," she wins over her charges with a pretty, instructional chant called "Do Re Mi"; soon afterward she recommends yodeling, instead of whistling, as the swiftest antidote to fear; and later, in an item that reminds one of the entry of the Siamese children played backwards, she teaches the adoring Trapps a song wherein they depart, singly or in pairs, for bed. Each departure, of course, is overwhelmingly quaint. When the Baron displays erotic interest in her, Maria recoils and gets her back to the nunnery. The abbess, rousingly sung by Patricia Neway, refuses to readmit the erring postulant, whom she exhorts, in a pointlessly muscular number, to "climb every mountain, ford every stream." In one respect, this rejection does signal damage to the parallel with *The King and I*. The Baron von Trapp is not a bald hero, but if Maria had been allowed to take her vows, we might at least have had a hairless heroine. As things are, she returns and marries the martinet, whose putative fiancée, a woman of notable wealth, has deserted him upon learning that he is determined to defy the invading Nazis. What follows is the story of how the Trapps escape the coercion of the Third Reich; they appear in a local music festival, nip away while the applause is at its height, seek sanctuary in a neighbouring abbey, and subsequently cross the Alps into Switzerland.

Thinking back, I do not know which aspect of the show to applaud least. The book is damp and dowdy, like a remaindered novelette. I cannot comment on the overture or the choreography, since there is no overture, and next to no dancing. The décor, by Oliver Smith, follows a familiar Edwardian pattern by alternating gaudy interiors with superfluous front-cloth episodes intended to distract our attention from the scrape and rumble of scenery being changed in the background. Robert Russell Bennett's orchestration makes elaborate use of woodwinds and an unmistakable tuba to evoke the lumbering skittishness that passes in our theatres for Viennese lyricism. Lauri Peters, as the eldest Trapp daughter, is the most credible of a riotously cute septet. Kurt Kasznar puts in some energetic shrugging as a comical concert promoter who is reclaimed at the last moment from collaborationism, and I must pay a sympathetic tribute to the way in which Mr. Bikel manages to convey a sense of moody exasperation with everything that is going on around him. To be sure, his role requires a certain amount of testiness. However, it also demands that he should behave like a dictator in the first act and oppose dictatorship in the second, which is enough in itself to make any actor moody, and I thought I detected in Mr. Bikel's performance an element of irritation that went far beyond the line of duty. I have already mentioned Miss Martin, whose buoyancy is corklike and enchanting, despite a tendency to address the members of the audience as if they, like the Trapps, were her stepchildren. Of the score there is little to be said, except that Mr. Rodgers has written three or four tunes—such as "My Favourite Things" and "You Are Sixteen"—that abound in childlike lilt, and that Mr. Hammerstein has equipped them with sweetly pubescent lyrics. I won't go into the religious aspects of the piece, which seems to me to belong in the same category as *J.B.* and *The Tenth Man;* i.e., it represents Broadway's spiritual response to the materialistic challenge of Sputnik. To sum up uncontroversially, *The Sound of Music* is a show for children of all ages, from six to about eleven and a half.

(1959)

A Loss of Roses, BY WILLIAM INGE, AT THE EUGENE O'NEILL.

The recent discovery of *A Loss of Roses,* a mid-twentieth-century playscript attributed to one William Inge, represents a notable, if slightly dull, contribution to Freudian archaeology. Many of its pages proved, on inspection, to have been defaced by scribbled comments and emendations of a scurrilous nature, probably indicating that the owner of the volume was a precocious rebel against the cult of Freudian infallibility. These "revisions," however, have been chemically erased, and the text now stands revealed as a ritual drama of semi-magical character, designed as a conventional act of homage to the memory of Freud, whose spirit is alleged in the course of the entertainment to have been immanent even in the rural districts of Kansas as long ago as 1933. The play, or interlude, thus takes its place, albeit a lowly one, in the cycle of Freudian Mysteries that formed the religious core of the winter theatre festivals held annually on the island of Manhattan for the benefit of the United Hospital Fund. Founded on the Freudian myth concerning the mischievous behaviour of the mind deity called Oedipus, or Funny Foot, the narrative (which may be no more than a fragment; certainly something appears to be missing) is composed in a halting, nondescript style that affords solid confirmation of the theory that most of the lesser plays in the cycle are the work of one hand, possibly that of a priest.

If we accept this hypothesis, internal evidence suggests that *A Loss of Roses* was written either very early or very late in the career of its industrious author. The plot, which deals with latent incestuous impulses in the relationship between a middle-aged widow and her twenty-one-year-old son, is dutifully Freud-centered—one might even say Freud-fearing—in conception, but the execution is tentative and halfhearted throughout, as if the author had not quite decided what he wanted to say, or whether, indeed, he wanted to say anything. Was this because he was a tyro, unversed in the techniques of religious drama? Or must we see him as an ageing propagandist whose faith had dimmed and who felt disillusioned and Freud-forsaken? We cannot be sure. What we do know is that the action of the play is minimal and that it tells us almost nothing about the First Great Depression, during which it is supposed to unfold. These facts, unfortunately, are of little help to us in ascertaining the author's age at the time of composition. From first to last, monolithic Freudianism subjected all its captive artists to a process of brainwashing that taught them to equate "introspection" with "action" and to regard the phrase "social environment" as meaningless at best and dangerously heretical at worst. My own hunch, unscientific though it may be, is to plump for 'teen-age authorship of *A Loss of Roses.* I picture a pink-faced acolyte with literary ambitions singling out the much-loved Funny Foot legend as the one most likely to win him preferment. Boldly he submits his play to the festival, in competition with established dramatists like Williams, MacLeish, and Kazan. His inexperience betrays him; the notorious Tribunal of Seven turns thumbs down, and he is consigned to the dreaded Doghouse—from which, as we know, he later emerged to write the series of gnomic texts that are among our richest sources of information about the short-lived epoch during which Freudianism held despotic sway over what used to be called "the Western World," though it has since come to be known as the Middle East. The texts to which I refer include, among many others, *A Clearing in the Woods, The Silver Cord, Cue for Passion, Oh, Men! Oh, Women!, Masquerade,* and *The Dark at the Top of the Stairs,* all of which derive from the doctrinaire school of Freudian drama that was founded by Barrie with *Peter Pan.* Despite the restrictions imposed on the self-styled Inge by his creed, archaeology owes a great debt to this dedicated scribe, whose . . .

In other words, if I may parachute down from this bumpy flight of fancy, the new William Inge play is a mess. Mother (Betty Field, far below her best) shares a bungalow outside Kansas City with her son (Warren Beatty), who works at a gas station. For reasons that are unspoken but unquestionably erotic, he cannot bring himself to abandon her and take a better job elsewhere. She feels much the same way about him, but has found outlets for her emotions in good works and religion. Into this uneasy ménage there irrupts an old friend of the family, who turns out to be a catalyst in disguise. This is Carol Haney, playing a brassy, pathetic actress-*cum*-hoofer, temporarily unemployed and in need of shelter. Swiftly sizing her up as a member of the age-group—forty and upward—that attracts him most, the boy makes a drunken pass at her. His first attempt fails, but before long he contrives to seduce the woman, a substitute mother if ever I saw one. This sexual triumph enables him at last to leave home. Miss Haney, shattered, attempts to commit suicide by slashing her wrists, but eventually departs on the arm of a brutish ex-lover to make blue movies in Kansas City. We are meant to infer from her experience that reality is pitiless and unchangeably hostile. "It's like the depression," she says wanly. "You've got to make the best of it." Yet the depression, unless my memory has run mad, was lifted by organized human effort; reality was changed, by a transfusion of practical pity.

Miss Haney tends to overplay, performing every scene in the same vein of corrosive urgency, but Mr. Beatty, sensual around the lips and pensive around the brow, is excellent as the boy, and there is nothing wrong with Daniel Mann's direction that a stronger script could not have remedied. The main fault of the piece lies elsewhere, and deeper. The truth is that you cannot write a first-rate play about the Oedipus complex alone. (*Oedipus Rex* is about a city that is languishing under a curse, and its hero does not suffer from an Oedipus complex.) A serious dramatist who analyzes personal problems without analyzing the social problems that encircle and partly create them is neglecting a good half of his job, though if he is writing at high pressure, with the fullest kind of insight, he may succeed in persuading us to forget about the other half. In *A Loss of Roses* Mr. Inge displays no such persuasive power. I commend to his attention what an English critic, the late Christopher Caudwell, once said about the limitations of an exclusively Freudian approach to human behaviour:

> It is as if a man, seeing a row of trees bent in various ways by the prevailing winds, were without studying the relation between growth and environment to deduce that a mysterious complex in trees caused them always to lean as the result of a death instinct attracting them to the ground, while eternal Eros bade them spring up vertically.

There is more to trees, and much more to us, than that.

(1959)

Five Finger Exercise, by Peter Shaffer, at the Music Box, New York.

Transplanted from London, where it has been running for ages, Peter Shaffer's *Five Finger Exercise* arrived last week in New York. As in the Inge piece, one of the central figures is a young man whose love for his mother goes far beyond the normal bounds of filial duty; the difference is that Mr. Shaffer has many things on his mind besides the Oedipus theme, which is merely one strand in the cat's cradle of intertwined relationships that he sets before us. The five characters in his play are all in need of love. With fiendish skill Mr. Shaffer shows us how each of them seeks it in the very quarter from which it is least likely to be forthcoming. His purpose, implicitly moral, is to expose the pain and the rage that ensue when one human being ignores another's plea, however ill-timed or misguided, for sympathy. The setting, handsomely laid out by Oliver Smith, is one of those oak-beamed country houses in which so many roguish English comedies have chortled their way to oblivion. Mr. Shaffer puts the old place to a new use. Here, in a state of mutual incomprehension, live the four members of the Harrington family. Mother is a fussy snob with intellectual pretensions and an undergraduate son whom she calls "Jou-jou" and *"mon petit* Cossack," like an empress addressing her latest lover. She regards her husband, a stolid furniture manufacturer, as a benighted vulgarian, rather to be pitied than rebuked for his plebeian insensitivity to culture; in the son's words, "The rift you may detect between them is the difference between the *salon* and the saloon." Father, meanwhile, is baffled by his wife and profoundly suspicious of his son, whom he thinks "arty-tarty" and a potential wastrel. There is also a teen-age daughter, who seems totally impervious to the clash of values that is going on around her; a buoyant girl, she shares with her brother a number of private jokes, some less whimsical than others, but the main reason for her existence has little to do with her sense of humour. She is a mechanical necessity, since without her there would be no pupil to be taught by the shy, blond German tutor whose impact on the household, inadvertently devastating, is the fulcrum of the action and the point of the play. Mrs. Harrington at once begins to flirt with him, but recoils in fury when he thanks her for behaving toward him with the warmth of a mother. (His own parents, as we learn later, are staunch and impenitent Nazis.) Like Mrs. Wilcox in *Howards End,* Mrs. Harrington is "one of the unsatisfactory people—there are many of them—who dangle intimacy and then withdraw it." Fuming, she succeeds in convincing her husband that the tutor has become too friendly with their daughter; secretly glad to be rid of the intruder, Mr. Harrington fires him, but his action ramifies in ways he could never have predicted. His son protests against the dismissal with a passion that has unmistakably homosexual overtones. The German, meanwhile, attempts suicide.

All the pieces of the puzzle interlock snugly and without strain, falling into place with a splendid, steely inevitability. Seeking comparisons, one's mind turns to Swiss watches or chess problems—especially the latter, since the contending forces in *Five Finger Exercise* take a long time to get to grips and the tension mounts very slowly. You will certainly be held, you may even be mesmerized, but you are not likely to be moved. The writing, expert though it is, has about it a curious bloodlessness, as you will see if you compare Mr. Shaffer's work with *A Month in the Country,* which also deals with the jealousy that overcomes a rural châtelaine when she fails to attract the affections of a hired tutor. Where Turgenev sprawls and smiles, Mr. Shaffer is tight-lipped and technical, constantly building up emotional climaxes that he lacks the verbal felicity to fulfil. The effect reminds one of a mountain range with all the peaks lopped off, or of a masterpiece of functional architecture from which the central heating has been inexplicably omitted. Despite these objections, *Five Finger Exercise* is the most accomplished new play Broadway has seen this wretched season. The acting, supervised by Sir John Gielgud, is superbly adroit. Father is Roland Culver, his face swagged in surly folds, with a monocle of wrinkles around each beady eye; as Mrs. Harrington, Jessica Tandy hits the right note of frayed edginess; and Juliet Mills, who plays the daughter, is a model of chubby common-sense. Even so, the boys come off best. Brian Bedford, as the son, steers his way through a part that is full of sarcasm and complaint without once sneering or whining, and Michael Bryant, as the tutor, gives a performance of the most audacious subtlety, speaking English in an accent so pure that it at once establishes him as a German. Among many other virtues, Mr. Bryant has the most authentic stammer I have ever heard on the stage.

(1959)

The Andersonville Trial, BY SAUL LEVITT, AT THE HENRY MILLER.

Hardly anything in the whole range of dramaturgy is more difficult than to write a dull trial scene. The playwright starts out with history and tradition lined up solidly on his side. The pattern of events is preordained and inexorable, and the essential conflict varies scarcely at all from place to place or from age to age. A spokesman for human guilt and a spokesman for human innocence are met to do battle for the life, the liberty, or at least the good name of a chosen prisoner. At once we are back among the bold simplifications of mediaeval drama; whatever the specific details of the case may be, the real question at issue is whether Everyman is to be damned or saved. The process whereby justice is seen to be done is one of the few forms of ritual theatre that survive in the Western world. In courtrooms we are all atavists, and the blood that runs in our veins is ancestral, if not actually tribal.

From the playwright's point of view, trials have several other advantages of a rather more mundane kind. For instance, he need not worry about providing excuses for entrances and exits; the witnesses appear when they are called and depart when they are told. Since most of the scenes are two-handed affairs, consisting of interrogation and response, the author is rarely bothered by the problems of orchestration that arise when three or more speakers are simultaneously involved, and matters are made still easier by the fact that the witnesses are legally compelled to give truthful answers to everything that is asked them. More crucially, they cannot leave without the judge's permission to do so. This, I am convinced, is a vital clue to the perennial fascination of courtroom plays. One human being is subjecting another to a bombardment of ferocious and painfully intimate questions. In ordinary circumstances the victim's natural impulse would be to say "The hell with this" and walk out, and that—unless the inquisitor was equipped with a gun or some other means of physical coercion—would be the end of the colloquy. But in a court of law the witness must stay and reply, and we, accordingly, stay and listen.

My purpose in composing this preamble is to prepare you for the news that Saul Levitt's *The Andersonville Trial* is a decently gripping piece of work. The entire action, which is based on historical record, takes place in the stuffy Washington courtroom where, during the late summer of 1865, a military tribunal convened to decide whether Henry Wirz, a Swiss immigrant who had served as commandant of the Confederate prison camp at Andersonville, Georgia, could be held criminally responsible for the inhuman treatment that led to the death of fourteen thousand Northern soldiers. Starvation and disease were rampant inside the stockade, and bullets and bloodhounds were available for those who sought to escape. Could Captain Wirz have done anything to mitigate the horror? Yes, says the prosecutor, ambitious for revenge and promotion. No, says the defense counsel, founding his case on the postulate that in every instance Wirz was obeying orders he received from a superior officer. This squabble occupies the first half of the play, and it becomes, as witness follows witness, more than a little redundant. Clearly, the prosecutor is a blackhearted villain, the defending attorney is a champion of the underdog, and the accused—a bewildered neurotic with suicidal leanings—is a pitiable scapegoat. Or so we are craftily led to believe. In the second act the balance excitingly shifts. Against the advice of the court, the prosecutor abandons the military question of what Wirz was permitted to do as a subordinate and takes up the moral question of what he ought to have done as a human being. By a sudden paradox, the members of the tribunal find themselves at one with the prisoner, in that both sides are committed to an absolute belief in the necessity of obedience to authority. Undeterred, the prosecutor forces the crumbling, moaning defendant to explain why he acted on instructions that would result, as he knew perfectly well, in multiple murder. Wirz can only iterate that he did as he was told and had no authority to do otherwise. In the course of a single cross-examination the victim becomes the villain, and Wirz is sentenced to death.

The Andersonville Trial deals with an Army officer who is accused of excessive obedience and condemned on the ground that he did not rebel. An obvious analogy is *The Caine Mutiny Court Martial,* which dealt with a naval officer who was accused of active disobedience and acquitted on the ground that his rebellion was justified. This may seem like the same situation turned inside out; the difference is that Mr. Levitt's play contains nothing comparable to the repulsive epilogue that disfigured Herman Wouk's, wherein the defendant's own attorney changed sides after the verdict was announced, and excoriated his client for having acted under the influence of unpatriotic intellectuals. It is seldom wise to take the anti-intellectual position, however patriotic its implications may be, and Mr. Levitt commits no such stupidity. He does, however, seem to be offering an indirect justification for the death sentences that were imposed at the Nuremberg war trials, and this is somewhat disturbing in an author who seems in other respects to be lodging an outraged complaint against violence. His writing, especially in the second half, is vivid and pertinent, but at the end I was left reflecting that a Confederate Beast of Belsen was perhaps too easy a target to destroy, and I could not help wondering how the author—and the audience—would have reacted to a play that used the same valid arguments against the men who, in strict obedience to orders, decimated Dresden and flattened Hiroshima.

I have already mentioned some of the advantages of courtroom drama. Its principal drawback is that it can show us nothing of the characters beyond their public behaviour; we can only guess what sort of people they are in private, what impulses they follow, what convictions they inwardly hold. As directed by José Ferrer, *The Andersonville Trial* contains a full load of red-blooded public acting, much of which would have benefited from a little cooling down and a few brisk injunctions to refrain from inundating the audience with molten lava. Herbert Berghof, as the doomed Wirz, resembles Lenin in his later years, and stews throughout in a state of suppressed uproar; he has some highly effective moments during his breakdown on the stand, but elsewhere he conforms to the demands of that modish acting technique, mistakenly associated with the teachings of Stanislavsky, whereby gesture precedes utterance by at least five seconds. In Mr. Berghof's case, the gesture is a stabbing movement of the index finger; in that of George C. Scott, who plays the prosecutor, it is a massaging of the forehead, as if the actor were in the grip of an uncontrollable migraine. Mr. Scott is an intense performer with a voice that can achieve maximum acceleration and minimum intelligibility more swiftly than any of its Broadway competitors, and a chronic indisposition to admit that there are any nuances of volume between whisper and yell. His eyes rove in a manner that recalls the German silent screen, and his profile has the steely, prehensile outline of an invariably victorious bottle-opener. His very presence breathes melodrama. It does, however, breathe, and I should like to see its vitality put to less febrile uses. My summing-up of the production is that it is full of impressive showmanship but that it too often fails to distinguish between showmanship and salesmanship. Perhaps, after all, there is no distinction.

(1960)

Caligula, BY ALBERT CAMUS, AT THE 54TH STREET THEATRE.

Albert Camus' *Caligula* is a cold, confused experience thet evoked in me the same kind of emotion that spectators at Cape Canaveral are said to feel when a rocket-launching fails. The aim is high, the ceremony tremendous, and the take-off full of flame and roaring. Then, suddenly, the missile shudders off course and centrifugally splinters, so that nothing is left but a hail of metallic fragments and the gentle, anticlimactic plop of a nose cone into the sea. The enterprise, in short, is mighty, but mightier still is the gap between aspiration and achievement. There is also, in much of *Caligula,* a curious discrepancy between manner and matter. What is being said seems strangely unrelated to what is being done. As often happens in philosophical drama, the drama and the philosophy are imperfectly wedded and appear at times to be scarcely more than nodding acquaintances. It is as if one were watching a silent Grand Guignol movie to which somebody had added, by way of dialogue, a sound track consisting of aphoristic excerpts from a series of lectures on the nature of power. At every turn one feels the presence of a restless mind and a supremely rebellious temperament, and these are qualities that must be saluted, on Broadway as anywhere else. Seldom, however, does one feel the presence of a dramatist. Wtih gnomic eloquence Camus speaks above, around, and beyond the action; he hardly ever permits the action to speak for itself. *Caligula* is the work of a man superbly endowed to be almost anything except a playwright.

It is also the work of a young man. In 1938, when he wrote it, Camus was only twenty-five years old and had just read Suetonius' *Lives of the Caesars*. Enthralled by the scabrous, gossipy charm of these unreliable biographical sketches, he decided to dramatize the brief imperial career of Caligula, the worst-behaved of the lot. Nearly twenty years later he came up with the following synopsis:

> Caligula, a relatively attractive prince up to then, becomes aware, on the death of Drusilla, his sister and mistress, that this world is not satisfactory. Thenceforth, obsessed with the impossible and poisoned with scorn and horror, he tries, through murder and the systematic perversion of all values, to practice a liberty that he will eventually discover not to be the right one. He challenges friendship and love, common human solidarity, good and evil. . . . Unfaithful to mankind through fidelity to himself, Caligula accepts death because he has understood that no one can save himself all alone and that one cannot be free at the expense of others. . . . For the dramatist, the passion for the impossible is just as valid a subject for study as avarice or adultery. Showing it in all its frenzy, illustrating the havoc it wreaks, bringing out its failure—such was my intention.

That is a fair and comprehensive summary of the play's theme. The trouble is that the play itself is rarely more enlivening than the passage I have quoted. Caligula sets out to demonstrate that unlimited personal freedom can be accomplished by the exercise of unlimited personal power. Abolishing the social bonds that link one human being with another, he robs, kills, and seduces, at whim and at random. He forces his courtiers to submit to the most grotesque humiliations and threatens them with death if they refuse to pay homage, both religious and financial, when he dons a gilded wig and effeminately claims to be the goddess Venus. He insists throughout that he wants the moon, and is fiercely incensed when he discovers that he cannot have it. As a final assertion of individuality, he strangles Caesonia, his long-suffering mistress, but even this does not bring him absolute satisfaction. He succumbs, shortly afterward, to the daggers of his enemies, moaning as he dies, "I'm still alive!" The professed purpose of all this bloodshed is to prove that it is fruitless, as well as inhuman, to use power for power's sake and that one cannot find oneself by slaughtering others.

My reaction to all this is easily stated. I couldn't agree more. I have heard the argument a thousand times, long ago from Lord Acton and every other day from Max Lerner, and although the text contains a good number of well-aimed homiletic barbs, none of them has the transfixing force of novelty, nor do they lend much profundity to Camus' recital of Caligula's atrocities. For a full and unbridled account of a tyrant's drive toward self-destruction, I still look to *Tamburlaine,* and *Peer Gynt* remains unrivalled as a study of the fallacy that is inherent in total dedication to self-fulfilment. In Marlowe, as in Ibsen, poetry and characterization are interlocked with—and inseparable from—ideas. Camus, who is no poet, cares about his characters only to the extent that he can impose ideas on them. This makes for an emotional climate that borders on the arctic. At one point Caligula displays fondness for a courageous young poet, at another he shows a certain amount of concern for a sincere and thoughtful adversary, but for the most part the people in the play have no human contact with each other. Instead, they describe themselves; they deliver introspective lectures, almost as if they were thinking of themselves in the third person; they analyze their motives and sensations with the detachment of onlookers from another planet. For each bloody deed Caligula has an accompanying aria of cerebration, and the arias get longer as the hour grows later. At the end we know little more about him than that his sense of humor is quaintly brutal and that omnipotence produces not absolute freedom but absolute loneliness. Compared with what we feel for him, it is a great deal.

Sidney Lumet has directed the play around a stark grey monolith flanked by sweeping Ziegfeld-type staircases and resting on a heart-shaped rostrum that juts boldly out toward the audience. (Will Steven Armstrong designed this soaring, formidable setting.) For Caligula, Mr. Lumet has obtained the services of Kenneth Haigh, the British actor whose bristling rhetorical energy contributed so much to the success of *Look Back in Anger*. Few players are as skilled as Mr. Haigh at portraying intelligent modern youth, especially in its moods of outrage and wry, puzzled resentment. His brow is commonly furrowed, sometimes to the point of peevishness, and he does not so much utter his lines as worry them, the way a dog worries a bone. He is courageous enough to take risks that most actors would avoid—as when, in *Caligula,* he strolls casually into a gathering of patricians, surveys them in contemptuous silence, turns to the audience, elaborately retches, and saunters out with unflurried aplomb. Yet, despite his manifold gifts, Mr. Haigh lacks two qualities that are essential if the incredible role of Caligula is to seem even momentarily believable. One is the ability to deliver outrageous commands as to the manner born; Mr. Haigh is deficient in this kind of effortless, fantastic arrogance. The other is the capacity to suggest maniacal obsession; however hard he tries, however wildly he squints, Mr. Haigh is unable to conceal the fact that he is not, *au fond,* a madman. He is an enormously talented performer, but ineradicably sane, and I extend to him the same sort of sympathy that one would offer to an expert motorist who had been inveigled into a chariot race. *Caligula,* I suspect, is one of those plays that come wholly to life only when the star is possessed of greater genius than the author. Since Camus is the author, this is a tallish order, and I do not blame Mr. Haigh for failing to fill it.

Like most of his colleagues, he suffers at times from the bewilderment that inevitably besets Anglo-Saxons when they try to interpret Parisian plays. French actors, who abhor realism and are baffled by the notion of psychological consistency, can switch in a flash from outright farce to wholehearted tragedy. English and American actors are less agile, and one feels a definite jolt when, for example, the fairground barking that opens the second act of *Caligula* is instantly followed by a serious discussion of blasphemy. Colleen Dewhurst, wearing a regal smirk, voluptuously plays Caligula's No. 1 mistress, and Philip Bourneuf gives the smoothest performance of the evening as Cherea, the Emperor's loyal, bearded, and implacably stubborn opposition. The crowd scenes, as one might have expected, are a disappointment. Except in musicals, Broadway directors are seldom called upon to handle more than a dozen actors on the same stage at the same time. It is not really Mr. Lumet's fault that his touch, elsewhere so assured, deserts him whenever a mob assembles. The explanation is simply lack of practice.

You may, in the foregoing, have discerned a touch of the petulance that critics are prone to display when a work that looked gigantic in conception falls short in execution. Let me make amends by declaring that, for all its evident flaws, *Caligula* is not a good bad play, like *Tobacco Road,* or a bad good play, like *Summer and Smoke*. It is something rarer, and therefore more to be cherished. *Caligula* is a bad great play.

(1960)

Greenwillow, by Frank Loesser, at the Alvin; *The Visit*, by Friedrich Dürrenmatt, at the City Centre.

Halfway through *Greenwillow,* a new-born calf is baptized. (This is God's truth. I wouldn't joke about such things.) The animal is then trundled around the stage in a sort of wheelbarrow while Gideon, Gramma, Martha, Micah, Sheby, and Jabez sing a jubilant roundelay entitled "Clang Dang the Bell." Jabez is a small boy whose pants keep falling down. Like the others, he belongs to a farming family, name of Briggs. Amos, the head of the household, is not on hand for the purification ceremony, since he suffers from a yearning in the blood that forces him to spend as much time away from home as possible. His son Gideon fears that he may be cursed with the same disease, though why he regards it as a curse it is hard to say, considering what is going on at home. At all events, Gideon believes that he is in imminent peril of succumbing to wanderlust, and for this reason he refuses to marry Dorrie Whitbred, the girl he loves. She loves him, too, as she explains with crystal clarity in a song called "Gideon Briggs, I Love You."

These honest rustics, with whom the hell, inhabit the hamlet of Greenwillow, which is an imaginary pastoral paradise that even Sir James Barrie might have found a little on the quaint side. You may get some notion of the rarefied atmosphere of the place when I tell you that it makes Glocca Morra look like a teeming slum. To put it another way, Brigadoon could be the Latin Quarter of Greenwillow. Fancifully, I picture the village cut-ups trooping into the corner apothecary's, where they linger disconsolately over their sugar muffins and dock-leaf cordials. Evening service is over, and there is nothing to do until milking time except sing madrigals. " 'Tis a handy-dandy night, and the moon rides high," says one of them, in the local *patois*. "Let's go over to Brigadoon and pick up some broads." Unfortunately, no such scamps as these are on view at the Alvin. All the same, I don't want you to go away with the idea that everyone in Greenwillow is a model of virtue; no, by Jimmy-go-jerkins and rum-tickle-ree—to coin an oath that the townsfolk themselves might have coined if any of them had ever got around to using foul language. Among the assembled peasantry there is at least one heavy, whom it is almost impossible to describe without exhuming the phrase "old curmudgeon." He hobbles about on a stick of spiral design, cheating his neighbours and sneering at young love, and he is stricken in the second half by a mortal attack of something called "the shrivelly fever." (As he expired, I had a sudden flash of revelation. If *Greenwillow* were to be rewritten, with the characters transformed into animals or dwarfs, it would make a wonderful subject for Walt Disney at his worst.) Owing to an episcopal error, the tiny parish church has two ministers, one of whom preaches hellfire and damnation, while the other—a far more representative citizen—believes that the key to the good life lies in bonhomous glee-singing, gambolling on the green, and wolfing as much glutinous confectionery as you can lay your hands on. The name of this amiable simpleton is the Reverend Birdsong. He carries flowers in his umbrella and keeps kittens in his pulpit, and if that doesn't give you the flavor of Greenwillow, I doubt whether anything will. I can't think what else to say about the place, except that it is elaborately bugged—the stage bristles with microphones—and that it slightly resembles Al Capp's Dogpatch, minus the satire and the sex. It is also intensely religious; the script is packed with references to sin and salvation. After Paddy Chayefsky's rabbis and Rodgers' and Hammerstein's nuns, we now have Frank Loesser's curates.

Frank Loesser wrote it. That is the astounding fact, and that is why I have dwelt on the show so long. It was he who chose the novel (by B. J. Chute) on which it is based, he who collaborated with Lesser Samuels on the book, and he, unaided, who composed the music and lyrics. Occasionally, in numbers like "Summertime Love" and the rowdy "Could've Been a Ring," the words and the melody seem inseparable, as if matched by a master, but on the whole it is barely credible that this simple-minded extravaganza is the work of the man who created *Guys and Dolls*. In the last ten years Mr. Loesser has travelled from urban ingenuity to grass-roots ingenuousness; with *Greenwillow* he has reached the end of the line, and we must all wish him a rapid recovery, followed by a speedy return to the asphalt jungle. His cast, smartly directed by George Roy Hill, behaves as well as can be expected in the circumstances, which are profoundly daunting. As the rival clergymen, Cecil Kellaway and William Chapman are respectively puckish and grim, and Ellen McCown makes a wistful, nondescript heroine. There is also a cow, unassumingly played by a cow. The hero is Anthony Perkins, who has acquired a splendid singing voice to back up his usual—but nonetheless effective—portrait of distraught young manhood. Mr. Perkins has to cope with several of Mr. Loesser's unhappiest lyrics, including a line that runs, "I hear the tea-kettle sing away, a-wee!" The tea-kettle, of course, sings nothing of the sort, and the man who says it does is either a liar or the slave of self-conscious naïveté. For a polite epitome of my feelings about *Greenwillow,* I must go to C. E. Montague, who once remarked that "the way to do big things in an art, as it is to get into the other parts of the Kingdom of Heaven, is to become as a little child, *so long as you do it without thinking all the time what an engaging child you are.*" The italics are mine, and in them my judgment is implicit. And with that we'll drop the subject, since I don't wish to twist the knife in the wound. As one of Mr. Loesser's characters says, "Suppose we all tippy-toe out for a biscuit and broth?"

After a taxing national tour, the Lunts have come home to New York with their celebrated production of Friedrich Dürrenmatt's *The Visit.* It closes on Sunday, and I urge you not to miss it, for there is nothing on Broadway of comparable power or penetration. The plot by now must be well known; a flamboyant, much-married millionairess returns to the Middle-European town where she was born and offers the inhabitants a free gift of a billion marks if they will consent to murder the man who, many years ago, seduced and jilted her. (Her birthplace is named Güllen. Like Greenwillow, it is meant to be a symbolic community of microcosmic significance. The difference between the two is that Greenwillow exists in a timeless nowhere, ruled only by romantic love, while Güllen belongs to the modern, industrial world and is subject to financial pressures that we can all understand and recognize.) Eventually, and chillingly, her chosen victim is slaughtered, but I quarrel with those who see the play merely as a satire on greed. It is really a satire on bourgeois democracy. The citizens of Güllen vote to decide whether the hero shall live or die, and he agrees to abide by their decision. Swayed by the dangled promise of prosperity, they pronounce him guilty. The verdict is at once monstrously unjust and entirely democratic. When the curtain falls, the question that Herr Dürrenmatt intends to leave in our minds is this: at what point does economic necessity turn democracy into a hoax? Miss Fontanne plays the super-capitalist with bloodcurdling aplomb, and Mr. Lunt, as her sacrifice, makes memorable use of his defeated shoulders, his beseeching hands, and the operatic bleat of his voice. With these unique performers, not a syllable is lost or a gesture wasted. They are nobly assisted by Thomas Gomez, Glenn Anders, and the astute direction of Peter Brook.

(1960)

Three Individualists: (1) *Garbo.*

What, when drunk, one sees in other women, one sees in Garbo sober. She is woman apprehended with all the pulsating clarity of one of Aldous Huxley's mescalin jags. To watch her is to achieve direct, cleansed perception of something which, like a flower or a fold of silk, is raptly, unassertively, and beautifully itself. Nothing intrudes between her and the observer except the observer's neuroses: her contribution is calm and receptiveness, an absorbent repose which normally, in women, coexists only with the utmost vanity. Tranced by the ecstasy of existing, she gives to each onlooker what he needs: her largesse is intarissable. Most actresses in action live only to look at men, but Garbo looks at flowers, clouds, and furniture with the same admiring compassion, like Eve on the morning of creation, and better cast than Mr. Huxley as Adam. Fame, by insulating her against a multitude of experiences which we take for granted, has increased rather than diminished her capacity for wonder. In England two years ago she visited Westminster Abbey, early one morning when no one was about, and in this most public of places found a source of enormous private enchantment. A walk along a busy street is for her a semi-mystical adventure. Like a Martian guest, she questions you about your everyday life, infecting you with her eagerness, shaming you into a heightened sensitivity. Conversing with her, you feel like Ramon Novarro, blinded in *Mata Hari,* to whom she said: "Here are your eyes," and touched her own.

I half-believed, until I met her, the old hilarious slander which whispered that she was a brilliant Swedish female impersonator who had kept up the pretence too long; behind the dark glasses, it was hinted, beneath the wild brown hair, there lurked the features of a proud Scandinavian diplomat, now proclaiming their masculinity so stridently that exposure to cameras was out of the question. This idle fabrication was demolished within seconds of her entering the room; sidelong, a little tentative, like an animal thrust under a searchlight, she advanced, put out a hand in greeting, murmured something muted and sibilant to express her pleasure, and then, gashing her mouth into a grin, expunged all doubt. This was a girl, all right. It is an indication of the mystery which surrounds her that I felt pleased even to have ascertained her sex.

"Are you all things to all men?" someone asks her in *Two-Faced Woman;* to which the honest reply (I forget the scripted one) would be: "To all men, women, and children." Garbo, Hepburn, and Dietrich are perhaps the only screen personalities for whom such a claim could seriously be made. "She has sex, but no particular gender," I once wrote of Dietrich, "her masculinity appeals to women, and her sexuality to men"; which is also true of Hepburn. Yet Garbo transcends both of them. Neither Hepburn nor Dietrich could have played Garbo's scenes with her son in *Anna Karenina;* something predatory in them would have forbidden such selfless maternal raptures. Garbo alone can be intoxicated by innocence. She turns her coevals into her children, taking them under her wing like a great, sailing swan. Her love is thus larger than Hepburn's or Dietrich's, which does not extend beyond the immediately desired object. It was Alistair Cooke who pointed out that in her films she seemed to see life in reverse and, because she was aware of the fate in store for them, offered the shelter of her sympathy to all around her. Through the cellophane *Kitsch* (how it dates!) of the Lubitsch touch she pierced, in *Ninotchka,* to affirm her pity for the human condition. The words were addressed to Melvyn Douglas, but we all knew for whom they were really intended, and glowed in the knowledge: "Bomps will fall, civilizations will crumble—but *not yet. . . . Give us our moment!"* She seemed to be pleading the world's cause, and to be winning, too. Often, during the decade in which she talked to us, she gave signs that she was on the side of life against darkness: they seeped through a series of banal, barrel-scraping scripts like code messages borne through enemy lines. Sometimes, uttering sentences that were plainly designed to speed the end of literature, she could convey her universal charity only in glimpses, such as, for instance, a half-mocking, half-despairing catch in the wine-dark voice. Round the militant bluster of M-G-M dialogue she wrapped a Red Cross bandage of humanity.

It is likely that too many volumes have been read into and written about her, and that every additional adulatory word reinforces the terror I am sure she feels at the thought of having to face us again and measure up to the legend. Possibly we exaggerated her intelligence from the beginning; perhaps she was perfectly happy with the velvet-hung, musk-scented tin lizzies that Salka Viertel and S. N. Behrman (among others) turned out as vehicles for her. Perhaps association with Lewis Stone and Reginald Owen, a stout pair of uncle-substitutes who crop up, variously bewigged, in many of her films, was vitally necessary to inspire her. Recall, too, that Carl Brisson and John Gilbert are known to have been high on her list of ideal men; and that we have no evidence that she has ever read a book. Except physically, we know little more about Garbo than we know about Shakespeare. She looks, in fact, about thirty-four, but her date of birth is disputable; the textbooks oscillate between 1905 and

1906, and one biography ungallantly plumps for 1903, which may, of course, be a wound left by an embittered typesetter. Stockholm cradled her, and, like Anna Christie, she was the daughter of an impoverished sailor. She had a brother and two sisters, left school at fourteen, entered the newly expanding Swedish film industry, and was discovered by Mauritz Stiller. After the completion of *Gösta Berling* in 1924, her life is a list of movies, twelve silent, fourteen talking, and a file of newspaper pictures catching her aghast and rain-coated, grey-faced and weirdly hatted, on the gangplanks of ships or the stairways to planes. We often know where she is going, but never why. Occasionally a man is with her, a sort of Kafkaesque guard, employed to escort her to her next inscrutable rendezvous. Baffled, we consult the astrologers, who tell us that those born, as she was, between the end of August and the end of September are almost bound to be perfectionists; but what, we are left sighing, is she perfecting?

She changed her name from Gustaffson to Garbo, the Swedish word for a sprite. I used to think the Spanish "garbo" an insult to her, having heard it applied to matadors whose work seemed to me no more than pretty or neat. A Hispanophile friend has lately corrected me: "garbo," he writes, "is animal grace sublimated—the flaunting of an assured natural charm, poise infected by *joie de vivre,* innate, high-spirited, controlled, the essentially female attribute (even in bullfighters). . . ." In short, "garbo" is Garbo without the melancholy, with no intimations of mortality. The word describes the embryo, the capital letter invests it with a soul. It is the difference between *Gösta Berling* and *Anna Karenina.*

But here again I am acquiescing in the myth of gloom. Long before the fit of hoarse hysterics that convulsed her when Melvyn Douglas fell off his chair, Garbo had laughed, even if it was only "wild laughter in the throat of death," and made us laugh too. She was never wholly austere. Posing as a man in the tavern scene of *Queen Christina,* how blithely she made us smile at her awkwardness when asked to share a bedroom with the Spanish ambassador! A secret heart-smile, with the lips drawn back as if bobbing for apples, was always her least resistible weapon. Her gaiety coalesced, to the dismay of academic distinctions, with plangency. Her retirement is unforgivable if only because it means that now we shall never see her as Masha in *The Three Sisters,* a part Chekhov might have written for her. It takes lesser actresses to express a single emotion, mirth or mirthlessness. Garbo's most radiant grins were belied always by the anxiety in the antennae-like eyebrows; and by the angle of her head she could effect a transition, not alone of mood, but of age. When it was tilted back, with the mouth sagging open, she was a child joyously anticipating a sweet; when it was tipped forward, the mouth still agape, she became a parent wide-eyed at her child's newest exploit.

Some of her impact, certainly, was derived from the exoticism of her accent; hers was probably the first Swedish voice that many a million filmgoers had ever heard. Anglo-Saxons are notoriously prone to ascribe messianic characteristics to any stranger with a Slavic, Teutonic, or Nordic intonation; Bergner and Bergman are examples that come to mind, and the history of the London stage is punctuated with shrieks of exultation over long-forgotten soubrettes with names like Marta Kling, Svenda Stellmar, or Ljuba Van Strusi. Garbo was unquestionably assisted by the fact that she had to be cast, more often than not, as an exile: how often, to go about her business of home-wrecking, she arrives by train from afar! The smoke clears, revealing the emissary of fate, hungrily licking her lips. The displaced person always inspires curiosity: who displaced her, what forces drove her from her native land? If it was Garbo's luck to provoke these enquiries, it was her gift which answered them. The impulse behind her voyages was romantic passion. Bergner might have left home to collect Pekes, Bergman to go on a hiking tour: Garbo could only have journeyed to escape or to seek a lover. Which is, as a line in *Ninotchka* has it, "a netchul impulse common to all."

Superficially, she changed very little in the course of her career; a certain solidity in her aspect suggested, at the very end, a spiritualised reworking of Irene Dunne, but that was all. She could still (and often did) fling her head flexibly back at right-angles to her spine, and she kissed as thirstily as ever, cupping her man's head in both hands and seeming very nearly to drink from it. And her appeal never lost its ambiguity. The after-dinner cooch-dance which drives Lionel Barrymore to hit the bottle in *Mata Hari* reveals an oddly androgynous physique, with strong-kneed legs as "capable," in their way, as the spatulate fingers: nothing is here of Herrick's "fleshie Principalities." Pectorally, the eye notes a subsidence hardly distinguishable from concavity: the art that conceals art could scarcely go further. If this undenominational temple-dance is seductive (and, like the swimming-pool sequence in *Two-Faced Woman,* it is), the explanation lies in our awareness that we are watching a real, imperfectly shaped human being, and not a market-fattened glamour-symbol.

I dwell on Garbo's physical attributes because I think the sensual side of acting is too often under-rated: too much is written about how actors feel, too little about how they look. Garbo's looks, and especially her carriage, always set up a marvellous dissonance with what she was saying. The broad ivory yoke of her shoulders belonged to a javelin-thrower; she walked obliquely, seeming to sidle even when she strode, like a middle-weight boxer approaching an opponent: how could this athletic port enshrine so frail and suppliant a spirit? Queen Christina, reputedly her favourite character, is encased for several reels in masculine garb, and when besought by her counsellors to marry, she replies: "I shall die a bachelor!" And think of: "I am Mata Hari—I am my own master!" To lines like these Garbo could impart an enigmatic wit which nobody else could have carried off. Deficient in all the surface frills of femininity, she replaced them with a male directness. Her Marie Walewska was as lion-hearted as Napoleon himself, and I have heard her described as "Charlemagne's Aunt." Her independence (in the last analysis) of either sex is responsible for the cryptic amorality of her performances. In most of the characters she played the only discernible moral imperative is loyalty, an animal rather than a human virtue—that "natural sense of honour" which, as Shaw says, "is nowhere mentioned in the Bible."

"Animal grace sublimated": I return to my correspondent's phrase. If it is true (as I think it is) that none of Garbo's clothes ever appear to be meant for her, much less to fit her, that is because her real state is not in clothes at all. Her costumes hamper her, whether they are stoles or redingotes or (as on one occasion) moiré, sequinned, principal-boy tights. She implies a nakedness which is bodily as well as spiritual. It is foolish to complain that, basically, she gave but one performance throughout her life. She has only one body, and in this incarnation that is all we can expect.

Through what hoops, when all is said and done, she has been put by Seastrom, Cukor, Clarence Brown, and the rest of her mentors! She has gone blonde for them, danced "La Chica-Choca" for them, played a travesty of Sarah Bernhardt for them, stood straight-faced by for them as Lewis Stone warned her of "a new weapon called The Tank." Can we ask for more self-abnegation? A life of Duse was once mooted for her—what an *éducation sentimentale,* one guesses, she would have supplied for D'Annunzio! Later she hovered over, but did not settle on, a mimed role in Lifar's ballet version of *Phèdre*. And at the last moment, when all seemed fixed, she sidestepped the leading part in Balzac's *La Duchesse de Langeais*. The most recent, least plausible rumour of all insisted that she would film *La Folle de Chaillot,* with Chaplin as the Rag-Picker. . . .

So it looks as if we were never to know whether or not she was a great actress. Do I not find the death scene of *Camille* or the bedroom-stroking scene of *Queen Christina* commensurate with the demands of great acting? On balance, no. The great actress, as G. H. Lewes declared, must show her greatness in the highest reaches of her art; and it must strictly be counted against Garbo that she never attemped Hedda, or Masha, or St. Joan, or Medea. We must acclaim a glorious woman who exhibited herself more profoundly to the camera than any of her contemporaries; but the final accolade must, if we are honest, be withheld.

(1953)

(2) *W. C. Fields.*

If you had been visiting Philadelphia in the winter of 1892 and had wanted to buy a newspaper, you would have stood a good chance of having mild hysterics and a story to dine out on in after years. W. C. Fields, then a frowning urchin of thirteen, was spending a few halcyon months peddling papers; and his manner of vending contained already the germs of a technique which later made him one of the two or three funniest men in the world. While other lads piped about wars and football, Fields would pick on a five-line fill-in at the bottom of a page and, quite disenchantedly, hawk it at the top of his voice. "Bronislaw Gimp acquires licence for two-year-old sheepdog!" he would bellow at passers-by, adding unnecessarily: "Details on page 26!" And by the tone of his voice, his latest biographer* tells us, you would gather that Gimp was an arch-criminal, for Fields trusted no one. A flabby scowl sat squarely on his face—the same scowl that we see in the curious portrait with which John Decker celebrated the comedian's sixtieth birthday: with a doily on his head and a silver salt-cellar balanced on top of that he sits, squinting dyspeptically at the camera, perfectly well aware of the profanity of the caption: "Sixty Years a Queen." Fields disliked and suspected most of his fellow creatures to the end of his life: his face would work in convulsive tics as he spoke of them. For sixty-seven years he played duck's back to their water, until on Christmas Day, 1946, the "fellow in the bright nightgown" (as he always referred to death) sneaked up on him and sapped him for good.

W. C. Fields: His Follies and Fortunes is certainly the best book we are likely to see about this droll and grandiose comic. Robert Lewis Taylor is a graduate of *The New Yorker,* and thus a master of the Harold Ross prose style—pungent and artless, innocently sly, superbly explicit:

* *W. C. Fields: His Follies and Fortunes,* by Robert Lewis Taylor.

what one would call low-falutin'. Like all *The New Yorker's* best profiles, this picture of Fields is composed with a sort of childish unsentimentality, the candour of a liquorous quiz kid. Taylor, having inscribed Fields' name glowingly on the roll of fame, beats him over the head with it. Except that he sometimes calls a mistress a "friend," he spares us little. We learn of Fields' astonishing consumption of alcohol (two quarts of gin a day, apart from wines and whisky); of his quite sincere cruelty (his favourite sequence was one in which he took his small niece to a fun fair and parked her "for safety" in the shooting gallery); of his never wholly cured habit of pilfering (on his first visit to England he strolled around stealing poultry hanging out in front of shops; it was his tribute to the salesmanship of the proprietors and, as he indignantly added: "You don't think I'd have stolen chickens in the Balkans, do you?"); of his jovial callousness towards his friends, towards most women, and towards the clergy. One rainy night Fields, fairly far gone, was driving home waving a gin bottle in his free hand, and generously gave a lift to a hitch-hiker. The man was outraged when Fields offered him a drink, and, explaining that he was a clergyman, went on to deliver a free sermon to the comedian—"I'll give you my number four," he said, "called 'The Evils of Alcohol.' " He was well into his stride when Fields nonchalantly pulled up alongside a hedge, kicked the man out, dropped a bottle of gin after him, and roared: "That's my number three —'How to keep warm in a ditch'!" Equally savage was his exchange with a bartender in *My Little Chickadee*. "You remember the time I knocked down Waterfront Nell?" he said. The barman, pretty angrily, replied: "Why, you didn't knock her down, *I* did." "Well," Fields went on, unperturbed, "I started kicking her first." He once genially condescended to teach an acquaintance of his, against whom he bore some slight grudge, a simple juggling trick requiring two paring knives. "I hope he worked at it," said Fields afterwards, "because if he did, he was almost certain to cut himself very painfully." Some of the managements for whom he worked complained about such jests as these. Fields never lost his temper on such occasions. "We must strive," he would say thoughtfully, "to instruct and uplift as well as entertain." And, eyeing them carefully, he would light a cigar.

About all this Mr. Taylor is quaintly frank; and he is even better at describing (for nobody could ever explain) the mysterious caverns of private humour in which Fields delighted. There was the two-reeler entitled *The Fatal Glass of Beer* which he did for Mack Sennett: it opened with Fields sitting on a campstool in a far Northern shack, wearing a coonskin coat and crooning to himself. From time to time he would get up, open the door, and cry: "Tain't a fit night out for man nor beast!" whereupon an extra would pelt him in the face with a handful of snow. There was hardly any other dialogue in the film.

Fields nearly always wrote his own stories (under pen-names such as Mahatma Kane Jeeves), and would drive studio chiefs to despair by his failure to understand that the fact that he appeared in every shot did not necessarily ensure continuity of plot-line. Still, he continued to scrawl plots on the backs of old laundry bills and to get $25,000 a time for them. Often he would wander through the streets wearing a false beard, a repulsive clip-in moustache, and an opera cape, and amble into any party he saw in progress, introducing himself as "Doctor Hugo Sternhammer, the Viennese anthropologist." He first did this during the 1914–18 war. "I remember telling one woman that the Kaiser was my third cousin," he mused; "she gave a little scream and ran like hell." His treatment of women often bordered on the fantastic: finding strange, unaccountable depths of hilarity in the Chinese, he made one of his mistresses dress in satin slippers and a split black skirt, and always called her "The Chinaman." Many of his letters to his last mistress and devoted nurse, Carlotta Monti, start out "Dear Chinese People" and are signed, even more bewilderingly, "Continental Person" or "Ampico J. Steinway." He liked ordering Chinese meals in his films: in *International House* (for Paramount in 1932) he called up room service and blandly asked for: "A couple of hundred-year-old eggs, boiled in perfume."

Fields enraged most people he worked with. Mae West still remembers how stunned she was when, in the middle of a take, he benignly ad-libbed: "And how is my little brood mare?" He worked first for Mack Sennett and later for Universal and M-G-M (most notoriously in *David Copperfield,* in which he was narrowly restrained from doing his entire juggling routine); but after he left Ziegfeld's *Follies* in 1921 we are probably most indebted to Paramount, who suffered under him through twenty-one movies, including *Tilly and Gus, If I Had a Million, Six of a Kind, Mrs. Wiggs of the Cabbage Patch, Mississippi,* and *The Man on the Flying Trapeze.* Much of the time they had to fight to keep him from cursing during takes: in retaliation he devised two expressions —"Godfrey Daniel!" and "Mother of Pearl!"—with which he baffled the Hays Office for more than a decade. They granted him a salary so spectacular that even Bing Crosby raised his eyebrows, and, by their unearthly tolerance, they allowed him to turn out a series of films which must rank amongst the least money-making comedy classics in cinema history. At last he left them, his powers quite unimpaired, and went to Universal for his last four pictures, *You Can't Cheat an Honest Man,*

My Little Chickadee, The Bank Dick, and the amazing *Never Give a Sucker an Even Break*—the last two of which probably represent the height of his achievement. They were made between 1938 and 1942, when Fields was moving reluctantly into his sixties. Someday they should be revived by the film societies, for in addition to being amongst the funniest films of a good period, they are splendid illustrations of the art of film-making without portfolio, or cinematic actor-management.

The function of a director in a Fields movie was clear right from the start. He either fought with or ignored them. He would reduce such men as Leo McCarey, Norman McLeod, George Marshall, and even George Cukor to impotent hysterics of rage by his incorrigible ad-libbing, his affectation of deafness whenever they suggested the slightest alteration in any of his lines or routines, and by his jubilant rudeness to anyone else who happened to be working in the neighbourhood. (Once, when it became known that Deanna Durbin was on a nearby lot and might be audible on clear days, Fields threatened "to get a good bead from the upstairs balcony and shoot her.") The only director to whose advice he ever paid attention was Gregory La Cava. "Dago bastard!" he would growl as, fretfully, he listened to La Cava's analyses of his gifts: yet he admitted that the director was in the right when he implored Fields not to work too hard for his laughs. What La Cava said is worth quoting, for it is acute and provides some sort of key to Fields' later methods. "You're not a natural comedian, Bill," he said. "You're a counter-puncher. You're the greatest straight man that ever lived. It's a mistake for you ever to do the leading. When you start to bawl out and ham around and trip over things, you're pushing. I hate to see it." He said that in 1934.

La Cava was correct, as Fields' maturer films show. Fields quiescent and smouldering is funnier than Fields rampant and yelling. He played straight man to a malevolent universe which had singled him out for siege and destruction. He regarded the conspiracy of fate through a pair of frosty little blue eyes, an arm flung up to ward off an imminent blow, and his shoulders instinctively hunched in self-protection. It is hard to imagine him without the "as I suspected" look with which he anticipates disaster. Always his face looked injured (as indeed it was: the nose was ruddy and misshapen not through drink, but from the beatings he received in his youth); he would talk like an old lag, watchfully, using his antic cigar almost as a cudgel. Puffy, gimlet-eyed, and magnificently alarmed, he would try to outwit the agents of calamity with sheer pomp, and invariably fail. Everything he says, even the most crushing insult, is uttered as if it were a closely guarded secret: he *admits* a line rather than speaks it. Only his alcoholic aplomb remains unpersecuted: that they cannot touch, these imps who plague him. Fields breakfasting with his screen family behaves with all the wariness of Micawber unexpectedly trapped in Fagin's thieves' kitchen. His face lights up only rarely, at the sight of something irresistibly and universally ludicrous, like a blind man. One remembers his efforts, in the general-store sequence of *It's a Gift,* to prevent a deaf and blind customer from knocking over things with his stick while Fields is attending to other clients. It was unforgettable, the mechanical enthusiasm of those brave, happy cries: "Sit down, Mr. Muckle, Mr. Muckle, please sit down!" (A stack of electric light bulbs crashes to the floor.) "Mr. Muckle, honey, *please sit down!*"

His nose, resembling a doughnut pickled in vinegar or an eroded squash ball, was unique; so, too, was his voice. He both looked and sounded like a cement-mixer. He would screw up his lips to one side and purse his eyes before committing himself to speech; and then he would roll vowels around his palate as if it were a sieve with which he was prospecting for nuggets. The noise that finally emerged was something quietly raucous, like the crowing of a very lazy cock. (If you substitute "Naw" for "No, Sir" and cast Fields as Johnson, most of Boswell becomes wildly amusing, as well as curiously characteristic.) Fields' voice, nasal, tinny, and massively bored, is that of a prisoner who has been uselessly affirming his innocence in the same court for centuries: when, in *It's a Gift,* he drives a carload of people straight into a large reproduction of the Venus de Milo, his response as he surveys the fragments is unhesitating. "Ran right in front of the car," he murmurs, a little wearily.

The recent revival of *It's a Gift* (Norman McLeod for Paramount, 1934) was received gratefully by students of Fields' middle period. He does little heavy wooing in it, and robs surprisingly few people, but most of his other traits are well represented. The cigar is there; so is the straw hat, which nervously deserts him at moments of crisis and has to be retrieved and jammed back on to the large, round head which squats, Humpty-Dumpty-like, on the oddly boyish shoulders. There is Fields' old rival Baby LeRoy to spill a barrel of molasses, described by the comedian in a famous line as the "spreadingest stuff I ever saw in m'life." (To a friend who enquired the name of his new co-star, Fields replied: "Fellow named LeRoy. Says he's a baby.") There is Kathleen Howard, the Fieldsian equivalent of Margaret Dumont, sneering with her wonderful baritone clarity at his "scheme to revive the celluloid collar." And there is the long and savoury sequence in which Fields, driven by Miss Howard's nocturnal scolding to seek sleep on the verandah, is kept awake by such things as a coconut rolling down a fire-escape, a squeaking clothes-line, an insurance salesman (who asks "Are you Mr. Karl LaFong, capital K small A small R small L capital L small A capital F small O small N small G?"), the whirr of bottles in a milk-crate, a "vegetable gentleman" selling calabashes, and, of course, by Master LeRoy, who drops grapes from above into the comedian's mouth. "Shades of Bacchus!" mutters Fields, removing the eleventh.

In the same programme as *It's a Gift* was a revival of *Monkey Business,* which the Fields section of the audience took in glacial silence, because this is script-bound comedy, the comedy of quotability. Groucho owes much to Perelman: Fields owes nothing to anyone, except dubiously Harry Tate. Fields strolls out of the frame into the theatre, while the Brothers remain silhouettes. Fields' fantasy has its roots in the robust soil of drunken reverie: theirs are in the hothouse of nightmare. They will resort to razors and thumbscrews to get laughs that Fields would have got with a rolled-up newspaper. Their comic style is comparable with his only in that, as Mr. Taylor notes, "most people harbour a secret affection for anyone with a low opinion of humanity." It is nowhere recorded what Fields thought of the Marx Brothers, but it is permissible to guess. Hearing them described: "Possibly a squad of gipsies," he might have grunted, pronouncing the "g" hard, as in gruesome.

Fields is pre-eminently a man's comedian. Women seldom become addicts of his pictures, and it is no coincidence that his closest friends (John Barrymore, Ben Hecht, Gene Fowler, Dave Chasen, Grantland Rice) were all men. He belongs inseparably to the poolroom and the barroom—though rarely to the smoking-room; and while he looked like a brimming Toby Jug, it was always clear that no mantelpiece would hold him. Few wives drag their husbands to see his films, which may partly explain their persistently low profits. Like Sid Field, he rejected pathos to the last, even when working with child stars: he refused to tap the feminine audience by the means that Chaplin used in *The Kid.* It is appalling, indeed, to reflect what Fields might have done to Jackie Coogan, a less resilient youth than LeRoy. Perhaps it is a final judgment on him that no self-respecting mother will ever allow her children to read Mr. Taylor's brilliant look—a chronicle of meanness, fraud, arrogance, and alcoholism.

We know, by the way, Fields' opinion of Chaplin. Late in life he was lured to a cinema where some of the little man's early two-reelers were being shown. The laughter inside was deafening, and halfway through Fields uneasily left. His companion found him outside in the car at the end of the show, and asked what he thought of Chaplin's work. "The son of a bitch is a ballet dancer," said Fields. "He's pretty funny, don't you think?" his friend went on doggedly. "He's the best ballet dancer that ever lived," said Fields, "and if I get a good chance I'll kill him with my bare hands."

(1952)

(3) *James Cagney.*

Twenty-one years ago James Cagney, playing in his first film, invented a new kind of screen character. In more than fifty subsequent appearances he has polished and complicated it, but the type has remained substantially unchanged; and it may now be time to investigate its extraordinary influence. Morally and psychologically, it could be maintained that the Cagney code and manners have come to dominate a whole tradition of American melodrama.

Before Cagney boffed Mae Clark with a grapefruit in *Public Enemy,* Hollywood had adhered to what was, by general consent, a reasonably stringent set of moral principles. The film is no exception to the other popular narrative arts: in its infancy it clings to a broad and exaggerated ethical system, based on pure blacks and whites. In the theatre this period is represented by the morality play, and was superseded by Marlowe, whose heroes were noble and wicked, fraudulent and pious, cruel and idealistic, at the same time. In the novel the period of oversimplification ended with the Romantics; and in the film it ended with Cagney.

This is not to say that the American movie before 1930 was never immoral: the very urgency of the need for a Hays Office demonstrates the contrary. But its immorality, however blatant, was always incidental and subordinate: a sheikh might flay his wives with scorpions to enliven the curious, but he would be sure to be trampled on, baked, or impaled in the last reel. He was always transparently evil, and the flayee transparently innocent. In the early Westerns there is no doubt who is the villain; he is the man leaning against the bar in black frock-coat, ribbon bow-tie, and pencilled moustache. He is a killer, charmless and unfunny, and suffers dreadfully by comparison with the bronzed hero on the white horse; his part, too, is much shorter than the star's. In the twenties there was not only a rigid distinction between the good characters and bad; they were also evenly balanced in numbers and fame. Vice and virtue proclaimed themselves irrevocably within the first hundred feet, or the director was failing at his job.

Cagney changed all this. In *Public Enemy* he presented, for the first time, a hero who was callous and evil, while being simultaneously equipped with charm, courage, and a sense of fun. Even more significantly, he was co-starred not with the grave young district attorney who would finally ensnare him, but with a bright, callow moll for him to slap. The result was that in one stroke Cagney abolished both the convention of the pure hero and that of approximate equipoise between vice and virtue. The full impact of this minor revolution was manifested in the 1942–7 period, when Ladd, Widmark, Duryea, and Bogart were able to cash in on Cagney's strenuous pioneering. It now becomes fascinating to trace the stages of development by which the Cagney villain (lover, brute, humorist, and killer) was translated into the Bogart hero (lover, brute, humorist, but non-killer). It is an involved story.

Probably it begins with the physical attributes of Cagney himself. One finds it hard to take such a small man seriously: how, after all, can a playful redhead of five feet eight inches really be a baron of vice? It is safe to say that if Cagney had been four inches taller, his popularity would be fathoms less than it is. Villains before him had tended to be huge; they loomed and slobbered, bellowed and shambled; you could see them coming. Cagney was and is spruce, dapper, and grinning. When he hits a friend over the ear with a revolver-butt, he does it as casually as he will presently press the elevator button on his way out. By retaining his brisk little smile throughout he makes one react warmly, with a grin, not coldly and aghast. Nobody in 1930, the year after Chicago's St. Valentine's Day massacre, at which Capone's lieutenants slaughtered nine men in a disused garage, would have tolerated any romanticisation of the gangster legend. When Muni played *Scarface* for Howard Hawks two years later, he presented the mob leader as an unhealthy, ungainly lout, a conception clearly in key with contemporary taste. Cagney unconsciously paved the way for the advent of the smooth, romantic gangster of the late 'thirties; he softened public opinion by sneaking up on it through a forgotten and unguarded loophole. He was never a romantic figure himself—at his height you can't be—nor was he sentimental—Cheshire cats never are—but he possessed, possibly in greater abundance than any other name star of the time, irresistible charm. It was a cocky, picaresque charm, the charm of pert urchins, the *gaminerie* of unlicked juvenile delinquents. Cagney, even with submachine-gun hot in hand and corpses piling at his ankles, can still persuade many people that it was not his fault. By such means he made gang law acceptable to the screen, and became by accident one of the most genuinely corrupting influences Hollywood has ever sent us. Cagney brought organised crime within the mental horizon of errand-boys, who saw him as a cavalier of the gutters—their stocky patron saint.

But before the actor comes the script. What literary circumstances were conspiring to produce a climate in which the brutal hero could flourish? It would be superficial to neglect Hemingway, who was beginning to project on to the American mind his own ideal of manhood—a noble savage, idly smoking, silhouetted against a background of dead illusions. Surveyed impartially, the Hemingway hero numbers among his principal characteristics that of extreme dumbness: he is the sincere fool who walks phlegmatically off the end of the pier. He is honourable, charmless, tough, and laconic; and he is always, in some sense, a pirate or an adventurer. What Cagney did was to extract the moral core from Hemingway's creation and put smartness in its place. The result was a character charmingly dishonourable, but saved from suavity or smugness by his brute energy and swift, impetuous speech. Perhaps the simplest point of departure is that, whereas the Hemingway man never hits a woman for fun, Cagney made a secure living out of doing just that.

The success of Cagney's methods made all sorts of variations possible, chief among them the *genre* popularised in the novels and films of Raymond Chandler. Here the central character is tough, cynically courageous, and predisposed towards brutality; he is in fact identical with the Cagney version in all save one vital respect—he is on the side of the law. The process is thus completed: the problem of how to retain the glamour of the killer without the moral obloquy of murder has been solved. Let your hero be a private eye, and he can slaughter just as insensitively in the name of self-defence.

Cagney himself has rarely compromised; at the height of his career he never lined up with the police or made any concessions to public morals beyond the token one of allowing himself to be killed at the end, as an indispensable but tiresome rubric. At his best (*Public Enemy, The Mayor of Hell, The G-Men, White Heat*) he flouts every standard of social behaviour with a disarming Irish pungency that makes murder look like an athletic exercise of high spirits and not a mean and easy transgression. He sweetened killing; and to have done this immediately after the Capone regime, during the era of the concentration camp and between two lacerating wars, is something of an achievement.

He was born in New York in 1904 and educated at Stuyvesant High School and Columbia University; his background was East Side, but not the slum and tenement area. He began his stage career, mysteriously, as a female impersonator in 1923, and thereafter for six years danced and understudied in vaudeville. He was mostly penniless. In

1929 William Keighley, then a Broadway director, saw Cagney and Joan Blondell in a romp called *Maggie the Magnificent* and starred them in *Penny Arcade;* the play was bought by First National, and all three went to Hollywood with it. Retitled *Sinners' Holiday,* it was released in 1930. Cagney made eight pictures with Joan Blondell in less than four years, and she proved a perfect punch-bag for his clenched, explosive talent; the best of the series, *Steel Highway,* started a revealing vogue for stories about men who work in dangerous proximity to death-dealing machines. These films invariably centred on a character who was happy only when close to sudden extinction, who enjoyed tight-roping along telegraph wires or lighting cigarettes around kegs of dynamite. For such parts Cagney was a natural, and Wellman, who directed *Steel Highway,* quickly exploited the new star's edgy gameness by putting him into *Public Enemy,* with Blondell and Mae Clark. When the film appeared in 1931, the age of the screen gangster had officially begun. Howard Hawks followed in 1932 with *Scarface,* which, though it had the advantage of one of Ben Hecht's best scripts, lacked Cagney's spearhead precision to hold it together. For ten years afterwards he led the gangster film to extraordinary box-office eminence, and four times appeared in the annual list of the ten top money-making stars. In 1932 Hawks made *The Crowd Roars* with Cagney and Blondell; in 1933 came *The Mayor of Hell;* in 1934 Michael Curtiz' *Jimmy the Gent;* in 1935 Keighley's expert and sombre *The G-Men;* and finally, feeling that things were becoming too easy for him, Warners teamed Cagney with Bogart in *Angels with Dirty Faces* (1938) and *The Roaring Twenties* (1939). At this point he had made thirty-two films in nine years; the association with Blondell had dissolved, and his most frequent sparring partner was Pat O'Brien.

Cagney was now maturely at his best. Even the most ascetic *cinéaste* will admit that it is impossible to forget how he looked and talked at the height of his popularity. The spring-heeled walk, poised forward on the toes; the fists clenched, the arms loosely swinging; the keen, roving eyes; the upper lip curling back in defiance and derision; the rich, high-pitched, hectoring voice; the stubby, stabbing index finger; the smug purr with which he accepts female attention—Cagney's women always had to duck under his guard before he would permit them to make love to him. He was practically unkillable; it would generally take a dozen Thompson guns and a bomb or two to bring him to his knees; and he would always die running at, not away from, his pursuers, in a spluttering, staggering zig-zag, ending with a solid and satisfying thump. He moved more gracefully than any other actor in Hollywood. And he had a beguiling capacity for reassuring while he murdered: he would wrinkle up his face into a chubby mask of sympathy and then let you have it in the stomach. His relaxation, even when springing, was absolute; he released his compact energy quite without effort. When circumstances forced him to shout, his face would register how distasteful he found it.

Cagney's first rival in the game of romantic murder appeared in 1936. Humphrey Bogart, five years Cagney's senior, had made half a dozen mediocre pictures since 1932, and had returned to the stage to play the escaping gangster, Duke Mantee, in *The Petrified Forest.* In 1936 the play was filmed and Bogart was established. It was a new style; speculative, sardonic, sourly lisping, he stood out in direct contrast to Cagney, who was agile, clean-cut, and totally unreflective. Bogart frequently appeared unshaven; Cagney, never; but the challenge was clear, for both men specialised in whimsical law-breaking and both commanded alarming sex-appeal. Cagney, who had captured several million infant hearts with pictures like *Here Comes the Navy, Devil Dogs of the Air,* and Howard Hawks' *Ceiling Zero,* had access to an audience to which Bogart never appealed; but Bogart split Cagney's female admirers, and was usually featured with bigger stars and better directors than Warners could offer Cagney. *Bullets or Ballots* (1936) followed *The Petrified Forest;* in 1937, after a brief and unsuccessful venture into legality as the D.A. in *Marked Woman,* Bogart made *San Quentin* and *Kid Galahad;* and he breasted the year with his superbly metallic playing of Baby-Face Morgan in Wyler's *Dead End.* He had added to the gangster film something which Cagney always avoided: the dimension of squalor. In Cagney's looting there had been an atmosphere, almost, of knight-errantry; Bogart, tired, creased, and gnarled, effectively debunked it. The two films they made together for Warners made an absorbing conflict of styles—with Cagney throwing his hard, twisting punches and Bogart lazily ducking them. Cagney's was the more accomplished exhibition of ring-craft, but Bogart's sewage snarl won him the decision. At times both men found themselves using the same tricks; each had perfected his own version of the fanged killer's smile, and a good deal of *The Roaring Twenties* developed into a sort of grinning contest.

The experience must have proved something to both Cagney and Warners, because he made no more gangster films for ten years. By then the war had begun, the mob was very small beer, and the echo of machine-guns across deserted lots had lost its fascination for movie audiences. Bogart graduated to the side of justice, and the second important change in the history of filmed mayhem had taken place. In 1941 he played Sam Spade for Huston in *The Maltese Falcon*—still the same wry brute, but more insidiously immoral, since now there was a righteous justification for his savagery. He repeated this performance in *Across the Pacific,* and when *The Big Sleep* appeared in 1945 it looked as if the pure gangster film was dead. In 1942 Paramount produced their answer to Bogart in *This Gun for Hire*—the soft and silky thuggishness of Alan Ladd; and Dick Powell entered what was by now a very competitive market with *Farewell, My Lovely* (1944) and *Cornered* (1945). Screen melodrama in this period was filled with ageing bandits, battering their way to glory under police protection. Meanwhile Cagney had not been idle, though films like *The Strawberry Blonde, Captains of the Clouds,* and *The Bride Came C.O.D.* (in which he daintily plucked cactus needles from Bette Davis' behind) were not materially helping his reputation. In 1942 Curtiz made *Yankee Doodle Dandy,* a masterpiece of heartfelt hokum, and Cagney won an Academy Award with his sturdy, chirpy pirouetting; but the shamelessness of his early days seemed to have vanished. The woman-slapping outlaws of the forties were performed by feature players, not by stars, and they were mostly in the hands of Dan Duryea, the impact of whose rancid and lascivious unpleasantness in *The Little Foxes* had been confirmed by his straw-hatted blackmailer in Lang's *Woman in the Window* (1944) and his raucous pimp in *Scarlet Street* (1945). The courage of nastiness had gone.

In 1942 Cagney formed his own production unit with his brother William, and in seven years made only four films—*Johnny Vagabond,* a philosophical failure; *Blood on the Sun,* a commonplace espionage thriller; *13 Rue Madeleine,* a documentary-style spy story; and *The Time of Your Life*—a shrug of a film, charmingly aimless and inexpensive, in which Cagney, as a talkative drinker, gave his best perfrmance since *Yankee Doodle Dandy*. The critics were suggesting that Cagney had agreed to accept middle-age and abandoned the orgiastic killing of his youth. Then, in 1950, he suddenly returned to Warners and, with Raoul Walsh, made *White Heat*.

The style in that amazing film was the man himself: Cagney had never been more characteristic—flamboyant, serio-comic, and tricky as a menagerie. It is not easy to decide why he came back to straight gangster vehicles, though I have the impression that Twentieth Century–Fox had much to do with it; they had begun, in 1947, an ambitious campaign to sell Richard Widmark to the public. His weedy, snickering murderer in *Kiss of Death* gave an unexpected lease of life to the gangster film. Playing within the semi-documentary convention, he could not be permitted to dominate his films as Cagney had in the lawless thirties, but he had the same gimlet appeal and was tapping the same love of clever violence. By 1949 his popularity was such that it must have persuaded Warners to disturb the retirement of their senior hoodlum.

Walsh and Cagney reverted in *White Heat* to the frankly artificial framework of *Public Enemy:* there were a few location sequences, but the main burden fell on the star's personality. The scenario made a genuflection to contemporary demand by giving its hero a mother-complex, and Cagney staggered even his devotees by acting it up to the hilt with a blind conviction which was often terrifying: he never let up. The film dealt with the breakdown of a killer's mind and his slow, unwitting, unadmitting approach to the long tunnel of insanity. Cagney never indulged in self-pity for a moment: if the script called for a fit, he would throw one, outrageous and full-blooded; and by a miracle his integrity never gave out. The result was a lesson in neurosis which ranks, in recent Hollywood memory, only with Richard Basehart's in *Fourteen Hours.* One cannot unlearn the sequence in which Cagney, attempting to ward off a mutiny in the mob, succumbs to one of his recurring blackouts and drags himself to the cover of a bedroom, moaning in deep thick sighs like a wounded animal. And, above all, the scene in the prison refectory. Word is passed down the table to Cagney that his mother has been killed: he stops eating, grins spasmodically, murmuring to himself, and then goes berserk, letting out strange, bestial cries and punching, punching at everyone with a compulsive defiance as he scampers the length of the hall. No other actor in Hollywood could have got away with that.

The older, crisper Cagney was there too; even he has never outdone, for sheer casualness, the murder of the stool-pigeon, whom he has locked up in the luggage-trap of his car. "Kinda stuffy in here," the prisoner complains. "Like some air?" says Cagney, cocking a wicked eyebrow; and, stopping only to pop a hot dog in his mouth, fires six shots into him through the body of the car. The climax was nerve-racking: cornered, he takes refuge in an explosives plant and is chased to the top of a huge circular vat of, presumably, T.N.T. Yelling: "On top of the world, Ma, on top of the world!" he sends his last bullet into it and is blown sky-high. It was audacious and incredible in retrospect, but such was the intensity of Cagney's playing that one refused to laugh. It is seldom easy to deride perfect stylists, even if one disapproves of the ends to which the style is being put. There could be no question, in this sequence, that a very remarkable actor had hit his full stride and was carrying his audience with him.

I do not mean, by all this, to suggest that the crime film deserves over-serious analysis: it has always been openly unreal in structure, depending for its excitement on jazzed dialogue and overstated photography. But its influence on scripting and camera-work has been incalculable, involving many of the most expert and adult intelligences in Hollywood—Hecht, Hawks, Wyler, Toland, Huston, Wellman, Lang, Chandler, and Hellinger among them—and it has provided an incomparable outlet for at least one unique acting talent. If it has had a pernicious social influence, that is probably Cagney's fault, and there is no space here to balance the old scales between art and morality. For myself, I do not mind walking the Edgware Road in peril as long as there is a Cagney picture at Marble Arch. A great deal of desperate urgency and attack would have been lost to the cinema if the gang film had not arrived, making fantastic technical demands on cameraman and electrician and recording engineer, with Cagney, safe and exulting, at the wheel of a bullet-riddled Cadillac.

(1952)

The Broadway Dilemma.

"That the most exalted of the arts should have fallen into the receivership of businessmen and gamblers is a situation parallel in absurdity to the conduct of worship becoming the responsibility of a herd of water buffaloes. It is one of those things that a man of reason had rather not think about until the means of redemption is more apparent."

Such, in the spring of 1944, was Tennessee Williams' opinion of the theatre in New York, expressed just a year before he had his first Broadway success with *The Glass Menagerie*. Today, fifteen springs and many hits later, Mr. Williams appears to have found his means of redemption: he has joined the ranks of the "businessmen and gamblers." He and his director, Elia Kazan, own between them seventy-five per cent of *Sweet Bird of Youth,* the latest Williams play to have reached and ravished Broadway. In this development there is a parable of a very American kind. No longer is the artist a mere suppliant in the market place; he is packaging and selling his own wares. A playwright of Mr. Williams' wealth and prestige can eliminate the middleman and share in the profits as well as collect his royalties—a privilege unknown to novelists or indeed to anyone who writes primarily for the printed page. This is the climax of the Broadway process, the fulfilment of the Broadway dream—the birth, you might say, of a salesman.

That a dramatist should thus turn tycoon is an event that may serve as a symbol of the fantastic, pragmatic island through which Broadway runs. No other city of comparable size and influence is devoted exclusively—as New York is—to earning and spending. The nation's laws are not made here, nor is the country governed from here; yet Manhattan, whose ticking heart is the Stock Exchange, is the cultural capital of America. This is a singular state of affairs. In European countries, politics and the arts almost invariably have their headquarters in the same place. (And when they don't, there is trouble, as in the case of West Germany, which has its seat of government at Bonn and its cultural heart in Berlin.) What is odd about New York, making it unique, as far as I know, among the great cities of history, is that it performs the function of an artistic capital in surroundings wholly dedicated to commerce. In such circumstances, it is not surprising that playwrights become producers, or that New York is the only theatrical centre on earth without a single legitimate playhouse run on non-commercial lines, free from the necessity of showing a profit.

The district around Times Square is New York in little, though writ extremely large: a barker's paradise, a shill's spawning ground, a wonder, a horror, and a surge of life. The square itself, where Broadway and Seventh Avenue converge and cross, is not a square at all. It is shaped like a diabolo, if you remember that ancient toy, and it looks appropriately diabolical. If you stand in the middle of it and turn slowly through 360 degrees, you will see (in the few seconds before you are mown down by a taxi) such things as Ripley's Odditorium, where malformed fellow creatures are on view beside tableaux of medieval torture; a large number of souvenir shops, where you can buy plastic excrement to surprise your guests; and about a dozen cinemas, several of which specialize in heavily cut movies about nudist colonies and white slavery. You can also, if you have X-ray vision, see the American theatre, most of which is born and dies within a few hundred yards of where you stand. In Paris, Berlin, and Moscow there is no "theatre district." The same, to a slightly lesser extent, is true of London; it would take at least twenty minutes by cab to travel from the Palladium to the Old Vic. The geographical compression of the New York theatre has no parallel anywhere. The twenty-eight Broadway houses cluster around Times Square like iron filings round a magnet, so closely that half of them are squeezed into two city blocks—from 44th Street to 46th, between Broadway and Eighth Avenue. For a similar concentration of entertainment, I have sometimes reflected, you would have to go to the bordello district of a Spanish port.

The concentration is more than physical; it is emotional as well. A

Broadway opening is a much tenser affair than all but the most important of London first nights. More money is at stake; *Sweet Bird of Youth,* for instance, cost $150,000 to produce, and a musical could run three times as high. You would have to divide these figures by five to get the rough British equivalents. But, apart from finance, the atmosphere in the theatre is different. A London opening often has the feeling of a party; you mix with friends in the lobbies, which are usually spacious and Edwardian, you drink in the theatre bars during intermissions, and often you can smoke in the auditorium. Broadway, by contrast, is functional, urgently focussed on the business in hand; frivolity is an absentee from these nervous gatherings in the West Forties. No bars, no smoking, and few lobbies large enough to permit much mingling; during intermission you either read the programme in your seat or elbow your way out to shuffle, and frequently to shiver, on the sidewalk. At London first nights the most popular question is: "Are you enjoying it?" In New York it is: "Do you think it'll go?"

Meanwhile, the seven daily critics are left to cerebrate undisturbed. One picks out Brooks Atkinson of the *Times,* with hat and coat on lap, looking gnomish, wily, and sedate; Walter Kerr of the *Herald Tribune,* who is toughly handsome, like a retired welterweight, and sometimes wears dark shirts that suggest both membership in the intelligentsia and allegiance to some nameless criminal syndicate; John McClain, the president of the Critics' Circle, beaming like the chairman of a business convention, and dressed to match; Richard Watts of the *Post,* genial, chuckling, and—to use his favorite critical epithet—engaging; Robert Coleman, whose flowing hair and Chestertonian bulk consort strangely with a prose style that goes in for expressions like "slam-bang comedy smash"; John Chapman, plum-coloured above the collar and generally sunk in reverie; and Frank Aston, wiry and white-thatched, the newest addition to the seven make-or-breakers. Most of them spend the intervals sitting and pondering; it is no light task to pronounce verdict, in less than an hour of writing time, on an enterprise that has probably been in preparation for a year and may easily, in the course of its casting, financing, rehearsing, and rewriting, have driven several of its participants to the edge of madness or beyond. The audience, aware that the show's statistical chances of success are about one in five, displays inordinate enthusiasm whenever the slimmest provocation is offered, applauding every new setting, every new entrance (right down to the cop in the third act), every demonstration of physical agility (like climbing on a table), and almost every exit. This hair-triggered responsiveness can be highly distracting. In retrospect, especially if the play has flopped, it reminds me of the ritual cheering with which observers on dry land offer encouragement to people on a sinking ship. When the curtain has fallen and the critics have fled up the darkened aisles to their typewriters, it takes a brave author to expose himself to the crowd as it spills into the lobby. James Thurber happened to find himself in this vulnerable position after the opening of *The Male Animal,* on which he collaborated with Elliott Nugent. The first man out was a critic he knew, who shrugged indecipherably and mumbled what sounded like: "Organ recital. Vested fever." The next was Marc Connelly, who told Thurber that he and Nugent had given Brahms' Fifth to a mandolin player. This upset Thurber considerably until he remembered that there is no Brahms' Fifth.

Even the more conventional course of going to Sardi's for supper strikes me as pretty courageous if you are the author or, indeed, anyone involved in the play. Unless the evening has been unrelieved calamity, you are sure to be applauded as you shamble into the restaurant. I have watched this curious rite many times, and I have reached a few tentative conclusions. If you are applauded only by those at your own table, it means nothing. If to their applause is joined that of backers, press agents, friends, and gallant ex-wives, it still means nothing. If a few strangers chime in, still nothing. It is only when a large number of strangers applaud *standing up* that you can be tolerably sure of one basic fact: your show will be running tomorrow. Assuming that you have chosen the Sardi's ordeal, there now follows an agony of waiting that goes on until half past midnight, when copies of the *Times* and the *Tribune* are ceremoniously distributed throughout the restaurant. For ten minutes the place rustles and crackles, while fingers fuss and get begrimed with newsprint; the whole room takes on the aspect of the ads about the Philadelphia newspaper that "nearly everybody reads." The Atkinson review, mostly composed in short, declarative sentences, is studied first; next, one dives into the more florid prose of Mr. Kerr, who favours opening sentences like—and I parody:

> Along about halfway through "The Flatbush Thunderbolt," a frolicsome ditty called "That Old Dented Pillow" finds actress Tansy Brittle pausing in the act of caroling her maidenly distaste for unmade beds long enough to sweep her honeycomb hair out of her cornflower eyes, favor us with a dazzlingly tooth-filled smile, and hiss at the conductor a mischievous: "What's with the tempo, bud?" I'm glad she asked that question. I'd been wondering the same thing all evening.

By current computation, if Atkinson plus Kerr plus any three other reviews are good, you have a hit; the same applies to Atkinson-or-Kerr plus Chapman plus Watts plus two others. Into such bizarre arithmetic does the Broadway industry conscript you.

More anxious effort and nervous energy go into New York openings than into theatrical productions anywhere else on earth. I stress the anxiety and the nerves because they are the principal difference between the atmosphere of a Broadway *première* and the atmosphere, say, that attends a new production at the Moscow Art Theatre. The latter will have been rehearsed not for a rigid four weeks but for as long as the director thinks fit, after which it will gradually be shoe-horned into the repertory of a company that worries a lot about art but very little about economics. Security of this sort is a virtue; its vice is apathy. The Broadway system of financial insecurity often induces the opposite vice of hysteria. Sometimes the hysteria can be creative, spurring people to ardours and self-discoveries of which they would not otherwise have been capable; only under the grimmest pressures are diamonds formed. But it can also be wasteful and neurotic; and it is never reassuring to watch.

I shall always remember, after an opening in Boston, going to the director's hotel suite and finding, instead of the exhausted conviviality I had expected, a small factory operating full blast. In one room a famous playwright (not the author of the play) was writing laughs into the first act; in another an even more famous playwright was gouging laughs out of the second act; and the director, leading me into the bathroom, asked me what I thought was wrong with the third. I said that it seemed to me to have come out of some other play. He said I was probably right, because he had written it. Meanwhile, in the living room, one of the producers was talking, long distance, to a man in California, who was making radical suggestions based on the evening's performance, which naturally he had not seen. A popular song-writer was also contributing ideas, many of which were eagerly snapped up, although the show was not a musical. After an hour of this the first review appeared. It was a good one, and for several minutes we downed tools and toasted each other. Suddenly the director stumbled in, his face the colour of an oyster, holding the next review—a bad one. Within seconds everyone was back at work. As I slipped away, I asked the director where the author was. "Joe?" he said. "Oh, Joe's in Palm Springs." He waved vaguely and went on rewriting.

The play whose parturition I briefly witnessed was a tragicomedy about back-yard sexual frustration and also a tremendous success. It was a bad play, but it came at a time when "mood" was all the rage, and it was bursting with "mood"—a sort of steamy, twilit *ambience* of pubescent yearning. That was several years ago, and the vogue for such plays—best represented by *The Glass Menagerie* and *The Member of the Wedding*—has waned. Its expiring sigh may be heard in the subsequent spate of dramatized anecdotes about maladjusted children unable to "get through" to their parents. The parallel, and considerably older, fashion for "social drama," usually dealing with individuals crushed and humbled by society, seems likewise to have vanished. Since Arthur Miller's *The Crucible,* no political play of any merit has been seen on Broadway.

To find out whether anything new is on its way in, it may be helpful to look at the theatre listings. As I write, twenty-six shows are running in New York, of which ten are playing to capacity. Five of the ten are musicals. In this department Broadway is still potent, although there is room for regret that the day of the great clown seems to be passing. A general display of ear-splitting good humour has replaced individual comic invention. The genius of Judy Holliday was recently visible in *Bells are Ringing,* but the occasion was exceptional, and seven years have passed since Broadway saw a great male comedian in a musical—I refer to Phil Silvers, whose gaudy ego permeated a boisterous show called *Top Banana* that may come to be regarded by historians as the last outpost of vaudeville. The sixth of the ten sell-outs is the French revue *La Plume de Ma Tante,* which may owe some of its success to nostalgia for the great days of the comic tradition. Two of the remaining four are domestic comedies safely spiced with sex. Both have a quality common on Broadway: built-in obsolescence. They will run for a season, to be scrapped and replaced by something identical in every respect, except that the next model may feature a new husky-voiced young actress, a new setting (like Cuba), a new thematic twist (like incest), or a new old movie star coaxed panting out of semi-oblivion.

So far, you notice, eight of the ten hits come under the heading of light entertainment. Yet a cab-driver complained to me the other day about the shortage of entertainment facilities in New York. "Take a couple who come in from out of town," he said. "Sure, the wife maybe wants to go a theatre, but the businessman wants to *relax.*" The implications here are frightening. One is that Broadway, despite its plethora of lighthearted hits, is still not relaxing enough for visiting males; the other is that plays of any kind are of interest mainly to sensitive, emotional, artistic people like women.

The two theatre-fillers I have not yet mentioned are what we call "serious" plays, meaning that they present a view of life from which the pain is not left out. The first is Lorraine Hansberry's *A Raisin in the Sun,* a humane tragicomedy that won the 1958–9 Critics' Circle Award; on the present Broadway horizon, this comes nearest to what I expect drama to be. It tells of an episode in the life of a poor, ambitious Negro family in Chicago, examining their reactions to a windfall of insurance money and their ultimate decision to buy a house in a white district. It is gay, earthy, thoughtful, and close to the facts—not the documentary facts so much as the facts of human feeling. It is not a masterpiece, but it has the quality without which no modern masterpiece is possible: it evokes a life that relates to ours and makes sympathy endemic.

The other "serious" play is Tennessee Williams' *Sweet Bird of Youth.* I won't go into the plot, except to say that it concerns a Southern gigolo who returns to his home town, accompanied by a decrepit movie queen who is alcoholic but far from anonymous, and allows himself to be castrated at the orders of a local political boss whose daughter, many years before, he has unwittingly infected with venereal disease. (The emasculation is timed to take place on Easter Monday, which probably implies that Mr. Williams means us to equate his hero with Attis, the ancient god who bled to death after castrating himself and whose symbolic rebirth was celebrated in Rome on roughly the same day as Christ's resurrection.) What interests me most about the play is what it has in common with Archibald MacLeish's *J.B.,* which won the Pulitzer Prize. Both are obsessed with personal guilt; both are written in a vein of inflated melodrama; and both were directed by Elia Kazan. The hero of *J.B.* is Job modernized, a prosperous businessman beset by a series of disasters culminating in a nuclear war that brings him out in a nasty (though happily non-lethal) rash. Although his misfortunes are clearly explicable in human terms, he insists on ascribing them to God, who periodically thunders at him over the public-address system. At the end, capriciously, the author turns about and asserts that there is no divine judge upstairs; there is simply conjugal love on earth. Since holocausts are inevitable, all we can do is try to get on better with our wives.

Both plays have a missing facet: neither admits any human responsibility for the human condition. We see man in relation to forces, either cosmic and external (*J.B.*) or neurotic and internal (*Sweet Bird*), that are utterly beyond his control. He is alienated from society, isolated and victimized, and nowhere is the possibility even considered that he might, in some madcap Utopia, be able to shape the circumstances in which he lives. Both heroes go through torments in expiation of sins they are hardly aware of having committed. It is as if suffering itself, in a vacuum and for no discernible purpose, were by definition heroic, useful, and even necessary.

I have heard reputable critics defend these plays on the grounds that they have "theatrical vitality," that they savagely assault the nerves, that they are hurricanes of emotion, and that they brutally lacerate the sensibilities. All I can say is that they represent, for me, wanton exploitations of human vulnerability, and that "theatrical vitality" without human relevance seems to me as unpleasant as a carefully planned car smash. I confess that I have little sympathy with those who regard an ideal theatrical experience as something akin to sitting in the direct path of a herd of stampeding elephants. Perhaps the most alarming thing about the two plays is that hardly any of the critics mentioned the brackish hollowness with which they are written; it was enough that they were block-busters. One felt, in many of the reviews, a hunger for Grand Subjects, for sonority and amplitude and universal repercussions—a hunger so intense that it seemed not only ready but eager to take the will for the deed. This appetite for grandeur, and its concomitant, a proneness to be deceived by pretentiousness, are not in themselves to be derided. What perturbs me is the nature of the themes and the quality of the emotions in which grandeur is sought and found. Their official acceptance paves the way for audiences composed rather of passive, masochistic *voyeurs* than of people seeking keys to the predicament of contemporary living.

I have said that Elia Kazan directed both plays. In the past few years Mr. Kazan has grown harsher and at the same time more sentimental—the latter epithet applies to any situation that is filled with more emotion, cruel or tender, than it can hold. It would be helpful if a committee could be formed to prohibit the warlike use of Kazan and to restrict him to peaceful purposes; for if his present tendency continues unchecked, it may mean the end of theatrical civilization as we know it. I spoke earlier of trends. There is only one trend in the Broadway theatre, and its name is Kazan. It is up to him whether he follows his current path of violence or returns to pursuits that befit the compassionate man who directed *A Streetcar Named Desire* and *Death of a Salesman,* the best American productions since World War II.

Broadway's problem is its economic need to appeal to the widest possible audience, instead of to the audience that a particular play may require. Since there are many playwrights who aim their work at a circle of spectators smaller than that which is required to make a Broadway hit, some other outlet had to be found. Hence Off-Broadway, the epidemic of little theatres that now surrounds Broadway on every side except the West. In a night club last year a straw-hatted comedian sang:

> Give my regards to Off-Broadway,
> Remember me to Sheridan Square.
> Tell all the gang at the Jan Hus Auditorium
> That I will soon be there. . . .

The movement is not new; it began before America's entry into World War I with the Provincetown Players, who staged the early work of Eugene O'Neill, and the Washington Square Players, who incubated the Theatre Guild and were incidentally responsible, in 1916, for the début of Katharine Cornell. In the Thirties and Forties, however, the downtown bloom went to seed; Off-Broadway was ignored by the critics and concentrated mainly on amateur shows. In 1949 there were only five companies operating away from the Orion's Belt of Broadway. Today there are twenty-four. The nourishment that hastened this startling proliferation was provided in 1952 by Brooks Atkinson, who wrote an enthusiastic review about a revival of Tennessee Williams' Broadway failure *Summer and Smoke* at the Circle-in-the-Square. Geraldine Page, who played the lead, was launched overnight; so was José Quintero, the director; and so was Off-Broadway. In 1953 the Phoenix Theatre on Second Avenue reopened its doors, under the direction of Norris Houghton and T. Edward Hambleton, and has stayed miraculously active ever since; for the most part it has staged revivals with visiting stars, though in 1954 it presented a non-star musical called *The Golden Apple* that won a Critics' Award and cost $75,000, which remains a record for Off-Broadway productions.

Since then New York's little theatres have spread across the city, up from the Village to the East Seventies, the West Eighties, and the 41st Street Theatre, on the very boundaries of Broadway. The Brecht-Weill *Threepenny Opera* opened at the Theatre de Lys in September 1955, and you can see it there still. Siobhan McKenna appeared in *Saint Joan,* and Franchot Tone in Chekhov; and a couple of years ago Tennessee Williams decided to have his double bill, *Garden District,* unveiled Off-Broadway, at the York Theatre on First Avenue. Apart from Miss Page and Mr. Quintero, the movement has fledged such valuable talents as those of Kim Stanley, Ben Gazzara, Jack Palance, Joseph Anthony, Jason Robards, Jr., Fritz Weaver, William Ball, and Hal Holbrook, whose Mark Twain is the most convincing performance of an old man by a young one that I have ever witnessed. Off-Broadway has also presented an adventurous list of new foreign plays, among them works by Ionesco, Beckett, Genet, and Brendan Behan, and it has offered fresh and startling insights into plays that Broadway saw and rejected, such as O'Neill's *The Iceman Cometh,* Arthur Laurents' *A Clearing in the Woods,* and Miller's *The Crucible*.

I cannot imagine anybody seriously challenging me when I assert that Off-Broadway today is the most active little-theatre movement on earth. This is not to say that it is without dangers. Ten years ago, if a Broadway producer received an offbeat script that impressed him, although it clearly needed a lot of revamping, he would probably buy an option and encourage the author to work on it, with the result that it might reach Broadway within a season or two. Nowadays, faced with the same script, he might well say: "See how it goes Off-Broadway, and then we'll think again." What I mean is that Off-Broadway may become a convenient receptacle into which all experimental plays are glibly siphoned; and that would be a glum prospect.

Is there a place in New York where the idealism of Off-Broadway and the know-how of Broadway might wed? Not at present, I fear, but in 1963 there may be. That is the year in which the Repertory Theatre at the Lincoln Centre for the Performing Arts is due to open. Three million dollars have been contributed toward the building of the playhouse, which will seat twelve hundred and go up alongside a concert hall, a dance theatre, and the new Metropolitan Opera House. The Centre's president, John D. Rockefeller III, has appointed a committee to keep an advisory eye on the dramatic side of the project. The result could be a National Theatre, something unknown, though long sought, in American history.

How will it work? The chairman of the committee, a respected Broadway producer named Robert Whitehead, hopes to assemble a company of about twenty actors, under contract for not less than two years, and to stage six shows every season. One, or possibly two directors would be employed on a permanent basis. But where will the actors, directors, and authors come from? Who will pay them? Mr. Whitehead's guess is that the theatre will need a minimum of $750,000 to see it through its first year. After that, he thinks it will be able to pay its way.

To my thinking, this is a fatal error. If the Lincoln Square Theatre is to supply a full spectrum of the riches of American drama, alternating them on repertory lines, it can never show a profit, any more than the Louvre or the Comédie Française. It must not be asked to compete with Broadway on Broadway's terms, any more than the public library is asked to compete with Scribner's bookshop. It should be demanded of the new theatre that it should lose a solid, whacking sum of money each year, just as the Metropolitan Opera House makes an annual deficit of half a million dollars. The actors and directors should be paid well enough to lure them away from Broadway and Hollywood, and the same goes for scripts—the Lincoln Square Theatre should not have to go begging, cap in hand, for plays that Broadway has rejected.

To carry out this, the only conceivable policy for such a theatre, the first necessity is money, and I have no doubt that one or another of the larger foundations can be cajoled into coughing up. The second necessity is personal dynamism. There must somewhere be an artistic director with passion, zeal, and knowledge enough to create a tradition of repertory drama in a city—and a country—where it has never existed. His name might be Kazan; it might be Harold Clurman; it might be Lee Strasberg. It might even be an unfamiliar European name: Rudolf Bing, after all, came from Europe to reform the Metropolitan, and all the conductors of the New York Philharmonic before Leonard Bernstein were foreigners.

"The trouble with the whole thing," a Broadway producer remarked to me, *à propos* of the Lincoln Square Theatre, "is that there's nobody in on it who really gives a burning damn." He exaggerated, of course; but not, I think, absurdly. Many burning damns, in addition to a lot of money, will have to be given if this great chance is to be fully seized. The idea behind the project, according to Mr. Rockefeller, is that it should be "an enduring symbol of America's cultural maturity." This statement, I suggest, needs a little modification. It is the "cultural maturity" of modern capitalism, rather than of America, that will be on trial at Lincoln Square.

(1959)

Culture in Trouble.

Since this year ends in a nought and is thus divisible by ten, nearly all the leading American magazines have lately been firing at their readers such stark, factitious questions as "What Trends Will Guide Our Culture in the Coming Decade?" and "Have We a Viable Stance for the Sixties?" A man from a national weekly telephoned me a few weeks ago to ask the former question. He caught me at a bad time. I had just seen a TV programme in which Jacques Barzun, Lionel Trilling, and W. H.

Auden had discussed "The Crisis in Our Culture" with such fussy incoherence that they seemed to be not so much debating the crisis as embodying it. Mr. Barzun sat bolt upright and smirked, while Mr. Trilling leaned so far forward in cerebration that he appeared, in close shots, about to butt the camera. Mr. Auden, looking like a rumpled, bulkier version of Somerset Maugham, slumped in his chair and squinted gaily at everyone, flicking ash at random, grinning mysteriously in the manner of Mr. Amis' Professor Welch, and displaying throughout the show the sartorial hallmark of the middle-aged English intellectual—a collar tip curling up over the lapel of his jacket. From time to time he made eccentric interventions, as when he said he was ashamed to admit that he read newspapers, and when he suddenly asked Messrs. Trilling and Barzun how old they were. "Videowise," he emerged as a distinct individual with little to say; they, on the other hand, had plenty to say, but seemed devoid of individuality. They spoke with the corporate drone of a house organ (Mr. Barzun's "House of Intellect," no doubt), beside which Mr. Auden sounded like a mouth organ—i.e., a very human instrument, capable of expressing great skittishness and great melancholy, but difficult to integrate into an orchestra. Together they formed a triptych of official American culture, and their appeal, especially to intelligent viewers under forty, must have been almost nil.

What will happen to American culture at that level of punditry I would not care to predict. Yet elsewhere, in the theatre and among the younger writers, I do discern a trend—or, to be more exact, a strong and growing preoccupation with two themes. The first of these, mainly noticeable on Broadway, has to do with biography. Popular shows are tending more and more to be based on the careers of people still living or fairly recently dead. Two years ago we had Dore Schary's *Sunrise at Campobello*, which was concerned with Franklin Roosevelt's battle against polio; *Gypsy,* last season's biggest musical hit, explained how the youthful Gypsy Rose Lee became a successful stripper; and the most prosperous shows of the new season—*Fiorello!, The Miracle Worker,* and *The Sound of Music*—deal respectively with the early triumphs of Fiorello LaGuardia, Helen Keller's childhood struggle against physical handicaps, and the adventures of an Austrian family called Trapp, who escaped from the Nazis and became famous in America for their singing. We have also had a play founded on the efforts of Harry Golden, a Jewish editor living in the South, to fight segregation through ridicule; and before long Judy Holliday is to appear in a dramatized biography of Laurette Taylor, whose problem was the bottle.

I won't go into the quality of these shows, which, apart from *Gypsy* and *Fiorello!,* has so far been pretty poor; what concerns us here is their prevalence and popularity. In no other country has the theatre ever devoted itself so zealously to biographical studies of the recent national past. The trend began in Hollywood with films like *The Jolson Story, The Glenn Miller Story,* and their numerous successors, all of which offered quasi-factual proof that it was possible for anyone, given enough talent and energy, to rise from the utmost obscurity to the topmost celebrity. Broadway has now followed suit, and American drama, which has hitherto given most of its serious attention to fictional characters defeated by circumstance, appears to be changing its course; the new emphasis is on real-life characters who triumph over circumstances. The individual, spurred on by courage, faith, and good will, not only survives adversity but emerges from it an object of national admiration. And if we complain (as we might in the case of an ordinary play) that this picture of life is facile and wishfully optimistic, we are easily refuted, because: "It actually happened." American audiences, of course, have an unbounded faith in victorious individualism; all the same, it does their suspension of disbelief no harm to know that the victory in question can be historically verified.

Along with this interest in upbeat biography goes a second trend, which I hesitate to call religious or even spiritual, since in some of its manifestations it is neither. Less precisely, and therefore more accurately, it concerns the belief that what happens inside a human being is more important than what happens outside. This notion, of course, is usually expressed in Freudian terms: man is said to be ruled by the internal trinity of Ego, Superego, and Id. Sometimes, stated in another form, it declares that the summit of human aspiration and responsibility is achieved when one person learns to love another. The hero of *J.B.*, the modern Job play with which Archibald MacLeish won a Pulitzer Prize last year, sees no hope in politics, psychiatry, or organized religion; discarding all three, he "finds fulfilment," as they say, by loving his wife. A similar conclusion is reached in *The Tenth Man,* a heartily acclaimed new play by Paddy Chayefsky. The central character, a suicidal Jewish ex-Communist in the throes of analysis, is cured of his disenchantment with mankind by taking part in a ceremony held to exorcise a supposed demon from the body of a young girl. "It is better to believe in dybbuks," an old rabbi tells him, "than in nothing." This eminently disputable statement weans the hero away from nihilism, and he achieves personal salvation by falling in love with the girl.

In plays like this it is never suggested that society's relationship with man might be among the causes of his distress, and the idea that man might have a constructive relationship with society has clearly been abandoned as impossibly Utopian. Happiness lies within, and nowhere else; the world outside, brutal and immutable, is best ignored, since it can only bruise you and damage the inviolability of your soul. This doctrine of inner illumination crops up *passim* in contemporary American writing. J. D. Salinger's Glass family, for instance, is mainly composed of latter-day mystics and self-slaughtered saints whose offers of disinterested love are constantly being slapped down by a society which their humility forbids them to criticize. The Beat extremists go much further, dedicating themselves to reaching enlightenment through lysergic acid or opium; and the most memorable theatrical experience at present accessible in New York is an Off-Broadway play called *The Connection,* which deals, somewhat in the manner of *Waiting for Godot,* with the mystique and the technique of dope addiction, including the lassitude that precedes the "fix" and the illusion of spiritual insight, soaring and superhuman, that follows it. (The author's name is Jack Gelber.) Nor must I omit Norman Mailer and the philosophy of Hipsterism that he expounds in his controversial new book, *Advertisements for Myself,* which is partly a Mailer anthology and partly an exercise in self-revelation. Soon after he wrote *The Naked and the Dead* Mr. Mailer became an active Socialist; now, symptomatically, he has swung to the opposite extreme and embraced a religion of outright, psychopathic (his own word) egocentricity. The Hipster, in brief, is a man who has divorced himself from history as well as from society; who lives exclusively in the present; who thinks of himself as a white Negro; and whose aim is self-discovery through sexual pleasure, enhanced if need be by the aid of marijuana.

Christopher Caudwell, in his brilliant *Studies in a Dying Culture,* attributed the decline of bourgeois art to two forces:

> On the one hand there is production for the market—vulgarization, commercialization. On the other there is hypostatization of the art work as the goal of the art process, and the relation between art work and individual as paramount. This necessarily leads to a dissolution of those social values which make the art in question a social relation, and therefore ultimately results in the art work's ceasing to be an art work and becoming a mere private phantasy.

A ham-fisted paragraph, but not without relevance. Mr. Caudwell, who died more than twenty years ago, could not have predicted that Broadway, the theatre market, would take to selling the life stories of famous contemporaries; and if he had, it would merely have confirmed his opinion of commercialism. Meanwhile, what he says about art developing into "private phantasy" is disturbingly borne out by the cult of inner fulfilment that I have just described.

This movement, according to some observers, represents nothing more serious than—to quote one of them—"a transient reaction to Soviet atheism and materialism." I hope they are right. In fact, they had better be; American culture is tilting far too heavily in one direction, and it is becoming quite urgent that the balance should be restored.

(1960)

III: THE FRENCH THEATRE

Les Nuits de la Colère, by Armand Salacrou, and *Oedipe*, by André Gide; *Partage de Midi*, by Paul Claudel—at the St. James' Theatre, London.

M. Barrault's may be a grasshopper mind, but there is no denying its energy and versatility. It wears seven-league boots.

Salacrou's *Nuits de la Colère* smells, I am afraid, somewhat of the typewriter and the deadline. It is a tale of the Occupation, of a moral weakling who betrays his best friend to the Gestapo. One regrets that the dialogue is so often unsubtle and journalistic, so easily led into sentimentalism. The sheep (played with touching dignity by M. Jean Desailly) is not really a traitor: Salacrou shifts that responsibility to his wife, one of Mme. Renaud's piercing sketches of bourgeois frivolity. M. Barrault speaks for the hunted man with shrewd and sturdy competence—but how is it that five minutes after leaving the theatre one cannot recall this actor's voice?

Oedipe, played frankly and formally as an intellectual vaudeville turn, fares much better. M. Barrault syncopates it, jazz-fashion, substituting for Gide's lofty ironies a general mood of high good-humour. His own Oedipe is a ferocious sophisticate, squatting in angular boredom through Tiresias' admonitions, his pained eyebrows wriggling like serpents. He brings off one superbly hazardous thing in the last act: having blinded himself, he re-enters, stumbles towards his throne, bumps his eye against it, and recoils like a kitten from an electric fire. M. Barrault is hardly to blame if his costume and wig reminded me of Pocahontas. Among his prankishly incestuous children, the enchanting Elina Labourdette stands out, a frail and witty Ismène.

M. Barrault's most distinguished production to date is unquestionably Claudel's *Partage de Midi.* Set in and around China, this a very personal and oblique study of a self-wounding love. Mesa, a customs official, loves Ysé, a married woman; he arrives, through mortal sin, at an intense apprehension of God—a sequence in which one may trace the harsh growth of Claudel's own Catholicism. The performance (by a cast of four) is as lovely and mysterious to watch as a tank of tropical fish, and Félix Labisse's settings wonderfully enforce the mood. His first act, aboard ship, is particularly fine—a hothouse of canvas awnings alive with reflected ripples.

The evening's single weakness is M. Barrault's own exhibition as Mesa. Gripped by the necessity of communicating to us an aspiring spirit, he shuts tight his eyes, clenches his fists, and mimes "aspiration" with an increasingly exasperated curtness, feeling, how deeply, the importance of Mesa's plight, but never soaring, never (to use his own phrase) "taking off." But there is something more than compensation in Mme. Edwige Feuillère's Ysé: this is acting of a fragrance and fullness for which my memory cannot find a rival, unless it be Mme. Feuillère's Marguérite Gautier two Christmasses ago. Her voice, even in agony, strokes the forehead of every man in the audience, and she can fire it to violence with the suddenness and attack of a lioness. Her moment of union with Mesa, in the second act, left one line quivering in my mind like a dagger: *"Il n'y a plus d'Ysé!"* She speaks it, as Bernhardt is said to have spoken Pelléas' *"Moi! Moi! et Moi!"*, in the tones of a strangled dove.

(1951)

Thrice Blessed.

Theatrically, Paris makes us all sybarites. The English critic, accustomed to begging and yapping for the veriest crumb of quality, rapidly finds that his taste for caviare is regarded not as a bizarre craving but as a natural appetite which not to satisfy would be a gross discourtesy.

Consider those Temples of Dramatic Gastronomy, the three great repertory theatres of France. Most ancient and blessed is the Comédie-Française, whose twin shrines owe their dignity to the fact that, unlike any theatre in England, they are of the blood royal, created by Louis XIV's express decree. The English court patronised the theatre: the French court adopted it; and therein lies the difference. To support its company of thirty *sociétaires* (elected for twenty years) and fifty *pensionnaires* (engaged for a season), the Comédie receives an annual subsidy of some £380,000—more than twenty times the sum granted to the Old Vic—with which it is able not only to keep new plays and established classics permanently alternating in its repertoire, but also to stage *reprises* of lesser works applauded in their day and now revived to test their endurance, thereby ensuring that no masterpiece dies of neglect.

The point about the Comédie is that it is the touchstone, the standard of measurement, the guarantee of continuity, the rule which must be learned before it can be broken; the central blazing sun which, no matter how many satellites whirl off from its periphery, provides the dramatic universe with a constant *punctum referens*. Its acting style, clear as a chessboard and taut as a drum, blends the rhetorical past with the realistic present, welding the players together into an orchestra of concerted expertise. French is a language that easily petrifies into cliché and formula. The end of the world, when it arrives, will surely be announced in French; but this very hardness and finality of outline has forced the French to bend the language to their will by means of gesture and inflection. What their tongue prohibited, their temperament has achieved. By making an unnatural effort, they became "natural actors"; and the Comédie enshrines the result. To see its production of de Montherlant's *Port-Royal* is to feel a bridge of solid architecture beneath one's feet; to see anything at the Old Vic is to leap from one greasy stepping-stone of individual talent to another. True style is a weapon which, though it may split mountains, can also crack nuts. Witness Molière's *Les Amants Magnifiques,* the gracious frailty of which is exactly matched by Suzanne Lalique's settings, soaring and dissolving, shining in pearl and gold.

Beyond question it was the Comédie that created the audience for classical repertory on which Jean-Louis Barrault drew when he seceded in 1946 to set up the non-subsidised Compagnie Renaud-Barrault at the Marigny. This is another Temple, but one in which the high priest preaches too many of the sermons. Barrault, a born director of high intellectual vigour, lacks both the stature and the presence of a great actor. About Alceste in *Le Misanthrope* there must hang a ruinous Byronic grandeur: Barrault, unable to supply more than a petulant asperity, is acted out of sight by Pierre Bertin as Oronte, a bland pink trout of a poet *manqué*. Barrault's supreme virtue is that he will fly at anything; Shakespeare, Kafka, Fry—and even Chekhov, whose genius shrivels under the searchlight of the French language, which brusquely dispels his mists, sharpening his vague evocative outlines into razor-edged silhouettes. One yearned, in Barrault's production of *The Cherry Orchard,* for the looseness of English. Chekhov's vital third dimension is achieved only by Jean Desailly as Lopakhin, the only character in the play whose approach to life is calculated, realistic, and thoroughly French.

Any other nation would have been satisfied with two such repertories. France insisted on a third and got it: Jean Vilar's Théâtre National Populaire, installed at the Palais de Chaillot at a cost to the public of £55,000 a year. Low prices and a programme ranging from Corneille to Bertolt Brecht keep the gigantic fan-shaped auditorium regularly filled. I am myself antipathetic to the French classics; their starved vocabulary is a penance to my ear, and I agree with Stendhal that *"l'alexandrin est un cache-sottise."* For me Corneille's *Cid* does not flower, and I gloated when the audience failed to spot such transpositions as *"honneur"* for *"devoir"* and *"violence"* for *"impatience."* Yet from this prolonged display of baleful pomp one fact clearly emerged: that in Gérard Philipe the T.N.P. has the best *jeune premier* in the world, a limpid, lyrical young animal about whom the only reservation must be that animals seldom age well: an ideal Cid rarely grows up into an ideal Lear. About the T.N.P's production of Brecht's *Mère Courage* I have no reservations at all: a glorious performance of a contemporary classic which has been acclaimed everywhere in Europe save in London. Into this ribald epic of the Thirty Years' War the squalor of all wars is somehow compressed. Does Germaine Montero, as the sleazy, irresistible heroine, nag where she should dominate? Yes—but the play carries her. Never before have I seen a thousand people rise cheering and weeping in their seats.

The three Temples, as international in scope as only truly national theatres can be, cruelly expose our shortcomings. Next year M. Julien, the ebullient impresario of the Théâtre Sarah-Bernhardt, intends to repeat the international drama festival he held so successfully last summer. On that occasion the English contribution was a somewhat depleted company of *The Confidential Clerk*. M. Julien is already worried. How shall he find an English group fit to compete with the French, German, and Russian contingents? Where, in the absence of a national playhouse, is our best to be sought? Must we forever shrink from committing ourselves to a theatre which should enshrine our drama, cradle and nourish it, presenting eight times a week a performance of which we can say to our guests: "This is English acting. This is our style"? If it be argued that there is no audience for such an experiment, I answer in the traditional maxim of French actors: "The public always follows the crowd." And in any theatre, from Shakespeare's to our own, the intelligent public is ultimately the crowd.

(1955)

La Plume de Ma Tante, AT THE GARRICK, LONDON.

My allegiance to M. Robert Dhéry, the star and author of *La Plume de Ma Tante,* dates from a rainy evening in Paris last winter when I attended a revue of his devising called *Ah! Les Belles Bacchantes!* Within ten minutes I had entered a new dimension of comedy, the dimension of calamity.

Everything in the show went wrong: not loudly wrong but mildly, shiftily, provoking those tiny tremors that plague the nervous system when, in a large quiet room, a small object falls thunderously to the floor. While announcing the first item (a modest scena depicting the creation of the universe), the *compère* paused and stared, without comment but with immense disquiet, at something that was happening on the stage a few feet in front of him. Whatever it was (and he did not explain), it disturbed other members of the troupe as well; they would break off, in the middle of songs and sketches, to contemplate it. Glances of horror would be exchanged, and mute appeals flashed towards the wings. At length the truth transpired: what everyone on stage knew, and had determined to hide from us, was that gas was escaping from the footlights. No action was taken, because by now the cast had other things on its mind: a lion was at large in the backstage corridors, and one of the dressing-rooms was on fire.

M. Dhéry has been presenting shows like this for more than seven years, and I was a late-comer to the cult. In *La Plume de Ma Tante* he and his squadron of harassed stoics make their London début. Over some of their work, it must be admitted, there hangs a pall of slip-shod improvisation; and they are without their greatest clown, the irreplaceable Louis de Funès. Yet enough remains to throw serious doubt on the English definition of revue as an entertainment in which acid, modish people say acid, modish things. Nothing in the present show is satirical, and nothing is topical—how could it be, since M. Dhéry's sense of humour has no malice and is quite untethered to time and place? If we seek a parallel, we may find it in the films of M. Jacques Tati and nowhere else on earth.

The deviser himself takes part, with a touch of Chaplin in his method and of Commedia dell'Arte in his lineage. He treats his company, a bright-eyed troupe to whom ghastly things are constantly happening, with enormous compassion. I am not sure why he intruduces M. Christian Duvaleix as "my brother-in-law, Amsterdam," but when

M. Duvaleix slinks ogling into view, the penalty is swift: his electric guitar blows up in his face. At this he betrays absolutely no surprise. Imagine the convulsions with which an English comedian would greet a similar mischance and you have the measure of M. Dhéry's directorial tact, which amounts to a minor revolution in comic technique. Or consider Mlle. Colette Brosset's appearance as an understudy involved in a *pas de deux* with an Eton-cropped ballerina whose interest in her is not exclusively professional; vaguely aghast, Mlle. Brosset confides to the audience no more than a single, horrified whisper: "She must be *mad!*" And I have not yet mentioned the superb M. Jacques Legras, whose face is a fish-mask of utter despair and who eats dog-biscuits for solace; nor would it be fair to omit my delight in the brief item entitled "Domingo Blazes and His Courageous Latin-American Band." (Courageous in what sense I do not know, though I suppose it takes courage of a sort to work for a bandleader three feet high.) M. Gérard Calvi's music is wanly haunting, and the dances are led with long-limbed abandon by Mlle. Nicole Parent, who shows in a bullfight ballet that she really knows something about how bulls are fought.

M. Dhéry's speciality is the comedy of disaster, the gaiety of quiet desperation, and because of this he provides the perfect response to the alarming events of our time. He teaches us, when confronted with calamity, to react with only the faintest of shrugs. We may look foolish, but we have kept our dignity. His basic theme is embarrassment, the agony of a man discovered in a moment of private aberration, of anti-social lunacy; and he implies that such lunacy is not only funny, but healthy. I shall often return to the Garrick in the weeks to come, knowing that, however much I may chafe at the passing crudities, there will always be golden moments at which, suddenly and without warning, tears of laughter will stand in my eyes. Either M. Dhéry is a genius or the word has no meaning.

(1955)

Stars from the East.

The second Paris Drama Festival, now entering the seventh of its ten weeks, is already a resounding success. Every theatrical capital has sent a team except Moscow, and this will be remedied next year, when we are promised the Maly Theatre in Chekhov. One of the few flops has been Judith Anderson, playing *Medea* in a Widow Twankey wig and a style describable only as armpit rhetoric. One of my special joys was the great Neapolitan comedian Eduardo de Filippo, appearing in his own play *Questi Fantasmi!* and giving a performance that combined the urbane authority of Louis Jouvet with the deadpan melancholy of Buster Keaton. But Paris, so far, has kept its loudest cheers for the Berliner Ensemble of Bertolt Brecht and—*hors de catégorie*—the Peking Opera.

Brecht's troupe, a post-war phenomenon, is some twelve hundred years younger than the Chinese opera, yet both have much in common. They presage an era in which drama, ballet, and opera are no longer separate arts requiring separate critics. They mix dance, mime, speech, and song in the service of the ultimate god: narrative. And both are popular forms, untouched by anything esoteric. The Chinese programme, made up of excerpts from longer works, contains little we would call opera; most of it is brilliant tumbling, acrobatics put to the task of telling a good story. An old man takes a girl across a river in a punt, but there is no river and no punt: the performers mime the action, with the delicacy of cats. Two warriors fight in a darkened room, miming even the darkness (for the stage is brightly lit), missing each other by inches, prowling and swooping through fifteen minutes of ceaseless comic invention. You may object that nothing very profound takes place; but I cannot call superficial an art that explores, with entranced and exquisite love, the very wellsprings of physical movement, speaking the language of the body so ardently that a flexed arm becomes a simile and a simple somersault a metaphor.

Bertolt Brecht's Epic Theatre borrows heavily from the Chinese: the emphasis is classically on how events happen, not romantically on the emotions of the people they happen to. Once in a generation the world discovers a new way of telling a story. This generation's pathfinder is Brecht, both as playwright and as director of the Berliner Ensemble. Last year he electrified Paris with *Mother Courage;* this year he brought *The Caucasian Chalk Circle*. My first impression was of petrified amazement at the amount of money involved. From East Berlin Brecht has transported dozens of impressionistic settings, hundreds of costumes, a new revolving stage for the Sarah-Bernhardt, a new curtain, and seventy-six actors—scarcely more than half of his permanent company. Brecht has adapted the Oriental tale of the Chalk Circle to medieval Georgia. An army rebellion unseats the governor of a city, whose wife flees in panic, leaving her baby son behind; Grusha, her maid, protects the child, finds it a father, and then, when the revolt is quelled, disputes posssesion of it with the real mother, now returned to power. The judge gives the child to Grusha because, in Brecht's words: "Each thing belongs to him who can do it the most good." If I was unmoved by what Brecht had to say, I was overwhelmed by the way in which he said it. It is as shocking and revolutionary as a cold shower. In the British theatre everything is sacrificed to obtain sympathy for the leading characters. *Chez* Brecht, sympathy is nowhere; everything is sacrificed for clarity of narrative. No time is wasted on emotional climaxes. Situations which our playwrights would regard as cues for sentimental tirades are drowned by the clatter of horses' hooves or cut off by the whirr of the closing curtain. Three commentators, seated at the side of the stage, then outline in song what is going to happen next.

I have read a great deal about Brecht's theory of acting, the famous *Verfremdungseffekt,* or "alienation effect." What it boils down to in practice is something extremely simple. The small parts are all generalised. They wear masks down to their lips, fashioned like faces in Bosch or Brueghel and so exaggerated that we know at a glance what kind of people they are meant to be—drunken, prying, lecherous, miserly, what have you. We can thus concentrate on the principals, who wear no masks or make-up and play with absolute realism. These include Ernst Busch as the Judge and Angelica Hurwicz as Grusha (a fat girl, because Brecht does not want us to judge his characters on the easy grounds of physical attractiveness); but the supporting players are not neglected. Helene Weigel, the governor's wife, leaves no doubt that she is a great actress: she has eyes like the glint of hatchets, a clarion voice, and a physical technique as supple as that of Martha Graham.

The whole production is superb: a legend for today told in Flemish and Oriental terms. One sees why Brecht feels that our method is as different from his as driving a carriage-and-four is from driving a car. Unless we learn it soon, a familiar process will take place. Thirty years from now Brecht will be introduced to the English critics, who will at once decry him for being thirty years out of date. The ideal way of staging *Henry IV, Tamburlaine, Peer Gynt,* and a hundred plays yet unwritten will have been ignored; and the future of the theatre may have been strangled in its cot.

(1956)

Le Chien du Jardinier, BY LOPE DE VEGA; *Occupe-toi d'Amélie*, BY GEORGES FEYDEAU; AND *Le Misanthrope*, BY MOLIÈRE, AT THE PALACE, LONDON.

"Ils se moquent toujours de mon amour de la pantomime," said M. Barrault on Monday night, flashing his grin slantwise at the house. He was speaking of his colleagues, who had just queued up to recite, with prelusive ahemming, a number of French poems, and who now departed, leaving the stage free for M. Barrault to impersonate a horse.

The simulation was superb; nothing more equine has graced our theatre since the retirement of a certain Earl's Court *ingénue;* and yet, when the actor had pranced off into the wings, my heart was with the mockers. I had seen, that evening, altogether too much *haute-école* theatre. The troupe had dandy-minced it through *Le Chien du Jardinier,* a chilling triviality adapted from Lope de Vega; then had come the poems; and then the horse. In a way that he can scarcely have guessed, M. Barrault's climax was not quite inept. After two hours' demonstration of the dramatic uses of snaffle and curb, many of us, echoing Roy Campbell's quatrain, were beginning to wonder what had become of the horse.

These doubts persisted throughout the Renaud-Berrault company's first week in London. In the newer *mises en scène* one got a feeling of dehydrated Luntishness, of a husband-and-wife team bent on titillation rather than revelation; we were almost in the world of Julia Neilson and Fred Terry—an entirely respectable world, but poles apart from M. Barrault's avowed intent, "the cult of the Absolute." The creative éclat of ten years ago was distinctly dimmed. Some of the blame, no doubt, attaches to the bourgeois audiences of the Marigny Theatre; the rest lies with the mechanistic "robot" method to which M. Barrault has committed himself. It has led him into an increasing preoccupation with manner and an increasing carelessness of matter. The best of this week's productions, *Occupe-toi d'Amélie,* is as joyously volatile as it seemed seven years ago; Desailly and Bertin are superb, and M. Barrault's brief intervention as an aged clerk with a strangely pendulous right foot may well be his finest performance; but already, through its virtues, the limitations of the style are visible. It fits Feydeau's characters, obsessed automata who butt into each other like dodgem cars; it suits, indeed, all farce and much comedy. It can make a superficial play seem a masterpiece. It can also make a masterpiece seem superficial.

Le Misanthrope is a case in point. Desailly and Bertin, at ease in any style, rise readily to the challenge—especially Bertin, whose outsize portrait of Oronte owes more to the Comédie-Française than to the Marigny. Boobyish in looks and speech, the actor conceals beneath his pink, porpoise exterior a tremendous technical authority. And a dignity, too: a dignity gapingly absent from M. Barrault's Alceste. Though he has learned how to overcome his lack of inches, M. Barrault cannot coax his slim and foxy mask into the semblance of majesty. I do not say that Alceste is a tragic character, but I do say that he is trying to solve a profound and universal human dilemma—whether or not to accept the standards of the society into which one is born. Alceste decides to reject them; but where Molière chides him for going too far, M. Barrault derides him for ever having begun. His Alceste is a mannerless, egotistical upstart, a small man inflated by pride. Only his prevailing bad temper distinguishes him from the artful valets whom M. Barrault has made his own in Marivaux, Lope de Vega, and other plays by Molière. The part is cut down to fit the actor.

Similarly, Mme. Renaud's Celimène, guileful and undulant, replete with bubbling chuckles, is an exact facsimile of former performances in comparable plays; and she repeats it as the widowed countess in Lope's comedy, tantalising her secretary with hopes of bed. Next week, in Claudel and Giraudoux, I hope to find the company's range broader and deeper than at present I think it.

(1956)

Christophe Colomb, BY PAUL CLAUDEL, AND *Intermezzo*, BY JEAN GIRAUDOUX, AT THE PALACE, LONDON.

In an age top-heavy with cerebration, who can resist the innocent physical exuberance of Jean-Louis Barrault? "Once upon a stage . . ." he begins, and goes on to beguile us with a whole armoury of theatrical magic. His production of *Christophe Colomb* is a child's dream of what the playhouse should be: a home of ecstatic noise, sweeping movement, and miraculous conjuring tricks. In discipline and audacity it rivals Orson Welles' *Moby Dick*. The décor is a great slung sail, pendent over a rostrum; before it the chorus chants and swirls, whipping both halves of the story along—the triumphant, west-bound first half, ending when the sight of land converts mutiny into exultation, and the sobering return, ending in indigence and death. By using the sail as a cinema screen, M. Barrault makes the wooden O infinitely elastic: when the chorus speaks of doves (*colombes*), we see them wheeling and fluttering on the canvas.

Twice he extends the frontiers of the theatre by throwing on to the screen filmed close-ups of scenes that live actors are playing in the foreground, so that one's eye can choose between close shot and long shot. Surprise, both visual and aural, is exploited with stunning virtuosity; and the acting is pitched at a level of intensity that resembles *flamenco* singing in that it almost transcends the banality of the words it is called upon to utter. Almost, but not quite: one cannot wholly disguise banality as insistent as Claudel's. Those confident sages who find Brecht's chronicle plays *naïve* when judged by the standards of Western sophistication must surely have squirmed on Monday night, for Claudel's bombastic epic achieves a shallowness which not even an East German yokel could mistake for profundity. M. Barrault worships Copeau and fills his stage with doves, but only in a literal sense does the result resemble the Vieux Colombier. His style, being bold and explicit, works wonders with bold and explicit plays; but when it seeks to transmit the nuances of observable reality, it fails, as an archer would fail who sought to hit a goldfish. Its gesture is too broad; the air around it seems over-full of manual rhetoric. The flavour of life is condemned to death by underlining. It is as if a man were to expel into a recorder the amount of violently compressed air that is necessary to blow a trumpet. It is by puffing its cheeks too strenuously that the company fails in its greatest test, the Giraudoux *Intermezzo*.

I do not mean to imply that this is a realistic play: Giraudoux's kaleidoscopic prose is purple to the last semi-colon, pure anthology stuff; yet unless the actors keep one foot rooted in reality, the point of the piece is lost. The only road to death, says Giraudoux, is life: to fall in love with death without having first embraced life is the supreme crime. It is committed by a young schoolmistress who falls in love with a ghost, which bureaucracy condemns to immediate exorcism. The first climax, in which the ghost reveals that he is really alive and is instantly shot dead, is cheated of its proper poignancy because in M. Barrault's production everyone on stage seems just as unreal as the ghost. The second climax is similarly muffed. Life and death, the known world and the unknown, battle for the girl's allegiance; and the village chemist (who describes himself, exquisitely, as one chosen by destiny to carry out its transitions) tempts her back to life by besieging her ears with a seductive cacophony of everyday noises. She awakens an adult, reconciled at last to the impure tumult of reality.

In M. Barrault's production she awakens to a world of artifice. She awakens to Maurice Brianchon's settings, which are as dully stylised as Pierre Bertin's performance as the Government Inspector. She awakens to a betrayal of Giraudoux's message, which is that the atmosphere of life itself, however polluted and imperfect, is wonderfully worth breathing. Cleverly as Simone Valère plays her, she awakens to puppetry.

Jean Desailly, as her bureaucratic lover, shows once more his mastery of confusion, embarrassment, awkwardness, and perplexity, qualities that French playwrights demand so often of their male characters and so seldom of their women. Popular French drama, like French theatre troupes, is a matriarchy. It is primarily designed for the entertainment of sophisticated wives, and many are the talents that have been enfeebled by the necessity of wooing the blue-rinsed Parisian female audience. No French playwright would dare to humiliate a woman as Blanche is humiliated in *A Streetcar Named Desire;* and no Frenchwoman, as things turned out, was able to play the part properly. A few years ago George Jean Nathan asked one of his Paris colleagues whether Mistinguett was still alive. At the time she was, and the colleague said so. "And is Sarah Bernhardt still dead?" Nathan continued. The question is not as jocular as it sounds. Spiritually, Sarah lives on to dominate the French theatre, whose watchword is the gentle subjugation of the male. What names come to mind when you think of French acting? Not Coquelin or Lemaître, but Rachel, Réjane, Bernhardt, and Feuillère, each with her foot exquisitely planted on some masculine neck. If you wonder why French actors shrug so much, let me remind you that the shrug, a sign of bafflement or apology, is the only defence they have against the consistent brilliance of the lines written for French leading ladies.

One's summing-up of M. Barrault's theatre must be that it is balletic, comedic, mimetic, Dionysiac even, but essentially out of touch with life. Art preserve me from insisting that theatre should always be lifelike: that would be to fall into the old puritan error of condemning poetry on the grounds that it is all lies and feigning. My quarrel with M. Barrault is that he feigns too much and too exclusively; he has uprooted himself from the soil that should nourish him. He has lost contact with his base. Many plays respond to his treatment, but not *Intermezzo;* not the best.

(1956)

Pauvre Bitos, BY JEAN ANOUILH, AT THE THÉÂTRE MONTPARNASSE-GASTON BATY.

A sensation being bruited, I went last week to see M. Anouilh's new play, *Pauvre Bitos, ou Le Diner de Têtes,* which has split Paris into two camps—those who dislike it, and those who detest it. Mere dislike is the Right-Wing reaction, while active loathing issues from the Left: both camps, needless to say, are packing the theatre. Far more than *Antigone, Bitos* is M. Anouilh's political manifesto. It is a cruel, discordant work, as bitterly imagined as written, in mood as violent as that of a neurotic schoolboy locked up in a dormitory while his classmates frolic in the sun; and its conclusion lies somewhere between "A plague on both your houses" and "I'll be revenged on the whole pack of you." It is the blackest by far of M. Anouilh's plays. It is also the most cunningly constructed, a dirty act done with the utmost art, a torture-chamber designed by a master builder.

In shape it resembles a fox-hunt, except that the fox in this instance has envenomed teeth. A truer similitude, perhaps, would be the slow tearing of wings from a wasp. Maxime, an arrogant young landowner, has inherited a derelict priory where in 1793 the revolutionary tribunal condemned several of his ancestors to death. Thither he summons his rich friends to a dinner at which each must impersonate a figure of the Revolution. Their aim is to vilify and humiliate the guest-of-honour, a Communist deputy named Bitos, who was once a lowly scholarship boy at Maxime's school. His entrance, as Robespierre, is a stupefying *coup de théâtre*. The other guests are correctly clad in periwigs and ordinary dinner jackets; the ignorant Bitos arrives in full eighteenth-century fig, complete with knee-breeches and buckle-shoes. Atop his *perruque* there rests, absurdly, a bowler hat. Stifling his shame, he tries to pass off as high-born banter the increasingly savage gibes of his tormentors, who scorned him even as a child because, as Maxime icily observes, *"vous manquiez de grâce."* The charade now begins to bare its fangs, declaring its contempt for the common man and his pitiful efforts to set up "an aristocracy of mediocrity."

From taunts they proceed to direct intimidation. Robespierre was shot in the face on the eve of his execution; so a pistol, loaded with blanks, is fired at little Bitos, who promptly swoons. In a dream he relives Robespierre's life in counterpoint to his own, and finds that the melody is the same: both were sullen, unloved tots who grew up to condemn in others the qualities they lacked themselves. Unable to please, Bitos has devoted his life to denouncing pleasure. This explanation of revolutionary zeal is painfully familiar, but it has seldom been advanced so liverishly, and never with so complete an absence of pity. Michel Bouquet, rightly divining his author's wish, allows no hint of pathos to soften his portrait of Bitos as a smug and bloodless puppet. But M. Anouilh's spleen is far from spent. Out, in the last act, come the thumbscrews. The revived Bitos is plied with drink until he consents to accompany the jokers to a night-club, where they plan to involve him in an unsavoury brawl. They are unexpectedly foiled. As a wise insurance against the charge of total misanthropy, M. Anouilh has admitted to the cast two people in whom human feeling is not quite extinct. One of them, a young schoolteacher, leaves the dining-room with a short and half-hearted paean to what he vaguely calls *"le vrai peuple."* The other is a girl who now urges Bitos to quit the party before further ignominy befalls him. He takes her advice, but turns in the doorway to inform her, in a frenzy of spite, that nothing is as crushing as pity; and that it is she, in consequence, whom he will remember with the purest hatred.

As an essay in political thought, the play is imitative and negligible. As a study of human character, it is hysterical and often foul-mouthed. As a piece of dramatic architecture, it is, as I have said, exquisitely gripping. But it fascinates me most in another aspect: as an exercise in self-revelation. Whose side is the author on? The question has agitated Paris ever since the play opened a fortnight ago. To be sure, M. Anouilh's aristos are heartless sadists; but I have little doubt that his real enemy is Bitos, in whose wounds no knife is left unturned. This despised provincial upstart is drawn with an ugly, obsessive passion, almost as if he were a ghost that the haunted author were struggling to exorcise. The name Bitos called up an odd echo. I found myself thinking of the derisive nickname, "Anouilh le Miteux," that Jouvet bestowed on the young upstart from Bordeaux; scruffy Anouilh, at whose work the maestro laughed, saying that it reeked of old socks. In every Anouilh play there is mockery, and in many there is hatred; but in this one I smell self-hatred. Perhaps, as Max Beerbohm said of Ibsen's attack on the artistic temperament in *When We Dead Awaken,* "it is but another instance of his egoism that he has reserved his most vicious kick for himself." *Pauvre Jean,* in fact: but how brilliant, how distastefully brilliant!

(1956)

Twilight of a Critic.

In an age when there are more successful commentators than important events to be commented on, the temptation to become a critic is enormous. Ours is a minuscule era with a million microscopes trained on it, and the natural tendency is to become one of the watchers rather than one of the watched. After all, why bother to make history if you can earn a better living as a non-combatant observer? The argument is powerful but specious. Those whom it has seduced into espousing criticism as a career should study the case of M. Paul Léautaud, the second volume of whose *Journal Littéraire* has just appeared in Paris.

M. Léautaud, now eighty-three, was the illegitimate son of a prompter at the Comédie-Française. He became a critic in 1907 under the name of Maurice Boissard: witty, hawk-eyed, vehement, and a master of paradox. In matters of style he revered the swiftness and nonchalance of Stendhal; of prettiness, and style for style's sake, he had a horror. Shrewdly and sternly he reviled the excesses of French classical acting, and became quickly notorious. He loathed tragedy above all things, and quoted with approval the remark of Crébillon *fils* that French tragic drama, as exemplified by Corneille and Racine, was the most perfect farce ever invented by the wit of man. (*Andromaque,* which he liked, he defined as a brilliant psychological comedy.) *"Il n'y a de théâtre,"* he cried, *"que le théâtre comique,"* by which he meant to endorse the tragi-comic while excluding for ever the purely, relentlessly tragic. On and off, he flourished for more than thiry years, always candid and often querulous, in the best traditions of French polemic. Yet in 1941 he abandoned his craft and fled. Why?

His enemies say that his egotism had grown so unbridled that to sit in silence for three hours while actors declaimed had become a torture to him. Others hold that he took fright when a rancorous tragedian, sitting behind him at the Comédie-Française, set fire to his coat-tails. Whatever the reason, he retired with an army of pet cats to a tumbledown suburban house and locked himself in, like a wounded hermit crab. Warily, five years ago, he crept out to give a devastating series of broadcast talks about his private life. For a while he became fashionable, and no salon was complete without this dwarf cactus of a man, with his pockets full of cat's-meat and his mouth full of insults. Soon afterwards he shuffled back to his retreat, and nowadays to visit him is to court annihilation. At your approach an outpost or sentinel cat dashes indoors, presumably to warn its brethren to make the air hideous for your arrival. The door hangs on a rusted hinge, and the windows are broken and grey with dust. With a hopeful cry you announce yourself, and the response, from a high and smelly landing, is a strangled moan of grief. It comes from one who knew Zola, Huysmans, Péguy, Verlaine, and Rémy de Gourmont; it is the sound made by a critic at the end of his life. Do not mount the staircase: M. Léautaud lives at the top of it purely, they say, for the joy of kicking you down. He exists in imminent expectation of being blown to pieces. In this he sees no pathos. He wants no sympathy save that of his cats; it is only when human beings invade his hermitage that he grows petulant. And this is his chosen fate: logically, for his kind, there is no other. You would become a critic? Consider M. Léautaud, and think again.

(1956)

La Dame aux Camélias, BY ALEXANDRE DUMAS, AT THE DUKE OF YORK'S, LONDON.

It is the opinion of one of my colleagues that Mme. Edwige Feuillère is the greatest actress on earth. Lucky the man who can make such a claim! And as lucky he who, in another journal, confidently challenged it with his own contender, Dame Edith Evans! For here, surely, are critical eyes which have scanned the field and shrewdly concluded that where Mmes. Maria Casarès, Katina Paxinou, Helene Weigel, Anna Magnani, and Inga Tidblad (to name but five) won't do, Dame Edith and Mme. Feuillère will. Herein lies my embarrassment, and with it my envy, for I have seen only four of these seven ladies on the stage.

A short while ago I risked the assertion that Sir Laurence Olivier was the best actor alive, since when my desk has become a tournament of letters, from Greeks about their Minotis, from Germans about their Krauss. So let me now be circumspect. In assessing Mme. Feuillère's *La Dame aux Camélias,* I have taken care not to ignore what Paris thinks, which is that this actress is herself a permanent and changeless character in a permanent and changeless play disguised under several titles—*L'Aigle à Deux Têtes, Partage de Midi,* and the one we are considering.

Other actresses have discerned in Dumas' Marguérite Gautier traces of the *gamine,* even of the sensational slut; according to report, Miss Tallulah Bankhead made her die in a paroxysm of asthma, and Bernhardt hinted at her lack of education by hesitating before the word *"abnégation"* in M. Duval's letter. Mme. Feuillère will have none of this. In her *la classe des déclassées* finds its queen. This is a courtesan with no rough edges; she quilts the part with graciousness. Of Duse in the same role Shaw said that she was "exquisitely considerate"; "for this interesting actress," added Henry James, "the most beautiful thing is always the great thing." So with Mme. Feuillère. Every ripple of her voice, every line of her body is alive with the beauty of transience; her performance glows in the mind like a sunset. Some of the play's springtime charm necessarily disappears; "all champagne and tears," Henry James called it, but Mme. Feuillère gives us a riper, sweeter melancholy—Yquem and tears, perhaps. Besought by Armand's father to tell his son that she no longer loves him, she utters her riposte—*"Il ne me croira pas"*—not with youthful defiance but with a wise and rueful regret. Her death-fall, as sudden as the departure of a ghost at dawn, is mortally shocking.

Duse, said Sir Max, "never stoops to impersonation," and the same is true of Mme. Feuillère. All that is subtle and poetic in erotic love she contains; the image is perfect, but immutable. She never becomes Marguérite, she gathers up Marguérite into herself, as she gathered up Ysé in Claudel's play, another bloom for her bouquet. It were a blasphemy to subject beauty like this to the rigours of Ibsen, Racine, or Shakespearean tragedy. One sees in Mme. Feuillère no capacity to frighten, no ability to compel awe. I once knew a painter of miniatures who wanted to paint murals; having failed, he contented himself by boasting that he painted the largest miniatures in the world. This is Mme. Feuillère's case. Let me sum her up—and this must be understood as cancelling any rasher opinions I may formerly have expressed—as the best *romantic* actress I have ever seen. She has a powerful, if rather charmless, Armand in M. Jacques Dacqmine.

(1957)

Phèdre, BY RACINE, AT THE PALACE, LONDON.

"Poussez le rôle vers la douleur et non vers la fureur, tout le monde y gagnera, même Racine." That was Régnier's advice to Bernhardt when she first approached *Phèdre* in 1874, and Sarah heeded it. As well she might, for to adopt the "furious" reading would have been to court comparison with the apocalyptic performance of Rachel twenty years earlier. That this was an earthquake of acting nobody need doubt. Hear Lewes on

her entrance: "You felt that she was wasting away under the fire within, that she was standing on the verge of the grave with pallid face, hot eyes, emaciated frame—an awful, ghastly apparition. . . ." Her fourth act was a tempest, the actress being driven by a gale of emotion as horrifying as it was uncontrollable.

Since Sarah, however, the *"douleur"* interpretation has been in vogue: Phèdre is seen as the catspaw of the gods, more sinned against than sinning in her passion for her stepson. Arguing this case, the defence traditionally calls Racine himself, who insists in his preface to the play that his heroine, essentially virtuous, is the pitiable victim of destiny, not of her own desires. But here, surely, the author was simply insuring himself against possible charges of immorality, being fully aware that the woman he had created was not only the prey of Venus but an active collaborator as well. In short, though she knows she is doing wrong, she cannot help doing it; there is a tigress within her that must be fed. Without the tigress, the play has no motive force, and the calmer passages, with their anguished envy of innocence, go for nothing.

On Monday night Edwige Feuillère essayed the part for the first time, and it was soon clear that she favoured the passive, quietist reading. An imposing stillness, a tranquil desolation—these were the phrases that crept to mind. The last act was so delicately cadenced as to be almost inaudible, and the actress throughout made her most touching effects with those lines, expressive of romantic resignation, to which her talents naturally incline her. In the fourth-act tirades she came, very nearly, to the boil; her voice, until then strangely fuzzed and bottled, achieved vibrations of considerable intensity; but her only downright concession to the Grand Manner was her death-fall. No one drops dead like Mme. Feuillère. Shatteringly, she slumped, and there, almost before the eye could register it, was mortality.

Yet chance after chance was inexplicably missed.

Soleil! je te viens voir pour la dernière fois

was thrown away. Nothing was made of

On ne voit point deux fois le rivage des morts.

And the seizing of Hippolyte's sword, which should be tremendous, was most strangely fumbled, as if not a sword but a compromising letter were in question.

The plain truth is that this actress is wanting in the majestic attack that should compel awe. Never does she command the stage; rather than lead the action, she is led by it. Never is she eaten up with desire: one does not feel that the plague within her is ambitious and contagious. The part should be, in the literal meaning of the word, terrific. With Mme. Feuillère one gets no sense of danger. Her performance is an immensely graceful apology for Phèdre, a sort of obituary notice composed by a well-wishing friend; but it is never a life nakedly lived before our eyes.

On top of this, and through no remediable fault of her own, she fails to satisfy the *optique du théâtre*. The hunted, ravaged look of the great sufferers is beyond her means. She lacks the tragic mask. Her face is immovably serene, and it cannot, how grimly soever she purse her lips, how fiercely knit her eyebrows, assume the lineaments of total agony. For this reason, if for no other, the performance must be accounted a gallant failure. The Hippolyte, Jean-François Calvé, is game but immature, and the best feature of a somewhat stodgy supporting cast is the eloquent Thésée of Bernard Noel.

(1957)

Fin de Partie AND *Acte sans Paroles*, BY SAMUEL BECKETT, AT THE ROYAL COURT, LONDON.

> You began Catholic, that is to say, you began with a system of values in stark opposition to reality. . . . You really believe in chastity, purity and the personal God, and that is why you are always breaking out into cries of c___, s___ and hell. As I don't believe in these things except as quite provisional values, my mind has never been shocked to outcries by the existence of water closets—and undeserved misfortunes. . . . Your work is an extraordinary experiment and I would go out of my way to save it from destruction or restrictive interruption. It has its believers and its following. Let them rejoice in it. To me it is a dead end.

That is Wells, writing in 1928 to James Joyce. After seeing *Fin de Partie,* which closed last night, I offer it as an admonitory text to Samuel Beckett, formerly Joyce's friend. I do not wish to press too far the comparison between the two men. Their styles are utterly different: one gorges on Joyce and slims on Beckett. But they share an Irish gallows-humour, an absorption in psychiatry, and a grudge against God that the godless never feel. But above all, in Beckett's private world, one hears the cry that George Orwell attributed to Joyce: "Here is life without God. Just look at it!"

As produced in London, *Waiting for Godot* made Beckett's world valid and persuasive. Though deserted by God, the tramps survived, and did so with gaiety, dignity, and a moving interdependence; a human affirmation was made. I had heard, and discounted, rumours that Beckett disliked the London production. These rumours I now believe. The new play, directed by Roger Blin under the author's supervision, makes it clear that his purpose is neither to move nor to help us. For him, man is a pygmy who connives at his own inevitable degradation. There, says Beckett, stamping on the face of mankind: there, that is how life is. And when protest is absent, the step from "how life is" to "how life should be" is horrifyingly short.

Before going any further, I ought to explain what I think the play is about. I take it to be an analysis of the power-complex. The hero, a sightless old despot robed in scarlet, has more than a passing affinity with Francis Bacon's paintings of shrieking cardinals. He lives in a womb-shaped cell, attended by Clov, his shambling slave, on whose eyes he is totally dependent. His throne is flanked by two dust-bins, wombs within the womb, inhabited by his parents, Nagg and Nell. Eventually Nell dies, whereupon the tyrant asks Clov to see what Nagg is up to. *"Il pleure,"* says Clov. *"Donc,"* says the boss, *"il vit."* The curtain falls on a symbolic stalemate: King (Nagg) versus King and Knight (Boss and Clov). The boss is imprisoned for ever in the womb. He can never escape from his father.

Schopenhauer once said: "The will is the strong blind man who carries on his shoulders the lame man who can see." Beckett reverses the positions. It is the lame man, Clov—representing perception and imagination—who is bowed down by the blind bully of naked will. The play is an allegory about authority, an attempt to dramatise the neurosis that makes men love power. So far, so good. I part company with Beckett only when he insists that the problem is insoluble, that this is a deterministic world. *"Quelque chose suit son cours":* and there is nothing we can do about it. My interpretation may be incomplete, but it illuminates at least one of the play's facets. The blind irascible hero, Hamm, is working on an interminable novel: does this not bring to mind the blind "cantankerous Irishman" by whom Beckett was once employed? Hamm stands for many things: for the Church, the State, and even Godot himself; for all the forms of capricious authority. One of them may perhaps be Joyce.

When I read the play, I enjoyed long stretches of it—laconic exchanges that seemed to satirise despair, vaudeville *non-sequiturs* that savagely parodied logic. Within the dark framework I even discerned glimmers of hope. I now see that I was wrong. Last week's production, portentously stylised, piled on the agony until I thought my skull would split. Little variation, either of pace or emphasis, was permitted: a cosmic comedy was delivered as humourlessly as if its author had been Racine. Georges Adet, peeping gnome-like from his bin, performed with charming finesse; otherwise, moaning was the rule, to which Jean Martin (Clov) conformed with especial intensity. I suddenly realised that Beckett wanted his private fantasy to be accepted as objective truth. And that nothing less would satisfy him. For a short time I am prepared to listen in any theatre to any message, however antipathetic. But when it is not only disagreeable but forced down my throat, I demur.

I was influenced, I admit, by *Acte sans Paroles,* the solo mime which followed the play. Here Man (Deryk Mendel) is a shuffling puppet, obedient to the imperious blasts of a whistle which send him vainly clambering after a flask of water, lowered from above only to be whisked out of reach. He is foiled even when he tries to hang himself, and ends up inert, unresponsive to whistle and carafe alike. This kind of facile pessimism is dismaying in an author of Beckett's stature. It is not only the projection of a personal sickness, but a conclusion reached on inadequate evidence. I am ready to believe that the world is a stifling, constricting place—but not if my informant is an Egyptian mummy.

(1957)

France in Shadow.

There's always the acting—and on the acting, this melancholy Paris season, one is forced to fall back. The back-stage staffs of the national theatres are on strike, but you would scarcely notice it: these easy, various players do their own lighting and scene-painting with voice and gesture. Does this sometimes expose too clearly the fact that all French gestures, excepting those indicating oneself, are variants of the shrug? It does: but emphatically not in *Le Sexe Faible,* Edouard Bourdet's satire on fortune-hunting in the twenties, which the Comédie-Française has lately put to the test of revival. A conventionally cynical text is made to dance by spring-heeled playing. Gabrielle Dorziat presides at the head of a household of adventurers, whose victims include a lean, metallic Boston widow (Denise Noël, smart as a whip) and Denise Gence as a hennaed antique so withered by lubricity that she can hardly crawl. The wheels of the action are oiled by Jacques Charon, who plays a French

Jeeves with the omniscient repose of a great comic stylist. One is conscious throughout of a national company doing its job, part of which is to rescue plays like this from premature oblivion.

But when we leave the performers and consider what is being performed, the Paris scene clouds over. Several of the more audacious little theatres have closed, among them the Babylone, and the few that remain confine themselves exclusively to squibs of surrealism: lively enough, but escapist to the *n*th degree. In all the fifty theatres of Paris you will find not one play dealing seriously with contemporary French life. Marital farces, trumpery trompery, scuttle lifelessly through half of them, and imported successes fill most of the rest. There is no new Anouilh this year, but the other "respectable" commercial playwrights seem committed to his latter-day brand of stereotyped biliousness: *vide* Marcel Aymé's *La Mouche Bleue,* an anti-American satire of stupefying glibness.

Consumed by a sick mingling of xenophobia and self-disgust, of chauvinism and cynicism, the average French audience seems to me in grave danger of becoming an audience of neurotic simpletons. It is significant that the biggest popular and critical success of the season is *La Famille Hernandez,* a production sponsored by the state-run Centre Régional d'Art Dramatique d'Algérie. Performed by a company of non-Arab amateurs, it purports to depict scenes from ordinary life in Algeria today. To say the least, you would hardly recognise the old place. Algeria today, it seems, is a sun-kissed paradise full of happy, childlike people, mostly of Spanish origin, who sing and shout and work out new slapstick routines all day, worrying about nothing more vital than winning magazine contests and going to Hollywood; nobody has told them that there is a war on, conceivably because words like "atrocity" would be about three syllables too long for them. The production, like the play, is crude and chaotic: and it is somehow doubly depressing that nobody so far has risked saying so.

Elsewhere, plushy revivals are in vogue. M. Barrault is filling the vast barn of the Sarah-Bernhardt with *Madame Sans-Gêne,* Sardou's piece of Napoleonic tushery about the laundress who hob-nobbed with the great: lavish décor, lots of blue-chinned flunkeys in tie-wigs, and great fun for Madeleine Renaud; but a triviality all the same. The programme, as often with this troupe, is at least ten times as well written as the play. At the Athénée there is *La Mégère Apprivoisée,* a brisk adaptation of *The Taming of the Shrew:* Pierre Brasseur plays the tamer with ill-disguised impatience when others are speaking and with tyrannous complacency when they are not. At the T.N.P. we have Pirandello's

Henry IV. The keynote here is wintry monotony, set by Jean Vilar, who plays the lead in a voice like an amplified beehive, and relieved only by Jean Topart as his rival, a dapper and fascinating slug.

A public outcry has lately been caused by the revival of *La Reine de Césarée,* written seventeen years ago by Robert Brasillach, the notorious collaborationist and anti-Semite, who was executed immediately after the war. The play itself is negligible: a windy, tendentious bore about the abortive love affair between the Emperor Titus (Aryan) and the vanguished Bérénice (Jewish), which the author uses to advocate a vague sort of *apartheid,* urging even the nicer Jews to understand that, because of their unfortunate racial origins, their place is as far away as possible from solid Aryan citizens. The important thing is that, in spite of the riots that closed the piece after its first performance, it has since reopened and is playing to audiences of "paying guests," a euphemism for anyone who is not explicitly left-wing.

Yet Jean Genet's *Le Balcon,* which was announced for production at the Antoine, was cancelled at the first whisper of official disapproval: in which context it is worth remembering that, although there is no pre-production censorship in France, the police can shut any theatre where public performances may result in breaches of the peace. Nobody is willing to take that risk with M. Genet's play, and this is what provoked M. Sartre to a memorable burst of polemics in *L'Observateur*. He was, he said, in favour of theatrical liberty to express right-wing opinion, as long as there was similar liberty for the Left: and he concluded that in the French theatre that liberty no longer existed. It is hard, surveying the list of available plays, to disagree. There is a strike at the Comédie; there is also a lock-out on the part of the theatre owners of all dissident opinions, all controversy. I hope it is temporary, for otherwise one will be forced to conclude that this is the kind of theatre that a majority of the French people want.

(1958)

Phèdre, BY RACINE, AT THE THÉÂTRE NATIONAL POPULAIRE.

I am glad to announce that Jean Vilar and I have both overcome our resistance to Racine. M. Vilar, a Corneille man, has hitherto kept Racine off the stage of the T.N.P. But he has now changed his mind, and in so doing has shown me that the pompous monotony and narrow sensibility which have put me off former productions of the plays existed not so much in the text as in the actors.

Up to now I have always regarded *Phèdre* as a disappointing sequel to *A Midsummer Night's Dream.* M. Vilar has made me realise that it is in fact a high tragedy with a correspondingly high melting-point: that is to say, it remains cold and unyielding unless subjected to the fire of a great performance. At the T.N.P. it is plunged into a blast furnace. Making the stiff lines bend to her passion, forcing the frozen vowels to cry with her pain, Maria Casarès gave me at last a hint of what Rachel must have made of the part. Not once does she generalise; this is a particular woman devoured by a particular obsession; yet in the specific instance she implies, as the best acting always does, the general application. If you have ever looked within yourself and hated what you saw, you will respond to Mme. Casarès: at her best, she speaks for all of us at our worst.

Cocteau was right to cast her as Death in his film of *Orphée.* "Loosed out of hell to speak of horrors" is precisely how she comes before us, haggard with bewilderment and terror, her great eyes staring and her hands uncontrollably shaking with fright. I have never seen the imminence of suicide more powerfully conveyed. *"C'est Vénus toute entière à sa proie attachée":* with the line the actress became a vulture, and one felt the claws. The confession of love to her stepson was crowned by a single syllable: *"Donne,"* whereat she seized his sword in a frenzy of self-destruction that shocked the whole audience.

I do not know which to praise more, the stunned, stumbling walk that preceded her prayer to *"implacable Vénus"* or the helpless fervour, shamed beyond shame, with which it was delivered. *"Que fais-je? Où ma raison se va-t-elle égarer?"* told me more about the fear of madness than any Lear I have ever heard; and when the poison was swallowed and the queen quietly dead, one felt not only that a great storm had passed, but that a close friend had been horridly destroyed. It says much for Alain Cuny's resplendent Thésée that he held the stage for the remaining ten lines of the play without making anybody restive.

(1958)

The Chairs AND *The Lesson*, BY EUGÈNE IONESCO, AT THE ROYAL COURT.

The French theatre, about which I prophesied glumly some months ago, has now entered upon a state of emergency. An alarming article in the current issue of *Arts* reveals that during the first five months of this year the box-office receipts at Parisian theatres declined, compared with the same period last year, by nearly two fifths. The fact to be faced is brutal and simple: French audiences are drifting away from the theatre because they feel that the theatre is drifting away from them. They are frankly bored with it; and the immediate prospect reflects their boredom. Thirty-two theatres, an unprecedented number, will close this summer. Only twelve have elected to brave the drought, most of them peddling the theatrical equivalent of scented water-ices. *Cocktail Sexy* will hold the fort at the Capucines; at the Grand-Guignol, *L'École du Strip-tease*. At only one small theatre will you find, throughout the dog-days, the work of a French author of serious repute. Who is the man capable of inspiring such unique managerial confidence? Nobody but M. Ionesco, founder and headmaster of *l'école du strip-tease intellectuel, moral, et social*.

Faith in the drawing-power of this anarchic wag seems to be shared by the English Stage Company, who last week offered a double bill of *The Chairs* and *The Lesson*. Neither play is new to London. *The Chairs* is a Court revival, and the Arts Theatre taught us our lesson in 1955. The point of the programme is to demonstrate the versatility of Joan Plowright, who sheds seventy years during the interval, and to celebrate this nimble girl's return from Broadway, where she appeared in both plays under Tony Richardson's direction. Yet there was more in the applause than a mere welcome home. It had about it a blind, deafening intensity: one felt present at the consecration of a cult. Not, let me add, a Plowright cult—staggeringly though she played the crumbling hag in the first play, she simpered a little too knowingly as the crammer's prey in the second. No: this was an Ionesco cult, and in it I smell danger.

Ever since the Fry-Eliot "poetic revival" caved in on them, the ostriches of our theatrical intelligentsia have been seeking another faith. Anything would do as long as it shook off what are known as "the fetters of realism." Now the broad definition of a realistic play is that its characters and events have traceable roots in life. Gorki and Chekhov, Arthur Miller and Tennessee Williams, Brecht and O'Casey, Osborne and

Sartre have all written such plays. They express one man's view of the world in terms of people we can all recognize. Like all hard disciplines, realism can easily be corrupted. It can sink into sentimentality (N. C. Hunter), half-truth (Terence Rattigan), or mere photographic reproduction of the trivia of human behaviour. Even so, those who have mastered it have created the lasting body of twentieth-century drama: and I have been careful not to except Brecht, who employed stylised production techniques to set off essentially realistic characters.

That, for the ostriches, was what ruled him out of court. He was too real. Similarly, they preferred Beckett's *Fin de Partie,* in which the human element was minimal, to *Waiting for Godot,* which not only contained two tramps of mephitic reality but even seemed to regard them, as human beings, with love. Veiling their disapproval, the ostriches seized on Beckett's more blatant verbal caprices and called them "authentic images of a disintegrated society." But it was only when M. Ionesco arrived that they hailed a messiah. Here at last was a self-proclaimed advocate of *anti-théâtre:* explicitly anti-realist, and by implication anti-reality as well. Here was a writer ready to declare that words were meaningless and that all communication between human beings was impossible. The aged (as in *The Chairs*) are wrapped in an impenetrable cocoon of hallucinatory memories; they can speak intelligibly neither to each other nor to the world. The teacher in *The Lesson* can "get through" to his pupil only by means of sexual assault, followed by murder. Words, the magic innovation of our species, are dismissed as useless and fraudulent.

Ionesco's is a world of isolated robots conversing in cartoon-strip balloons of dialogue that are sometimes hilarious, sometimes evocative, and quite often neither, on which occasions they become profoundly tiresome. (As with shaggy-dog stories, few of M. Ionesco's plays survive a second hearing. I felt this particularly with *The Chairs.*) This world is not mine, but I recognise it to be a valid personal vision, presented with great imaginative aplomb and verbal audacity. The peril arises when it is held up for general emulation as the gateway to the theatre of the future, that bleak new world from which the humanist heresies of faith in logic and belief in man will for ever be banished.

M. Ionesco certainly offers an "escape from realism," but an escape into what? A blind alley, perhaps, adorned with *tachiste* murals. Or a self-imposed vacuum, wherein the author ominously bids us observe the absence of air. Or, best of all, a fun-fair ride on a ghost train, all skulls and hooting waxworks, from which we emerge into the far more intimidating clamour of diurnal reality. M. Ionesco's theatre is pungent and exciting, but it remains a diversion. It is not on the main road: and we do him no good, nor the drama at large, to pretend that it is.

(1958)

Postscript on Ionesco.

The position towards which M. Ionesco is moving is that which regards art as if it were something different from and independent of everything else in the world; as if it not only did not but *should* not correspond to anything outside the mind of the artist. The end of that line, of course, is Action Painting. M. Ionesco has not yet gone so far. He is stuck in an earlier groove, the groove of cubism, which has fascinated him so much that he has begun to confuse ends and means. The cubists employed distortion to make discoveries about the nature of objective reality. M. Ionesco, I fear, is on the brink of believing that his distortions are more valid and important than the external world it is their proper function to interpret. To adapt Johnson, I am not yet so lost in drama criticism as to forget that plays are the daughters of earth, and that things are the sons of heaven. But M. Ionesco is in danger of forgetting; of locking himself up in that hall of mirrors which in philosophy is known as solipsism.

Art is parasitic on life, just as criticism is parasitic on art. M. Ionesco and his followers are breaking the chain, applying the tourniquet, aspiring as writers to a condition of stasis. At their best, of course, they don't succeed; the alarming thing is that they try. As in physiology, note how quickly the brain starved of blood produces hallucinations and delusions of grandeur. "A work of art," says M. Ionesco, "is the source and the raw material of ideologies to come." O *hubris!* Art and ideology often interact on each other, but the plain fact is that both spring from a common source. Both draw on human experience to explain mankind to itself; both attempt, in very different ways, to assemble coherence from seemingly unrelated phenomena; both stand guard for us against chaos. They are brothers, not child and parent. To say, as M. Ionesco has said, that Freud was inspired by Sophocles is the direst nonsense. Freud merely found in Sophocles confirmation of a theory he had formed on the basis of empirical evidence. This does not make Sophocles a Freudian, or vice versa: it is simply a pleasing instance of fraternal corroboration.

You may wonder why M. Ionesco is so keen on this phantom notion of art as a world of its own, answerable to none but its own laws. Wonder no more: he is merely seeking to exempt himself from any kind of value-judgment. His aim is to blind us to the fact that we are all in some sense critics, who bring to the theatre not only those "nostalgias and anxieties" by which, as he rightly says, world history has largely been governed, but also a whole series of new ideas—moral, social, psychological, political—through which we hope some day to free ourselves from the rusty hegemony of *Angst*. These fond ideas, M. Ionesco, quickly assures us, do not belong in the theatre. Our job, as critics, is just to hear the play and "simply say whether it is true to its own nature." Not, you notice, whether it is true to ours, or even relevant; for we, as an audience, have forfeited our right to a hearing as conscious, sentient beings. "Clear evidence of cancer here, sir." "Very well, leave it alone: it's being true to its own nature."

Whether M. Ionesco admits it or not, every play worth serious consideration is a statement. It is a statement addressed in the first person singular to the first person plural; and the latter must retain the right of dissent. I am rebuked in the current issue of *Encounter* for having disagreed with the nihilistic philosophy expressed in Strindberg's *Dream Play*. "The important thing," says my interviewer, "seems to me to be not the rightness of Strindberg's belief, but rather how he has expressed it. . . ." Strindberg expressed it very vividly, but there are things more important than that. If a man tells me something I believe to be an untruth, am I forbidden to do more than congratulate him on the brilliance of his lying?

Cyril Connolly once said, once and wanly, that it was closing time in the gardens of the West; but I deny the rest of that suavely cadenced sentence, which asserts that "from now on an artist will be judged only by the resonance of his solitude or the quality of his despair." Not by me he won't. I shall, I hope, respond to the honesty of such testimonies, but I shall be looking for something more, something harder: for evidence of the artist who is not content with the passive role of a symptom, but concerns himself, from time to time, with such things as healing. M. Ionesco correctly says that no ideology has yet abolished fear, pain, or sadness. Nor has any work of art. But both are in the business of trying. What other business is there.?

(1958)

Summing-Up: 1959.

The office of André Malraux, Minister of State in Charge of Cultural Affairs in General de Gaulle's government, overlooks the courtyard of the Palais Royal and commands a splendid rear view of the Comédie-Française, which backs on to the other side of the great enclosed plaza. When escorting visitors on to his balcony, the Minister is apt to fling up one elbow in a mock-defensive gesture, as if he expected at any moment to be picked off by a sniper from the House of Molière. This jocular piece of mime, as few Parisians would need to be told, has its origin in the celebrated press conference of April 9, 1959, at which M. Malraux analyzed, briskly and tartly, the faults of the Comédie and announced his scheme for setting them right. A weak administration, he said, had allowed effective control of the company to pass into the hands of a clique of expert light comedians who had concentrated on farce while neglecting the French heritage of classical tragedy; during the six months that ended in February, the troupe had given a hundred and thirteen performances of Labiche and only six of Racine. As a sort of punishment for imbalance, for offending against the sacred principle of equilibrium, one of its two theatres was to be taken away from the company; the Salle Luxembourg, renamed the Théâtre de France, would be handed over to Jean-Louis Barrault in the fall, whereafter the Comédie would confine its Parisian activities to the Salle Richelieu. The present administrator was to be summarily replaced by Claude Bréart de Boisanger, a career diplomat with no theatrical experience. As if these bombshells were not enough for one spring morning, M. Malraux went on to explode several more. The current standard of productions at the Opéra and the Opéra-Comique reminded him, he said, of the Comédie-Française in the twenties, or even in the nineties; henceforth, the *théâtres lyriques* were to be united under the leadership of A.-M. Julien, the bustling founder of the Paris International Drama Festival. Two more prizes remained to be distributed. The Théâtre Récamier, a smart little Left Bank playhouse, was to be given to Jean Vilar, the director of the Théâtre National Populaire, as a showcase for apprentice playwrights, and Albert Camus was to have a theatre of his own, in which to produce spurned, forgotten, or undiscovered masterpieces. Finally, M. Malraux explained the purpose of his plan: he hoped to attract to the national theatres those members of the younger generation who had come to believe that live drama was dull, archaic, and no longer their concern.

The repercussions began at once, and are still noisily audible. The Comédie was up in arms; one of its former administrators, writing as temperately as he could, bade M. Malraux remember that, except in the epochs of great actresses such as Rachel and Bernhardt, tragedy had never been very popular with the company's audiences, while a talent for comedy, he added, did not strike him as undesirable in a theatre dedicated to the name of Molière. *L'Express* came out with a cartoon depicting a lachrymose M. Malraux addressing the spectators at the Salle Richelieu with the words *"Aux larmes, citoyens."* The accompanying article supported the plan as a whole, but was dubious about some of its implications. The author feared that state aid for *avant-garde* theatres (i.e., those of Camus and Vilar) might inhibit the true spirit of experiment and induce conformism and self-censorship. Moreover, since there was no evidence that the Ministry of Finance intended to increase its annual theatrical allotment, the Malraux proposals, with their exclusively Parisian emphasis, might constitute a setback for the provincial theatre. The five National Centres of Drama outside Paris were already in a shaky financial condition; needing more money, they might, under the new dispensation, get even less, and the best they could hope for was the continuation of an unsatisfactory *status quo*. These doubts were echoed and amplified by members of the theatrical Left, who declared that a cultural dictatorship was imminent; what M. Malraux wanted, they said, was a safe, centralized theatre that could be bribed into connivance with Gaullism. "André Malraux," one young writer said to me, adapting Cocteau's famous remark about Victor Hugo, "is a madman who thinks he's André Malraux." The most exciting productions in France, he went on, were being staged in Lyon at the Théâtre de la Cité de Villeurbanne, directed by Roger Planchon, an avowed disciple of Bertolt Brecht. "Malraux says he admires Planchon, but will he dare to subsidize him?" Meanwhile, the traditionalists are complaining that the new set-up bestows too many favours on people of Leftist sympathies, such as MM. Vilar, Camus, and Julien. Accused by the conservatives of being a revolutionary and by the Leftists of tendencies toward Fascism, M. Malraux thus finds himself between two fires. The situation is fascinating and in one respect unique: for the first time in history, official responsibility for a country's cultural health has been placed in the hands of an internationally respected man of letters. Can an artist work for a government without letting that government's policies colour his view of art? Are intellectuals capable of translating theory into action? The results of the Malraux plan will provide answers, partial but empirical, to questions like these.

Most people I met in Paris this summer agreed with the Minister on two points: that the Comédie-Française was ripe for reform, and that youth had lost interest in drama. Françoise Sagan was undoubtedly speaking for many of her contemporaries when she said to me, "I never go to the theatre. I don't know anyone who does." I almost apologized for having brought the subject up; the tone of her voice, decorously bored, made me feel as if I had confessed to some tedious minor eccentricity, like collecting bus tickets. For Mlle. Sagan and her coevals, the cinema is the only performing art that counts. Even so, the fact that Paris has around sixty stages on which live actors appear nightly suggests that the theatre is not exactly moribund. After two weeks of intense playgoing I had a long, informal conversation with M. Malraux, in order to match my impressions against his. Darkly dressed, compulsively blinking, and snorting with sinus, he talked readily and electrically. Here, grouped under various headings, is a contrapuntal account of what I saw and what he said:

(1) The Comédie-Française. I spent an evening at *Le Dindon,* one of Georges Feydeau's hotel-bedroom farces, which was directed by Jean Meyer and played with slippery glibness by a cast that included Robert Hirsch and the wonderfully effusive Jacques Charon. MM. Meyer, Hirsch, and Charon are founder-members of the cabal that M. Malraux holds responsible for the company's decadence. Accomplished though they are, one understands his objections. It is idiotic, as he said, to devote 600,000,000 francs ($1,200,000) a year to bolstering the reputations of Feydeau and Labiche. I also saw a revival of François Mauriac's *Les Mal-Aimés,* a sombre closet drama about a rich alcoholic who, deserted by his wife, employs emotional blackmail to force his elder daughter into staying with him and giving up the man she loves to her younger sister; the point of the play is to show the terrible skill with which people who cannot command love revenge themselves on people who can. I thought the production admirable, in a slightly musty way, but I can't say I relished the round of applause that greeted the father's description of French politics as a squalid zoo badly in need of an animal trainer—*"Tant qu'en France il n'y aura pas de dompteur, je me désintéresserai de la ménagerie."*

Mauriac's plays are among the few in the French repertoire that occupy the middle ground between stylized tragedy and stylized comedy (or satire); in other words, they belong in the realistic tradition, which, despite its success in Russia, Scandinavia, Germany, Britain, and the United States, never really took root in the French theatre. I asked M. Malraux why this was so. He replied that Corneille and Racine had created, in the seventeenth century, a form of drama that resembled, in the dignity of its proportions and the magnitude of its moral architecture, a palace, and that this image had dominated the French theatre ever since. What appalled Voltaire about Shakespeare was, *au fond,* that he made no attempt to be "palatial" in the manner of Racine. Whenever the French wrote plays, said M. Malraux, they were trying—often without knowing it—to "rediscover the palace." Even comedy was regarded as a palace annex. He added that this theory would have to be modified a little to fit Claudel, whom he considers a modern giant. (As he put it, Claudel may be a cathedral, but he certainly isn't a palace.) I suggested that this aversion to realism applied to actors as well as to playwrights; one seldom saw a good French performance of Chekhov or Ibsen. M. Malraux agreed, but he thought that this was a Latin, rather than a peculiarly French, characteristic. Latin civilizations were made up of people who behaved as if they were permanently on stage. Their idea of a great man was *"une conception de parade,"* involving large gestures and romantic display, and they felt the same way about great acting. It would have been impossible, he said, for Bernhardt to play a Chekhov heroine, because her conception, not so much of the role as of the whole purpose of acting, would have been alien and inappropriate.

Since realistic drama presented such problems, and since he had already committed himself on the subject of farce, I wondered what plays, apart from the French classics, M. Malraux would like to see in the programme of the Comédie. Neatly side-stepping, he said that the choice of plays was not his business but that of the new administration. He himself was not especially enamoured of Racine; he merely hoped that more use might be made of tragediennes like Annie Ducaux and Marie Bell. It did not matter enormously that neither of these actresses was a Rachel, because nowadays the appeal of tragedy depended not on star performers but on star productions, as Jean Vilar had shown at the T.N.P. The grand objective, M. Malraux repeated, was to bring young people into the national theatre, and he would go to any lengths to achieve it. Public funds would be used to make good seats cheaply available to youth; efforts were being made to sign up Maurice Chevalier for a season of Molière; and whenever the home company was away on tour, its place would be taken by visiting troupes from the provincial centres. At worst, I decided, the Malraux plan could do no harm to the Comédie-Française, and at best it could do a vast amount of good.

(2) The Compagnie Renaud-Barrault, which will open at the Salle Luxembourg in October, operating on an annual subsidy of 130,000,-000 francs, to be deducted from the former Comédie-Française allow-

ance of 600,000,000. M. Barrault, who left the Comédie after the war to form the company he now co-directs with his wife, Madeleine Renaud, has in recent years shown a weakness for whimsy that cannot wholly be blamed on the necessity of pleasing the fashionable bourgeois audience. An actor whose charm is as boundless as his emotional range is limited, he has too often played parts—such as Alceste in *Le Misanthrope*—for which he patently lacks the guns, while the talents of his wife, a twinkling adept in all the caprices and condescensions of high comedy, have been seen in too many nearly identical roles. All the same, M. Barrault's directorial energy is immense, and he has a rare cementing power that has enabled him, over more than a decade, to command the allegiance of such gifted players as Simone Valère, Jean Desailly, and Pierre Bertin. Last season, at the Palais Royal, he revived Offenbach's *La Vie Parisienne* with such verve and aplomb that it has filled the theatre ever since; the whole company sang and danced as buoyantly as it spoke, and free rein was given to the antic genius of Jean Parédès, a fleshy, fish-eyed droll, debonair as a sea-lion, who played three parts under as many wigs and convinced me, not for the first time, that he was the funniest actor in France. I am certain, however, that what endeared M. Barrault to M. Malraux was not *La Vie Parisienne* but his production, at the same theatre, of Claudel's *Le Soulier de Satin.* When M. Barrault moves into the Salle Luxembourg, his inaugural task will be the staging of *Tête d'Or,* an early Claudel play that has never been publicly performed. This will be followed by Jean Anouilh's *La Petite Molière,* which was tried out by the Barrault company at the Bordeaux Music Festival at the beginning of June.

The latter piece has a bizarre history. Some years ago M. Anouilh wrote a film script about the life of Molière; the front office rejected it, whereupon he sent it to M. Barrault, wondering whether it might somehow be revamped into a play. He got a startling reply: M. Barrault declared himself perfectly willing to stage it unchanged—long shots, close-ups, and all. And that, more or less, is what he did in Bordeaux. The text is trite and fact-bound: Molière the artist is weaned away from tragedy to comedy while Molière the man moves from happiness to misery, deserting his mistress to marry her convent-trained sister, who promptly and casually cuckolds him. I liked the moment when Molière, played by Barrault, sonorously remarks that *"L'homme est un animal inconsolable et gai,"* and, when asked who said that, retorts that, of course, he did—the joke being that the phrase was coined by the hero of *L'Hurluberlu,* M. Anouilh's latest Paris success. But most of the evening's pleasure comes from the stagecraft. No sooner has a group of live actors left an inn than a gilded frame drops into sight, behind which we see a miniature facsimile of the inn's exterior and the surrounding landscape; tiny puppets trot out of the door and drive off in a tiny coach. This is the long shot. Immediately afterward another picture frame slides down and we get the close-up—three actors sitting and jogging in the back seat while a painted avenue of trees recedes behind them. It is all very clever, and all very superficial. At dinner a few nights later I badgered M. Barrault about his obsession with stylized trickery. He smiled, like an artful urchin caught sticky-fingered in the act of filching candy, and then got down to definitions. There were, he said, three possible ways of staging a play, of which two were valid. "To explain how the three differ," he went on, "let us take a chair." Realism, which was good, meant a real chair in a real setting. Stylization, which was bad, meant a deformed chair in a deformed setting. Transposed realism, which was better than either, meant a real chair in an unreal setting. He implied that Stanislavsky and Brecht, whom one associates, respectively, with the first and last categories, had it over the Surrealists and Expressionists, who are sandwiched together in the second. As a theory, this is unexceptionable; all that remains is for M. Barrault to put it into practice. I felt a passing twinge of alarm, however, when he told me that his third production at the Salle Luxembourg would be *Le Rhinocéros,* by Eugène Ionesco, the king of the Surrealist conjurors.

(3) The Théâtre National Populaire. Jean Vilar has done some tremendous things at the Palais de Chaillot—I think of Germaine Montero in *Mother Courage* and Maria Casarès as Phèdre—but that colossal auditorium, with its wasteland of a stage, is a great destroyer of subtlety, and the company has long needed a second, smaller home in which to try its hand at intimacy and close quarters. The Théâtre Récamier, M. Malraux's gift, looks like an ideal choice.

I have just mentioned M. Ionesco, and this may be the place to say something about his *Tueur sans Gages,* which was the last independent production to be presented at the Récamier. Apart from *Le Rhinocéros,* as yet unseen, this is the only full-length play M. Ionesco has written, and it confirmed my opinion of him as a brilliant, anarchic sprinter unfitted by temperament for the steady, provident mountaineering of the three-act form. The first two hours are a tiresome blur. An architect, symbolizing bureaucracy, escorts the hero, a Chaplinesque innocent, around a Utopian city whose peace has been shattered by a series of unexplained murders. Determined to solve them, the innocent is frustrated, Kafka-fashion, by the police, who care about nothing but traffic control, and by politics, in the person of a raging harridan who, quoting Orwell without acknowledgement, bawls that under her regime war will be called peace, tyranny liberty, and misery happiness. The play comes to life only in the last half-hour, during which, ironically, it also comes to death. The killer appears, squat-nosed, slack-lipped, cretinous, clad in jeans and swaying gently back and forth on the soles of his shoes. The hero begs him to give up killing, to which he makes no reply beyond a quiet, detached, commiserating snicker. And as the scene progresses, we realize that this is no murderer but death himself, the unslaked and unbribable principle of mortality. Jean Saudray played the part, and I saw no better performance in Paris.

(4) Albert Camus. Many European theatres are named after famous playwrights, and many fine companies have had resident dramatists, as the Moscow Art Theatre had Chekhov and the Compagnie Louis Jouvet had Giraudoux, but for a government to engage a celebrated author to direct his own playhouse is something unknown since Molière. The nearest modern analogy, I suppose, would be Bertolt Brecht's Berliner-Ensemble, and even there the parallel is not precise, because the titular head of the troupe was not Brecht himself but his wife, Helene Weigel, who has continued to run it since his death. For all pertinent purposes, M. Camus will be working without precedents. Whatever happens, I feel pretty sure that the emphasis will be on words and ideas rather than on *mise en scène*. I base this prediction on the adaptation of Dostoevsky's *The Possessed* that M. Camus wrote and directed in Paris last season. Considering the length and complexity of the novel, I thought it a surprisingly successful job; I don't know when I last saw on the stage such an elaborate study of the motives that impel non-proletarians to become revolutionaries, or of the ways in which such motives, if imperfectly comprehended, may lead to actions that are inhuman, self-destructive, or both. On the one hand we have Pierre, the plotter and fanatic, who is quite unaware that his reasons for executing the student Shatov are founded on personal resentment and not, as he imagines, on revolutionary zeal. This very lack of self-knowledge is what makes Pierre indestructible; he survives through ignorance. Stavrogin, on the other hand, whom Pierre worships, achieves a sort of self-knowledge and commits suicide, realizing that the savage, nihilistic behavior for which he is notorious arises out of an expiatory need to be regarded as an unpardonable monster—a need that, in turn, springs from a moment in his past when he felt himself responsible for the death of a twelve-year-old girl. Stavrogin, in fact, is the literary progenitor of Arthur Koestler's hero in *Arrival and Departure,* who discovered that he was doing the right revolutionary things for the wrong psychological reasons. There is

a lot to carp at in M. Camus' dramatization. Although it goes on for nearly four hours, many of the domestic and romantic relationships are left scamped or nebulous, and the end is a concertina of catastrophe, with the deaths of Shatov, Pierre's father, and Stavrogin following on each other's heels like melodramatic clockwork. The best performance was that of Michel Bouquet as Pierre—pallid and gimlet-eyed, his hair like a combed mop that had been dyed jet black, and shuffling around the stage on tiptoe, as if fearful of making full pedal contact with the earth. My high opinion of M. Bouquet may be partly due to the fact that he had the most self-absorbed role; impregnable egotism is the quality that French actors play most easily. (If you doubt this, go to a comedy in Paris. You will find the leading performers so enchanted by their own voices that they will cut short their own laughs rather than allow the audience to usurp the floor; they regard laughter as a form of heckling.) After seeing *The Possessed* I decided that M. Camus had attempted the impossible with a great deal of literary skill; that he was an uneven director of actors; and that he had a lot to learn about lighting and stage illusion. My mind looks forward to his new venture rather more eagerly than my eyes and ears.

As far as it goes, therefore—and I needn't add that it goes infinitely further than any British or American scheme for helping the theatre has ever gone—the Malraux plan seems to me provocative and invigorating. I wish, however, that it had found room for the Théâtre de la Cité de Villeurbanne, directed by Roger Planchon, whose remarkable productions of both parts of Shakespeare's *Henry IV* I attended at the Théâtre Montparnasse-Gaston Baty. Like Brecht, his mentor, M. Planchon sees drama as a public statement of something useful, and believes in the beauty of useful things. Also like Brecht, he is quite prepared to take a text and slash, paraphrase, and reshuffle it to make a contemporary impact. He did this with the two Henrys. No translator was named in the programme, but the plays were boiled down to the bare social bones; each point was made, coolly and pungently, on a rostrum backed by a map of medieval England, and each scene was prefaced by a caption, projected on to a screen, that summed up the import of what we were about to see. Individual characterization was subjected to the larger image of declining feudalism. The result was not Shakespeare; it was abundance reduced to relevance, riches cut down to a living wage, a jungle turned into a cartographical survey. The audience was held not so much by what was happening to the characters as by what was happening to the whole society. I admired what I saw, and understood why Arthur Adamov, the leading Socialist in the theatrical *avant-garde,* thinks M. Planchon the best director in France. He is not alone in his opinion. Soon after I left Paris, M. Planchon presented Marivaux's *La Seconde Surprise de l'Amour* in a production that was described by the critic of *Arts,* an ostentatiously neutral weekly, as a revelation. Henceforth, it would be impossible, said the review, to stage Marivaux without reference to M. Planchon's *mise en scène,* which was, apparently, bold enough to suggest that the servants in the play led lives as vivid and vital as those of their masters and mistresses.

Meanwhile, the commercial theatre is tenuously prosperous, most of the right-bank houses being occupied by comedies with titles like *Déshabillez-vous, Madame.* Sterner stuff runs up against the problem of apathy. Tennessee Williams' *Orpheus Descending* was playing, when I saw it, to dwindling audiences, despite the faunlike magnetism of Jean Babilée as the martyred hero, the cluttered eloquence of Lila de Nobili's set, and the detailed control of Raymond Rouleau's direction. (Apart from MM. Rouleau, Barrault, Planchon, Vilar, and André Barsacq, few French directors pay much attention to detail.) The Swedish Lars Schmidt, who produced *Orpheus Descending,* has lately become the most active Parisian backer of American plays; in the past two seasons *Cat on a Hot Tin Roof, The Diary of Anne Frank, Twelve Angry Men,* and *Two for the Seesaw* have opened under his patronage. He is a soft, anxious, harassed man. Production costs, he says, are as high in Paris as in London; *Orpheus* ran up a bill of ten million francs before the curtain rose. On top of that, the Société des Auteurs insists that managements stage at least as many native plays as foreign ones, and the opportunities created by the Malraux plan will make it even more difficult to get hold of new manuscripts. Even so, I am not madly worried about Mr. Schmidt's solvency. Against rising costs, for instance, one must set the fact that theatre rents in Paris amount to no more than fifteen per cent of the box-office take, whereas in London the figure is forty per cent.

The two great popular hits of the last Paris season were Félicien Marceau's *La Bonne Soupe* and M. Anouilh's *L'Hurluberlu; ou Le Réactionnaire Amoureux.* I can't say I was bowled over by either of them. The latter, a windy and posturing work, sets out to be a sort of moralizing farce, which involves the author in a certain amount of unfairness, as when the *jeune premier,* having behaved toward a young woman as cynically as farce tradition demands, is treated to a serious lecture on the vileness of cynicism. The whole play is ambiguous; we are never sure whether we are listening to Anouilh the boulevard Thersites or Anouilh the right-bank conformist. His hero is a retired general who has resigned from the Army in disgust and settled in the country, where he plots ineffectively against the established order. His grandiose plans for governing the nation are contrasted with his incompetence at running his own family—his daughter is seduced and abandoned by a young idler who reads radical papers, and he suspects his wife of having taken a lover. Throughout the play M. Anouilh uses the general as his mouthpiece to attack those aspects of modern life that affluent French theatregoers find most distasteful. On one occasion the hero inquires, at thunderous length, why the opinion of a million imbeciles should be regarded as sacred; this anti-democratic tirade brought the house down, and I felt I must have been one of the few people present who questioned the infallibility of retired generals when it comes to deciding who is an imbecile and who is not. Again (and again and again), M. Anouilh's spokesman asserts that France must regain her sense of honour. Life must be made harder; there must be obedient effort and respect for authority, with no more nonsense about social security. It is true that in the second half many of the general's ideals are shown to be unworkable, but there is no doubt that M. Anouilh wants us to sympathize with them, just as he wants us to detest the oafish milkman who dashes in from time to time, bawling about the rights of the workers. I thought, as I watched the play, of Cyril Connolly's remark about right-wing satire—that it was doomed to ultimate peevishness because it was directed at a moving staircase from a stationary one. There are odd flashes of the earlier, better Anouilh, especially when the subject is marriage. The production was notable for the kind of décor, not uncommon in Paris, that confuses slapdash fragility with visual poetry, and for a lot of effective, loudmouthed acting.

In *La Bonne Soupe,* as in *L'Oeuf,* his great success of the season before last, M. Marceau tells the story of an obscure member of society who beats the system at its own game and comes out on top. Also as in *L'Oeuf,* the action is composed of a multitude of short scenes narrated in the first person by the central character. In this case the protagonist is a shopgirl from Carcassonne who runs away to Paris with a married man and ends up, after a number of ticklish reverses, as a highly prosperous *grande cocotte*. The heroine, rampageously played by Marie Bell, tells her tale to a croupier at a casino; she is on stage throughout, commenting on the action. Nicole Courcel appears as her younger self, a provincial *ingénue* slowly donning the armour of urban cynicism. The play is not without virtues; I remember a speech that superbly conveyed the atmosphere of a prostitutes' hotel, which reminds Mlle. Courcel, in its silence, its secrecy, its perpetual twilight, and the lethargic motion of its inhabitants, of a film she once saw about the bottom of the sea. And I think of a moment in the last act when the narrator announces that it is time for her to replace Mlle. Courcel. Rising from the roulette table, Mme. Bell interrupts the scene and tells the girl to withdraw, which she does, slowly and calmly, moving backward as she waves farewell. *"Adieu, ma jeunesse,"* murmurs Mme. Bell, and briskly, drying her tears, takes over. There are several scenes as affecting as this; unfortunately, there are many more that are crude and naïve, so that the play's pseudo-sophistication appears as *voulu* and false as magenta lipstick on a ten-year-old schoolgirl. I must add that André Barsacq's staging is impeccably speedy and does everything possible to give the piece the raffish poetry it aims at and misses.

If I had to choose the best French play of the year, I would probably go for *Tchin-Tchin,* by a young writer named François Billetdoux, which I saw at a pocket theatre in Montparnasse. From the title and the locale, you might forgivably imagine it to be an experimental work of the kind that one associates with M. Ionesco and Samuel Beckett. In fact, it is a simple tragicomedy, composed in a style that can only, if drably, be described as poetic realism. The two main characters are a guarded young-middle-aged Englishwoman called Mrs. Puffy-Picq, whose husband has just left her, and Cesareo, a rueful Italian whose wife has just run off with Mr. Puffy-Picq. The Italian pays a nervous visit to the Englishwoman. Tentatively, they drink. They drink a lot; hence the title. Gradually, hopelessly, they try to complete the classic pattern by falling in love themselves. It doesn't work; they mistrust each other too much, and, anyway, the equation doesn't balance. Yet by the end of the play they have achieved, after a series of violent ups and downs, something that approaches consolation. Neither of them will now collapse or commit suicide, though it is likely that both will go on drinking quite heavily. They remain, to the end, essentially comic characters, and that is what makes them moving; they will survive without sentimentality, suspecting that they may be fairly silly and not caring very much if they are. The curtain falls on a note of true, hard-earned optimism, which I prefer to the facile pessimism of so much left-bank writing. The leading roles are beautifully played by Katharina Renn, as the bereft wife, and by the author, as the bereft husband. M. Billetdoux is in his early thirties and has plenty of time to lure the younger French playwrights out of the blind alley into which Messrs. Beckett and Ionesco have beguiled them. To assert that all communication between human beings is impossible is rather like putting on a strait jacket and then complaining about the impossibility of shaking hands. If I understand him rightly, M. Billetdoux is saying that communication is desperate and rare, always difficult and seldom total; but possible, with whatever qualifications; possible, all the same.

(1959)

IV: THE RUSSIAN THEATRE

Theatre in Moscow.

Last November, having signed a customs form vouching that my baggage contained no antelope horns, Manchurian deer, hashish, "negatives or clichés," I entered Russia via Leningrad. A company of British actors, directed by Peter Brook, had been invited by the Ministry of Culture to perform *Hamlet* in Moscow. For the first time since the October Revolution, English was to be spoken on a Russian stage; and I took advantage of the cultural thaw to ride in on the actors' wake and take a firsthand look at the Moscow theatre.

The city itself had first to be digested. Its very layout is dramatic, monumentally gaunt and gaping, like a convention of huge warehouses held on an open plain. The new university soars upward like Rockefeller Centre in New York, though the Russians do not thank you for making the comparison; and by night the city suggests America, fantastically stripped of bars and grills and ads. How comforting, in memory, is neon lighting, symbol of salesmanship and hence of ingratiation! By day the great impersonal squares unfold: there must be half a dozen open places in the centre of Moscow where the battle of Waterloo could be fought without breaking a single window. For colour one looks at the domes and minarets of St. Basil's Cathedral, which is Brighton Pavilion in war paint and, as far as I could see, the only thing in Moscow that wears make-up. The squares surge with wind-bruised, shiny-cheeked people conversing in condensed steam. There are thousands of Chinese faces, many of them belonging to Chinese. Wandering unescorted, you rapidly get lost, for maps and 'phone books are as closely guarded as the two embalmed dynasts in the bakelite mausoleum on Red Square. In Moscow, as in most other great cities, the best landmarks are the theatres.

Seven of these are occupied by music hall, puppetry, opera, operetta, and ballet; the rest—twenty-one in number—are legitimate theatres, including three entirely devoted to plays for children. The same principles of organization apply to all of them. Every theatre has a permanent company of between eighty and a hundred and fifty actors, recruited in most cases from an affiliated drama school; and a repertoire of some twenty plays, so alternated that the same piece is never performed for more than two consecutive nights. This means that in any given week the visitor has a choice of about a hundred and fifty different shows. The thought of playing the same part night after night fills Russian actors with horror and incredulity; the idea of a "long run" exists only in the theatres of London, Paris, and New York, and can scarcely be expressed in the Russian language.

And here let me pause to shatter a popular fallacy. With two exceptions, the Moscow theatre is not supported by government money. State subsidies were withdrawn in 1948 from every playhouse except the Bolshoi (meaning "big") and the Maly (meaning "little"). These are the two repositories of theatrical tradition. The Bolshoi is the home of opera and ballet, a gaudy pleasure dome where no fantasy goes unindulged; before your eyes the river Neva bursts its banks and a whole palace, staircase and all, subsides in flames. Nowhere on earth is the art of theatrical magic more extravagantly practised. The Maly, founded in 1824, is the oldest straight theatre in Moscow, and is known as the "House of Ostrovsky" in much the same way as the Comédie-Française is known as the House of Molière. All the other theatres are autonomous and self-supporting. This seems unbelievable, in view of the splendour of the productions and the size of the companies, until you remember that they pay no theatre rent or entertainment tax, and that it is a rare season when average attendances drop below ninety-five per cent of capacity.

The British *Hamlet,* a middling specimen of West End Shakespeare, had its *première* at the second house of the Moscow Art Theatre; or, to give it its full title, the Affiliated House of the Moscow Academic Art Theatre in the Name of Gorky. The audience reactions were immensely revealing. Accustomed to constant changes of scenery, they were baffled when the curtain rose again and again on the same gray permanent setting. Nor, in a theatre where doubling is unknown, could they comprehend why so many members of the cast were playing more than one part apiece. During the interval one critic expressed his delight at the subtle stroke of interpretation whereby the same actor played the Player Queen and the Second Gravedigger, and I had not the heart to tell him that the reason for this was not theatrical invention but economic necessity. Some of the older Russian actors were shocked at the speed with which the verse was spoken. "Cinema technique!" moaned one. "Is

Shakespeare not allowed to draw breath in Britain?" The admiring comments made by many people on the relative cheapness of the production must, I imagine, have fallen rather brutally on the ears of the producer, Hugh Beaumont, for it was one of the most costly shows he had ever backed. Physically, the acting looked wooden and inexpressive beside the rich mobility of Russian players; but if the audience thought so, it kept its counsel, and the applause at the end was long and stormy.

Russian directors have of course made *Hamlet* very much their own property. To Akimov in 1932 he was a revolutionary who staged a fake ghost in order to overthrow the tyrant Claudius; and in the spring of 1955 Nikolai Okhlopkov, with a cast of a hundred and eighty and a full orchestra booming Tchaikowsky, directed a Hamlet who represented Renaissance Man casting off the fetters of the Middle Ages. Paul Scofield's British Hamlet, by contrast, represented only Paul Scofield, which struck some Russian theorists as a trifle meagre. The director of the Maly Theatre, however, called it "a three-octave performance," and *Pravda* congratulated the actor on seeing Hamlet as a positive, dynamic hero rather than as a pessimistic weakling. At the British Embassy reception after the first night much else emerged, and I was able to piece together a picture of the Russian attitude toward drama as a whole.

To begin with, our notion of an opening night as a nerve-racked occasion on which everything depends is quite inexplicable to a Russian. In Moscow plays are rehearsed for many months with at least two separate casts; and the critics are expected to see the new production several times before reviewing it, which gives them time to ponder the relative contributions of author, actors, and director. Bad notices never mean unemployment; if the new show fails to draw, it is dropped, and that is that; the repertoire rolls on unhindered. I made the childish errror of asking an actor to name the star of his company, and my interpreter gently signified to me that the concept of a "star" was something his language was incapable of rendering. Outside Russian theatres the names of the plays are billed, but never the names of the actors. Against each important character the programme usually lists two or three names, with a penciled tick beside the one who will be playing it at that particular performance.

Maturity and consistent excellence are rewarded with the title of Honoured Artist of the Soviet Union, which is as close as Russia gets to the idea of a "star." Even so, you will see Honoured Artists playing Lear on Tuesday and a three-line bit part on Wednesday. The great drawing card in Moscow is not the actor but the theatre he works for.

Above all, the Embassy reception showed me that the great gulf of sensibility which in London makes it almost impossible for an actor to converse intelligibly with a politician simply did not exist in Moscow. In Russia man is assumed to be a political animal, and the theatre to be a limb of the body politic; and the politician who cannot talk theatre is regarded as culpably myopic.

Yet much less of the theatre than I had expected is politically slanted. The classics are no longer twisted to make debating points; Shaw, Wilde, and Dickens are played with absolute fidelity to the letter and spirit of the text. And nothing could be falser than the Western idea that the Russians treat Chekhov as a satirical farce: he is handled with the solemn respect due to a classic. Propaganda in the Moscow theatre (which is about one tenth of it) seeks primarily to stimulate enthusiasm for hard work. One of our most popular philosophers once remarked regretfully: "Man is the only animal that works"; in Moscow it would be said triumphantly. Life in the town is Spartan, as befits the training camp of a heavyweight contender; and the basic tenet of all propaganda is that life imitates art. You work because art shows you the pleasures of work, and this is even true of the Children's Theatres, where dashing new plays urge the young to leave home and build community centres in Siberia.

But for some Russian tastes the theatre has grown too hortatory of late. People have been complaining that art ought to imitate life a little more. In the past year, and for the first time since the Revolution, some theatres have been reporting empty seats; and too many bad playwrights, it has been hinted, are getting preferential treatment purely because they toe the party line. In November Mr. Mikhailov, the Minister of Culture, called a public meeting to find out what had gone wrong. One speaker recalled the great days when squads of police had to be summoned to control the queues outside the Art Theatre. Now, he added bitterly, you could sometimes get seats by walking in on the day of perfromance. The case for more imitation of life was strongly pressed, especially by a woman called Engineer Ginsburg, who said: "We want to see ordinary people on the stage. The villains now are too black, and the heroes are like the dishes in a dietetic restaurant—no salt, no pepper, nothing with a tang to it." Another speaker reminded the audience that plays critical of the régime were now approved, such as the one in which a commissar's daughter forms a decadent yearning for jeans, jazz, and pony-tail hairdos; but the consensus was that the revolutionary theatre needed more realistic fuel. In a speech a few days later Mr. Mikhailov roundly condemned those theatre directors and playwrights who had failed to come through with their quota of new plays, and exhorted them to go out and look at life in the raw.

At present the revolutionary theatre of experiment has almost ceased to exist, except at the little Satirical Theatre. Vakhtangov, Meyerhold, and Tairov are dead; Okhlopkov directs very seldom; and the only active survivor of the pre-war group is the sixty-four-year-old Alexei Popov, who has been in charge of the Red Army Theatre since 1936. The great Russian theatres today are homes of the solid bourgeois virtues, performing nineteenth-century plays in surroundings of weighty scenic opulence; the Maly, for instance, and the Moscow Art. The joy of seeing master craftsmen working in unison, with the humane poetry and not just the neurotic trimmings of naturalism is something I had never known until I saw these perdurable players. This is Stanislavsky without Freud, physiological acting without the psychiatric glosses beloved of so many American "Method" actors; it has subtlety and absolute inevitability, plus what Stark Young once described as "a magnificent dignity and grave, warm beauty like nature's." To say that youth is not at the helm of the Russian theatre is an understatement: it is lucky if it is allowed to scrub the decks. The power and the glory of Soviet theatre resides in its older actors, who are by far the finest I have ever seen.

With age they do not wither or grow frail, as our actors often do. They expand in mind and muscle, a formidable parade of which every member resembles Blake's Ancient of Days. There is a simple reason for this continuity of development: economic security. Once an actor has been accepted by a company and proved himself in it, he has no financial worries. Variation of repertoire keeps him from going stale or gaga; he is seldom asked to act more than four times a week, and when he retires the state steps in with a liberal pension. Compare the plight of the old actor in England, ashamed of his age and doubtful whether he can learn his lines in three weeks' rehearsal.

In Moscow age is a badge of merit, and there is time for certainty and for perfection. To see an Ostrovsky play at the Maly is like spending a week-end with old friends. Onto the stage the giants trundle, hawk-eyed spectacular dowagers like Turchaninova, ancient intriguers like Vladislavsky, all playing with a selfless economy and precision that recalls a group of champions at a chess tournament. It is the same at the Moscow Art Theatre; ripe in years, robust as oaks, beaming in their beards and their supreme authority, the masters play together as Stanislavsky taught them and as they can still teach the world. Tonight Konsky, sardonic and lantern-jawed, will delight you in *An Ideal*

Husband. The next night, in Tolstoy, it is Gribov, as a jaundiced, fish-eyed *moujik,* who sets you cheering; a day later Zhiltsov, with his effortless barrel-chested thunder, will transfix you, or Tarassova, who weeps as readily as most British actresses simper.

Finally, in Gorki's *The Lower Depths* a dozen new faces will be thrust before you, faces from a Bosch crucifixion, crapulous faces, swollen and condemned. Every step that is taken has beneath it, you feel, a tradition of immortal rock; the characters' roots are sunk deep into the stage. These players tend to sit heavily (I saw a chair break under one of them at the Maly: he instantly turned the mishap to theatrical advantage). They fan themselves, gesture with their eyebrows and fingertips, and never lose the thread of the tapestry they are weaving. Theirs is the greatness that can come only to actors who do not need to worry about how great they are. The surfaces of life, audible and visible, are flawlessly captured: every moment a sudden, eccentric, but obviously *right* gesture catches your eye, yet each fragment fits smoothly into the general mosaic.

If their actors are older than ours, their audiences are younger. Nevertheless, the system has its drawbacks. The old actors tend to cling to the roles of their youth, and surrender them to younger players only under considerable pressure. Mr. Mikhailov made this point when he said in a recent speech that the dearth of new Russian plays was partly due to the necessity of writing parts for middle-aged actors. Yet there are other reasons for the thinness of contemporary Soviet drama. One is the cultural iron curtain.

The only American playwrights known in Russia are Howard Fast, Lillian Hellman, and Arthur Miller. The only French author performed is Jean-Paul Sartre. His *Edmund Kean* is already in rehearsal, and *The Respectful Prostitute* was a sensation last winter because it portrayed a tart with something approaching realism. In Paris the play was a virulent one-act squib lasting just over an hour; in Moscow it lasts over three hours, has six settings, and ends with a heroic tableau in which the tart and the Negro, hand in hand, look forward into a new dawn of enlightenment. This was greeted with cheers. My interpreter said, and I agreed with him, that all culture needed a strain of naïveté to survive; but the whole point of the original play was its sophisticated irony. This had been banished at the author's suggestion. It was ruin by consent.

The real reason for the lack of new plays lies in the basis of Communism as a whole. By definition, the U.S.S.R. has abolished nostalgia. Nobody looks back on the past with regret, which means that there can be no more playwrights like Turgenev and Chekhov, who half-loathed the old way of life yet were half-committed to it. That delicate tension has gone. At the same time the Western sense of humour strikes Russians as gloomy or macabre. I showed a few old *New Yorkers* to a Russian actor, and his comment was that things in the west couldn't be as bad as that. To him the cartoons were either unintelligible (jokes about advertising, sugar daddies, and commercial TV) or unimaginably cynical. Thurber's humour of quiet desperation only made him sigh with compassion; he could not see why we laughed at anything so close to despair. The comedy of surrealism has no meaning in Moscow. Revolutionary comedy is always moral, which is to say that it is never pure comedy but always satire.

The most imaginative production I saw was of a satire, Mayakovsky's *Klop* (*The Bedbug*), written in 1929. Yutkevich has restaged it at the Satirical Theatre with an ebullient technique compounded of vaudeville, revue, and cartoon film. Its hero is a backsliding worker who reverts to bourgeois habits once the first stage of the revolution is completed and he has money to spend—not, of course, to multiply, for in Russia you cannot make money breed. Deserting his proletarian sweetheart, he marries into a family of social climbers, from whom he learns vulgarity, the inevitable by-product of class distinctions. The willing oaf is taught to overdress ("But don't wear two ties at once, especially of different colours!") and to dance the tango with his little finger crooked. To symbolize its loyalty to the revolution, the family holds a winter wedding party dressed and lit entirely in shades of red. This develops into a nightmare orgy, rather like a parody of *The Boy Friend* held in a brothel. With the rout at its height, fire breaks out, and the guests perish in a scabrous cartoon sequence, brilliantly filmed; we see their wigs and eyelashes going up in flames and their cosmetic-laden faces melting down like wax dummies. Only the hero survives, frozen in a block of ice as the firemen's hoses play on him. Fifty years later he is discovered and defrosted by a world which, now having reached the final stage of Communism, regards him as an alien monster or zoological specimen. His vodka-tainted breath prostrates all who approach him, and six electric fans whirr to keep the air pure. If he touches a dog, it is at once infected with the plague of servility and will do nothing thereafter but sit up and beg. In consequence he is placed in a zoo, where his atavistic habits of smoking, gambling, drinking, and singing sentimental songs are watched rather as we in London watch the chimpanzees' tea party.

The comedian playing the "bedbug" was a fine low comic rather like Bert Lahr, and I relished the production until the hero's jilted fiancée, now an old woman, said: "And to think I nearly killed myself for filth like that!" Compassion, I suddenly realized, was banished, even for this misguided moon-calf. *Saeva indignatio* was the correct reaction. We were not to pity him, since that would imply some degree of identification and might even lead to our tolerating him. At once my tainted heart was with him in his cage, beside his vodka, his cigarettes, and his ukulele; and it remained there to the end, though my mind acknowledged the impact of a staggeringly clever production. On the way out of the theatre I lit a cigarette, feeling as defiant as if I were peroxiding my hair.

But if pure comedy is rare, pure tragedy is nonexistent. To our mind, the spectacle of a man hounded and suffering, defeated by society or strangled by fate, constitutes tragedy, from which we derive a refinement of our knowledge of the human condition. But in Utopia that kind of tragedy is impossible. Since there is always a way out, no one can ever be trapped. Mr. Zubov, the director of the Maly Theatre, put the case to me quite frankly. Domestic tragedy, he said, was still conceivable, though it was fast disappearing; but social tragedy was unthinkable. In Soviet society a man could never be crushed. He quoted Vishnevsky's *An Optimistic Tragedy* as an example of Soviet tragedy in that it had a happy ending. I mentioned *Hamlet*. He smiled.

"Ah," he said, "that is a golden page of the past." He added that in Russia the circumstances necessary to create the anguish of a Hamlet or Lear simply did not exist. "In our society," he concluded, "there may be occasional collisions, but there are no defeats." That is the attitude, and the theatre reflects it. A generation of actors has thus grown up whose only acquaintance with tragic emotion is restricted to the classics. Another theatre director, going still further, explained to me why Communists regarded individualism, in our eyes the wellspring of tragedy, as a doubtful social virtue. "You think of artists as crazy individuals," he said, "and you do not mind sacrificing a whole generation as long as a few individual rebels turn out a few poems of suffering and despair. We would rather save the generation and do without the poets."

Our conception of the artist as an individual rebel was, I realized, badly in need of revaluation. If Russia is right, the pressures which produce lyric artists, passionately affirming their own selfhood, are inexorably being removed. Collective art is taking their place, for how can one *épater les bourgeois* when there are no *bourgeois* to *épater?* J. D. Salinger's latest story, "Raise High the Roofbeam, Carpenters," is a gloriously moving piece of writing about the martyrdom of a saint in a vulgarized society. The saint eventually, and with tremendous pathos, commits suicide. But in Utopia, one asks, what would Mr. Salinger write about?

There are many bad plays in Moscow today. Many breasts are beaten, many flags wagged, and many lectures read. But there are no plays that are merely, in Mr. Zubov's phrase, "aids to digestion." The theatre of mindless farce and meaningless melodrama is unknown. One would like to see a Western theatre organized on Russian lines without Russian ideology; but without some ideology or other the theatres would never be built and the organization never imposed.

I was revolving these things in my mind as my plane rose, bearing me away from the shashlik territory, across the *boeuf Stroganoff* belt into the Schnitzel country. I landed for a while at Prague—sour word, which rhymes with nothing. At Brussels vulgarity and fecklessness started to flow back into my system. By the time we reached London my moral disintegration was complete; yet I felt an individual once more, a little lost and purposeless perhaps, but still an individual, going to hell in my own way instead of to heaven in somebody else's. I felt specific, and no longer generic.

For this freedom I paid the ultimate price. My first duty on leaving the airport was to attend the first night of a farce about pre-marital sex. It satirized the future (universal television and progressive education) where Russian plays satirize the past. By Russian standards it had scarcely been rehearsed at all, yet it looked over-rehearsed to the point of seeming mechanical. The actors imitated not life but other actors; the sets drew their inspiration not from the world but from other sets. If it was a success the management might, in six months' time, be tempted to gamble some of its profits on a play of moderate intelligence. I thought of Moscow, swallowed my doubts, and decided that ours was just a difference of approach. Just a simple difference of approach.

(1956)

The Cherry Orchard AND *Three Sisters*, BY ANTON CHEKHOV, AT SADLER'S WELLS, LONDON.

The great thing about the Moscow Art Theatre's production of *The Cherry Orchard* is that it blows the cobwebs off the play. And who put them there? Why, we ourselves. We have remade Chekhov's last play in our image just as drastically as the Germans have remade *Hamlet* in theirs. Our *Cherry Orchard* is a pathetic symphony, to be played in a mood of elegy. We invest it with a nostalgia for the past which, though it runs right through our culture, is alien to Chekhov's. His people are country gentry: we make them into decadent aristocrats.

Next, we romanticise them. Their silliness becomes pitiable grotesquerie; and at this point our hearts warm to them. They are not Russians at all: they belong in the great line of English eccentrics. The upstart Lopakhin, who buys up their heritage, cannot be other than a barbarous bounder. Having foisted on Chekhov a collection of patrician mental cases, we then congratulate him on having achieved honorary English citizenship. Meanwhile the calm, genial sanity of the play has flown out of the window. In M. Stanitsyn's production it is magnificently restored. Common-sense is not a quality we like to attribute to our artists; we prefer them slightly deranged; but Chekhov had it in full measure, and so have his present, peerless interpreters. Did I say this was Chekhov without the cobwebs? It is more: it is a total spring-cleaning.

Part of its freshness comes from the fact that it is a brand-new production, with new décor and several newly graduated players: on this tour the Art Theatre is clearly experimenting with youth. But there is more to it than that. The real novelty lies in its attitude towards Mme. Ranevsky's feckless household. This is not the old régime, crazily expiring with a pathetic jest on its lips. It is a real family, capricious perhaps and irresponsible, but essentially normal and undoomed. The play becomes what Chekhov called it: a comedy. "In places, even a farce," he added, but M. Stanitsyn does not go as far as that. He simply treats the characters as recognisable human beings in a mess, rather than as freaks trapped in a tragic *impasse*.

M. Massalsky's Gayev, for example, is no crumbling dodderer but the man of "suavity and elegance" whom Chekhov imagined: the decay is internal and moral. Nor is there anything of the neurotic spinster in Mlle. Lennikova's Varya: she is a practical, good-hearted girl who blushes too much to be easily marriageable; and her collapse, when Lopakhin lets her down, is the more moving for its lack of neurotic preparation. Lopakhin himself behaves, as Chekhov demanded, "with the utmost courtesy and decorum": no thrusting vulgarity here, but a mature impatience which rises, in the third-act announcement that he is the master now, to an astonishing climax of dismayed exasperation. The actor, M. Lukyanov, plays like a master throughout.

One crucial test remains: what does the production invite us to make of Trofimov, the eternal student with his vision of a transformed Russia? The English habit is to present him as a hare-brained booby whom no one could possibly take seriously. Yet the Czarist censor took him seriously enough to expunge several of his more critical speeches. M. Gubanov's performance is delicately right: a bundle of nerves, forever fingering his spectacles, and a fumbler in matters of emotion, but intelligent and sincere withal—a true misfit, but also a true prophet. This is straight Chekhov, not propagandist distortion. It is we who, by turning the other members of Ranevsky's household into caricatures of high-born futility, have infected the text with unnecessary social significance.

There are many more actors to salute—it is in the nature of this glowing troupe that it bats all the way down the list. I think of M. Leonidov's Yasha, more cad's cad than gent's gent, embracing the maid Dunyasha and blowing cigar-smoke into her eyes as she smiles at him. Of M. Yanshin's earth-larding Pischchik, frantically feeling for his purse after the conjuring tricks have been played. Of M. Kornukov's plump Epikhodov, pocketing an apple to make up for his rejection by Dunyasha. And I have not yet mentioned Alexis Gribov, one of the great actors of the world, who plays the tiny part of Firs, the ancient butler—fixed like a statue, in jaundiced petrifaction, and held upright only by handy walking-sticks or tables. Are there no weaknesses? For me, yes: I thought Mme. Tarassova inexpressive and unmoving. This is not a failure of conception; Chekhov expressly forbade the romantic agonies which most actresses bring to Mme. Ranevsky. It is a failure of execution. The actress is simply monotonous.

Peter Ustinov contends that team-work and Chekhov are, in acting terms, incompatible. The characters, he maintains, are all soloists who occasionally interrupt each other's monologues but never listen to what anyone else is saying. They are deaf and blind to the world outside them —which is why they are funny and also why they are appalling. Fair comment, and in *Three Sisters,* a much more complex work than *The Cherry Orchard,* this technique is carried as far as it can go without blowing the play centrifugally apart. The very theme is estrangement: a brief brushing of lips is as close as anyone ever gets to another's soul. Of the three girls yearning for Moscow, Olga will never marry, Masha has married badly, and Irina is cheated of marriage by a tragic duel. Their brother, Andrey, is yoked to a prolific and faithless shrew. Two nihilists look on: one active—the savage Solyony, who scents his hands because, like Lear's, they smell of mortality—and the other passive: Chebutikin, the doctor, jilted by the girls' mother and now drunk past caring. And so all sit, mourning and mumbling, making out of their inconsequence a choral lament on human isolation.

The Moscow production, based on the original staging by Nemirovich-Dantchenko, gets all of this and infuses it with that strange dynamic apathy that is Chekhov's greatest demand on his actors. The sisters themselves are new to the roles and as yet unsettled in them: Mlle.

Yurieva's Masha comes nearest to the wry fatalism we are looking for. Her Vershinin, M. Massalsky, is unduly restrained, tarred with the pomade of the *matinée* idol; but the elder parts are filled to overflowing with beard and rasp and detail. M. Gribov's Chebutikin, in particular, is all I had heard of it; encrusted with corruption, a ponderous fish-eyed shrug of a man, he is yet capable, while remembering his dead love, of a sudden and transfixing pathos. The last act is, I suppose, the high-water mark of twentieth-century drama, yet this superb company meets its challenge as if opening the door to an old friend. The sound-effects and lighting are brilliant throughout: we weep, apart from anything else, for a lost world so lovingly revived. How these actors eat; and listen; and fail to listen; and grunt and exist, roundly and egocentrically exist! They have become, with long rehearsal, the people they are playing: they do not need, as our actors do, to depend on the lines alone for their characterisation. We act with our voices, they with their lives. Where we leave off, they begin. Don't be deterred by the language barrier. This is not verbal acting, like ours, but total acting: Stanislavsky often made his players rehearse without words, to be sure that their faces and bodies were performing as well. Read the play before going, and you will be safe. Safe, and enriched.

By a shaming coincidence, our theatre last week offered what should have been its best: Edith Evans, John Gielgud, and Harry Andrews in *Henry VIII* at the Old Vic. This sprawling chronicle has four good scenes: Buckingham's downfall and Wolsey's, and Katharine's trial and death. The rest slumps without galvanic direction, which here it doesn't get. The style is ceremonial and listless, bogged down by leaden costumes and drab settings. The end of an era, I thought during the first act, when Dame Edith and Mr. Andrews, ludicrously under-rehearsed, were groping for lines like children playing at blind-man's-buff. And though Sir John made good use of his poker back and door-knob face, he never for a moment suggested Wolsey the self-made "butcher's cur": all was rigid declamation, issuing from a tense and meagre tenor.

Certes, he wept: which is to say, he moved himself. Dame Edith, by contrast, moved me. Her death scene lifted her to those serene, unassertive heights where at her best she has no rivals. The quiet, large face, with its prehensile upper lip, shifted and quaked according to the dictates of the character, an unabashed queen in great extremity. Dame Edith ignored the "verbal music," and thereby made a truer music, having to do with the experience of dying. Alone in the company at what foreigners are wrongly encouraged to regard as our national theatre, she could have wandered on to the stage at Sadler's Wells and seemed at home.

(1958)

Uncle Vanya, BY ANTON CHEKHOV, AND *The Troubled Past*, BY RAKHMANOV, AT SADLER'S WELLS, LONDON.

In *Uncle Vanya* Chekhov created one of the most improbable and least playable heroes in dramatic literature. Everything about him is either negative or ridiculous. Vanya has wasted his life running the estate for his brother-in-law, a transparent old fraud whom he once mistook for a literary genius. His fumbling advances to the dotard's second wife have been wearily repelled. His status in the household is that of a tolerated clown. About all of this he grumbles incessantly, yet does nothing; nothing, that is, until the ancient locust proposes to sell the estate from under him: whereat we plunge into the farce of his botched suicide attempt and the pot-shot that fails even to wing his intended victim. Self-pitying in repose, ineffectual in action, how can we take him seriously? Yet if we don't, the play collapses. I expected the Moscow Art Theatre to have solved the problem, but I could never have guessed how. M. Orlov and his director, M. Kedrov, have found in Vanya a wholly unsuspected quality: dignity.

On the surface this Vanya is a man of weight and substance. His aspect is grave, and his beard, though a lightish brown, is none the less a serious beard. The tie gives us our first hint of weakness—it is somehow too fussy—and his voice, when he addresses his mother, gets a little too petulant for comfort. Yet the external man is robustly mature. Only in flashes do we glimpse the man within, an adolescent who can neither be his age nor live up to his looks. It is a lightweight who peers out through the pale eyes of the heavyweight face. He knows he has squandered his life on an old humbug; knows he has lost the power to live for himself; yet always he keeps up appearances. Dignity never deserts him. He clings to it even in the shooting spree, which becomes in its mad way a matter of honour, an assertion of principle rather than a display of temperament; and in tenacity like this there is a kind of heroism. M. Orlov's clumsy nobility puts us in mind, as it should, of Don Quixote. This Vanya always looks capable of tragedy: his tragedy is that he is capable only of comedy.

Around this superb performance a constellated production revolves. M. Khtorov misses nothing of Serebryakov, a literary lion in the last stages of mange; and instead of the glittering *mondaine* our actresses like to make of Elena (or any other part, given half a chance), Mlle. Anastasieva gives us both a credible wife for the old beast and a woman to whom Vanya and Astrov can be drawn without looking too much like doomed moths. The Astrov himself (M. Gubanov, so good as Trofimov in *The Cherry Orchard*) is a failure, partly because the actor is too young and partly because he falls too readily into that vein of stolid, sententious rhetoric which tempts even the best Russian players from time to time. Of course Astrov sees through the phoneys around him, and of course he has visions of a revived Russia: but he is also a self-disgusted cynic and a hard drinker, and of these M. Gubanov shows us nothing. Against this signal disappointment I can set Mlle. Lennikova's shining Sonya and the Telyegin, plump and wheezing, of M. Yanshin, whose performance as Mr. Pickwick must be as perfect as Moscow says it is.

But the true stars of the show, M. Orlov apart, are the second-act storm and the dawn that succeeds it. This is a storm with a personality of its own; a special, authentic, Stanislavsky-trained storm, not just a shaking of thundersheets and a dribble of peas in a drum. It begins far off, with a premonitory rumble and a hiss of light rain. The curtains faintly billow. Then, with a catarrhal explosion that makes the theatre throb, it is upon us: the curtains flare like flags, and the rain pelts down, so savagely that we can hear it splashing off the porch into its own puddles. Capriciously, it subsides, and as capriciously resumes, without for an instant distracting our attention from the actors. It is followed by the gaunt electric blue of dawn, which seeps across the room from the drenched garden and finally, when the first spikes of sunlight reinforce it, persuades even Chekhov's night-long talkers to go to bed. Technicians, as much as actors, make up the magic of the M.A.T. ensemble: and my main complaint about the production is that, by setting the first act indoors instead of out, it cheated us of seeing and hearing what these unseen *virtuosi* could make of a garden at sunset.

It is by their last acts that most of us will remember this Chekhov cycle: all three plays end with protracted and desolate leave-takings. The fourth production, Rakhmanov's *The Troubled Past,* also ends on a farewell, but this time the mood is triumphant: the revolutionary army of 1918 is marching off to repulse the invading capitalist hordes. This pedestrian play, written in 1935, celebrates the decision of the eminent Russian naturalist Timiryazev to throw in his lot with the rebels. The old man's instinctive faith is contrasted with the qualms of his assistant, who thinks the intelligentsia should stay aloof; but "intelligentsia," says the professor, is a "bragging, boastful word," since it implies a separation of the intellectual from the worker to whom he must be allied if social progress is to be made.

The conclusion is unexceptionable: what is dismaying is the absence of argument that precedes it. Nobody challenges the professor's points, everything is taken as read, and the dialectic passion that lights up the best propaganda plays is totally lacking. The piece is frankly designed to remind students and *savants* of their duty to support the régime: and the congratulatory phone-call from Lenin which the hero receives at the end is a clear promise of official laurels for all who heed the message. I see no reason why a Soviet company should not bring over a play with a Soviet emphasis, but I wish they could have picked a better one. Needless to say, the M.A.T. humanises the text magnificently: M. Koltsov's professor is a sharp, querulous creature of eccentric impulse, and Mme. Androvskaya positively embraces the role of his aghast, admiring wife—this is the couple out of Angus Wilson's *The Mulberry Bush,* long before they became darling dodos.

People who wonder exactly what this company stands for should note that two of the tiniest crowd-parts in *The Troubled Past* are played by Mlle. Maximova and M. Gubanov, both of whom play leads in the Chekhovs. It is also worth remembering that, while the touring troupe is appearing in London, the M.A.T. is keeping two Moscow theatres open with a full repertory of plays. Theatre on this scale is something we in England have not even begun to contemplate. I wish the M.A.T. had brought us their version of Dickens or their resplendent production of Wilde's *Ideal Husband,* both of which were suggested by Moscow but rejected by the host-impresario, Peter Daubeny: an error, I feel sure, for the comparisons would have been instructive. But I am niggling. We have entered an Aladdin's cave of acting to which, without Mr. Daubeny, we would never have had access at all. I feel pelted with pearls.

(1958)

A Western Approach.

Under the appallingly jovial title of *Broadway, U.S.S.R.* Faubion Bowers has assembled a pile of information about the performing arts in the Soviet Union today. Most of it was gleaned at first hand, which is one point in the book's favour; another is the fact that the author speaks Russian. Judging from the style, which frequently subsides into cliché, I suspect—or hope—that Mr. Bowers was writing in haste. Whether he was or not, a little more checking here and there would not have come amiss. For example, I assumed a sceptical squint when Mr. Bowers asserts, *à propos* of a Russian production of *Hamlet,* that Laertes' return to Elsinore had been directorially distorted. According to Mr. Bowers, Laertes "appears at the head of a popular rebellion, and the angry proletariat clamber up the iron grille, pounding on it, trying to break into the palace"; so far from being a distortion, this is exactly what Shakespeare demands in the text. There are also a few confessions of ignorance that make one a touch dubious about Mr. Bowers' scholarship. Having mentioned Goldoni in a list of playwrights whose work can be seen in Moscow, he adds, "To me that is an obscure name"—an odd comment, surely, on one of the two or three greatest Italian dramatists.

In general, though, Mr. Bowers is a thorough and informed reporter. He writes in detail and at length about such obvious landmarks as the Bolshoi, the Moscow Art Theatre, and Obraztsov's puppets, and he is properly aware of the departures from official realism that distinguish the Satirical Theatre's audacious production of Mayakovsky's *Bedbug.* His curiosity took him to places that most tourists miss, such as the Operetta Theatre, where he saw several bizarre musical comedies of the thirties, in one of which, *The Ball at the Savoy,* green chartreuse was drunk out of a whisky bottle at nine o'clock in the morning. (The setting was Cannes.) He went to Vladimir Durov's Animal Theatre, just outside Moscow, where the cast included a skunk, a raccoon, a crow, a baboon, and a trio of foxes. At the Variety Theatre he was delighted by Arkadi Raikin, a famous Leningrad comedian, whom he likens to Danny Kaye and cites as a proof that the spirit of Soviet vaudeville is not dead.

Mr. Bowers found, on the whole, much less overt propaganda than he had expected. What he did find was a propensity toward didacticism, based on the belief that it is the artist's business to teach, as well as to distract, his contemporaries. Until the last century, of course, this view of art as "instruction through delight" was so completely accepted as to be universal, and it is an illustration of how far, and how swiftly, we have moved away from it when Mr. Bowers can write, of a performance at Obraztsov's theatre, that "the dilemma of keeping you amused and informed at the same time [detracts] from the development of a pure art form." This statement would have been meaningless to both Aristotle and Johnson, and it would have seemed highly controversial to most good writers until well into the nineteenth century. A few pages later Mr. Bowers says something equally revealing: "Russia as a whole has a curious lack of what we in the West associate with pleasure. There are only theatres and concerts, sports and chess, books and walks." (He omits television.) It is a moot point whether this indicates that we are over- or they under-entertained.

Mr. Bowers' most valuable contribution to our knowledge of trans-Curtain drama is beyond doubt the section he devotes to new plays. Where tragedy is concerned, the Party line appears to be as inflexible as ever; in Soviet drama the tragic hero, hounded and crushed by circumstance, simply does not exist. Elsewhere in the theatre Mr. Bowers discerns heartening evidences of thaw. He observes that "scripts no longer have to be submitted to government agencies"; in theory at least, theatre censorship has been abolished. Nikolai Pogodin, the *doyen* and senior trimmer of Soviet dramatists, has lately had a huge success with a piece called *Sonnet of Petrarch,* which Mr. Bowers describes as being "sprinkled with subtle venom against the Party and its heartless discipline." In another popular play "the only entirely unsympathetic character . . . is the Party bureaucrat." Mr. Bowers' conclusion is that "nowadays the Russians have a good measure of freedom of speech and the right to criticize the Communist Party." Above all, he points to the flood of new plays dealing with personal relationships—such as young love, marital problems, and even divorce—that were formerly subordinated to the all-important relationship between the individual and the state. Unless Mr. Bowers has been grotesquely deceived, the Soviet drama is opening its doors to something very much like humanism.

His book is not without passages of astonishing aberrancy, as witness his assault on the repertory system that operates in all Russian and most Continental theatres. He doubts, first of all, whether an actor can go on re-creating "a stream of important roles with sufficient brilliance to hold the prolonged attention of sophisticated audiences," and feels that without new faces "a staleness, a tiredness, creeps in." To reply briefly and temperately to a statement based on so many false premises is a stiff task; I might, however, mention that in the repertory system no actor performs every night, and few actors appear more than four times a week; that most repertory theatres constantly draw new blood from affiliated drama schools; and that I can conceive of no staleness staler than that of a Western actor who has been uttering the same lines nightly for a year or more. On the question of persuading senior performers to be their age Mr. Bowers is more pertinent. It is often hard, unless the director is a man of exceptionally strong will, to dislodge elder players from roles they have clearly outgrown. But as an instance of over-age casting, Mr. Bowers singles out Victor Stanitsyn, who, "in his sixties, plays Gaev in *The Cherry Orchard*"—an oddly unglaring example, I should have thought, since Gaev himself is in his fifties. Nor can I go along with Mr. Bowers when he argues that the repertory system leads to standards of staging that are lower than ours; how can this be, when the great Continental theatres can afford a multiplicity of stagehands and a plurality of devices, such as lifts and revolves, that are almost non-existent on Broadway? On the same page, as it happens, Mr. Bowers contradicts himself by asserting that Soviet playwrights are corrupted by "the endless resources of the Russian stage." They can have as many sets, and as many actors, as they wish. There follows this sentence, which is in the strict sense egregious:

> The playwright who has never known the discipline of writing three acts within one set has, in my opinion, missed one of the most valuable exercises in intellectual concentration the theatre offers.

All one can say is that Shakespeare missed it; so did Chekhov and Sophocles, and, indeed, every dramatist who lived too early to savour the strait-jacket tyranny which is imposed by the box office and which Mr. Bowers so assiduously espouses.

(1959)

V: THE GERMAN THEATRE

A Touch of the Poet, by Eugene O'Neill, at the Stadttheater, Düsseldorf.

There it all was: a large civic subsidy, a permanent company, an enlightened policy, and a new playhouse, built since the war, in which to deploy all three. I am speaking—indeed, shouting—of Düsseldorf, whose Stadttheater I lately visited at the invitation of Karl Heinz Stroux, its Intendant. It is a majestic structure, which seats twelve hundred people and has backstage facilities second to none; yet no sooner had I seen it than my hosts began apologising for it. "Just a temporary building, of course. The *real* theatre will be over there"—and they pointed to a site big enough for Wembley Stadium. "It may take a year to build. Or even more," they added, bravely determined to give me the whole sorry picture of official apathy. And, finally, with a gallant shrug: "You know how it is."

I said I did, but I lied. I do *not* know how it is to live in a city where the construction of a civic playhouse is regarded not as a wild caprice of municipal bounty but as a basic, almost niggardly, cultural minimum. I do *not* know how it is to belong to a community where a theatre as palatial as Düsseldorf's could be considered a makeshift. Coventry's new Belgrade Theatre, which opens later this month, has been built entirely out of public money: as such it will be unique in post-war Britain. But in post-war Germany, East as well as West, Herr Stroux's theatre is part of the normal civic landscape, as indispensable as the public library or the railway station. In Düsseldorf, a provincial city slightly smaller than Sheffield, the Stadttheater offers a repertoire of plays ranging from Shakespeare to Brecht, together with a company of ninety actors to perform them and an annual subsidy of £100,000 to pay for them. In spite of films and television, there is seldom an empty seat.

The excuse for my trip was the German *première* of Eugene O'Neill's last completed play, *A Touch of the Poet*. As with much late O'Neill, its mood is an odd, inimitable fusion of charity and misanthropy.

The hero is a pompously drunken Irish officer, late of Wellington's army, who has emigrated to America along with his peasant wife and pretty daughter, both of whom he despises. He scoffs at his daughter's plan to marry a young local swell; but his derision turns to outrage when the boy's parents try to prevent the betrothal with a straight offer of cash. He seeks a duel: from which he returns bloody and beaten, his treasured uniform soiled and ripped. The test of reality has bruised beyond repair his dream of himself as a godlike military snob, and he goes back to the bottle utterly defeated. Even his daughter, who has hitherto hated him and still means to marry her lover, cannot help asking her mother: "Why do I mourn for him?"

The play is often weak, notably in the flabby melodramatic blarney of its period Irish dialogue; but it is strong where O'Neill at his best is unbeatable—in the creation of a family held together as much by hate as by love, a Strindbergian household whose every member stares at the others with a hypnotised, horrified pity. The scenes between father and daughter have a special intensity, and I do not blame Herr Stroux for spicing them with a dash of incest. And the Düsseldorf troupe gave the play as a whole the sort of solid, flexible, mature performance that in London we sometimes get but can never count on. Ralph Richardson could probably play the hero more imaginatively than Alfred Schieske; but whereas we have but one Richardson, Germany has not fewer than a dozen Schieskes, regularly performing in a dozen great cities. And I can think of no British actress who could begin to rival the bodily bravura, vocal attack, and sad, commiserating eyes of Nicole Heesters, who plays the daughter.

I have seen many productions as good as this in London, but never consecutively, month after month, at the same theatre; and London, remember, is a capital city, which Düsseldorf is not. The stock objection to a subsidised theatre is that it can afford to be good. To which I reply that it cannot afford to be anything else. The subsidy may be withheld, or the director changed. It is harder by far to live up to a subsidy than to play down to the box-office.

(1958)

Berlin at Play.

West Berlin, now busy with its annual arts festival, is superficially gayer than the denuded Eastern sector of the city, and one has to guard against the pathetic fallacy of judging the spirit of a place by the energy of its advertising industry. Over the Kurfürstendamm the slim street-lights lean like sea-serpents, illuminating a long, low avenue that is all dressed up for a party to which no one appears to be going. Here there are no visiting trippers to pack the pavements, and by midnight the Berliners are mostly in bed. Half a mile to the east begins the great dust bowl that separates the two camps. The Reichstag, as befits a senior ruin, presides over the chaos, staring across unkempt parkland at a smashed railway station, where flowers grow between the tracks. The man-made horizons are hereabouts limitless. Those two shallow steps, leading nowhere, are the Reich Chancellery; that drunkenly tilted cone of bricks in the back yard is the Bunker—only now the whole district is back yard. Presumably in a mood of what-the-hell, the East Germans themselves demolished the Imperial Palace, thereby knocking two squares into one to make Marx-Engels-Platz. It is the largest in Europe, and the loneliest.

How has this flattened, sundered city managed to re-establish itself as the European capital of serious drama? It has no playwrights of stature now that Brecht is dead, and many of its best actors are working in Hamburg, Düsseldorf, and elsewhere. What holds its theatre together is something very German: a tenacious belief that great plays belong in great playhouses as surely as great paintings belong in great museums, and that it is a public responsibility to keep them there. Germany long ago outgrew the folly of trying to make plays pay; besides Berlin's broad canvas, the London theatre resembles a pigmy boudoir *vignette*. We call our system democratic because it submits every new production to the test of popular opinion; in fact it is a dictatorship, ruled by economic pressure. In the West End all plays are equal, but farces and melodramas are more equal than others.

The lesson of Berlin is that there is no theatrical freedom without theatrical subsidies. The Western Sector has seven legitimate playhouses, two of which are directly state-aided, while the rest are subsidised indirectly by the Volksbühne, a municipal organisation that distributes seats at cut prices to a myriad subscribers. (The situation is roughly the same in the East.) The result is a repertory which makes some Western critics feel that their theatre is, if anything, too free: it stages too many great plays. One sees their point. Swollen with *haute cuisine* (Ibsen, Strindberg, Büchner, O'Neill, Lorca, Miller, Shaw, Giraudoux, Molière, Schnitzler, Faulkner, and Shakespeare were on the menu last week), a man might well yearn for a doughnut.

Very loosely, you might say that West Berlin likes its plays to be introspective and retrospective; the East prefers a more extrovert drama. In the West one's first stop is the Schiller-Theater, which is London Airport with good acoustics—a functional paradise, hushed by pile carpets, where at once one feels a respected guest, not just a source of income. Its new production of *Measure for Measure,* a rather formal, choreographic affair, has both the vices and the virtues of West German taste. The major vice, probably incurable, is a submerged hysteria in the acting. Whenever a famous speech comes up, there bursts through the façade that shrieking teutonic demon that Brecht tried so hard to exorcise. The compensating virtue is an intense imaginative thoroughness. The director (Sellner) must have read the text to tatters before it yielded up a simple question which, as far as I know, has never been asked before: how old is Angelo? Traditionally he is middle-aged. Sellner, with startling logic, sees him as a vain, attractive youngster, an interpretation which makes sense of the part, sense of the relationship with Mariana, and sense of the play.

The veteran director Erwin Piscator, who invented "Epic Theatre" in the twenties, is curtly dismissed by many Berlin intellectuals as a back number. By local standards, they may be right; by ours, his production of *Danton's Death* is wildly exciting. The setting (by Caspar Neher, still the *doyen* of German designers) is a wide curved ramp spiralling up to a height of about fifteen feet and then spiralling centrally down again; at the highest point stands the guillotine. Symbolic? Yes: but capable of presenting crowd scenes worthy of Eisenstein, and of showing us, as it spins on the revolve, a revolution that has got out of hand and forgotten that violence is self-perpetuating.

In Büchner's masterpiece the disillusioned Danton ("We haven't made the Revolution: the Revolution has made us") and the doctrinaire Robespierre are both drawn with equal sympathy. Piscator slants his production against both of them. Danton is played as a bombastic sensualist and Robespierre as a frigid fanatic: the play becomes an attack on the principle of revolution, rather than a sad dissection of revolutionary practice. Still, this production is a gauntlet flung down by Piscator to Brecht; and Brecht has done some slanting in his time.

Brecht's heir apparent as the kingpin of Berlin theatre seems to be

Oscar Fritz Schuh, who runs the Theater am Kurfürstendamm. His festival offering is the German *première* of Eugene O'Neill's posthumous play *Long Day's Journey into Night*—four hours of introspection, "written," as the preface unpromisingly bodes, "in tears and blood." At greater length and in greater depth than usual, this is the familiar American tragedy of two sons alienated from their father. The younger son is Edmund (O'Neill himself), who has T.B. His brother secretly hates him, and his father is a miser; all three drink heavily. Mother, meanwhile, takes dope in the attic. The play is a throbbing, repetitive essay in self-justification: it goes round and round the family circle to prove that Edmund's weaknesses are entirely due to the wickedness of his relations. The translation, even in a city where translating is a large minor industry, misses the Irishness of the text, and the sinister, gauzy setting (Neher again) suggests a household wrongly akin to the Mannons of *Mourning Becomes Electra*. Schuh's handling of the actors, however, is miraculous. I shall never forget the haggard, twitching, elderly child that Grete Mosheim makes of Mama; and the hectic fragility of Hans Christian Blech's Edmund is astounding in an actor whose temperament and appearance are those of a young James Cagney.

(1956)

Berlin Postscript.

"Our theatre," an East Berlin actor said to me, "looks at the state of the world and asks: why? The Western theatre shrugs and says: why not?"

But nothing in Berlin is as simple and clear-cut as that. The East accuses the West of clinging to the star system, forgetting that there are star personalities even in that holy of Eastern holies, the Berliner Ensemble itself. The West retorts that the East irons out all individuality, forgetting that teamwork is so deeply rooted in German theatre that no actor, whatever his politics, can escape it. The only safe truths are these: that Berlin has no knockdown stars like Olivier or Edith Evans; that its actors have never developed that elaborate technique of charm with which French and English actors make bad plays commercial; and that its general theatrical level is higher than anywhere west of Moscow's best.

The Brechtless Berliner Ensemble maintains a standard of production unbeaten in either sector. The plays it produces are sometimes another matter. One, written by the Minister of Culture, yawningly chronicles the Nazi defeat outside Moscow—sad stuff, redeemed only by Brechtian stagecraft and settings that seem to have been broken off from naked reality by a giant hand. Visually, their *Playboy of the Western World* (renamed *The* Hero *of the Western World*) is equally ravishing, down to the last pecking hen and hunk of peat, but all the poetry has gone from Synge's text, which is interpreted as a satire on the Western cult of violence. (Hitler and Mickey Spillane are mentioned tersely in the programme.) The acting style, of course, is as deft and clear as ever. The question is whether it, and the company, will hold together now that their great energumen is dead. Their average age is already perilously low, and some of the older actors are on the brink of defecting.

The West has two answers to the Berliner Ensemble. One is the director Oscar Fritz Schuh, whom I discussed last week. The other is the entire repertory of the Schlosspark-Theater, the smaller of the two state playhouses. Here one sees plays for which we London critics are frankly out of training. Strindberg's *Road to Damascus,* for instance, the whole massive trilogy trimmed to fit into a single evening. Its hero is an unnamed Stranger (the author, lightly disguised) pursued by fantasies of guilt: at first he rejects the consolation of religion, since it would compel him to hate his neighbour as himself, but later undergoes a half-hearted, quasi-Pauline conversion. Dank and arid, I thought it; yet I was glad to have seen it, and gladder still to acclaim Martin Held, in the dual role of the Beggar and the Confessor, as a supreme mimetic talent, with the repose of a lizard and the attack of a lion.

Next day I saw William Faulkner's *Requiem for a Nun,* staged by Piscator in black and white for the rather dreary reason that the leading characters are a spade and a spook—a Negress, that is to say, and a white woman. The Negress is to die for the murder of her mistress's baby, and the play's purpose is to show that the real responsibility for the crime lies with the nymphomaniac mother. I never expected to relish the droning stammer of Faulkner's style, but Joana Maria Gorvin almost converted me, a haunting actress with a pinched face, eyes full of dread, and a downhearted-frail voice that carried me with her at least halfway to expiation.

And at the Schlosspark last Monday I survived the most drastic emotional experience the theatre has ever given me. It had little to do with art, for the play was not a great one; yet its effect, in Berlin, at that moment of history, transcended anything that art has yet learned to achieve. It invaded the privacy of the whole audience: I tried hard to stay detached, but the general catharsis engulfed me. Like all great theatrical occasions, this was not only a theatrical occasion: it involved the world outside. The first page of the programme prepared one: a short, stark essay on collective guilt. Turn over for the title: *The Diary of Anne Frank,* directed by Boleslaw Barlog, *première* performance. It is not a vengeful dramatisation. Quietly, often gaily, it re-creates the daily life of eight Jews who hid for two years in an Amsterdam attic before the Gestapo broke in. Otto Frank was the sole survivor: Anne was killed in Belsen.

When I saw the play in New York, it vaguely perturbed me. There seemed no *need* to do it: it smacked of exploitation. The Berlin actors (especially Johanna von Koczian and Walter Franck) were better, on the whole, and devouter than the Americans, but I do not think that was why the play seemed so much more urgent and necessary on Monday night. After the interval the man in front of me put his head in his hands and did not afterwards look at the stage. He was not, I believe, Jewish. It was not until the end that one fully appreciated Barlog's wisdom and valour in using an entirely non-Jewish cast. Having read the last lines of the diary, which affirm, movingly and irrationally, Anne Frank's unshattered trust in human goodness, Otto Frank closes the book and says, very slowly: "She puts me to shame."

Thus the play ended. The house-lights went up on an audience that sat drained and ashen, some staring straight ahead, others staring at the ground, for a full half-minute. Then, as if awakening from a nightmare, they rose and filed out in total silence, not looking at each other, avoiding even the customary nods of recognition with which friend greets friend. There was no applause, and there were no curtain-calls.

All of this, I am well aware, is not drama criticism. In the shadow of an event so desperate and traumatic, criticism would be an irrelevance. I can only record an emotion that I felt, would not have missed, and pray never to feel again.

(1956)

The Caucasian Chalk Circle AND *Mother Courage*, BY BERTOLT BRECHT; *Trumpets and Drums*, ADAPTED BY BERTOLT BRECHT FROM GEORGE FARQUHAR'S *The Recruiting Officer*, AT THE PALACE, LONDON.

When the house-lights went up at the end of *The Caucasian Chalk Circle,* the audience looked to me like a serried congress of tailor's dummies. I probably looked the same to them. By contrast with the blinding sincerity of the Berliner Ensemble, we all seemed unreal and stagey. Many of us must have felt cheated. Brecht's actors do not behave like Western actors; they neither bludgeon us with personality nor woo us with charm; they look shockingly like people—real potato-faced people such as one might meet in a bus-queue.

Let me instance the peasant wedding in *The Caucasian Chalk Circle,* a scene more brilliantly directed than any other in London. A tiny cell of a room, ten by ten, is cumulatively jammed with about two dozen neighbours and a sottish monk. The chances for broad farce are obvious, but they are all rejected. Reality is preferred, reality of a memorable and sculptural ruggedness. I defy anyone to forget Brecht's stage pictures. No steps or rostra encumber the platform; the dominant colours are browns and greys; and against a high, encircling, off-white backcloth we see nothing but solid, selected objects—the twin gates in *The Caucasian Chalk Circle* or Mother Courage's covered wagon. The beauty of Brechtian settings is not of the dazzling kind that begs for applause. It is the more durable beauty of *use*.

The same applies to the actors. They look capable and practical, accustomed to living in the open air. Angelica Hurwicz is a lumpy girl with a face as round as an apple. Our theatre would cast her, if at all, as a fat comic maid. Brecht makes her his heroine, the servant who saves the governor's child when its mother flees from a palace rebellion. London would have cast a gallant little waif, pinched and pathetic: Miss Hurwicz, an energetic young woman too busy for pathos, expresses petulance where we expect her to "register" terror, and shrugs where other actresses would more likely weep. She strengthens the situation by ignoring its implications: it is by what it omits that we recognise hers as a great performance.

As Eric Bentley said, "Brecht does not believe in an inner reality, a higher reality or a deeper reality, but simply in reality." It is something for which we have lost the taste: raised on a diet of gin and goulash, we call Brecht ingenuous when he gives us bread and wine. He wrote morality plays and directed them as such, and if we of the West End and Broadway find them as tiresome as religion, we are in a shrinking minority. There is a world elsewhere. "I was bored to death," said a bright Chelsea girl after *Mother Courage.* "Bored to life" would have been apter.

The famous "alienation effect" was originally intended to counterbalance the extravagant rhetoric of German classical acting: to a debauched emotionalism, Brecht opposed a rigorous chastity. *Mother Courage* cries out for rich and rowdy performances. Brecht has staged it in a style light, swift, and ironic. In the central part Helene Weigel is never allowed to become a bawdy and flamboyant old darling: her performance is casual and ascetic: we are to observe but not to embrace her. Twice, and agonisingly, she moves us: elsewhere, even in Paul Dessau's magnificent songs, we must never sympathise with Mother Courage. She has battened on the Thirty Years' War, and must suffer for her complicity by losing her daughter and both her sons. But the clearest illustration of the "A-effect" comes in the national anthem, which the Berliner Ensemble have so arranged that it provokes, instead of patriotic ardour, laughter. The melody is backed by a trumpet *obbligato* so feeble and pompous that it suggests a boy bugler on a rapidly sinking ship. The orchestration is a criticism of the lyrics, and a double flavour results, the ironic flavour which is "A-effect."

Irony crops up throughout *Trumpets and Drums,* Brecht's expansion of Farquhar's *The Recruiting Officer,* advanced by a hundred years so as to coincide with the American Revolution. This involves propaganda, but it is propaganda as blithe and irrefutable as the remark made by an American wit on first seeing the playing-fields of Eton: "Here," he cried, "is where the battle of Yorktown was lost!" Farquhar's text has been surveyed by cool new eyes, against the larger vista of England at war, and there is evidence that the director (Benno Besson) does not find enforced recruitment particularly hilarious.

Captain Plume is the kind of role in which, formerly, John Clements was wont to cut a charming dash. Dieter Knaup plays him realistically, as a sallow and calculating seducer. The costumes look as if people and not puppets had worn them, and the settings, shiny Hogarthian etchings suspended on wires, are amusing without being "amusing." And to show that Brecht can throw his bonnet over the windmill, we have Wolf Kaiser as Captain Brazen, who does just that, entering every time with a new hat which he whips off and flings irretrievably over the nearest rooftop.

Is it mere decadence that makes us want more of this, more attack, more abandon? I think not. Brecht's rejection of false emotions sometimes means that the baby is poured out with the bath-water: the tight-wire of tension slackens so much that the actors fall off, and instead of single-mindedness, we have half-heartedness. Yet as a corrective he is indispensable. It is possible to enter the Palace Theatre wearing the familiar British smile of so-unsophisticated-my-dear-and-after-all-we've-rather-*had*-Expressionism (what *do* such people think Expressionism was?) and it is possible to leave with the same faint smile intact. It is possible: but not pleasant to contemplate.

(1956)

Summing Up: 1959.

Drama in Germany is a wounded art, still recovering from the casualties it suffered between 1933 and 1945. Exile accounts for some of them, death for the rest. In the case of the refugees, the damage was measurable and vast; with the coming of Hitler, Germany lost many of its best writers, directors, and actors, and for a decade and more its theatre resembled a decapitated giant with a megaphone instead of a mind. But there is no way of calculating how much potential talent was killed off in the war. Travelling around German theatres today, you rapidly notice that something is missing, and before long you realize what it is. A whole age group has almost disappeared; there are hardly any actors in their forties.

The wartime losses were, of course, architectural as well as human; most of the great playhouses were shattered by bombs. After twelve years of sickness a cultural tradition had to be revived amid ruins, with rubble still smoking underfoot. It is customary, when discussing the post-war German theatre, to applaud its technical efficiency and the speed of its recuperation, and then to complain that it has turned out no new playwrights of any importance. The complaint is accurate, but niggling. It is remarkable enough that post-war Germany has an organized theatre at all; what is astonishing, not to say eerie, is that in range of repertoire and general excellence of production there is no theatre in Europe to match it. I am not speaking in terms of individual talent. The finest actor in Europe is not a German; several other countries have directors as good as Germany's best; and in the matter of living dramatists the French and the British hold an authoritative lead. Where the German theatre scores, and ultimately wins, is in versatility, consistency, and national extensiveness. From one end of the sundered country to the other, every town big enough to have an art gallery and a public library also has a municipal playhouse, which automatically gets a civic subsidy, since the Germans believe that if a citizen has a right to good paintings, good sculpture, and good books, he has a right to good drama as well. Every such theatre has an *Intendant,* or administrator, who engages the company and selects the plays, most of which he is likely to direct himself; an average season's repertoire consists of around half a dozen new productions, augmented by a few left over from previous years. In any given week you can usually see at least four different shows, and sometimes as many as six. The lucky Düsseldorfers, I noticed as I flashed through their city this summer, could take in Schiller, Molière, and *Waiting for Godot* on consecutive nights at the local *Stadttheater,* and there are fewer Düsseldorfers than there are inhabitants of Buffalo.

To the outsider, the most flabbergasting thing about the German theatre is its eclecticism; the country we associate most closely with nationalism is the one that offers the widest international choice of plays. This was true thirty years ago, and it is even truer now that Germany is split. On both sides of the East-West border the European classics are the backbone of the repertory; but while the West performs contemporary French, English, and American plays that are seldom seen in the East, the East puts on modern Russian, Chinese, Hungarian, Rumanian, Polish, and Czech plays that are seldom, if ever, staged in the West. The result, *in toto,* is theatre of a diversity unparalleled anywhere in the world. The Federal Republic has a number of "private" (i.e., commercially run) playhouses, which have no counterparts in the Eastern Zone. Otherwise, both Germanys adhere to a principle much older than their latter-day antagonisms; namely, that it is a permanent public responsibility to make serious professional drama readily available, by means of subsidy, to everyone who wants to see it.

A few statistics, and we can get down to particulars. At the last count, West Germany, with a population of 53,000,000, had 121 theatres, or one to every 430,000 people. The equivalent figures for the East are 18,000,000 inhabitants and 86 theatres, or one to every 209,000. Just why the East should be so much more saturated theatrically is something that has never been fully explained to me. Its supporters say that Marxism and culture, its opponents that Marxism and propaganda, are synonymous.

Berlin is a city with two centres—the cluster of expensive hotels, bars, cinemas, shops round the Memorial Church, a sparkling nucleus of light, like a sham diamond, in the shabby twilight of the town; and the self-conscious civic centre of buildings round the Unter den Linden. . . .

This admirable description of the city today was written in 1932 by Christopher Isherwood—a fact that rather makes one doubt the validity of pointing modern political morals by contrasting the glittering opulence of the Western sector with the bureaucratic austerity of the East. Berlin seems always to have been split—once atmospherically and now geographically. Despite its bisected nature, it remains the artistic capital of the nation as a whole. In some ways, competition between the two sectors has had a stimulating effect on the theatre; in others, it has created enervating tensions. If, for instance, a West Berlin actor takes a job in an East Berlin production of an anti-capitalist play, he is liable to be reviled by the West-sector press. Similarly, an East Berlin director would have very ambiguous feelings if one of his shows got a rave review from a reactionary West Berlin critic. On one point, however, civic pride overrules political rivalry. Few West Berliners, no matter how rabid their allegiance to the Bonn government, would deny that the finest productions in the city are those of the Berliner Ensemble, which operates at the Theater am Schiffbauerdamm, in the East. Founded and inspired by the late Bertolt Brecht, this celebrated troupe was described in the London *Spectator* as "the only theatre that can be named in the same breath with the Moscow Arts or the Abbey at the height of their powers"—a judgment with which I concur, and on which I shall enlarge later.

Being Germany in little, Berlin offers a theatrical diet that is an open incitement to gluttony. The Western sector has six legitimate playhouses, the Eastern sector five—not counting the Theater der Freundschaft, which puts on plays for children. During a sample week in June the West was doing Sophocles, Calderón, Goldoni, Chekhov, Giraudoux, and John Osborne, while the East was busy with Shakespeare, Jonson, Goethe, Lessing, Shaw, Synge, and Brecht. And in both sectors, inevitably, there were productions of Molière and Schiller. Most of the serious work in West Berlin takes place at the Schiller-Theater, a great gray pleasure dome that has been rebuilt since the war, and at its affiliated suburban house, the Schlosspark; their joint Intendant, Boleslaw Barlog, receives an annual grant of four million marks—just over $950,000—on which to struggle through the season. Understandably, he manages to keep up a fairly high standard, with plenty of room for experiment. This summer I saw an extremely far-out production, at the Schiller, of Sophocles' *Trachiniae,* in a German version of Ezra Pound's brisk colloquial translation. On the stage, which projected jaggedly out into the auditorium, there was a lopsided abstract construction in polished steel, a long ramp that went zigzagging up into distant darkness, and practically nothing else except the cast. The choral bits were intoned by a group of young women in green gym tunics, who carried out, from time to time, little choreographic stunts reminiscent of a eurythmics class celebrating the opening of the new playing field. Yet, despite these vagaries, the tragedy came across like thunder. The Heracles (Fritz Eberth) never went off into the daemonic, shrieking, self-hypnotized trance that is the plague of so many German actors, not to mention politicians, when they are faced with a solid patch of rhetoric, and Hilde Krahl was memorably guilt-ravaged as the slave bride who gives her husband the corrosive, undoffable shirt of Nessus, under the impression that it is a garment magically endowed with the power of preserving love. I felt at the end, as I seldom do after watching, say, *Medea,* that I knew several marriages exactly like that. Next day the company presented *The Madwoman of Chaillot,* Giraudoux's ravishing fantasy about a flamboyant old beldam who saves Paris from destruction at the hands of an oil combine by walling up the entire board of directors in a sewer. This, I'm afraid, is the kind of play the Germans do least well. As performers, they are incomparable in logic, clarity, and head-on emotional impact; call upon them, however, for elegance, grace, and the subtler nuances of charm, and you will often be disappointed. It is not by chance that there are no German ballet companies. The Schiller production missed none of Giraudoux's points, but blunted many; lyricism, like a bird frightened by traps set to snare it, flew out of the window. The leading role was played—graciously, though slothfully—by a venerable actress in her eighties, making what was probably her farewell appearance. I decided that I pitied her. The German theatre is predominantly a male province; Moissi, Krauss, Bassermann, Deutsch, and Gründgens are the players whose names come first to mind. (In France, of course, acting is female; one thinks of Rachel, Bernhardt, Feuillère.) At the Schiller the central character in *The Madwoman* was not the Madwoman but the Ragpicker, performed with overwhelming zest and dynamism by Martin Held, the best all-round actor in Germany today. A sturdy, pink-faced man in his forties (a decimated age group, as I've said), he has enormous pathos and an attacking style full of the simplicity that we sometimes, and stupidly, call naïveté. In the Giraudoux he played not only the Ragpicker, who is a proletarian droll, but the president of the oil company—a brilliant trick worthy of Pirandello, since it is the Rag-picker who volunteers, during the second act, to impersonate the president at a mock trial, wherein he improvises a riotous defence of money-making as a healthy way of life. We thus hear the same actor twice extolling the mystique of wealth—first sincerely, then tongue in cheek.

At the Schlosspark I saw a production, by Hans Lietzau, of John Osborne's *The Entertainer* that made me radically reconsider my strictures on the play as it was presented in London and New York. I had formerly maintained that the role of Jean, Archie Rice's disillusioned daughter, was ineffectual and underwritten. The last act tapered off, I had snarled; the girl's part came to nothing. I have now changed my mind. To be sure, the German version lacked an Olivier, but not without reason; there is no music-hall tradition in Germany, and hence no model for the seedy, bawdy raconteur that Sir Laurence played. Martin Held compromised by making Archie a German-Cabaret m.c., cruder and sweatier than Olivier, and drunker, too, in a stiff-backed, stolid way, emphasizing his jokes with a ghastly, crowing laugh. A lot of subtleties were lost, but the play as a whole took on, almost by default, much more cogency and shape. In Lietzau's production the centre of the stage was occupied by daughter Jean, a tight-lipped blonde, forever watching her father, and reacting with tremors of pity and disgust to each new evidence of disintegration, each new proof that the man was spiritually dead. We saw the action through her eyes, and the play achieved a unity I had never thought it possessed.

The Schiller-Schlosspark pattern of variety, thoroughness, and efficiency recurs all over the country. In a short week-end at Hamburg—a city for whose green, water-girt beauty I was, by the way, completely unprepared, having expected Pittsburgh with mud-wrestling—I was able to see three first-rate works at the Schauspielhaus, which is run by the veteran Gustav Gründgens, and to spend an evening at the local experimental theatre, which advertised something called *Mississippi-Melodie,* by Tennessee Williams (not, as I'd hoped, a minstrel show culled from Mr. Williams' juvenilia but a quadruple bill, dowdily cast, of his better-known one-act plays). The Schauspielhaus presented Schiller's *Mary Stuart,* which was played with thumping soundness, despite someone's decision to garb Queen Elizabeth in a negligée trimmed with pink marabou; the first part of Goethe's *Faust,* in a lively new staging by Gründgens; and Brecht's *Saint Joan of the Stockyards,* which had had its world *première* at the same theatre earlier in the season. Written just after the 1929 unpleasantness, Brecht's piece is a bitter attempt to illustrate the interdependence of capitalism and religion, or—to put it more precisely—of profiteering and charity. It revolves around the friendship between Pierpont Mauler, a sentimental Chicago meat king, and a Salvation Army girl named Joan Dark. Warmed at first by Mauler's private good-heartedness, Joan slowly discovers that in an economic pinch he will go to any lengths to safeguard his profits, whereafter she realizes that by distributing soup and moral sustenance to the poor she is not alleviating hardship but accepting it as an immutable fact of life, and therefore encouraging its perpetuation. With this message on her lips, she returns to the mission hall, which Mauler and his friends have equipped with a gaudy new golden-piped organ. But her voice is drowned by the choir; exhausted by tramping the winter streets, she collapses and dies, and is thereupon hailed by the meat king's spokesman as "a fighter, and a sacrifice in the service of God." As a portrait of Chicago, the play is less than convincing, but as a satire on the relationship between those who take and those who give, its pungency is tremendous; it was by far the most successful show of the Hamburg season.

Wherever you go in Germany, Brecht is inescapable. Frankfurt, which has staged five Brecht plays since 1952, added a sixth last spring, to critical applause so tumultuous that it made half a column in the *New York Times*. The occasion was the West German *première* of *Schweik in the Second World War,* Brecht's version of the adventures that might have befallen Jaroslav Hašek's Good Soldier had he been conscripted by the Nazis to fight against Russia. Schweik, the beaming innocent who makes authority look most foolish when most he seems to embrace it, had an abiding appeal for Brecht, who once said that Hašek's book was one of the three literary works of this century most likely to become classics. In Brecht's play, as Schweik blunders into the Army and toward Stalingrad, the action is constantly interrupted by Hitler and his lieutenants, on a platform high above the stage; the Führer persistently, and pathetically, inquires whether Schweik, the little man, still loves him, because without the love of the little man he cannot go on. Finally, Schweik rejects his advances with unctuous obscenity. Although it is embellished with some of the loveliest lyrics Brecht ever wrote, the text is rough, acid, and brutally contemptuous of Nazi sympathizers. The night I was there, the Frankfurt audience cheered it.

The ubiquity and the influence of Brecht have been growing ever since his death, three years ago, at the age of fifty-eight. In the 1957–8 season he set a record; for the first time in the history of the German theatre a contemporary native playwright was among the four dramatists whose works were most often performed in the German-speaking countries. Shakespeare, as always, came first, with 2,674 performances, and he was followed by Schiller, with 2,000; Goethe, with 1,200; and Brecht, with 1,120. (Molière, Shaw, and Hauptmann, in that order, were the runners-up.) It is doubtful whether any dramatist in history has made a greater impact on his own country in his own era than this stubby, ribald Marxist, who spent his mature creative years—from 1933 to 1948—away from home, exiled and almost penniless, first in Scandinavia and then in the United States.

I have paid many visits to Brecht's Berliner Ensemble in the five years since it took up residence at the Theater am Schiffbauerdamm, but whenever I approach the place, I still feel a *frisson* of expectation, an anticipatory lift, that no other theatre evokes. Western taxis charge double to go East, since they are unlikely to pick up a returning fare, but the trip is worth it: the arrow-straight drive up to the grandiose, bullet-chipped pillars of the Brandenburg Gate, the perfunctory salutes of the guards on both sides of the frontier; the short sally past the skinny trees and bland neo-classical façades of Unter den Linden (surely the emptiest of the world's great streets), and the left turn that leads you across the meagre, oily stream of the Spree and into the square-*cum*-parking-lot where the theatre stands, with a circular neon sign—"BERLINER ENSEMBLE"—revolving on its roof like a sluggish weather vane. You enter an unimposing foyer, present your ticket, buy a superbly designed programme, and take your seat in an auditorium that is encrusted with gilt cupids and cushioned in plush. When the curtain, adorned with its Picasso dove, goes up, one is usually shocked, so abrupt is the contrast between the baroque prettiness of the house and the chaste, stripped beauty of what one sees on the expanses, relatively enormous, of the stage. No attempt is made at realistic illusion. Instead of being absorbed by a slice of life, we are sitting in a theatre while a group of actors tell us a story that happened some time ago. By means of songs, and captions projected on to a screen, Brecht explains what conclusions he draws from the tale, but he wants us to quarrel with him—to argue that this scene need not have ended as it did, or that this character might have behaved otherwise. He detested the reverence of most theatre audiences, much preferring the detached, critical expertise that he noted in spectators at sporting events. Theatrical trickery, such as lighting and scene changes, should not, he felt, be concealed from the customer. In his own words,

> . . . don't show him too much
> But show something. And let him observe
> That this is not magic but
> Work, my friends.

Always, as a director, he told his actors that the mere fact of passing through a stage door did not make them separate, sanctified creatures cut off from the mass of humanity—hence his practice, which is still followed to some extent by the Ensemble, of allowing outsiders to wander into rehearsals, as long as they kept quiet. He abhorred the idea that the production of plays is a secret, holy business, like the nurture of some rare hothouse plant. If actors can spend their spare time watching ditchdiggers, he said, why shouldn't ditchdiggers watch actors? Initially, the Ensemble actors were embarrassed by this open-door policy; later, however, they realized how much it had helped them to shed inhibitions. A cast that has rehearsed for weeks before strangers is unlikely to dread an opening night.

I arrived at the theatre this year during a rehearsal, and one that was loaded with nostalgia. *The Threepenny Opera,* Brecht's first decisive success, was being prepared for revival on the same stage that had seen its *première* thirty-one years earlier, with the same director in charge—Erich Engel, now looking gaunt and unwell, despite the jaunty cocksureness of his beret. As I entered, somebody was singing "Mack the Knife" with the tinny, nasal vibrato that one remembers from the old Telefunken records. Engel and two young assistants interrupted from time to time, talking with the easy, probing frankness that comes of no haste, no pressure, no need to worry about publicity, deadlines, or out-of-town reviews. I noticed that Mr. Peachum, a part usually given to a rubicund butterball, was being played by Norbert Christian, a slim soft-eyed actor in his thirties. Brecht, I reflected, would have liked that; he always detested physical type-casting. In Brecht's theatre it is what people do, not what they feel or how they look, that counts. Action takes precedence over emotion, fact over fantasy. *"Die Wahrheit ist konkret"* ("Truth is concrete") was Brecht's favourite maxim; for him there could be no such thing as abstract truth. Somebody once asked him what the purpose of a good play ought to be. He answered by describing a photograph he had seen in a magazine, a double-page spread of Tokyo after the earthquake. Amid the devastation, one building remained upright. The caption consisted of two words: "Steel Stood." That, said Brecht, was the purpose of drama—to teach us how to survive.

The rehearsal continued, the patient denuding process that would ultimately achieve the naked simplicity and directness on which the Ensemble prides itself. To encourage the players to look at themselves objectively, a large mirror had been placed in the footlights, and throughout the session photographers were taking pictures of everything that happened, providing a visual record that would afterward be used to point out to the actors just where, and how, they had gone wrong. One of the most impressive women alive had meanwhile come to sit beside me—Helene Weigel, Brecht's widow, who has directed the Ensemble since its inception ten years ago and plays several of the leading roles. At sixty, she has a lean, nut-brown face that suggests, with its high cheekbones, shrewdly hooded eyes, and total absence of make-up, a certain kind of Spanish peasant matriarch; her whole manner implies a long life of commanding and comforting, of which she clearly regrets not an instant. Her warmth is adventurous, her honesty contagious, and her sophistication extreme, and that is the best I can do to sum up a woman who would, I think, be proud to be called worldly, since a scolding, tenacious affection for the world is the main article of her faith. The Weigel—to adopt the German manner of referring to an actress—has no real counterpart in the American theatre; in appearance, and in dedication, she resembles Martha Graham, but a Martha Graham altogether earthier and more mischievous than the one Americans know. At the end of the rehearsal we exchanged gifts and greetings. I got a scarf, designed by Picasso in the company's honour; a book about the Ensemble's seminal production, *Mother Courage;* a photographic dossier comparing the performances of Charles Laughton and Ernst Busch in the title role of Brecht's *The Life of Galileo;* and—unexpectedly—a complicated game of the do-it-yourself variety, invented by Mozart to teach children how to compose country dances by throwing dice. The Weigel, alas, got only a cigarette lighter. Talking about the state of the company, she said, "When Brecht died, I was afraid this place might become a museum." Her fears have turned out to be unjustified. It is true that the Ensemble mostly performs Brecht plays, but the plays are acted and directed by people steeped in the Brecht spirit. Throughout the theatre his ghost is alive and muscular.

Or, rather, his ghosts, because there were many different Brechts, as I discovered while reading John Willett's invaluable book *The Theatre of Bertolt Brecht* and Martin Esslin's biographical study, *Brecht: A Choice of Evils*. The early Brecht was a touchy child, with a Bavarian accent, whose father ran a paper mill in Augsburg. After serving as a medical orderly in the First World War—an experience that inspired his lifelong hatred of militarism—Brecht plunged into the German *avant-garde* of the twenties, making a name for himself as an outspoken, nihilistic poet-playwright with a gift for turning gutter idiom into poetry. In Germany, where literature had always spoken a high-flying language unknown to human tongues, this was something new; as Ernest Borneman lately remarked in the *Kenyon Review,* "There was no precedent (a) for colloquial poetry; (b) for plain storytelling. There was no German equivalent to writers like Kipling, Mark Twain, or Hemingway." Brecht was impressed by, and freely borrowed from, the work of writers as disparate as Villon, Rimbaud, Büchner, Wedekind, Shakespeare, Kipling, and Luther, and he positively welcomed the charge of plagiarism, retorting that in literature, as in life, he rejected the idea of private property. Through the mouth of Herr Keuner, an imaginary character on whom he fathered many anecdotes and aphorisms, he scoffed at authors whose egotism compelled them to exclude from their work all notions and phrases that were not of their own invention: "They know no larger buildings than those a man can build by himself." (In this respect, as in several others, Brecht resembles Picasso, who once remarked, "To copy others is necessary, but to copy oneself is pathetic." In the early Montmartre days, according to Roland Penrose's recent biography, Picasso's reading matter included Verlaine, Rimbaud, Diderot, and the adventures of Sherlock Holmes, Nick Carter, and Buffalo Bill; the same list, or one very similar, would serve for the young Brecht. In addition, both men embraced Communism, yet expressed themselves in styles that were utterly antipathetic to Socialist realism; both revolutionized the arts of their choice; and both, despite shortness of stature and slovenliness of dress, were immoderately attractive to women.)

Brecht's early manner was summed up in 1922 by the German critic Herbert Ihering:

> This language can be felt on the tongue, on the palate, in one's ears, in one's spine. . . . It is brutally sensuous and melancholically tender. It contains malice and bottomless sadness, grim wit, and plaintive lyricism.

A little later there was the Brecht who, in collaboration with Kurt Weill, revolutionized the popular musical stage with *The Threepenny Opera* and *The Rise and Fall of the City of Mahagonny,* using the rhythms and slang of a depressed urban society to lacerate Western decadence, and bringing into the "serious" theatre the sardonic street-corner poetry of post-war Berlin. Already he was moving toward the vantage point that he was to make his own—"that interesting and largely neglected area," as Mr. Willett describes it, "where ethics, politics, and economics meet." In 1926 Brecht read *Das Kapital* for the first time. Marxism supplied a corrective to his anarchic tendencies, a remedy for his disgust with the world around him, and a mental discipline that delighted his love of logic and paradox. Hence, after 1928 we get Brecht the Communist didact, writing instructional plays in a new, sparse, bony style:

> When I address you
> Cold and broadly
> In the driest terms
> Without looking at you
> (I apparently fail to recognize you,
> Your particular manner and difficulties),
>
> I address you merely
> Like reality itself
> (Sober, incorruptible, thanks to your manner,
> Tired of your difficulties),
> Which you seem to me to be disregarding.

From this period come *Die Massnahme,* an austere analysis of revolutionary self-abnegation that is, intellectually, the masterpiece of Communist drama, and *Die Mütter,* Brecht's stage adaptation of the famous Gorki novel. Both plays were savagely attacked in the Marxist press—the latter for being out of touch with working-class reality, the former because it denied the thesis that a good Communist is never torn between the claims of reason and emotion. (Brecht's failure to reconcile these rival claims accounts, in Mr. Esslin's view, for the fascinating ambiguity that runs through his work. The bald statement he wants to make and the poetry with which he makes it often pull in different directions; matter and manner are exquisitely at odds.) Like many of his Leftist contemporaries, Brecht was seeking a method whereby economic processes could be effectively dramatized; he hoped to see money and food some day displace power and sex as the drama's major themes. With most bourgeois writers, he said, "the fact that moneymaking is never the subject of their work makes one suspect that . . . it may be the object instead."

The next Brecht was the director who practised, and the theorist who preached, "Epic Theatre"—a phrase he borrowed from Erwin Piscator in the twenties and went on defining until the end of his life. This, perhaps, is the Brecht who is best known in America, thanks to the energetic proselytizing of Eric Bentley. For every American who has seen a Brecht production, there are probably a thousand who are armchair experts on the "alienation effect," the abolition of suspense, the prefacing of scenes with projected captions, the use of music not to intensify emotion but to neutralize it, the rejection of "atmospheric" lighting in favour of general illumination, and the outright ban on costumes and props that do not look worn or handled.

> Of all works, my favourite
> Are those which show usage.
> The copper vessels with bumps and dented edges,
> The knives and forks whose wooden handles are
> Worn down by many hands: such forms
> To me are the noblest.

Brecht's opposition to naturalistic acting was really, as he often insisted, a return to the older forms of popular theatre, including (the list is Mr. Esslin's) "the Elizabethan, the Chinese, Japanese, and Indian theatre, the use of the chorus in Greek tragedy, the techniques of clowns and fairground entertainers, the Austrian and Bavarian folk play, and many others." His refusal to permit actors to "identify" with their roles, and thus to create strongly individualized characters, sprang from his conviction that human identity is not fixed but infinitely mutable, dependent on particular social and economic circumstances; this is the left-wing equivalent of Pirandello's theories, at once frivolous and despondent, about the many-faceted impermanence of the human ego. What Pirandello fatalistically accepted, Brecht sought to explain. His loathing of stage emotionalism is more easily accounted for. It was a violent reaction against the bombast of the conventional German theatre. Life in a Brecht production is laid out before you as comprehensively as in a Brueghel painting, and with many of the same colours—browns, greys, and off-whites. It does not seize you by the lapel and yell secrets into your ear; humanity itself, not the romantic individualist, is what it is seeking to explore. In 1936 Brecht stated his attitude:

> The spectator of the *dramatic* theatre says: "Yes, I have felt the same. I am just like this. This is only natural. It will always be like this. This human being's suffering moves me because there is no way out for him. This is great art; it bears the mark of the inevitable. I am weeping with those who weep on the stage, laughing with those who laugh."
>
> The spectator of the *epic* theatre says: "I should never have thought so. That is not the way to do it. This is most surprising, hardly credible. This will have to stop. This human being's suffering moves me because there would have been a way out for him. This is great art; nothing here seems inevitable. I am laughing about those who weep on the stage, weeping about those who laugh."

Nobody of any critical intelligence who is familiar with what passes for "great art" in London or New York could fail to applaud this succinct, startling, and unforgettable distinction between the audience that is all heart and nerves and the audience that tempers feeling with knowledge and observation.

Two more Brechts, and the outline is complete. One was the mellow playwright who reached the peak of his creativity in exile. Between 1937 and 1945 Brecht wrote eleven plays, among them *The Life of Galileo, Mother Courage, The Good Woman of Setzuan, Puntila* and *The Caucasian Chalk Circle.* By that time the ideological element was assumed or implied more often than it was stated. The five works I have named all deal with the tension between instinct, love, and emotion, on the one hand, and, on the other, a society that perverts or exploits all three. The church defeats Galileo by playing on his weakness for the good, sensual life. Mother Courage tries to protect her family by making money out of the Thirty Years' War, but the war, in the end, destroys her children. Shen Te, of Setzuan, finds that you cannot help those you love without injuring your neighbours. The landowner Puntila, all charity and generosity when drunk, is an efficient businessman during bouts of cold-blooded sobriety, from which, unavailingly, he begs to be delivered. In the last of the great plays, *The Caucasian Chalk Circle,* good-heartedness defeats the system. Grusha, the maid, is brought to trial for having kidnapped a high-born baby, but the judge decrees that the child belongs to her, since everything should belong to those who serve it best.

The last Brecht was the sage of East Berlin, at once the pride and the embarrassment of the Communist regime, which saw him laurelled in the West (especially at the Paris International Theatre Festivals of 1954 and 1955) and accused in Russia of being a "formalist" opponent of Socialist realism. Mr. Esslin's book goes deeply into Brecht's ambivalent relationship with the Party when he returned to Germany in 1948 after an inconclusive velitation with the Un-American Activities Committee. Before moving to East Berlin, he not only contrived, with characteristic guile, to obtain an Austrian passport, which would allow him easy access to the West, but gave the copyrights of his works to a West German publisher, who still owns them. When someone asked him, toward the end of his life, why he had elected to stay in the East, he is said to have likened himself to a doctor with a limited supply of drugs who is forced to choose between two patients—a syphilitic old roué and a diseased prostitute who is, however, pregnant. It seems clear, too, that Brecht's acquaintance with Hitlerism had left him with very little faith in the possibility of turning Germany into a true democracy overnight;

hence he felt able to support an authoritarian government that, whatever its faults, was at least anti-Nazi and anti-capitalist. (I suddenly remember the occasion when I took Helene Weigel to the West Berlin *première,* three years ago, of *The Diary of Anne Frank.* At the final curtain the audience sat shocked and motionless; Frau Weigel's face was rigid and masklike. Shortly afterward, in the restaurant next door to the theatre, she wept; and I should think she weeps seldom. Wiping her eyes, she shook her head and said firmly, "I know my dear Germans. They would do this again. Tomorrow.")

Early in 1949, in collaboration with his old friend Erich Engel, Brecht staged *Mother Courage* at the Deutsches-Theater in East Berlin. The style—light, relaxed, and ascetically spare—set the pattern for all his subsequent productions. As the tireless old protagonist, dragging her canteen wagon across the battlefields of the Thirty Years' War, Helene Weigel played in a manner that shrank utterly from flamboyance; her performance was graphic yet casual, like a shrug. At two carefully selected moments she was piercingly and unforgettably moving—first in the soundless cry that doubles her up when her son is executed, and again when, to avoid incriminating herself, she must pretend not to recognize his body. She walks over to the stretcher, wearing a feigned, frozen smile that does not budge from her lips until she has surveyed the corpse, shaken her head, and returned to her seat on the other side of the stage. Then she turns to the audience, and we see for an instant the drained, stone face of absolute grief. These moments apart, the production achieved a new kind of theatrical beauty, cool and meaningful, by deliberately avoiding climaxes of individual emotion; with *Mother Courage* the broad canvas and the eagle's-eye view of humanity were restored to European drama after too long an absence.

That autumn the company formally adopted the name Berliner Ensemble, and for the next five years it spent most of its time on tour. In 1952 a detailed, illustrated account of its first six presentations, complete with an analysis of the acting techniques and methods of stagecraft, was published in a huge volume of well over four hundred pages, laconically entitled *Theaterarbeit* (*Theatre Work*). In the spring of 1954 the Ensemble moved into the Theater am Schiffbauerdamm, and Brecht celebrated his homecoming with an extraordinary production of *The Caucasian Chalk Circle,* which opened in June and later astonished Paris and London. A concave white curtain covered the back of the stage, a convex white curtain swept to and fro across the front; between them, the vast revolve whirled around, bearing fragmentary settings for the journeying heroine to encounter, and long silken sheets adorned with

Oriental landscapes came billowing down to indicate place and climate. Lee Strasberg, the artistic director of the Actors' Studio and a passionate upholder of Stanislavsky's quest for emotional truth in acting, as opposed to the social truth sought by Brecht, saw the play while the Ensemble was in London. He concluded that what Brecht practised was by no means incompatible with what Stanislavsky preached, and declared that the production was one of the best half-dozen he had ever witnessed.

I met Brecht, for the first and only time, in Paris during the summer of 1955, the year before his death. Ovally built, and blinking behind iron-rimmed glasses, he sported a grey tunic of vaguely Russian cut and conversed in wry, smiling obliquities, puffing on a damp little cigar. To judge by Ernest Borneman's description of him in the twenties, exile had changed his appearance hardly at all: "He was an eccentric in behaviour, speech, and dress, as well as in politics. He wore clothes that kept a neat balance between those of a soldier, a workman, and a hobo. . . . The hair was sliced off abruptly after two or three inches growth, all around the head, and hung down . . . like the coiffure you see on busts of Roman emperors." Max Frisch, the Swiss playwright and novelist, has set down perhaps the best portrait of Brecht in his later years, and I am indebted to Mr. Esslin for introducing me to it. Brecht met Frisch in Zurich in 1947 and would often, when the latter was embarking on a train journey, go to the station to see him off:

> Avoiding the crowd, he leaves the platform with rapid, short, rather light steps, his arms hardly swinging, his head held slightly sideways, his cap drawn on to the forehead as if to conceal his face, half conspiratorially, half bashfully. . . . He gives the impression of a workman, a metalworker; yet he is too slight, too graceful for a workman, too much awake for a peasant . . . reserved, yet observant, a refugee who has left innumerable stations, too shy for a man of the world, too experienced for a scholar, too knowing not to be anxious, a stateless person . . . a passer-by of our time, a man called Brecht, a scientist, a poet without incense.

After the Master's death many people in the company, as well as outside it, wondered whether it could survive without his fiery presence. An interim answer was supplied by the Ensemble's triumphant East Berlin presentation, in January 1957, of *The Life of Galileo*—a production begun by Brecht and finished by Engel. I saw it again this summer, and the play still seems to me, as it did at the first night, an incomparable theatrical statement of the social responsibilities of the intellectual. At the outset it looks as if we were in for a straight fight between religious obscurantism and scientific discovery. The only progressive art, says Galileo, is "the art of doubt," a remark that echoes Brecht's own dictum: "Scepticism moves mountains." But before long we arrive at the author's real purpose, which is to condemn Galileo for cowardice. Intimidated by the threat of torture, cajoled by the promise of a cossetted life, he abjectly recants, and emerges from the Inquisition chamber to be shunned by his pupils, one of whom shouts at him, "Unhappy is the land that lacks a hero!" Wanly, Galileo responds, "Unhappy is the land that needs a hero." Brecht goes on to show how one such concession brings a hundred in its train; within months Galileo is backing the Church in social and political, as well as scientific and theological, affairs. The final tableau epitomizes the argument: in the foreground a choir polyphonously hymns the power of science, while in the background Galileo wolfs a fat roast goose. The play contains two scenes that exemplify, as sharply as anything Brecht ever wrote, his ability to make an intellectual position visible and tangible. In the first of them a provincial ballad singer hails Galileo's challenge to Rome. As he does so, a riotous procession, reminiscent of a painting by Hieronymus Bosch, streams across the stage. Some of the marchers are clad in obscene masks, and coax a jangling music out of saucepans and brass bedsteads; others toss a straw effigy of a cardinal in a blanket; one, a child, is attired as the earth, with water squirting from its eyes at the loss of its position at the centre of the universe; another clumps in horrendously on twenty-foot stilts, surmounted by a gigantic facsimile, acclaimed on all sides, of Galileo's head. The second scene that sticks in my mind is the one in which the liberal Cardinal Barberini, newly installed as Pope, turns against Galileo. At first, skinny in his underwear, waiting to be robed, Barberini refuses to countenance the Inquisitor's demand that the scientist be brought to trial, but as the robing proceeds and he is draped, encased, and almost buried in the ceremonial vestments of his office, the Pope grows more and more receptive to the Inquisitor's plea, to which, at last, he consents. It is instructive, by the way, to contrast Brecht's attitude toward Galileo with Arthur Koestler's in *The Sleepwalkers*—bearing in mind, of course, that Mr. Koestler's Marxism was once as deeply ingrained as Brecht's. According to the Koestler version, Galileo's pride brought about a disastrous and unnecessary breach between science and religion. Brecht, on the other hand, accuses Galileo of not having had enough pride (or self-respect) to make a breach that was healthy and necessary. Koestler wants to reconcile the physical with the metaphysical; Brecht strives to keep them apart. But, whatever one thinks of the argument, it is impossible to deny the unassertive loveliness of Caspar Neher's décor for *The Life of Galileo*—three towering panelled walls of darkly glowing copper, enclosing an area into which informatively beautiful objects, such as Roman bas-reliefs and silver models of the Aristotelian universe, are occasionally lowered. The production proved that the spheres of the Ensemble would continue to revolve without the animating zeal of their great mover. Brecht thus demonstrated, posthumously, the truth of his own apothegm that no man is indispensable, or, if he is, he is up to no good.

The Ensemble today consists of sixty-two actors, plus a staff of administrators, office workers, stagehands, musicians, designers, dressmakers, scene builders, electricians, ushers, waitresses, and cooks that brings the grand total of employees up to nearly three hundred. Its yearly subsidy, paid by the Ministry of Culture, amounts to more than three million marks. Rehearsals, in this happy set-up, may go on for anything between two and six months; when I was there in June, the cast of *The Threepenny Opera* was already wearing full costume and make-up, although the opening was not scheduled until October. It sometimes worries Helene Weigel that in all its ten years of operation the Ensemble has presented no more than twenty-five plays. She need not disturb herself unduly, because the main reason for the company's low output is, quite simply, its fame. Its productions are being reverently filmed for the East Berlin archives, it is constantly being invited to foreign countries (Hungary and Rumania this summer, Scandinavia in the fall, England and China next year), and it spends a lot of time polishing and recasting its existing repertoire.

This summer I attended two productions I had not seen before. One was *Die Mutter,* Brecht's expansion of the Gorky novel about an illiterate Russian mother who begins by urging her son to abandon his revolutionary activities and ends up, after he has been shot, a convinced supporter of the cause. The play is outright *agitprop,* a mosaic of Marxist exhortations, and the last scene shows the whole cast singing in praise of Communism while a film projector fills the backcloth with newsreel shots of Lenin, Khrushchev, Mao Tse-tung, and even—fleetingly—Stalin. It all sounds crudely hysterical until one sees the stealth and subtlety of the performance. There are no exaggerated Czarist villains, no exuberantly heroic proletarians; everyone acts with a detached calm that, if anything, reinforces the message. Weigel plays the mother as a quiet but relentless nagger. ("I picked out the nagging and decided to use it all through," she told me later. "I wanted to show that nagging could be constructive as well as nasty.") Looking like Nefertiti lined by years of labour over a hot stove, she permits herself one moment of pure lyricism. Her son, who has escaped from Siberia, appears without warning at a house where his mother is employed as housekeeper. Entering from the kitchen, she sees him and instinctively registers chiding disapproval; then, uncontrollably, she flies to his arms, as weightlessly as Ulanova's Juliet flies to Romeo, letting both legs swing round the boy's waist as he catches her. Throughout the evening one feels Brecht's passion for objects that have been durably used—a sofa, a soup tureen, a hand-operated printing press. Once, in a poem, he said that his wife chose her props with the same loving precision as that with which a poet chooses his words. Weigel's props, he declared, were selected

> . . . for age, purpose, and beauty
> By the eyes of the knowing,
> The hands of the bread-baking, net-weaving,
> Soup-cooking comprehender
> Of reality.

After this, one of the company's oldest productions, I went to see the newest—*The Resistible Rise of Arturo Ui,* described in the program as *"ein Gangster-Spektakel von Bertolt Brecht."* Written in 1941, it is a jagged, raucous parody of Hitler's rise to power, told in terms of Chicago in the twenties, composed mostly in blank verse, and including several malicious revampings of scenes from Shakespeare and Goethe. Hitler-Ui is a small-time thug who, taking advantage of a falling market, blackmails the mayor of the city (Hindenburg) into allowing him to organize a really prosperous protection racket. When the mayor dies, Ui succeeds him. His plans to take over the suburb of Cicero (Austria) are disputed by some of the mob; he slaughters the dissidents with as merry a lack of compunction as Hitler showed in disposing of Ernst Roehm and his friends on the Night of the Long Knives. In the final scene Ui is the boss, high on a rostrum spiky with microphones, through which he shrieks an oration that is cacophonously reproduced, at intervals of roughly half a second, by loudspeakers all over the theatre. The whole play is performed in a style that is somewhere between Erich von Stroheim and the Keystone Cops. The Roehm murders are staged like the St. Valentine's Day massacre; a truck drives into a garage, its headlights blazing straight at the audience, and silhouetted gunmen mow down the victims. The entire cast wears the sort of distorted make-up that one associates with puppets; the revolve whizzes around; and squalling Dixieland jazz interlards the scenes. Macabre farce on this level of inventiveness was something I had never struck before in any theatre. Its quality was condensed in the performance of Ekkehard Schall as Ui—one of the most transfixing human experiments I have ever seen on a stage, and a perfect image of Brechtian acting. Schall, who is under thirty, plays Ui with a ginger moustache, a ginger forelock, a trench coat, and a hat with the brim completely turned down. He invests the part with all the deadpan gymnastic agility of the young Chaplin: clambering on to the back of a hotel armchair and toppling abruptly out of sight; biting his knuckles, and almost his whole fist, when momentarily frustrated; indulging, when left alone with women, in displays of ghastly skittishness; and learning, from a hired ham actor, that the golden rule of public speaking is to preserve one's chastity by shielding—as Hitler always did—the lower part of one's belly. Yet Schall can change gears without warning, swerving from pure knockabout to sudden glooms of fearful intensity; from Chaplin, one might say, to Brando; for the virtue of Brechtian training, as of Brechtian thinking, is that it teaches the infinite flexibility of mankind. The play itself is rowdy and Chaplinesque. What the production—and Schall, above all—has added to it is a fever, a venom, and a fury that make laughter freeze, like cold sweat, on one's lips.

> In me are contending
> Delight at the apple trees in blossom
> And horror at the house-painter's speeches.
> But only the second
> Drives me to my desk.

Thus Brecht; and this production makes one glad that he was so driven. Its directors—Peter Palitzsch and Manfred Wekwerth—are both, like Schall, young men who were shaped by his tuition. The tradition, I would hazard, is safe.

(1959)

PERORATION

A speech delivered in 1958 at the National Film Theatre, London.

Ever since the Greeks we have been told that drama is a social art, a communal experience, and we still accept as fact what is nowadays mostly a fiction. For most people today the theatre is a place where *we* go—if we go at all—to see and hear *them,* the others, the glittering sealed-off people who provide what is called "art" for us to wonder at. That "they" belong to the same mundane world as "us" and are subject to the same stresses and dismays is a notion that all too seldom bothers us. What we have lost, in the commercal theatre as a whole, with its talk of playgoing as "an occasion," is the vital sense that we make drama: it is about us: and the moment it ceases to be about us, it ceases to be drama.

The opposition to this simple sentiment is deeply entrenched, even among comparatively literate people. I lately received a letter from a well-known Irish writer chastising me for my heresies. I had written somewhere that since art had a bearing on life, it was capable of influencing life, and that it was one of its functions to do so. Sadly, he rebuked me. To say that art could influence life, he asserted, was like saying that cricket could influence sport. Art, he went on, was as much a part of life as toad-in-the-hole or lipstick: it was something special and unique, a compartment of living rather than an interpretation of life. My correspondent is a sane and normally rational man, but on this subject he had fallen inadvertently into the dangerous midst of those who would segregate art from life, them from us. De Quincey was nearer to the truth when he defined art as *idem in alio*—the same thing in another form—by which he meant that art was parasitic on life. A statue is a man in clay or marble: a play is a human situation projected in theatrical terms. And the sculpture could no more exist without the man than the play could exist without the human situation. The *idem,* which art transmutes *in alio,* is reality—our reality. What we have to decide is whether we want our drama to batten on the lipstick of life or on the blood of it.

If drama is to play a part in human advancement, we must keep this in mind: are we studying the relevance of a text to philology or the relevance of a human experience to our lives? In most schools drama is taught as a suspiciously amusing branch of literature: we would gain much if it were taught as an offshoot of sociology. To study Shakespeare is not enough: to understand the sources of drama it would help if pupils were encouraged to improvise and write plays of their own based on current events in the world and their own lives. Shakespeare, as we all know, was not for an age but for all time; but the fact that he was so deeply of his own age is one of the reasons for his timelessness. The secret of theatrical longevity is neither to care about the past nor to worry over the future: it is to relate to the present.

I have to underline this platitude because the contemporary trend is to deny it. The idea of drama as an *alternative* to life is embedded in the modern psyche. The play that distracts is extolled at the expense of the play that focuses; and the play that supplies nourishment as well as entertainment will be lucky if the critics bestow on it no phrase more damning than "strong meat" or "not for the squeamish." A *Daily Mail* editorial, entitled "Cobblers and Lasts," appeared in March 1958 and stated in brisk, uncompromising terms the case for undernourished and undernourishing drama. The "Let 'Em Eat Chips" school has rarely exposed itself so nakedly. The column began by quoting John Osborne, who had somewhere complained that London playgoers used the theatre "as a sort of pleasant indigestion pill." It continued:

"Now we, in our ignorance, always imagined that that was what the theatre was for. It was something to do after dinner. It is a diversion. It is a relaxation.

"If the theatre is not that it is nothing. It should certainly not be a vehicle for propaganda, nor a lecture hall, nor a substitute for a revival meeting. Such things are better done elsewhere.

"The stage is an ingenious device intended simply and solely to entertain. . . ."

This vein, once embarked on, is almost unstoppable, and the writer went on to applaud the "boisterous, bawdy and beautiful plays" of Shakespeare, who "did not go to the theatre with a Message"; and ended with a smart pull-up-your-socks exhortation to Mr. Osborne and the "other members of the psycho-analytical school of literature" to put their talent to its proper use—i.e., to be resolutely trivial and lay off subjects they really feel strongly about. I am not aware that a "psycho-analytical school" of playwrights exists, or that Mr. Osborne would belong to it if it did; but if psycho-analysis means the unravelling of mental processes, it is certainly the stuff of drama, just as much as politics, sex, revivalism, or anything else. And I am perfectly sure that a playwright has as much right to sound off on politics as a political-leader writer has to sound off on drama. Yet this astounding editorial was not challenged by any of the *Mail's* readers. Some of them must have been aware that the best plays, from Aeschylus to Arthur Miller, were more than diversions; that we read and see them not only for their turns of phrase but because they distil for us the living essence of societies and their problems; because they relate to us and speak, at their finest, to our whole souls, convincing us that what is happening on the stage, however far removed from us in time or geography, is not different in kind from what is happening in our hearts and habitual lives. Some *Mail* readers may have felt this to the extent of writing letters about it; if so, none was published. The editor clearly saw no need to print them. It is one of the tragedies of our culture that the cause of serious majority drama is supported only by a tiny minority. Many others, who might support it, are discouraged by being subjected night and day to the kind of propaganda for drivelling irresponsibility of which the editorial I have quoted is only one example.

I am not advocating a revolution: merely a return to the ancient idea that drama concerns all of us, that it is an extension and an illumination of our experience, not something different and "artistic" and relaxingly apart. A French painter recently declared that, since nothing in nature precisely resembled anything else, he proposed to destroy all of his paintings which resembled anything that already existed. He became an abstractionist and is now immensely rich. Whether he is still, in any sense known to me, an artist, I cannot say. But I am sure that he was moving in the wrong direction, even for a painter; and even more for a playwright, since abstract, non-representational drama is, thanks to the stubborn physical reality of actors, almost impossible to achieve.

Stanislavsky talked once of the methods by which an actor's imagination could be kindled and excited. "How can it be done?" he asked, and answered himself: "By relating the subject of the play and its separate moments to real life as it unfolds today before our eyes. Learn to see and hear. Love life. Learn to bring it into art." The advice applies not only to actors, but to playwrights and audiences as well; and that excludes none of us, even critics.

INDEX

KENNETH TYNAN

was born in Birmingham, England, in 1927. After receiving a degree in literature from Magdalen College, Oxford, he acted, directed and produced for the British theatre and television. He joined *The Spectator* in 1951 as drama critic. The next year he served as drama critic for the *Evening Standard,* and the following year for the *Daily Sketch.* He went to *The Observer* in 1954, remaining four years as drama critic. From 1956 to 1958 he was also script editor for Ealing Films. In 1958, Mr. Tynan joined the staff of *The New Yorker* magazine as drama critic. He returned to *The Observer* in 1960. He has published four books, among them a biography, *Alec Guinness,* and *Bull Fever,* which was published in the United States in 1955.